# Thesaurus for Graphic Materials

## TGM I: Subject Terms

## TGM II: Genre and Physical Characteristic Terms

Compiled and edited by
Prints and Photographs Division
Library of Congress

Library of Congress
Cataloging Distribution Service
Washington, D.C.
1995

Library of Congress Cataloging-in-Publication Data


Library of Congress.  Prints and Photographs Division.
    Thesaurus for graphic materials / compiled by Prints and Photographs Division,
Library of Congress.
             p.      cm.
    Rev. ed. of 2 works.  First work originally published: LC thesaurus for graphic
materials / compiled by Elisabeth Betz Parker.  Washington, D.C. : Cataloging Distribution
Service, Library of Congress, 1987.  Second work originally published: Descriptive terms for
graphic materials / compiled and edited by Helena Zinkham and Elisabeth Betz Parker.
Washington, D.C. : Cataloging Distribution Service, Library of Congress, 1986.
    Includes bibliographical references.
    Contents: 1. Topical terms for subject access -- 2. Genre and physical characteristic
terms.
---- ------ Copy 3 Z663.39 .T48  1994
    1. Cataloging of graphic materials.  2. Cataloging of pictures.  3.  Subject headings.
I. Parker, Elisabeth Betz.  LC thesaurus for graphic materials.  II. Zinkham, Helena.
Descriptive terms for graphic materials.  III. Title.
Z695.27.L52  1995
025.3'47--dc20                                   94-40967
                                            CIP


ISBN 0-8444-0889-1

-------------------------------------------------------------------------

For sale by the Cataloging Distribution Service,
Library of Congress, Washington, D.C. 20541
202-707-6100

# THESAURUS FOR GRAPHIC MATERIALS

# TABLE OF CONTENTS

## PREFACE

The first edition of the *Thesaurus for Graphic Materials* was, in fact, two separate volumes published in 1986 and 1987. The second editions were intended to be separate volumes again. As publication plans were being made, it became clear that the two tools are so often used together that a single volume comprising the two separate thesauri would be more practical and cost effective. The parts are referred to as *TGM I: Subject Terms* and *TGM II: Genre and Physical Characteristic Terms*. Each part retains its own introductory text, examples, and thesauri.

# TGM I:

## Subject Terms

The following code has been assigned to this thesaurus for the MARC format.  It must be entered in subfield 2 of field 650:


**lctgm**

# TGM I
## TABLE OF CONTENTS

# ACKNOWLEDGMENTS

Demand for access to pictorial collections has increased dramatically over the last decade, as have opportunities to build automated catalogs and to share catalog records.  In response to numerous requests from custodians of picture collections for a published list of terms to guide them in subject indexing and retrieval, I prepared <u>Subject Headings Used in the Library of Congress Prints and Photographs Division</u>, a preliminary list issued in 1980.  This list could not, however, translate readily into the environment of more sophisticated access and integrated systems.  It was Jackie Dooley who convinced me in 1984 that it was time to revise and expand the preliminary list.

I would like most of all to thank the catalogers in the Prints and Photographs Division, who provided a steady supply of terms and questions about scope and application that led to the formulation of public and cataloger's notes, as well as the guidelines outlined in the introduction.  For their stimulation and enthusiasm as I pursued this monumental task, I am grateful to Mary Goss, Marilyn Ibach, Jane Dunbar Johnson, Barbara C. Orbach, and Helena Zinkham.  Helena Zinkham also helped by reading the entire thesaurus during final review.

The staff of the Chicago Historical Society, who have worked with draft copies of the thesaurus, also made comments which resulted in the addition of notes and guidelines.

I am greatly indebted to Jackie Dooley, who undertook the writing of the introduction, even after she moved from LC to the University of California at San Diego.  It is not easy trying to explain in the abstract how pictures are subject cataloged.  I wish also to thank Barbara Orbach for helping with the editing of the introduction.

Prasad Nair of Project Management, Inc., and the Library of Congress Automated Systems Office provided technical support for LEXICO, the software used to produce this thesaurus. Without automation, the task could never have been accomplished.

I am grateful to Henriette Avram, Lucia Rather, and Mary K. Pietris of the Library of Congress Processing Services Department for their support, which is of the utmost importance in such an endeavor. I also thank Stephen E. Ostrow, Renata V. Shaw, and the Prints and Photographs Division staff for their patience during this long process.

Elisabeth Betz Parker
Picture Cataloging Specialist
Prints and Photographs Division
March 1987

## ACKNOWLEDGMENTS FOR THE SECOND EDITION

Many people both in the Prints and Photographs Division (P&P) of the Library of Congress and in other institutions were involved with the preparation of the second edition of the *Thesaurus for Graphic Materials I: Subject Terms (TGM I)*. Elisabeth Betz Parker, Assistant Chief, and Helena Zinkham, Head, Processing Section, gave their experienced guidance and advice throughout the editing process. P&P Reference Librarian Barbara Orbach Natanson revised the introduction, reflecting new indexing practices as of January 1994. P&P Cataloger Karen Chittenden, with P&P Curators Ford Peatross and Cristina Carbone, developed new hierarchies of architectural terms. In addition to working on thesauri issues, Judith Terpstra, with BP Exploration (Alaska), edited the appendices, and P&P Cataloger Marcy Flynn proofread the thesaurus.

Other P&P catalogers and processing staff provided valuable input and advice on key questions, and reference and curatorial staff offered valuable consultation on terminology. Outside reviewers for the final draft included John Bye, North Dakota Institute for Regional Studies, North Dakota State University Archives; Beth Delaney, Albany Institute of History and Art; Jackie Dooley, Getty Art History Information Program, Janet Murray, Photography Collection, Miriam & Ira D. Wallach Division of Art, Prints and Photographs, New York Public Library. LEXICO software developers, Prasad Nair and Lyn Neal (Project Management, Inc.), provided an easy to use and flexible thesaurus maintenance system. The Library of Congress Information Technology Services and Automation Planning and Liaison Office also provided technical support. The Cataloging and Distribution Service arranged the publication and marketing of the thesaurus, in coordination with P&P Cataloger Sarah Rouse.

Barbara Orbach Natanson                        Arden Alexander
Reference Librarian and                        Cataloger (Pictorial Collections) and
editor for *TGM I*, 1989-1994                  editor for *TGM I*, 1993-

November 1994

## TGM I: INTRODUCTION

## I. *TGM I*: SUMMARY OF FEATURES

### I.A. SCOPE AND PURPOSE

The *Thesaurus for Graphic Materials I: Subject Terms* (*TGM I*) provides a substantial body of terms for subject indexing of pictorial materials, particularly the large general collections of historical images which are found in many libraries, historical societies, archives, and museums. Developed to support the cataloging and retrieval needs of the Library of Congress Prints and Photographs Division, *TGM I* is offered to other institutions in the hope that it will fill similar needs and will promote standardization in image cataloging. *TGM I* is primarily designed for automated cataloging and indexing systems and is authorized for use in MARC (Machine-Readable Cataloging) records. The vocabulary can also be used, however, in manual indexing systems, whether card catalogs or vertical files of pictures.

*TGM I* may be used to index subjects represented in a variety of still image media and formats, including prints, photographs, drawings, posters, architectural drawings, cartoons, and pictorial ephemera. The thesaurus provides a controlled vocabulary for describing a broad range of subjects depicted in such materials, including activities, objects, types of people, events, and places. *TGM I* includes subject categories only. Thus, proper noun names of people, organizations, events, and geographic places are excluded.[1] Art historical and iconographical concepts are not included either, but *TGM I* does supply terms for abstract ideas represented in certain types of images, such as allegorical prints and editorial cartoons.

*TGM I* is designed as a tool both for those who create catalog records and for those who search for them. Entry vocabulary and scope notes are designed to serve a dual purpose: assisting indexers in selecting terms for indexing and helping researchers find appropriate terms with which to search for pictures. At present, *TGM I* contains 5,504 authorized ("postable") terms, and 4,324 cross-reference ("non-postable") terms, giving it a very high ratio of entry vocabulary and increasing the ease with which searchers can translate their own terminology into the language of *TGM I*.

*TGM I* adheres to the American National Standards Institute (ANSI) guidelines for thesaurus construction.[2] In developing *TGM I*, emphasis has been placed on providing easily readable notations, logical hierarchical relationships, terms structured in natural language order, clearly distinguishable public notes and cataloger's notes, and modern American spelling conventions.[3]

Although the primary purpose of *TGM I* is to serve as a source of terminology for topics represented in graphic materials, it also offers indexing guidelines. Indexers trained to analyze textual materials may not know how basic indexing practices can be applied to pictorial indexing. It is hoped that the guidelines presented in this introduction will help in this regard and lead to consistent application of *TGM I*.

---

[1] An exception has been made in the case of five commonly used ethnic group headings from *LCSH*, which have been included in *TGM I*'s alphabetical listing for ease of look-up: **Afro-Americans, Blacks, Indians of North America, Indians of Central America,** and **Indians of South America.**

[2] American National Standards Institute. *American National Standard Guidelines for Thesaurus Structure, Construction, and Use: Approved June 30, 1980.* (New York: ANSI, 1980). ANSI Z39.19-1980.

[3] The UNISIST *Guidelines for the Establishment and Development of Monolingual Thesauri.* 2nd rev. ed. (Paris: UNESCO, 1981), which offers detailed guidance on establishing relationships among terms, has also been useful in the development of *TGM I*.

## I.B. TERM SELECTION AND FORMULATION

Developing and maintaining a large subject thesaurus is a major effort; it is one that the Library of Congress Prints and Photographs Division (P&P) undertakes out of an ongoing need not fulfilled by other tools. Understanding the origins and evolution of P&P's thesaurus work, the primary sources and characteristics of terminology included in *TGM I*, as well as *TGM I*'s relationship to other thesauri, may help in evaluating its usefulness for particular applications.

*TGM I* is built from a base of vocabulary that has been used to provide subject access to P&P's collections in the course of over 50 years of cataloging and indexing. The terms found in *TGM I* thus reflect the diversity of the subject matter found in materials held by P&P, which range from documentary photographs to architectural drawings to editorial cartoons to fine prints. Since terms are added to *TGM I* only as the topic is encountered in the course of cataloging and indexing, not all possible topics are represented in the thesaurus. Likewise, *TGM I* vocabulary is quite specific in some topic areas and remains very general in others because of the varying nature of P&P's indexing activities. Depending upon the situation, the indexing may cover anything from a single item to an entire collection.

The first comprehensive, systematic listing of P&P's subject terminology was compiled by Elisabeth Betz Parker and was issued in 1980 as a preliminary list entitled *Subject Headings Used in the Library of Congress Prints and Photographs Division* (*SHP&P*). The first edition of *TGM I* (published in 1987 and referred to then by the acronym *LCTGM*) incorporated the topical terms that were found in *SHP&P*. But *TGM I* excluded the proper names (e.g., **Halloween, Ku Klux Klan, Niagara Falls, Virgin Mary, War of 1812**) that had been included in the earlier list.[4] In conformity with the ANSI standard, *TGM I* also eliminated *SHP&P*'s inverted and compound term structures and shifted from constructing strings composed of broader and narrower terms (e.g., **Animals--Camels, Animals--Cats**) to showing the relationship among broader and narrower terms (as well as other term relationships) using ANSI standard thesaurus notation.

Another development was in the handling of terms for visual genre and physical characteristics and techniques (e.g., **Daguerreotypes, Memorial prints, Posters**), many of which had been included in the preliminary list. Because of the distinctive nature of this vocabulary, it was developed before *TGM I* within the framework of a separate thesaurus, *Descriptive Terms for Graphic Materials: Genre and Physical Characteristics Headings* (*GMGPC*). The first edition of *TGM I* included all of the terms and cross-references that appeared in *GMGPC* for ease of reference and for use in cases where types and formats of graphic materials constitute the <u>subjects</u> of images (see Section II.E). That practice is continued in this edition; postable and non-postable terms found in *Thesaurus for Graphic Materials II: Genre and Physical Characteristic Terms* (the second edition of the *Descriptive Terms* thesaurus) as of October 1994 are included in *TGM I*. These terms are identifiable by the statement "TCM II term" that appears in the cataloger's note (CN).

P&P's thesauri not only complement each other, they also complement other published thesauri and subject heading lists. While many of the topics covered by *TGM I* are no different from those that occur in other media, some of the more specific, visual concepts, such as **Children playing in sand, Document signings, Dormers, Hammer & sickle, Moonlight, Shaking hands,** and **Ship of state,** occur much more frequently as subjects of images than as subjects of books or other formats. Such terms are, therefore, not found in thesauri geared to

---

[4] Including proper noun names in the subject heading list was, without question, a helpful feature for researchers, but integrating proper names with the other sorts of relationships indicated in the thesaurus, and maintaining the ever-growing list of names grew cumbersome. P&P turned to the LC Name Authority File and *LCSH* (both of which serve as national authority files) as sources for proper names. It was decided that the time spent maintaining the names within the thesaurus framework (and adjusting them whenever they were altered in the authority files) could be better devoted to developing a cohesive universe of topical terms.

indexing non-pictorial materials. Conversely, thesauri or subject heading lists designed for indexing other media, especially textual materials, include many topics that cannot be expressed visually. *TGM I* attempts to aid indexers and users of visual materials by constructing a cohesive network of terms representing subjects commonly expressed in still images.

Many institutions provide access to materials in a variety of media, with indexing supplied from diverse sources and, therefore, must maintain databases which include terminology from multiple subject thesauri. In order that terminology might be as compatible as possible in such an environment, *TGM I* incorporates terms from other standard thesauri whenever possible.

The encyclopedic *Library of Congress Subject Headings* (*LCSH*), which (as of the end of 1993) includes 206,300 postable terms devised primarily in the course of cataloging textual, book-length materials, is the major thesaurus used by the Library of Congress and numerous other institutions.[5] As such, it is the most frequent source of terminology for *TGM I*. *LCSH* terms are used without alteration whenever possible, but term syntax or spelling is at times changed in order to conform to the ANSI standard. As necessary, cross references are made from *LCSH* terms to corresponding *TGM I* terms.

It should be noted that *TGM I* does not utilize two techniques authorized in *LCSH* for indexing publications concerned with or consisting chiefly of pictures. The *LCSH* free-floating form subdivision "Pictorial works" would be applicable to all pictorial materials and is far too broad to be a meaningful form heading for original and historical graphics. In addition, the technique of establishing a phrase heading "[topic] in art" (e.g., **Cathedrals in art**) is used in *LCSH* to designate textual materials which discuss or illustrate a specific subject as an artistic theme. Applying such a phrase to original materials would imply a value judgment about the particular work as "art" and would blur the distinction between objective subject analysis and iconographical analysis. For collections consisting largely or entirely of pictorial works, both of these techniques lose their meaning.

Lack of textual documentation frequently makes it difficult for a picture indexer to determine which aspect of a multifaceted subject best applies to the image in hand. In a thesaurus as extensive as *LCSH*, for example, one finds both scientific and popular names for plants and animals, as well as a variety of terms expressing closely related elements of a concept or phenomenon (e.g., **Arbitration, Industrial**; **Collective bargaining**; **Industrial relations**; **Labor contracts**; **Labor disputes**; **Mediation & conciliation, Industrial**). In some cases, elements occur so regularly together when represented in visual form that they need not be separately indexed. In order to guide picture indexers in their choice of terms and thereby improve the consistency of their indexing, *TGM I* selects from the rich vocabulary of *LCSH*, limiting the choice among overlapping terms (i.e., there are fewer to choose from) and attempting to make their specific application clear by means of notes and relationships.

The *Legislative Indexing Vocabulary* (*LIV*), developed for the Congressional Research Service at the Library of Congress, focuses on contemporary political and social issues.[6] *LIV* is consulted in compiling *TGM I* because the types of terms *LIV* includes have been found to be useful for indexing pictorial materials such as posters and cartoons that relate to social and political issues.

Another valuable source of terminology is the *Art and Architecture Thesaurus* (*AAT*). Since the *AAT* is often compared to *TGM I*, it may be useful to clarify here differences in the scope, purpose, and method of compilation of the two thesauri. The *AAT* provides terminology "for art and architecture of the Western world from

---

[5] Library of Congress. Cataloging Policy and Support Office. *Library of Congress Subject Headings*. 17th ed. Washington, D.C.: Library of Congress Cataloging Distribution Service, 1994.

[6] *Legislative Indexing Vocabulary: The CRS Thesaurus*. 20th ed. [Washington, D.C.]: Library Services Division, Congressional Research Service, Library of Congress, 1991.

antiquity to the present."[7]  It is intended for use in indexing objects as well as textual and pictorial materials, incorporating highly specific concepts as well as the more general categories in which those concepts belong.  The *AAT* includes an array of terms useful for indexing pictures of the built environment, furnishings and equipment, and manifestations of visual and verbal communication, as well as "supporting terminology" for the physical attributes, persons, and concepts that relate to the creation and appreciation of art and architecture.  Lying outside the *AAT*'s scope, however, are the broader range of people, events, and activities which are equally important aspects of general picture collections.  The *AAT* is regularly consulted in adding art and architecture-related terms to *TGM I* and has been influential in thinking through relationships among *TGM I* terms.

The *AAT* is constructed independently of the cataloging operations of any single institution.  *AAT* vocabulary has been developed to a considerable level of specificity in constructing the logical arrays of terms--the hierarchies--that compose it.  In contrast, the terms included in *TGM I* are there, for the most part, because they have been needed in the course of cataloging the collections of the Prints and Photographs Division or a contributing institution.  Occasionally a "gathering term" is added to *TGM I* when it is deemed useful for bringing out relationships among a cluster of narrower terms, but not all of the logically related terms or levels of hierarchy are incorporated unless they are needed for cataloging.  This operating method partially accounts for the fact that the hierarchies that appear in *TGM I* are neither so "deep" nor so elaborate as those that have been developed for the *AAT*.  Moreover, as the compilers of the *AAT* have pointed out, terms for abstract concepts are more difficult to classify than those for concrete objects.[8]  When no place for such terms can be found in an existing *TGM I* hierarchy, they are left as "orphans" (i.e., with no broader term designation) and an effort is made to lead the user to associated concepts through related term (RT) relationships.

In addition to the indexing tools mentioned above, standard tools which aid in term selection and definition include *Webster's Third New International Dictionary*, *Webster's New Collegiate Dictionary*, and the *Encyclopedia Americana*.  The expertise of specialists in the Prints and Photographs Division, other divisions of the Library of Congress, and other institutions has also been tapped to identify commonly accepted terminology, define terms, and discern relationships among terms.  In all cases, *TGM I* strives to avoid vocabulary which would imply subjective assumptions on the part of the indexer.

---

[7] *Art & Architecture Thesaurus* (New York: Oxford University Press, 1990), vol. 1, p. 25.  (A second edition of the *AAT* is scheduled to be published in 1994.)

[8] *AAT*, vol. 1, p. 11.

## I.C. STRUCTURE AND SYNTAX

### I.C.1. Relationships

  *TGM I* is a thesaurus in alphabetical format. As stated previously, *TGM I* conforms to the ANSI standard for structure and syntax. "Postable" terms (terms that are authorized for indexing) and "non-postable" terms (cross references pointing from unauthorized to authorized terms) are interfiled. Under each authorized term, the reference structure includes unauthorized terms (UF), broader terms (BT), narrower terms (NT), and related terms (RT). For each relationship that is established in the thesaurus, its reciprocal relationship can be found at another point in the thesaurus.

Example:   **Building dedications**        (authorized term)
       UF   Dedication of buildings  (term not authorized)
       BT   Dedications          (broader authorized term)
       NT   Church dedications    (narrower authorized terms)
             Cornerstone laying
       RT   Buildings            (related authorized terms)
             Groundbreaking ceremonies
             Toppings out

       Dedication of buildings
        USE  Building dedications   (cross reference from unauthorized term to authorized term)

Used for (UF):  A term that is not authorized for indexing.  UF terms are listed primarily for editorial purposes, but they may help searchers by clarifying the scope or meaning of a term.  The reciprocal is USE.

Use (USE):  A cross reference that points catalogers and searchers to an authorized term.  USE references may be made from synonyms, near synonyms, antonyms, inverted phrases, or other closely related terms or phrases.  The reciprocal is UF.

Broader term (BT):  An authorized term which indicates the more general class to which a term belongs.  Everything that is true of a term is also true of its broader term(s).

Narrower term (NT):  An authorized term which is narrower in scope and a member of the general class represented by the broader term under which it is listed.  The reciprocal is BT.

Related term (RT):  An authorized term which is closely related to the term under which it is listed, but the relationship is not a hierarchical one.  The reciprocal is also RT.

Although no precise rules dictate when related term references should be supplied, some typical situations include:

• Near synonyms
• Overlapping meanings
• Discipline and the object of study
• Persons and their occupations
• Products and industries
• Whole/part relationships

*TGM I* tends to be generous in supplying related term references. This is partly because relationships that would be implicit in a hierarchical display of the terms are less apparent when the terms appear in an alphabetical display. In accordance with thesaurus construction guidelines, however, related term references are never made to two terms at different levels in the same hierarchy.

Example:    **Game industry**     NOT    **Game industry**
        RT   Games             RT  Games
                                   Board games   [a narrower term to **Games**]

More detailed definitions and discussion of hierarchical and related term relationships can be found in the ANSI standard.

## I.C.2. <u>Syntax</u>

In accordance with the ANSI standard, terms are selected based on common usage and are established using natural language word order and modern American spelling conventions.

### I.C.2.a. Single terms

Headings for concrete concepts are established in the plural.

Example:    **Theaters**
           **Watermelons**

Headings for abstract concepts are established in the singular.

Example:    **Civilization**

Headings for activities are established as gerunds.

Example:    **Banking**
           **Running**

## I.C.2.b.  Compound terms

Compound terms are established (1) when a single concept is expressed by multiple words in natural language, (2) when it would be difficult or unnecessary for an indexer to differentiate between two closely related concepts, and (3) when splitting them into single terms to be placed in separate fields would lead to retrieval of irrelevant material.

Example:    **Artificial flowers**
**Cattle ranches**
**Children playing outdoors**
**Educational organizations**
**Real estate development**
**Tobacco industry**

Compound terms are always expressed in natural language order, never inverted.

Example:    **Protestant churches**    NOT    **Churches, Protestant**

Compound terms which include the word "and" are used when two terms occur together with such frequency that it would be undesirable to establish them separately.  Such terms are constructed with an ampersand (&) in order to differentiate in retrieval systems between the use of "and" as a Boolean operator and the use of "&" as part of an indexing term.

Example:    **Doors & doorways**
**Good & evil**

## I.C.2.c.  Parenthetical qualifiers

Qualifiers are used to differentiate between homographs.

Example:    **Camouflage (Biology)**
**Camouflage (Military science)**

## I.C.3.  Facet indicators

Facet indicators, which appear in brackets directly underneath authorized terms, signal that a term may be subdivided by geographic and/or nationality designations.

Example:    **Military camps**
--[nationality]--[country or state]--[city]

These indicators have been included on a systematic basis with certain categories of headings; with other types of headings, they are added as need arises in P&P's cataloging.  (See Section III for further information about using geographic, nationality, and other types of subdivisions.)

## I.C.4.  Notes

*TGM I* uses several kinds of notes to help catalogers apply terms consistently and to help researchers find appropriate search terms.

**I.C.4.a.  Public note**

The public note (PN) defines a term, explains its scope, or helps a user understand the structure of the thesaurus.

Example:   **Ships**
       PN   Includes steamships that are ocean-going vessels.  Search under STEAMBOATS for steamships that are used on inland or coastal waters.

**I.C.4.b.  Cataloger's note**

The cataloger's note (CN) clarifies how to use a term or when to use it in conjunction with another term ("double indexing").

Example:   **Sick bays**
       CN   Double index under type of vessel.

The note "TGM II term," which occurs frequently throughout *TGM I*, refers to terms which also appear in *Thesaurus for Graphic Materials II: Genre and Physical Characteristic Terms*.  (See Section II.E. for guidance on application of these terms.)

Example:   **Stereographs**
       CN   TGM II term.

Notes beginning with the phrase "Used in a note under ..." are of value primarily in editing and maintaining the thesaurus.

Example:   **Religious services**
       CN   Used in a note under RELIGIOUS FACILITIES.

**I.C.4.c.  History note**

The history note (HN) records the fact that a change has taken place in a term or the status of a term since the publication of the first edition of *TGM I*.  This may prove useful to searchers since it suggests terms that may have been in use formerly and that should be checked to retrieve older catalog records.  Generally, if one term has been completely replaced by another term, the older term appears as a "UF."

Example:   **Draft**
       HN   Changed 11/1987 from COMPULSORY MILITARY SERVICE.

**I.C.5.  Filing conventions**

The thesaurus maintenance software (LEXICO) used to produce *TGM I* follows ASCII filing rules.  Thus,

- Ampersands file before hyphens
- Hyphens file before Arabic numerals
- Arabic numerals file before letters of the alphabet
- Uppercase letters file before lowercase letters

## I.D.  RELATION TO OTHER CATALOGING TOOLS

*TGM I* has been developed to complement other tools used for cataloging pictures.  Descriptive cataloging records for pictorial items and groups can be prepared with guidance from the 2nd edition of the *Anglo-American Cataloguing Rules* (*AACR2*, revised 1988)[9], supplemented by the manual *Graphic Materials*.[10]  The latter set of rules expands and interprets AACR2 for descriptive cataloging of graphics in historical and archival collections.  To aid in the identification and retrieval of pictures by their physical type and format, *Thesaurus for Graphic Materials II: Genre and Physical Characteristic Terms* (*TGM II*) may be used.[11]  As noted above, *TGM I* incorporates terminology from this thesaurus, but *TGM II* itself should be consulted for the most current vocabulary, for information about the definition and scope of specific terms, and for guidance in the relationships among *TGM II* terms.

Whether an institution's system is manual or automated, access to graphic materials will be greatly improved through widespread application of a set of standard tools.  The *USMARC Format for Bibliographic Description* (a standard for communicating bibliographic data in machine readable form) accommodates the use of all of the tools mentioned here.[12]

## I.E.  MARC CODING

*TGM I* is one of several standard thesauri authorized for use in the 650 field of MARC records.  *TGM I* terms are entered in the subfield ǂa of the 650 field.  The Library of Congress has assigned the code "lctgm" to this thesaurus.  The source of each term is made apparent by the field indicator 7 and subfield ǂ2 code, which are required elements.

Example:    650 -7 ǂa [*TGM I* term]. ǂ2 lctgm

650 -7 ǂa **Cheerleading.** ǂ2 lctgm

Subdivisions are entered in other subfields in the 650 field: general (topical and nationality) subdivisions are entered in subfield ǂx; geographic subdivisions are entered in subfield ǂz; chronological subdivisions are entered in subfield ǂy.

Example:    650 -7 ǂa **Soldiers** ǂx **Italian** ǂy **1940-1950.** ǂ2 lctgm
**Soldiers--Italian--1940-1950.** lctgm

Example:    650 -7 ǂa **Schools** ǂz **Illinois** ǂz **Chicago** ǂy **1890-1900.** ǂ2 lctgm
**Schools--Illinois--Chicago--1890-1900.** lctgm

(For further information on subdivisions, see Section III below.)

---

[9] *Anglo-American Cataloguing Rules.* 2nd ed., 1988 revision.  Ottawa: Canadian Library Association; Chicago: American Library Association, 1988.

[10] Elisabeth Betz Parker, *Graphic Materials: Rules for Describing Original Items and Historical Collections.* Washington, D.C.: Library of Congress, 1982.

[11] The second part of this publication, beginning on page 473.

[12] *USMARC Format for Bibliographic Data: Including Guidelines for Content Designation.* Washington, D.C.: Cataloging Distribution Service, Library of Congress, 1988- .

## I.F.  SIGNIFICANT DIFFERENCES FROM THE FIRST EDITION

Probably the most significant change in *TGM I* has been in the addition of 1,937 postable and 1,755 non-postable terms.  Additions and changes to the vocabulary are a direct outgrowth of the cataloging that has been going on in P&P and a few contributing organizations over the past seven years.  The cataloging of groups of photographs, including many relating to Native Americans, and a program to catalog single items for which orders for reproduction have been received--ranging from Currier & Ives prints and Civil War drawings and photographs to 20th century fine prints and World War II posters--have resulted in many new terms.  Other recent projects have focused on cataloging groups of architectural drawings and architectural photographs.  These cataloging ventures have resulted in the addition of more specific vocabulary (**Houses** has been added as a narrower term to **Dwellings**, for instance).  Coinciding as they did with the publication of the *AAT*, such projects have also spurred a re-examination of the terms used for buildings and sites and of the relationships that exist among them.  Appropriately enough, this has resulted in a new structure, founded on the concept of **Facilities**, a broader concept than **Buildings**.  This new structure attempts to incorporate many terms that were previously "orphans" (i.e., they had no broader term), while remaining flexible enough to be used in situations that show combinations of site, structure, and activities characteristic of a particular type of facility.  A corresponding structure for **Architectural and site components** has also been developed.

Changes in terminology, while inevitable, can be time-consuming to implement in indexing systems or, if not fully implemented, can place burdens on the users who must then search under old and new terms.  While some term changes have been necessary, particularly in the context of the work on **Facilities**, an attempt has been made to keep major changes to a minimum and to alert users of *TGM I* to changes that have occurred by recording history notes under changed terms.

The lists of topical subdivisions used by P&P have been restructured and expanded since the first edition; they include, for the first time, subdivisions used with names of corporate bodies and names of wars (see Appendices A through D).  Other differences from the first edition include greater allowance for geographic and nationality subdivision (see Section III for a discussion of subdivision practice).  Public and cataloger's notes that were found to be too local or limited in their application have been eliminated or altered.  Cataloging examples have been added to illustrate some of the indexing principles and practices employed by P&P catalogers.

## II.  INDEXING IMAGES: SOME PRINCIPLES

It is desirable to follow standard indexing practice when using *TGM I*, especially in MARC records that will be integrated with cataloging of non-pictorial materials.  This section focuses on techniques which are particularly relevant to pictorial indexing.[13]  These guidelines assume that *TGM I* will be applied primarily within a cataloging environment that allows for a variety of topical subject access points to be appended to a descriptive cataloging record for either a single graphic item or for a group of graphic items.  (See Section IV for guidance in indexing for vertical file systems.)

## II.A.  WHAT TO INDEX?

Subject indexing of textual materials such as books and journal articles is usually aided by the availability of several convenient sources of information--title, table of contents, abstract, or index--from which to determine the

---

[13] For an in-depth treatment of issues relating to subject indexing of pictures, see Sara Shatford, "Analyzing the Subject of a Picture: A Theoretical Approach," *Cataloging & Classification Quarterly* 6 (Spring 1986): 39-61.

author's scope and purpose and the overall subject of the work. Several specific headings usually can be selected to describe the content of the book or article.

Picture indexers frequently have no such convenient sources. There may not be any written documentation accompanying the material by which to identify the "Who? What? Where? When? and Why?" of its creation and purpose. A cataloger may, therefore, have to invest some time in research in order to answer these questions before describing and indexing images.

The task of devising a title often falls to the cataloger as well, since many pictorial items and groups lack them; *Graphic Materials* offers guidance in devising descriptive titles. The information supplied in the title is usually expanded in a Summary Note (MARC field 520), which more fully outlines the subject of the images at hand, particularly for group-level records. Composition of the title and summary data are closely linked to assignment of subject terms, since all subject access points should be substantiated in the body of the descriptive cataloging record.

Catalogers should consider some additional questions when trying to decide which subjects to index. How historically significant is the subject matter of the images? Is the subject matter widely depicted, or are there novel aspects which are rarely found in pictorial collections? If a subject is not prominently or clearly shown in an image, can it be omitted in indexing because it is better represented elsewhere? How does the material relate to other collections in the institution? How can such significant relationships be highlighted through consistent description and indexing from one collection to the next? Does a group of images demonstrate that the creator had a particular point of view or message in mind, thus providing a rationale for indexing for the context as well as the content? It is often important to remember that the images being cataloged may, in fact, be unique primary evidence of a particular time and place.

## II.B.  "OF" AND "ABOUT"

By their very nature, most pictures are "of" something; that is, they depict an identifiable person, place, or thing. The most obvious exceptions are abstract works of art which depict different things in the eyes of different viewers. In addition, pictorial works are sometimes "about" something; that is, there is an underlying intent or theme expressed in addition to the concrete elements depicted. This is often true of works of art and cartoons; it is frequently harder to discern with documentary works.

Subject cataloging must take into account both of these aspects if it is to satisfy as many search queries as possible. Indexers should examine images, their captions, and accompanying documentation carefully to determine both the most salient concrete aspects (what the picture is "of") and any apparent themes or authorial intents (what the picture is "about"), taking care not to read into the images any subjective aspects which are open to interpretation by the viewer.

Example:  A political cartoon depicting a basketball game in which the players are dribbling a globe is "of" **Basketball** and "about" **International relations**.

Example:  Dorothea Lange's photograph known as "Migrant Mother," which depicts a Dust Bowl migrant worker and her children, is "of" **Mothers & children** and **Migrant laborers**. In this case, it would be overly subjective to assign terms for "aboutness," since the caption fails to tell us whether the photographer's focus was poverty, despair, hardship, survival, or other abstract concepts.

If determining what an image is intended to be about poses challenges, determining what an image is of-- what its focus is for indexing purposes--can often be no less challenging. This is particularly true when an image shows aspects of a subject that are commonly depicted together. In cases where the focus of an image is not readily apparent, P&P catalogers consider the questions listed in Section II.A., using two additional questions to try out the terms towards which they are leaning: "Is this image informative regarding [possible term]?" "If I were a researcher interested in [possible term], would I appreciate being brought to this image?"

Example: A photograph showing a bowling alley with people at several lanes engaged in the game. The indexer may decide that **Bowling alleys** and **Bowling** are both warranted, because the image provides plenty of detail about both the site and the activity, but **Bowlers** may be unnecessary, since the image does not show very clearly the types of people playing the game, what they wore, etc.

## II.C.  PROPER NAME INDEXING

Picture researchers usually find geographical and biographical access useful in addition to topical subjects. Therefore, picture repositories may want to index under the name of a person, organization, or place in cases where these are represented in an image and identified.

As described in Section I, *TGM I* does not include proper noun name headings for people, organizations, events, structures, or geographic places; its scope is limited to subject categories only. In most cases, proper name headings can be found in either the Library of Congress Name Authority File (personal names and corporate bodies) or *Library of Congress Subject Headings* (geographic features, structures, events, etc.). The Prints and Photographs Division utilizes the headings found in these sources and contributes headings as necessary to these national authority files. Institutions that do not have access to the Library of Congress authority files will most likely want to create local or shared authority files of commonly used proper names in order to maintain consistency in indexing proper name subjects of pictures.

In certain cases, the Prints and Photographs Division appends subdivisions to names taken from or added to one of the authority files cited above in order to specify what aspects of the subject are covered by an image. Topical subdivisions are drawn from the lists given in Appendices A through D. Further information about subdivision practice may be found in Section III below.

## II.D.  GENERIC AND SPECIFIC

*TGM I* terms should be applied following the principle of "specificity," which requires that the most specific term possible be used to describe a subject. That is, an image of a rose is indexed under **Roses**, not under the broader term **Flowers**, and not under both terms.

When an image is indexed under a proper name heading, however, both the name heading and a generic subject term can be applied. For example, **Department of the Interior Building (Washington, D.C.)** and **Government facilities; Knights Templar (Masonic order)** and **Fraternal organizations; Langtry, Lillie, 1853-1929**, and **Actresses**. This double indexing practice is useful because, while for some types of research, picture searchers seek names of specific people, places, and things, for other types of research, they want generic examples of a subject (i.e., not a particular named example) to illustrate a concept. It would be asking a lot to expect researchers to think of the names of all organizations, actresses, or government buildings that might be represented. Indexing for both generic topics and specific instances is the most satisfactory solution to this problem.

Unfortunately, always indexing under both generic and specific instances of a subject can become highly impractical, particularly when a catalog record requires many subject headings, or when an institution can ill afford the expense of authority work necessary to establish headings for proper names. Responding to the questions posed in Section II.A. and II.B. may help a cataloger decide where to economize in the assignment of headings. That is, rather than automatically assigning both generic and specific headings in every case, the usefulness of each should be evaluated in advance; only those headings which provide access to the most significant characteristics of images being cataloged should be assigned.

When double indexing is desirable but not feasible, a tool such as *LCSH*, in which there are often cross references between generic topics and named instances (e.g., **Holidays** see also **Arbor Day**), may compensate and guide users among generic and specific terms.

## II.E.  SUBJECT HEADINGS AS COMPARED WITH GENRE AND PHYSICAL CHARACTERISTIC HEADINGS

Some pictorial materials are important as much for their artifactual value as for their subject content.  The distinction between topical terms and genre or physical characteristic terms is critical in describing such materials, since researchers often know with great certainty whether they wish to see examples of formats and physical types or images in which formats or physical types constitute the subject.  When a pictorial item is an example of a format or physical type, this may be indexed by selecting the appropriate term from *Thesaurus for Graphic Materials II: Genre and Physical Characteristic Terms* (*TGM II*) (entered in MARC field 655 or 755).  When an image depicts recognizable types of graphic materials, a term from *TGM II* may be used as a topical heading (entered in MARC field 650).

Example:  A stereograph of a family viewing stereographs is indexed with: (650) **Stereographs** (for the subject of the image); (755) **Stereographs** (for the physical characteristic of the item).

Example:  A self-portrait of an artist making a self-portrait is indexed with: (650) **Self-portraits** (for the subject of the image); (655) **Self-portraits** (for the format of the item).

The *TGM II* introduction provides guidelines for construction and use of 655 and 755 fields.

## III.  SUBJECT HEADING STRINGS AND SUBDIVISIONS

*TGM I* terms are suited to postcoordinate indexing: terms from the thesaurus may be listed separately to cover all aspects of the subjects represented in the image without indicating any relationships that may exist among the subjects; searchers may then combine terms at the searching stage.  For example, an image showing women involved in sports activities might be assigned two separate headings: **Women** and **Sports**.  *TGM I* terms may also be used as elements in subject heading "strings" in order to bring out relationships among topics, as in the subject heading string: **Women--Sports**.[14]  A number of factors must be weighed in determining whether to rely on the single term or the subject heading string approach, including the data entry, retrieval, and display features of the system in which the terms will be used and the kinds of knowledge and skills that will be required of indexers and users of the system.

Subject heading strings that link aspects of the subject covered (e.g., names, topics, time periods, places) and succinctly display these relationships have long been used in manual indexing systems.[15]  Even in an age when many institutions use automated systems with Boolean and keyword searching capabilities that enable searchers to

---

[14] The term **Women** is one of the few *TGM I* terms identified for use with topical subdivisions.  See Section III.D.1 and Appendix A.

[15] This type of indexing is generally referred to as "precoordinate" indexing.  Lois Mai Chan offers the following distinction between precoordinate and postcoordinate indexing: "In a precoordinate system, terms for a topic and its aspects are linked at the time of indexing, with prepositions or other devices (punctuation or the structure of the string) showing how the terms interrelate.  In a postcoordinate system, terms for the main subject and its aspects are simply listed separately." *Library of Congress Subject Headings: Principles and Application.* 2nd ed. (Littleton, Colorado: Libraries Unlimited, Inc., 1986), 37.

specify desired combinations of subject characteristics at the searching stage, subject heading strings can still prove of value. Explicitly linking together aspects of a subject may help searchers avoid, or at least more quickly identify and weed out, "false drops"--retrieval results where the relation between two or more subjects specified by the searcher is not what the searcher intended. The researcher interested in images of women engaging in sports may find a number of records that include the subjects **Women** and **Sports**, including images of women watching sports and images of women picketing sports events; the subject heading string **Women--Sports**, however, enables the researcher to identify quickly those images that show women <u>doing</u> sports. Linkage of this sort can be particularly useful when a single catalog record covers multiple subjects taking place in multiple locations at multiple times, as is sometimes the case in records for groups of images.[16]

Searchers should not have to construct and enter long strings of terms and subdivisions just to see what might be available on their topic. But such strings can be useful in orienting the searcher when a large result is returned in response to a keyword search. Although there is some evidence that multiple screens of subdivided headings confuse users of online catalogs, it is also true that well-designed, easily browsed displays of subject heading strings can help users to (1) develop a conceptual framework of how information in the catalog is organized and (2) winnow large sets of results down to the material most appropriate to the searcher's need.[17] For instance, a display such as:

**Women--Political activity**
**Women--Social life**
**Women--Spiritual life**
**Women--Sports**

might be doubly useful to the researcher interested in depictions of women, making it possible to hone in on the particular aspect of the topic most of interest and, at the same time, suggesting possible related aspects.

Significant as the virtues of precoordinated terms may be for retrieval and display, some institutions may find that their system is not designed to take advantage of the benefits. Others may find that the benefits are outweighed by the effort required to maintain consistency in the elements and sequence of elements included in strings or by the extra data entry involved in repeating geographic and chronological subdivisions under multiple topical headings in the same record. Outlined below are some of the subdivision practices employed by the Prints and Photographs Division. Use of nationality, geographic, chronological, and topical subdivisions, however, is **optional**.

---

[16] Martha Yee deftly handles this topic, particularly in relation to the first edition of *TGM I* in "Subject Access to Moving Image Materials in a MARC-Based Online Environment," in *Beyond the Book: Extending MARC for Subject Access*, ed. by Toni Petersen and Pat Molholt (Boston: G.K. Hall & Co., 1990), 102-103.

[17] For discussions of browsable displays, see, for example, Mia Massicotte, "Improved Browsable Displays for Online Subject Access," *Information Technology and Libraries* 7 (Dec. 1988): 373-380; Dorothy McGarry and Elaine Svenonius, "More on Improved Browsable Displays for Online Subject Access" *Information Technology and Libraries* 10 (Sept. 1991): 185-191.

## III.A.  NATIONALITY SUBDIVISIONS

A facet indicator for nationality is added selectively to terms for certain occupations, activities, and objects. The facet is used to indicate a national association, particularly in cases where the subject either operates on behalf of a nation or where its occurrence outside its nation of origin is likely to be of interest.  Nationality terms are drawn, wherever possible, from *LCSH*.

Examples:  [Thesaurus]        **Soldiers--[nationality]**
           [Indexing string]  **Soldiers--Italian**

           [Thesaurus]        **Automobiles--[nationality]**
           [Indexing string]  **Automobiles--Japanese.**

(Note: Because of P&P's extensive American Civil War holdings, the nationality facet has been added to a number of headings in order to be able to append the "nationality" designation "--Confederate" or "--Union.")

MARC coding: Nationality subdivisions are assigned subfield code "x."

## III.B.  GEOGRAPHIC SUBDIVISIONS

Important geographical information may be embodied in images.  A number of questions commonly arise regarding the best means of providing geographic access, partly because the MARC format offers a number of fields in which geographic designations may be encoded.  Use of geographic subdivisions has been expanded in this edition of *TGM I* because in a MARC record environment it is, at present, one of the best methods for (1) providing hierarchical access to places, enabling keyword retrieval by specific place name as well as by the larger geographic entity in which the place is located and (2) making a clear linkage between topic and place, so as to avoid confusion when multiple topics and multiple places are recorded in a single catalog record.[18]  P&P does not employ a technique found in *LCSH* for subdividing place names by topics (e.g., Chicago (Ill.)--Commerce) because this does not offer as predictable a form of hierarchical place name access; moreover, constructing such headings requires additional indexing effort with little added benefit in systems featuring keyword retrieval and for a collection that comprises all areas of the world.  The [place]--[topic] technique may be of more value in manual systems or automated systems that do not have keyword searching capability.  It may also be useful in geographically oriented collections where it is important to be able to browse under place name for all aspects of a particular geographic place.  Institutions that are trying to match headings that are used on records for books and other materials cataloged using *LCSH* may also find it desirable to follow this practice.[19]

A facet indicator for geographic subdivision is added to terms for natural geographical features, structures, and objects which have fixed locations; to most activity terms; as well as to other terms where locale is deemed both a distinguishable and a distinguishing feature.  The geographic subdivision is understood to indicate place of depiction (as opposed to, for example, place of origin), unless a cataloger's note specifies otherwise.  (Users of *TGM I* may find terms that do not have a geographic facet indicator, although a geographic subdivision may seem

---

[18]  There has been some discussion of modifying an existing USMARC field or creating a new one in order to make it possible to provide hierarchical geographic subject access, perhaps down to the street address level. As new methods are developed for providing hierarchical access to places represented in images and for linking topic and place elements, there may be less need for geographic subdivisions.

[19]  For discussion of the [place]--[topic] indexing technique, see Library of Congress.  Office for Subject Cataloging Policy, *Subject Cataloging Manual: Subject Headings*.  (Washington, D.C.: Cataloging Distribution Service, Library of Congress, 1991), sections H1140, H1145.5, and H1845.

appropriate. To make sure geographic subdivisions are used consistently, indexers may wish to annotate their copies of the thesaurus if they decide to use a geographic subdivision with a heading where the geographic facet indicator does not presently appear.)

Following *LCSH* practice, geographic subdivisions are constructed in indirect order (i.e., broader place name preceding narrower place name). The facet indicator [country or state]--[city] merely suggests the general pattern; as appropriate, catalogers substitute names of regions or specific geographic features. Geographic names are taken from *LCSH* and the LC Name Authority File, or are formulated according to guidelines on choice of name found in the *Anglo-American Cataloguing Rules*. The Library of Congress' *Subject Cataloging Manual: Subject Headings* (Section H 830) specifies subdivision practice for various types of geographic entities. For instance, sites in the United States are subdivided first by state (not by country) and then by the lowest appropriate geographic jurisdiction or feature (other than named sections of cities). Geographic features that span more than two jurisdictions are entered without interposing a broader geographic name.

| Examples: | [Thesaurus] | **Marine terminals** |
|---|---|---|
| | | --[country or state]--[city] |
| | [Indexing string] | **Marine terminals--California--San Diego** |
| | | |
| | [Thesaurus] | **Steamboats** |
| | | --[country or state]--[city] |
| | [Indexing string] | **Steamboats--Mississippi River** |

MARC coding: Geographic subdivisions are assigned subfield code "z."

## III.C. CHRONOLOGICAL SUBDIVISIONS

Consistent use of chronological subdivisions is an aid to organizing images or descriptions of images of a particular subject in an ascending or descending date order, resulting in a file arrangement that presents the evolution of the subject over time.

All *TGM I* terms may be subdivided chronologically. P&P has generally based the chronological subdivision on the year of execution, i.e., the year that the material being cataloged was created. When an image portrays a subject whose chronological orientation is significantly different from the year in which the original image was made (for instance, a lithograph made in 1924 depicting a scene from the American Revolution), it may be desirable to base the subdivision on the year of depiction.

Since all terms may be subdivided chronologically, this facet is not enumerated under each term in the thesaurus. Each institution must determine its own scheme for chronological subdivision. In order to provide a predictable set of dates in systems which do not feature truncation or range-searching, P&P has adopted a practice of subdividing by the decade(s) span that encompasses the year(s) of execution/depiction.

Example:  Photograph taken of lion hunting in Africa in 1933.

       [Thesaurus]        **Lion hunting**
       [Indexing string]  **Lion hunting--Africa--1930-1940**

Example:  Engraving made between 1822 and 1865 that shows a theater in Atlanta.

       [Thesaurus]        **Theaters**
                        **--[country or state]--[city]**
       [Indexing string]  **Theaters--Georgia--Atlanta--1820-1870**

Example:  Cartoon drawn in 1955 showing a Confederate general during the Civil War.

       [Thesaurus]        **Generals**
                        **--[nationality]--[country or state]--[city]**
       [Indexing string]  **Generals--Confederate--1860-1870**

MARC coding: Chronological subdivisions are assigned subfield code "y."

### III.D.  TOPICAL SUBDIVISIONS

The Prints and Photographs Division has devised topical subdivisions to be used in combination with four categories of Name headings from *LCSH* or the LC Name Authority File and with six *TGM I* headings for classes of persons. These subdivisions have been included in Appendices A through D for the convenience of users of Prints and Photographs Division records and for other institutions that might find them useful.

(1) Appendix A: Subdivisions Used With Names of Ethnic, Racial, and Regional Groups and With Classes of Persons (e.g., **Hawaiians, Indians of North America, Mexican Americans**) and six particular classes of persons (**Aged persons; Children; Handicapped persons; Indigenous peoples; Men;** and **Women**). Names of ethnic, racial, and regional groups come from *LCSH*; the six classes of persons are terms found in *TGM I*. The subject heading strings are entered in MARC field 650.

(2) Appendix B: Subdivisions Used With Names of Persons (e.g., **Elizabeth I, Queen of England, 1533-1605; Washington, George, 1732-1799**). Names are taken from the Library of Congress Name Authority File or formulated according to AACR2 guidelines. The subject heading strings are entered in MARC field 600.

(3) Appendix C: Subdivisions Used With Names of Wars (e.g., **Spanish American War, 1898; United States-- History--Civil War, 1861-1865; World War, 1939-1945**). The names come from *LCSH*. Depending on the nature of the heading, the subject heading strings are entered in MARC field 650 or 651.

(4) Appendix D: Subdivisions Used With Corporate Bodies and Named Events (e.g., **Fort Monroe (Va.); National Association for the Advancement of Colored People; United States. Army, Cavalry, 6th; World's Columbian Exposition (1893 : Chicago : Ill.)**). Names come from the Library of Congress Name Authority File. Depending on the nature of the heading, the subject heading strings are entered in MARC field 610, 611, 650, or 651.

Institutions using *TGM I* may decide, for a variety of reasons, not to make use of these topical subdivisions. Since public notes (PN's) appearing under many terms in the thesaurus mention related subdivisions to search under, institutions that do not use the subdivisions will probably want to alert their users to this fact.

The question sometimes arises whether the [proper name]--[subdivision] combination and the corresponding *TGM I* topical term from the main thesaurus list should both be used in the same record. P&P's practice is generally to supply the [proper name]--[subdivision] combination for the broad subject matter of the image and to supply *TGM I* terms for the specific "of's" and "about's."

Example:  Image of airplane production in Fort Worth, Texas, during World War II.

> **World War, 1939-1945--Economic & industrial aspects--Texas--Fort Worth**
> **Airplane industry--Texas--Fort Worth--1940-1950**

> NOT

> **World War, 1939-1945--Economic & industrial aspects--Texas--Fort Worth**
> **Industrial aspects of war--Texas--Forth Worth--1940-1950**

MARC coding: When topical subdivisions from *TGM I* are used with a heading from *LCSH* or the LC Name Authority File, the second indicator is "4" ("source not specified"). The topical subdivision is assigned subfield code "x."

Example:    **650 -4 ǂa World War, 1939-1945 ǂx Economic & industrial aspects ǂz Texas**

### III.E.  COMBINING SUBDIVISIONS

In general, any and all subdivisions appropriate for an image or group of images are used. Chronological subdivisions may be eliminated, however, from certain types of subject heading strings that commonly include specific dates, such as headings for wars and other events, in order to avoid redundancy and potential confusion. P&P catalogers supply nationality and geographic subdivisions depending upon what is known from caption information--research is not usually conducted to discover this information. Subdivisions for both nationality and country are used, even when they refer to the same nation, because each conveys a different type of information (national affiliation in the one case, place of depiction in the other). Moreover, despite the apparent redundancy, using each type of subdivision consistently leads to greater predictability in retrieval.

The order of elements in the subject heading string is: [term]--[topical subdivision]--[nationality]--[country or state]--[city]--[chronological subdivision]. Elements not accounted for are simply left out.

Examples:    **Arms & armament--Italian--Italy--1910-1920**
             **International economic assistance--American--Greece--1940-1950**
             **Women--Employment--New York (State)--Albany--1920**

(See instructions in the appendices for further information on usage.)


### IV.  INDEXING FOR MANUAL FILES

In manual systems, whether in the form of a card catalog or a vertical file of pictures, only the first word in the subject heading string can be searched. Alternative indexing techniques may be needed to enable researchers to retrieve an image by its various aspects and to find it in close proximity to related images. These techniques might include indexing separately for topical and geographic aspects of the image and double indexing images at more than one level of a hierarchy of terms. For example, a beach scene in Santa Monica, California, could be indexed under **Santa Monica (Calif.)**; **California**; and **Beaches--California--Santa Monica**. Automated systems that feature keyword searching would require only the last heading in order to make all three concepts fully accessible.

Institutions may also find it useful to subdivide selected broad terms (BT) by their narrower terms (NT) in order to collocate related materials in browsing files, as well as to subdivide generic *TGM I* terms by proper names rather than double indexing in the manner described in Section II.D. These techniques are <u>not</u> authorized for use in MARC records, but may be used in local card catalogs and vertical files.

<u>Example</u>:     **Animals**
                    NT     Tapirs
*becomes*     Animals--Tapirs

<u>Example</u>:     **Industry**
                    NT     **Tobacco industry**
*becomes*     Industry--Tobacco industry

<u>Example</u>:     **Fraternal organizations**
*becomes*     Fraternal organizations--Knights Templar (Masonic order)

<u>Example</u>:     **Religious groups**
*becomes*     Religious groups--Buddhists

If this technique is used, it may be helpful to searchers who begin by looking under specific terms if cross-references are supplied to point them to the broader topic under which they should search.


## V.  <u>PROPOSALS FOR NEW TERMS AND CHANGES</u>

Although there is no formal program for submitting new terms and requests for changes to *TGM I*, the thesaurus editor welcomes users' comments and questions. Proposals for new terms are considered, if their application is clear and general enough to be useful in indexing collections of historical images such as those found in P&P. Inquiries should be addressed to: *TGM I* Editor, Processing Section, Prints and Photographs Division, Library of Congress, Washington, D.C. 20540-4840.


## VI.  <u>FUTURE PROSPECTS FOR *TGM I*</u>

*TGM I* has been developed using available technologies to support P&P's cataloging and reference activities. As such, it forms one component of P&P's long-term vision of promoting access to still images. That vision includes linking P&P's bibliographic records to its thesauri (and, wherever possible, electronic images). Such linkage would promote both indexing and retrieval. Ideally it would include a searching capability that takes advantage of the links provided in *TGM I* among broader, narrower and related terms. This would enable a researcher to request, for instance, all images of musical instruments, including those indexed with the term **Musical instruments** as well as those indexed with terms that are cited as narrower terms to **Musical instruments** (**Lutes**, **Pianos**, etc.). Similarly, the researcher who finds nothing relevant under the term **Navigation** could request the system to search under the RTs cited in *TGM I* in order to see if more useful material turns up.

Some institutions that may be closer to realizing such a goal have requested *TGM I* in machine-readable form.  In the near future, automated editions of *TGM I* are expected to become available through one or more of the following avenues: Internet, as a text file; Internet, with Lexico software; Cataloger's Desktop, a CD-ROM; ASCII text file on a diskette.  No work has begun, however, to convert the terms to the MARC Authority Format. Expressions of interest in a particular automated format would be appreciated.

## TGM I: SAMPLE CATALOG RECORDS AND ILLUSTRATIONS

The following catalog records and illustrations demonstrate how *TGM I* and *TGM II* terms, *TGM I* appendix subdivisions, and headings from the LC authority files are used in combination to provide subject and genre/form access to images in Library of Congress collections.  The examples (shown with MARC format field tags) represent both item-level and group-level cataloging and a variety of material: photographs, prints, political cartoons, and architectural drawings. The captions highlight application guidelines discussed in the Introduction. Wherever possible, the sample record on the left-hand page corresponds to the image in the same position on the opposite page.

**Example 1: Subdivisions (Topical and geographic)**

        :001 92-522637 PP

        :050 Item in LOT 12342-7 <P&P>

        :245 Another preparedness measure that society is taking up seriously [graphic].

        :260 1917 March 21.

        :300 1 photographic print.

        :500 National Photo Company Collection.

        :520 Mr. J. Leon Phillips holding yarn for his wife as she knits for war effort in Palm Beach, Florida.

(1)    :600 Phillips, J. Leon--Family.

        :650 Knitting--Florida--Palm Beach--1910-1920. [lctgm]

(1)    :650 World War, 1914-1918--Social aspects--Florida--Palm Beach.

(2)    :655 Portrait photographs--1910-1920. [gmgpc]

(2)    :655 Group portraits--1910-1920. [gmgpc]

(2)    :755 Photographic prints--1910-1920. [gmgpc]

        :037 LC-USZ62-106947 DLC (b&w film copy neg.)

(1) Topical subdivisions from *TGM I* appendices may be used with a personal name and the name of a war.

(2) *TGM II* terms (portrait photographs, group portraits, and photographic prints) are in 655 and 755 fields.

**Example 2: "Of" and "about" indexing.**

        :001 92-513368 PP

        :050 CD 1 - Koerner, no. 1 (A size) <P&P>

        :100 Koerner, W. H. D. (William Henry Dethlef), 1878-1938, artist.

        :245 Spring house cleaning -- why not? [graphic] / Koerner.

        :260 [19]14.

        :300 1 drawing.

        :520 Cartoon showing large broom "womans suffrage" sweeping woman, gambler, and bartender.

        :500 Title on verso of piece.

        :581 Published in: Evening journal (Wilmington, Delaware)

(1)    :650 Women's suffrage--United States--1910-1920. [lctgm]

(1)    :650 Sweeping & dusting--1910-1920. [lctgm]

(1)    :650 Prohibition--United States--1910-1920. [lctgm]

        :650 Gambling--United States--1910-1920. [lctgm]

        :655 Editorial cartoons--American--1910-1920. [gmgpc]

        :755 Drawings--1910-1920. [gmgpc]

        :037 LC-USZ62-105106 DLC (b&w film copy neg.)

See Introduction, Section II.B for more detailed discussion of "of" and "about" indexing.

(1) The image depicts sweeping, thus the cataloger assigned the subject term "Sweeping & dusting" to reflect what the image is "of." However, the cartoon is actually "about" women's suffrage and prohibition, and thus the cataloger also has included these index terms in the record.

**Example 1.**

**Example 2.**

**Example 3: Subdivisions (Nationality and geographic).**

    :001  90-712283 PP
    :050  FP 2 - Chadbourne, no. 133 (D size) <P&P>
    :100  Utagawa, Yoshikazu, fl. 1848-1863, artist.
    :245  [Picture of foreign parade in Yokohama] [graphic].
    :260  [Japan : Izumi Ichi, 1861]
    :300  1 print : woodcut, color.
    :500  Title translated from Japanese.
    :520  Military parade led by soldier carrying American flag, Japanese bystanders looking on.
    :650  Military parades & ceremonies--Japan--Yokohama-shi--1860-1870. [lctgm]
(1)    :650  Soldiers--American--Japan--Yokohama-shi--1860-1870. [lctgm]
    :755  Woodcuts--Japanese--Color--1860-1870. [gmgpc]
    :037  LC-USZC4-1627 DLC (color film copy transparency)
    :037  LC-USZ62-72 DLC (b&w film copy neg.)

(1)  This record demonstrates how both the geographic and nationality subdivisions may be used with the subject term "Soldiers."

**Example 4: Genre terms as subjects.**

    :001  91-794884 PP
    :050  Item in LOT 2220  <P&P>
    :245  How U.S. movies are made. First step in set construction is artist's sketch [graphic].
    :260  1943?
    :300  1 photographic print.
    :500  Black Star photo.
    :500  No. 1.
    :500  Part of Portrait of America, no. 120.
    :520  Man sketching shot for movie showing man gesturing toward the couch on which he hopes to sleep.
    :650  Motion picture industry--1940-1950. [lctgm]
    :650  Drawing--1940-1950. [lctgm]
(1)    :650  Set design drawings--1940-1950. [lctgm]
    :755  Photographic prints--1940-1950. [gmgpc]
    :037  LC-USZ62-95601 DLC (b&w film copy neg.)

(1) The subject heading "Set design drawings" is a *TGM II* term, usually found in the 655 and 755 fields.  However, in this record, the cataloger used it as a subject heading (650 field) because the photograph is <u>about</u> the making of set design drawings; the image is not, itself, a set design drawing.

**Example 3.**

**Example 4.**

**Example 5: Chronological subdivision.**

```
        :001  90-713269 PP
        :050  ADE - Unit 1807, no. 4 (E size) <P&P>
        :100  Waterman, Thomas Tileston, 1900- .
        :245  [Front elevation of Governor's Palace, Williamsburg] [graphic].
        :260  1930 Sept. 12.
        :300  1 drawing on tracing paper : graphite.
        :500  "Preliminary for budget estimate only," "Floor heights and window heights from Jefferson data."
        :610  Governor's Palace (Williamsburg, Va.)
(1)     :650  Official residences--Virginia--Williamsburg--1930. [lctgm]
(1)     :655  Architectural drawings--1930. [gmgpc]
(1)     :755  Graphite drawings--1930. [gmgpc]
        :037  LC-USZ62-101650 DLC (b&w film copy neg.)
        :037  LC-USZC4-2500 DLC (color film copy transparency)
        :037  LC-USZ62-107451 DLC (b&w film copy neg.)
```

(1) The date of the drawing is used rather than the date of the building because the drawing documents the appearance of an 18th century building in 1930.

**Example 6: People vs. activity headings.**

```
        :001  92-522309 PP
        :050  FP - XVII - Visscher (C.), no. 8 (B size) <P&P>
        :100  Visscher, Cornelis, 1629-1658, artist.
        :245  [Le Vendeur de mort aux rats]. Fele fugas mures ...  [graphic] / Clemendt de Jonghe excudit.
        :260  [1655]
        :300  1 print : engraving.
        :510  Le Blanc 155 (4th state)
        :520  Ratcatcher with live and dead rats, a dog and a boy.
(1)     :650  Ratcatchers--1650-1660. [lctgm]
        :650  Rats--1650-1660. [lctgm]
        :755  Engravings--1650-1660. [gmgpc]
        :037  LC-USZ62-106909 DLC (b&w film copy neg.)
```

(1) The "people" heading "Ratcatcher" is more appropriate than an activity heading "Ratcatching," because the activity of ratcatching is not shown. The image focuses on the ratcatcher and the tools of his trade.

**Example 5.**

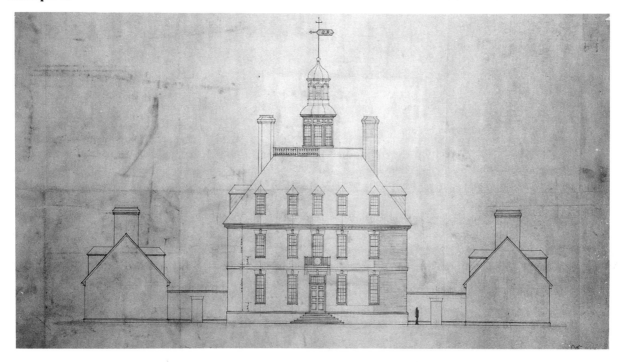

**Example 6.**

**Example 7: Group-level record.**

:001  92-510420 PP r943
:050  LOT 13024 (H) <P&P>
:100  Gentile, Charles, 1835-1893, photographer.
:245  Series of photographic views and portraits of Arizona and Arizona Indian tribes [graphic].
:260  1870-1872.
:300  1 album (41 albumen photographic prints) :  26 x 21 cm. (album).

:500  Captions and photo numbers written under each image by photographer, Charles Gentile.  Gentile's handwriting identified by Dr. Cesare Marino, Smithsonian Institution. Some captions identify sitters.
:500  Written on front cover before title: "No. 1." Written on front cover after title: "photographed by Charles Gentile and published by William H. Mardock & Co., No. 15 Amily (?) St., New York. This series to be copyrighted."
:500  Copyright office label on inside cover states that no copyright information was found in 1906 before album was transferred to the Division of Prints. No copyright information was found in the Library of Congress Copyright Office, General Index, 1870-1897.
:500  Additional information about the album is available in the Collections File, Prints & Photographs Division, Library of Congress. Caption list located with album.

:520 SUBJECT: Images of Mohave, Yuma, Maricopa, Yavapai, Pima, and Apache people in Arizona and one image of California Native Americans. Includes portraits of Pretty Bird, a Mohave "captain"; two Tonto Apache girls; Apache and Yavapai prisoners in shackles at Camp Verde; Juana, a Pima woman with baskets and pottery; an Apache warrior with a Mexican captive; Juan Chivaria, a Maricopa leader and his family; and others. Also includes images of the "first Indian school in Arizona" with students and Euro-American couple in front of building; San Xavier del Bac mission; Tumacacori mission; the commanding officers' quarters at Camp Colorado; Camp Apache in the White Mountains; Hohokam ruins at Casa Grande; Maricopa Wells; a posed image of US soldiers "repulsing" an attack of Apaches; and bearded man, possibly Gentile, posed in rocks with wagon.
:541  Transfer, Copyright Office, 1906 July 14.

:610  Mission San Xavier del Bac (Tucson, Ariz.).
:650  Mexicans--Arizona--1870-1880.
(1)     :650  Indians of North America--Clothing & dress--California--1870-1880.
(1)     :650  Indians of North America--Clothing & dress--Arizona--1870-1880.
:650  Indians of North America--Capture & imprisonment--Arizona--1870-1880.
:650  Indians of North America--Arts & crafts--Arizona--1870-1880.
:650  Indians of North America--Children--Arizona--1870-1880.
:650  Indians of North America--Education--Arizona--1870-1880.
:650  Indians of North America--Women--Arizona--1870-1880.
:650  Pima Indians--1870-1880.
:650  Yavapai Indians--1870-1880.
:650  Mohave Indians--1870-1880.
:650  Apache Indians--1870-1880.
:650  Yuma Indians--1870-1880.
:650  Maricopa Indians--1870-1880.
(2)     :650  Missions--Arizona--1870-1880. [lctgm]
:650  Tribal chiefs--United States--1870-1880. [lctgm]
(2)     :650  Prisoners--Arizona--1870-1880. [lctgm]
:650  Officers' quarters--Arizona--1870-1880. [lctgm]
:650  Indian reservations--Arizona--1870-1880. [lctgm]

|       | :650 | Military facilities--Arizona--1870-1880. [lctgm] |
| (2)   | :650 | Schools--Arizona--1870-1880. [lctgm] |
|       | :650 | Ruins--Arizona--1870-1880. [lctgm] |
|       | :651 | Tumacacori National Monument (Ariz.)--1870-1880. |
|       | :651 | Maricopa Wells (Ariz.)--1870-1880. |
|       | :655 | Portrait photographs--1870-1880. [gmgpc] |
|       | :655 | Group portraits--1870-1880. [gmgpc] |
|       | :655 | Photograph albums--1870-1880. [gmgpc] |
|       | :755 | Albumen prints--1870-1880. [gmgpc] |

This is a group-level catalog record for 41 images. Multiple geographical subdivisions and subjects are often necessary when cataloging more than one item in the same record.

(1) Multiple geographical subdivisions (Arizona and California).

(2) Multiple subjects (missions, schools, prisoners).

# TGM I: SUBJECT TERMS

3-legged racing
USE Three-legged racing
**4-H clubs**
--[country or state]--[city]
PN   Includes activities and structures.
CN   Double index under ORGANIZATIONS'
FACILITIES (or NTs) for images that focus
on facilities.
UF   Four-H clubs
BT   Clubs
Youth organizations
RT   Children
Farmers' groups
**A la poupée prints**
CN   TGM II term.
UF   Poupée prints
**A trois crayons drawings**
CN   TGM II term.
UF   Three chalk drawings
Trois crayons drawings
Äac prints
USE Photochrom prints
Abaca
USE Manila hemp
**Abandoned buildings**
--[country or state]--[city]
PN   For vacant, possibly delapidated,
buildings. Search under RUINS for the
remains of structures.
CN   Used in a note under
ARCHAEOLOGICAL SITES and RUINS.
UF   Deserted buildings
Vacant buildings
BT   Buildings
RT   Building deterioration
Ghost towns
Ruins
**Abandoned children**
--[country or state]--[city]
UF   Deserted children
Exposed children
BT   Children
RT   Abused children
Orphans
Abandoned towns
USE Ghost towns
**Abbeys**
--[country or state]--[city]
BT   Religious facilities
RT   Convents
Monasteries
Abdication
CN   Used only as a subdivision with names of
persons (Appendix B).
Abductions
USE Kidnappings
**Ablution fountains**
--[country or state]--[city]
UF   Fountains, Ablution
BT   Religious architectural elements
RT   Bathing
Fountains

**Ablution fountains (cont.)**
Rites & ceremonies
Abnormalities
USE Birth defects
Human curiosities
**Abolition movement**
--[country or state]--[city]
PN   For the subject of the abolition of slavery
in general.
UF   Anti-slavery movement
Free soil movement
BT   Protest movements
RT   Abolitionists
Civil rights
Slavery
Underground railroad system
**Abolitionists**
PN   Search under ABOLITION MOVEMENT
for the subject of abolitionism in general and
the activities of abolitionists.
BT   People associated with politics &
government
RT   Abolition movement
Activists
Aborigines
USE Indigenous peoples
**Abortions**
--[country or state]--[city]
UF   Terminations of pregnancy
RT   Birth control
Health care
Pregnancy
Abrasive wheels
USE Grinding wheels
Absence from work
USE Absenteeism (Labor)
**Absenteeism (Labor)**
--[country or state]--[city]
UF   Absence from work
Work, Absence from
RT   Employment
Hours of labor
Abstinence
USE Temperance
**Abstract drawings**
CN   TGM II term.
**Abstract paintings**
CN   TGM II term.
**Abstract photographs**
CN   TGM II term.
**Abstract prints**
CN   TGM II term.
**Abstract works**
CN   TGM II term.
**Abused children**
--[country or state]--[city]
UF   Battered children
Child abuse victims
Maltreated persons
Victims of abuse
BT   Children
Victims

---

BT  Broader term                                          RT  Related term                                        PN  Public Note
NT  Narrower term                                        UF  Used for                                             +   Term has NTs
HN  History Note                                         CN  Catalogers Note                                    --[ ] May subdivide

**Abused children (cont.)**
  RT  Abandoned children
       Crimes
       Violence
**Abused women**
       --[country or state]--[city]
  UF  Battered women
       Maltreated persons
       Victims of abuse
       Wife abuse victims
  BT  Victims
       Women
  RT  Crimes
       Violence
       Women's shelters
Abused women's shelters
  USE Women's shelters
Academic processions
  USE Graduation ceremonies
**Acanthi**
       --[country or state]--[city]
  PN  Sculptured ornamentations (as in a
       Corinthian capital) representing or suggesting
       the leaves of the acanthus.
  BT  Architectural decorations & ornaments
  RT  Corinthian order
       Leaves
Accelerators, Particle
  USE Particle accelerators
Accessories
  USE Clothing & dress
**Accidents**
       --[country or state]--[city]
  PN  Includes the event and any resulting
       damage.
  UF  Collisions
       Damage to property
       Property damage
       Wrecks
  BT  Events
  NT  Aircraft accidents
       Hunting accidents
       Marine accidents +
       Mine accidents
       Railroad accidents +
       Traffic accidents
  RT  Clumsiness
       Danger
       Disasters
       Electrocutions
       Insurance
       Rescue work
       Safety
       Wounds & injuries
**Accordions**
  PN  Includes the activity of playing
       accordions.
  BT  Keyboard instruments
       Wind instruments
Accusing
  USE Blaming
Aces (Fighter pilots)

Aces (Fighter pilots) (cont.)
  USE Fighter pilots
**Acetate negatives**
  CN  TGM II term.
  UF  Cellulose acetate negatives
       Cellulose diacetate negatives
       Cellulose triacetate negatives
       Diacetate negatives
       Triacetate negatives
Aches
  USE Pain
**Acorn decorations**
       --[country or state]--[city]
  BT  Architectural decorations & ornaments
  RT  Nuts
**Acoustical engineering**
       --[country or state]--[city]
  PN  For the subject of acoustical engineering in
       general and the activities of acoustical
       engineers.
  BT  Engineering
Acqueducts
  USE Aqueducts
Acquisition of territory
  USE Annexations
**Acrobatics**
       --[country or state]--[city]
  BT  Entertainment
  RT  Acrobats
       Aerialists
       Circus performers
       Circuses & shows
       Gymnastics
**Acrobats**
  BT  People associated with entertainment &
       sports
  RT  Acrobatics
       Aerialists
       Circus performers
**Acrylic paintings**
  CN  TGM II term.
Action comics
  USE Adventure comics
**Action & adventure dramas**
  PN  For images representing dramatic
       productions or scenes (theatrical, film, radio,
       or television) which consist of swordplay,
       fighting, or other forms of combat.  Can also
       include activities that involve danger and
       risk.
  RT  Campaigns & battles
       Danger
       Motion pictures
       Radio broadcasting
       Television broadcasting
       Theatrical productions
**Actions & defenses**
       --[country or state]--[city]
  UF  Defense (Law)
       Lawsuits
       Litigation
       Suits (Law)

---

BT Broader term      RT Related term      PN Public Note
NT Narrower term      UF Used for      + Term has NTs
HN History Note      CN Catalogers Note      --[ ] May subdivide

**Actions & defenses (cont.)**
- BT  Law & legal affairs
- RT  Judicial proceedings

**Activists**
- --[nationality]--[country or state]--[city]
- UF  Demonstrators
  - Militants
  - Political activists
  - Protesters
- BT  People associated with politics & government
- NT  Counterrevolutionaries
  - Draft resisters
  - Pickets
  - Rebels
  - Revolutionaries
  - Suffragists
- RT  Abolitionists
  - Civil disobedience
  - Civil rights leaders
  - Demonstrations
  - Dissenters
  - Guerrillas
  - Lobbying
  - Pacifists
  - Petitions
  - Political organizations
  - Political participation
  - Political prisoners
  - Protest movements
  - Rebellions
  - Terrorism

**Actors**
- PN  For male actors alone or groups of male and female actors. Search also under subdivision --PERFORMANCES used with names of persons (Appendix B).
- CN  Used in a note under COSTUMES and ACTRESSES.
- UF  Movie stars
- BT  Entertainers
- RT  Actresses
  - Auditions
  - Men
  - Motion picture industry
  - Opera singers
  - Television industry
  - Theatrical productions

**Actresses**
- PN  For female actresses. For groups of males and females use ACTORS. Search also under the subdivision --PERFORMANCES used with names of persons (Appendix B).
- CN  Used in a note under COSTUMES and ACTORS.
- UF  Movie stars
- BT  Entertainers
  - Women
- RT  Actors
  - Auditions
  - Motion picture industry
  - Opera singers

**Actresses (cont.)**
- Television industry
- Theatrical productions

**Acupuncture**
- --[country or state]--[city]
- BT  Health care
- NT  Acupuncture anesthesia
- RT  Pain

**Acupuncture anesthesia**
- BT  Acupuncture
  - Anesthesia

**Adages**
- USE Proverbs

**Adaptive reuse**
- USE Recycled structures

**Addiction to alcohol**
- USE Alcoholism

**Addiction to drugs**
- USE Drug abuse

**Addiction to tobacco**
- USE Tobacco habit

**Adding machine industry**
- USE Calculator industry

**Adding machines**
- USE Calculators

**Addresses**
- USE Public speaking

**Adherence**
- USE Allegiance

**Adhesives**
- USE Glue

**Adieus**
- USE Farewells

**Adiposity**
- USE Obesity

**Administrative agencies**
- --[country or state]--[city]
- UF  Agencies, Administrative
  - Executive departments
  - Federal agencies
  - Government agencies
  - Regulatory agencies
- BT  Organizations
- RT  Civil service

**Admirals**
- --[nationality]--[country or state]--[city]
- BT  Military officers
- RT  Ship captains

**Adobe buildings**
- --[country or state]--[city]
- BT  Buildings distinguished by material
- RT  Pueblos

**Adolescent pregnancy**
- USE Teenage pregnancy

**Adolescents**
- USE Children

**Adoration**
- PN  Profound veneration, devotion, or love whether in a spiritual or non-spiritual context.
- UF  Worship
- BT  Mental states

BT  Broader term                     RT  Related term                     PN  Public Note
NT  Narrower term                    UF  Used for                         +  Term has NTs
HN  History Note                     CN  Catalogers Note                  --[ ]  May subdivide

**Adoration (cont.)**
RT Rites & ceremonies
**Adult education**
--[country or state]--[city]
PN Includes activities and structures.
CN Double index under EDUCATIONAL
FACILITIES (or NTs) for images that focus
on facilities.
BT Education
Adulterations
USE Food adulteration & inspection
**Adultery**
--[country or state]--[city]
UF Extra-marital sex
Infidelity, Marital
Marital infidelity
BT Interpersonal relations
RT Lust
Marriage
Adults & children
USE Children & adults
**Adventure comics**
CN TGM II term.
UF Action comics
**Advertisements**
--[country or state]--[city]
PN For objects used to advertise. Search
under ADVERTISING for the general activity
of calling attention to something, usually by
announcement.
CN Used in a note under ADVERTISING.
TGM II term.
NT Sandwich boards
RT Advertising
Cigar store Indians
Logos
Publicity
Signs
Slogans
Window displays
**Advertising**
--[country or state]--[city]
PN For the general activity of advertising
(calling attention to something, usually by
announcement). Search under
ADVERTISEMENTS for objects used to
advertise.
CN Used in a note under
ADVERTISEMENTS.
BT Communication
NT False advertising
RT Advertisements
Advertising agencies
Logos
Publicity
**Advertising agencies**
--[country or state]--[city]
PN Includes activities and structures.
BT Service industry facilities
RT Advertising
**Advertising cards**
CN TGM II term.

**Advertising cards (cont.)**
UF Insert cards
Tradecards
Trading cards
**Advertising mail**
CN TGM II term.
UF Direct-mail advertising
Junk mail
**Aerial bombings**
--[country or state]--[city]
PN For images of military bombardment by
bombs dropped from the air. Search under
BOMBARDMENT for sustained military
attacks on cities, military positions, and other
places with bombs, shells, rockets, or other
explosive missiles. Search under BOMBINGS
for the use of explosive devices for the
purposes of political terrorism, protest, etc.
Search under ORDNANCE TESTING for
test bombs.
CN Used in a note under AIR WARFARE,
BOMBINGS, and BOMBARDMENT.
BT Air warfare
RT Air raid drills
Air raid shelters
Bombardment
Bombings
War blackouts
Aerial dusting in agriculture
USE Crop dusting
Aerial passenger lift bridges
USE Transporter bridges
**Aerial photographs**
CN TGM II term.
Aerial spraying in agriculture
USE Crop dusting
Aerial tankers
USE Airtankers
**Aerial tramways**
--[country or state]--[city]
UF Suspended railroads
Tramways
BT Cable railroads
**Aerial views**
CN TGM II term.
UF Air views
Balloon views
Views, Aerial
Aerial warfare
USE Air warfare
**Aerialists**
UF High wire performers
Tightrope performers
Trapeze artists
BT Entertainers
RT Acrobatics
Acrobats
Circus performers
Aerobatics
USE Stunt flying
Aeronautical accidents
USE Aircraft accidents

BT Broader term
NT Narrower term
HN History Note

RT Related term
UF Used for
CN Catalogers Note

PN Public Note
+ Term has NTs
--[ ] May subdivide

**Aeronautics**

--[country or state]--[city]

PN  Science, art, or practice of aircraft operation and/or aerial navigation.

UF  Aviation

RT  Air shows
Air traffic control
Aircraft
Aviation mechanics (Science)
Flight crews
Flight testing
Flight training
Flights around the world
Navigation
Space flight
Spin (Aerodynamics)
Stunt flying
Wind tunnels

Aerostats
  USE Airships

Affection
  USE Friendship

Affective states
  USE Mental states

African Americans
  USE Afro-Americans

**Afro-Americans**

--[country or state]--[city]

PN  For permanent residents of the United States of black African descent, including black slaves in the U.S. Search under BLACKS for blacks who are not permanent residents of the U.S., including citizens of other countries who temporarily reside in the U.S., such as students from abroad.

CN  Although it is a proper name, this Library of Congress Subject Headings term is included in TGM I for ready reference. As appropriate, subdivide by subdivisions used with names of ethnic, racial, and regional groups, and with classes of persons (Appendix A).

UF  African Americans
Black Americans
Negroes

Afterlife
  USE Heaven

**Agave plantations**

--[country or state]--[city]

PN  Includes activities and structures.

CN  As appropriate, double index under HARVESTING.

BT  Plantations

RT  Agaves

**Agaves**

--[country or state]--[city]

UF  Century plants
Magueys
Sisal plants

BT  Plants

RT  Agave plantations
Henequen

**Age & employment**

RT  Aged persons
Employment
Retirements
Youth

**Aged persons**

--[country or state]--[city]

PN  This heading may be further subdivided by the subdivisions used for classes of persons (Appendix A).

CN  As appropriate, subdivide by subdivisions used for classes of persons (Appendix A).

UF  Elderly persons
Older persons
Senior citizens

BT  People

RT  Age & employment
Gerontology
Grandparents
Human life cycle
Longevity
Medicare
Middle age
Pensions
Rejuvenation
Rest homes
Retirements

Agencies
  USE Organizations

Agencies, Administrative
  USE Administrative agencies

Agfacolor transparencies
  USE Dye coupler transparencies

Agony
  USE Distress
    Pain

Agreements
  USE Contracts
    Treaties

Agricultural assistance, Economic
  USE Farm relief

Agricultural assistance, International
  USE International agricultural assistance

Agricultural buildings
  USE Agricultural facilities

Agricultural equipment
  USE Agricultural machinery & implements

**Agricultural exhibits**

--[country or state]--[city]

PN  For displays of agricultural products and technology in the context of an exhibition.

BT  Exhibitions

RT  Agriculture
Fairs
Farm produce

**Agricultural facilities**

--[country or state]--[city]

HN  Changed 1/1993 from AGRICULTURAL BUILDINGS.

UF  Agricultural buildings
Farm buildings

BT  Facilities

BT  Broader term
NT  Narrower term
HN  History Note

RT  Related term
UF  Used for
CN  Catalogers Note

PN  Public Note
+  Term has NTs
--[ ]  May subdivide

Agricultural facilities (cont.)
  NT  Animal housing +
      Barns
      Farms +
      Food storage buildings +
      Horticultural buildings +
      Ranches +
  RT  Agriculture
Agricultural groups
  USE Farmers' groups
Agricultural laborers
      --[nationality]--[country or state]--[city]
  UF  Farm workers
      Farmworkers
      Field laborers
  BT  Laborers
  NT  Cotton pickers
      Migrant agricultural laborers
  RT  Agricultural laborers' unions
      Farmers
      Peasants
Agricultural laborers' unions
      --[country or state]--[city]
  BT  Labor unions
  RT  Agricultural laborers
Agricultural machinery & implements
  HN  Changed 11/1992; formerly two separate
      terms: AGRICULTURAL MACHINERY and
      AGRICULTURAL EQUIPMENT.
  UF  Agricultural equipment
      Farm equipment
      Farm machinery
  NT  Harvesting machinery +
      Pitchforks
      Plows
      Scythes
  RT  Equipment
      Machinery
      Tractors
Agricultural price supports
      --[country or state]
  UF  Farm price supports
  BT  Economic policy
  RT  Price regulation
Agricultural productivity
      --[country or state]--[city]
  UF  Efficiency, Agricultural
      Productivity, Agricultural
  BT  Economic & social conditions
  RT  Agriculture
      Farm produce
      Farm relief
      International agricultural assistance
Agricultural products
  USE Farm produce
Agricultural societies
  USE Farmers' groups
Agriculture
      --[country or state]--[city]
  PN  For the production of plants and animals
      for purposes of human consumption in some
      form.

Agriculture (cont.)
  NT  Farming +
      Horticulture +
  RT  Agricultural exhibits
      Agricultural facilities
      Agricultural productivity
      Biological pest control
      Farm produce
      Food industry
      Forestry
      Irrigation
      Livestock
Ague
  USE Malaria
Aid (Relief)
  USE Assistance
Ailments
  USE Diseases
Air
  CN  For allegorical images of air.
  BT  Natural phenomena
Air aces
  USE Fighter pilots
Air bases
      --[nationality]--[country or state]--[city]
  PN  Bases of operations for military aircraft.
  UF  Air stations, Military
  BT  Military facilities
  RT  Air forces
      Airports
      Military air pilots
      Military air shows
Air compressors
  UF  Compressors, Air
  BT  Machinery
Air conditioners
      --[country or state]--[city]
  BT  Appliances
  RT  Air conditioning industry
      HVAC systems
Air conditioning industry
      --[country or state]--[city]
  CN  Double index under INDUSTRIAL
      FACILITIES (or NTs) for images that focus
      on facilities.
  BT  Heating & ventilation industry
  RT  Air conditioners
Air conditioning, heating & ventilating drawings
  USE HVAC drawings
Air crews
  USE Flight crews
Air forces
      --[nationality]--[country or state]--[city]
  BT  Military organizations
  RT  Air bases
Air line industry
  USE Airline industry
Air lines
  USE Airline industry
Air mail service
      --[country or state]--[city]
  UF  Airmail service

---

BT  Broader term              RT  Related term              PN  Public Note
NT  Narrower term             UF  Used for                  +   Term has NTs
HN  History Note              CN  Catalogers Note           --[ ]  May subdivide

**Air mail service (cont.)**
  BT  Postal service
  RT  Airplanes
Air operations
  CN  Used only as a subdivision with names of
       wars (Appendix C).
**Air pilots**
       --[nationality]--[country or state]--[city]
  UF  Airline pilots
       Aviators
       Pilots (Aeronautics)
  BT  People associated with transportation
  NT  Balloonists
       Military air pilots +
  RT  Aircraft
       Airline industry strikes
       Astronauts
       Fighter pilots
       Flight crews
**Air pollution**
       --[country or state]--[city]
  BT  Air quality
       Pollution
**Air pumps**
  BT  Pumps
**Air quality**
       --[country or state]--[city]
  NT  Air pollution
  RT  Ecology
       Pollution
**Air raid drills**
       --[country or state]--[city]
  BT  Civil defense
  RT  Aerial bombings
       Air raid shelters
**Air raid shelters**
       --[country or state]--[city]
  UF  Bomb shelters
  BT  Shelters
  RT  Aerial bombings
       Air raid drills
       Bombproof construction
       Civil defense
**Air refueling**
Air rescue service
  USE Search & rescue operations
Air ships
  USE Airships
**Air shows**
       --[country or state]--[city]
  UF  Airshows
  BT  Events
  NT  Military air shows
  RT  Aeronautics
       Aircraft
Air stations, Military
  USE Air bases
Air tattoos
  USE Military air shows
**Air traffic control**
       --[country or state]--[city]
  RT  Aeronautics

**Air traffic control (cont.)**
       Aircraft accidents
       Navigation
       Safety
**Air travel**
  BT  Travel
  RT  Aircraft
       Airports
Air views
  USE Aerial views
**Air warfare**
       --[country or state]--[city]
  PN  Includes all aspects of aerial combat.
       Search under AERIAL BOMBINGS for
       images that focus on military bombardment
       by bombs dropped from the air.  Search also
       under the subdivision --AIR OPERATIONS
       used with names of wars (Appendix C).
  CN  Prefer the subdivision.
  UF  Aerial warfare
  BT  Military art & science
  NT  Aerial bombings
  RT  Aircraft accidents
       Aircraft carriers
       Bombers
       Campaigns & battles
       Fighter pilots
       Fighter planes
**Airbrush works**
  CN  TGM II term.
**Aircraft**
       --[nationality]--[country or state]--[city]
  BT  Vehicles
  NT  Airplanes +
       Airships
       Autogiros
       Balloons (Aircraft) +
       Helicopters
  RT  Aeronautics
       Air pilots
       Air shows
       Air travel
       Aircraft accidents
       Aircraft carriers
       Airports
       Flight crews
       Flight testing
       Hangars
       Kites
       Mooring
       Navigation
       Rockets
       Unidentified flying objects
**Aircraft accidents**
       --[country or state]--[city]
  HN  Changed 11/1993 from
       AERONAUTICAL ACCIDENTS.
  UF  Aeronautical accidents
       Airplane crashes
  BT  Accidents
  RT  Air traffic control
       Air warfare

---

BT  Broader term
NT  Narrower term
HN  History Note

RT  Related term
UF  Used for
CN  Catalogers Note

PN  Public Note
+  Term has NTs
--[ ]  May subdivide

**Aircraft accidents (cont.)**
  Aircraft
**Aircraft carriers**
      --[nationality]--[country or state]--[city]
  UF  Airplane carriers
      Carriers (Warships)
      Carriers, Aircraft
  BT  Warships
  RT  Air warfare
      Aircraft
Aircraft crews
  USE Flight crews
Aircraft testing
  USE Flight testing
**Airline industry**
  PN  Includes activities and structures.
  CN  Double index under TRANSPORTATION
      FACILITIES (or NTs) for images that focus
      on facilities.
  UF  Air line industry
      Air lines
      Aviation industry
  BT  Business enterprises
  RT  Airplanes
**Airline industry strikes**
      --[country or state]--[city]
  UF  Pilots' strikes
  BT  Strikes
  RT  Air pilots
Airline pilots
  USE Air pilots
Airmail service
  USE Air mail service
Airplane carriers
  USE Aircraft carriers
Airplane crashes
  USE Aircraft accidents
**Airplane engines**
  UF  Airplane motors
  BT  Engines
  RT  Airplane equipment
**Airplane equipment**
  UF  Airplane rigging
  BT  Equipment
  NT  Airplane propellers
      Airplane wings
  RT  Airplane engines
      Airplanes
Airplane hangars
  USE Hangars
**Airplane industry**
      --[country or state]--[city]
  PN  Includes activities and structures.
  CN  Double index under INDUSTRIAL
      FACILITIES (or NTs) for images that focus
      on facilities.
  BT  Transportation industry
  RT  Airplanes
Airplane motors
  USE Airplane engines
**Airplane propellers**
  UF  Propellers, Airplane

**Airplane propellers (cont.)**
  BT  Airplane equipment
**Airplane racing**
      --[country or state]--[city]
  BT  Racing
  RT  Airplanes
Airplane rigging
  USE Airplane equipment
**Airplane wings**
  UF  Wings, Airplane
  BT  Airplane equipment
**Airplanes**
      --[nationality]--[country or state]--[city]
  PN  Includes commercial, private, and military
      airplanes.
  BT  Aircraft
  NT  Airtankers
      Biplanes
      Bombers
      Convertiplanes
      Fighter planes
      Gliders
      Seaplanes
      Transport planes
  RT  Air mail service
      Airline industry
      Airplane equipment
      Airplane industry
      Airplane racing
      Autogiros
      Crop dusting
      Helicopters
      Model airplanes
      Parachuting
      Stunt flying
**Airports**
      --[country or state]--[city]
  BT  Transportation facilities
  RT  Air bases
      Air travel
      Aircraft
      Hangars
      Runways (Aeronautics)
**Airships**
      --[nationality]--[country or state]--[city]
  PN  Lighter-than-air aircraft having a
      propelling system and a means for controlling
      the direction of motion.
  UF  Aerostats
      Air ships
      Blimps
      Dirigibles
      Zeppelins
  BT  Aircraft
  RT  Balloons (Aircraft)
Airshows
  USE Air shows
**Airtankers**
      --[nationality]--[country or state]--[city]
  UF  Aerial tankers
      Tanker aircraft
  BT  Airplanes

---

BT Broader term
NT Narrower term
HN History Note

RT Related term
UF Used for
CN Catalogers Note

PN Public Note
+ Term has NTs
--[ ] May subdivide

**Airtankers (cont.)**
RT  Air refueling
Air-sea rescues
USE Search & rescue operations
**Air-supported structures**
--[country or state]--[city]
UF  Inflatable structures
BT  Buildings
RT  Portable buildings
Aisles
USE Passageways
**Alarm clocks**
BT  Clocks & watches
RT  Sleeping
Albertypes
USE Collotypes
**Albinos**
CN  As appropriate, double index under
HUMAN CURIOSITIES.
RT  Birth defects
Human curiosities
**Album cards**
CN  TGM II term.
**Album covers**
CN  TGM II term.
UF  Covers, Album
Covers, Record
Jackets, Record
Record covers
Record jackets
Sleeves, Record
Albumen photoprints
USE Albumen prints
**Albumen prints**
CN  TGM II term.
UF  Albumen photoprints
**Albumen transparencies**
CN  TGM II term.
UF  Hyalotypes
**Albums**
CN  TGM II term.
**Alchemy**
--[country or state]--[city]
PN  For the subject of alchemy in general and
the activities of alchemists.
UF  Transmutation of metals
RT  Chemistry
Gold
Magic
Alcohol abuse
USE Alcoholism
Alcoholic beverage industry
USE Brewing industry
Distilling industries
Wine industry
**Alcoholic beverages**
UF  Liquor
BT  Beverages
NT  Beer
Gin
Whiskey
Wine +

**Alcoholic beverages (cont.)**
RT  Bars
Blue laws
Drunk driving
Hangovers
Intoxication
Liquor stores
Prohibition
**Alcoholism**
--[country or state]--[city]
PN  Search under INTOXICATION for
images of drunk persons.
UF  Addiction to alcohol
Alcohol abuse
Dipsomania
Drinking problem
Liquor problem
BT  Diseases
Drug abuse
RT  Intoxication
Temperance
**Alcoves**
PN  A small recessed section of a room.
UF  Nooks
Recesses (Architecture)
BT  Interiors
Aldermen
USE City council members
**ALF**
USE Extraterrestrial life
**Alfalfa**
--[country or state]--[city]
BT  Plants
**Alidades**
PN  Telescopic sighting devices used as part of
a ship's navigational equipment for taking
bearings.
BT  Telescopes
RT  Navigation
**Alien laborers**
--[nationality]--[country or state]--[city]
PN  For laborers who seek work outside their
own country. Search under MIGRANT
LABORERS for those who regularly migrate
within the same country.
CN  Used in a note under MIGRANT
LABORERS.
UF  Foreign workers
BT  Aliens
Laborers
Alien life forms
USE Extraterrestrial life
**Aliens**
--[nationality]--[country or state]--[city]
PN  For persons who are not citizens of the
country in which they reside.
UF  Enemy aliens
Foreigners
BT  People
NT  Alien laborers
Illegal aliens
RT  Deportations

---

BT  Broader term
NT  Narrower term
HN  History Note

RT  Related term
UF  Used for
CN  Catalogers Note

PN  Public Note
+  Term has NTs
--[ ] May subdivide

**Aliens (cont.)**
   Emigration & immigration
   Exiles
   Immigrants
   Minorities
   Refugees
   Repatriation
Aliens (Space)
 USE Extraterrestrial life
**Allegiance**
   --[country or state]--[city]
 PN Devotion or loyalty to a cause, group, or
   person.
 UF Adherence
   Fidelity
   Loyalty, Political
   Political loyalty
 BT Mental states
 RT Patriotism
   Pledges of allegiance
   Solidarity
**Allegorical drawings**
 CN TGM II term.
**Allegorical paintings**
 CN TGM II term.
**Allegorical photographs**
 CN TGM II term.
**Allegorical prints**
 CN TGM II term.
**Allegories**
 CN TGM II term.
Allergic diseases
 USE Allergies
**Allergies**
   --[country or state]--[city]
 UF Allergic diseases
 RT Diseases
**Alleys**
   --[country or state]--[city]
 PN Narrow lanes between buildings,
   especially through the middle of city blocks,
   giving access to the rear of buildings; also,
   for those which are residential cul-de-sacs.
 BT Streets
 RT Backyards
Alleys, Bowling
 USE Bowling alleys
Alliances
 USE Treaties
Alliances, Temporary
 USE Coalition (Social sciences)
Allies, War
 USE War allies
**Alligator hunting**
   --[country or state]
 BT Hunting
 RT Alligators
**Alligators**
   --[country or state]--[city]
 BT Reptiles
 RT Alligator hunting
Allowances, Children's

Allowances, Children's (cont.)
 USE Children's allowances
**Allusions**
 CN TGM II term.
Alms
 USE Charity
Almsgiving
 USE Charity
**Almshouses**
   --[country or state]--[city]
 PN Privately financed homes for the poor.
   Includes activities and structures.
 UF Poor farms
   Poorhouses
   Workhouses (Poorhouses)
 BT Welfare facilities
 RT Poor persons
**Alpacas**
   --[country or state]
 BT Animals
**Alphabets (Writing systems)**
 UF Letters of the alphabet
 BT Writing systems
 NT Initials
   Phonetic alphabets
**Altarpieces**
   --[country or state]--[city]
 UF Predellas
   Reredos
   Retables
 BT Religious architectural elements
 RT Altars
   Art
   Churches
**Altars**
   --[country or state]--[city]
 BT Religious architectural elements
 RT Altarpieces
   Churches
   Pulpits
Altruists
 USE Philanthropists
Aluminium
 USE Aluminum
**Aluminum**
 UF Aluminium
 BT Metals
 RT Aluminum industry
**Aluminum industry**
   --[country or state]--[city]
 PN Includes activities and structures.
 CN Double index under INDUSTRIAL
   FACILITIES (or NTs) for images that focus
   on facilities.
 BT Metallurgical industry
 RT Aluminum
**Alumni & alumnae**
   --[country or state]--[city]
 UF Alumnus
   Graduates
 BT People associated with education &
   communication

---

BT Broader term    RT Related term    PN Public Note
NT Narrower term    UF Used for     + Term has NTs
HN History Note     CN Catalogers Note   --[ ] May subdivide

**Alumni & alumnae (cont.)**
RT   Students
     Universities & colleges
**Alumnus**
USE Alumni & alumnae
**Amateur radio**
USE Children & radio
     Radio broadcasting
**Amateur works**
CN   TGM II term.
**Ambassadors**
     --[nationality]--[country or state]--[city]
CN   Subdivide by nationality of country
     ambassador represents.
BT   Diplomats
**Ambrotypes**
CN   TGM II term.
UF   Cased photographs
     Collodion positive photographs
**Ambulances**
     --[nationality]--[country or state]--[city]
BT   Vehicles
RT   Emergency medical services
     Health care facilities
     Mobile health units
**Amendments, Constitutional**
USE Constitutional amendments
**Ammunition**
NT   Bullets
     Cannon balls
RT   Ammunition dumps
     Arms & armament
     Bullet holes
     Caissons (Vehicles)
     Magazines (Military buildings)
**Ammunition depots**
USE Magazines (Military buildings)
**Ammunition dumps**
     --[country or state]--[city]
RT   Ammunition
     Magazines (Military buildings)
**Ammunition magazines**
USE Magazines (Military buildings)
**Amnesty**
     --[country]
CN   Subdivide by country granting amnesty.
UF   Political amnesty
BT   Law & legal affairs
**Amphibian tractors**
USE Tracked landing vehicles
**Amphibians**
     --[country or state]
BT   Animals
NT   Frogs
     Toads
RT   Aquatic animals
**Amphibious automobiles**
USE Amphibious vehicles
**Amphibious operations**
CN   Used only as a subdivision with names of
     wars (Appendix C).
**Amphibious vehicles**

**Amphibious vehicles (cont.)**
     --[nationality]--[country or state]--[city]
UF   Amphibious automobiles
     Motor vehicles, Amphibious
BT   Vehicles
NT   Tracked landing vehicles
RT   Landing craft
     Military vehicles
**Amphitheaters**
     --[country or state]--[city]
PN   For natural or man-made oval,
     semicircular, or circular areas formed by
     slopes or rising tiers of seats around an open
     space used for various public events. Search
     under AUDITORIUMS for facilities used for
     public gatherings. Search under STADIUMS
     for large, often unroofed structures in which
     athletic events are held.
CN   Used in a note under AUDITORIUMS.
BT   Open-air theaters
RT   Stadiums
**Amputation**
USE Surgery
**Amputees**
     --[country or state]--[city]
BT   Handicapped persons
RT   Artificial limbs
     Dismemberment
**Amulets**
UF   Charms
     Fetishes
BT   Magical devices
RT   Jewelry
     Magic
     Preventive medicine
     Talismans
     Witchcraft
**Amusement parks**
     --[country or state]--[city]
PN   Includes activities and structures.
UF   Carnivals (Circus)
     Parks, Amusement
     Side shows
BT   Sports & recreation facilities
RT   Amusement piers
     Amusement rides
     Circuses & shows
     Fairs
     Human curiosities
     Miniature railroads
**Amusement piers**
     --[country or state]--[city]
UF   Recreation piers
BT   Sports & recreation facilities
RT   Amusement parks
     Amusement rides
     Boardwalks
     Piers & wharves
**Amusement rides**
     --[country or state]--[city]
UF   Rides, Amusement
BT   Sports & recreation facilities

---

BT Broader term                    RT Related term                 PN Public Note
NT Narrower term                   UF Used for                     + Term has NTs
HN History Note                    CN Catalogers Note              --[ ] May subdivide

**Amusement rides (cont.)**
- NT Ferris wheels
  - Merry-go-rounds
  - Roller coasters
- RT Amusement parks
  - Amusement piers
  - Fairs
  - Water slides

**Anaglyphs**
- CN TGM II term.

Analysis of food
- USE Food adulteration & inspection

**Anamorphic images**
- CN TGM II term.

**Anarchism**
- --[country or state]--[city]
- PN For the subject of anarchism in general.
- UF Anarchy
- BT Economic & political systems
- RT Anarchists
  - Government regulation
  - Libertarianism

**Anarchists**
- PN Search under ANARCHISM for the subject of anarchism in general and the activities of anarchists.
- BT People associated with politics & government
- RT Anarchism

Anarchy
- USE Anarchism

**Anatomy**
- --[country or state]--[city]
- PN For the subject of anatomy in general and the activities of anatomists.
- BT Biology

Ancestors
- USE Families

Anchorage
- USE Mooring

Anchorites
- USE Hermits

**Anchors**
- BT Equipment
- RT Mooring
  - Ship equipment & rigging
  - Vessels

**Andirons**
- PN Pairs of metal firewood supports used on a hearth, usually made of horizontal bars mounted on short legs.
- UF Fire dogs
- BT Furnishings
- RT Fireplaces

**Anesthesia**
- UF Ether
- NT Acupuncture anesthesia
- RT Medicines
  - Surgery

**Angels**
- UF Cherubim
  - Seraphim

**Angels (cont.)**
- BT Supernatural beings
- RT Heaven
  - Religion

**Anger**
- UF Indignation
  - Wrath
- BT Mental states
- RT Deadly sins
  - Quarreling
  - Shaking
  - Swearing

**Anglican churches**
- --[country or state]--[city]
- PN For images that focus on buildings, as well as the associated grounds.
- UF Episcopal churches
- BT Churches
- RT Cathedrals

Angling
- USE Fishing

Angst
- USE Anxiety

Anguish
- USE Distress

Animal acts
- USE Trained animals

**Animal attacks**
- --[country or state]--[city]
- UF Attacks by animals
- BT Animal behavior
- RT Animals
  - Bites & stings

**Animal auctions**
- --[country or state]--[city]
- PN For animal auctions of all types.
- CN Double index under type of animal.
- BT Auctions
- RT Livestock

**Animal behavior**
- --[country or state]--[city]
- UF Behavior of animals
- NT Animal attacks
- RT Animals
  - Stampedes

Animal bites
- USE Bites & stings

Animal cleaning
- USE Animal grooming

**Animal experimentation**
- --[country or state]--[city]
- UF Experimental animals
  - Laboratory animals
- RT Animal treatment
  - Animals
  - Dissections
  - Experiments
  - Science

**Animal feeding**
- --[country or state]--[city]
- PN Includes feeding of pets, livestock, etc.
- UF Feeding of animals

---

| BT Broader term | RT Related term | PN Public Note |
|---|---|---|
| NT Narrower term | UF Used for | + Term has NTs |
| HN History Note | CN Catalogers Note | --[ ] May subdivide |

**Animal feeding (cont.)**
> Feeding of pets
> Pet feeding
> RT Animals

**Animal grooming**
> PN Human tending, cleaning, brushing, etc. of animals.
> UF Animal cleaning
> BT Grooming
> RT Animals

Animal hospitals
> USE Veterinary hospitals

**Animal housing**
> --[country or state]--[city]
> BT Agricultural facilities
> NT Aviaries
> Beehives
> Birdhouses +
> Kennels
> Poultry houses
> Stables
> RT Animal shelters
> Animals

**Animal locomotion**
> BT Locomotion
> RT Animals

**Animal shelters**
> --[country or state]--[city]
> UF Dog pounds
> Pounds (Animal)
> BT Welfare facilities
> RT Animal housing
> Animal treatment
> Animal welfare organizations
> Animals
> Dogcatching

**Animal shows**
> --[country or state]--[city]
> BT Exhibitions
> NT Dog shows
> Horse shows
> RT Animals

Animal skins
> USE Hides & skins

**Animal teams**
> --[country or state]--[city]
> NT Dog teams
> Horse teams
> Ox teams
> Packtrains
> RT Carriages & coaches
> Carts & wagons
> Pack animals
> Sleds & sleighs
> Yokes

**Animal tracks**
> --[country or state]
> UF Tracks, Animal
> RT Animals
> Footprints
> Hunting

**Animal training**

**Animal training (cont.)**
> --[country or state]--[city]
> UF Field trials
> Training of animals
> RT Trained animals

**Animal traps**
> UF Traps, Animal
> BT Fishing & hunting gear
> NT Fishing weirs
> Flypaper
> Mousetraps
> RT Animals

**Animal treatment**
> --[country or state]--[city]
> UF Protection of animals
> NT Dogcatching
> RT Animal experimentation
> Animal shelters
> Animal welfare organizations
> Animals
> Ethics
> Wildlife conservation

**Animal welfare organizations**
> --[nationality]--[country or state]--[city]
> PN Includes activities and structures.
> CN Double index under ORGANIZATIONS' FACILITIES (or NTs) for images that focus on facilities.
> UF Humane societies
> BT Organizations
> RT Animal shelters
> Animal treatment
> Animals

**Animals**
> --[country or state]--[city]
> PN Search also under the subdivision --ANIMALS & PETS used with names of persons (Appendix B). Search also under the subdivision --ANIMALS used with names of wars (Appendix C).
> NT Alpacas
> Amphibians +
> Animals in human situations
> Anteaters
> Apes +
> Aquatic animals +
> Armadillos
> Badgers
> Bats
> Bears +
> Birds +
> Bison
> Buffaloes +
> Camels
> Cats
> Cheetahs
> Dead animals
> Deer +
> Dogs +
> Donkeys
> Elephants +
> Extinct animals +

---

BT Broader term
NT Narrower term
HN History Note

RT Related term
UF Used for
CN Catalogers Note

PN Public Note
+ Term has NTs
--[ ] May subdivide

**Animals (cont.)**
- Foxes
- Game & game birds
- Giraffes
- Goats +
- Hippopotamuses
- Horses +
- Hyenas
- Insects +
- Kangaroos
- Leopards
- Lions
- Livestock +
- Llamas
- Lynx
- Moles (Animals)
- Mongooses
- Monkeys +
- Mules
- Muskox
- Opossums
- Otters +
- Pack animals
- Pandas
- Panthers
- Peccaries
- Pets
- Platypuses
- Pumas
- Raccoons
- Reptiles +
- Rhinoceroses
- Rodents +
- Seals (Animals) +
- Sheep +
- Sloths
- Snails
- Swine +
- Tapirs
- Tigers
- Trained animals
- Weasels
- Wolverines
- Wolves +
- Worms
- Zebras
- RT  Animal attacks
- Animal behavior
- Animal experimentation
- Animal feeding
- Animal grooming
- Animal housing
- Animal locomotion
- Animal shelters
- Animal shows
- Animal tracks
- Animal traps
- Animal treatment
- Animal welfare organizations
- Camouflage (Biology)
- Children & animals
- Food

**Animals (cont.)**
- Fossils
- Herding
- Hibernation
- Hides & skins
- Mascots
- Milking
- Monsters
- Nature
- Packtrains
- Ranches
- Rookeries
- Stampedes
- Veterinary hospitals
- Veterinary medicine
- Watering troughs
- Zoos

**Animals in human situations**
- BT  Animals

**Animation cels**
- CN  TGM II term.
- UF  Cartoon cels
- Cels, Animation

**Annexations**
- --[country or state]--[city]
- CN  Subdivide geographically by area being annexed.
- UF  Acquisition of territory
- Cession of territory
- Territory, Annexation of
- BT  Law & legal affairs
- RT  Boundaries
- International relations
- Military occupations

**Anniversaries**
- --[country or state]--[city]
- PN  Search also under the subdivision --COMMEMORATION used with names of ethnic, racial, and regional groups and classes of persons (Appendix A); with names of persons (Appendix B); with names of wars (Appendix C); and with corporate bodies and named events (Appendix D).
- UF  Jubilees
- BT  Events
- NT  Birthdays
- RT  Celebrations
- Commemoration
- Festivals
- Founders' Day commemorations
- Historical reenactments
- Holidays
- Reunions

**Announcements**
- --[country or state]--[city]
- CN  TGM II term.
- UF  Proclamations
- BT  Communication
- Events
- RT  Broadsides
- Heralds
- Invitations

---

BT Broader term          RT Related term          PN Public Note
NT Narrower term         UF Used for              + Term has NTs
HN History Note          CN Catalogers Note       --[ ] May subdivide

Annual leave
  USE Employee vacations
**Anteaters**
     --[country or state]
  BT  Animals
**Antelope hunting**
     --[country or state]
  BT  Big game hunting
  RT  Antelopes
**Antelopes**
     --[country or state]
  BT  Deer
  NT  Gazelles
  RT  Antelope hunting
**Anthelmintics**
  UF  Vermifuges
      Worm medicines
  BT  Patent medicines
**Anthemia**
     --[country or state]--[city]
  PN  Ornaments consisting of floral or foliated
      forms arranged in a radiating cluster but
      always flat.
  UF  Honeysuckle ornaments
  BT  Architectural decorations & ornaments
Anthems, National
  USE National songs
Anthracite mining
  USE Coal mining
Anthropological photographs
  USE Ethnographic photographs
**Anthropology**
     --[country or state]--[city]
  PN  For the subject of anthropology in general
      and the activities of anthropologists.
  BT  Social science
  RT  Archaeology
      Bertillon system
Anticommunism
  USE Anti-communism
Antipathy
  USE Prejudice
**Antipersonnel weapons**
  PN  Weapons designed for use against military
      personnel.
  BT  Arms & armament
Antique shops
  USE Antique stores
**Antique stores**
     --[country or state]--[city]
  PN  Includes activities and structures.
  HN  Changed 1/1993 from ANTIQUE
      DEALERS.
  UF  Antique shops
  BT  Stores & shops
**Antiquities**
     --[nationality]
  PN  Relics of ancient times, such as coins or
      statues. Search under ARCHAEOLOGICAL
      SITES for ancient structures or remains of
      ancient structures. Search also under the
      subdivision --ANTIQUITIES &

**Antiquities (cont.)**
      ARCHAEOLOGICAL SITES used with
      names of ethnic, racial, and regional groups
      and with classes of persons (Appendix A).
  CN  Used in a note under
      ARCHAEOLOGICAL SITES.
  RT  Archaeological sites
      Archaeology
      Ruins
Antiquities & archaeological sites
  CN  Used only as a subdivision with names of
      ethnic, racial, and regional groups and with
      classes of persons (Appendix A).
**Antisemitism**
     --[country or state]--[city]
  BT  Racism
**Antitrust law**
     --[country or state]
  BT  Law & legal affairs
  RT  Government regulation
      Industrial trusts
**Anti-communism**
     --[country or state]--[city]
  PN  For anti-communism in general as well as
      rhetoric or activities directed against
      communism.
  HN  Prior to 4/1991, COMMUNISM was used
      for both communism and anti-communism.
  UF  Anticommunism
      Anti-communist movements
  RT  Communism
      McCarthyism
Anti-communist movements
  USE Anti-communism
Anti-slavery movement
  USE Abolition movement
Anti-war
  USE Pacifism
      Peace
Anti-war movements
  USE Protest movements
**Ants**
     --[country or state]
  BT  Insects
**Anxiety**
  UF  Angst
  BT  Mental states
  RT  Fear
      Perspiration
      Stress
      Worry
**Apartheid**
     --[country or state]--[city]
  PN  For the political, economic, and social
      policies of the government of South Africa
      designed to keep racial groups in South
      Africa and Namibia separated.
  UF  Separate development (Race relations)
  BT  Economic & political systems
  RT  Race relations
      Segregation
Apartment complexes

---

BT  Broader term                    RT  Related term                    PN  Public Note
NT  Narrower term                   UF  Used for                        +   Term has NTs
HN  History Note                    CN  Catalogers Note                 --[ ] May subdivide

Apartment complexes (cont.)
  USE Housing developments
**Apartment houses**
       --[country or state]--[city]
  PN  For apartment house structures; search
       under APARTMENTS for single units within
       apartment houses or living units not in
       apartment houses.
  CN  Used in a note under APARTMENTS.
  UF  Flats
       High rise apartment buildings
  BT  Dwellings
  NT  Tenement houses
  RT  Apartments
       Houses
       Penthouses
**Apartments**
       --[country or state]--[city]
  PN  For single units within apartment houses
       or living units not in apartment houses; search
       under APARTMENT HOUSES for
       apartment house structures.
  CN  Used in a note under APARTMENT
       HOUSES.
  UF  Flats
  BT  Interiors
  RT  Apartment houses
       Penthouses
**Apathy**
  UF  Impassiveness
       Indifference
  BT  Mental states
  NT  Voter apathy
  RT  Boredom
       Obliviousness
**Apes**
       --[country or state]
  PN  Distinguished from the other higher
       primates, the monkeys, by their complete lack
       of external tail and by their more complex
       brains.
  BT  Animals
  NT  Gorillas
Aphorisms
  USE Proverbs
Apothecaries
  USE Druggists
Apothecary shops
  USE Drugstores
Apparel
  USE Clothing & dress
Apparitions
  USE Ghosts
**Apple orchards**
       --[country or state]--[city]
  CN  As appropriate, double index under
       HARVESTING.
  BT  Orchards
  RT  Apple trees
       Apples
**Apple trees**
       --[country or state]--[city]

**Apple trees (cont.)**
  BT  Trees
  RT  Apple orchards
       Apples
**Apples**
       --[country or state]--[city]
  BT  Fruit
  RT  Apple orchards
       Apple trees
       Bobbing for apples
**Appliance stores**
       --[country or state]--[city]
  PN  Includes activities and structures.
  BT  Stores & shops
  NT  Light fixture stores
  RT  Appliances
       Furniture stores
       Hardware stores
       Home furnishings stores
**Appliances**
  PN  Instruments or devices (as electric stoves,
       fans, or refrigerators) operated by gas or
       electric current.
  UF  Domestic appliances
       Home appliances
  BT  Equipment
  NT  Air conditioners
       Dishwashing machines
       Refrigerators +
       Toasters
       Vacuum cleaners
       Washing machines
  RT  Appliance stores
       Irons (Pressing)
       Light fixtures
       Ovens
       Sewing machines
       Stoves
Appointments, Presidential
  USE Presidential appointments
**Apportionment**
       --[country or state]--[city]
  UF  Reapportionment
  BT  Politics & government
  RT  Census
       Political elections
       Political representation
**Apprentices**
       --[country or state]--[city]
  BT  People
  RT  Child labor
       Children
       Vocational education
Appropriations
  USE Economic policy
**Apses**
       --[country or state]--[city]
  BT  Interiors
  RT  Basilicas
       Churches
Aquaducts
  USE Aqueducts

---

BT  Broader term              RT  Related term              PN Public Note
NT  Narrower term             UF  Used for                  +  Term has NTs
HN History Note               CN  Catalogers Note           --[ ] May subdivide

**Aquariums**
--[country or state]--[city]
BT   Exhibition facilities
RT   Aquatic animals

**Aquatic animals**
--[country or state]
PN   For animals that live entirely in the water.
UF   Fauna, Marine
     Marine animals
     Marine life
     Ocean life
     Sea animals
     Sea life
     Water animals
BT   Animals
NT   Dolphins
     Fish +
     Jellyfishes
     Octopuses
     Shellfish +
     Sponges
     Squids
     Whales
RT   Amphibians
     Aquariums
     Sea otters
     Seas
     Shells
     Tide pools

**Aquatic sports**
--[country or state]--[city]
UF   Water sports
BT   Sports
NT   Shooting rapids
     Surfing
     Water skiing
RT   Diving
     Swimming

**Aquatints**
CN   TGM II term.

**Aqueducts**
--[country or state]--[city]
PN   Structures for conveying a canal over a
     river or hollow.
UF   Acqueducts
     Aquaducts
     Conduits, Water
     Water conduits
BT   Hydraulic facilities
RT   Bridges
     Canals

Arab-Jewish relations
USE Jewish-Arab relations

Arbitration of industrial disputes
USE Industrial arbitration

Arboretums
USE Botanical gardens

**Arbors (Bowers)**
--[country or state]--[city]
PN   Leafy shelters of boughs, vines, etc.
UF   Bowers
BT   Landscape architecture facilities

**Arbors (Bowers) (cont.)**
NT   Pergolas
     Trellises

**Arcades (Architectural components)**
--[country or state]--[city]
PN   For images that focus on series of arches.
     Search under ARCADES (SHOPPING
     FACILITIES) for covered passageways or
     avenues along which are located rows of
     shops.
CN   Used in a note under ARCADES
     (SHOPPING FACILITIES).
BT   Architectural elements
RT   Arcades (Shopping facilities)
     Arches
     Loggias
     Walls

**Arcades (Shopping facilities)**
--[country or state]--[city]
PN   For covered passageways or avenues along
     which are located rows of shops. Search
     under ARCADES (ARCHITECTURAL
     COMPONENTS) for images that focus on
     series of arches.
CN   Used in a note under ARCADES
     (ARCHITECTURAL COMPONENTS).
UF   Shopping arcades
BT   Mercantile facilities
RT   Arcades (Architectural components)
     Shopping centers

Arcades, Penny
USE Penny arcades

Arch blocks
USE Voussoirs

**Archaeological sites**
--[country or state]--[city]
PN   For ancient structures still largely intact
     and remains of ancient structures; also
     includes active excavations. Search under
     ANTIQUITIES for relics (coins, etc.) of
     ancient times. Search under RUINS for
     remains of structures not of ancient times and
     under ABANDONED BUILDINGS for
     vacant, possibly dilapidated buildings. Search
     also under the subdivision --ANTIQUITIES &
     ARCHAEOLOGICAL SITES used with
     names of ethnic, racial, and regional groups,
     and with classes of persons (Appendix A).
UF   Excavation sites
BT   Historic sites
RT   Antiquities
     Archaeology
     Cliff dwellings
     Ruins

**Archaeology**
--[country or state]--[city]
PN   For the subject of archaeology in general
     and the activities of archaeologists.
BT   Science
RT   Anthropology
     Antiquities
     Archaeological sites

BT   Broader term                          RT   Related term                      PN Public Note
NT   Narrower term                         UF   Used for                          + Term has NTs
HN   History Note                          CN   Catalogers Note                   --[ ] May subdivide

Archbishops
  USE Bishops
**Archery**
      --[country or state]--[city]
  BT  Shooting
      Sports
  RT  Arrows
      Bows (Archery)
      Crossbows
      Martial arts
      Targets (Sports)
**Arches**
      --[country or state]--[city]
  BT  Architectural elements
  RT  Arcades (Architectural components)
      Memorial arches
      Tympana
      Voussoirs
Arches, Rock
  USE Rock formations
Archipelagoes
  USE Islands
**Architects**
  BT  People
  RT  Architects' offices
      Architecture
**Architects' offices**
      --[country or state]--[city]
  PN  Includes activities and structures.
  HN  Changed 1/1993 from
      ARCHITECTURAL OFFICES.
  UF  Architectural offices
  BT  Service industry facilities
  RT  Architects
      Offices
**Architectural decorations & ornaments**
      --[country or state]--[city]
  UF  Motifs, Architectural
      Ornaments, Architectural
  BT  Architectural elements
  NT  Acanthi
      Acorn decorations
      Anthemia
      Architectural sculpture +
      Chimneypieces
      Festoons
      Friezes (Ornamental bands)
      Medallions (Ornament areas)
      Quatrefoils
      Rosettes
      Trophies (Architectural ornaments)
  RT  Decorations
Architectural details
  USE Architectural elements
**Architectural drawings**
  CN  TGM II term.
  UF  Drawings, Architectural
**Architectural elements**
  PN  Individual parts of a structure that play a
      functional or decorative role.
  UF  Architectural details
      Details, Architectural

**Architectural elements (cont.)**
  BT  Architectural & site components
  NT  Arcades (Architectural components)
      Arches
      Architectural decorations & ornaments +
      Architectural orders +
      Architraves
      Awnings
      Balustrades
      Batteries (Weaponry) +
      Battlements
      Capitals (Columns)
      Cartouches (Architecture)
      Ceilings +
      Chimneypieces
      Chimneys +
      Coffers (Ceilings) +
      Colonnades +
      Columns +
      Consoles
      Coping
      Cornerstones
      Cornices
      Courses (Wall components) +
      Cupolas
      Domes +
      Doors & doorways +
      Dormers +
      Entablatures
      Finials
      Fireplaces
      Floors
      Friezes (Entablature components)
      Gables +
      Gargoyles
      Girders
      Grilles
      Lanterns (Architecture)
      Light courts
      Lintels
      Locks (Hydraulic engineering)
      Mantels
      Moats
      Moldings +
      Newels
      Niches
      Ovens
      Parapets
      Pediments
      Pilasters
      Pylons (Bridges)
      Quoins
      Rafters
      Railings +
      Religious architectural elements +
      Roofs +
      Roundels
      Shutters
      Spandrels
      Spires
      Stairways
      Steeples

BT  Broader term              RT  Related term              PN  Public Note
NT  Narrower term             UF  Used for                  +   Term has NTs
HN  History Note              CN  Catalogers Note           --[ ] May subdivide

**Architectural elements (cont.)**
  Structural systems +
  Trusses +
  Tympana
  Vaults (Architecture)
  Voussoirs +
  Wainscoting
  Walls +
  Weather vanes
  Window boxes
  Window seats
  Windows +
RT Mirrors
  Screens
  Towers

**Architectural follies**
  --[country or state]--[city]
UF Eye catchers
  Follies, Architectural
BT Landscape architecture facilities
RT Mimetic buildings
  Recycled structures
  Visionary architecture

**Architectural models**
PN Miniature relief or three-dimensional
  representations in scale of structures or parts
  of structures made for the purpose of showing
  the result of actual architectural construction
  plans. Search under BUILDING MODELS
  for miniature representations of real or
  imaginary buildings. Search under MODEL
  HOUSES for full-scale representations of
  houses planned to be constructed.
CN Used in a note under BUILDING
  MODELS and MODEL HOUSES.
UF Design models
BT Models
RT Building models
  Construction industry

Architectural offices
  USE Architects' offices

**Architectural orders**
  --[country or state]--[city]
PN In classical architecture, particular styles
  of columns with their entablatures having
  standardized details.
UF Orders, Architectural
BT Architectural elements
NT Corinthian order
  Doric order
  Ionic order
RT Capitals (Columns)
  Columns
  Entablatures

**Architectural photographs**
CN TGM II term.
Architectural polychromy
  USE Color in architecture

**Architectural sculpture**
  --[country or state]--[city]
PN Sculture that is integral to a structure.
BT Architectural decorations & ornaments

**Architectural sculpture (cont.)**
  Sculpture
NT Bas-reliefs

**Architectural & site components**
  --[country or state]--[city]
PN Elements that, together, contribute to the
  make-up and appearance of structures.
NT Architectural elements +
  Building divisions +
  Building systems +
  Site elements +
RT Architecture
  Facilities

**Architecture**
  --[country or state]--[city]
PN For the subject of architecture (style,
  design, etc.) in general and the activities of
  architects. Search under FACILITIES (and
  NTs) and ARCHITECTURAL & SITE
  COMPONENTS for images that focus on
  structures and sites or elements thereof,
  under CONSTRUCTION for the process of
  building, and under CONSTRUCTION
  INDUSTRY for the construction business.
NT Visionary architecture
RT Architects
  Architectural & site components
  Color in architecture
  Facilities

**Architraves**
  --[country or state]--[city]
PN The lowermost elements of a classical
  entablature and similar elements when carried
  around doorways and openings.
UF Epistyles
BT Architectural elements
RT Entablatures

**Archives**
  --[country or state]--[city]
UF Depositories
  Manuscript repositories
  Record repositories
  Repositories
RT Documents
  Government facilities
  Libraries
  Recording & registration

Argot
  USE Slang
Arguments
  USE Debates
  Quarreling
Aristocracy
  USE Upper class

**Aristotypes**
  CN TGM II term.
Arithmetic
  USE Mathematics

**Armadillos**
  --[country or state]
BT Animals
Armament

| | | |
|---|---|---|
| BT Broader term | RT Related term | PN Public Note |
| NT Narrower term | UF Used for | + Term has NTs |
| HN History Note | CN Catalogers Note | --[ ] May subdivide |

Armament (cont.)
  USE Arms & armament
Armed forces
  USE Military organizations
**Armies**
        --[nationality]--[country or state]--[city]
  BT   Military organizations
  NT   Artillery (Troops)
       Cavalry
       Infantry
  RT   Draft
       Troop movements
**Armistices**
  PN   Temporary suspensions of hostilities by
       agreement between opponents. Search also
       under the subdivisions --ARMISTICES and
       --PEACE used with names of wars (Appendix
       C).
  UF   Ceasefires
       Truces
  RT   Campaigns & battles
       Peace
       Peace negotiations
**Armor**
  BT   Arms & armament
       Clothing & dress
  NT   Shields
  RT   Armorers
       Helmets
       Knights
**Armored trains**
        --[nationality]--[country or state]--[city]
  PN   Trains with protective covering, usually
       steel plates. Includes exteriors and interiors.
  BT   Armored vehicles
       Railroad cars
**Armored vehicle industry**
        --[country or state]--[city]
  PN   Includes activities and structures.
  CN   Double index under INDUSTRIAL
       FACILITIES  (or NTs) for images that focus
       on facilties.
  BT   Ordnance industry
       Transportation industry
  RT   Armored vehicles
**Armored vehicles**
        --[nationality]--[country or state]--[city]
  PN   Vehicles with protective covering, usually
       steel plates.
  BT   Vehicles
  NT   Armored trains
       Armored vessels +
       Tanks (Military science)
  RT   Armored vehicle industry
       Arms & armament
       Military art & science
       Military vehicles
**Armored vessels**
        --[nationality]--[country or state]--[city]
  PN   For the first armored warships built during
       the revolution in naval architecture in the
       second half of the 19th century.

Armored vessels (cont.)
  UF   Broadsides (Warships)
       Casements
       Ironclads
       Iron-clad vessels
  BT   Armored vehicles
       Warships
  NT   Turret ships
  RT   Floating batteries
**Armorers**
  BT   People associated with manual labor
  RT   Armor
**Armorial bookplates**
  CN   TGM II term.
  UF   Heraldic bookplates
**Armories**
        --[nationality]--[country or state]--[city]
  PN   Buildings used for military training or the
       storage and manufacture of military
       equipment or weapons.
  UF   Arsenals
  BT   Military facilities
  RT   Arms & armament
       Military depots
       Ordnance industry
**Arms control**
  PN   For international action placing limitations
       on armed forces, armaments, and military
       expenditures. Includes restrictions on the use,
       levels, or deployment of weapons or forces.
  UF   Control of arms
       Disarmament
  BT   International relations
  RT   Arms race
       Arms & armament
       International security
       Militarism
       Peace
       Rearmament
Arms policy
  USE Military policy
Arms production
  USE Ordnance industry
**Arms race**
  PN   For reciprocal build-up in the quality or
       quantity of the military power of two
       opponents, caused by each striving to
       maintain or achieve a desired military posture
       relative to the other.
  RT   Arms control
       Arms & armament
Arms smuggling
  USE Illegal arms transfers
Arms trafficking
  USE Illegal arms transfers
**Arms (Anatomy)**
  RT   Human body
**Arms & armament**
        --[nationality]--[country or state]--[city]
  CN   Nationality subdivision indicates place
       where arms were manufactured. Geographic
       subdivision indicates place where arms are

BT Broader term                RT Related term                PN Public Note
NT Narrower term               UF Used for                    + Term has NTs
HN History Note                CN Catalogers Note             --[ ] May subdivide

**Arms & armament (cont.)**
    depicted.
  UF  Armament
       Ordnance
       Weapons
  BT  Equipment
  NT  Antipersonnel weapons
       Armor +
       Artillery (Weaponry) +
       Battering rams
       Bayonets
       Bombs
       Crossbows
       Daggers & swords
       Firearms +
       Mines (Warfare)
       Nightsticks
       Nuclear weapons
       Spears
       Throwing sticks +
       Torpedoes
  RT  Ammunition
       Armored vehicles
       Armories
       Arms control
       Arms race
       Arrows
       Axes
       Bows (Archery)
       Chevaux-de-frise
       Explosives
       Fishing & hunting gear
       Illegal arms transfers
       Knives
       Military art & science
       Ordnance industry
       Powder kegs
       Rearmament
       Tear gas
       Trophies (Architectural ornaments)
       Warships
Army jeeps
  USE Jeep automobiles
Army schools
  USE Military education
**Army-Navy stores**
    --[country or state]--[city]
  PN  Includes activities and structures.
  UF  Military surplus stores
       Surplus stores, Military
       War surplus stores
  BT  Stores & shops
Around the world voyages
  USE Voyages around the world
Around-the-world flights
  USE Flights around the world
Arrests
  USE Law enforcement
**Arrivals & departures**
    --[nationality]--[country or state]--[city]
  UF  Departures
       Landings (Arrivals)

**Arrivals & departures (cont.)**
       Leave-takings
  NT  Homecomings
  RT  Emigration & immigration
       Farewells
       Internal migration
       Salutations
**Arrows**
  BT  Equipment
  RT  Archery
       Arms & armament
       Bows (Archery)
**Arroyos**
    --[country or state]--[city]
  BT  Land
  RT  Streams
Arsenals
  USE Armories
**Art**
  PN  Search also under the subdivision --ARTS
       & CRAFTS used with names of ethnic,
       racial, and regional groups, and with classes
       of persons (Appendix A).
  NT  Calligraphy
       Children drawing & painting
       Drawing
       Modeling (Sculpture)
       Murals
       Painting
       Printmaking
       Rock art
       Sculpture +
       Stained glass
       Textile art
  RT  Altarpieces
       Art auctions
       Art clubs
       Art collectors
       Art dealers
       Art education
       Art exhibitions
       Art festivals
       Art objects
       Art thefts
       Artists
       Artists' materials
       Graffiti
       Sandpaintings
       Surrealism
**Art auctions**
    --[country or state]--[city]
  UF  Painting auctions
  BT  Auctions
  RT  Art
Art by children
  USE Children's art
**Art clubs**
    --[country or state]--[city]
  CN  Double index under ORGANIZATIONS'
       FACILITIES (or NTs) for images that focus
       on facilities.
  UF  Art societies

---

BT  Broader term        RT  Related term        PN  Public Note
NT  Narrower term        UF  Used for        +  Term has NTs
HN  History Note        CN  Catalogers Note        --[ ]  May subdivide

**Art clubs (cont.)**
 BT Clubs
 RT Art
  Camera clubs
**Art collectors**
  --[country or state]--[city]
 BT Collectors
 RT Art
  Art dealers
**Art colonies**
 USE Artist colonies
**Art critics**
 USE Critics
**Art dealers**
  --[country or state]--[city]
 UF Dealers, Art
 BT People associated with commercial
  activities
 RT Art
  Art collectors
  Commercial art galleries
**Art education**
  --[country or state]--[city]
 PN Includes activities and structures.
 CN Double index under EDUCATIONAL
  FACILITIES (or NTs) for images that focus
  on facilities.
 UF Art schools
 BT Education
 RT Art
**Art exhibition posters**
 USE Exhibition posters
**Art exhibitions**
  --[country or state]--[city]
 PN Includes activities, structures, and sites.
 BT Exhibitions
 RT Art
  Photography
**Art festivals**
  --[country or state]--[city]
 UF Arts festivals
 BT Festivals
 RT Art
**Art galleries, Commercial**
 USE Commercial art galleries
**Art materials**
 USE Artists' materials
**Art objects**
 UF Bric-a-brac
  Objects, Art
 NT Jade art objects
 RT Art
  Jewelry
  Religious articles
**Art reproductions**
 CN TGM II term.
**Art schools**
 USE Art education
**Art societies**
 USE Art clubs
**Art supplies**
 USE Artists' materials

**Art thefts**
  --[country or state]--[city]
 BT Robberies
 RT Art
**Artesian wells**
  --[country or state]--[city]
 BT Wells
**Artichokes**
  --[country or state]--[city]
 BT Plants
**Artificial butter**
 USE Margarine
**Artificial flower industry**
  --[country or state]--[city]
 PN Includes activities and structures.
 CN Double index under INDUSTRIAL
  FACILITIES (or NTs) for images that focus
  on facilities.
 BT Industry
 RT Artificial flowers
**Artificial flowers**
 RT Artificial flower industry
  Flowers
**Artificial limbs**
 UF Prosthetics
 BT Medical equipment & supplies
 RT Amputees
**Artificial pollination**
 UF Pollination, Artificial
 RT Biology
**Artificial respiration**
 BT Lifesaving
**Artificial rubber industry**
  --[country or state]--[city]
 PN Includes activities and structures.
 CN Double index under INDUSTRIAL
  FACILITIES (or NTs) for images that focus
  on facilities.
 UF Synthetic rubber industry
 BT Chemical industry
 RT Rubber industry
**Artificial satellites**
  --[nationality]--[country or state]--[city]
 UF Earth satellites
  Orbiting vehicles
  Satellite vehicles
  Sputniks
 BT Vehicles
 RT Space flight
**Artificial weather control**
 USE Weather control
**Artillery (Troops)**
  --[nationality]--[country or state]--[city]
 BT Armies
 RT Artillery (Weaponry)
**Artillery (Weaponry)**
  --[nationality]--[country or state]--[city]
 PN For missile engines and weapons, as well
  as mounted guns as distinct from small arms.
 HN Changed 10/1992 from ARTILLERY.
 UF Guns
 BT Arms & armament

---

BT Broader term
NT Narrower term
HN History Note

RT Related term
UF Used for
CN Catalogers Note

PN Public Note
+ Term has NTs
--[ ] May subdivide

**Artillery (Weaponry) (cont.)**
  NT  Cannons +
        Horse artillery
        Mortars (Ordnance)
        Railroad artillery
  RT  Artillery (Troops)
        Batteries (Weaponry)
        Bombs
        Firearms
        Gun turrets
        Quaker guns
        Rockets

**Artist colonies**
      --[country or state]--[city]
  UF  Art colonies
        Colonies, Artist
  BT  Settlements
  RT  Artists
        Collective settlements

**Artists**
  BT  People
  NT  Cartoonists
  RT  Art
        Artist colonies
        Artists' models
        Artists' studios
        Photographers

**Artists' devices**
  CN  TGM II term.
  UF  Symbols, Artists
        Symbols, Artists'

**Artists' early works**
  USE Juvenilia

**Artists' materials**
  UF  Art materials
        Art supplies
  BT  Equipment
  NT  Palettes
  RT  Art

**Artists' models**
  UF  Models, Artists'
  RT  Artists
        Fashion models

**Artists' proofs**
  CN  TGM II term.

**Artists' signatures**
  CN  TGM II term.

**Artists' studios**
      --[country or state]--[city]
  BT  Studios
  RT  Artists
        Photographic studios
        Potteries

**Artotypes**
  USE Collotypes

**Arts festivals**
  USE Art festivals

**Arts & crafts**
  CN  Used only as a subdivision with names of
      ethnic, racial, and regional groups, and with
      classes of persons (Appendix A).

**Asbestos mining**

**Asbestos mining (cont.)**
      --[country or state]--[city]
  PN  Includes activities and sites.
  BT  Mining

**Ash disposal**
      --[country or state]--[city]
  BT  Refuse disposal

**Asiatic cholera**
  USE Cholera

**Asparagus**
      --[country or state]--[city]
  BT  Vegetables

**Aspirations, Student**
  USE Student aspirations

**Assassinations**
      --[country or state]--[city]
  PN  For murders of prominent persons. Search
      also under the subdivisions
      --ASSASSINATION or --ASSASSINATION
      ATTEMPTS used with names of persons
      (Appendix B).
  UF  Political murders
        Political violence
        Violence, Political
  BT  Homicides

**Assemblies**
  USE Legislative bodies

**Assembly halls**
  USE Auditoriums

**Assembly-line methods**
      --[country or state]--[city]
  CN  Double index under the industry.
  UF  Production-line methods
  RT  Industry

**Asses**
  USE Donkeys

**Assistance**
      --[country or state]--[city]
  PN  Search also under the subdivision
      --ECONOMIC & INDUSTRIAL ASPECTS
      used with names of wars (Appendix C).
  CN  Subdivide geographically by place in
      which assistance is given. Used in a note
      under SCARCITY.
  UF  Aid (Relief)
        Economic assistance
        Federal subsidies
        Government lending
        Government subsidies
        Grants
        Monetary assistance
        Public welfare
        Relief (Aid)
        Subsidies
        Welfare
  NT  Clothing relief
        Disaster relief +
        Domestic economic assistance +
        Farm relief
        Food relief +
        International agricultural assistance
        International economic assistance

---

BT Broader term      RT Related term      PN Public Note
NT Narrower term      UF Used for      + Term has NTs
HN History Note      CN Catalogers Note      --[ ] May subdivide

**Assistance (cont.)**
> Legal aid
> Military assistance
>> RT Asylums
>> Charitable organizations
>> Charity
>> Cooperation
>> Economic policy
>> International organizations
>> Philanthropy
>> Poor persons
>> Public service organizations
>> Scarcity
>> Welfare facilities

**Associated objects**
> CN Used only as a subdivision under names of persons (Appendix B).

**Associations**
> USE Organizations

**Astrological signs**
> USE Zodiac

**Astrology**
> --[country or state]--[city]
> PN For the subject of astrology in general and the activities of astrologers.
> BT Supernatural practices
> RT Astronomy
>> Celestial bodies
>> Divination
>> Fortune telling
>> Prophecy
>> Stargazing
>> Zodiac

**Astronauts**
> --[nationality]--[country or state]--[city]
> UF Cosmonauts
> BT People associated with transportation
> RT Air pilots
>> Flight crews
>> Space flight

**Astronomical observation**
> USE Astronomy
>> Stargazing

**Astronomical observatories**
> --[country or state]--[city]
> PN For images that focus on facilities. Search under ASTRONOMY for activities.
> UF Observatories
> BT Research facilities
> RT Astronomy
>> Planetaria
>> Telescopes

**Astronomy**
> --[country or state]--[city]
> PN For the subject of astronomy in general and the activities of astronomers.
> CN Used in a note under ASTRONOMICAL OBSERVATORIES.
> UF Astronomical observation
> RT Astrology
>> Astronomical observatories
>> Celestial bodies

**Astronomy (cont.)**
> Cosmology
> Eclipses
> Galaxies
> Sextants
> Stargazing
> Zodiac

**Asylums**
> --[country or state]--[city]
> PN Institutions for the protection or relief of some class of destitute, afflicted, or otherwise unfortunate persons. Includes activities and structures. Search under MENTAL INSTITUTIONS for insane asylums.
> UF Benevolent institutions
>> Charitable institutions
>> Homes (Institutions)
> BT Welfare facilities
> RT Assistance
>> Charitable organizations
>> Foster home care
>> Institutional care
>> Mental institutions

**Asylum, Right to**
> USE Right to asylum

**As-built drawings**
> CN TGM II term.
> UF Drawings, As-built

**Athenaeums**
> --[country or state]--[city]
> PN Includes activities and structures.
> UF Atheneums
> BT Cultural facilities
> RT Libraries

**Atheneums**
> USE Athenaeums

**Athletes**
> --[nationality]--[country or state]--[city]
> CN Geographical subdivision indicates place where team or athletes are based.
> UF Sports teams
>> Teams, Sports
> BT People associated with entertainment & sports
> NT Baseball players
>> Basketball players
>> Bowlers
>> Boxers (Sports)
>> Fencers
>> Football players
>> Jockeys
>> Rowers
>> Runners (Sports)
>> Softball players
>> Wrestlers +
> RT Athletic clubs
>> Coaching (Athletics)
>> Sports
>> Sports & recreation facilities
>> Swimmers
>> Tennis players

**Athletic clubs**

| | | |
|---|---|---|
| BT Broader term | RT Related term | PN Public Note |
| NT Narrower term | UF Used for | + Term has NTs |
| HN History Note | CN Catalogers Note | --[ ] May subdivide |

**Athletic clubs (cont.)**
      --[country or state]--[city]
   CN  Double index under ORGANIZATIONS'
       FACILITIES (or NTs) for images that focus
       on facilities.
   UF  Sports clubs
       Turnvereine
   BT  Clubs
   RT  Athletes
       Locker rooms
       Sports
Athletic equipment
   USE Sporting goods
**Athletic fields**
      --[country or state]--[city]
   BT  Sports & recreation facilities
   RT  Playgrounds
Atolls
   USE Islands
Atom smashers
   USE Particle accelerators
Atomic bombing victims
   USE Nuclear weapons victims
Atomic bombs
   USE Nuclear weapons
Atomic power
   USE Nuclear power
Atomic weapons
   USE Nuclear weapons
**Atriums**
      --[country or state]--[city]
   PN  Includes modern atriums that are
       enclosed.
   UF  Interior courtyards
   BT  Rooms & spaces
   RT  Courtyards
**Atrocities**
      --[nationality]--[country or state]--[city]
   PN  Search also under the subdivision
       --MORAL & ETHICAL ASPECTS used with
       names of wars (Appendix C).
   CN  Subdivide by nationality of those
       committing the atrocity.
   BT  Punishment & torture
   NT  Genocide
       Massacres
   RT  Crimes
       Executions
       War crimes
Attacks by animals
   USE Animal attacks
**Attics**
      --[country or state]--[city]
   UF  Garrets
   BT  Interiors
Attitudes
   USE Mental states
Attorneys
   USE Lawyers
**Auction catalogs**
   CN  TGM II term.
**Auctions**

**Auctions (cont.)**
      --[country or state]--[city]
   BT  Commerce
       Meetings
   NT  Animal auctions
       Art auctions
   RT  Slave trade
**Audiences**
      --[country or state]--[city]
   PN  Groups or assemblies of listeners.
   BT  People
   NT  Motion picture audiences
       Theater audiences
   RT  Concerts
       Crowds
       Events
       Spectators
**Audiovisual materials**
   NT  Motion pictures +
       Sound recordings
**Auditions**
      --[country or state]--[city]
   UF  Tryouts
   RT  Actors
       Actresses
       Rehearsals
       Theatrical productions
**Auditoriums**
      --[country or state]--[city]
   PN  For facilities used for public gatherings.
       Search under AMPHITHEATERS for flat or
       gently sloping outdoor areas surrounded by
       slopes on which spectators can sit.
   CN  Used in a note under
       AMPHITHEATERS.
   UF  Assembly halls
   BT  Cultural facilities
   RT  Concert halls
       Social & civic facilities
       Stages (Platforms)
       Theaters
Augury
   USE Divination
Auricular confession
   USE Confession
**Auroras**
      --[country or state]--[city]
   UF  Northern lights
   BT  Natural phenomena
**Authors**
   UF  Writers
   BT  People associated with education &
       communication
   NT  Dramatists
       Poets
   RT  Literature
Authors' rights
   USE Copyright
Auto courts
   USE Motels
Auto mechanics
   USE Mechanics (Persons)

---

BT  Broader term              RT  Related term              PN  Public Note
NT  Narrower term             UF  Used for                  +  Term has NTs
HN  History Note              CN  Catalogers Note            --[ ] May subdivide

Auto parts
  USE Automobile equipment & supplies
Auto parts stores
  USE Automobile equipment & supplies stores
Auto washes
  USE Car washes
**Autochromes**
  CN  TGM II term.
**Autogiros**
      --[nationality]--[country or state]--[city]
  UF  Gyroplanes
  BT  Aircraft
  RT  Airplanes
Autograph sessions
  USE Autographing
**Autographing**
      --[country or state]--[city]
  UF  Autograph sessions
      Book signings
      Signing autographs
  RT  Autographs
      Celebrities
      Celebrity touring
      Document signings
      Writing
**Autographs**
  CN  TGM II term.
  RT  Autographing
Automatic data processing equipment
  USE Calculators
      Computers
Automatons
  USE Robots
**Automats**
      --[country or state]--[city]
  BT  Restaurants
  RT  Coin operated machines
Automobile accessories
  USE Automobile equipment & supplies
**Automobile dealerships**
      --[country or state]--[city]
  PN  Includes activities and structures.
  UF  Dealerships, Automobile
      Used car lots
  BT  Business enterprises
      Mercantile facilities
  RT  Automobile equipment & supplies stores
      Automobiles
**Automobile driving**
      --[country or state]--[city]
  UF  Driving, Automobile
  BT  Transportation
  NT  Children driving
      Stunt driving
  RT  Automobiles
      Drunk driving
      Parking
      Recreation
**Automobile equipment & supplies**
  UF  Auto parts
      Automobile accessories
  BT  Equipment

**Automobile equipment & supplies (cont.)**
  RT  Automobile equipment & supplies stores
      Automobiles
      Dashboards
      License plates
      Steering wheels
**Automobile equipment & supplies stores**
      --[country or state]--[city]
  PN  Includes activities and structures.
  UF  Auto parts stores
  BT  Stores & shops
  RT  Automobile dealerships
      Automobile equipment & supplies
      Automobile industry
      Vehicle maintenance & repair
**Automobile industry**
      --[country or state]--[city]
  PN  Includes activities and structures.
  CN  Double index under INDUSTRIAL
      FACILITIES (or NTs) for images that focus
      on facilities. Used in a note under
      WELDING.
  BT  Transportation industry
  RT  Automobile equipment & supplies stores
      Automobile industry unions
      Automobiles
      Truck industry
**Automobile industry strikes**
      --[country or state]--[city]
  BT  Strikes
  RT  Automobile industry unions
**Automobile industry unions**
      --[country or state]--[city]
  BT  Labor unions
  RT  Automobile industry
      Automobile industry strikes
**Automobile inspections**
      --[country or state]--[city]
  RT  Automobiles
      Safety
Automobile license plates
  USE License plates
Automobile mechanics
  USE Mechanics (Persons)
**Automobile racing**
      --[country or state]--[city]
  CN  Used in note under AUTOMOBILE
      RACING DRIVERS.
  UF  Car racing
  BT  Racing
  RT  Automobiles
      Racing automobiles
**Automobile racing drivers**
  PN  For automobile racing drivers not engaged
      in the activity of racing. Search under
      AUTOMOBILE RACING for activities.
  UF  Drag racers
**Automobile service stations**
      --[country or state]--[city]
  PN  Includes gasoline pumps which are part of
      a service station.
  CN  Used in a note under GASOLINE and

BT  Broader term         RT  Related term         PN Public Note
NT  Narrower term        UF  Used for             + Term has NTs
HN  History Note         CN  Catalogers Note      --[ ] May subdivide

**Automobile service stations (cont.)**
    GASOLINE PUMPS.
  UF  Commercial garages
    Filling stations
    Garages, Commercial
    Gas stations
    Service stations
  BT  Business enterprises
    Transportation facilities
  RT  Automobiles
    Gasoline
    Gasoline pumps
    Vehicle maintenance & repair
Automobile tags
  USE License plates
**Automobiles**
    --[nationality]--[country or state]--[city]
  UF  Cars
  BT  Vehicles
  NT  Convertible automobiles
    Electric automobiles
    Limousines
    Racing automobiles
    Steam automobiles
    Three wheel automobiles
  RT  Automobile dealerships
    Automobile driving
    Automobile equipment & supplies
    Automobile industry
    Automobile inspections
    Automobile racing
    Automobile service stations
    Car washes
    Chauffeurs
    Convertiplanes
    Driver education
    Drive-in restaurants
    Drive-in theaters
    Garages
    Hearses
    Jeep automobiles
    Model cars
    Traffic accidents
Automobiles, Coaster
  USE Coaster cars
**Autonomy**
    --[country or state]
  UF  Home rule
    Independence
    Self-government
  BT  Economic & political systems
  NT  Municipal home rule
  RT  National liberation movements
Autosuggestion
  USE Hypnotism
Autos-da-fé
  USE Auto-da-fé sermons
Autotypes
  USE Carbon prints
**Auto-da-fé sermons**
    --[country or state]--[city]
  PN  Ceremonies at which judgment was

**Auto-da-fé sermons (cont.)**
    pronounced on those convicted of heresy by
    the Spanish Inquisition.
  UF  Autos-da-fé
  BT  Rites & ceremonies
  RT  Religious meetings
**Autumn**
    --[country or state]--[city]
  UF  Fall
  BT  Seasons
**Avalanches**
    --[country or state]
  BT  Landslides
  RT  Mountains
    Snow
Avant des lettres prints
  USE Proofs before letters
**Avarice**
  UF  Covetousness
    Greed
  BT  Mental states
  RT  Deadly sins
    Miserliness
    Wealth
Avenues
  USE Streets
**Aviaries**
    --[country or state]--[city]
  BT  Animal housing
  RT  Birds
    Zoos
Aviation
  USE Aeronautics
Aviation industry
  USE Airline industry
Aviation mechanics (Persons)
  USE Mechanics (Persons)
**Aviation mechanics (Science)**
  UF  Mechanics, Aviation (Science)
  BT  Science
  RT  Aeronautics
Aviation personnel
  USE Flight crews
Aviators
  USE Air pilots
    Fighter pilots
Awaking
  USE Waking
**Awards**
  UF  Prizes
    Rewards
    Rewards & prizes
    Trophies
  NT  Nobel prizes
  RT  Contests
    Medals
    Military decorations
    Rites & ceremonies
Awards of merit
  USE Rewards of merit
**Awnings**
    --[country or state]--[city]

---

BT  Broader term      RT  Related term      PN  Public Note
NT  Narrower term    UF  Used for       +  Term has NTs
HN  History Note      CN  Catalogers Note    --[ ] May subdivide

**Awnings (cont.)**
  BT  Architectural elements
**AWOL**
  USE Military deserters
**Axes**
  UF  Hatchets
  BT  Equipment
  NT  Tomahawks
  RT  Arms & armament
Axis powers
  USE War allies
**Axonometric projections**
  CN  TGM II term.
**Azaleas**
        --[country or state]--[city]
  BT  Rhododendrons
A-bombs
  USE Nuclear weapons
Babies
  USE Infants
**Baboons**
        --[country or state]
  BT  Monkeys
**Baby carriages**
        --[country or state]--[city]
  UF  Perambulators
  BT  Vehicles
  RT  Infants
Baby sitting
  USE Babysitting
**Babysitting**
  UF  Baby sitting
  RT  Children
        Day care
**Bachelors**
        --[country or state]--[city]
  BT  Men
  RT  Marriage
        Single women
Back yards
  USE Backyards
**Back (Anatomy)**
  RT  Human body
Backdrops
  USE Studio props
**Backgammon**
  BT  Board games
**Backyards**
        --[country or state]--[city]
  UF  Back yards
  BT  Sites
  RT  Alleys
        Dwellings
        Gardens
        Outbuildings
**Bacteria**
  UF  Germs
        Microbes
  RT  Diseases
        Microorganisms
**Badgers**
        --[country or state]

**Badgers (cont.)**
  BT  Animals
**Badges**
  CN  TGM II term.
  UF  Button badges
        Ribbon badges
  RT  Medals
**Badminton**
        --[country or state]--[city]
  BT  Sports
Baggage
  USE Luggage
**Bagpipes**
  PN  Includes the activity of playing bagpipes.
  BT  Wind instruments
**Bags**
  CN  TGM II term.
  UF  Sacks
**Bailiffs**
        --[country or state]--[city]
  UF  Law enforcement officers
  BT  People
  RT  Law enforcement
        Police
**Baked products**
        --[country or state]--[city]
  PN  Search under BAKING for activities.
  CN  Subdivide by location of national or
        regional association, as appropriate.
  BT  Food
  NT  Bread +
        Cakes
        Crackers
        Doughnuts
        Pies
        Pretzels
  RT  Bakeries
        Baking
        Baking powder
**Bakeries**
        --[country or state]--[city]
  PN  For images that focus on facilities. Search
        under BAKING for activities.
  UF  Bakery shops
  BT  Stores & shops
  RT  Baked products
        Baking
Bakery shops
  USE Bakeries
**Baking**
        --[country or state]--[city]
  PN  Includes both commercial and domestic
        activities.
  CN  Used in a note under BAKED
        PRODUCTS and BAKERIES.
  BT  Cookery
  RT  Baked products
        Bakeries
        Baking powder
        Ovens
**Baking powder**
  RT  Baked products

---

BT Broader term                    RT Related term                    PN Public Note
NT Narrower term                   UF Used for                        + Term has NTs
HN History Note                    CN Catalogers Note                 --[ ] May subdivide

**Baking powder (cont.)**
      Baking
**Balalaikas**
  PN  Includes the activity of playing balalaikas.
  BT  Stringed instruments
Balance of nature
  USE Ecology
**Balconies**
      --[country or state]--[city]
  PN  For platforms (usually unroofed) that
      project from the wall of a building, enclosed
      by a parapet or railing.
  BT  Rooms & spaces
  RT  Galleries (Rooms & spaces)
      Loggias
      Porches
Bald eagles
  USE Eagles
**Baldness**
  RT  Hairstyles
      Scalps
**Ball bearings**
      --[country or state]--[city]
  RT  Machinery
**Ball dresses**
  UF  Balldresses
  BT  Clothing & dress
  RT  Ballroom dancing
**Ball & chain**
  PN  Symbol of something that severely
      restricts a person's activity; usually
      oppressively.
  BT  Symbols
  RT  Prisoners
      Shackles
**Ballads**
  BT  Songs
Balldresses
  USE Ball dresses
**Ballerinas**
  BT  Dancers
      Women
  RT  Ballet
**Ballet**
      --[nationality]--[country or state]--[city]
  PN  For the subject of ballet in general and the
      activity of  ballet dancing.
  BT  Dancing
  RT  Ballerinas
**Balloon racing**
      --[country or state]--[city]
  BT  Racing
  RT  Balloons (Aircraft)
Balloon views
  USE Aerial views
      Bird's-eye views
      Panoramic views
**Balloonists**
      --[nationality]--[country or state]--[city]
  BT  Air pilots
  RT  Balloons (Aircraft)
**Balloons**

**Balloons (cont.)**
  PN  For balloons other than vehicles.
  RT  Balloons (Aircraft)
      Festive decorations
      Toys
**Balloons (Aircraft)**
      --[nationality]--[country or state]--[city]
  UF  Hot air balloons
  BT  Aircraft
  NT  Captive balloons +
  RT  Airships
      Balloon racing
      Balloonists
      Balloons
Ballot counting
  USE Vote counting
Ballot tabulation
  USE Vote counting
**Ballots**
  CN  TGM II term.
  UF  Election tickets
**Ballroom dancing**
      --[country or state]--[city]
  PN  For dancing at balls (large and formal
      assemblies for social dancing).
  BT  Dancing
  RT  Ball dresses
      Ballrooms
      Balls (Parties)
**Ballrooms**
      --[country or state]--[city]
  BT  Interiors
  RT  Ballroom dancing
**Balls (Parties)**
      --[country or state]--[city]
  PN  For formal dances; search under DANCE
      PARTIES for less formal dances.
  CN  Used in a note under DANCE PARTIES.
  UF  Cotillions
  BT  Parties
  RT  Ballroom dancing
Baltic hemp
  USE Flax
**Balustrades**
      --[country or state]--[city]
  BT  Architectural elements
  RT  Railings
      Roofs
**Bamboo**
      --[country or state]--[city]
  BT  Plants
**Banana peels**
  RT  Bananas
**Banana plantations**
      --[country or state]--[city]
  PN  Includes activities and structures.
  CN  As appropriate, double index under
      HARVESTING.
  BT  Plantations
  RT  Banana plants
      Bananas
**Banana plants**

---

BT  Broader term                    RT  Related term                    PN  Public Note
NT  Narrower term                   UF  Used for                        +   Term has NTs
HN  History Note                    CN  Catalogers Note                 --[ ] May subdivide

**Banana plants (cont.)**
--[country or state]--[city]
BT  Plants
RT  Banana plantations
    Bananas
**Bananas**
--[country or state]--[city]
BT  Fruit
RT  Banana peels
    Banana plantations
    Banana plants
**Band uniforms**
--[country or state]--[city]
BT  Uniforms
RT  Bands
Band wagons
USE Bandwagons
Bandits
USE Criminals
Bandmasters
USE Conductors
**Bands**
UF  Brass bands
BT  Music ensembles
NT  Marching bands
    Military bands
    Rock groups
    Youth bands
RT  Band uniforms
    Bandstands
    Bandwagons
    Brass instruments
    Wind instruments
**Bandstands**
--[country or state]--[city]
BT  Cultural facilities
RT  Bands
    Gazebos
**Bandwagons**
UF  Band wagons
RT  Bands
    Carts & wagons
**Banjos**
PN  Includes the activity of playing banjos.
BT  Stringed instruments
**Bank note vignettes**
CN  TGM II term.
UF  Security engravings
**Bank notes**
CN  TGM II term.
Bank runs
USE Business panics
**Bankers**
--[country or state]--[city]
BT  People associated with commercial
    activities
RT  Banking
    Banks
**Banking**
--[country or state]--[city]
PN  For activities. Search under BANKS for
    images that focus on buildings.

**Banking (cont.)**
CN  Used in a note under BANKS.
BT  Business & finance
RT  Bankers
    Banks
    Credit
**Banks**
--[country or state]--[city]
PN  For images that focus on facilities. Search
    under BANKING for activities.
CN  Used in a note under BANKING and
    BANKERS.
UF  Depositories
BT  Financial facilities
RT  Bankers
    Banking
    Coin banks
    Safes
    Vaults (Strong rooms)
**Banners**
--[country or state]--[city]
CN  TGM II term.
BT  Signs
RT  Drapery
    Flags
**Banquet camera photographs**
CN  TGM II term.
**Banquet halls**
--[country or state]--[city]
BT  Interiors
RT  Banquets
**Banquets**
--[country or state]--[city]
UF  Feasts
BT  Events
RT  Banquet halls
    Eating & drinking
**Banyan trees**
--[country or state]--[city]
PN  East Indian trees, the branches of which
    send out numerous trunks that grow down to
    the soil so that a single tree covers a large
    area.
BT  Trees
**Baobab**
--[country or state]--[city]
BT  Trees
**Baptismal certificates**
CN  TGM II term.
Baptismal fonts
USE Fonts
**Baptisms**
--[country or state]--[city]
UF  Christenings
    Immersions, Baptismal
BT  Rites & ceremonies
RT  Fonts
    Preaching
    Religious services
Baptism, Sailors'
USE Shellbacks
**Baptist churches**

---

BT  Broader term
NT  Narrower term
HN  History Note

RT  Related term
UF  Used for
CN  Catalogers Note

PN  Public Note
+   Term has NTs
--[ ]  May subdivide

**Baptist churches (cont.)**
>--[country or state]--[city]
- PN   For images that focus on buildings, as well as the associated grounds.
- BT   Protestant churches

**Barabans**
- USE Drums (Domes)

**Barbary corsairs**
- USE Pirates

**Barbary sheep**
- USE Mountain sheep

**Barbecue grilles**
- RT   Barbecues
>Cookery

**Barbecues**
>--[country or state]--[city]
- RT   Barbecue grilles
>Eating & drinking
>Outdoor cookery

**Barbed wire**
- RT   Barbed wire industry
>Fences

**Barbed wire industry**
>--[country or state]--[city]
- PN   Includes activities and structures.
- CN   Double index under INDUSTRIAL FACILITIES (or NTs) for images that focus on facilities.
- BT   Industry
- RT   Barbed wire

**Barbering**
>--[country or state]--[city]
- PN   For activities outside of barbershops.
- CN   Used in a note under BARBERSHOPS.
- BT   Hairdressing
- RT   Barbershops
>Barbers' strikes
>Shaving

**Barbershop quartets**
- UF   Quartets, Barbershop
- BT   Music ensembles
- RT   Singing

**Barbershops**
>--[country or state]--[city]
- PN   Search under BARBERING for activities outside of shops.
- BT   Service industry facilities
- RT   Barbering
>Beauty shops

**Barbers' strikes**
>--[country or state]--[city]
- BT   Strikes
- RT   Barbering

**Bards**
- BT   Entertainers
- RT   Harps
>Minstrels
>Poets
>Singers

**Bareback riding**
>--[country or state]--[city]
- BT   Horseback riding

**Bareback riding (cont.)**
- RT   Circuses & shows
>Trick riding

**Barges**
>--[nationality]--[country or state]--[city]
- UF   Riverboats
- BT   Boats
- NT   Whalebacks
- RT   Shipping

**Barley**
>--[country or state]--[city]
- BT   Grains

**Barns**
>--[country or state]--[city]
- BT   Agricultural facilities
- RT   Stables

**Barometers**
- BT   Scientific equipment
- RT   Weather

**Baronage**
- USE Peerage

**Barracks**
>--[nationality]--[country or state]--[city]
- UF   Quarters, Military
- BT   Dwellings
>Military facilities
- RT   Officers' quarters

**Barrage balloons**
>--[nationality]--[country or state]--[city]
- PN   Small captive balloons used to support wires or nets as protection against air attacks.
- BT   Captive balloons

**Barrel organ players**
- USE Organ grinders

**Barrels**
>--[country or state]--[city]
- UF   Casks
- BT   Containers

**Barricades**
>--[country or state]--[city]
- UF   Ramparts
- NT   Chevaux-de-frise
- RT   Electric fences
>Forts & fortifications
>Military art & science

**Barrier reefs**
- USE Reefs

**Barrooms**
>--[country or state]--[city]
- UF   Tap rooms
>Taprooms
- BT   Interiors
- RT   Bars

**Bars**
>--[country or state]--[city]
- PN   Includes activities and structures.
- UF   Juke joints
>Public houses
>Pubs
>Saloons
>Taverns
- BT   Eating & drinking facilities

---

BT  Broader term
NT  Narrower term
HN  History Note

RT  Related term
UF  Used for
CN  Catalogers Note

PN  Public Note
+  Term has NTs
--[ ]  May subdivide

**Bars (cont.)**
- NT  Speakeasies
- RT  Alcoholic beverages
-      Barrooms
-      Beer halls
-      Hotels
-      Nightclubs
-      Restaurants
-      Taverns (Inns)

Bars (Sand)
- USE Sandbars

**Barter**
-      --[country or state]--[city]
- UF  Exchange (Barter)
- BT  Commerce
- RT  Money

Base exchanges
- USE Military exchanges

**Baseball**
-      --[country or state]--[city]
- PN  Includes organizations and activities.
- CN  Used in a note under BASEBALL
  PLAYERS.
- BT  Sports
- NT  Water baseball
- RT  Baseball players
-      Softball

**Baseball cards**
- CN  TGM II term.

**Baseball managers**
-      --[country or state]--[city]
- CN  Geographical subdivision indicates place
  where manager is based.
- BT  People associated with entertainment &
  sports

**Baseball players**
-      --[country or state]--[city]
- CN  Geographical subdivision indicates place
  where team or player is based.
- BT  Athletes
- RT  Baseball
-      Softball players

**Basements**
-      --[country or state]--[city]
- UF  Cellars
- BT  Interiors

**Basilicas**
-      --[country or state]--[city]
- BT  Churches
- RT  Apses

**Basins**
-      --[country or state]--[city]
- UF  Washbasins
- BT  Containers
- RT  Cleaning

**Basins (Bodies of water)**
-      --[country or state]--[city]
- BT  Bodies of water

**Basket making**
-      --[country or state]--[city]
- BT  Handicraft
- RT  Baskets

**Basket making (cont.)**
-      Weaving

**Basketball**
-      --[country or state]--[city]
- PN  Includes organizations and activities.
- BT  Sports
- RT  Basketball players

**Basketball players**
-      --[country or state]--[city]
- CN  Geographical subdivision indicates place
  where team or player is based.
- BT  Athletes
- RT  Basketball

**Baskets**
- BT  Containers
- RT  Basket making

**Bass**
-      --[country or state]
- BT  Fish

**Bassinets**
- USE Children's furniture

**Bassoons**
- PN  Includes the activity of playing bassoons.
- BT  Wind instruments

Bastardy
- USE Illegitimacy

**Bas-reliefs**
-      --[country or state]--[city]
- PN  Works of sculpture in which the projection
  of figures, ornaments, etc., from the
  background is slight, no part being entirely
  detached.
- BT  Architectural sculpture
-      Sculpture

Bath chairs
- USE Wheeled chairs

Bath houses
- USE Bathhouses

**Bathhouses**
-      --[country or state]--[city]
- PN  Public facilities containing dressing
  rooms. Includes activities and structures.
  Search under PUBLIC BATHS for public
  buildings for bathing.
- CN  Used in a note under PUBLIC BATHS.
- UF  Bath houses
-      Bathing pavilions
-      Beach changing-rooms
-      Pool houses
- BT  Sports & recreation facilities
- NT  Cabanas
- RT  Bathing
-      Beaches
-      Public baths
-      Shelters
-      Swimming

**Bathing**
-      --[country or state]--[city]
- UF  Baths
- NT  Children bathing
- RT  Ablution fountains
-      Bathhouses

---

BT Broader term          RT Related term          PN Public Note
NT Narrower term        UF Used for             + Term has NTs
HN History Note          CN Catalogers Note      --[ ] May subdivide

**Bathing (cont.)**
        Bathrooms
        Bathtubs & showers
        Grooming
        Hygiene
        Public baths
        Therapeutic baths
**Bathing beaches**
  USE Beaches
**Bathing beauties**
  BT   Women
  RT   Bathing suits
        Beauty contests
**Bathing houses**
  USE Public baths
**Bathing pavilions**
  USE Bathhouses
**Bathing suits**
  PN   For images in which swimming attire is
        prominent.
  UF   Swimsuits
  BT   Clothing & dress
  RT   Bathing beauties
        Beaches
        Swimming
**Bathrooms**
        --[country or state]--[city]
  UF   Lavatories
        Restrooms
        Washrooms
  BT   Interiors
  RT   Bathing
        Bathtubs & showers
        Privies
        Public comfort stations
        Toilets
**Baths**
  USE Bathing
**Baths, Bird**
  USE Birdbaths
**Bathtubs & showers**
        --[country or state]--[city]
  UF   Showers
        Tubs, Bath
  BT   Plumbing fixtures
  RT   Bathing
        Bathrooms
        Furniture
**Bathyspheres**
  PN   Strongly built diving spheres used for
        deep-sea observation and study.
  BT   Scientific equipment
**Batiks**
  BT   Textiles
**Baton twirling**
        --[country or state]--[city]
  CN   Used in a note under DRUM MAJORS
        and DRUM MAJORETTES.
  RT   Drum majorettes
        Drum majoring
        Drum majors
        Parades & processions

**Bats**
        --[country or state]
  BT   Animals
**Battercakes**
  USE Pancakes & waffles
**Battered children**
  USE Abused children
**Battered women**
  USE Abused women
**Batteries (Weaponry)**
        --[country or state]--[city]
  BT   Architectural elements
  NT   Floating batteries
  RT   Artillery (Weaponry)
        Forts & fortifications
        Military art & science
**Batteries, electric**
  USE Electric batteries
**Battering rams**
  UF   Rams, Battering
  BT   Arms & armament
**Battle flags**
  USE Military standards
**Battle reenactments**
  USE Historical reenactments
**Battlefields**
        --[country or state]--[city]
  PN   Battle sites after the time of fighting.
        Search under CAMPAIGNS & BATTLES
        and under the names of conflicts for images
        at the time of battles. Search also under the
        subdivision --BATTLEFIELDS used with
        names of wars (Appendix C).
  CN   Used in a note under CAMPAIGNS &
        BATTLES.
  BT   Historic sites
  RT   Campaigns & battles
        War damage
**Battlements**
        --[country or state]--[city]
  PN   Parapets consisting of alternate solid parts
        and open spaces that surmount a wall.
  UF   Embattlements
  BT   Architectural elements
  RT   Forts & fortifications
        Parapets
**Battles**
  USE Campaigns & battles
**Battleships**
        --[nationality]--[country or state]--[city]
  UF   Dreadnoughts
        Pocket battleships
  BT   Warships
**Bay windows**
        --[country or state]--[city]
  UF   Jut windows
        Oriel windows
  BT   Windows
  NT   Bow windows
**Bayoneting**
  USE Bayonets
**Bayonets**

---

BT Broader term           RT Related term           PN Public Note
NT Narrower term         UF Used for             + Term has NTs
HN History Note           CN Catalogers Note      --[ ] May subdivide

**Bayonets (cont.)**
  --[nationality]--[country or state]--[city]
  UF  Bayoneting
  BT  Arms & armament
  RT  Rifles
**Bayous**
  --[country or state]--[city]
  PN  Distributaries of streams, bounded by
      natural levees, through which water is
      channeled by repeated divisions into swamps,
      then marshes of a delta, and ultimately into
      the ocean.
  BT  Streams
**Bays**
  --[country or state]
  UF  Coves
      Estuaries
      Gulfs
      Inlets
      Sounds (Geomorphology)
  BT  Bodies of water
  NT  Fjords
  RT  Harbors
      Seas
**Bazaars**
  --[country or state]--[city]
  PN  Markets consisting of rows of shops or
      stalls often found in Middle Eastern or
      Islamic countries.
  UF  Oriental bazaars
      Souks
      Suqs
  BT  Markets
Beach changing-rooms
  USE Bathhouses
**Beaches**
  --[country or state]--[city]
  CN  Used in a note under CHILDREN
      PLAYING IN SAND and CHILDREN
      PLAYING IN WATER.
  UF  Bathing beaches
      Boat landings
      Seashores
      Strands
  BT  Land
      Waterfronts
  RT  Bathhouses
      Bathing suits
      Boardwalks
      Bodies of water
      Children playing in sand
      Children playing in water
      Dunes
      Resorts
      Sand sculpture
      Surf fishing
      Swimming
**Beacons**
  --[country or state]--[city]
  BT  Communication devices
  RT  Lighthouses
      Navigation

**Bead & reel moldings**
  --[country or state]--[city]
  UF  Reel & bead moldings
  BT  Moldings
Beams
  USE Girders
Beano
  USE Bingo
**Beans**
  --[country or state]--[city]
  BT  Vegetables
  NT  Soybeans
**Bear hunting**
  --[country or state]
  BT  Big game hunting
  RT  Bears
**Beards**
  UF  Whiskers
  RT  Hairstyles
**Bears**
  --[country or state]
  BT  Animals
  NT  Grizzly bears
      Polar bears
  RT  Bear hunting
**Beating**
  --[country or state]--[city]
  BT  Punishment & torture
  NT  Spanking
      Whipping
Beatniks
  USE Bohemians
Beautification of cities & towns
  USE Urban beautification
**Beauty contestants**
  --[country or state]--[city]
  CN  Geographical subdivision indicates place
      where contestant is based.
  UF  Beauty queens
      Contestants, Beauty
  BT  Women
  RT  Beauty contests
**Beauty contests**
  --[country or state]--[city]
  UF  Beauty pageants
  BT  Contests
  RT  Bathing beauties
      Beauty contestants
Beauty pageants
  USE Beauty contests
Beauty parlors
  USE Beauty shops
Beauty queens
  USE Beauty contestants
**Beauty shops**
  --[country or state]--[city]
  UF  Beauty parlors
      Salons, Beauty
  BT  Service industry facilities
  RT  Barbershops
      Grooming
**Beaver dams**

BT  Broader term                RT  Related term            PN  Public Note
NT  Narrower term               UF  Used for                +  Term has NTs
HN  History Note                CN  Catalogers Note         --[ ] May subdivide

**Beaver dams (cont.)**
--[country or state]
RT    Beavers
Bodies of water
Dams
**Beavers**
--[country or state]
BT    Rodents
RT    Beaver dams
**Bedbugs**
--[country or state]
BT    Insects
**Bedrooms**
--[country or state]--[city]
BT    Interiors
RT    Beds
Boudoirs
Dormitories
Staterooms
**Beds**
BT    Furniture
RT    Bedrooms
Sleeping
**Bee culture**
--[country or state]--[city]
UF    Beekeeping
RT    Beehives
Bees
Beefcake photographs
USE Glamour photographs
**Beehives**
UF    Hives, Bee
BT    Animal housing
RT    Bee culture
Bees
Honeycombs
Wasps' nests
Beekeeping
USE Bee culture
**Beer**
--[country or state]--[city]
CN    Double index under EATING &
DRINKING for the activity of beer drinking.
BT    Alcoholic beverages
RT    Beer halls
Brewing industry
**Beer halls**
--[country or state]--[city]
BT    Eating & drinking facilities
RT    Bars
Beer
Nightclubs
Restaurants
Beer industry
USE Brewing industry
**Bees**
--[country or state]
UF    Bumble bees
BT    Insects
RT    Bee culture
Beehives
Honeycombs

**Bees (Cooperative gatherings)**
--[country or state]--[city]
PN    Social gatherings where people combine
work, competition, and amusement.
BT    Events
Manners & customs
NT    Quilting bees
RT    Country life
Beet sugar
USE Sugar
**Beets**
--[country or state]--[city]
UF    Sugar beets
BT    Vegetables
RT    Sugar
Sugar industry
Before & after views
USE Then & now comparisons
**Beggars**
--[country or state]--[city]
BT    Poor persons
RT    Tin cups
Tramps
Begging (Pleading)
USE Pleading (Begging)
Beginnings
USE Creation
Behavior of animals
USE Animal behavior
Behavior of children
USE Child behavior
Beheadings
USE Decapitations
Behinds (Human body)
USE Buttocks
Belching
USE Burping
Bell buoys
USE Buoys
Bell peppers
USE Peppers
**Bell towers**
--[country or state]--[city]
UF    Campaniles
BT    Towers
RT    Bells
Bellmen's verses
USE Carriers' addresses
**Bellows**
PN    Instruments or machines that by alternate
expansion and contraction or by rise and fall
of the top draws in air through a valve or
orifice and expels it more or less forcibly
through a tube.
RT    Equipment
Machinery
**Bells**
PN    Includes the activity of ringing bells.
BT    Percussion instruments
NT    Chimes
RT    Bell towers
Communication devices

---

BT  Broader term            RT  Related term         PN  Public Note
NT  Narrower term           UF  Used for             +  Term has NTs
HN  History Note            CN  Catalogers Note      --[ ] May subdivide

**Bells (cont.)**
     Liberty bell
Belt courses
    USE Stringcourses
**Belt industry**
     --[country or state]--[city]
    PN  Includes activities and structures.
    CN  Double index under INDUSTRIAL
         FACILITIES (or NTs) for images that focus
         on facilities.
    BT  Industry
**Belts (Clothing)**
    BT  Clothing & dress
Belvederes
    USE Gazebos
**Benches**
     --[country or state]--[city]
    BT  Seating furniture
    NT  Window seats
    RT  Pews
Benches, Windows
    USE Window seats
**Benedictions**
     --[country or state]--[city]
    PN  For the blessing of objects and persons and
         the act of blessing as a liturgical function.
    UF  Blessings
    BT  Rites & ceremonies
    RT  Preaching
         Religious services
Benefits (Fund raising)
    USE Fund raising
Benefits, Employee
    USE Employee fringe benefits
Benefits, Veterans'
    USE Veterans' benefits
Benevolence
    USE Charity
Benevolent institutions
    USE Asylums
Benevolent societies
    USE Fraternal organizations
Bequests
    USE Inheritance & sucession
**Berries**
     --[country or state]--[city]
    BT  Fruit
    NT  Cranberries
         Raspberries
         Strawberries
Berthing
    USE Mooring
**Bertillon system**
    PN  Identification of criminals through records
         of their physical characteristics.
    RT  Anthropology
         Criminals
         Human body
         Investigation
Betting
    USE Gambling
         Wagers

Bevel siding
    USE Clapboard siding
**Beverage industry**
     --[country or state]--[city]
    PN  Includes activities and structures.
    CN  Double index under INDUSTRIAL
         FACILITIES (or NTs) for images that focus
         on facilities.
    BT  Food industry
    NT  Brewing industry
         Coffee industry
         Distilling industries
         Tea industry
         Wine industry
    RT  Beverage industry strikes
         Beverages
         Dairy products industry
         Dairying
**Beverage industry strikes**
     --[country or state]--[city]
    BT  Strikes
    RT  Beverage industry
**Beverages**
     --[country or state]--[city]
    UF  Drinks
    BT  Food
    NT  Alcoholic beverages +
         Bitters
         Carbonated beverages +
         Cider
         Coffee
         Mineral waters
         Tea
    RT  Beverage industry
         Drinking vessels
         Eating & drinking
         Eating & drinking facilities
         Pitchers
Bias (Psychology)
    USE Prejudice
**Bible cards**
    CN  TGM II term.
    UF  Scripture cards
         Sunday school cards
**Bible societies**
     --[country or state]--[city]
    PN  Societies concerned with the publication
         and distribution of the Bible. Includes
         activities and structures.
    CN  Double index under ORGANIZATIONS'
         FACILITIES (or NTs) for images that focus
         on facilities.
    BT  Organizations
    RT  Bibles
         Publishing industry
Bible stories
    USE Biblical events
**Bibles**
     --[country or state]--[city]
    BT  Religious books
    RT  Bible societies
         Biblical events

---

BT  Broader term            RT  Related term           PN  Public Note
NT  Narrower term         UF  Used for              +  Term has NTs
HN  History Note           CN  Catalogers Note      --[ ]  May subdivide

**Biblical events**
UF   Bible stories
BT   Events
NT   End of the world
RT   Bibles
        Crèches (Nativity scenes)
        Noah's ark
Bicentennials
   USE Centennial celebrations
**Bicycle racing**
        --[country or state]--[city]
BT   Cycling
        Racing
RT   Bicycles & tricycles
**Bicycle shops**
        --[country or state]--[city]
PN   Includes activities and structures.
BT   Stores & shops
RT   Bicycles & tricycles
**Bicycles & tricycles**
        --[nationality]--[country or state]--[city]
UF   Tricycles
        Velocipedes
BT   Vehicles
RT   Bicycle racing
        Bicycle shops
        Children riding bicycles & tricycles
        Cycling
        Motorcycles
        Wheeled chairs
Bicycling
   USE Cycling
**Big business**
        --[country or state]--[city]
PN   Conduct of commercial activities
        involving economic groups consisting of
        large profit-making corporations, especially
        with regard to their influence on social and
        political policy.
UF   Economic concentration
BT   Business & finance
NT   Industrial trusts
        Monopolies
RT   Special interests
**Big game fishing**
        --[country or state]
UF   Deep-sea fishing
BT   Fishing
NT   Shark fishing
**Big game hunting**
        --[country or state]
BT   Hunting
NT   Antelope hunting
        Bear hunting
        Bison hunting
        Elephant hunting
        Elk hunting
        Kangaroo hunting
        Lion hunting
        Mountain goat hunting
        Mountain sheep hunting
        Puma hunting

**Big game hunting (cont.)**
RT   Safaris
Big top
   USE Circuses & shows
        Show tents
**Bigamy**
        --[country or state]--[city]
PN   Multiple marriage as a criminal offense.
        Search under POLYGAMY for the practice
        of having more than one spouse.
CN   Used in a note under POLYGAMY.
UF   Multiple marriage
BT   Crimes
        Marriage
RT   Polygamy
Biggest
   USE Curiosities & wonders
Bighorn sheep
   USE Mountain sheep
Bigotry
   USE Prejudice
Bill paying
   USE Paying bills
**Billboard posters**
CN   TGM II term.
**Billboards**
        --[country or state]--[city]
BT   Signs
**Billheads**
CN   TGM II term.
Billiard halls
   USE Billiard parlors
**Billiard parlors**
        --[country or state]--[city]
PN   Search under BILLIARDS for images that
        focus on the game.
UF   Billiard halls
        Parlors, Billiard
        Pool halls
        Pool parlors
        Poolrooms
BT   Sports & recreation facilities
RT   Billiard rooms
        Billiards
**Billiard rooms**
        --[country or state]--[city]
PN   Search under BILLIARDS for images that
        focus on the game.
BT   Recreation rooms
RT   Billiard parlors
        Billiards
**Billiard table industry**
        --[country or state]--[city]
PN   Includes activities and structures.
CN   Double index under INDUSTRIAL
        FACILITIES (or NTs) for images that focus
        on facilities.
BT   Furniture industry
RT   Billiards
**Billiards**
        --[country or state]--[city]
CN   Used in a note under BILLIARD ROOMS

---

BT  Broader term                           RT  Related term                           PN Public Note
NT  Narrower term                          UF  Used for                               + Term has NTs
HN History Note                            CN Catalogers Note                         --[ ] May subdivide

**Billiards (cont.)**
　　　　and BILLIARD PARLORS.
　　UF　Carom billiards
　　　　Pool
　　BT　Games
　　NT　Children playing billiards
　　RT　Billiard parlors
　　　　Billiard rooms
　　　　Billiard table industry
Bills of fare
　　USE Menus
Bills (Legislation)
　　USE Legislation
Billy clubs
　　USE Nightsticks
**Bimetallism**
　　PN　Use of two metals (such as gold and
　　　　silver) jointly as a monetary standard with
　　　　both constituting legal tender at a
　　　　predetermined ratio.
　　BT　Economic policy
　　RT　Silver question
Binding twine
　　USE Twine
**Bingo**
　　　　--[country or state]--[city]
　　UF　Beano
　　BT　Games
　　RT　Gambling
**Binoculars**
　　BT　Optical devices
Biological mechanics
　　USE Biomechanics
**Biological pest control**
　　　　--[country or state]--[city]
　　PN　Use of natural predators or parasites to
　　　　control insects and related pests.
　　BT　Pest control
　　RT　Agriculture
　　　　Biology
　　　　Plant parasites
**Biology**
　　　　--[country or state]--[city]
　　PN　For the subject of biology in general and
　　　　the activities of biologists.
　　BT　Science
　　NT　Anatomy
　　　　Botany
　　　　Embryology
　　　　Zoology
　　RT　Artificial pollination
　　　　Biological pest control
　　　　Biomechanics
　　　　Camouflage (Biology)
　　　　Dissections
　　　　Evolution
　　　　Longevity
　　　　Pest control
**Biomechanics**
　　PN　For the study of the mechanics of
　　　　biological and especially muscular activity.
　　UF　Biological mechanics

**Biomechanics (cont.)**
　　BT　Physics
　　RT　Biology
　　　　Locomotion
**Biplanes**
　　　　--[nationality]--[country or state]--[city]
　　BT　Airplanes
Birch trees
　　USE Birches
**Birches**
　　　　--[country or state]--[city]
　　UF　Birch trees
　　BT　Trees
Bird baths
　　USE Birdbaths
Bird cages
　　USE Birdcages
Bird dogs
　　USE Hunting dogs
Bird houses
　　USE Birdhouses
Bird hunting
　　USE Game bird hunting
Bird nests
　　USE Birds' eggs & nests
**Bird watching**
　　　　--[country or state]--[city]
　　UF　Birding (Bird watching)
　　　　Birdwatching
　　RT　Birds
**Birdbaths**
　　　　--[country or state]--[city]
　　UF　Baths, Bird
　　　　Bird baths
　　BT　Yard ornaments
　　RT　Birds
**Birdcages**
　　UF　Bird cages
　　BT　Cages
　　RT　Birds
　　　　Pets
**Birdhouses**
　　　　--[country or state]--[city]
　　UF　Bird houses
　　　　Houses, Bird
　　BT　Animal housing
　　NT　Dovecotes
　　RT　Birds
　　　　Birds' eggs & nests
Birding (Bird watching)
　　USE Bird watching
**Birds**
　　　　--[country or state]
　　UF　Chicks
　　　　Nestlings
　　BT　Animals
　　NT　Birds of prey +
　　　　Bulbuls
　　　　Chickadees
　　　　Coots
　　　　Cormorants
　　　　Cranes (Birds)

BT Broader term　　　　　　RT Related term　　　　　　PN Public Note
NT Narrower term　　　　　　UF Used for　　　　　　　　+ Term has NTs
HN History Note　　　　　　　CN Catalogers Note　　　　--[ ] May subdivide

**Birds (cont.)**
        Crows
        Ducks
        Flamingos
        Geese
        Grouse
        Gulls
        Herons
        Hummingbirds
        Ibis
        Kingfishers
        Loons
        Magpies
        Ostriches
        Parrots +
        Partridges
        Peafowl +
        Pelicans
        Penguins
        Pheasants
        Pigeons +
        Poultry +
        Prairie hens
        Quails +
        Ravens
        Robins
        Sandpipers
        Snipes
        Starlings
        Storks
        Swallows
        Swans
        Titmice
        Toucans
        Turkeys
        Vultures
        Woodcocks
        Woodpeckers
  RT  Aviaries
        Bird watching
        Birdbaths
        Birdcages
        Birdhouses
        Birds' eggs & nests
        Cockfighting
        Extinct birds
        Feathers
        Firebird (Mythical bird)
        Game bird hunting
        Game & game birds
        Phoenix (Mythical bird)

**Birds of prey**
        --[country or state]
  UF  Prey, Birds of
  BT  Birds
  NT  Eagles
        Hawks +
        Ospreys
        Owls

**Birds' eggs & nests**
  UF  Bird nests
        Nestlings

**Birds' eggs & nests (cont.)**
        Nests
  RT  Birdhouses
        Birds
        Eggs

**Birdwatching**
  USE Bird watching

**Bird's-eye view prints**
  CN  TGM II term.
  UF  Panoramic maps

**Bird's-eye views**
  CN  TGM II term.
  UF  Balloon views
        Views, Bird's-eye

**Birth certificates**
  CN  TGM II term.

**Birth control**
        --[country or state]--[city]
  NT  Sterilization
  RT  Abortions
        Births
        Medicine
        Population control
        Women

**Birth defects**
  UF  Abnormalities
        Malformations
  RT  Albinos
        Births
        Handicapped persons
        Human curiosities

**Birthday cards**
  CN  TGM II term.

**Birthday parties**
        --[country or state]--[city]
  BT  Parties
  RT  Birthdays
        Children's parties

**Birthdays**
        --[country or state]--[city]
  PN  Search also under the subdivision
        --COMMEMORATION used with names of
        persons (Appendix B).
  BT  Anniversaries
  RT  Birthday parties

**Birthplaces**
        --[country or state]--[city]
  PN  Search also under the subdivision
        --BIRTHPLACE used with names of persons
        (Appendix B).
  CN  Used in a note under DWELLINGS.
  BT  Historic sites
  RT  Dwellings

**Births**
        --[country or state]--[city]
  UF  Childbirth
        Home births
  BT  Events
  RT  Birth control
        Birth defects
        Human life cycle
        Illegitimacy

---

**Births (cont.)**
      Maternity hospitals
      Midwives
      Pregnancy
Births, Multiple
  USE Quadruplets
      Quintuplets
      Triplets
      Twins
**Bishops**
      --[country or state]--[city]
  UF  Archbishops
  BT  Clergy
  NT  Popes
**Bison**
      --[country or state]
  PN  For the American buffalo. Search under
      BUFFALOES for buffaloes of the eastern
      hemisphere.
  CN  Used in a note under BUFFALOES.
  BT  Animals
  RT  Bison hunting
      Buffaloes
      Cattle
**Bison hunting**
      --[country or state]
  BT  Big game hunting
      Hunting
  RT  Bison
**Bites & stings**
  UF  Animal bites
      Insect bites
      Stings & bites
  BT  Wounds & injuries
  RT  Animal attacks
      Insects
**Bitters**
      --[country or state]--[city]
  BT  Beverages
  RT  Patent medicines
**Bittersweet**
      --[country or state]--[city]
  BT  Plants
Black Americans
  USE Afro-Americans
Black art (Witchcraft)
  USE Witchcraft
Black light works
  USE Luminous works
Black line prints
  USE Diazo prints
**Black lung**
      --[country or state]--[city]
  PN  Lung disease caused by coal dust
      inhalation.
  BT  Diseases
  RT  Coal mining
**Black market**
      --[country or state]--[city]
  UF  Contraband trade
      Gray market
  BT  Commerce

**Black market (cont.)**
  RT  Consumer rationing
      Price regulation
      Smuggling
**Black power**
      --[country or state]--[city]
  PN  Movement of Afro-Americans to gain
      control of the political, social, economic, and
      cultural institutions that effect them. Term
      especially used in the 1960s and 1970s.
  BT  Power (Social sciences)
  RT  Political participation
**Black sheep**
  PN  Member of a group who stands in
      conspicuous and unfavorable contrast to the
      other members, especially by reason of
      socially undesirable characteristics.
  UF  Sheep, Black
  BT  People
      Symbols
**Blackboards**
  UF  Chalkboards
  RT  Furniture
Blackface entertainment
  USE Minstrel shows
Blackmail
  USE Extortion
**Blacks**
      --[country or state]--[city]
  PN  For blacks who are permanent residents of
      countries other than the United States.
      (Images relating to black people in countries
      whose racial composition is predominantly
      black are assigned headings appropriate for
      the country as a whole, without the use of the
      heading BLACKS.) Search under
      AFRO-AMERICANS for permanent
      residents of the U.S. of black African
      descent, including black slaves in the U.S.
  CN  Although it is a proper name, this Library
      of Congress Subject Headings term is
      included in TGM I for ready reference. As
      appropriate, subdivide by subdivisions used
      with names of ethnic, racial, and regional
      groups, and with classes of persons
      (Appendix A).
  UF  Negroes
Blacksmith shops
  USE Forge shops
**Blacksmithing**
      --[country or state]--[city]
  CN  Used in a note under BLACKSMITHS.
  UF  Horse shoeing
      Horseshoeing
  BT  Forging
  RT  Blacksmiths
      Horseshoes
**Blacksmiths**
      --[country or state]--[city]
  BT  People associated with manual labor
  RT  Blacksmithing
Black-and-white prints

---

BT  Broader term
NT  Narrower term
HN  History Note

RT  Related term
UF  Used for
CN  Catalogers Note

PN  Public Note
+  Term has NTs
--[ ]  May subdivide

Black-and-white prints (cont.)
USE Photographic prints
**Blaming**
UF Accusing
Censuring
Fault finding
Pointing the finger
Reproaching
BT Interpersonal relations
RT Quarreling
Scapegoats
**Blankets**
BT Textiles
RT Clothing & dress
Furnishings
Blast furnaces
USE Furnaces
Bleeding (Therapy)
USE Phlebotomy
Blessings
USE Benedictions
Blimps
USE Airships
Blind embossed prints
USE Inkless intaglio prints
**Blind man's bluff**
BT Games
**Blind persons**
--[country or state]--[city]
BT Handicapped persons
RT Blindness
Braille
**Blind stamps**
CN TGM II term.
UF Stamps, Blind
**Blindness**
--[country or state]--[city]
PN For the physical condition of being
without sight and the quality of mental or
moral blindess.
RT Blind persons
Mental states
Vision disorders
**Blizzards**
--[country or state]--[city]
PN Includes the event and any resulting
damage.
UF Snowstorms
BT Storms
RT Snow
Block prints
USE Relief prints
**Blockade running**
--[country or state]--[city]
RT Blockades
Ships
Smuggling
War relief
**Blockades**
--[nationality]--[country or state]--[city]
PN Barriers set up by troops or ships to
prevent ingress or egress; also restrictive

Blockades (cont.)
measures to obstruct communication and cut
off commerce with an enemy.
CN Subdivide by nationality of those
imposing the blockade.
BT Military art & science
RT Blockade running
Embargoes
**Blockhouses**
--[nationality]--[country or state]--[city]
BT Military facilities
RT Forts & fortifications
Martello towers
**Blocks (Toys)**
UF Building blocks (Toys)
BT Toys
Blocks, Printing
USE Printing blocks
**Blood**
RT Blood donations
Cardiovascular system
Human body
Phlebotomy
Blood circulation
USE Cardiovascular system
**Blood donations**
--[country or state]--[city]
UF Donations of blood
RT Blood
Medicine
Phlebotomy
Blood letting
USE Phlebotomy
Blood pressure, High
USE Hypertension
Bloodletting
USE Phlebotomy
**Bloody shirt**
PN Means employed to stir up or revive party
or sectional animosity.
UF Waving the bloody shirt
BT Symbols
RT Clothing & dress
Prejudice
Sectionalism (United States)
**Bloomers**
BT Clothing & dress
RT Underwear
Blossoms
USE Flowers
Blue collar workers
USE Laborers
Blue collar (Social class)
USE Working class
**Blue laws**
--[country or state]--[city]
BT Laws
RT Alcoholic beverages
Prohibition
Blue line prints
USE Diazo prints
**Bluefish**

---

BT Broader term
NT Narrower term
HN History Note

RT Related term
UF Used for
CN Catalogers Note

PN Public Note
+ Term has NTs
--[ ] May subdivide

**Bluefish (cont.)**
      --[country or state]
  BT  Fish
**Blueprints**
  CN  TGM II term.
**Blues music**
      --[country or state]--[city]
  BT  Music
  RT  Blues singers
**Blues singers**
  UF  Blues vocalists
  BT  Singers
  RT  Blues music
Blues vocalists
  USE  Blues singers
Bluffs
  USE  Cliffs
**Board games**
      --[country or state]--[city]
  BT  Games
  NT  Backgammon
        Checkers
        Chess
        Mah jong
Board rooms
  USE  Conference rooms
Boarding houses
  USE  Lodging houses
Boardrooms
  USE  Conference rooms
**Boards of trade**
      --[country or state]--[city]
  PN  In the United States, bodies organized for
      the advancement and protection of business
      interests. Includes activities and structures.
  BT  Commercial organizations
  RT  Chambers of commerce
**Boardwalks**
      --[country or state]--[city]
  BT  Walkways
  RT  Amusement piers
        Beaches
        Penny arcades
        Streets
        Waterfronts
**Boars**
      --[country or state]
  BT  Swine
Boasting
  USE  Bragging
Boat building
  USE  Boat & ship industry
**Boat clubs**
      --[country or state]--[city]
  PN  Includes activities and structures.
  CN  Double index under ORGANIZATIONS'
      FACILITIES (or NTs) for images that focus
      on facilities.
  BT  Clubs
  NT  Yacht clubs
**Boat engines**
  UF  Motorboat engines

**Boat engines (cont.)**
      Ship engines
  BT  Engines
**Boat graveyards**
      --[country or state]--[city]
  UF  Graveyards, Boat
  BT  Junkyards
  RT  Vessels
Boat landings
  USE  Beaches
       Piers & wharves
Boat people
  USE  Refugees
Boat racing
  USE  Regattas
       Steamboat racing
**Boat & ship companies**
      --[country or state]--[city]
  PN  Includes activities and structures.
  BT  Business enterprises
  RT  Vessels
**Boat & ship industry**
      --[country or state]--[city]
  PN  Includes activities and structures.
  CN  Double index under INDUSTRIAL
      FACILITIES (or NTs) for images that focus
      on facilities.
  UF  Boat building
        Boatyards
        Dockyards
        Dry docks
        Shipbuilding
        Shipyards
  BT  Transportation industry
  RT  Boat & ship industry strikes
        Construction industry
        Launchings
        Naval yards & naval stations
        Vessels
**Boat & ship industry strikes**
      --[country or state]--[city]
  BT  Strikes
  RT  Boat & ship industry
**Boathouses**
      --[country or state]--[city]
  PN  A building usually built partly in the water
      for the housing or storing of boats.
  BT  Transportation facilities
  RT  Sports & recreation facilities
Boating
  USE  Boats
**Boats**
      --[nationality]--[country or state]--[city]
  UF  Boating
  BT  Vessels
  NT  Barges +
        Canal boats +
        Canoes +
        Dhows
        Dories (Boats)
        Ferries +
        Fireboats

---

BT  Broader term           RT  Related term           PN Public Note
NT  Narrower term          UF  Used for             + Term has NTs
HN  History Note           CN  Catalogers Note     --[ ] May subdivide

**Boats (cont.)**
    Flatboats
    Glass bottom boats
    Houseboats +
    Iceboats
    Junks
    Keelboats
    Lifeboats
    Longboats
    Motorboats +
    Pilot boats
    Racing shells
    Rafts +
    Rowboats
    Sailboats
    Sampans
    Tugboats
  RT  Portages
    Regattas
    Ships
**Boatyards**
  USE Boat & ship industry
    Naval yards & naval stations
**Bobbing for apples**
    --[country or state]--[city]
  BT  Games
  RT  Apples
**Bobsleds**
    --[country or state]--[city]
  PN  Includes the activity of bobsledding.
  HN  Changed 7/1989 from BOBSLEDDING.
  BT  Sleds & sleighs
**Bobwhites**
    --[country or state]
  BT  Quails
**Bodies**
  USE Dead animals
    Dead persons
**Bodies of water**
    --[country or state]--[city]
  UF  Water, Bodies of
  NT  Basins (Bodies of water)
    Bays +
    Channels
    Harbors
    Lakes & ponds +
    Seas +
    Springs
    Streams +
    Territorial waters
    Tide pools
    Waterfalls
  RT  Beaches
    Beaver dams
    Floods
    Hydraulic facilities
    Land
    Nature
    Oases
    Reflections
    Wading
    Water pollution

**Bodies of water (cont.)**
    Waterfronts
    Wetlands
    Whirlpools
**Body marking**
  USE Body-marking
**Bodybuilders**
  USE Strong men
**Bodybuilding**
  USE Weight lifting
**Body, Human**
  USE Human body
**Body-marking**
    --[country or state]--[city]
  UF  Body marking
  NT  Tattoos
  RT  Manners & customs
**Bogs**
  USE Wetlands
**Bohemians**
    --[country or state]--[city]
  UF  Beatniks
    Nonconformists
  BT  People
  RT  Hippies
    Manners & customs
**Boiler industry**
    --[country or state]--[city]
  PN  Includes activities and structures.
  CN  Double index under INDUSTRIAL
    FACILTIES (or NTs) for images that focus
    on facilities.
  BT  Industry
  RT  Boilers
**Boilers**
  BT  Equipment
  RT  Boiler industry
**Bolshevism**
  USE Communism
**Bolts & nuts**
  UF  Nuts (Hardware)
  BT  Hardware
**Bomb attacks**
  USE Bombings
**Bomb damage**
  USE War damage
**Bomb shelters**
  USE Air raid shelters
**Bombardment**
    --[country or state]--[city]
  PN  Sustained military attacks on cities,
    military positions, and other places with
    bombs, shells, rockets, or other explosive
    missiles.  Search under AERIAL BOMBING
    for images of military bombardment by
    bombs dropped from the air and under
    BOMBINGS for the use of explosive devices
    for the purposes of political terrrorism,
    protest, etc.
  CN  Used in a note under BOMBINGS and
    AERIAL BOMBINGS.
  BT  Military art & science

---

BT Broader term      RT Related term      PN Public Note
NT Narrower term     UF Used for      + Term has NTs
HN History Note       CN Catalogers Note    --[ ] May subdivide

**Bombardment (cont.)**
RT   Aerial bombings
      Bombings
**Bombers**
      --[nationality]--[country or state]--[city]
BT   Airplanes
RT   Air warfare
**Bombings**
      --[country or state]--[city]
PN   For the use of explosive devices for the
      purposes of political terrorism, protest, etc.
      Search under AERIAL BOMBINGS for
      images of military bombardment by bombs
      dropped from the air and under
      BOMBARDMENT for sustained military
      attacks on cities, military positions, and other
      places with bombs, shells, rockets, or other
      explosive missiles.
CN   Used in a note under AERIAL
      BOMBINGS and BOMBARDMENT.
UF   Bomb attacks
RT   Aerial bombings
      Bombardment
      Bombs
      Explosions
      Nuclear weapons
      Ordnance testing
      Terrorism
**Bombproof construction**
      --[country or state]--[city]
UF   Bomb-proof buildings
      Building, Bombproof
BT   Construction
RT   Air raid shelters
      Forts & fortifications
**Bombs**
      --[nationality]--[country or state]--[city]
BT   Arms & armament
      Explosives
RT   Artillery (Weaponry)
      Bombings
      Nuclear weapons
Bomb-proof buildings
   USE Bombproof construction
Bondage
   USE Physical restraints
**Bonds (Financial records)**
CN   TGM II term.
RT   Saving & investment
      War bonds & funds
Bone fractures
   USE Fractures
**Bones**
RT   Death's head
      Fractures
      Skeletons
**Bones (Musical instrument)**
BT   Percussion instruments
**Bonnets**
PN   Head coverings for women or small
      children made of cloth or straw usually tied
      under the chin with ribbons or strings and

**Bonnets (cont.)**
      made with or without a brim.
UF   Poke bonnets
      Sunbonnets
BT   Hats
**Book burning**
      --[country or state]--[city]
UF   Burning of books
BT   Censorship
RT   Books
      Fires
Book cases
   USE Bookcases
**Book clubs**
      --[country or state]--[city]
PN   Includes activities and structures.
CN   Double index under CLUBHOUSES or
      ORGANIZATIONS' FACILITIES (or NTs)
      for images that focus on facilities.
BT   Clubs
RT   Book talks
      Books
      Reading
**Book covers**
CN   TGM II term.
**Book ends**
BT   Equipment
RT   Bookcases
      Books
Book exhibitions
   USE Book fairs
**Book fairs**
      --[country or state]--[city]
PN   Includes activities, structures, and sites.
UF   Book exhibitions
BT   Exhibitions
RT   Bookselling
      Publishing industry
**Book illustrations**
CN   TGM II term.
UF   Pamphlet illustrations
**Book jackets**
CN   TGM II term.
UF   Dust jackets
      Jackets, Book
Book plates
   USE Bookplates
Book signings
   USE Autographing
**Book talks**
      --[country or state]--[city]
BT   Events
      Public speaking
RT   Book clubs
      Books
      Libraries
      Reading
Book trade
   USE Bookselling
      Publishing industry
**Book & magazine posters**
CN   TGM II term.

---

BT  Broader term             RT  Related term             PN  Public Note
NT  Narrower term          UF  Used for                +  Term has NTs
HN  History Note           CN  Catalogers Note       --[ ]  May subdivide

**Book & magazine posters (cont.)**
- UF   Magazine posters
-      Newspaper posters
-      Periodical posters

**Bookbinding**
- RT   Books
-      Handicraft
-      Leather industry

**Bookcases**
-      --[country or state]--[city]
- UF   Book cases
-      Bookshelves
-      Cases, Book
- BT   Furniture
-      Shelving
- RT   Book ends
-      Bookstacks

**Booklets**
- USE   Leaflets
-      Pamphlets
-      Viewbooks

**Bookmarks**
- CN   TGM II term.

**Bookmobiles**
-      --[nationality]--[country or state]--[city]
- BT   Vehicles
- RT   Libraries

**Bookplates**
- CN   TGM II term.
- UF   Book plates
-      Ex libris

**Books**
- PN   For images that focus on books. Search under READING for activities.
- CN   TGM II term.
- NT   Encyclopedias & dictionaries
-      Religious books +
-      Telephone directories
- RT   Book burning
-      Book clubs
-      Book ends
-      Book talks
-      Bookbinding
-      Bookstacks
-      Bookstores
-      Libraries
-      Publishing industry
-      Registers
-      Secondhand bookstores

**Bookselling**
-      --[country or state]--[city]
- PN   For bookselling outside of bookstores.
- UF   Book trade
-      Colportage
- RT   Book fairs
-      Bookstores
-      Publishing industry
-      Secondhand bookstores

**Bookshelves**
- USE   Bookcases

**Bookstacks**
-      --[country or state]--[city]

**Bookstacks (cont.)**
- PN   For sets of shelves or bookcases usually separated by narrow aisles, used for compactly storing books.
- UF   Stacks, Book
- BT   Furniture
- RT   Bookcases
-      Books
-      Libraries

**Bookstores**
-      --[country or state]--[city]
- PN   Includes activities and structures.
- BT   Stores & shops
- NT   Secondhand bookstores
- RT   Books
-      Bookselling

**Boomerangs**
- BT   Throwing sticks

**Boot industry**
- USE   Shoe industry

**Boot making**
- USE   Shoemaking

**Bootblacks**
- USE   Shoe shiners

**Booting**
- USE   Kicking

**Bootlegging**
- USE   Prohibition
-      Stills (Distilleries)

**Boots**
- PN   Footwear usually of leather or rubber that covers the foot and part or all of the legs.
- HN   Changed 8/1988 from non-postable term (Use SHOES).
- BT   Footwear

**Booty**
- USE   War destruction & pillage

**Borders**
- USE   Boundaries

**Boredom**
- UF   Ennui
- BT   Mental states
- RT   Apathy
-      Fatigue

**Borers**
- USE   Drilling & boring machinery

**Boring**
-      --[country or state]--[city]
- PN   For cutting of holes in earth or rocks to determine the nature of the strata penetrated or to create an outlet for oil, water, or gas. Search under DRILLING for drilling of holes in metal or wood for construction and manufacturing purposes.
- CN   Used in a note under DRILLING.
- NT   Underwater drilling
- RT   Construction
-      Drilling
-      Drilling & boring machinery
-      Excavation
-      Petroleum industry

**Boring machinery**

---

Boring machinery (cont.)
  USE Drilling & boring machinery
Botanical drawings
  USE Botanical illustrations
**Botanical gardens**
         --[country or state]--[city]
  UF  Arboretums
  BT  Gardens
**Botanical illustrations**
  CN  TGM II term.
  UF  Botanical drawings
       Drawings, Botanical
**Botany**
         --[country or state]--[city]
  PN  For the subject of botany in general and
       the activities of botanists.
  BT  Biology
  RT  Paleontology
       Plants
**Bottle industry**
         --[country or state]--[city]
  PN  Includes activities and structures.
  CN  Double index under INDUSTRIAL
       FACILITIES (or NTs)  for images that focus
       on facilities.
  BT  Industry
  RT  Bottles
Bottled ships
  USE Ship models in bottles
**Bottles**
  BT  Containers
  RT  Bottle industry
       Glassware
       Ship models in bottles
**Boudoir card photographs**
  CN  TGM II term.
Boudoir photographs
  USE Glamour photographs
**Boudoirs**
         --[country or state]--[city]
  PN  Women's bedrooms, dressing rooms, or
       private sitting rooms.
  UF  Dressing rooms
  BT  Interiors
  RT  Bedrooms
       Living rooms
**Boulders**
         --[country or state]
  PN  Detached and rounded or much-worn
       masses of rock.
  RT  Rock formations
**Boundaries**
         --[country or state]
  UF  Borders
  RT  Annexations
       Geography
**Bouquets**
  RT  Festive decorations
       Flowers
Bourgeoisie
  USE Middle class
**Bow windows**

Bow windows (cont.)
         --[country or state]--[city]
  PN  Bay windows that are curved in plan.
  UF  Windows, Bow
  BT  Bay windows
Bowers
  USE Arbors (Bowers)
**Bowing**
  BT  Etiquette
**Bowlers**
         --[country or state]--[city]
  CN  Geographical subdivision indicates place
       where team or player is based.
  UF  Bowling leagues
       Bowling teams
  BT  Athletes
  RT  Bowling
       Bowling alleys
**Bowling**
         --[country or state]--[city]
  CN  Used in a note under BOWLING
       ALLEYS.
  BT  Sports
  RT  Bowlers
       Bowling alleys
       Pinsetting
**Bowling alleys**
         --[country or state]--[city]
  PN  Search under BOWLING for activities.
  UF  Alleys, Bowling
       Lanes, Bowling
  BT  Sports & recreation facilities
  RT  Bowlers
       Bowling
       Pinsetting
Bowling leagues
  USE Bowlers
Bowling teams
  USE Bowlers
**Bowls (Tableware)**
  BT  Tableware
**Bows (Archery)**
  BT  Equipment
  NT  Crossbows
  RT  Archery
       Arms & armament
       Arrows
Box cars
  USE Railroad freight cars
**Box industry**
         --[country or state]--[city]
  PN  Includes activities and structures.
  CN  Double index under INDUSTRIAL
       FACILITIES (or NTs) for images that focus
       on facilities.
  UF  Paper box industry
       Wooden box industry
  BT  Industry
  RT  Boxes
Box irons
  USE Irons (Pressing)
**Boxers (Sports)**

---

BT  Broader term
NT  Narrower term
HN  History Note

RT  Related term
UF  Used for
CN  Catalogers Note

PN  Public Note
+  Term has NTs
--[ ] May subdivide

**Boxers (Sports) (cont.)**
    --[country or state]--[city]
CN  Geographical subdivision indicates place
    where player is based.
BT  Athletes
RT  Boxing
**Boxes**
BT  Containers
RT  Box industry
**Boxing**
    --[country or state]--[city]
UF  Prizefighting
BT  Sports
RT  Boxers (Sports)
    Fighting
    Martial arts
**Boycotts**
    --[nationality]--[country or state]--[city]
CN  Subdivide by nationality of those
    imposing the boycott.
BT  Events
RT  Commerce
    Strikes
**Boys**
    --[country or state]--[city]
PN  Males, ages 0-16.
HN  Changed 7/1991 from non-postable term
    (Use CHILDREN). For earlier cataloging,
    search under CHILDREN.
BT  Children
RT  Men
Boys' gangs
  USE Gangs
Braces
  USE Orthopedic braces
Brackets (Consoles)
  USE Consoles
**Bragging**
UF  Boasting
RT  Pride
**Braids (Hairdressing)**
UF  Pigtails
BT  Hairstyles
**Braille**
BT  Writing systems
RT  Blind persons
Branches
  USE Tree limbs
Branding of cattle
  USE Cattle branding
Brass bands
  USE Bands
**Brass industry**
    --[country or state]--[city]
PN  Includes activities and structures.
CN  Double index under INDUSTRIAL
    FACILITIES (or NTs) for images that focus
    on facilities.
BT  Metallurgical industry
RT  Copper industry
**Brass instruments**
PN  Includes the activity of playing brass

**Brass instruments (cont.)**
    instruments.
BT  Wind instruments
NT  Bugles
    Cornets
    Trombones
    Trumpets
    Tubas
RT  Bands
Bravery
  USE Courage
**Bread**
    --[country or state]--[city]
BT  Baked products
NT  Tortillas
RT  Sandwiches
**Bread & soup lines**
    --[country or state]--[city]
UF  Food lines
    Soup lines
BT  Food relief
    Queues
Break crops
  USE Crop rotation
Breakers
  USE Seas
Breakers (Machinery)
  USE Coal mining
Breakfast cereals
  USE Prepared cereals
**Breakfast rooms**
    --[country or state]--[city]
BT  Interiors
RT  Eating & drinking facilities
Breakwaters
  USE Jetties
Breast beams
  USE Lintels
**Breast feeding**
    --[country or state]--[city]
UF  Breastfeeding
    Nursing (Infant feeding)
BT  Children eating & drinking
RT  Infants
    Mothers & children
Breastfeeding
  USE Breast feeding
**Breasts**
UF  Mammary glands
RT  Human body
Breeding grounds
  USE Rookeries
**Brethren churches**
    --[country or state]--[city]
PN  For images that focus on buildings, as
    well as the associated grounds.
UF  Dunkard churches
BT  Protestant churches
Breweries
  USE Brewing industry
**Brewing industry**
    --[country or state]--[city]

---

BT  Broader term
NT  Narrower term
HN  History Note

RT  Related term
UF  Used for
CN  Catalogers Note

PN  Public Note
+  Term has NTs
--[ ]  May subdivide

**Brewing industry (cont.)**
  PN  Includes activities and structures.
  CN  Double index under INDUSTRIAL
      FACILITIES (or NTs) for images that focus
      on facilities.
  UF  Alcoholic beverage industry
      Beer industry
      Breweries
  BT  Beverage industry
  RT  Beer
      Hops

**Bribery**
      --[country or state]--[city]
  RT  Corruption

**Brick industry**
      --[country or state]--[city]
  PN  Includes activities and structures.
  CN  Double index under INDUSTRIAL
      FACILITIES (or NTs)  for images that focus
      on facilities.
  BT  Building materials industry
      Clay industries
  RT  Kilns

**Bricklayers' unions**
      --[country or state]--[city]
  BT  Labor unions
  RT  Bricklaying

**Bricklaying**
      --[country or state]--[city]
  BT  Masonry
  RT  Bricklayers' unions
      Brickwork

**Brickwork**
      --[country or state]--[city]
  RT  Bricklaying

Bric-a-brac
  USE Art objects

Bridal gowns
  USE Wedding costume

Bridegrooms
  USE Grooms (Weddings)

**Brides**
  PN  For images which focus on persons, search
      under WEDDINGS for activities.
  RT  Grooms (Weddings)
      Wedding costume
      Weddings

**Bridge construction**
      --[country or state]--[city]
  BT  Civil engineering
      Construction
  RT  Bridges
      Road construction

**Bridge failures**
      --[country or state]--[city]
  UF  Collapse of bridges
  BT  Disasters
  RT  Bridges
      Pier & wharf failures

**Bridge (Game)**
  BT  Card games

**Bridges**

**Bridges (cont.)**
      --[country or state]--[city]
  PN  Structures erected over a depression or
      obstacle, as over a river, gorge, roadway,
      etc., carrying a roadway and/or walkway for
      vehicles or persons. Search under SWING
      BRIDGES for bridges that move horizontally
      and under VERTICAL LIFT BRIDGES for
      bridges that lift vertically.
  UF  Viaducts
  BT  Transportation facilities
  NT  Covered bridges
      Drawbridges
      Pedestrian bridges
      Pile bridges
      Pontoon bridges
      Railroad bridges
      Suspension bridges
      Swing bridges
      Toll bridges
      Transporter bridges
      Vertical lift bridges
  RT  Aqueducts
      Bridge construction
      Bridge failures
      Culverts
      Elevated highways
      Moving of structures
      Pylons (Bridges)
      Trestles
      Trusses

Bridges, Natural
  USE Rock formations

Bridle paths
  USE Trails & paths

**Broadcasting**
      --[country or state]--[city]
  PN  Search also under the subdivision
      --COMMUNICATIONS used with the names
      of wars (Appendix C).
  BT  Communication
  NT  Radio broadcasting
      Television broadcasting
  RT  Newsrooms
      Reporters
      Sound recording

Broadsheets
  USE Broadsides

**Broadsides**
  CN  TGM II term.
  UF  Broadsheets
  RT  Announcements

Broadsides (Warships)
  USE Armored vessels

Brochures
  USE Leaflets

**Broken glass**
  UF  Glass, Broken
  RT  Glassware

Bromide prints
  USE Silver gelatin prints

Bromoil photoprints

---

BT  Broader term
NT  Narrower term
HN  History Note

RT  Related term
UF  Used for
CN  Catalogers Note

PN Public Note
+ Term has NTs
--[ ] May subdivide

Bromoil photoprints (cont.)
  USE Bromoil prints
**Bromoil prints**
  CN  TGM II term.
  UF  Bromoil photoprints
**Broncos**
       --[country or state]--[city]
  UF  Bucking broncos
  BT  Horses
  RT  Cowboys
       Rodeos
       Trick riding
**Bronze industry**
       --[country or state]--[city]
  CN  Double index under INDUSTRIAL
       FACILITIES (or NTs) for images that focus
       on facilities.
  BT  Metallurgical industry
  RT  Copper industry
Brooks
  USE Streams
**Broom & brush industry**
       --[country or state]--[city]
  PN  Includes activities and structures.
  CN  Double index under INDUSTRIAL
       FACILITIES (or NTs) for images that focus
       on facilities.
  BT  Industry
  RT  Brooms & brushes
**Brooms & brushes**
  PN  For brooms and brushes not in the process
       of being used. Search under SWEEPING &
       DUSTING for activities.
  UF  Brushes
  BT  Equipment
  RT  Broom & brush industry
       Sweeping & dusting
**Brothels**
       --[country or state]--[city]
  UF  Houses of prostitution
       Whorehouses
  BT  Service industry facilities
  RT  Prostitution
Brotherly love
  USE Interpersonal relations
Brothers
  USE Families
Brownies
  USE Fairies
Brownprints
  USE Diazo prints
       Kallitypes
**Brush works**
  CN  TGM II term.
Brushes
  USE Brooms & brushes
Bubble blowing
  USE Bubbles
       Children blowing bubbles
Bubble gum cards
  USE Sports cards
**Bubbles**

Bubbles (cont.)
  UF  Bubble blowing
  RT  Children blowing bubbles
Bubonic plague
  USE Plague
Buccaneers
  USE Pirates
Buck passing
  USE Passing the buck
Buckets
  USE Pails
Bucking broncos
  USE Broncos
**Buckwheat**
       --[country or state]--[city]
  BT  Grains
**Buddhas**
       --[country or state]--[city]
  BT  Buddhist gods
  RT  Religious articles
       Sculpture
**Buddhist gods**
  BT  Gods
  NT  Buddhas
  RT  Buddhist temples
**Buddhist temples**
       --[country or state]--[city]
  BT  Temples
  RT  Buddhist gods
       Wats
Budget
  USE Economic policy
Budget freezes
  USE Government spending reductions
Budget reductions
  USE Government spending reductions
**Buffaloes**
       --[country or state]
  PN  For buffaloes of the eastern hemisphere.
       Search under BISON for the American
       buffalo.
  CN  Used in a note under BISON.
  UF  Oxen, Wild
       Wild oxen
  BT  Animals
  NT  Water buffaloes
  RT  Bison
       Cattle
**Buffets (Cookery)**
       --[country or state]--[city]
  RT  Cookery
**Buffets (Furniture)**
  UF  Credenzas
       Sideboards
  BT  Furniture
Buggies
  USE Carriages & coaches
**Bugles**
  PN  Valveless brass instruments that resemble
       trumpets and are used especially for military
       calls. Includes the activity of playing bugles.
  BT  Brass instruments

---

BT  Broader term                    RT  Related term                    PN Public Note
NT  Narrower term                   UF  Used for                        +  Term has NTs
HN  History Note                    CN  Catalogers Note                 --[ ] May subdivide

**Bugles (cont.)**
  RT  Communication devices
       Trombones
       Trumpets
       Tubas
**Bugs**
  USE Insects
**Bugs (Electronic surveillance)**
  USE Electronic surveillance
**Building**
  USE Construction
**Building blocks (Toys)**
  USE Blocks (Toys)
**Building construction**
      --[country or state]--[city]
  CN  As appropriate, double index under the
       type of building. Used in a note under
       BUILDINGS.
  HN  Term established 2/90. Earlier cataloging
       used CONSTRUCTION INDUSTRY and the
       type of structure involved.
  BT  Construction
  RT  Buildings
       Cornerstone laying
       Toppings out
**Building dedications**
      --[country or state]--[city]
  UF  Dedication of buildings
  BT  Dedications
  NT  Church dedications
       Cornerstone laying
  RT  Buildings
       Ground breaking ceremonies
       Toppings out
**Building deterioration**
      --[country or state]--[city]
  UF  Decay of buildings
       Deterioration of buildings
       Dilapidation of buildings
       Weathering of buildings
  BT  Deterioration
  RT  Abandoned buildings
       Building failures
       Erosion
       Slums
       Vandalism
**Building divisions**
      --[country or state]--[city]
  BT  Architectural & site components
  NT  Pavilions (Building divisions)
       Penthouses
       Rooms & spaces +
       Wings (Building divisions)
  RT  Buildings
**Building failures**
      --[country or state]--[city]
  UF  Collapse of buildings
       Roof collapses
  BT  Disasters
  RT  Building deterioration
       Buildings
**Building guards**

**Building guards (cont.)**
  USE Watchmen
**Building materials**
  NT  Clapboard siding
       Concrete
       Laths
  RT  Building materials industry
       Laminated plastics
       Tiles
**Building materials industry**
      --[country or state]--[city]
  PN  Includes activities and structures.
  CN  Double index under INDUSTRIAL
       FACILITIES (or NTs) for images that focus
       on facilities.
  BT  Industry
  NT  Brick industry
       Cement industries
       Concrete products industry
       Nail industry
  RT  Building materials
       Ceramic industries
       Construction industry
       Glass industry
       Lumber industry
**Building models**
  PN  Miniature relief or three-dimensional
       representations of real or imaginary
       buildings. Search under ARCHITECTURAL
       MODELS for miniature representations in
       scale of structures or parts of structures made
       for the purpose of showing the result of actual
       architectural construction plans. Search under
       MODEL HOUSES for full-scale
       representations of houses planned to be
       constructed.
  CN  Used in a note under ARCHITECTURAL
       MODELS.
  BT  Models
  NT  Dollhouses
  RT  Architectural models
       Buildings
**Building plaques**
  USE Plaques
**Building systems**
      --[country or state]--[city]
  PN  Assemblies of integrated building
       subsystems satisfying the functional
       requirements of a building.
  BT  Architectural & site components
  NT  Conveying systems +
       Mechanical systems +
       Mechanical systems components +
  RT  Intercommunication systems
       Lighting
       Public address systems
**Buildings**
      --[country or state]--[city]
  PN  For buildings in general; includes
       buildings with indeterminate functions and
       buildings distinguished by attributes other
       than function.  Search under other

BT  Broader term                RT  Related term                PN Public Note
NT  Narrower term             UF  Used for                     + Term has NTs
HN History Note                CN Catalogers Note           --[ ] May subdivide

**Buildings (cont.)**
FACILITIES NTs for buildings that serve particular functions (e.g., AGRICULTURAL FACILITIES). Search also under the subdivision -- STRUCTURES used with ethnic, racial, and regional groups, and classes of persons (Appendix A). Search also under the subdivision --BUILDINGS used with names of corporate bodies and named events (Appendix D).
BT   Facilities
NT   Abandoned buildings
      Air-supported structures
      Buildings distinguished by form +
      Buildings distinguished by material +
      Gatehouses
      Historic buildings
      Office buildings
      Outbuildings +
      Portable buildings
      Prefabricated buildings
      Recycled structures
      Temporary buildings
RT   Building construction
      Building dedications
      Building divisions
      Building failures
      Building models
      Moving of structures

**Buildings distinguished by form**
CN   This heading is not used for indexing.
BT   Buildings
NT   Circular buildings
      Distyle-in-antis buildings
      Greek cross buildings
      Hexagonal buildings
      Latin cross buildings
      Lean-tos
      Mimetic buildings
      Octagonal buildings
      Skyscrapers
      Towers +

**Buildings distinguished by material**
CN   This heading is not used for indexing.
BT   Buildings
NT   Adobe buildings
      Half-timbered buildings
      Sod buildings
      Stone buildings
      Wooden buildings +

Building, Bombproof
USE Bombproof construction

**Built-in furniture**
--[country or state]--[city]
BT   Furniture

Bulbs, Light
USE Light bulbs

**Bulbuls**
--[country or state]
BT   Birds

**Bulldozers**
BT   Machinery

**Bulldozers (cont.)**
RT   Steam shovels
      Tracklaying vehicles
      Tractors

**Bullet holes**
BT   Holes
RT   Ammunition
      Bullets
      Firearms
      Shooting

**Bullets**
BT   Ammunition
RT   Bullet holes
      Firearms

**Bullfighters**
--[country or state]--[city]
UF   Matadors
      Toreadors
      Toreros
BT   People associated with entertainment & sports
RT   Bullfighting

**Bullfighting**
--[country or state]--[city]
BT   Sports
RT   Bullfighters

Bullocks
USE Cattle

**Bulls**
--[country or state]
BT   Cattle
RT   Cows

**Bull's eye windows**
--[country or state]--[city]
PN   Round or oval windows, usually with glazing bars radiating from a circular center.
UF   Oeil-de-boeuf windows
      Oxeye windows
BT   Windows

Bull's-eyes
USE Targets (Sports)

Bumble bees
USE Bees

**Bumper stickers**
CN   TGM II term.

**Bundling (Packing)**
--[country or state]--[city]
PN   The activity of assembling or binding material in a group.
UF   Ricking
RT   Shipping

**Bungalows**
--[country or state]--[city]
PN   One-story frame houses or summer cottages, often surrounded by covered verandas.
BT   Houses

**Buoys**
UF   Bell buoys
BT   Communication devices
RT   Navigation

Bureaucratic paperwork

---

BT Broader term        RT Related term        PN Public Note
NT Narrower term      UF Used for           + Term has NTs
HN History Note         CN Catalogers Note     --[ ] May subdivide

Bureaucratic paperwork (cont.)
  USE Paperwork
Bureaucratic red tape
  USE Red tape
Bureaus (Furniture)
  USE Clothes chests
Burglar alarms
  USE Security systems
Burglaries
  USE Robberies
Burial vaults
  USE Tombs & sepulchral monuments
Burials
  USE Funeral rites & ceremonies
**Burials at sea**
  BT  Funeral rites & ceremonies
Burlesque posters
  USE Theatrical posters
**Burlesque shows**
       --[country or state]--[city]
  PN  For theatrical entertainments characterized
       by broad humor, consisting of comic skits,
       slapstick, striptease acts, and songs and
       dances performed by soloists or a chorus.
  BT  Theatrical productions
  RT  Music
       Music halls
Burning
  USE Fire
**Burning at the stake**
       --[country or state]--[city]
  UF  Burnt at the stake
  BT  Executions
  RT  Fires
**Burning coal veins**
       --[country or state]--[city]
  RT  Coal
       Fire
Burning in effigy
  USE Executions in effigy
Burning of books
  USE Book burning
Burning the dead
  USE Cremation
**Burns & scalds**
  UF  Scalds
  NT  Sunburns
Burnt at the stake
  USE Burning at the stake
Burnt offerings
  USE Sacrifices
**Burping**
  UF  Belching
  RT  Manners & customs
Burros
  USE Donkeys
Bus stations
  USE Bus terminals
**Bus stops**
       --[country or state]--[city]
  BT  Site elements
  RT  Bus terminals

Bus stops (cont.)
       Buses
**Bus terminals**
       --[country or state]--[city]
  UF  Bus stations
  BT  Transportation facilities
  RT  Bus stops
       Buses
**Buses**
       --[nationality]--[country or state]--[city]
  UF  Omnibuses
  BT  Vehicles
  NT  Double-decker buses
  RT  Bus stops
       Bus terminals
       Mass transit
Bushes
  USE Shrubs
Business agreements
  USE Deals
**Business cards**
  CN  TGM II term.
  UF  Tradecards
Business deals
  USE Deals
**Business districts**
       --[country or state]--[city]
  PN  Areas in towns or cities used for
       commerical purposes; usually defined and
       limited by zoning ordinances.
  UF  Central business districts
       Commercial districts
       Districts, Business
       Downtown districts
  BT  Commercial facilities
  RT  Commercial streets
**Business education**
       --[country or state]--[city]
  PN  Includes activities and structures.
  CN  Double index under EDUCATIONAL
       FACILITIES (or NTs) for images that focus
       on facilities.
  UF  Business schools
  BT  Education
  RT  Business & finance
**Business enterprises**
       --[country or state]--[city]
  PN  For organizations and undertakings
       concerned with the supply and distribution of
       goods and services. Search under
       COMMERCIAL FACILITIES (and NTs) for
       facilities where goods and services are
       bought and sold.
  HN  Scope note changed 1/1993.  Formerly
       included both organizations involved in
       supply and distribution of goods and services
       and the facilities where goods and services
       are bought and sold, including stores and
       shops.
  UF  Companies
       Enterprises, Business
       Firms

---

BT  Broader term          RT  Related term          PN Public Note
NT  Narrower term        UF  Used for               + Term has NTs
HN  History Note          CN  Catalogers Note      --[ ] May subdivide

**Business enterprises (cont.)**
- BT Commercial organizations
- NT Airline industry
  - Automobile dealerships
  - Automobile service stations
  - Boat & ship companies
  - Clock & watch making
  - Food vendors
  - Fuel trade
  - Insurance companies
  - Interior decoration firms
  - Mail-order businesses
  - Monument builders
  - Motion picture industry
  - Moving & storage trade
  - Plumbing industry
  - Printing industry
  - Public utility companies
  - Publishing industry +
  - Railroad companies
  - Real estate business +
  - Stationery trade
  - Telephone companies
- RT Businessmen
  - Commerce
  - Commercial facilities
  - Cooperatives
  - Customer relations
  - Deals
  - Fur trade
  - Home labor
  - Industry
  - Merchandise displays
  - Military exchanges
  - Occupations
  - Offices
  - Real estate development
  - Secondhand sales
  - Shoe shining
  - Sutlers

**Business ethics**
- USE Ethics

**Business machines**
- USE Office equipment & supplies

**Business panics**
- --[country or state]--[city]
- UF Bank runs
  - Financial panics
  - Money crises
- BT Economic & social conditions
  - Events

**Business schools**
- USE Business education

**Business & finance**
- --[country or state]--[city]
- UF Finance
- NT Banking
  - Big business +
  - Commerce +
  - Credit
  - Debt +
  - Paying bills

**Business & finance (cont.)**
- Saving & investment
- Usury
- RT Business education
  - Commercial facilities
  - Discounts
  - Economic aspects of war
  - Economic policy
  - Economic & social conditions
  - Financial disclosure
  - Insurance
  - Money
  - Mortgages

**Businessmen**
- --[nationality]--[country or state]--[city]
- UF Entrepreneurs
  - Executives
  - Manufacturers
- BT People associated with commercial activities
- NT Merchants
- RT Business enterprises

**Busing (School integration)**
- --[country or state]--[city]
- UF School busing (Integration)
  - Student busing (School integration)
- RT Education
  - Minorities
  - Race relations
  - Schools
  - Segregation
  - Transportation

**Buskers**
- USE Street entertainers

**Butcher shops**
- --[country or state]--[city]
- PN Includes activities and structures.
- BT Stores & shops
- RT Meat cutting
  - Meat industry

**Butter**
- BT Dairy products
- RT Butter making
  - Churns
  - Margarine

**Butter churns**
- USE Churns

**Butter making**
- --[country or state]--[city]
- PN For domestic activities. Search under DAIRYING for large scale or commercial activities.
- UF Churning
- BT Home food processing
- RT Butter
  - Churns
  - Dairying

**Butterflies**
- --[country or state]
- BT Insects
- RT Butterfly nets

Butterfly chairs

---

Butterfly chairs (cont.)
   USE Hardoy chairs
**Butterfly nets**
   UF   Nets, Butterfly
   BT   Nets
   RT   Butterflies
**Buttes**
        --[country or state]
   BT   Land
   RT   Hills
        Mountains
**Buttocks**
   UF   Behinds (Human body)
        Butts (Human body)
        Derrieres
   RT   Human body
Button badges
   USE Badges
**Buttonhole industry**
        --[country or state]--[city]
   PN   Includes activities and structures.
   CN   Double index under INDUSTRIAL
        FACILITIES (or NTs) for images that focus
        on facilities.
   UF   Buttonhole-cutter industry
   BT   Clothing industry
   RT   Buttons
Buttonhole-cutter industry
   USE Buttonhole industry
**Buttons**
   BT   Clothing & dress
   RT   Buttonhole industry
Butts (Human body)
   USE Buttocks
Buzzards
   USE Vultures
Cab drivers
   USE Taxicab drivers
**Cabanas**
        --[country or state]--[city]
   PN   Shelters resembling cabins usually with an
        open side facing a beach.
   BT   Bathhouses
Cabarets
   USE Nightclubs
**Cabbage**
        --[country or state]--[city]
   BT   Vegetables
Cabinet card photographs
   USE Cabinet photographs
Cabinet cards
   USE Cabinet photographs
Cabinet making
   USE Cabinetmaking
**Cabinet officers**
        --[country or state]
   PN   For the subject of the office in general and
        for incumbents.
   CN   Subdivide geographically by the
        jurisdiction (e.g. state, nation) of the cabinet
        officer.
   BT   Government officials

**Cabinet officers (cont.)**
   NT   Prime ministers
   RT   Cabinet officers' spouses
**Cabinet officers' spouses**
        --[country or state]
   CN   Subdivide geographically by the
        jurisdiction (e.g., state, nation) of the cabinet
        officer.
   BT   Spouses
   RT   Cabinet officers
**Cabinet photographs**
   CN   TGM II term.
   UF   Cabinet card photographs
        Cabinet cards
**Cabinetmaking**
        --[country or state]--[city]
   PN   Skilled work of cutting, shaping, and
        assembling high-grade articles of furniture
        requiring fine finish.
   UF   Cabinet making
   BT   Handicraft
   RT   Carpentry
        Furniture
        Joinery
        Woodworking
Cabinets
   USE Cupboards
**Cabins**
        --[country or state]--[city]
   PN   A simple one-story house or hut, often of
        logs.
   UF   Cottages, Resort
        Resort cottages
   BT   Houses
   NT   Log cabins
   RT   Resorts
Cabins, Ship
   USE Crew quarters
        Staterooms
Cable cars
   USE Cable railroads
**Cable industry**
        --[country or state]--[city]
   PN   Includes activities and structures.
   CN   Double index under INDUSTRIAL
        FACILITIES (or NTS)  for images that focus
        on facilities.
   UF   Wire cable industry
   BT   Industry
**Cable railroads**
        --[country or state]--[city]
   PN   For railroads powered by cable. These
        railroads were situated underground in most
        cities; such systems were largely abandoned
        in most U.S. cities after the mid 1890s in
        favor of street railroads running on overhead
        electric wires.
   CN   Used in a note under STREET
        RAILROADS.
   UF   Cable cars
        Funicular railroads
   BT   Railroads

---

BT  Broader term                            RT  Related term                            PN Public Note
NT  Narrower term                           UF  Used for                                + Term has NTs
HN  History Note                            CN  Catalogers Note                         --[ ] May subdivide

**Cable railroads (cont.)**
  NT  Aerial tramways
  RT  Inclined railroads
       Mountain railroads
       Street railroads
**Cables, Submarine**
  USE Submarine cables
**Cables, Telecommunication**
  USE Telecommunication cables
**Cabooses**
  USE Railroad cabooses
**Cabs**
  USE Taxicabs
**Cabs, Hansom**
  USE Carriages & coaches
**Cacao**
      --[country or state]--[city]
  PN  For cacao trees and culture.
  UF  Chocolate-trees
  BT  Trees
  RT  Chocolate industry
       Cocoa industry
**Caches**
      --[country or state]--[city]
  PN  Hiding places, especially for concealing or
       preserving provisions or implements.
  UF  Hidden property
       Loot
  RT  Treasure-trove
**Cactus**
      --[country or state]--[city]
  BT  Plants
**CAD drawings**
  USE Computer-aided designs
**Cadavers**
  USE Dead animals
       Dead persons
**Caddies**
      --[country or state]--[city]
  UF  Golf caddies
  BT  People associated with manual labor
  RT  Golf
**Cadets**
      --[country or state]--[city]
  UF  Military students
  BT  People associated with military activities
  RT  Military education
       Military training
       Students
**Caduceus**
  PN  Symbol of the medical profession.
  BT  Symbols
  RT  Medicine
**Cafes**
      --[country or state]--[city]
  PN  Usually small and informal establishments
       serving various refreshments, often partly
       outdoors.
  BT  Restaurants
  RT  Coffeehouses
**Cafeterias**
      --[country or state]--[city]

**Cafeterias (cont.)**
  PN  Self-service food establishments.
  UF  Lunchrooms
       Self-service restaurants
  BT  Restaurants
  RT  School meals
**Cages**
      --[country or state]--[city]
  PN  Includes enclosures resembling a cage in
       form or purpose.
  NT  Birdcages
  RT  Containers
       Jails
**Cairns**
      --[country or state]--[city]
  PN  For heaps of stones piled up as
       monuments or landmarks.
  UF  Rock cairns
  RT  Monuments & memorials
       Stonework
**Caissons (Vehicles)**
      --[nationality]--[country or state]--[city]
  BT  Carts & wagons
  RT  Ammunition
**Cakes**
      --[country or state]--[city]
  CN  As appropriate, subdivide by place with
       which cakes are associated.
  BT  Baked products
       Confections
**Calamities**
  USE Disasters
**Calculating machines**
  USE Calculators
**Calculator industry**
      --[country or state]--[city]
  PN  Includes activities and structures.
  CN  Double index under INDUSTRIAL
       FACILITIES (or NTs) for images that focus
       on facilities.
  UF  Adding machine industry
  RT  Calculators
**Calculators**
  PN  For present-day calculators, as well as
       calculators and mechanical computers of
       pre-1945 vintage. Search under
       COMPUTERS for modern electronic
       computers first developed after 1945.
  CN  Used in a note under COMPUTERS.
  UF  Adding machines
       Automatic data processing equipment
       Calculating machines
       Data processing equipment
       Mechanical computers
  BT  Office equipment & supplies
  RT  Calculator industry
       Computers
       Punched card systems
       Weights & measures
**Calendars**
  CN  TGM II term.
**Calico**

---

BT  Broader term          RT  Related term          PN  Public Note
NT  Narrower term       UF  Used for            +  Term has NTs
HN  History Note        CN  Catalogers Note     --[ ] May subdivide

**Calico (cont.)**
BT  Textiles
California crazy
  USE Mimetic buildings
**California poppies**
      --[country or state]--[city]
UF  Poppies, California
BT  Flowers
**Calisthenics**
      --[country or state]--[city]
PN  Exercise without apparatus or with light
     hand apparatus to promote strength and
     gracefulness.
RT  Physical education
     Physical fitness
Calla
  USE Lilies
Calligrams
  USE Letter pictures
**Calligraphy**
      --[country or state]--[city]
CN  TGM II term.
BT  Art
     Writing
Calling cards
  USE Visiting cards
**Calliopes**
PN  Includes the activity of playing calliopes.
BT  Keyboard instruments
Callitypes
  USE Kallitypes
**Caloric engines**
UF  Hot-air engines
BT  Engines
**Calotypes**
CN  TGM II term.
UF  Talbotypes
     Water paper negatives
     Waxed paper negatives
**Calumets**
      --[country or state]--[city]
CN  Changed 11/1993 from PEACE PIPES.
UF  Peace pipes
BT  Tobacco pipes
RT  Peace
Calumny
  USE Libel & slander
Calves
  USE Cattle
**Camels**
      --[country or state]
BT  Animals
RT  Caravans
**Camera clubs**
      --[country or state]--[city]
CN  Double index under ORGANIZATIONS'
     FACILITIES (or NTs) for images that focus
     on facilities.
UF  Photography clubs
BT  Clubs
RT  Art clubs
     Photography

**Camera lucida works**
CN  TGM II term.
**Camera obscura works**
CN  TGM II term.
**Cameras**
BT  Photographic apparatus & supplies
**Camouflage (Biology)**
RT  Animals
     Biology
**Camouflage (Military science)**
PN  Search also under the subdivision
     --CAMOUFLAGE used with names of wars
     (Appendix C).
BT  Military art & science
Camp cookery
  USE Outdoor cookery
Camp life
  USE Military life
**Camp meetings**
      --[country or state]--[city]
PN  Religious gatherings held, usually by
     Methodists, for conducting a series of
     religious services in the open air or in some
     removed spot. Includes activities and sites.
UF  Campmeetings
BT  Religious services
RT  Outdoor religious services
     Revivals
Camp stoves
  USE Stoves
Campaign funds
  USE Political campaign funds
Campaign posters
  USE Political posters
Campaigning, Whistle-stop
  USE Whistle-stop campaigning
**Campaigns & battles**
      --[country or state]--[city]
PN  For images at the time of fighting. Search
     under BATTLEFIELDS for sites of
     previously fought battles. Search also under
     the subdivision --CAMPAIGNS & BATTLES
     used with names of wars (Appendix C).
CN  Also index under name of specific battle
     when known.
UF  Battles
     Campaigns, Military
     Combat
     Invasions
BT  Events
RT  Action & adventure dramas
     Air warfare
     Armistices
     Battlefields
     Foxholes
     Gas warfare
     Lancers
     Massacres
     Military art & science
     Mine warfare
     Naval warfare
     Night warfare

BT  Broader term        RT  Related term        PN Public Note
NT  Narrower term      UF  Used for        + Term has NTs
HN  History Note       CN  Catalogers Note     --[ ] May subdivide

**Campaigns & battles (cont.)**
        Trench warfare
        War
Campaigns, Membership
  USE Membership campaigns
Campaigns, Military
  USE Campaigns & battles
Campaigns, Political
  USE Political elections
Campaigns, Scrap
  USE Scrap drives
Campaniles
  USE Bell towers
**Campfires**
  BT  Fire
  RT  Camping
      Camps
      Outdoor cookery
**Camping**
      --[country or state]--[city]
  PN  For camping outside of organized camps
      and without permanent shelters. Search under
      CAMPS for organized camps and camping
      within permanent structures.
  CN  Used in a note under CAMPS.
  RT  Campfires
      Camps
      Recreation
      Tents
      Tourist camps & hostels
Campmeetings
  USE Camp meetings
**Camps**
      --[country or state]--[city]
  PN  Includes activities and sites. Search under
      PRIVATE CAMPS for retreats, complexes of
      cabins, boathouses, etc., for families and
      friends. Search under CAMPING for camping
      outside of organized camps and without
      permanent shelters.
  CN  Used in a note under PRIVATE CAMPS
      and CAMPING.
  UF  Organized camps
      Summer camps
  BT  Sports & recreation facilities
  NT  Private camps
  RT  Campfires
      Camping
      Indian encampments
      Lodges
      Military camps
      Work camps
Camps, Internment
  USE Concentration camps
      Relocation camps
Camps, Military
  USE Military camps
Campus disorders
  USE Student movements
Campus schools
  USE Laboratory schools
**Can industry**

**Can industry (cont.)**
      --[country or state]--[city]
  PN  Includes activities and structures.
  CN  Double index under INDUSTRIAL
      FACILITIES (or NTs)  for images that focus
      on facilities.
  BT  Industry
  RT  Cans
**Canal boats**
      --[nationality]--[country or state]--[city]
  BT  Boats
  NT  Gondolas
  RT  Canals
**Canal construction**
      --[country or state]--[city]
  BT  Civil engineering
      Construction
  RT  Canals
**Canals**
      --[country or state]--[city]
  BT  Hydraulic facilities
  RT  Aqueducts
      Canal boats
      Canal construction
      Erosion protection works
      Locks (Hydraulic engineering)
      Millraces
**Cancellation proofs**
  CN  TGM II term.
  UF  Cancelled plate prints
Cancelled plate prints
  USE Cancellation proofs
**Cancer**
      --[country or state]--[city]
  BT  Diseases
**Candelabras**
  BT  Light fixtures
  RT  Candles
Candidates, Political
  USE Political elections
Candidates, Presidential
  USE Presidential elections
**Candlemaking**
      --[country or state]--[city]
  PN  For small businesses and domestic
      activities.
  RT  Candles
      Industry
**Candles**
  RT  Candelabras
      Candlemaking
      Lighting
      Sconces
**Candy**
      --[country or state]--[city]
  CN  As appropriate, subdivide by place with
      which candy is associated.
  BT  Confections
  RT  Chewing gum
Candy making
  USE Cookery
Candy stores

---

BT  Broader term                RT  Related term                PN  Public Note
NT  Narrower term            UF  Used for                        + Term has NTs
HN  History Note             CN  Catalogers Note           --[ ] May subdivide

Candy stores (cont.)
USE Confectioneries
Cane sugar
USE Sugar
Canes
USE Staffs (Sticks)
Canneries
USE Food industry
**Cannibalism**
--[country]
RT Manners & customs
Shrunken heads
Canning & preserving
USE Food industry
Home food processing
**Cannon balls**
UF Cannonballs
BT Ammunition
RT Cannons
Cannonballs
USE Cannon balls
**Cannons**
BT Artillery (Weaponry)
NT Howitzers
RT Cannon balls
Canoeing
USE Canoes
**Canoes**
--[nationality]--[country or state]--[city]
UF Canoeing
Kayaks
BT Boats
NT Outrigger canoes
RT Shooting rapids
**Canopies**
--[country or state]--[city]
BT Roofs
RT Landscape pavilions
Marquees
Tents
**Cans**
UF Milk cans
BT Containers
NT Sardine cans
RT Can industry
**Cantaloupes**
--[country or state]--[city]
BT Melons
Canteens (Employee)
USE Employee eating facilities
**Canteens (Wartime, emergency, etc.)**
--[country or state]--[city]
PN Temporary establishments which provide
members of the armed forces and, in
emergencies, civilians with food and
recreation.
BT Sports & recreation facilities
RT Disaster relief
Restaurants
USO clubs
**Cantilevered roofs**
--[country or state]--[city]

**Cantilevered roofs (cont.)**
UF V-support roofs
BT Roofs
**Canvassing**
--[country or state]--[city]
UF Door-to-door selling
Traveling salesmanship
BT Selling
RT Peddlers
Canvassing, Political
USE Political elections
**Canyons**
--[country or state]--[city]
PN For valleys between precipitous walls.
Search under CLIFFS for very steep,
perpendicular, or overhanging faces of rock,
earth, or glacial ice of considerable height.
CN Used in a note under CLIFFS.
UF Chasms
Gorges
Gulches
Gullies
Ravines
BT Valleys
RT Cliffs
**Capes (Coasts)**
--[country or state]
UF Coastlines
Headlands
Necks (Coasts)
Points (Coasts)
BT Land
RT Peninsulas
Waterfronts
Capital punishment
USE Executions
Capital sins
USE Deadly sins
**Capitalism**
--[country or state]--[city]
PN For the subject of capitalism in general.
BT Economic & political systems
**Capitals (Columns)**
--[country or state]--[city]
PN Molded or carved tops of columns.
BT Architectural elements
RT Architectural orders
Capitol buildings
USE Capitols
**Capitol pages**
UF Congressional pages
Pages, Congressional
BT Children
RT Legislators
**Capitols**
--[country or state]--[city]
UF Capitol buildings
Parliament buildings
State houses
Statehouses
BT Government facilities
Capitulations, Military

---

BT Broader term
NT Narrower term
HN History Note

RT Related term
UF Used for
CN Catalogers Note

PN Public Note
+ Term has NTs
--[ ] May subdivide

Capitulations, Military (cont.)
  USE Surrenders
Caps
  USE Hats
Captains, Ship
  USE Ship captains
**Captive balloons**
    --[nationality]--[country or state]--[city]
  BT  Balloons (Aircraft)
  NT  Barrage balloons
**Captives**
    --[nationality]--[country or state]--[city]
  BT  Prisoners
Capture & imprisonment
  CN  Used only as a subdivision with names of
      ethnic, racial, and regional groups, and with
      classes of persons (Appendix A) and with
      names of persons (Appendix B).
Captures
  USE Confiscations
Car mechanics
  USE Mechanics (Persons)
Car racing
  USE Automobile racing
**Car washes**
    --[country or state]--[city]
  UF  Auto washes
      Carwashes
  BT  Service industry facilities
  RT  Automobiles
**Caravans**
    --[country]
  RT  Camels
      Caravansaries
      Commerce
      Packtrains
      Transportation
**Caravansaries**
    --[country]
  BT  Public accommodation facilities
  RT  Caravans
Carbines
  USE Rifles
Carbon photoprints
  USE Carbon prints
**Carbon prints**
  CN  TGM II term.
  UF  Autotypes
      Carbon photoprints
      Chromotypes
      Lambertypes
**Carbon transparencies**
  CN  TGM II term.
**Carbonated beverages**
  UF  Soda water
      Soft drinks
  BT  Beverages
  NT  Sarsaparilla
Carbro photoprints
  USE Carbro prints
**Carbro prints**
  CN  TGM II term.

Carbro prints (cont.)
  UF  Carbro photoprints
      Ozobrome photoprints
**Card catalogs**
    --[country or state]--[city]
  BT  Catalogs
  RT  Cards
**Card games**
    --[country or state]--[city]
  PN  For the activity of playing cards.
  UF  Card playing
  BT  Games
  NT  Bridge (Game)
  RT  Card tricks
      Gambling
      Playing cards
**Card photograph albums**
  CN  TGM II term.
  UF  Cartes de visite albums
**Card photographs**
  CN  TGM II term.
Card playing
  USE Card games
**Card tricks**
    --[country or state]--[city]
  BT  Magic
  RT  Card games
      Playing cards
**Cardinals**
  BT  Clergy
**Cardiovascular system**
  UF  Blood circulation
      Circulatory system
      Vascular system
  RT  Blood
      Human body
**Cards**
  CN  TGM II term.
  RT  Card catalogs
Cards, Charge
  USE Credit cards
Cards, Credit
  USE Credit cards
Careers
  USE Occupations
Cargo
  USE Shipping
Cargo handling
  USE Shipping
**Cargo holds**
  UF  Freight holds
      Holds, Cargo
  BT  Interiors
  RT  Cargo ships
Cargo planes
  USE Transport planes
**Cargo ships**
    --[nationality]--[country or state]--[city]
  UF  Freight ships
      Freighters
  BT  Ships
  NT  Tankers

BT Broader term    RT Related term    PN Public Note
NT Narrower term    UF Used for    + Term has NTs
HN History Note    CN Catalogers Note    --[ ] May subdivide

**Cargo ships (cont.)**
   RT   Cargo holds
        Shipping
**Caricatures**
   CN  TGM II term.
   UF  Stereotypes
**Caricaturists**
   USE Cartoonists
**Carnations**
       --[country or state]--[city]
   BT  Flowers
**Carnival posters**
   USE Circus posters
**Carnivals (Circus)**
   USE Amusement parks
**Carnivals, Winter**
   USE Winter carnivals
**Caroling**
       --[country or state]--[city]
   BT  Singing
   RT  Holidays
**Carom billiards**
   USE Billiards
**Carousels**
   USE Merry-go-rounds
**Carpenter shops**
       --[country or state]--[city]
   PN  For images that focus on facilities. Search
        under CARPENTRY for activities.
   CN  Used in a note under CARPENTRY.
   BT  Workshops
   RT  Carpentry
**Carpenters**
       --[country or state]--[city]
   BT  People associated with manual labor
   RT  Carpenters' unions
        Carpentry
**Carpenters' unions**
       --[country or state]--[city]
   BT  Labor unions
   RT  Carpenters
**Carpentry**
       --[country or state]--[city]
   PN  Building with wood, especially in the
        construction of buildings and other
        structures.
   CN  Used in a note under CARPENTER
        SHOPS.
   BT  Construction
   RT  Cabinetmaking
        Carpenter shops
        Carpenters
        Chisels & mallets
        Joinery
        Woodworking
**Carpet tacks**
   USE Tacks
**Carpets**
   USE Floor coverings
**Carriage drivers**
   USE Coach drivers
**Carriage houses**

**Carriage houses (cont.)**
       --[country or state]--[city]
   UF  Coach houses
   BT  Transportation facilities
   RT  Residential facilities
        Storage facilities
**Carriages & coaches**
       --[nationality]--[country or state]--[city]
   PN  Vehicles, drawn by animals, used
        primarily for the transport of people.
   CN  Used in a note under CARTS &
        WAGONS.
   UF  Buggies
        Cabs, Hansom
        Coaches
        Hansom cabs
        Turnouts
   BT  Vehicles
   NT  Goat carts
        Pony carts
        Stagecoaches
   RT  Animal teams
        Carts & wagons
        Chariots
        Coach drivers
        Hearses
        Howdahs
        Wheeled chairs
**Carrier pigeons**
   USE Homing pigeons
**Carriers (Warships)**
   USE Aircraft carriers
**Carriers, Aircraft**
   USE Aircraft carriers
**Carriers' addresses**
   CN  TGM II term.
   UF  Bellmen's verses
        Newscarriers' addresses
        Newsmen's presents
**Carries**
   USE Portages
**Carrots**
       --[country or state]--[city]
   BT  Vegetables
**Carrying & lifting**
   USE Lifting & carrying
**Cars**
   USE Automobiles
**Cartes de visite**
   CN  TGM II term.
**Cartes de visite albums**
   USE Card photograph albums
**Cartes de visite (Visiting cards)**
   USE Visiting cards
**Cartography**
   USE Map making
**Cartoon cels**
   USE Animation cels
**Cartoon characters**
   USE Fictitious characters
**Cartoon patterns**
   USE Cartoons (Working drawings)

---

BT Broader term        RT Related term        PN Public Note
NT Narrower term      UF Used for           + Term has NTs
HN History Note        CN Catalogers Note    --[ ] May subdivide

Cartoon strips
  USE Comics
**Cartoonists**
  UF  Caricaturists
  BT  Artists
Cartoons
  USE Cartoons (Commentary)
**Cartoons (Commentary)**
  CN  TGM II term.
  UF  Cartoons
      Comic pictures
**Cartoons (Working drawings)**
  UF  Cartoon patterns
**Cartouches**
  CN  TGM II term.
**Cartouches (Architecture)**
  PN  An ornamental tablet often inscribed or
      decorated, and framed with elaborate
      scroll-like carving.
  BT  Architectural elements
**Carts & wagons**
      --[nationality]--[country or state]--[city]
  PN  Vehicles, drawn by animal or man or
      pushed, primarily for the transportation of
      goods. Search under CARRIAGES &
      COACHES for vehicles used primarily to
      transport people.
  CN  Used in a note under CARRIAGES &
      COACHES.
  UF  Delivery wagons
      Freight wagons
      Wagons
  BT  Vehicles
  NT  Caissons (Vehicles)
      Chuckwagons
      Covered wagons
      Hoover wagons
  RT  Animal teams
      Bandwagons
      Carriages & coaches
      Ox teams
      Portable darkrooms
      Shipping
      Wagon sheds
**Carving**
      --[country or state]--[city]
  UF  Sculpting
      Sculpturing
  BT  Handicraft
  NT  Ivory carving
      Stone carving
      Wood carving
  RT  Sculpture
Carvings
  USE Sculpture
Carwashes
  USE Car washes
Cascades
  USE Waterfalls
Cased photographs
  USE Ambrotypes
      Daguerreotypes

Cased photographs (cont.)
      Photograph cases
**Casein paintings**
  CN  TGM II term.
Casement doors
  USE French doors
Casements
  USE Armored vessels
Cases, Book
  USE Bookcases
Cases, Display
  USE Showcases
Cases, Show
  USE Showcases
**Cash registers**
  BT  Office equipment & supplies
  RT  Money
**Casinos**
      --[country or state]--[city]
  BT  Sports & recreation facilities
  RT  Gambling
      Hotels
      Resorts
      Slot machines
Caskets
  USE Coffins
Casks
  USE Barrels
Cassons
  USE Coffers (Ceilings)
**Cast ironwork**
      --[country or state]--[city]
  UF  Pig ironwork
  BT  Ironwork
**Cast paper prints**
  CN  TGM II term.
**Castaways**
      --[nationality]--[country or state]--[city]
  RT  Shipwrecks
**Castles & palaces**
      --[country or state]--[city]
  UF  Chateaux
      Palaces
  BT  Houses
  RT  Forts & fortifications
      Moats
      Official residences
Casualties
  CN  Used only as a subdivision with names of
      wars (Appendix C).
Casualties, War
  USE War casualties
**Catacombs**
      --[country or state]--[city]
  PN  Subterranean cemeteries consisting of
      galleries or passages with side recesses for
      tombs.
  BT  Cemeteries
  RT  Tombs & sepulchral monuments
Catalog order businesses
  USE Mail-order businesses
**Catalogs**

---

BT Broader term      RT Related term      PN Public Note
NT Narrower term      UF Used for      + Term has NTs
HN History Note      CN Catalogers Note      --[ ] May subdivide

**Catalogs (cont.)**
- CN  TGM II term.
- UF  Catalogues
- NT  Card catalogs

Catalogues
- USE Catalogs

Cataracts
- USE Waterfalls

Catastrophes
- USE Disasters

**Caterpillars**
- --[country or state]
- BT  Insects

Caterpillar-type machinery
- USE Tracklaying vehicles

**Catfish**
- --[country or state]
- BT  Fish

**Cathedrals**
- --[country or state]--[city]
- PN  For images that focus on buildings, as well as the associated grounds.
- BT  Churches
- RT  Anglican churches
-      Catholic churches

**Catholic churches**
- --[country or state]--[city]
- PN  For images that focus on buildings, as well as the associated grounds.
- BT  Churches
- RT  Cathedrals

**Cats**
- --[country or state]
- UF  Kittens
- BT  Animals

Catstep gables
- USE Crow-stepped gables

**Cattle**
- --[country or state]
- PN  Includes domesticated calves, heifers, oxen, and steers. Also includes mixed groups of cattle and cows and bulls, if their sex cannot be determined.
- UF  Bullocks
-      Calves
-      Heifers
-      Oxen
-      Steers
- BT  Livestock
- NT  Bulls
-      Cows
- RT  Bison
-      Buffaloes
-      Cattle branding
-      Cattle herding
-      Cattle raids
-      Cattle ranches
-      Corrals
-      Dairy farming
-      Dairying
-      Ox teams
-      Rodeos

**Cattle branding**
- --[country or state]--[city]
- UF  Branding of cattle
- RT  Cattle
-      Cowboys

**Cattle herding**
- --[country or state]
- UF  Round-ups
- BT  Herding
- RT  Cattle
-      Cowboys

Cattle markets
- USE Meat industry
-      Stockyards

Cattle pens
- USE Stockyards

**Cattle raids**
- --[country or state]--[city]
- BT  Crimes
- RT  Cattle

**Cattle ranches**
- --[country or state]--[city]
- BT  Ranches
- RT  Cattle

**Cauliflower**
- --[country or state]--[city]
- BT  Vegetables

Causes
- CN  Used only as a subdivision with names of wars (Appendix C).

**Causeways**
- --[country or state]
- PN  Raised ways across wet ground or water.
- BT  Roads

**Cavalry**
- --[nationality]--[country or state]--[city]
- UF  Dragoons
- BT  Armies
- RT  Horse artillery
-      Horses
-      Lancers

**Cave churches**
- --[country or state]--[city]
- PN  For images that focus on structures, as well as the associated grounds.
- BT  Churches
- RT  Caves

**Cave drawings**
- --[country or state]
- UF  Pictographs
- RT  Caves
-      Murals
-      Rock art

**Cave dwellers**
- --[country or state]
- UF  Cavemen
- BT  People
- RT  Cave dwellings
-      Caves

**Cave dwellings**
- --[country or state]--[city]
- BT  Dwellings

---

BT Broader term              RT Related term             PN Public Note
NT Narrower term           UF Used for                  + Term has NTs
HN History Note               CN Catalogers Note        --[ ] May subdivide

**Cave dwellings (cont.)**
  RT  Cave dwellers
       Caves
**Cavemen**
  USE Cave dwellers
**Caverns**
  USE Caves
**Caves**
       --[country or state]
  PN  Includes the activity of exploring caves.
  UF  Caverns
       Caving
       Grottoes
       Spelunking
  BT  Land
  RT  Cave churches
       Cave drawings
       Cave dwellers
       Cave dwellings
       Rock formations
       Stalactites & stalagmites
**Caving**
  USE Caves
**Cavities**
  USE Holes
**Ceasefires**
  USE Armistices
**Ceibas**
       --[country or state]--[city]
  UF  Silk-cotton trees
  BT  Trees
**Ceilings**
       --[country or state]--[city]
  BT  Architectural elements
  NT  Suspended ceilings
  RT  Coffers (Ceilings)
       Paneling
       Vaults (Architecture)
**Celebrations**
       --[country or state]--[city]
  PN  Includes festivities associated with major events and holidays, as well as smaller festivities such as birthday parties. Search also under the subdivision --COMMEMORATION used with the names of ethnic, racial, and regional groups, and classes of persons (Appendix A); with names of persons (Appendix B); with names of wars (Appendix C); and with corporate bodies and named events (Appendix D).
  BT  Events
  NT  Centennial celebrations
       Political pageantry
       Victory celebrations
  RT  Anniversaries
       Commemoration
       Fairs
       Festivals
       Holidays
       Pageants
       Parades & processions
       Parties

**Celebrations (cont.)**
       Reunions
       Rites & ceremonies
**Celebrities**
       --[country or state]--[city]
  BT  People
  RT  Autographing
       Celebrity touring
       Entertainers
       Fame
       Socialites
**Celebrity**
  USE Fame
**Celebrity touring**
       --[country or state]--[city]
  PN  For performance or publicity tours by celebrities. Search also under the subdivision --JOURNEYS used with names of persons (Appendix B).
  UF  Touring, Celebrity
  BT  Travel
  RT  Autographing
       Celebrities
       Whistle-stop campaigning
**Celery**
       --[country or state]--[city]
  BT  Vegetables
**Celestial bodies**
  NT  Moon
       Planets +
       Stars
       Sun
  RT  Astrology
       Astronomy
       Galaxies
       Zodiac
**Cellars**
  USE Basements
**Cellocuts**
  CN  TGM II term.
**Cellos**
  USE Violoncellos
**Cells (Biology)**
**Cellulose acetate negatives**
  USE Acetate negatives
**Cellulose diacetate negatives**
  USE Acetate negatives
**Cellulose nitrate negatives**
  USE Nitrate negatives
**Cellulose triacetate negatives**
  USE Acetate negatives
**Cels, Animation**
  USE Animation cels
**Cembalos**
  USE Harpsichords
**Cement industries**
       --[country or state]--[city]
  PN  Includes activities and structures.
  CN  Double index under INDUSTRIAL FACILITIES (or NTS) for images that focus on facilities.
  BT  Building materials industry

---

BT Broader term       RT Related term       PN Public Note
NT Narrower term      UF Used for          + Term has NTs
HN History Note        CN Catalogers Note    --[ ] May subdivide

**Cement industries (cont.)**
Ceramic industries
**Cemeteries**
--[nationality]--[country or state]--[city]
PN   Search also under the subdivision
--CEMETERIES used with names of wars
(Appendix C).
UF   Graveyards
BT   Funerary facilities
NT   Catacombs
RT   Gravedigging
Graves
Tombs & sepulchral monuments
**Censored works**
CN   TGM II term.
**Censorship**
--[nationality]--[country or state]--[city]
PN   Search also under the subdivision
--COMMUNICATIONS used with names of
wars (Appendix C).
UF   Intellectual freedom
NT   Book burning
RT   Freedom of information
Freedom of speech
National security
Politics & government
Censuring
USE Blaming
**Census**
--[country or state]--[city]
UF   Population surveys
RT   Apportionment
Surveying
**Centennial celebrations**
--[country or state]--[city]
UF   Bicentennials
Tercentennials
Tricentennials
BT   Celebrations
RT   Exhibitions
History
Centers, Visitors'
USE Visitors' centers
Central American Indians
USE Indians of Central America
Central business districts
USE Business districts
Century plants
USE Agaves
**Ceramic industries**
--[country or state]--[city]
PN   Includes activities and structures.
CN   Double index under INDUSTRIAL
FACILITIES (or NTs) for images that focus
on facilities.
BT   Industry
NT   Cement industries
Clay industries +
Glass industry
RT   Building materials industry
Pottery industry
**Ceramic photographs**

**Ceramic photographs (cont.)**
CN   TGM II term.
UF   Photoceramics
Porcelain photographs
Ceramics
USE Pottery
**Cereal products**
--[country or state]--[city]
NT   Prepared cereals
RT   Food
Grain industry
Grains
**Ceremonial dancers**
--[country or state]--[city]
PN    Search also under the subdivision
--DANCE used with names of ethnic, racial,
and regional groups, and classes of persons
(Appendix A).
UF   Tribal dancers
BT   Dancers
People associated with religion
RT   Rites & ceremonies
**Ceremonial maces**
BT   Staffs (Sticks)
Symbols
RT   Power (Social sciences)
**Ceremonial rooms**
--[country or state]--[city]
BT   Interiors
NT   Reception rooms
Ceremonial-civic buildings
USE Social & civic facilities
Ceremonies
USE Rites & ceremonies
**Certificates**
CN   TGM II term.
Cession of territory
USE Annexations
**Chain gangs**
--[country or state]--[city]
BT   Prison laborers
Chain stores
USE Stores & shops
**Chains**
RT   Hoisting machinery
Shackles
Chains (Shackles)
USE Shackles
**Chairs**
BT   Seating furniture
NT   Hardoy chairs
Rocking chairs
Stools
Thrones
RT   Sedan chairs
Wheelchairs
Wheeled chairs
**Chalets**
--[country or state]--[city]
PN   A timber house often found in the Alps,
distinguished by the exposed and decorative
use of structural members, balconies, and

---

BT  Broader term                                      RT  Related term                                      PN Public Note
NT  Narrower term                                   UF  Used for                                           + Term has NTs
HN History Note                                     CN Catalogers Note                                --[ ] May subdivide

**Chalets (cont.)**
  stairs. Upper floors usually project beyond
  the stories below.
 BT Houses
**Chalices**
 UF Communion-cups
 BT Drinking vessels
 RT Religious articles
**Chalk drawings**
 CN TGM II term.
Chalkboards
 USE Blackboards
**Chambers of commerce**
  --[country or state]--[city]
 PN Associations of businessmen who promote
  commercial and industrial interests in the
  community. Includes activities and
  structures.
 BT Commercial organizations
 RT Boards of trade
**Champagne (Wine)**
  --[country or state]--[city]
 BT Wine
Chanceries
 USE Embassies
  Judicial proceedings
**Chandeliers**
 BT Light fixtures
Change purses
 USE Purses
Changing rooms
 USE Locker rooms
**Channels**
  --[country or state]--[city]
 UF River channels
  Sounds (Geomorphology)
  Straits
 BT Bodies of water
 RT Moats
  Streams
**Chapels**
  --[country or state]--[city]
 PN For chapels within churches or other
  buildings. Search under CHURCHES for
  chapels that are separate buildings.
 UF Oratories
 BT Interiors
 RT Churches
Characters, Fictitious
 USE Fictitious characters
**Charcoal**
  --[country or state]--[city]
 RT Charcoal making
  Fuel
**Charcoal drawings**
 CN TGM II term.
**Charcoal making**
  --[country or state]--[city]
 PN The activity of making charcoal in
  small-scale operations.
 RT Charcoal
Charge cards

Charge cards (cont.)
 USE Credit cards
**Chariot racing**
  --[country or state]--[city]
 BT Horse racing
 RT Chariots
**Chariots**
  --[country or state]--[city]
 BT Vehicles
 RT Carriages & coaches
  Chariot racing
Charitable institutions
 USE Asylums
**Charitable organizations**
  --[country or state]--[city]
 PN Includes activities and structures.
 CN Double index under ORGANIZATIONS'
  FACILITIES (or NTs) for images that focus
  on facilities.
 UF Charities
 BT Organizations
 RT Assistance
  Asylums
  Charity
  Clubs
  Community service
  Fraternal organizations
  Philanthropy
  Public service
  Thrift shops
Charitable work
 USE Community service
Charities
 USE Charitable organizations
**Charity**
  --[country or state]--[city]
 UF Alms
  Almsgiving
  Benevolence
 BT Interpersonal relations
 RT Assistance
  Charitable organizations
  Community service
  Ethics
  Philanthropy
  Poor persons
Charlatans
 USE Quacks
**Charleston (Dance)**
  --[country or state]--[city]
 BT Dancing
Charms
 USE Amulets
  Talismans
**Charters**
  --[country or state]--[city]
 PN Instruments in writing, creating and
  defining the franchises of a city, educational
  institution, or corporation.
**Charts**
 CN TGM II term.
**Chasing**

BT Broader term  RT Related term  PN Public Note
NT Narrower term  UF Used for  + Term has NTs
HN History Note  CN Catalogers Note  --[ ] May subdivide

**Chasing (cont.)**
  UF   Pursuing
  BT   Locomotion
  RT   Running
Chasms
  USE Canyons
**Chastity belts**
  UF   Girdles of chastity
  BT   Clothing & dress
Chateaux
  USE Castles & palaces
**Chauffeurs**
        --[country or state]--[city]
  BT   People associated with transportation
  RT   Automobiles
**Chautauquas**
        --[country or state]--[city]
  PN   Includes activities, structures, and sites.
  BT   Meetings
  RT   Education
        Entertainment
**Chauvinism & jingoism**
        --[nationality]
  UF   Jingoism
        Warmongering
  RT   Imperialism
        Militarism
        Nationalism
        Patriotism
Chauvinism, Male
  USE Sexism
**Checkers**
  BT   Board games
Cheer leading
  USE Cheerleading
**Cheering**
        --[country or state]--[city]
  RT   Cheerleading
        Excitement
Cheerleaders
  USE Cheerleading
**Cheerleading**
        --[country or state]--[city]
  UF   Cheer leading
        Cheerleaders
  BT   Communication
  RT   Cheering
        Sports
**Cheese**
  BT   Dairy products
Cheesecake photographs
  USE Glamour photographs
**Cheetahs**
        --[country or state]
  UF   Chittahs
  BT   Animals
Chefs
  USE Cooks
Chemical abuse
  USE Drug abuse
**Chemical industry**
        --[country or state]--[city]

**Chemical industry (cont.)**
  PN   Includes and activities and structures.
  CN   Double index under INDUSTRIAL
        FACILITIES (or NTs) for images that focus
        on facilities.
  BT   Industry
  NT   Artificial rubber industry
        Fertilizer industry
        Paint industry
        Pharmaceutical industry
        Phosphate industry
        Soda industry
        Sulphur industry
        Sulphuric acid industry
        Turpentine industry
  RT   Chemicals
        Gums & resins
**Chemicals**
  NT   Nitrates
        Tear gas
  RT   Chemical industry
        Chemistry
**Chemistry**
        --[country or state]--[city]
  PN   For the subject of chemistry in general and
        the activities of chemists.
  BT   Science
  RT   Alchemy
        Chemicals
**Cherries**
        --[country or state]--[city]
  BT   Fruit
  RT   Cherry orchards
        Cherry trees
**Cherry orchards**
        --[country or state]--[city]
  CN   As appropriate, double index under
        HARVESTING.
  BT   Orchards
  RT   Cherries
        Cherry trees
**Cherry trees**
        --[country or state]--[city]
  UF   Japanese flowering cherry trees
  BT   Trees
  RT   Cherries
        Cherry orchards
Cherubim
  USE Angels
**Chess**
  BT   Board games
**Chestnuts**
  BT   Nuts
**Chests**
  BT   Furniture
  NT   Clothes chests
Cheval-de-frise
  USE Chevaux-de-frise
**Chevaux-de-frise**
        --[country or state]--[city]
  PN   Defensive obstacle composed of spikes or
        barbed wire attached to a wooden frame.

---

BT  Broader term          RT  Related term          PN  Public Note
NT  Narrower term         UF  Used for              +  Term has NTs
HN  History Note          CN  Catalogers Note       --[ ] May subdivide

**Chevaux-de-frise (cont.)**
UF   Cheval-de-frise
BT   Barricades
RT   Arms & armament
      Trench warfare
**Chewing gum**
UF   Gum, Chewing
RT   Candy
      Chewing gum industry
**Chewing gum industry**
      --[country or state]--[city]
PN   Includes activities and structures.
CN   Double index under INDUSTRIAL
      FACILITIES (or NTs) for images that focus
      on facilities.
BT   Food industry
RT   Chewing gum
Chewing tobacco
      USE Smokeless tobacco
**Chiaroscuro woodcuts**
CN   TGM II term.
**Chickadees**
      --[country or state]
BT   Birds
Chicken coops
      USE Poultry houses
Chicken houses
      USE Poultry houses
**Chicken industry**
      --[country or state]--[city]
PN   Includes activities and structures.
CN   Double index under INDUSTRIAL
      FACILITIES (or NTs) for images that focus
      on facilities.
BT   Industry
RT   Chickens
**Chickens**
      --[country or state]--[city]
UF   Chicks
BT   Poultry
NT   Roosters
RT   Chicken industry
Chicks
      USE Birds
         Chickens
Chief justices
      USE Supreme Court justices
Chiefs, Tribal
      USE Tribal chiefs
Child abuse victims
      USE Abused children
**Child behavior**
      --[country or state]--[city]
UF   Behavior of children
NT   Children misbehaving
RT   Child discipline
      Child rearing
      Children
Child custody
      USE Custody of children
**Child discipline**
      --[country or state]--[city]

**Child discipline (cont.)**
UF   Disciplinary action
      Disciplining children
      Punishment of children
NT   School discipline
RT   Child behavior
      Child rearing
      Children
      Punishment & torture
**Child labor**
      --[country or state]--[city]
PN   For images about or depicting child labor.
HN   Changed 3/1989 from non-postable term
      (use CHILDREN-- WORK).
BT   Employment
RT   Apprentices
      Child laborers
**Child laborers**
      --[country or state]--[city]
BT   Children
      Laborers
RT   Child labor
Child raising
      USE Child rearing
**Child rearing**
      --[country or state]--[city]
PN   Images related to the principles and
      techniques of raising children.
UF   Child raising
      Raising of children
      Rearing of children
RT   Child behavior
      Child discipline
      Children & adults
      Children's allowances
Childbirth
      USE Births
Childhood & youth
CN   Used only as a subdivision with names of
      persons (Appendix B).
**Children**
      --[country or state]--[city]
PN   Includes ages 0-16. This heading may be
      further subdivided by the subdivisions used
      for classes of persons (Appendix A). Search
      also under the subdivision --CHILDREN used
      with names of ethnic, racial, and regional
      groups (Appendix A), and with names of
      wars (Appendix C). Search also under other
      headings beginning with CHILDREN.
CN   As appropriate, subdivide by the
      subdivisions used for classes of persons
      (Appendix A).
UF   Adolescents
      Schoolchildren
      Teenagers
BT   People
NT   Abandoned children
      Abused children
      Boys
      Capitol pages
      Child laborers

---

BT Broader term        RT Related term        PN Public Note
NT Narrower term        UF Used for            + Term has NTs
HN History Note         CN Catalogers Note     --[ ] May subdivide

**Children (cont.)**
        Children dressing
        Children performing in theatrical productions
        Children reading & writing
        Children sailing boats
        Children sculpting
        Children stealing
        Children using telephones
        Choirboys
        Delivery boys
        Girls
        Infants
        Juvenile delinquents
        Newspaper carriers
        Orphans
        Pin boys
        School children
        Sick children
  RT  4-H clubs
        Apprentices
        Babysitting
        Child behavior
        Child discipline
        Children & money
        Children & safety
        Cupids
        Day care
        Foster home care
        Gangs
        Governesses
        Human life cycle
        Nurseries
        Schools
        Teenage pregnancy
        Young adults
        Youth
        Youth bands
**Children bathing**
        --[country or state]--[city]
  BT  Bathing
**Children blowing bubbles**
        --[country or state]--[city]
  UF  Bubble blowing
  BT  Children playing
  RT  Bubbles
**Children cooking**
        --[country or state]--[city]
  BT  Cookery
**Children crying**
        --[country or state]--[city]
  BT  Crying
**Children dancing**
        --[country or state]--[city]
  BT  Dancing
  RT  Children performing in theatrical
        productions
**Children doing housework**
        --[country or state]--[city]
  UF  Children's chores
  BT  Housework
  RT  Domestic life
**Children drawing & painting**

**Children drawing & painting (cont.)**
        --[country or state]--[city]
  UF  Children painting
  BT  Art
  RT  Children sculpting
        Drawing
        Painting
**Children dressing**
        --[country or state]--[city]
  BT  Children
  RT  Clothing & dress
**Children driving**
        --[country or state]--[city]
  BT  Automobile driving
**Children eating & drinking**
        --[country or state]--[city]
  BT  Eating & drinking
  NT  Breast feeding
  RT  School meals
**Children exercising**
  BT  Physical fitness
  RT  Children playing
**Children fighting**
        --[country or state]--[city]
  BT  Fighting
**Children fishing**
        --[country or state]--[city]
  BT  Fishing
**Children flying kites**
        --[country or state]--[city]
  BT  Children playing outdoors
  RT  Kites
**Children gambling**
        --[country or state]--[city]
  BT  Gambling
**Children golfing**
        --[country or state]--[city]
  BT  Golf
**Children jumping**
        --[country or state]--[city]
  BT  Children playing
        Jumping
**Children kissing**
        --[country or state]--[city]
  BT  Kissing
Children making telephone calls
  USE Children using telephones
**Children misbehaving**
        --[country or state]--[city]
  UF  Children playing tricks
        Misbehaving children
  BT  Child behavior
  RT  Practical jokes
        Spanking
Children operating radios
  USE Children & radio
Children painting
  USE Children drawing & painting
**Children performing in theatrical productions**
        --[country or state]--[city]
  BT  Children
  RT  Children dancing

---

BT Broader term          RT Related term          PN Public Note
NT Narrower term        UF Used for           + Term has NTs
HN History Note         CN Catalogers Note     --[ ] May subdivide

**Children performing in theatrical productions (cont.)**
    Children singing
**Children pillow fighting**
    --[country or state]--[city]
UF   Pillow fighting
BT   Children playing
**Children playing**
    --[country or state]--[city]
UF   Play
BT   Recreation
NT   Children blowing bubbles
    Children jumping
    Children pillow fighting
    Children playing adults +
    Children playing billiards
    Children playing outdoors +
    Children playing table tennis
    Children playing tennis
    Children playing with marbles
    Children playing with toys +
    Children riding bicycles & tricycles
RT   Children exercising
    Games
    Rope skipping
    School recesses
    Sports
    Toys
**Children playing adults**
    --[country or state]--[city]
UF   Children playing house
BT   Children playing
NT   Children playing doctors
    Children playing soldiers
RT   Children playing with dolls
**Children playing billiards**
    --[country or state]--[city]
BT   Billiards
    Children playing
**Children playing doctors**
    --[country or state]--[city]
BT   Children playing adults
RT   Physicians
Children playing house
USE Children playing adults
**Children playing in mud**
BT   Children playing outdoors
RT   Mud
**Children playing in sand**
    --[country or state]--[city]
CN   Use BEACHES and CHILDREN
    PLAYING OUTDOORS for children at the
    beach.
BT   Children playing outdoors
RT   Beaches
**Children playing in snow**
    --[country or state]--[city]
BT   Children playing outdoors
RT   Snow
    Snowballs
    Snowmen
**Children playing in water**
    --[country or state]--[city]

**Children playing in water (cont.)**
CN   Use BEACHES and CHILDREN
    PLAYING OUTDOORS for children at the
    beach.
BT   Children playing outdoors
RT   Beaches
    Children sailing boats
    Children swimming
    Swimming
**Children playing musical instruments**
    --[country or state]--[city]
BT   Musical instruments
**Children playing outdoors**
    --[country or state]--[city]
CN   Used in a note under CHILDREN
    PLAYING IN SAND and CHILDREN
    PLAYING IN WATER.
BT   Children playing
NT   Children flying kites
    Children playing in mud
    Children playing in sand
    Children playing in snow
    Children playing in water
    Children swinging
RT   Playgrounds
**Children playing soldiers**
    --[country or state]--[city]
BT   Children playing adults
RT   Soldiers
**Children playing table tennis**
    --[country or state]--[city]
BT   Children playing
    Table tennis
**Children playing tennis**
    --[country or state]--[city]
BT   Children playing
    Tennis
Children playing tricks
USE Children misbehaving
**Children playing with dolls**
    --[country or state]--[city]
PN   Includes children posed with dolls.
BT   Children playing with toys
RT   Children playing adults
    Dolls
**Children playing with marbles**
    --[country or state]--[city]
UF   Marble playing
BT   Children playing
**Children playing with toys**
    --[country or state]--[city]
PN   Includes children posed with toys.
HN   Changed 10/92 from Children & toys.
UF   Children & toys
BT   Children playing
NT   Children playing with dolls
    Children sailing boats
**Children praying**
    --[country or state]--[city]
BT   Prayer
**Children reading & writing**
    --[country or state]--[city]

---

BT  Broader term               RT  Related term             PN Public Note
NT  Narrower term            UF  Used for                 + Term has NTs
HN  History Note              CN Catalogers Note        --[ ] May subdivide

**Children reading & writing (cont.)**
- BT Children
- RT Letters to Santa Claus
  - Reading
  - Writing

**Children riding bicycles & tricycles**
- --[country or state]--[city]
- BT Children playing
  - Cycling
- RT Bicycles & tricycles

**Children riding horses**
- --[country or state]--[city]
- UF Children riding ponies
- BT Children & animals
  - Horseback riding

Children riding ponies
USE Children riding horses

**Children sailing boats**
- --[country or state]--[city]
- BT Children
  - Children playing with toys
- RT Children playing in water
  - Model ships
  - Sailboats

**Children sculpting**
- --[country or state]--[city]
- BT Children
- RT Children drawing & painting
  - Modeling (Sculpture)

**Children sewing**
- --[country or state]--[city]
- BT Sewing

**Children singing**
- --[country or state]--[city]
- BT Singing
- RT Children performing in theatrical
  - productions
  - Choirboys

**Children sleeping**
- --[country or state]--[city]
- BT Sleeping

**Children smoking**
- --[country or state]--[city]
- BT Smoking

**Children stealing**
- --[country or state]--[city]
- UF Stealing
- BT Children
- RT Robberies

**Children swimming**
- --[country or state]--[city]
- BT Swimming
- RT Children playing in water

**Children swinging**
- --[country or state]--[city]
- PN For the activity of swinging, whether or
  not on a swing, e.g., swinging on a rope.
  Search under SWINGS when just the swing is
  depicted.
- CN Used in a note under SWINGS.
- BT Children playing outdoors
- RT Swings

**Children telling stories**
- --[country or state]--[city]
- BT Storytelling

Children using radios
USE Children & radio

**Children using telephones**
- --[country or state]--[city]
- UF Children making telephone calls
- BT Children
- RT Telephones

**Children walking**
- --[country or state]--[city]
- BT Walking

**Children & adults**
- --[country or state]--[city]
- PN Search under FAMILIES for children and
  adults who are related.
- UF Adults & children
- BT People
- RT Child rearing
  - Custody of children
  - Families
  - Fathers & children
  - Intergenerational relations
  - Men
  - Mothers & children
  - Women

**Children & animals**
- --[country or state]--[city]
- NT Children riding horses
- RT Animals
  - Pets

**Children & money**
- RT Children
  - Children's allowances
  - Money

**Children & radio**
- --[country or state]--[city]
- UF Amateur radio
  - Children operating radios
  - Children using radios
  - Ham radio
  - Radio & children
- RT Radio broadcasting
  - Radios

**Children & safety**
- RT Children
  - Safety

Children & toys
USE Children playing with toys

**Children's allowances**
- UF Allowances, Children's
- RT Child rearing
  - Children & money
  - Money

**Children's art**
- CN TGM II term.
- UF Art by children
  - Juvenile art

Children's chores
USE Children doing housework

Children's clothing & dress

---

Children's clothing & dress (cont.)
HN   Changed 12/1992 to non-postable term.
Use CHILDREN with Appendix A
subdivision --Clothing & dress.
**Children's furniture**
UF   Bassinets
Cradles
Cribs
BT   Furniture
**Children's parties**
BT   Parties
NT   Children's tea parties
RT   Birthday parties
**Children's rights**
--[country or state]--[city]
BT   Civil rights
Children's rooms
USE Nurseries
Playrooms
**Children's tea parties**
BT   Children's parties
Tea parties
RT   Tea
**Chimes**
BT   Bells
Chimney pieces
USE Chimneypieces
**Chimney sweeping**
--[country or state]--[city]
BT   Sweeping & dusting
RT   Chimney sweeps
Chimneys
**Chimney sweeps**
--[country or state]--[city]
BT   People associated with manual labor
RT   Chimney sweeping
**Chimneypieces**
--[country or state]--[city]
PN   Ornamental constructions over and around
fireplaces that include the mantel.
UF   Chimney pieces
Mantelpieces
BT   Architectural decorations & ornaments
Architectural elements
RT   Fireplaces
Mantels
**Chimneys**
--[country or state]--[city]
BT   Architectural elements
NT   Smokestacks
RT   Chimney sweeping
Fireplaces
China
USE Porcelain
Tableware
**Chine collé prints**
CN   TGM II term.
Chinese junks
USE Junks
**Chinese lanterns**
PN   Collapsible lanterns of thin colored paper.
BT   Lanterns

**Chisels & mallets**
UF   Mallets
BT   Equipment
RT   Carpentry
Stone cutting
Woodworking
Chittahs
USE Cheetahs
**Chivalry**
BT   Manners & customs
RT   Knights
Chloride prints
USE Photographic prints
Chloro-bromide prints
USE Silver gelatin prints
**Chocolate industry**
--[country or state]--[city]
CN   Double index under INDUSTRIAL
FACILITIES (or NTs) for images that focus
on facilities.
BT   Food industry
RT   Cacao
Cocoa industry
Confections
Chocolate-trees
USE Cacao
**Choirboys**
BT   Children
Singers
RT   Children singing
Choirs (Music)
Religious services
**Choirs (Music)**
BT   Music ensembles
RT   Choirboys
Religious services
Singing
Choking
USE Strangling
**Cholera**
--[country or state]--[city]
UF   Asiatic cholera
BT   Communicable diseases
Chopping wood
USE Woodcutting
**Choreography**
RT   Dancers
Dancing
**Chorus girls**
BT   Entertainers
Women
RT   Chorus girls' unions
Musical revues & comedies
**Chorus girls' unions**
--[country or state]--[city]
BT   Labor unions
RT   Chorus girls
Choruses
USE Singers
**Chow chows (Dogs)**
--[country or state]
UF   Spitz dogs

---

BT Broader term
NT Narrower term
HN History Note

RT Related term
UF Used for
CN Catalogers Note

PN Public Note
+ Term has NTs
--[ ] May subdivide

**Chow chows (Dogs) (cont.)**
  BT   Dogs
Christenings
  USE Baptisms
Christian
  USE Christianity
**Christian Science churches**
       --[country or state]--[city]
  PN   For images that focus on buildings, as
       well as the associated grounds.
  BT   Protestant churches
**Christian vacation schools**
       --[country or state]--[city]
  UF   Vacation Bible schools
  BT   Church schools
  RT   Christianity
**Christianity**
       --[country or state]--[city]
  UF   Christian
  BT   Religion
  RT   Christian vacation schools
       Clergy
       Confession
       Evangelists
       Gospel music
       Missionaries
       Monks
       Nuns
       Saints
       Stations of the Cross
**Christmas cards**
  CN   TGM II term.
Christmas crèches
  USE Crèches (Nativity scenes)
**Christmas decoration stores**
       --[country or state]--[city]
  PN   Includes activities and structures.
  BT   Stores & shops
  RT   Christmas decorations
       Decorations
**Christmas decorations**
  BT   Festive decorations
  RT   Christmas decoration stores
       Holidays
**Christmas seals**
  RT   Fund raising
       Postage stamps
**Christmas stockings**
  BT   Festive decorations
  RT   Gifts
       Hosiery
**Christmas trees**
       --[country or state]--[city]
  BT   Festive decorations
       Trees
**Chromolithographs**
  CN   TGM II term.
Chromotypes
  USE Carbon prints
Chromo-photographs
  USE Crystoleum photographs
Chronometers

Chronometers (cont.)
  USE Clocks & watches
Chronophotographs
  USE Motion study photographs
**Chrysanthemums**
       --[country or state]--[city]
  BT   Flowers
**Chuckwagons**
       --[country or state]--[city]
  UF   Cook cars
  BT   Carts & wagons
  RT   Kitchens
       Outdoor cookery
**Church dedications**
       --[country or state]--[city]
  UF   Consecration of churches
  BT   Building dedications
  RT   Churches
**Church schools**
       --[country or state]--[city]
  PN   For elementary and secondary schools
       operated under church auspices, control, or
       support. Includes activities and structures.
  BT   Schools
  NT   Christian vacation schools
       Sunday schools
  RT   Religious education
       Religious facilities
Church services
  USE Religious services
**Church vestments**
  BT   Clothing & dress
  RT   Clergy
**Church & education**
       --[country or state]
  RT   Education
       Religion
**Church & state**
       --[country or state]
  UF   State & church
  BT   Politics & government
  RT   Religion
       Secularism
       Theocracy
**Churches**
       --[country or state]--[city]
  PN   For images that focus on buildings, as
       well as the associated grounds.
  CN   Used in a note under CHAPELS.
  UF   Churchyards
  BT   Religious facilities
  NT   Anglican churches
       Basilicas
       Cathedrals
       Catholic churches
       Cave churches
       Mission churches
       Mormon churches
       Orthodox churches
       Protestant churches +
  RT   Altarpieces
       Altars

---

BT  Broader term          RT  Related term          PN  Public Note
NT  Narrower term         UF  Used for              +  Term has NTs
HN  History Note          CN  Catalogers Note       --[ ] May subdivide

**Churches (cont.)**
>    Apses
>    Chapels
>    Church dedications
>    Clerestories
>    Fonts
>    Greek cross buildings
>    Latin cross buildings
>    Mosques
>    Organ lofts
>    Parish houses
>    Pews
>    Sacristies
>    Synagogues
>    Tabernacles
>    Temples

Churchyards
>  USE Churches

Churning
>  USE Butter making

**Churns**
>  PN   Machine which agitates cream or whole
>         milk, turning it into butter.
>  UF   Butter churns
>  BT   Equipment
>  RT   Butter
>         Butter making

Cibachrome prints
>  USE Dye destruction prints

**Cider**
>  BT   Beverages
>  RT   Wine

**Cigar industry**
>         --[country or state]--[city]
>  PN   Includes activities and structures.
>  CN   Double index under INDUSTRIAL
>         FACILTIES (or NTs)  for images that focus
>         on facilities.
>  BT   Tobacco industry
>  RT   Cigars

**Cigar store Indians**
>         --[country or state]--[city]
>  BT   Wood carvings
>  RT   Advertisements

**Cigarette cards**
>  CN   TGM II term.
>  UF   Tobacco cards

**Cigarette industry**
>         --[country or state]--[city]
>  PN   Includes activities and structures.
>  CN   Double index under INDUSTRIAL
>         FACILITIES (or NTs) for images that focus
>         on facilities.
>  BT   Tobacco industry
>  RT   Cigarettes

**Cigarette papers**
>  UF   Rolling papers
>  RT   Cigarettes

**Cigarettes**
>  BT   Tobacco products
>  RT   Cigarette industry
>         Cigarette papers

**Cigarettes (cont.)**
>         Smoking

**Cigars**
>  BT   Tobacco products
>  RT   Cigar industry
>         Smoking

Cinema
>  USE Motion pictures

**Cinematography**
>         --[country or state]--[city]
>  PN   For the subject of cinematography in
>         general and the activities of
>         cinematographers.
>  UF   Motion picture photography
>  BT   Photography
>  RT   Motion picture cameras

Cinerary urns
>  USE Urns

**Circular buildings**
>         --[country or state]--[city]
>  UF   Round buildings
>  BT   Buildings distinguished by form
>  RT   Rotundas

**Circular rooms**
>         --[country or state]--[city]
>  UF   Round rooms
>  BT   Interiors
>  RT   Rotundas

**Circulars**
>  CN   TGM II term.

Circulatory system
>  USE Cardiovascular system

Circumnavigation
>  USE Voyages around the world

Circus entertainers
>  USE Circus performers

**Circus parades**
>         --[country or state]--[city]
>  BT   Parades & processions
>  RT   Circuses & shows

**Circus performers**
>  UF   Circus entertainers
>  BT   Entertainers
>  RT   Acrobatics
>         Acrobats
>         Aerialists
>         Circuses & shows
>         Clowns
>         Daredevils

**Circus posters**
>  CN   TGM II term.
>  UF   Carnival posters
>         Wild west show posters

**Circuses & shows**
>         --[country or state]--[city]
>  UF   Big top
>         Shows
>         Side shows
>         Specialty acts
>  BT   Entertainment
>  NT   Medicine shows
>         Wild west shows

---

**Circuses & shows (cont.)**
  RT   Acrobatics
        Amusement parks
        Bareback riding
        Circus parades
        Circus performers
        Human curiosities
        Juggling
        Midways
        Rodeos
        Show tents
        Trained animals
        Trick riding
Cirkut camera photographs
  USE Panoramic photographs
Citadels
  USE Forts & fortifications
Citations, Traffic
  USE Ticketing
**Cities & towns**
        --[country or state]
  PN   For images that focus on structures and
        sites.  Search under CITY & TOWN LIFE for
        images that focus on activities.
  BT   Settlements
  RT   City & town life
        Streets
        Villages
Citizen participation
  USE Community service
        Political participation
**Citizenship**
        --[country]
  BT   Politics & government
  RT   Naturalization
        Repatriation
**Citrus fruit**
        --[country or state]--[city]
  BT   Fruit
  NT   Grapefruit
        Lemons
        Limes
        Oranges
  RT   Citrus fruit industry
**Citrus fruit industry**
        --[country or state]--[city]
  PN   Includes activities and structures.
  CN   Double index under INDUSTRIAL
        FACILITIES (or NTs)  for images that focus
        on facilities.
  UF   Citrus industry
        Citrus trade
  BT   Fruit industry
  RT   Citrus fruit
        Orange orchards
Citrus industry
  USE Citrus fruit industry
Citrus trade
  USE Citrus fruit industry
City beautification
  USE Urban beautification
**City council members**

**City council members (cont.)**
        --[country or state]--[city]
  UF   Aldermen
        Council members, City
  BT   Municipal officials
City dumps
  USE Refuse
        Refuse disposal
City gates
  USE Gates
City halls
  USE City & town halls
City officials
  USE Municipal officials
**City planning**
        --[country or state]--[city]
  UF   Planning, City
        Urban planning
  RT   Housing
        Land subdivision
        Land use
        Municipal services
        Urban beautification
        Urban growth
City planning drawings
  USE Planning drawings
City views
  USE Cityscapes
**City walls**
        --[country or state]--[city]
  RT   Forts & fortifications
        Walls
**City & town halls**
        --[country or state]--[city]
  UF   City halls
        Guildhalls (Municipal buildings)
        Town halls
        Village halls
  BT   Government facilities
**City & town life**
        --[country or state]--[city]
  PN   For images that focus on activities. Search
        under CITIES & TOWNS for images that
        focus on structures and sites. Search under
        STREETS for thoroughfares in cities, towns,
        and villages.
  CN   Used in a note under STREETS and
        CITIES & TOWNS.
  UF   Street life
        Town life
        Urban life
  BT   Manners & customs
  RT   Cities & towns
        Economic & social conditions
        Ethnic neighborhoods
        Markets
        Peddlers
        Slums
        Street entertainers
        Streets
        Town criers
        Town meetings

---

| BT Broader term | RT Related term | PN Public Note |
| NT Narrower term | UF Used for | + Term has NTs |
| HN History Note | CN Catalogers Note | --[ ] May subdivide |

**City & town life (cont.)**
      Traffic accidents
      Traffic congestion
**Cityscape drawings**
  CN  TGM II term.
**Cityscape paintings**
  CN  TGM II term.
**Cityscape photographs**
  CN  TGM II term.
**Cityscape prints**
  CN  TGM II term.
**Cityscapes**
  CN  TGM II term.
  UF  City views
      Skyline views
      Topographic views
      Townscapes
      Views, City
Civic buildings
  USE Social & civic facilities
**Civil defense**
      --[country or state]--[city]
  PN  Search also under the subdivision --CIVIL
      DEFENSE used with names of wars
      (Appendix C).
  UF  Civilian defense
      Defense, Civil
      Emergency preparedness
  BT  National security
      Preparedness
  NT  Air raid drills
  RT  Air raid shelters
      Evacuations
      War
      War blackouts
**Civil disobedience**
      --[country or state]--[city]
  UF  Government, Resistance to
      Noncooperation
      Political violence
      Resistance to government
      Violence, Political
  NT  Passive resistance
  RT  Activists
      Civil rights leaders
      Political prisoners
      Protest movements
Civil disorders
  USE Riots
**Civil engineering**
      --[country or state]--[city]
  PN  For the subject of civil engineering in
      general and the activities of civil engineers.
  BT  Engineering
  NT  Bridge construction
      Canal construction
      Dam construction
      Excavation +
      Reclamation of land +
      Road construction
  RT  Pilings (Civil engineering)
      Surveying

**Civil liberties**
      --[nationality]--[country or state]--[city]
  PN  For the rights of individuals. Search under
      CIVIL RIGHTS for the constitutional and
      legal status and treatment of minority groups
      that are distinguished from the majority by
      race, religion, sex, national origin, etc.
  CN  Used in a note under CIVIL RIGHTS.
  UF  Human rights
  BT  Liberty
  NT  Civil rights +
      Freedom of information
      Freedom of religion
      Freedom of speech +
      Right of property
      Suffrage +
  RT  Employee rights
      Firearms control
**Civil rights**
      --[country or state]--[city]
  PN  Search also under the subdivision --CIVIL
      RIGHTS used with names of ethnic, racial,
      and regional groups and classes of persons
      (Appendix A).
  CN  Used in a note under CIVIL LIBERTIES.
  UF  Civil rights movements
      Freedom from discrimination
      Rights, Civil
  BT  Civil liberties
  NT  Children's rights
      Gay rights
      Veterans' rights
      Women's rights +
  RT  Abolition movement
      Civil rights leaders
      Discrimination
      Legal aid
      Minorities
      Segregation
      Slavery
**Civil rights leaders**
      --[country or state]
  PN  For officials and other individuals
      involved in organizing to promote civil
      rights.
  UF  Civil rights workers
  BT  People
  RT  Activists
      Civil disobedience
      Civil rights
      Demonstrations
      Political participation
      Protest movements
Civil rights movements
  USE Civil rights
Civil rights workers
  USE Civil rights leaders
**Civil service**
      --[country or state]--[city]
  PN  For the subject of employment in branches
      of the public service which are not military,
      naval, legislative, or judicial.

---

BT Broader term              RT Related term              PN Public Note
NT Narrower term           UF Used for                  + Term has NTs
HN History Note            CN Catalogers Note         --[ ] May subdivide

**Civil service (cont.)**
- CN  Used in a note under PUBLIC SERVICE EMPLOYMENT.
- UF  Federal employment
      Merit system
- BT  Employment
      Politics & government
- RT  Administrative agencies
      Civil service reform
      Government employees
      Government officials
      Public service
      Public service employment

**Civil service reform**
    --[country or state]--[city]
- BT  Reform
- RT  Civil service
      Government reorganization

Civil war envelopes
    USE Patriotic envelopes

**Civil wars**
    --[country or state]--[city]
- BT  War
- RT  Rebellions
      Revolutions

Civilian defense
    USE Civil defense

Civilian war relief
    USE War relief

Civilians, Evacuation of
    USE Evacuations

**Civilization**
- PN  For the subject of and symbolic representations of civilization.
- RT  Creation
      Evolution
      History

**Clams**
    --[country or state]
- BT  Shellfish

**Clapboard siding**
    --[country or state]--[city]
- UF  Bevel siding
      Siding, Bevel
      Siding, Clapboard
      Weatherboard siding
- BT  Building materials

Classes (Social)
    USE Social classes

**Classrooms**
    --[country or state]--[city]
- UF  School classrooms
      Schoolrooms
- BT  Interiors
- RT  Educational facilities
      School children
      School overcrowding
      Students
      Teachers

Clavicembalos
    USE Harpsichords

**Clay industries**

**Clay industries (cont.)**
    --[country or state]--[city]
- PN  Includes activities and structures.
- CN  Double index under INDUSTRIAL FACILITIES (or NTs)  for images that focus on facilities.
- BT  Ceramic industries
- NT  Brick industry
      Pottery industry
      Tile industry
- RT  Clay mining

**Clay miners**
    --[country or state]--[city]
- BT  Miners
- RT  Clay mining

**Clay mining**
    --[country or state]--[city]
- PN  Includes activities and sites.
- BT  Mining
- RT  Clay industries
      Clay miners

Clay modeling
    USE Modeling (Sculpture)

**Cleaning**
    --[country or state]--[city]
- UF  Washing
- NT  Dishwashing
      Refuse disposal +
      Snow removal
      Street cleaning
      Sweeping & dusting +
      Window cleaning
- RT  Basins
      Household soap
      Housework
      Wash tubs
      Washboards

**Cleaning establishments**
    --[country or state]--[city]
- PN  Includes activities and structures.
- CN  Used in a note under LAUNDRIES (ROOMS & SPACES).
- UF  Dry cleaners
      Laundries (Commercial establishments)
- BT  Service industry facilities
- RT  Laundry
      Laundry workers' strikes

**Clearing of land**
    --[country or state]--[city]
- PN  Removal of timber and bushes from land. Search under RECLAMATION OF LAND for bringing wild, waste, or marshy land into a condition for cultivation or other use.
- CN  Used in a note under RECLAMATION OF LAND.
- UF  Land clearing
- BT  Reclamation of land
- RT  Cutover lands
      Mowing
      Real estate development

Clearstories
    USE Clerestories

---

BT  Broader term
NT  Narrower term
HN  History Note

RT  Related term
UF  Used for
CN  Catalogers Note

PN Public Note
+ Term has NTs
--[ ] May subdivide

Clenched fists
  USE Fists
**Clerestories**
      --[country or state]--[city]
  UF  Clearstories
  RT  Churches
**Clergy**
      --[country or state]--[city]
  HN  Changed 12/1992 from CLERGYMEN.
  UF  Clergymen
      Clerics
      Ministers of the gospel
  BT  People associated with religion
  NT  Bishops +
      Cardinals
      Patriarchs
      Priests +
      Rabbis
  RT  Christianity
      Church vestments
      Missionaries
      Religion
      Religious orders
      Religious services
      Spiritual leaders
      Theological seminaries
Clergymen
  HN  Changed 12/1992 from postable term.
  USE Clergy
Clerical workers
  USE Office workers
Clerics
  USE Clergy
Clerks' strikes
  USE Retail trade strikes
**Clichés-verre**
  CN  TGM II term.
  UF  Glass prints
**Cliff dwellings**
      --[country or state]--[city]
  BT  Dwellings
  RT  Archaeological sites
      Cliffs
**Cliffs**
      --[country or state]
  PN  Very steep, perpendicular, or overhanging
      faces of rock, earth, or glacial ice of
      considerable height. Search under CANYONS
      for images that focus on valleys between
      cliffs.
  CN  Used in a note under CANYONS.
  UF  Bluffs
      Escarpments
      Palisades
      Precipices
  BT  Land
  RT  Canyons
      Cliff dwellings
      Mountains
Climate
  USE Weather
**Climbing**

Climbing (cont.)
      --[country or state]--[city]
  BT  Locomotion
  NT  Mountaineering
Climbing plants
  USE Vines
**Clinics**
      --[country or state]--[city]
  PN  Health care facilities for treatment of
      non-resident patients.
  UF  Free clinics
  BT  Health care facilities
  RT  Infirmaries
      Mobile health units
**Clipper ship cards**
  CN  TGM II term.
  UF  Yankee clipper cards
**Clipper ships**
      --[country or state]--[city]
  BT  Sailing ships
**Clippings**
  CN  TGM II term.
  UF  Newspaper clippings
      Press clippings
Clips, Paper
  USE Paper clips
**Clock towers**
      --[country or state]--[city]
  BT  Towers
  RT  Clocks & watches
**Clock & watch industry**
      --[country or state]--[city]
  PN  Includes activities and structures. Search
      under CLOCK & WATCH MAKING for
      small businesses.
  CN  Double index under INDUSTRIAL
      FACILITIES (or NTs) for images that focus
      on facilities. Used in a note under CLOCK &
      WATCH MAKING.
  UF  Watch industry
  BT  Industry
  RT  Clock & watch making
      Clocks & watches
**Clock & watch making**
      --[country or state]--[city]
  PN  For small businesses. Search under
      CLOCK & WATCH INDUSTRY for factory
      work.
  CN  Used in a note under CLOCK & WATCH
      INDUSTRY.
  UF  Watch making
  BT  Business enterprises
  RT  Clock & watch industry
      Clocks & watches
**Clocks & watches**
  UF  Chronometers
      Watches
  NT  Alarm clocks
      Cuckoo clocks
  RT  Clock towers
      Clock & watch industry
      Clock & watch making

---

BT  Broader term        RT  Related term        PN Public Note
NT  Narrower term      UF  Used for          + Term has NTs
HN  History Note        CN Catalogers Note    --[ ] May subdivide

**Clocks & watches (cont.)**
    Furnishings
    Hourglasses
    Jewelry
    Longcase clocks
    Sundials
    Time
**Cloisonné**
  RT  Jewelry
    Pottery
Cloisters
  USE Convents
    Monasteries
Closed seas
  USE Freedom of the seas
**Closets**
    --[country or state]--[city]
  UF  Clothing closets
    Linen closets
    Wardrobes
  BT  Furniture
  RT  Clothing & dress
    Cupboards
Cloth
  USE Textiles
Cloth labels
  USE Textile labels
**Cloth photographs**
  CN  TGM II term.
  UF  Collodion positive photographs
**Cloth prints**
  CN  TGM II term.
**Clothes chests**
    --[country or state]--[city]
  UF  Bureaus (Furniture)
    Dressers (Furniture)
  BT  Chests
Clothes washing
  USE Laundry
**Clotheslines**
    --[country or state]--[city]
  BT  Equipment
  RT  Laundry
Clothing closets
  USE Closets
**Clothing industry**
    --[country or state]--[city]
  PN  Includes activities and structures.
  CN  Double index under INDUSTRIAL
    FACILITIES (or NTs) for images that focus
    on facilities.
  BT  Industry
  NT  Buttonhole industry
    Hat industry
    Hosiery industry
    Neckwear industry
    Shoe industry
    Shoestring industry
  RT  Clothing industry unions
    Clothing & dress
    Mannequins
    Sewing

**Clothing industry (cont.)**
    Tailoring
    Textile industry
**Clothing industry strikes**
    --[country or state]--[city]
  UF  Garment workers' strikes
  BT  Strikes
  RT  Clothing industry unions
    Textile industry strikes
**Clothing industry unions**
    --[country or state]--[city]
  BT  Labor unions
  RT  Clothing industry
    Clothing industry strikes
    Textile industry unions
Clothing reform
  USE Dress reform
**Clothing relief**
    --[nationality]--[country or state]--[city]
  PN  Subdivide by nationality only when relief
    provided to another country.
  BT  Assistance
  RT  Clothing & dress
    Disaster relief
    Disaster victims
**Clothing stores**
    --[country or state]--[city]
  PN  Includes activities and structures.
  BT  Stores & shops
  NT  Shoe stores
  RT  Mannequins
    Millinery
**Clothing & dress**
    --[country or state]--[city]
  PN  Search also under groups of people
    associated with particular types of clothing,
    e.g., FLAPPERS and COWBOYS. Search
    also under the subdivision --CLOTHING &
    DRESS used with names of ethnic, racial, and
    regional groups, and with classes of persons
    (Appendix A).
  UF  Accessories
    Apparel
    Costume
    Dress
    Fashion
    Garments
  NT  Armor +
    Ball dresses
    Bathing suits
    Belts (Clothing)
    Bloomers
    Buttons
    Chastity belts
    Church vestments
    Coats +
    Collars
    Costumes
    Crowns
    Diving suits
    Footwear +
    Fur garments +

---

BT Broader term          RT Related term          PN Public Note
NT Narrower term        UF Used for              + Term has NTs
HN History Note          CN Catalogers Note      --[ ] May subdivide

**Clothing & dress (cont.)**
    Gloves
    Handbags
    Handkerchiefs
    Hats +
    Hosiery
    Jewelry +
    Kilts
    Masks +
    Miniskirts
    Neckties
    Purses
    Sleepwear
    Trousers +
    Tuxedoes
    Underwear +
    Uniforms +
    Veils
    Wedding costume
RT   Blankets
    Bloody shirt
    Children dressing
    Closets
    Clothing industry
    Clothing relief
    Cross dressing
    Dandies
    Dress reform
    Eye patches
    Fashion models
    Fashion shows
    Hairstyles
    Laundry
    Leis
    Staffs (Sticks)
    Umbrellas
**Cloud seeding**
USE Rain making
**Clouds**
BT   Natural phenomena
**Clowns**
BT   Entertainers
RT   Circus performers
    Comedians
    Fools & jesters
**Club women**
USE Clubwomen
**Clubhouses**
    --[country or state]--[city]
BT   Organizations' facilities
RT   Clubs
    Fraternal lodges
    Sports & recreation facilities
**Clubs**
    --[country or state]--[city]
PN  Search also under the subdivision
    --ORGANIZATIONS used with names of
    racial, ethnic, and regional groups and with
    classes of persons (Appendix A).
CN  Double index under ORGANIZATIONS'
    FACILITIES (or NTs) for images that focus
    on facilities.

**Clubs (cont.)**
BT   Organizations
NT   4-H clubs
    Art clubs
    Athletic clubs
    Boat clubs +
    Book clubs
    Camera clubs
    Country clubs
    Drama clubs
    Hunting & fishing clubs
    USO clubs
RT   Charitable organizations
    Clubhouses
    Fraternal organizations
    Patriotic societies
**Clubwomen**
    --[country or state]--[city]
PN  For women identified as being active in
    formally established societies or clubs.
UF  Club women
BT   Women
RT   Socialites
**Clumsiness**
RT   Accidents
    Falling
    Locomotion
**Coach drivers**
UF  Carriage drivers
    Coachmen
BT   People associated with transportation
RT   Carriages & coaches
**Coach houses**
USE Carriage houses
**Coaches**
USE Carriages & coaches
**Coaching (Athletics)**
    --[country or state]--[city]
RT   Athletes
    Physical education
    Sports
**Coachmen**
USE Coach drivers
**Coal**
    --[country or state]--[city]
BT   Fuel
    Minerals
NT   Coke
RT   Burning coal veins
    Coal mining
    Ore industry
**Coal miners**
    --[country or state]--[city]
BT   Miners
RT   Coal mining
**Coal mining**
    --[country or state]--[city]
PN  Includes activities and sites.
CN  Double index under STRIP MINING, as
    appropriate. Used in a note under STRIP
    MINING.
UF  Anthracite mining

---

BT Broader term           RT Related term           PN Public Note
NT Narrower term         UF Used for                + Term has NTs
HN History Note           CN Catalogers Note       --[ ] May subdivide

**Coal mining (cont.)**
    Breakers (Machinery)
  BT  Mining
  RT  Black lung
    Coal
    Coal miners
**Coalition (Social sciences)**
  UF  Alliances, Temporary
  BT  Power (Social sciences)
**Coaster cars**
    --[nationality]--[country or state]--[city]
  UF  Automobiles, Coaster
    Soap box derby racers
  BT  Vehicles
  RT  Racing automobiles
**Coastlines**
  USE Capes (Coasts)
    Waterfronts
**Coats**
  UF  Jackets
    Overcoats
  BT  Clothing & dress
  NT  Fur coats
**Coats of arms**
  CN  TGM II term.
**Cobblers**
  USE Shoemakers
**Cobblestone roads**
  USE Cobblestone streets
**Cobblestone streets**
    --[country or state]--[city]
  HN  Changed 1/1993 from COBBLESTONE
    ROADS.
  UF  Cobblestone roads
  BT  Streets
**Cobwebs**
  UF  Spiderwebs
  RT  Spiders
**Cockatoos**
    --[country or state]
  BT  Parrots
**Cockfighting**
    --[country or state]--[city]
  BT  Sports
  RT  Birds
**Cocktail waitresses**
  USE Waitresses
**Cocoa industry**
    --[country or state]--[city]
  PN  Includes activities and structures.
  CN  Double index under INDUSTRIAL
    FACILITIES (or NTs) for images that focus
    on facilities.
  BT  Food industry
  RT  Cacao
    Chocolate industry
**Coconut palms**
  USE Palms
**Coconut plantations**
    --[country or state]--[city]
  PN  Includes activities and structures.
  CN  As appropriate, double index under

**Coconut plantations (cont.)**
    HARVESTING.
  BT  Plantations
  RT  Coconuts
    Palms
**Coconuts**
    --[country or state]--[city]
  BT  Fruit
  RT  Coconut plantations
    Palms
**Codfish**
    --[country or state]
  BT  Fish
**Codicils**
  USE Wills
**Coffee**
    --[country or state]--[city]
  PN  Includes the activity of coffee drinking.
  CN  Double index under EATING &
    DRINKING for the activity of coffee
    drinking.
  BT  Beverages
  RT  Coffee plantations
    Coffee plants
    Coffeehouses
    Coffeepots
**Coffee industry**
    --[country or state]--[city]
  PN  Includes activities and structures.
  CN  Double index under INDUSTRIAL
    FACILITIES (or NTs) for images that focus
    on facilities.
  BT  Beverage industry
  RT  Coffee plantations
**Coffee plantations**
    --[country or state]--[city]
  PN  Includes activities and structures.
  CN  As appropriate, double index under
    HARVESTING.
  BT  Plantations
  RT  Coffee
    Coffee industry
    Coffee plants
**Coffee plants**
    --[country or state]--[city]
  BT  Plants
  RT  Coffee
    Coffee plantations
**Coffee pots**
  USE Coffeepots
**Coffee tables**
  UF  Tables, Coffee
  BT  Tables
**Coffeehouses**
    --[country or state]--[city]
  PN  Enterprises serving coffee and other
    refreshments, and that commonly serve as an
    informal club or forum for political
    discussion.
  BT  Eating & drinking facilities
  RT  Cafes
    Coffee

BT Broader term
NT Narrower term
HN History Note

RT Related term
UF Used for
CN Catalogers Note

PN Public Note
+ Term has NTs
--[ ] May subdivide

**Coffeepots**
UF   Coffee pots
BT   Containers
RT   Coffee
Teapots

**Coffers (Ceilings)**
--[country or state]--[city]
PN   For recessed panels, especially forming
with other panels a continuous pattern in a
vault, ceiling, or soffit.
UF   Cassons
BT   Architectural elements
NT   Dome coffers
RT   Ceilings
Paneling

**Coffins**
UF   Caskets
BT   Containers
NT   Sarcophagi
RT   Dead persons
Funeral rites & ceremonies
Lying in state

Cog railroads
USE Mountain railroads

Coiffures
USE Hairstyles

Coigns
USE Quoins

Coillons
USE Quoins

**Coin banks**
UF   Piggy banks
BT   Containers
RT   Banks
Coins

**Coin counting machines**
PN   Device used in banks, mints, and financial
institutions for counting coins.
UF   Counting devices
BT   Machinery
RT   Weights & measures

**Coin operated machines**
--[country or state]--[city]
UF   Machines, Coin operated
BT   Machinery
NT   Jukeboxes
Pinball machines
Slot machines
Vending machines
RT   Automats

Coin purses
USE Purses

**Coins**
--[country]
UF   Specie
BT   Money
RT   Coin banks
Silver question

Coins (Wall components)
USE Quoins

**Coke**
BT   Coal

**Coke (cont.)**
RT   Coke industry

**Coke industry**
--[country or state]--[city]
PN   Includes activities and structures.
CN   Double index under INDUSTRIAL
FACILITIES (or NTs) for images that focus
on facilities.
BT   Industry
RT   Coke

**Cold**
RT   Heat
Ice
Temperature

Collaboration
USE Fraternization

**Collages**
CN   TGM II term.

**Collagraphs**
CN   TGM II term.
UF   Collographs

Collapse of bridges
USE Bridge failures

Collapse of buildings
USE Building failures

Collapse of piers & wharves
USE Pier & wharf failures

**Collars**
BT   Clothing & dress

**Collecting cards**
CN   TGM II term.
UF   Trading cards

**Collective farms**
--[country or state]--[city]
UF   Collectives
BT   Farms

Collective security
USE International security

**Collective settlements**
--[country or state]--[city]
PN   For formally organized communal
ventures, usually based on ideological,
political, or religious affiliation.
UF   Collectives
Communal settlements
Utopian communities
BT   Settlements
RT   Artist colonies
Cooperatives
Cults
Religious communities

Collectives
USE Collective farms
Collective settlements

**Collectors**
--[country or state]--[city]
BT   People
NT   Art collectors
RT   Hobbyists

**Collectors' marks**
CN   TGM II term.

**College administrators**

---

BT  Broader term                    RT  Related term                    PN  Public Note
NT  Narrower term                   UF  Used for                        +  Term has NTs
HN  History Note                    CN  Catalogers Note                 --[ ]  May subdivide

**College administrators (cont.)**
    UF   College officials
         University administrators
    BT   People associated with education &
         communication
    RT   Universities & colleges
College fraternities
    USE Fraternities & sororities
College officials
    USE College administrators
College students
    USE Students
College unions
    USE Student unions
Colleges
    USE Universities & colleges
College, Electoral
    USE Electoral college
Collisions
    USE Accidents
         Disasters
Collodion dry plate negatives
    USE Dry collodion negatives
Collodion negatives
    USE Dry collodion negatives
         Wet collodion negatives
Collodion positive photographs
    USE Ambrotypes
         Cloth photographs
         Collodion transparencies
         Leather photographs
         Tintypes
Collodion printing-out paper photoprints
    USE Collodion printing-out paper prints
**Collodion printing-out paper prints**
    CN   TGM II term.
    UF   Collodion printing-out paper photoprints
         Collodio-chloride prints
**Collodion transparencies**
    CN   TGM II term.
    UF   Collodion positive photographs
Collodio-chloride prints
    USE Collodion printing-out paper prints
Collographs
    USE Collagraphs
**Collonnettes**
         --[country or state]--[city]
    PN   Conspicuously small columns.
    BT   Columns
**Collotypes**
    CN   TGM II term.
    UF   Albertypes
         Artotypes
         Heliotypes
Colonialism
    USE Imperialism
**Colonies**
         --[nationality]--[country or state]--[city]
    PN   For the subject of colonies and
         colonialism.
    CN   Subdivide by colonizing country.
    RT   Colonists

**Colonies (cont.)**
         Emigration & immigration
         National liberation movements
         White man's burden
Colonies, Artist
    USE Artist colonies
**Colonists**
         --[nationality]--[country or state]--[city]
    CN   Used in a note under COLONIES.
    BT   People
    RT   Colonies
         Emigration & immigration
         Frontier & pioneer life
**Colonnades**
         --[country or state]--[city]
    PN   Rows of columns supporting an
         entablature.
    BT   Architectural elements
    NT   Peristyles
    RT   Columns
         Entablatures
Color guards
    USE Flag bearers
**Color in architecture**
         --[country or state]--[city]
    UF   Architectural polychromy
         Polychromy, Architecture
    RT   Architecture
Color screen transparencies
    USE Screen color film transparencies
         Screen color glass transparencies
**Color separation negatives**
    CN   TGM II term.
    UF   Separation negatives
**Color separation positives**
    CN   TGM II term.
    UF   Color separation transparencies
         Postitives, Color separation
         Postives, Color separation
         Separation positives, Color
         Separation transparencies, Color
Color separation transparencies
    USE Color separation positives
Coloring
    USE Dyeing
Colportage
    USE Bookselling
Colts
    USE Horses
**Columns**
         --[country or state]--[city]
    PN   Includes both supporting pillars and
         free-standing shafts.
    CN   Used in a note under ARCHITECTURAL
         ORDERS.
    UF   Pillars
    BT   Architectural elements
    NT   Collonnettes
    RT   Architectural orders
         Colonnades
         Distyle-in-antis buildings
         Obelisks

---

BT  Broader term             RT  Related term             PN  Public Note
NT  Narrower term           UF  Used for                +  Term has NTs
HN  History Note            CN  Catalogers Note        --[ ]  May subdivide

**Columns (cont.)**
>    Pedestals
>    Pilasters
>    Totem poles

Combat
>    USE Campaigns & battles

Combination prints
>    USE Composite photographs

**Combines (Agricultural machinery)**
>    BT    Harvesting machinery

**Combs**
>    BT    Dressing & grooming equipment
>    RT    Hairdressing

**Comedians**
>    BT    Entertainers
>    RT    Clowns
>          Comedies

**Comedies**
>    PN    For images representing dramatic
>          productions or scenes (theatrical, film, radio,
>          or television) which have humorous or
>          amusing intent.
>    RT    Comedians
>          Motion pictures
>          Musical revues & comedies
>          Radio broadcasting
>          Television broadcasting
>          Theatrical productions

Comedies, Musical
>    USE Musical revues & comedies

Comfort stations
>    USE Public comfort stations

**Comic books**
>    CN    TGM II term.

**Comic cards**
>    CN    TGM II term.

Comic characters
>    USE Fictitious characters

Comic pictures
>    USE Cartoons (Commentary)
>          Humorous pictures

Comic strips
>    USE Comics

**Comics**
>    CN    TGM II term.
>    UF    Cartoon strips
>          Comic strips

Coming out
>    USE Debutantes

Command of troops
>    USE Military leadership

**Commemoration**
>          --[country or state]--[city]
>    PN    Acts in honor or remembrance of an
>          individual, a category of persons, or an event.
>          Search also under the subdivision
>          --COMMEMORATION used with names of
>          ethnic, racial, and regional groups, and with
>          classes of persons (Appendix A); with names
>          of persons (Appendix B); with names of wars
>          (Appendix C); and with corporate bodies and
>          named events (Appendix D).

**Commemoration (cont.)**
>    CN    Used in a note under CELEBRATIONS,
>          MEMORIAL RITES & CEREMONIES, and
>          MONUMENTS & MEMORIALS.
>    RT    Anniversaries
>          Celebrations
>          Historical reenactments
>          Impersonation
>          Memorial rites & ceremonies
>          Reunions

**Commemorative prints**
>    CN    TGM II term.

Commencements
>    USE Graduation ceremonies

**Commerce**
>          --[nationality]
>    PN    Search also under the subdivision
>          --COMMERCE used with names of ethnic,
>          racial, and regional groups, and with classes
>          of persons (Appendix A).
>    UF    Exports
>          Foreign trade
>          Imports
>          Trade
>    BT    Business & finance
>    NT    Auctions +
>          Barter
>          Black market
>          Free trade & protection +
>          Fur trade
>          Selling +
>          Slave trade
>          Tourist trade
>    RT    Boycotts
>          Business enterprises
>          Caravans
>          Commercial organizations
>          Commercialism
>          Consuls
>          Consumers
>          Customs houses
>          Embargoes
>          International competition
>          Shipping
>          Surplus commodities
>          Tariffs

Commercial art design drawings
>    USE Graphic design drawings

**Commercial art galleries**
>          --[country or state]--[city]
>    PN    Includes activities and structures.
>    UF    Art galleries, Commercial
>    BT    Mercantile facilities
>    RT    Art dealers
>          Galleries & museums

Commercial buildings
>    USE Commercial facilities

Commercial catalogs
>    USE Sales catalogs

Commercial districts
>    USE Business districts

**Commercial facilities**

---

**Commercial facilities (cont.)**
--[country or state]--[city]
PN   For facilities associated with the various activities involved in conducting business or trade.
HN   Changed 2/1993 from COMMERCIAL BUILDINGS.
UF   Commercial buildings
BT   Facilities
NT   Business districts
Eating & drinking facilities +
Financial facilities +
Mercantile facilities +
Service industry facilities +
RT   Business enterprises
Business & finance
Office buildings
Parking garages
**Commercial garages**
USE Automobile service stations
**Commercial organizations**
--[country or state]--[city]
BT   Organizations
NT   Boards of trade
Business enterprises +
Chambers of commerce
Cooperatives
RT   Commerce
**Commercial streets**
--[country or state]--[city]
HN   Made postable 2/90. Earlier cataloging used STREETS and/or BUSINESS ENTERPRISES or COMMERCIAL BUILDINGS.
BT   Streets
RT   Business districts
Shopping
**Commercialism**
PN   Excessive emphasis on profit or financial success.
RT   Commerce
War profiteering
**Commerical art design drawings**
USE Graphic design drawings
**Commissaries, Military**
USE Military exchanges
**Commissions of inquiry**
USE Governmental investigations
**Committee rooms**
USE Conference rooms
**Committees**
--[nationality]--[country or state]--[city]
PN   Body of persons appointed for a special function.
BT   Organizations
RT   Delegations
Governmental investigations
Juries
**Commodities, Surplus**
USE Surplus commodities
**Commodity exchanges**
--[country or state]--[city]

**Commodity exchanges (cont.)**
PN   Includes activities and structures.
CN   As appropriate, double index under the industry.
UF   Exchanges
Produce exchanges
BT   Financial facilities
RT   Merchants' exchanges
Stock exchanges
**Common graves**
USE Mass burials
**Common markets**
USE International economic integration
**Commons (Social order)**
USE Working class
**Communal settlements**
USE Collective settlements
**Communicable diseases**
--[country or state]--[city]
PN   Illnesses caused by living beings (both microscopic or submicroscopic, such as viruses, bacteria, and protozoa, and visible, such as certain disease-producing mites and worms) that invade the body.
UF   Contagious diseases
Epidemics
Infectious diseases
Pestilences
BT   Diseases
NT   Cholera
Hookworm disease
Leprosy
Malaria
Measles
Plague
Poliomyelitis
Rabies
Sexually transmitted diseases
Smallpox
Trench mouth
Tuberculosis
Typhus fever
Yellow fever
RT   Quarantines
Vaccinations
**Communication**
PN   Search also under the subdivision --COMMUNICATION used with names of ethnic, racial, and regional groups, and classes of persons (Appendix A). Search also under the subdivision --COMMUNICATIONS used with names of wars (Appendix C).
NT   Advertising +
Announcements
Broadcasting +
Cheerleading
Conversation
Correspondence +
Debates
Discussion
Filibustering

---

BT Broader term
NT Narrower term
HN History Note

RT Related term
UF Used for
CN Catalogers Note

PN Public Note
+ Term has NTs
--[ ] May subdivide

**Communication (cont.)**
    Flattery
    Hog calling
    International communication
    Interviews
    Journalism +
    Peace negotiations
    Pleading (Begging)
    Press conferences
    Propaganda
    Public opinion
    Public speaking +
    Publicity
    Questioning
    Sign language
    Silence
    Slang
    Sound recording
    Storytelling +
    Writing +
    Writing systems +
  RT  Communication devices
    Communication facilities
    Confession
    Eavesdropping
    Interpersonal relations
    Messengers
    Press
    Sounds
    Speech therapy
    Town criers
**Communication cables**
  USE Telecommunication cables
**Communication devices**
  NT  Beacons
    Buoys
    Heliographs (Apparatus)
    Horns (Communication devices)
    Hotlines (Communication)
    Intercommunication systems
    Megaphones
    Phonographs +
    Public address systems
    Radiophones
    Radios
    Signal flags
    Signal lights +
    Signs +
    Telecommunication cables +
    Telecommunication lines +
    Telegraph
    Telephones
    Televisions
  RT  Bells
    Bugles
    Communication
    Communication facilities
    Pneumatic tubes
    Writing materials
**Communication facilities**
    --[country or state]--[city]
  PN  For structures housing communication

**Communication facilities (cont.)**
    devices and/or activities.
  BT  Facilities
  NT  Radio stations
    Signal stations
    Signal towers +
    Telegraph offices
    Telephone booths
  RT  Communication
    Communication devices
    Lighthouses
    Stockrooms
**Communication with the dead**
  USE Spiritualism
**Communications**
  CN  Used only as a subdivision with names of
    wars (Appendix C).
**Communion**
  UF  Eucharist
    Holy Communion
    Lord's Supper
    Sacrament of the Altar
  BT  Rites & ceremonies
  RT  Preaching
    Religious services
**Communion-cups**
  USE Chalices
**Communism**
    --[country or state]--[city]
  PN  For the subject of communism in general.
  UF  Bolshevism
    Leninism
    Maoism
    Marxism
  BT  Economic & political systems
  RT  Anti-communism
    Communists
    Hammer & sickle
    McCarthyism
    Totalitarianism
**Communists**
    --[country or state]--[city]
  PN  Search under COMMUNISM for the
    subject of communism in general and the
    activities of communists.
  BT  People associated with politics &
    government
  RT  Communism
**Communities, Religious**
  USE Religious communities
**Community beautification**
  USE Urban beautification
**Community centers**
    --[country or state]--[city]
  BT  Social & civic facilities
  RT  Sports & recreation facilities
**Community property**
  BT  Law & legal affairs
  RT  Marriage
**Community service**
    --[country or state]--[city]
  UF  Charitable work

---

BT Broader term                  RT Related term                  PN Public Note
NT Narrower term                UF Used for                       + Term has NTs
HN History Note                 CN Catalogers Note            --[ ] May subdivide

**Community service (cont.)**
>      Citizen participation
>      Service, Community
>      Volantarism
>      Volunteer work
> BT  Public service
> NT  Scrap drives
> RT  Charitable organizations
>      Charity

**Commuters**
>      --[country or state]--[city]
> PN  For persons who travel regularly between
>      one place and another. Search under
>      PASSENGERS for general travelers.
> CN  Used in a note under PASSENGERS.
> BT  People associated with transportation
> RT  Passengers

Companies
> USE Business enterprises

Company police
> USE Private police

Comparisons, Then & now
> USE Then & now comparisons

**Compasses**
> BT  Scientific equipment
> RT  Navigation

Compensation for war damage
> USE Reparations

Compensation for work
> USE Wages

Compensatory spending
> USE Deficit financing

**Competition drawings**
> CN  TGM II term.
> UF  Drawings, Competition

**Competition (Psychology)**
> UF  Rivalry
> BT  Mental states
> RT  Cooperation
>      Interpersonal relations

Competitions
> USE Contests
>      Sports

**Composers**
> BT  Musicians

**Composite photographs**
> CN  TGM II term.
> UF  Combination prints
>      Simulated images

Composite prints
> USE Photomontages

Composition cases
> USE Union cases

Composition (Printing)
> USE Typesetting

Compressors, Air
> USE Air compressors

Compulsory military service
> USE Draft

**Computer graphics**
> CN  TGM II term.
> UF  Digital images

**Computer graphics (cont.)**
>      Electronic images
>      Simulated images

**Computers**
> PN  For modern electronic computers first
>      developed after 1945. Search under
>      CALCULATORS for present-day
>      calculators, as well as calculators and
>      mechanical computers of pre-1945 vintage.
> CN  Used in a note under CALCULATORS.
> UF  Automatic data processing equipment
>      Data processing equipment
>      Electronic calculating machines
> BT  Office equipment & supplies
> RT  Calculators
>      Robots

**Computer-aided designs**
> CN  TGM II term.
> UF  CAD drawings

Concealed camera photographs
> USE Detective camera photographs

**Concentration camps**
>      --[country or state]--[city]
> UF  Camps, Internment
>      Internment camps
> BT  Detention facilities
> RT  Political prisoners
>      Prisoners of war
>      Relocation camps
>      Settlements
>      War

**Concert halls**
>      --[country or state]--[city]
> UF  Symphony halls
> BT  Cultural facilities
> NT  Music halls
>      Opera houses
> RT  Auditoriums
>      Concerts

**Concert posters**
> CN  TGM II term.
> UF  Music posters

**Concerts**
>      --[country or state]--[city]
> BT  Entertainment
> RT  Audiences
>      Concert halls
>      Conductors
>      Music
>      Music festivals
>      Musical instruments
>      Orchestras

**Concourses**
>      --[country or state]--[city]
> PN  For large open spaces or halls in buildings
>      where crowds come together and circulate, as
>      in a railroad station or airport.
> BT  Interiors
> RT  Passageways
>      Transportation facilities

**Concrete**
>      --[country or state]--[city]

---

| BT  Broader term | RT  Related term | PN  Public Note |
| NT  Narrower term | UF  Used for | +  Term has NTs |
| HN  History Note | CN  Catalogers Note | --[ ] May subdivide |

**Concrete (cont.)**
  BT   Building materials
  RT   Reinforced concrete construction
**Concrete products industry**
       --[country or state]--[city]
  CN   Double index under INDUSTRIAL
       FACILITIES (or NTs) for images that focus
       on facilities.
  BT   Building materials industry
**Condiments**
  BT   Food
  RT   Spices
**Condominiums**
       --[country or state]--[city]
  UF   Condos
  BT   Dwellings
Condos
  USE Condominiums
Conductor heads
  USE Leader heads
**Conductors**
  PN   For images that focus on conductors and
       for conductors away from the context of their
       work.
  UF   Bandmasters
  BT   Musicians
  RT   Concerts
       Music ensembles
Conductors, Railroad
  USE Railroad employees
Conduits, Water
  USE Aqueducts
       Culverts
       Penstocks
Conestoga wagons
  USE Covered wagons
**Confectioneries**
       --[country or state]--[city]
  PN   Includes activities and structures.
  UF   Candy stores
  BT   Stores & shops
  RT   Confections
**Confections**
       --[country or state]--[city]
  PN   Sweet edibles, including candies, cakes,
       pastries, and other mixtures of sugar, fruit, or
       nuts.
  CN   As appropriate, subdivide by place with
       which confections are associated.
  UF   Sweetmeats
       Sweets
  BT   Food
  NT   Cakes
       Candy
  RT   Chocolate industry
       Confectioneries
**Conference rooms**
       --[country or state]--[city]
  UF   Board rooms
       Boardrooms
       Committee rooms
       Convention halls (Rooms)

**Conference rooms (cont.)**
       Meeting rooms
  BT   Interiors
  RT   Meetings
Conferences
  USE Meetings
Conferences, Press
  USE Press conferences
**Confession**
  UF   Auricular confession
  RT   Christianity
       Communication
       Confessionals
       Religion
**Confessionals**
       --[country or state]--[city]
  BT   Furnishings
       Religious architectural elements
  RT   Confession
**Confirmations**
       --[country or state]--[city]
  BT   Rites & ceremonies
**Confiscations**
       --[country or state]--[city]
  PN   Search also under the subdivision
       --DESTRUCTION & PILLAGE used with
       names of wars (Appendix C).
  UF   Captures
       Seizures
  RT   Foraging
       Police raids
       War
Conflagrations
  USE Fires
**Conformity**
  RT   Individuality
       Interpersonal relations
**Confucian temples**
       --[country or state]--[city]
  BT   Temples
Congestion, Traffic
  USE Traffic congestion
**Congregational churches**
       --[country or state]--[city]
  PN   For images that focus on buildings, as
       well as the associated grounds.
  BT   Protestant churches
Congress & presidents
  USE Presidents & the Congress
Congresses
  USE Legislative bodies
       Meetings
Congressional investigations
  USE Governmental investigations
Congressional pages
  USE Capitol pages
**Congressional privileges & immunities**
  UF   Immunities, Congressional
       Privileges, Congressional
  RT   Law & legal affairs
       Legislators
       Political patronage

BT  Broader term                          RT  Related term                          PN  Public Note
NT  Narrower term                         UF  Used for                              +   Term has NTs
HN  History Note                          CN  Catalogers Note                       --[ ] May subdivide

Congressional spouses
  USE Legislators' spouses
Congressmen
  USE Legislators
**Conjectural works**
  CN   TGM II term.
  UF   Historical studies
       Imaginary views
       Recreations (Conjectural works)
  RT   Forecasting
       Visionary architecture
Conjurers
  USE Magicians
Conjuring
  USE Magic
**Conscientious objectors**
       --[country or state]--[city]
  BT   People
  RT   Draft
       Draft resisters
       Freedom of religion
       Moral aspects of war
       Pacifists
Consciousness, Loss of
  USE Loss of consciousness
Conscription, Military
  USE Draft
Consecration of churches
  USE Church dedications
**Conservation of natural resources**
       --[country or state]--[city]
  UF   Environmental protection
       Natural resource conservation
  NT   Recycling
       Soil conservation
       Wildlife conservation
  RT   Ecology
       Fish ladders
       Land use
       Water supply
       Water use
**Conservation & restoration**
       --[country or state]--[city]
  PN   For restoration work on structures, as well
       as conservation of objects, e.g., books.
  UF   Restoration
  RT   Construction
       Recycled structures
       Remodeling
**Conservatism**
       --[country or state]--[city]
  UF   Neo-conservatism
       New Right
       Reactionism
  BT   Economic & political systems
Conservatories (Greenhouses)
  USE Greenhouses
Conservatories, Home
  USE Garden rooms
Conservatories, Musical
  USE Music education
**Consoles**

Consoles (cont.)
       --[country or state]--[city]
  PN   Projecting, scroll-shaped members serving
       as brackets or corbels.
  UF   Brackets (Consoles)
  BT   Architectural elements
**Constitutional amendments**
  UF   Amendments, Constitutional
  BT   Law & legal affairs
  NT   Equal rights amendments
  RT   Constitutions
**Constitutional conventions**
       --[country or state]--[city]
  BT   Meetings
  RT   Constitutions
**Constitutions**
       --[country or state]
  BT   Law & legal affairs
  RT   Constitutional amendments
       Constitutional conventions
**Construction**
       --[country or state]--[city]
  PN   For the process of building and types of
       construction.  Search under
       CONSTRUCTION INDUSTRY for the
       construction business.  Search also under the
       subdivision --ENGINEERING &
       CONSTRUCTION used with names of wars
       (Appendix C).
  CN   Used in a note under ARCHITECTURE
       and CONSTRUCTION INDUSTRY.
  HN   Usage altered 2/90. In earlier cataloging,
       CONSTRUCTION was used only for
       small-scale building operations.
  UF   Building
  NT   Bombproof construction
       Bridge construction
       Building construction
       Canal construction
       Carpentry
       Dam construction
       Fire-resistive construction
       Reinforced concrete construction
       Road construction
  RT   Boring
       Conservation & restoration
       Construction industry
       Demolition
       Drilling
       Excavation
       Maintenance & repair
       Masonry
       Railroad construction workers
       Railroad construction & maintenance
       Remodeling
       Steeplejacks
       Structural systems
**Construction camps**
       --[country or state]--[city]
  PN   Mobile camps for construction workers.
  BT   Labor housing
  RT   Construction industry

---

BT  Broader term                    RT  Related term                    PN  Public Note
NT  Narrower term                   UF  Used for                        +  Term has NTs
HN  History Note                    CN  Catalogers Note                 --[ ] May subdivide

**Construction industry**
--[country or state]--[city]
PN   For the construction business, including finance, planning, management, and skills. Search under CONSTRUCTION or its NTs for the process of building and types of construction.
CN   Used in a note under ARCHITECTURE and CONSTRUCTION. Double index under INDUSTRIAL FACILITIES (or NTs) for images that focus on facilities.
HN   Usage altered 2/90. In earlier cataloging, CONSTRUCTION INDUSTRY was used for large-scale building operations.
BT   Industry
RT   Architectural models
     Boat & ship industry
     Building materials industry
     Construction
     Construction camps
     Engineering
     Model houses
     Plumbing industry
     Real estate development
     Steeplejacks
     Surveying

**Construction progress photographs**
USE Progress photographs

**Consuls**
--[nationality]--[country or state]--[city]
CN   Subdivide by nationality of country consul represents.
BT   Diplomats
RT   Commerce

**Consumer cooperatives**
USE Cooperatives

**Consumer protection**
--[country or state]--[city]
BT   Law & legal affairs
RT   Consumers
     Food adulteration & inspection
     Government regulation

**Consumer rationing**
--[country or state]--[city]
UF   Rationing, Consumer
BT   Government regulation
RT   Black market
     Economic aspects of war
     Government spending policy
     Scarcity

**Consumers**
--[country or state]--[city]
BT   People associated with commercial activities
RT   Commerce
     Consumer protection
     Customer relations

**Consumption (Disease)**
USE Tuberculosis

**Contact sheets**
CN   TGM II term.

**Contagious diseases**

**Contagious diseases (cont.)**
USE Communicable diseases

**Containers**
NT   Barrels
     Basins
     Baskets
     Bottles
     Boxes
     Cans +
     Coffeepots
     Coffins +
     Coin banks
     Crates
     Drinking vessels +
     Fuel tanks
     Ice buckets
     Mailboxes
     Musical instrument cases
     Pails
     Pitchers
     Plant containers +
     Powder kegs
     Samovars
     Septic tanks
     Spittoons
     Teapots
     Tin cups
     Urns
     Vats
     Wash tubs
     Watering troughs
RT   Cages
     Cornucopias
     Vases

**Conté crayon drawings**
USE Crayon drawings

**Contentment**
BT   Mental states

**Contestants, Beauty**
USE Beauty contestants

**Contests**
--[country or state]--[city]
UF   Competitions
BT   Events
NT   Beauty contests
     Marathons +
     Spelling bees
     Tournaments +
RT   Awards
     Exhibitions
     Manners & customs
     Sports
     Victories
     World records

**Contraband trade**
USE Black market
    Prohibition
    Smuggling

**Contract drawings**
CN   TGM II term.
UF   Drawings, Contract

**Contract laborers**

BT Broader term              RT Related term           PN Public Note
NT Narrower term             UF Used for               + Term has NTs
HN History Note              CN Catalogers Note        --[ ] May subdivide

**Contract laborers (cont.)**
 --[nationality]--[country or state]--[city]
 UF Coolies
 BT Laborers
**Contracts**
 UF Agreements
 BT Law & legal affairs
 NT Defense contracts
   Insurance +
   Mortgages
 RT Deals
Contras
 USE Counterrevolutionaries
Control of arms
 USE Arms control
Control of guns
 USE Firearms control
Control of pests
 USE Pest control
Convalescent camps
 USE Medical aspects of war
Convalescent homes
 USE Nursing homes
   Rest homes
Convalescents
 USE Medical aspects of war
   Sick persons
Convenience stations
 USE Public comfort stations
**Convenience stores**
 --[country or state]--[city]
 PN Includes activities and structures.
 UF Fast food stores
 BT Stores & shops
Convention halls
 USE Social & civic facilities
Convention halls (Rooms)
 USE Conference rooms
Conventions
 USE Treaties
Conventions (Congresses)
 USE Meetings
**Convents**
 --[country or state]--[city]
 PN For local communities or houses of nuns.
 UF Cloisters
   Nunneries
 BT Religious communities
 RT Abbeys
   Monasteries
   Nuns
   Religious orders
**Conversation**
 PN For images of persons engaged in casual talk.
 CN Used in a note under DISCUSSION.
 UF Gossip
   Speaking
   Talking
 BT Communication
 RT Interviews
   Reminiscing

**Conversation (cont.)**
   Whispering
Converted structures
 USE Recycled structures
**Convertible automobiles**
 --[nationality]--[country or state]--[city]
 UF Convertibles (Automobiles)
 BT Automobiles
**Convertible furniture**
 BT Furniture
Convertibles (Automobiles)
 USE Convertible automobiles
**Convertiplanes**
 --[nationality]--[country or state]--[city]
 BT Airplanes
 RT Automobiles
Conveying machinery
 USE Conveying systems
**Conveying systems**
 --[country or state]--[city]
 HN Changed 1/1993 from CONVEYING MACHINERY.
 UF Conveying machinery
 BT Building systems
 NT Dumbwaiters
   Elevators
   Pneumatic tubes
Convict laborers
 USE Prison laborers
Convicts
 USE Prisoners
Cook cars
 USE Chuckwagons
**Cookery**
 --[country or state]--[city]
 UF Candy making
   Cooking
   Food preparation
 NT Baking
   Children cooking
   Home food processing +
   Military cookery
   Outdoor cookery
 RT Barbecue grilles
   Buffets (Cookery)
   Cooking utensils
   Cooks
   Dietary laws
   Eating & drinking
   Food
   Home economics
   Housework
   Kitchens
   Stoves
   Street kitchens
   Toasters
Cooking
 USE Cookery
**Cooking utensils**
 UF Kitchen utensils
 BT Equipment
 NT Kettles

---

BT Broader term   RT Related term   PN Public Note
NT Narrower term   UF Used for    + Term has NTs
HN History Note   CN Catalogers Note  --[ ] May subdivide

**Cooking utensils (cont.)**
- RT Cookery
  - Silverware
  - Tableware

**Cooks**
- UF Chefs
- BT People
- RT Cookery
  - Restaurant workers

Coolies
- USE Contract laborers

Coons
- USE Raccoons

**Cooperation**
- --[country or state]--[city]
- PN For the association of persons or living things for their common good.
- RT Assistance
  - Competition (Psychology)
  - Cooperatives
  - International organization
  - International organizations
  - Interpersonal relations
  - Solidarity

**Cooperatives**
- --[country or state]--[city]
- PN Enterprises or organizations owned by and operated for the benefit of those using their services. Includes activities and structures.
- UF Consumer cooperatives
  - Marketing cooperatives
- BT Commercial organizations
- RT Business enterprises
  - Collective settlements
  - Cooperation

**Coots**
- --[country or state]
- BT Birds

Copies
- USE Reproductions

**Coping**
- PN Protective caps, tops, or covers of a wall, parapet, or other structure, often of stone, terra cotta, or metal.
- BT Architectural elements
- RT Parapets
  - Walls

**Copper industry**
- --[country or state]--[city]
- PN Includes activities and structures.
- CN Double index under INDUSTRIAL FACILITIES (or NTs) for images that focus on facilities.
- BT Metallurgical industry
- RT Brass industry
  - Bronze industry
  - Copper ingots
  - Copper mining

**Copper ingots**
- --[country or state]--[city]
- UF Ingots, Copper
- RT Copper industry

**Copper miners**
- --[country or state]--[city]
- PN For persons not actually engaged in mining work. Search under COPPER MINING for activities.
- BT Miners
- RT Copper mining

**Copper mining**
- --[country or state]--[city]
- PN Includes activities and sites.
- BT Mining
- RT Copper industry
  - Copper miners

**Copy art**
- CN TGM II term.
- UF Xerographic art

**Copying machines**
- BT Office equipment & supplies

Copying rooms
- USE Scriptoria

**Copyright**
- UF Authors' rights
- BT Law & legal affairs

Corbel gables
- USE Crow-stepped gables

Corbiestepped gables
- USE Crow-stepped gables

Cordons
- USE Stringcourses

**Corduroy roads**
- --[country or state]
- PN Roads built of logs laid side by side transversely.
- BT Roads

**Corinthian order**
- --[country or state]--[city]
- BT Architectural orders
- RT Acanthi

**Cork**
- --[country or state]--[city]
- RT Trees

**Cormorants**
- --[country or state]
- BT Birds

**Corn**
- --[country or state]--[city]
- BT Grains
- NT Popcorn
- RT Corn cribs
  - Corn husking

**Corn cribs**
- --[country or state]--[city]
- UF Corncribs
  - Cribs, Corn
- BT Food storage buildings
- RT Corn

**Corn husking**
- --[country or state]--[city]
- UF Corn shucking
  - Husking bees
- RT Corn
  - Farm life

---

BT Broader term            RT Related term            PN Public Note
NT Narrower term           UF Used for                + Term has NTs
HN History Note            CN Catalogers Note          --[ ] May subdivide

Corn shucking
  USE Corn husking
Corncribs
  USE Corn cribs
**Corner cards**
  CN   TGM II term.
Corner stones
  USE Cornerstones
**Cornerstone laying**
        --[country or state]--[city]
  UF   Foundation stones, Laying of
  BT   Building dedications
  RT   Building construction
        Cornerstones
**Cornerstones**
        --[country or state]--[city]
  PN   Stones forming part of corners or angles in
        walls, especially lying at the foundation of a
        principal angle.
  UF   Corner stones
        Pillar stones
  BT   Architectural elements
  RT   Cornerstone laying
**Cornets**
  PN   Includes the activity of playing cornets.
  BT   Brass instruments
  RT   Trombones
        Trumpets
        Tubas
**Cornices**
        --[country or state]--[city]
  PN   Molded projections that can either serve as
        uppermost division of an entablature, run
        around the walls of a room just below the
        ceiling, or serve as exterior trim at the
        meeting of wall and roof.
  BT   Architectural elements
  RT   Entablatures
        Moldings
**Cornucopias**
  UF   Horns of plenty
  BT   Symbols
  RT   Containers
        Prosperity
**Coronations**
        --[country]
  PN   Search also under the subdivision
        --CORONATION used with names of
        persons (Appendix B).
  CN   Prefer the subdivision.
  BT   Rites & ceremonies
  RT   Crowns
        Rulers
Corporal punishment devices
  USE Punishment devices
Corpses
  USE Dead persons
Corpulence
  USE Obesity
**Corrals**
        --[country or state]--[city]
  RT   Cattle

Corrals (cont.)
        Fences
        Horses
Correctional facilities
  USE Prisons
        Reformatories
**Correspondence**
  UF   Letters
        Mail
  BT   Communication
  NT   Hate mail
        Letters to Santa Claus
        Love letters
  RT   Postal service
        Telegrams
**Correspondence schools**
        --[country or state]--[city]
  PN   Includes activities and structures.
  CN   Double index under EDUCATIONAL
        FACILITIES (or NTs) for images that focus
        on facilities.
  BT   Education
Correspondents
  USE Reporters
Corridors
  USE Passageways
**Corruption**
        --[country or state]--[city]
  UF   Graft
        Political corruption
        Political scandals
        Scandals, Political
  RT   Bribery
        Crimes
        Ethics
        Gerrymandering
        Muckraking
        Vice
        War profiteering
Corsairs
  USE Pirates
**Corsets**
  BT   Lingerie
**Cosmetics industry**
        --[country or state]--[city]
  PN   Includes activities and structures.
  CN   Double index under INDUSTRIAL
        FACILITIES (or NTs) for images that focus
        on facilities.
  BT   Industry
  RT   Cosmetics & soap
**Cosmetics stores**
  BT   Stores & shops
  RT   Cosmetics & soap
**Cosmetics & soap**
  UF   Makeup (Cosmetics)
        Soap
        Toilet articles
        Toiletries
  NT   Perfumes
  RT   Cosmetics industry
        Cosmetics stores

---

BT Broader term              RT Related term              PN Public Note
NT Narrower term             UF Used for                  + Term has NTs
HN History Note              CN Catalogers Note           --[ ] May subdivide

**Cosmetics & soap (cont.)**
>   Dressing & grooming equipment
>   Grooming
>   Hair preparations

**Cosmology**
>   RT   Astronomy
>        Creation
>        Extraterrestrial life

Cosmonauts
>   USE Astronauts

Cost of living
>   USE Cost & standard of living

Cost of war
>   USE Economic aspects of war

**Cost & standard of living**
>   UF   Cost of living
>        Living standard
>        Standard of living
>   BT   Economic & social conditions
>   RT   Discounts
>        Inflation
>        Poverty
>        Prices
>        Social classes
>        Wages
>        Wealth

Costume
>   USE Clothing & dress

Costume balls
>   USE Masquerades

**Costume design drawings**
>   CN   TGM II term.

**Costume prints**
>   CN   TGM II term.

**Costumes**
>   --[nationality]
>   PN   For clothing used to disguise or to take on
>        another identity, including clothing of
>        another time or place. Search also under
>        THEATRICAL PRODUCTIONS, as well as
>        ACTORS and ACTRESSES for people in
>        costume.  Search also under the subdivision
>        CLOTHING & DRESS used with names of
>        ethnic, racial, and regional groups, and with
>        classes of persons (Appendix B).
>   CN   Subdivide by nationality for national
>        costumes.
>   UF   National costumes
>        Theater costumes
>   BT   Clothing & dress
>   RT   Masks
>        Masquerades
>        Mumming
>        Wigs

Cotillions
>   USE Balls (Parties)

Cottages
>   USE Dwellings

Cottages, Resort
>   USE Cabins

**Cotton**
>   PN   For images that focus on the usually white

**Cotton (cont.)**
>   downy substance produced by various plants.
>   BT   Fibers
>   RT   Cotton gins
>        Cotton industry
>        Cotton plantations
>        Plants

**Cotton gins**
>   BT   Machinery
>   RT   Cotton
>        Cotton industry

**Cotton industry**
>   --[country or state]--[city]
>   PN   Includes activities of processing raw
>        cotton and weaving cotton into cloth, and
>        associated structures.
>   CN   Double index under INDUSTRIAL
>        FACILITIES (or NTs)  for images that focus
>        on facilities.
>   UF   Cotton mills
>   BT   Textile industry
>   RT   Cotton
>        Cotton gins
>        Cotton plantations

Cotton mills
>   USE Cotton industry

**Cotton pickers**
>   --[country or state]--[city]
>   BT   Agricultural laborers
>   RT   Cotton plantations

**Cotton plantations**
>   --[country or state]--[city]
>   PN   Includes activities and structures.
>   CN   As appropriate, double index under
>        HARVESTING.
>   BT   Plantations
>   RT   Cotton
>        Cotton industry
>        Cotton pickers

**Couches**
>   PN   Long seating furniture with a back support
>        and one end, generally used for reclining, not
>        sitting.
>   BT   Seating furniture
>   RT   Sofas

Cougars
>   USE Pumas

**Coughing**
>   RT   Health
>        Sneezing

Council members, City
>   USE City council members

Countenances
>   USE Faces

**Counterbalances**
>   BT   Hardware
>   RT   Weights & measures

**Counterfeiting**
>   --[country or state]--[city]
>   BT   Crimes
>   RT   Fraud
>        Money

---

BT Broader term                    RT Related term                    PN Public Note
NT Narrower term                   UF Used for                        + Term has NTs
HN History Note                    CN Catalogers Note                 --[ ] May subdivide

Counterfeits
USE Forgeries
**Counterproofs**
CN   TGM II term.
**Counterrevolutionaries**
--[country or state]--[city]
CN   Used in a note under
COUNTERREVOLUTIONS.
HN   Prior to 5/1992 the term
COUNTERREVOLUTIONISTS was used.
UF   Contras
Counterrevolutionists
BT   Activists
RT   Counterrevolutions
Counterrevolutionists
USE Counterrevolutionaries
**Counterrevolutions**
--[country or state]--[city]
PN   For the subject of counterrevolutions in
general. Search under
COUNTERREVOLUTIONISTS for images
that focus on real persons.
BT   Events
RT   Counterrevolutionaries
Revolutions
Counting devices
USE Coin counting machines
Counting of votes
USE Vote counting
**Country clubs**
--[country or state]--[city]
PN   Includes activities and structures.
CN   Double index under ORGANIZATIONS'
FACILITIES (or NTs) for images that focus
on facilities.
BT   Clubs
Country elevators
USE Grain elevators
**Country life**
--[country or state]--[city]
UF   Rural life
BT   Manners & customs
NT   Farm life
Frontier & pioneer life
RT   Bees (Cooperative gatherings)
Economic & social conditions
Home food processing
Square dancing
Country stores
USE General stores
County fairs
USE Fairs
**County government**
--[country or state]--[city]
BT   Politics & government
**Couples**
--[country or state]--[city]
PN   For couples not known to be husband and
wife.
BT   People
RT   Courtship
Love

**Couples (cont.)**
Romances
Spouses
**Coupon stores**
--[country or state]--[city]
PN   Includes activities and structures.
UF   Premium stores
BT   Stores & shops
RT   Premiums
**Courage**
UF   Bravery
BT   Mental states
RT   Cowardice
Heroes
**Courses (Wall components)**
--[country or state]--[city]
PN   Layers of masonry units running
horizontally in a wall or over an arch.
BT   Architectural elements
NT   Stringcourses
RT   Walls
Courses, Belt
USE Stringcourses
Court houses
USE Courthouses
Court martial
USE Courts martial & courts of inquiry
Courtesies
USE Etiquette
**Courthouses**
--[country or state]--[city]
PN   For images that focus on facilities. Search
under JUDICIAL PROCEEDINGS for
activities.
UF   Court houses
BT   Government facilities
RT   Courtrooms
Judicial proceedings
Courting
USE Courtship
Courtroom art
USE Courtroom sketches
Courtroom illustrations
USE Courtroom sketches
**Courtroom sketches**
CN   TGM II term.
UF   Courtroom art
Courtroom illustrations
Trial sketches
**Courtrooms**
--[country or state]--[city]
BT   Interiors
RT   Courthouses
Judicial proceedings
Courts
USE Judicial proceedings
**Courts martial & courts of inquiry**
--[country or state]--[city]
UF   Court martial
Courts of inquiry
Inquiry, Military courts of
Investigations, Military

BT  Broader term          RT  Related term          PN  Public Note
NT  Narrower term         UF  Used for               +  Term has NTs
HN  History Note          CN  Catalogers Note       --[ ] May subdivide

**Courts martial & courts of inquiry (cont.)**
- BT  Investigation
-      Judicial proceedings
- RT  Military art & science

**Courts of inquiry**
- USE Courts martial & courts of inquiry

**Courtship**
- HN  Changed 11/1992 from COURTSHIP & LOVE.
- UF  Courting
-      Flirtation
-      Wooing
- BT  Interpersonal relations
-      Manners & customs
- NT  Marriage proposals
- RT  Couples
-      Cupids
-      Free love
-      Kissing
-      Love
-      Love letters
-      Lovers' lanes
-      Marriage
-      Relations between the sexes
-      Romances

**Courts, Tennis**
- USE Tennis courts

**Courtyards**
- --[country or state]--[city]
- BT  Rooms & spaces
- RT  Atriums
-      Patios
-      Quadrangles (Courtyards)
-      Walls

**Cove lighting**
- --[country or state]--[city]
- PN  Lighting from sources which are out of sight.
- BT  Lighting

**Covered bridges**
- --[country or state]--[city]
- BT  Bridges

**Covered wagons**
- --[country or state]--[city]
- UF  Conestoga wagons
- BT  Carts & wagons
- RT  Wagon trains

**Covered walks**
- --[country or state]--[city]
- UF  Porticoes (Covered walks)
- BT  Walkways

**Covers (Illustration)**
- CN  TGM II term.
- UF  Illustrated covers

**Covers, Album**
- USE Album covers

**Covers, Illustrated**
- USE Pictorial envelopes

**Covers, Magazine**
- USE Magazine covers

**Covers, Patriotic**
- USE Patriotic envelopes

**Covers, Record**
- USE Album covers

**Covert operations**
- --[nationality]--[country or state]--[city]
- PN  For activities, subversive or otherwise, performed surreptitiously, usually for political or military purposes. Search also under the subdivision --COVERT OPERATIONS used with names of wars (Appendix C).
- CN  Subdivide by nationality of those initiating the operation.
- UF  Operations, Covert
- RT  Military intelligence
-      Secret service
-      Spying

**Coves**
- USE Bays

**Covetousness**
- USE Avarice

**Cow milking**
- USE Milking

**Cowardice**
- BT  Mental states
- RT  Courage
-      Fear

**Cowboys**
- --[country or state]--[city]
- CN  Subdivide geographically for the place cowboys are depicted.
- UF  Stockmen (Animal industry)
- BT  Men
- NT  Gauchos
- RT  Broncos
-      Cattle branding
-      Cattle herding
-      Cowgirls
-      Ranches
-      Rodeos
-      Westerns
-      Wild west shows

**Cowgirls**
- --[country or state]--[city]
- CN  Subdivide geographically for place where cowgirls are depicted.
- BT  Women
- RT  Cowboys
-      Ranches
-      Rodeos
-      Westerns
-      Wild west shows

**Cows**
- --[country or state]
- BT  Cattle
- RT  Bulls

**Coyns**
- USE Quoins

**Coyote hunting**
- --[country or state]
- BT  Hunting
- RT  Coyotes

**Coyotes**

---

Coyotes (cont.)
    --[country or state]
  BT  Wolves
  RT  Coyote hunting
Crabs
    --[country or state]
  BT  Shellfish
Crackers
  BT  Baked products
Cradleboards
    --[country or state]--[city]
  BT  Equipment
  RT  Infants
Cradles
  USE Children's furniture
Crafts (Handicraft)
  USE Handicraft
Cranberries
    --[country or state]--[city]
  BT  Berries
Cranes
  USE Hoisting machinery
Cranes (Birds)
    --[country or state]
  UF  Whooping cranes
  BT  Birds
Crap
  USE Feces
Craps
  USE Gambling
Crate labels, Fruit
  USE Fruit crate labels
Craters
    --[country or state]
  BT  Land
Crates
    --[country or state]--[city]
  BT  Containers
  RT  Shipping
Cravats
  USE Neckties
Crawling & creeping
  UF  Creeping
  BT  Locomotion
Crayon drawings
  CN  TGM II term.
  UF  Conté crayon drawings
Crayon enlargements
  CN  TGM II term.
  UF  Crayon photographic prints
       Crayon prints
Crayon manner prints
  CN  TGM II term.
Crayon photographic prints
  USE Crayon enlargements
Crayon prints
  USE Crayon enlargements
Crazes
  USE Fads
Creation
  UF  Beginnings
       Origins

Creation (cont.)
  RT  Civilization
       Cosmology
       Evolution
       Human life cycle
       Inventions
Crèches (Nativity scenes)
    --[country or state]--[city]
  UF  Christmas crèches
       Manger scenes (Crèches)
       Nativity scenes (Crèches)
  BT  Festive decorations
  RT  Biblical events
Credenzas
  USE Buffets (Furniture)
Credit
  PN  Amount or limit to which a person or body
      may receive goods or money on trust of
      future repayment.
  BT  Business & finance
  RT  Banking
       Credit cards
       Debt
       Usury
Credit cards
  UF  Cards, Charge
       Cards, Credit
       Charge cards
  RT  Credit
Creeks
  USE Streams
Creeping
  USE Crawling & creeping
Cremation
    --[country or state]--[city]
  PN  Search under CREMATORIUMS for
      images that focus on facilities.
  CN  Used in a note under CREMATORIUMS.
  UF  Burning the dead
  RT  Crematoriums
       Death
       Funeral rites & ceremonies
       Undertaking
Crematoriums
    --[country or state]--[city]
  PN  For images that focus on buildings. Search
      under CREMATION for activities.
  BT  Funerary facilities
  RT  Cremation
       Morgues & mortuaries
       Undertaking
Crew quarters
  CN  Double index under type of vessel.
  UF  Cabins, Ship
  BT  Interiors
  RT  Officers' quarters
       Vessels
Crew rowing
  USE Team rowing
Crewing
  USE Team rowing
Crews

---

BT  Broader term
NT  Narrower term
HN  History Note

RT  Related term
UF  Used for
CN  Catalogers Note

PN  Public Note
+  Term has NTs
--[ ]  May subdivide

Crews (cont.)
USE Sailors
Criblée prints
USE Dotted prints
Cribs
USE Children's furniture
Cribs, Corn
USE Corn cribs
**Cricket**
--[country or state]--[city]
BT Sports
Criers
USE Peddlers
**Cries**
CN TGM II term.
UF Street cries
Crime photographs
USE Forensic photographs
Crime syndicates
USE Organized crime
**Crimes**
--[country or state]--[city]
NT Bigamy
Cattle raids
Counterfeiting
Embezzlement
Extortion
Homicides +
Illegal arms transfers
Kidnappings
Poaching
Rapes
Robberies +
Sabotage
Sedition
Smuggling
Terrorism
Treason
Vandalism
RT Abused children
Abused women
Atrocities
Corruption
Criminal investigations
Criminals
Gambling
Impeachments
Law enforcement
Libel & slander
Organized crime
Prostitution
Rebellions
Security systems
Self-defense
Sexual harassment
Threats
Vice
Violence
**Crimes of passion**
--[country or state]--[city]
UF Crimes passionel
BT Homicides

Crimes passionel
USE Crimes of passion
**Criminal investigations**
--[country or state]--[city]
BT Investigation
RT Crimes
Informers
**Criminals**
--[country or state]--[city]
UF Bandits
Delinquents
Desperadoes
Gangsters
Highwaymen
Offenders
Outlaws
Robbers
BT People
NT Pirates
RT Bertillon system
Crimes
Gangs
Juvenile delinquents
Military deserters
Organized crime
Prisoners
Punishment devices
Punishment & torture
Crippled persons
USE Handicapped persons
**Critics**
UF Art critics
Literary critics
BT People
RT Pundits
**Crocheting**
BT Sewing
RT Yarn
Crockery
USE Pottery
**Crocodiles**
--[country or state]
BT Reptiles
**Crop dusting**
--[country or state]--[city]
UF Aerial dusting in agriculture
Aerial spraying in agriculture
BT Pest control
RT Airplanes
Farming
Crop picking
USE Harvesting
**Crop rotation**
--[country or state]--[city]
UF Break crops
Rotation of crops
BT Farming
**Croplands**
--[country or state]--[city]
PN Land that is suited to or used for crops.
CN Double index under crop as appropriate.
UF Fields (Agriculture)

---

BT Broader term
NT Narrower term
HN History Note

RT Related term
UF Used for
CN Catalogers Note

PN Public Note
+ Term has NTs
--[ ] May subdivide

**Croplands (cont.)**
  BT  Land
  RT  Farms
      Land use
      Meadows
Crops
  USE Farming
      Plants
**Croquet**
      --[country or state]--[city]
  BT  Games
**Cross dressing**
      --[country or state]--[city]
  PN  For persons dressing as if they were
      members of the opposite sex, regardless of
      purpose.
  UF  Men in women's clothing
      Transvestism
      Women in men's clothing
  BT  Impersonation
  RT  Clothing & dress
      Female impersonators
      Relations between the sexes
**Crossbows**
  BT  Arms & armament
      Bows (Archery)
  RT  Archery
**Crosscut saws**
  BT  Saws
  RT  Lumber industry
      Woodcutting
**Crossed fingers**
  BT  Fingers
**Crosses**
      --[country or state]--[city]
  RT  Crucifixions
      Stations of the Cross
      Swastika
Crossings, Low water
  USE Fords (Stream crossings)
Crossings, Railroad
  USE Railroad crossings
**Crossroads**
      --[country or state]--[city]
  PN  Place where two or more roads intersect.
  BT  Roads
**Crossword puzzles**
  BT  Puzzles
Cross-country journeys
  USE Transcontinental journeys
**Crowbars**
  BT  Equipment
**Crowds**
      --[country or state]--[city]
  UF  Mobs
  BT  People
  RT  Audiences
      Events
      Queues
      Rites & ceremonies
      Spectators
**Crowfooted gables**

Crowfooted gables (cont.)
  USE Crow-stepped gables
**Crown of thorns**
  BT  Symbols
  RT  Crowns
      Wreaths
**Crowns**
  BT  Clothing & dress
  RT  Coronations
      Crown of thorns
      Jewelry
      Rulers
**Crows**
      --[country or state]
  BT  Birds
**Crow-stepped gables**
      --[country or state]--[city]
  UF  Catstep gables
      Corbel gables
      Corbiestepped gables
      Crowfooted gables
      Step gables
  BT  Gables
**Crucifixions**
      --[country or state]--[city]
  BT  Executions
  RT  Crosses
      Stations of the Cross
Cruciform (Latin) buildings
  USE Latin cross buildings
**Cruisers (Warships)**
      --[nationality]--[country or state]--[city]
  BT  Warships
Cruises
  USE Ocean travel
**Crying**
  UF  Weeping
  NT  Children crying
  RT  Mental states
      Temper tantrums
Crystal ball gazing
  USE Fortune telling
**Crystal balls**
  RT  Fortune telling
      Magic
**Crystal glass**
  BT  Glassware
**Crystals**
      --[country or state]--[city]
  BT  Minerals
  RT  Quartz
**Crystoleum photographs**
  CN  TGM II term.
  UF  Chromo-photographs
**Cuckoo clocks**
  BT  Clocks & watches
**Cucumbers**
      --[country or state]--[city]
  BT  Vegetables
Cultivation of soils
  USE Farming
**Cults**

---

BT Broader term              RT Related term              PN Public Note
NT Narrower term             UF Used for                  + Term has NTs
HN History Note              CN Catalogers Note           --[ ] May subdivide

**Cults (cont.)**
   --[country or state]--[city]
  BT  Organizations
  RT  Collective settlements
      Religious groups
**Cultural buildings**
  USE Cultural facilities
**Cultural facilities**
   --[country or state]--[city]
  HN  Changed 1/1993 from CULTURAL
      BUILDINGS.
  UF  Cultural buildings
  BT  Facilities
  NT  Athenaeums
      Auditoriums
      Bandstands
      Concert halls +
      Libraries +
      Theaters +
      Visitors' centers
  RT  Galleries & museums
**Cultural relations**
  UF  Intercultural relations
  RT  International relations
      Interpersonal relations
**Culverts**
   --[country or state]--[city]
  PN  For arched drains or sewers.
  UF  Conduits, Water
  BT  Hydraulic facilities
  RT  Bridges
**Cuneiform**
  BT  Writing systems
**Cunes**
  USE Quoins
**Cupboards**
   --[country or state]--[city]
  UF  Cabinets
      Dressers, Kitchen
      Dressers, Pantry
      Kitchen cabinets
      Kitchen dressers
      Pantry dressers
  BT  Furniture
  RT  Closets
**Cupids**
  BT  Symbols
  RT  Children
      Courtship
      Love
**Cupolas**
   --[country or state]--[city]
  PN  Rounded vaults raised on a circular or
      other base and forming a roof or ceiling.
  BT  Architectural elements
  RT  Domes
      Drums (Domes)
      Roofs
**Cups**
  USE Drinking vessels
**Curb markets**
  USE Stock exchanges

**Cures**
  USE Healing
**Curing (Healing)**
  USE Healing
**Curing (Preservation)**
   --[country or state]--[city]
  RT  Fish drying
      Food drying
      Hides & skins
      Home food processing
      Smokehouses
**Curiosities & wonders**
   --[country or state]--[city]
  UF  Biggest
      Extremes
      Largest
      Oddities
      Smallest
      Trivia
      Wonders
  RT  Firsts
      Human curiosities
      World records
**Curling**
   --[country or state]--[city]
  BT  Sports
**Currency**
  USE Money
**Currency question**
  UF  Fiat money
      Free coinage
      Monetary question
  NT  Silver question
  RT  Economic policy
      Money
**Cursing**
  PN  For calling upon supernatural powers to
      send injury upon someone.  Use SWEARING
      for use of profane language.
  UF  Execration
      Imprecation
      Malediction
  RT  Prayer
      Supernatural practices
      Superstitions
**Curtain walls**
   --[country or state]--[city]
  UF  Enclosure walls
      Window walls
  BT  Walls
  RT  Windows
**Curtains**
  USE Drapery
**Curtsying**
  BT  Etiquette
**Cuspidors**
  USE Spittoons
**Custody of children**
   --[country or state]--[city]
  UF  Child custody
  BT  Law & legal affairs
  RT  Children & adults

BT Broader term       RT Related term       PN Public Note
NT Narrower term     UF Used for         + Term has NTs
HN History Note       CN Catalogers Note    --[ ] May subdivide

**Custody of children (cont.)**
      Divorce
      Families
**Custom houses**
  USE Customs houses
**Customer relations**
  RT   Business enterprises
      Consumers
**Customs**
  USE Manners & customs
**Customs duties**
  USE Tariffs
**Customs houses**
      --[country or state]--[city]
  UF  Custom houses
  BT  Government facilities
  RT  Commerce
      Customs inspections
**Customs inspections**
      --[country or state]--[city]
  UF  Inspections, Customs
  RT  Customs houses
      Investigation
      Searching
      Tariffs
**Cut paper works**
  USE Paper cutouts
**Cutlery industry**
      --[country or state]--[city]
  PN  Includes activities and structures.
  CN  Double index under INDUSTRIAL
      FACILITIES (or NTs) for images that focus
      on facilities.
  BT  Equipment industry
  RT  Knives
      Silverware
      Tableware
**Cutover lands**
      --[country or state]
  PN  Land on which most of the salable timber
      has been cut.
  UF  Logged-off lands
  BT  Land
  RT  Clearing of land
      Forestry
      Lumber industry
**Cyanotypes**
  CN  TGM II term.
**Cycling**
      --[country or state]--[city]
  UF  Bicycling
  BT  Locomotion
  NT  Bicycle racing
      Children riding bicycles & tricycles
  RT  Bicycles & tricycles
      Sports
      Unicycles
**Cyclones**
      --[country or state]--[city]
  PN  Includes the event and any resulting
      damage.
  CN  Used in a note under STORMS.

**Cyclones (cont.)**
  BT  Storms
  RT  Hurricanes
      Tornadoes
**Cyclopedias**
  USE Encyclopedias & dictionaries
**Cynicism**
  BT  Pessimism
**Cypresses**
  BT  Trees
**Dadoes (Walls)**
  USE Wainscoting
**Daffodils**
      --[country or state]--[city]
  UF  Jonquils
      Narcissus
  BT  Flowers
**Daggers & swords**
  UF  Swords
  BT  Arms & armament
**Daguerreotypes**
  CN  TGM II term.
  UF  Cased photographs
**Dairy farming**
      --[country or state]--[city]
  PN  For the care, breeding, feeding, and
      milking of dairy cattle. Search under
      MILKING for the milking of cows away from
      the context of dairy farms. Search under
      DAIRYING for the production, processing,
      and manufacture of milk and its products.
  CN  Used in a note under MILKING.
  BT  Farming
  RT  Cattle
      Dairying
      Milking
**Dairy products**
  BT  Food
  NT  Butter
      Cheese
      Ice cream & ices
      Milk
  RT  Dairy products industry
      Dairying
**Dairy products industry**
      --[country or state]--[city]
  PN  Includes activities and structures.
  CN  Double index under INDUSTRIAL
      FACILITIES (or NTs) for images that focus
      on facilities.
  BT  Food industry
  RT  Beverage industry
      Dairy products
      Dairying
**Dairy stores**
      --[country or state]--[city]
  BT  Stores & shops
**Dairying**
      --[country or state]--[city]
  PN  For the production, processing, and
      manufacture of milk and its products.
      Includes activities and structures.

---

BT Broader term          RT Related term          PN Public Note
NT Narrower term        UF Used for             + Term has NTs
HN History Note          CN Catalogers Note     --[ ] May subdivide

**Dairying (cont.)**
  CN  Double index under AGRICULTURAL
       FACILITIES (or NTs) for images that focus
       on facilities. Used in a note under BUTTER
       MAKING and DAIRY FARMING.
  UF  Milk industry
  BT  Food industry
  RT  Beverage industry
       Butter making
       Cattle
       Dairy farming
       Dairy products
       Dairy products industry
       Goats

**Dais**
  USE Podiums

**Daisies**
       --[country or state]--[city]
  BT  Flowers

Dall sheep
  USE Mountain sheep

**Dam construction**
       --[country or state]--[city]
  BT  Civil engineering
       Construction
  RT  Dams

Damage to property
  USE Accidents
       Disasters
       Sabotage
       Vandalism
       War damage
       War destruction & pillage

**Dams**
       --[country or state]--[city]
  BT  Hydraulic facilities
  RT  Beaver dams
       Dam construction
       Erosion protection works
       Hydroelectric power
       Power plants
       Reservoirs
       Spillways

Dance
  CN  Used only as a subdivision with names of
       ethnic, racial, and regional groups, and with
       classes of persons (Appendix A).

**Dance cards**
  CN  TGM II term.

**Dance halls**
       --[country or state]--[city]
  PN  For images that focus on facilities. Search
       under DANCING for activities.
  BT  Sports & recreation facilities
  RT  Dancing
       Discotheques

**Dance marathons**
       --[country or state]--[city]
  BT  Dancing
       Marathons

**Dance parties**
       --[country or state]--[city]

**Dance parties (cont.)**
  PN  For less formal dances; search under
       BALLS (PARTIES) for formal dances.
  CN  Used in a note under BALLS (PARTIES).
  UF  Dances
  BT  Parties
  NT  Hoedowns (Parties)
  RT  Dancing

**Dance posters**
  CN  TGM II term.

**Dancers**
  PN  Search also under the subdivision
       --DANCE used with ethnic, racial, and
       regional groups and with classes of persons
       (Appendix A).
  BT  People
  NT  Ballerinas
       Ceremonial dancers
  RT  Choreography
       Dancing
       Entertainers

Dances
  USE Dance parties

**Dancing**
       --[country or state]--[city]
  PN  For the subject of dance in general and the
       activity of dancing. Search also under the
       subdivision --DANCE used with names of
       ethnic, racial and regional groups, and with
       classes of persons (Appendix A).
  CN  Used in a note under DANCE HALLS.
  BT  Locomotion
  NT  Ballet
       Ballroom dancing
       Charleston (Dance)
       Children dancing
       Dance marathons
       Folk dancing +
       Ghost dance
       Hula dancing
       Jitterbug dancing
       Minuets
       Modern dancing
       Rock & roll dancing
       Round dancing
       Snake dance
       Square dancing
       Tap dancing
  RT  Choreography
       Dance halls
       Dance parties
       Dancers
       Discotheques
       Entertainment
       May poles
       Music
       Recreation
       Rites & ceremonies

**Dandies**
       --[nationality]--[country or state]--[city]
  UF  Fops
  BT  Men

---

BT Broader term            RT Related term            PN Public Note
NT Narrower term          UF Used for               + Term has NTs
HN History Note           CN Catalogers Note        --[ ] May subdivide

**Dandies (cont.)**
RT Clothing & dress
**Danger**
UF Hazard
Peril
RT Accidents
Action & adventure dramas
Disasters
Fear
Horror dramas
Rescues
Safety
Threats
Warnings
**Daredevils**
UF Stuntmen
BT Entertainers
RT Circus performers
Stunt flying
Darkrooms, Portable
USE Portable darkrooms
Dart & egg moldings
USE Egg & dart moldings
**Darts**
BT Games
Darwinism
USE Evolution
**Dashboards**
UF Instrument panels
BT Equipment
RT Automobile equipment & supplies
Data processing equipment
USE Calculators
Computers
**Date orchards**
--[country or state]--[city]
CN As appropriate, double index under
HARVESTING.
BT Orchards
RT Dates
Palms
Date palms
USE Palms
**Dates**
--[country or state]--[city]
BT Fruit
RT Date orchards
Palms
Daughters
USE Families
Dawn
USE Sunrises & sunsets
**Day care**
RT Babysitting
Children
**Daydreaming**
RT Dreaming
Fantasy
**Daylight savings**
BT Time
Days of rest
USE Sabbaths

**Dead animals**
--[country or state]
UF Bodies
Cadavers
BT Animals
RT Death
Hunting
Hunting trophies
Skeletons
Taxidermy
**Dead persons**
--[country or state]--[city]
UF Bodies
Cadavers
Corpses
Deceased
BT People
NT Drowning victims
Mummies
RT Coffins
Death
Deathbeds
Executions
Funeral rites & ceremonies
Seances
Skeletons
Undertaking
War casualties
**Deadly sins**
PN The seven capital sins (pride,
covetousness, lust, anger, gluttony, and
sloth), considered fatal to spiritual progress.
UF Capital sins
Seven deadly sins
Sins, Deadly
RT Anger
Avarice
Envy
Gluttony
Laziness
Lust
Pride
Vice
**Deaf persons**
--[country or state]--[city]
BT Handicapped persons
RT Hearing aids
Sign language
Dealerships, Automobile
USE Automobile dealerships
Dealers, Art
USE Art dealers
**Dealers' marks**
CN TGM II term.
**Deals**
UF Business agreements
Business deals
RT Business enterprises
Contracts
Deaneries (Buildings)
USE Religious dwellings
**Death**

---

BT Broader term                RT Related term                PN Public Note
NT Narrower term               UF Used for                    + Term has NTs
HN History Note                CN Catalogers Note             --[ ] May subdivide

**Death (cont.)**
--[country or state]--[city]
PN   Search also under the subdivisions
--DEATH & BURIAL, --DEATH MASK
used with names of persons (Appendix B).
RT   Cremation
Dead animals
Dead persons
Dismemberment
Drowning
Funeral rites & ceremonies
Graves
Heaven
Homicides
Human life cycle
Inheritance & sucession
Inheritance & transfer taxes
Massacres
Tombs & sepulchral monuments
Wills

**Death certificates**
CN   TGM II term.

Death duties
USE Inheritance & transfer taxes

Death mask
CN   Used only as a subdivision with names of persons (Appendix B).

Death penalty
USE Executions

Death & burial
CN   Used only as a subdivision with names of persons (Appendix B).

**Deathbeds**
PN   Search also under the subdivision
--DEATH & BURIAL used with names of persons (Appendix B).
UF   Last words
RT   Dead persons
Last rites

**Death's head**
UF   Skull & crossbones
BT   Symbols
RT   Bones
Skulls

**Debates**
--[country or state]--[city]
PN   Includes the activity of engaging in formal debate.
UF   Arguments
Debating
BT   Communication
Events
RT   Discussion
Political participation
Public speaking

Debating
USE Debates

Debs
USE Debutantes

**Debt**
--[country or state]--[city]
UF   IOUs

**Debt (cont.)**
BT   Business & finance
NT   Public debt
RT   Credit
Pawnshops
Paying bills
Usury

**Debutantes**
--[country or state]--[city]
UF   Coming out
Debs
BT   Women
RT   Manners & customs

**Decals**
CN   TGM II term.

**Decapitations**
--[country or state]--[city]
UF   Beheadings
BT   Executions
RT   Guillotines

Decay
USE Deterioration

Decay of buildings
USE Building deterioration

Deceased
USE Dead persons

Deceit
USE Deception

**Deception**
--[nationality]--[country or state]--[city]
CN   Subdivide by nationality of deceivers when the deception is perpetrated by one nation on another.
UF   Deceit
Subterfuge
BT   Ethics
RT   False advertising
Fraud
Honesty
Impersonation

**Decks (Rooms & spaces)**
--[country or state]--[city]
UF   Sun decks
BT   Rooms & spaces
RT   Sunspaces

**Declarations of war**
--[nationality]
CN   Subdivide by nationality of country making declaration.
BT   Events
RT   War

Decline
USE Deterioration

**Decorations**
--[country or state]--[city]
CN   Also TGM II term.
UF   Ornaments
NT   Dried plant arrangements +
Festive decorations +
Wreaths
RT   Architectural decorations & ornaments
Christmas decoration stores

---

BT Broader term
NT Narrower term
HN History Note

RT Related term
UF Used for
CN Catalogers Note

PN Public Note
+ Term has NTs
--[ ] May subdivide

**Decorations (cont.)**
    Interior decoration
    Leis
    Table settings & decorations
    Yard ornaments
Decorations, Festive
  USE Festive decorations
Decorations, Military
  USE Military decorations
Decorations, Window
  USE Window displays
Decoration, Interior
  USE Interior decoration
Decorative plasterwork
  USE Plasterwork
**Decoys (Hunting)**
  UF  Duck decoys
  BT  Fishing & hunting gear
  RT  Game bird hunting
       Wood carvings
Decrepitude
  USE Deterioration
Dedication of buildings
  USE Building dedications
**Dedications**
    --[country or state]--[city]
  UF  Ribbon-cutting ceremonies
  BT  Rites & ceremonies
  NT  Building dedications +
       Ground breaking ceremonies
Deep-sea fishing
  USE Big game fishing
**Deer**
    --[country or state]
  BT  Animals
  NT  Antelopes +
       Elk
       Moose
       Musk deer
       Reindeer
  RT  Deer hunting
**Deer hunting**
    --[country or state]
  BT  Hunting
  NT  Moose hunting
  RT  Deer
Defamation
  USE Libel & slander
**Defense budgets**
    --[country or state]
  UF  Defense spending
  BT  Economic policy
  RT  Defense industry
       Economic aspects of war
       Military art & science
       Military policy
       National security
**Defense contracts**
    --[country or state]--[city]
  BT  Contracts
  RT  Defense industry
       Economic aspects of war

**Defense industry**
    --[country or state]--[city]
  PN  Includes activities and structures.
  CN  Double index under type of industry.
       Double index under INDUSTRIAL
       FACILITIES (or NTs) for images that focus
       on facilities.
  UF  War industry
       War production
  BT  Industry
  NT  Ordnance industry +
  RT  Defense budgets
       Defense contracts
       Defense industry strikes
       Economic aspects of war
       Military policy
       War
       War rallies
**Defense industry strikes**
    --[country or state]--[city]
  BT  Strikes
  RT  Defense industry
Defense policy
  USE Military policy
Defense spending
  USE Defense budgets
Defense (Law)
  USE Actions & defenses
Defenses
  USE Forts & fortifications
Defense, Civil
  USE Civil defense
Defense, National
  USE National security
**Deficit financing**
    --[country or state]--[city]
  CN  Subdivide geographically as appropriate to
       indicate national, state, or local level.
  UF  Compensatory spending
       Spending, Deficit
  BT  Economic policy
  RT  Public debt
Dehydration of food
  USE Food drying
Deities
  USE Goddesses
      Gods
Dejection
  USE Depression (Mental state)
      Sadness
**Delegations**
    --[country or state]--[city]
  PN  Groups of persons chosen to represent
       others.
  BT  People
  NT  Electoral college
  RT  Committees
       Meetings
       Political representation
**Delicatessens**
    --[country or state]--[city]
  PN  Includes activities and structures.

BT Broader term          RT Related term          PN Public Note
NT Narrower term        UF Used for             + Term has NTs
HN History Note          CN Catalogers Note     --[ ] May subdivide

**Delicatessens (cont.)**
  UF  Delis
  BT  Stores & shops
  RT  Grocery stores
       Restaurants
Delinquents
  USE Criminals
       Juvenile delinquents
Delis
  USE Delicatessens
**Delivery boys**
      --[country or state]--[city]
  BT  Children
  RT  Messengers
       Newspaper carriers
Delivery trucks
  USE Trucks
Delivery wagons
  USE Carts & wagons
**Deltas**
      --[country or state]--[city]
  UF  River deltas
  BT  Land
  RT  Rivers
Delusions
  USE Hallucinations & illusions
       Superstitions
Demobilizations
  USE Military demobilizations
**Democracy**
      --[country]
  PN  For the subject of democracy in general.
  UF  Self-government
  BT  Economic & political systems
  RT  Monarchy
       Political representation
       Referendums
**Demolition**
      --[country or state]--[city]
  UF  Wrecking
  RT  Construction
**Demons**
  UF  Devils
       Satan
  BT  Supernatural beings
  RT  Exorcism
       Hell
Demonstration houses
  USE Model houses
Demonstration schools
  USE Laboratory schools
**Demonstrations**
      --[country or state]--[city]
  PN  Public displays, usually by a crowd, either
       in sympathy with or antagonism toward a
       cause, event, product, etc. Search also under
       the subdivision --RIOTS &
       DEMONSTRATIONS used with corporate
       bodies and named events (Appendix D).
  UF  Marches, Political
       Protests
       Public demonstrations

**Demonstrations (cont.)**
       Public protest
       Sit-ins
       Smoke-ins
  BT  Events
  NT  Strikes +
  RT  Activists
       Civil rights leaders
       Meetings
       Pickets
       Protest movements
       Riots
       Student movements
Demonstrators
  USE Activists
Denominational schools
  USE Religious education
**Dens**
      --[country or state]--[city]
  PN  Comfortable, usually secluded rooms in
       dwellings for study, reading, or leisure.
  BT  Interiors
  RT  Libraries (Rooms)
       Living rooms
**Dental education**
      --[country or state]--[city]
  PN  Includes activities and structures.
  CN  Double index under EDUCATIONAL
       FACILITIES (or NTs) for images that focus
       on facilities.
  UF  Dental schools
  BT  Medical education
  RT  Dentistry
**Dental equipment & supplies**
  UF  Dental instruments
       Dental supplies
  BT  Medical equipment & supplies
  RT  Dentistry
**Dental hygiene**
      --[country or state]--[city]
  BT  Health care
       Hygiene
  RT  Dentistry
       Teeth
       Trench mouth
Dental instruments
  USE Dental equipment & supplies
**Dental offices**
      --[country or state]--[city]
  UF  Dentists' offices
  BT  Service industry facilities
  RT  Dentistry
       Health care facilities
       Medical offices
Dental schools
  USE Dental education
Dental supplies
  USE Dental equipment & supplies
**Dentistry**
      --[country or state]--[city]
  PN  For the subject of dentistry in general and
       the activities of dentists.

---

BT Broader term          RT Related term          PN Public Note
NT Narrower term        UF Used for             + Term has NTs
HN History Note          CN Catalogers Note     --[ ] May subdivide

**Dentistry (cont.)**
- BT   Medicine
- RT   Dental education
-      Dental equipment & supplies
-      Dental hygiene
-      Dental offices

Dentists' offices
- USE Dental offices

**Department stores**
-      --[country or state]--[city]
- PN   Includes activities and structures.
- BT   Stores & shops
- RT   Dry goods stores
-      General stores

Departures
- USE Arrivals & departures

Dependencies (Buildings)
- USE Outbuildings

**Deportations**
-      --[country]
- PN   Acts to remove, from a country, aliens not lawfully there or considered inimical to the public welfare.
- CN   Subdivide geographically by country from which persons are being deported.
- UF   Expulsions
-      Removals
- BT   Law & legal affairs
- RT   Aliens
-      Emigration & immigration
-      Exiles

Depositories
- USE Archives
-      Banks
-      Safes

Depots
- USE Railroad stations

Depots, Military
- USE Military depots

**Depression (Mental state)**
- UF   Dejection
-      Despondency
-      Gloom (Mental state)
-      Melancholy
-      Unhappiness
- BT   Mental states
- RT   Despair
-      Distress
-      Grief
-      Sadness

**Depressions**
-      --[country or state]--[city]
- BT   Economic & social conditions
- RT   Poverty
-      Prosperity
-      Unemployed

Derailments
- USE Railroad accidents

Derricks
- USE Hoisting machinery

Derrieres
- USE Buttocks

Dervishes
-      --[country or state]--[city]
- BT   People associated with religion
- NT   Fakirs

Desegregation
- USE Segregation

Deserted buildings
- USE Abandoned buildings

Deserted children
- USE Abandoned children

Deserted towns
- USE Ghost towns

Deserters, Military
- USE Military deserters

**Deserts**
-      --[country or state]
- BT   Land
- RT   Dunes
-      Oases

**Design drawings**
- CN   TGM II term.
- UF   Drawings, Design
-      Production drawings

Design models
- USE Architectural models

**Desks**
- BT   Furniture
- RT   Writing materials

**Despair**
- UF   Despondency
-      Hopelessness
-      Loss of hope
- BT   Mental states
- RT   Depression (Mental state)
-      Distress
-      Optimism

Desperadoes
- USE Criminals

Despondency
- USE Depression (Mental state)
-      Despair
-      Sadness

Destruction of property
- USE Sabotage
-      Vandalism
-      War damage
-      War destruction & pillage

Destruction & pillage
- CN   Used only as a subdivision with names of wars (Appendix C).

**Details**
- CN   TGM II term.

Details, Architectural
- USE Architectural elements

Detection
- USE Investigation

**Detective camera photographs**
- CN   TGM II term.
- UF   Concealed camera photographs
-      Vest camera photographs

**Detectives**
-      --[country or state]--[city]

BT Broader term      RT Related term      PN Public Note
NT Narrower term      UF Used for      + Term has NTs
HN History Note      CN Catalogers Note      --[ ] May subdivide

**Detectives (cont.)**
  PN  For persons who investigate private,
      especially illegal or illicit affairs; includes
      private law enforcement agents as well as
      police investigators.
  UF  Private detectives
      Private eyes
      Sleuths
  RT  Investigation
      Police
**Détente**
  PN  A relaxing of strained relations between
      nations.
  BT  International relations
**Detention facilities**
      --[country or state]--[city]
  PN  Search also under the subdivision
      --DETENTION FACILITIES used with
      names of wars (Appendix C).
  BT  Facilities
  NT  Concentration camps
      Jails
      Prisons
      Reformatories
      Relocation camps
  RT  Dungeons
      Justice facilities
      Prison hospitals
      Slave ships
Detergent, Household
  USE Household soap
**Deterioration**
      --[country or state]--[city]
  UF  Decay
      Decline
      Decrepitude
  BT  Economic & social conditions
  NT  Building deterioration
  RT  Progress
      Rake's progress
Deterioration of buildings
  USE Building deterioration
Developments, Housing
  USE Housing developments
Devilfish
  USE Octopuses
Devils
  USE Demons
**Devotional images**
  CN  TGM II term.
  UF  Holy cards
      Religious pictures
Devotional objects
  USE Religious articles
**Dhows**
      --[country or state]--[city]
  PN  For lateen-rigged Arabian vessels.
  BT  Boats
Diacetate negatives
  USE Acetate negatives
**Diagrams**
  CN  TGM II term.

**Diagrams (cont.)**
  UF  Production drawings
      Technical drawings
**Diamond miners**
      --[country or state]--[city]
  BT  Miners
  RT  Diamond mining
      Diamonds
**Diamond mining**
      --[country or state]--[city]
  PN  Includes activities and sites.
  BT  Mining
  RT  Diamond miners
      Diamonds
**Diamonds**
      --[country or state]--[city]
  BT  Gems
  RT  Diamond miners
      Diamond mining
Diazo photoprints
  USE Diazo prints
**Diazo prints**
  CN  TGM II term.
  UF  Black line prints
      Blue line prints
      Brownprints
      Diazo photoprints
      Diazotypes
      Dyelines
      Ozalids
      Primuline process prints
      Whiteprints
Diazotypes
  USE Diazo prints
Dice
  USE Gambling
Dictagraphs
  USE Dictating machines
Dictaphones
  USE Dictating machines
**Dictating machines**
  UF  Dictagraphs
      Dictaphones
      Dictographs
  BT  Office equipment & supplies
  RT  Sound recording
**Dictators**
      --[country]
  UF  Tyrants
  BT  Rulers
  RT  Fascism
      Military regimes
      Totalitarianism
Dictionaries
  USE Encyclopedias & dictionaries
Dictographs
  USE Dictating machines
Die industry
  USE Tool & die industry
**Dietary laws**
      --[country or state]--[city]
  PN  Religious laws that permit and prohibit

---

BT Broader term            RT Related term            PN Public Note
NT Narrower term            UF Used for                + Term has NTs
HN History Note             CN Catalogers Note         --[ ] May subdivide

**Dietary laws (cont.)**
          certain foods, or specify methods of food
          preparation.
   RT   Cookery
        Eating & drinking
        Kosher food industry
        Religion
Dieting
   USE Reducing
**Digging**
        --[country or state]--[city]
   NT   Gravedigging
   RT   Excavation
        Shovels
        Spades
        Steam shovels
Digging graves
   USE Gravedigging
Digital images
   USE Computer graphics
        Space photographs
        Transmitted images
**Dikes (Engineering)**
        --[country or state]--[city]
   UF   Dykes
   BT   Hydraulic facilities
   RT   Erosion protection works
        Levees
        Reclamation of land
        Sea walls
Dilapidation of buildings
   USE Building deterioration
Diners (Railroad cars)
   USE Railroad dining cars
**Diners (Restaurants)**
        --[country or state]--[city]
   PN   Includes activities and structures.
   BT   Restaurants
Dining
   USE Eating & drinking
Dining cars
   USE Railroad dining cars
**Dining rooms**
        --[country or state]--[city]
   BT   Interiors
   NT   Mess halls
   RT   Dining tables
        Eating & drinking facilities
        Employee eating facilities
        Tables
**Dining tables**
   UF   Tables, Dining
   BT   Tables
   RT   Dining rooms
        Eating & drinking
**Dinosaurs**
   BT   Extinct animals
        Reptiles
Diocletian windows
   USE Palladian windows
**Dioramas**
        --[country or state]--[city]

**Dioramas (cont.)**
   BT   Exhibitions
   RT   Galleries & museums
Diplomacy
   USE International relations
**Diplomas**
   CN   TGM II term.
**Diplomats**
        --[nationality]--[country or state]--[city]
   CN   Subdivide by nationality of country
        diplomat represents.
   UF   Ministers (Diplomatic agents)
   BT   Government employees
   NT   Ambassadors
        Consuls
   RT   International relations
Dipsomania
   USE Alcoholism
Directors, Theatrical
   USE Theatrical producers & directors
Direct-mail advertising
   USE Advertising mail
Dirigibles
   USE Airships
Disabled persons
   USE Handicapped persons
**Disabled veterans**
        --[nationality]
   BT   Handicapped persons
        Veterans
   RT   War casualties
Disarmament
   USE Arms control
Disaster housing
   USE Emergency housing
**Disaster relief**
        --[country or state]--[city]
   BT   Assistance
   NT   War relief
   RT   Canteens (Wartime, emergency, etc.)
        Clothing relief
        Disaster victims
        Disasters
        Emergency medical services
        Evacuations
        Food relief
        Relief ships
        Rescue work
**Disaster victims**
        --[country or state]--[city]
   CN   Double index under type of disaster. Used
        in a note under REFUGEES.
   BT   Victims
   RT   Clothing relief
        Disaster relief
        Disasters
        Evacuations
        Food relief
        Rescue work
**Disasters**
        --[country or state]--[city]
   PN   Includes the event and any resulting

---

BT  Broader term      RT  Related term      PN  Public Note
NT  Narrower term      UF  Used for      +  Term has NTs
HN  History Note      CN  Catalogers Note      --[ ]  May subdivide

**Disasters (cont.)**
  damage. Search also under the subdivision
  --DISASTERS used with corporate bodies
  and named events (Appendix D).
  CN  Used in a note under RUINS.
  UF  Calamities
      Catastrophes
      Collisions
      Damage to property
      Property damage
      Wrecks
  NT  Bridge failures
      Building failures
      Droughts
      Famines
      Pier & wharf failures
      Shipwrecks
  RT  Accidents
      Danger
      Disaster relief
      Disaster victims
      Earthquakes
      Emergency housing
      Explosions
      Fires
      Floods
      Landslides
      Lightning strikes
      Rescue work
      Storms
      Tidal waves
      Volcanic eruptions
**Discharges, Military**
  USE  Military discharges
**Disciplinary action**
  USE  Child discipline
       Punishment & torture
**Disciplining children**
  USE  Child discipline
**Disclosure of personal finances**
  USE  Financial disclosure
**Discos**
  USE  Discotheques
**Discotheques**
  --[country or state]--[city]
  UF  Discos
  BT  Sports & recreation facilities
  RT  Dance halls
      Dancing
      Nightclubs
**Discounts**
  RT  Business & finance
      Cost & standard of living
**Discoverers**
  USE  Explorers
       Inventors
**Discoveries**
  USE  Discovery & exploration
       Inventions
       Patents
**Discovery & exploration**
  --[nationality]--[country or state]--[city]

**Discovery & exploration (cont.)**
  CN  Subdivide by nationality of those doing
      the discovery & exploration.
  UF  Discoveries
      Exploration
      Journeys
  NT  Expeditions & surveys
      Westward movement
  RT  Events
      Explorers
      Frontier & pioneer life
      Guides & scouts
      Investigation
      Prospecting
      Travel
**Discrimination**
  --[country or state]--[city]
  PN  For overt discrimination. Search under
      PREJUDICE for the subject of prejudiced
      attitudes in general.
  CN  Used in a note under PREJUDICE.
  NT  Race discrimination
      Segregation
      Sexual harassment
  RT  Civil rights
      Ethics
      Prejudice
**Discs, Sound**
  USE  Sound recordings
**Discus throwing**
  --[country or state]--[city]
  BT  Track athletics
**Discussion**
  PN  Search under CONVERSATION for
      casual talking.
  UF  Group discussion
      Panel discussions
      Speaking
      Talking
  BT  Communication
  RT  Debates
      Meetings
      Public speaking
**Disease prevention**
  USE  Preventive medicine
**Diseases**
  --[country or state]--[city]
  PN  Search under SICK PERSONS for images
      of persons affected with unspecified
      ailments. Search also under the subdivision
      --HEALTH & WELFARE used with names
      of ethnic, racial and regional groups, and with
      classes of persons (Appendix A).
  UF  Ailments
      Illnesses
      Maladies
      Sickness
  NT  Alcoholism
      Black lung
      Cancer
      Communicable diseases +
      Hypertension

---

**Diseases (cont.)**
          Sickle cell anemia
          Vision disorders
   RT   Allergies
          Bacteria
          Drug abuse
          Healing
          Health
          Sick persons

**Disgrace**
   UF   Ignominy
          Shame
   BT   Mental states

Dishes
   USE Tableware

Dishonesty
   USE Honesty

Dishonorable discharges
   USE Military discharges

Dishwashers
   USE Dishwashing machines

**Dishwashing**
          --[country or state]--[city]
   UF   Washing dishes
   BT   Cleaning
   RT   Dishwashing machines

**Dishwashing machines**
          --[country or state]--[city]
   UF   Dishwashers
   BT   Appliances
   RT   Dishwashing

Disks, Sound
   USE Sound recordings

**Dismemberment**
   RT   Amputees
          Death
          Executions
          Punishment & torture

**Dismissal of employees**
          --[country or state]--[city]
   UF   Employee dismissal
          Firing of employees
          Layoffs
          Terminations of employment
   RT   Employment
          Resignations
          Unemployed

Displaced persons
   USE Refugees

Displaced persons camps
   USE Refugee camps

**Display cards**
   CN   TGM II term.

Display cases
   USE Showcases

Display drawings
   USE Presentation drawings

Display rooms
   USE Showrooms

Display windows
   USE Show windows
          Window displays

Displays of merchandise
   USE Merchandise displays

Disposal of refuse
   USE Refuse disposal

Disposal of waste
   USE Sewerage

**Dissections**
          --[country or state]--[city]
   RT   Animal experimentation
          Biology
          Experiments

**Dissenters**
   PN   For those who express nonconcurrence
          with reigning opinion, beliefs, or decisions.
   UF   Dissidents
          Nonconformists
   BT   People
   RT   Activists
          Freedom of religion
          Freedom of speech
          Individuality
          Opposition (Political science)
          Rebels

Dissidents
   USE Dissenters

Distance running
   USE Marathon running

Distillation apparatus
   USE Stills (Distilleries)

Distilleries
   USE Distilling industries

**Distilling industries**
          --[country or state]--[city]
   PN   Includes activities and structures.
   CN   Double index under INDUSTRIAL
          FACILITIES (or NTs) for images that focus
          on facilities.
   UF   Alcoholic beverage industry
          Distilleries
          Liquor industry
   BT   Beverage industry
   RT   Retorts (Equipment)
          Stills (Distilleries)

**Distress**
   PN   Search under PAIN for physical distress.
   CN   Used in a note under PAIN.
   UF   Agony
          Anguish
          Misery
          Suffering
   BT   Mental states
   RT   Depression (Mental state)
          Despair
          Pain
          Sadness
          Stress

Distribution of wealth
   USE Wealth

Districts, Business
   USE Business districts

**Distyle-in-antis buildings**
          --[country or state]--[city]

---

**Distyle-in-antis buildings (cont.)**
 BT Buildings distinguished by form
 RT Columns
**Divination**
 --[country or state]--[city]
 PN Art or practice that seeks to foresee or
 foretell future events or discover hidden
 knowledge usually by the interpretation of
 omens or by the aid of supernatural powers.
 UF Augury
 Predictions
 Soothsaying
 BT Supernatural practices
 RT Astrology
 Divining rods
 Fortune telling
 Prophecy
**Diving**
 --[country or state]--[city]
 PN For diving into water, as from a diving
 board.
 RT Aquatic sports
 Pearl fishing
 Skin diving
 Swimming
**Diving suits**
 BT Clothing & dress
 RT Skin diving
**Divining rods**
 UF Water witches
 BT Magical devices
 RT Divination
Divinity schools
 USE Theological seminaries
**Divorce**
 --[country or state]--[city]
 BT Law & legal affairs
 RT Custody of children
 Marriage
**Dizziness**
 UF Giddiness
 Lightheadedness
 RT Mental states
Dock hands
 USE Longshoremen
Docks
 USE Piers & wharves
Docks, Loading
 USE Loading docks
Dockyards
 USE Boat & ship industry
 Naval yards & naval stations
Doctors
 USE Physicians
Doctors' offices
 USE Medical offices
Doctors' surgeries
 USE Medical offices
**Document signings**
 --[country or state]--[city]
 UF Signing of documents
 BT Events

**Document signings (cont.)**
 RT Autographing
 Documents
 Petitions
 Writing
**Documents**
 UF Records (Information)
 RT Archives
 Document signings
 Paperwork
 Petitions
 Recording & registration
**Dodos**
 --[country or state]
 BT Extinct birds
Doffing
 USE Textile industry
Dog catching
 USE Dogcatching
Dog mushing
 USE Dogsledding
Dog pounds
 USE Animal shelters
**Dog shows**
 --[country or state]--[city]
 BT Animal shows
 RT Dogs
Dog sledding
 USE Dogsledding
**Dog teams**
 --[country or state]--[city]
 BT Animal teams
 RT Dogs
 Dogsledding
**Dogcatching**
 --[country or state]--[city]
 UF Dog catching
 BT Animal treatment
 RT Animal shelters
 Dogs
Doghouses
 USE Kennels
**Dogs**
 --[country or state]--[city]
 UF Puppies
 BT Animals
 NT Chow chows (Dogs)
 Hunting dogs
 Working dogs
 RT Dog shows
 Dog teams
 Dogcatching
 Dogs of war
 Dogsledding
 Kennels
**Dogs of war**
 BT Symbols
 RT Dogs
 War
**Dogsledding**
 UF Dog mushing
 Dog sledding

BT Broader term   RT Related term   PN Public Note
NT Narrower term   UF Used for   + Term has NTs
HN History Note   CN Catalogers Note   --[ ] May subdivide

**154**

**Dogsledding (cont.)**
     Sledding, Dog
  RT  Dog teams
     Dogs
     Sleds & sleighs
**Dollar signs**
  BT  Punctuation
     Symbols
**Dollhouses**
  UF  Miniature houses
  BT  Building models
  RT  Dolls
     Dwellings
**Dollies (Moving equipment)**
  BT  Equipment
  RT  Moving & storage trade
**Dolls**
  BT  Toys
  RT  Children playing with dolls
     Dollhouses
**Dolphins**
     --[country or state]
  BT  Aquatic animals
**Dome coffers**
     --[country or state]--[city]
  BT  Coffers (Ceilings)
  RT  Domes
**Domes**
     --[country or state]--[city]
  BT  Architectural elements
  NT  Onion domes
  RT  Cupolas
     Dome coffers
     Drums (Domes)
     Roofs
     Rotundas
Domestic appliances
  USE Appliances
**Domestic economic assistance**
     --[country or state]--[city]
  UF  Domestic lending
  BT  Assistance
  NT  Medicaid
     Medicare
     Public service employment
  RT  Social security
Domestic lending
  USE Domestic economic assistance
**Domestic life**
     --[country or state]--[city]
  PN  For activities in a home-like setting.
     Search also under the subdivision
     --DOMESTIC LIFE used with names of
     ethnic, racial, and regional groups, and with
     classes of persons (Appendix A).
  UF  Home life
  BT  Manners & customs
  RT  Children doing housework
     Economic & social conditions
     Families
     Home economics
     Housework

**Domestic life (cont.)**
     Laundry
Domestics
  USE Servants
Donations
  USE Gifts
Donations of blood
  USE Blood donations
**Donkeys**
     --[country or state]
  UF  Asses
     Burros
  BT  Animals
  RT  Mules
     Pin-the-tail-on-the-donkey
Donuts
  USE Doughnuts
Door fittings
  USE Keyholes
Door windows
  USE French doors
**Doors & doorways**
     --[country or state]--[city]
  UF  Doorways
     Entrances
     Portals
  BT  Architectural elements
  NT  Folding doors
     French doors
     Revolving doors
  RT  Gates
     Grilles
     Lintels
     Millwork
     Passageways
Doorways
  USE Doors & doorways
Door-to-door selling
  USE Canvassing
     Peddlers
**Doric order**
     --[country or state]--[city]
  BT  Architectural orders
**Dories (Boats)**
     --[country or state]--[city]
  PN  For small, narrow, flat-bottomed fishing
     boats with high sides and sharp prows.
  BT  Boats
**Dormers**
     --[country or state]--[city]
  PN  Gabled extensions of attic rooms through a
     sloping roof to allow for vertical window
     openings.
  BT  Architectural elements
  NT  Shed dormers
  RT  Roofs
     Windows
**Dormitories**
     --[country or state]--[city]
  UF  Halls of residence
     Residence halls
  BT  Dwellings

---

**Dormitories (cont.)**
RT   Bedrooms
**Dotted prints**
CN   TGM II term.
UF   Criblée prints
     Manière criblée prints
**Double-decker buses**
     --[nationality]--[country or state]--[city]
BT   Buses
Doubt
USE Suspicion
**Doughnuts**
UF   Donuts
BT   Baked products
**Dovecotes**
     --[country or state]--[city]
UF   Houses, Pigeon
     Pigeon houses
BT   Birdhouses
RT   Doves
**Doves**
     --[country or state]
CN   Used in a note under SYMBOLS.
BT   Pigeons
RT   Dovecotes
Down
USE Feathers
Down spouts
USE Downspouts
**Downspouts**
     --[country or state]--[city]
UF   Down spouts
     Down-pipes
     Rainwater pipes
BT   Mechanical systems components
RT   Leader heads
     Pipes
     Roofs
Downtown districts
USE Business districts
Down-pipes
USE Downspouts
**Draft**
     --[country]
HN   Changed 11/1987 from COMPULSORY
     MILITARY SERVICE.
UF   Compulsory military service
     Conscription, Military
     Selective service
BT   Military service
RT   Armies
     Conscientious objectors
     Draft resisters
Draft dodgers
USE Draft resisters
**Draft resisters**
     --[nationality]--[country or state]--[city]
UF   Draft dodgers
BT   Activists
RT   Conscientious objectors
     Draft
     Moral aspects of war

Drafting
USE Drawing
     Writing
Drag queens
USE Female impersonators
Drag racers
USE Automobile racing drivers
Dragging
USE Pulling
Dragon flies
USE Dragonflies
**Dragonflies**
     --[country or state]
UF   Dragon flies
BT   Insects
**Dragons**
BT   Supernatural beings
Dragoons
USE Cavalry
Drainage
USE Sewerage
**Drama clubs**
     --[country or state]--[city]
CN   Double index under ORGANIZATIONS'
     FACILITIES (or NTs) for images that focus
     on facilities.
BT   Clubs
RT   Theatrical productions
Dramas
USE Theatrical productions
**Dramatists**
UF   Playwrights
BT   Authors
**Drapery**
UF   Curtains
BT   Textiles
RT   Banners
     Festive decorations
     Furnishings
**Drawbridges**
     --[country or state]--[city]
PN   Search under SWING BRIDGES for
     bridges that move horizontally and under
     VERTICAL LIFT BRIDGES for bridges that
     move vertically.
UF   Lift bridges
     Movable bridges
BT   Bridges
**Drawing**
     --[country or state]--[city]
UF   Drafting
BT   Art
RT   Children drawing & painting
**Drawing rooms**
     --[country or state]--[city]
UF   Withdrawing rooms
BT   Interiors
RT   Parlors
     Reception rooms
**Drawings**
CN   TGM II term.
Drawings, Architectural

---

BT  Broader term                    RT  Related term                    PN  Public Note
NT  Narrower term                   UF  Used for                        +  Term has NTs
HN  History Note                    CN  Catalogers Note                 --[ ] May subdivide

Drawings, Architectural (cont.)
  USE Architectural drawings
Drawings, As-built
  USE As-built drawings
Drawings, Botanical
  USE Botanical illustrations
Drawings, Competition
  USE Competition drawings
Drawings, Contract
  USE Contract drawings
Drawings, Design
  USE Design drawings
Drawings, Electrical systems
  USE Electrical systems drawings
Drawings, Engineering
  USE Engineering drawings
Drawings, Exploded
  USE Exploded drawings
Drawings, Framing
  USE Framing drawings
Drawings, Landscape architecture
  USE Landscape architecture drawings
Drawings, Measured
  USE Measured drawings
Drawings, Mechanical
  USE Mechanical drawings
Drawings, Mechanical systems
  USE Mechanical systems drawings
Drawings, Medical
  USE Medical illustrations
Drawings, Naval architecture
  USE Naval architecture drawings
Drawings, Patent
  USE Patent drawings
Drawings, Planning
  USE Planning drawings
Drawings, Presentation
  USE Presentation drawings
Drawings, Structural systems
  USE Structural systems drawings
Drawings, Working
  USE Working drawings
Dreadnoughts
  USE Battleships
      Government vessels
**Dreaming**
  HN  Changed 4/1988 from DREAMS.
  UF  Nightmares
  BT  Mental states
  RT  Daydreaming
      Sleeping
      Somnambulism
**Dredging**
      --[country or state]--[city]
  BT  Excavation
  RT  Underwater drilling
Dress
  USE Clothing & dress
**Dress reform**
      --[country or state]--[city]
  UF  Clothing reform
  BT  Reform

**Dress reform (cont.)**
  RT  Clothing & dress
Dressers (Furniture)
  USE Clothes chests
Dressers, Kitchen
  USE Cupboards
Dressers, Pantry
  USE Cupboards
Dressing bureaux
  USE Dressing tables
Dressing rooms
  USE Boudoirs
**Dressing tables**
  UF  Dressing bureaux
      Tables, Dressing
      Vanities
  BT  Tables
  RT  Dressing & grooming equipment
      Grooming
**Dressing & grooming equipment**
      --[country or state]--[city]
  UF  Grooming equipment
      Toilet articles
      Toiletries
  BT  Equipment
  NT  Combs
      Shaving equipment +
  RT  Cosmetics & soap
      Dressing tables
      Grooming
Dressmaking
  USE Sewing
      Tailoring
**Dried plant arrangements**
  BT  Decorations
  NT  Skeleton leaf arrangements
  RT  Flowers
      Plants
**Drill halls**
      --[country or state]--[city]
  PN  Spacious halls used for drill by military or
      other drill teams.
  BT  Military facilities
Drill presses
  USE Drilling & boring machinery
**Drilling**
      --[country or state]--[city]
  PN  For drilling of holes in metal, wood, and
      other materials, as carried out for construction
      and manufacturing purposes. Search under
      BORING for the cutting of holes in earth or
      rocks to determine the nature of the strata
      penetrated or to create an outlet for oil, water,
      or gas.
  CN  Used in a note under BORING.
  RT  Boring
      Construction
      Drilling & boring machinery
      Drills (Equipment)
**Drilling & boring machinery**
  UF  Borers
      Boring machinery

---

BT  Broader term          RT  Related term          PN  Public Note
NT  Narrower term          UF  Used for               +  Term has NTs
HN  History Note           CN  Catalogers Note        --[ ]  May subdivide

**Drilling & boring machinery (cont.)**
>        Drill presses
>        Drills (Machinery)
>    BT    Machinery
>    RT    Boring
>        Drilling

Drilling, Underwater
>    USE Underwater drilling

**Drills (Equipment)**
>    PN    Hand-held tools for making holes in firm
>        objects.
>    BT    Equipment
>    RT    Drilling

Drills (Machinery)
>    USE Drilling & boring machinery

Drills, Military
>    USE Military training

Drinking
>    USE Eating & drinking

Drinking facilities
>    USE Eating & drinking facilities

Drinking problem
>    USE Alcoholism

**Drinking vessels**
>    UF    Cups
>        Goblets
>        Mugs
>        Tankards
>    BT    Containers
>        Tableware
>    NT    Chalices
>    RT    Beverages
>        Eating & drinking
>        Glassware
>        Tin cups

Drinks
>    USE Beverages

Drive ways
>    USE Driveways

**Driver education**
>        --[country or state]--[city]
>    BT    Education
>    RT    Automobiles

Drives, Membership
>    USE Membership campaigns

Drives, Scrap
>    USE Scrap drives

**Driveways**
>        --[country or state]--[city]
>    PN    Private roads giving access from a public
>        way to a building on abutting grounds.
>    UF    Drive ways
>    BT    Roads
>    RT    Streets

**Drive-in restaurants**
>        --[country or state]--[city]
>    PN    Includes activities and structures.
>    BT    Fast food restaurants
>    RT    Automobiles

**Drive-in theaters**
>        --[country or state]--[city]
>    BT    Motion picture theaters

**Drive-in theaters (cont.)**
>    RT    Automobiles

Driving while intoxicated
>    USE Drunk driving

Driving, Automobile
>    USE Automobile driving

Drop ceilings
>    USE Suspended ceilings

**Droughts**
>        --[country or state]
>    BT    Disasters
>    RT    Rain
>        Scarcity
>        Water supply

**Drowning**
>        --[country or state]--[city]
>    RT    Death
>        Lifesaving

**Drowning victims**
>        --[country or state]--[city]
>    BT    Dead persons
>        Victims
>    RT    Marine accidents

**Drug abuse**
>        --[country or state]--[city]
>    PN    For abuse or misuse of drugs in a broad
>        sense, such as aspirin, bromides, caffeine,
>        sedatives, alcohol, LSD, marihuana, and
>        narcotics.
>    CN    As appropriate, double index under the
>        drug.
>    UF    Addiction to drugs
>        Chemical abuse
>        Drug addiction
>        Narcotic habit
>        Substance abuse
>    NT    Alcoholism
>    RT    Diseases
>        Narcotics
>        Tobacco habit

Drug addiction
>    USE Drug abuse

Drug stores
>    USE Drugstores

Drug trade
>    USE Drugstores
>        Medicine shows
>        Pharmaceutical industry

**Druggists**
>    UF    Apothecaries
>        Pharmacists
>    BT    People associated with health & safety
>    RT    Drugstores
>        Health care
>        Medicines
>        Pharmaceutical industry

Drugs
>    USE Medicines
>        Narcotics

**Drugstores**
>        --[country or state]--[city]
>    PN    Retail stores where medicines are

---

**Drugstores (cont.)**
    compounded and dispensed and
    miscellaneous articles, e.g. food, cosmetics,
    and film, are sold. Includes activities and
    structures.
  HN  Prior to 5/1991, PHARMACIES was used
    for places where medicines are compounded,
    dispensed, and sold.
  UF  Apothecary shops
    Drug stores
    Drug trade
    Pharmacies
  BT  Stores & shops
  RT  Druggists
    Medicines
    Soda fountains

**Drum majorettes**
    --[country or state]--[city]
  PN  Search under DRUM MAJORING or
    BATON TWIRLING for images that focus on
    activities.
  UF  Majorettes, Drum
  RT  Baton twirling
    Drum majoring
    Drum majors
    Parades & processions

**Drum majoring**
    --[country or state]--[city]
  CN  Used in a note under DRUM MAJORS
    and DRUM MAJORETTES.
  RT  Baton twirling
    Drum majorettes
    Drum majors
    Parades & processions

**Drum majors**
    --[country or state]--[city]
  PN  Search under DRUM MAJORING or
    BATON TWIRLING for images that focus on
    activities.
  UF  Majors, Drum
  RT  Baton twirling
    Drum majorettes
    Drum majoring
    Parades & processions

**Drums**
  PN  Includes the activity of playing drums.
  BT  Percussion instruments
  NT  Tambourines

**Drums (Domes)**
    --[country or state]--[city]
  PN  Vertical walls that are circular or
    polygonal and carry a cupola or dome.
  UF  Barabans
  RT  Cupolas
    Domes

**Drunk driving**
    --[country or state]--[city]
  UF  Driving while intoxicated
    Drunken driving
    DWI
  RT  Alcoholic beverages
    Automobile driving

**Drunk driving (cont.)**
    Intoxication
    Traffic regulations

**Drunken driving**
  USE Drunk driving

**Drunkenness**
  USE Intoxication

**Dry cleaners**
  USE Cleaning establishments

**Dry collodion negatives**
  CN  TGM II term.
  UF  Collodion dry plate negatives
    Collodion negatives

**Dry docks**
  USE Boat & ship industry
    Naval yards & naval stations

**Dry goods stores**
    --[country or state]--[city]
  PN  Stores in which textiles, ready to wear
    clothing, and notions are sold. Includes
    activities and structures.
  UF  Fancy goods stores
  BT  Stores & shops
  RT  Department stores
    General stores

**Dry paintings**
  USE Sandpaintings

**Dry plate negatives**
  CN  TGM II term.
  UF  Gelatin dry plate negatives
    Silver gelatin glass negatives

**Drying of fish**
  USE Fish drying

**Drying of food**
  USE Food drying

**Drying sheds**
    --[country or state]--[city]
  PN  For structures used to dry material (e.g.,
    paper, textiles) by means of air flow.
  UF  Sheds, Drying
  BT  Sheds
    Storage facilities

**Drypoints**
  CN  TGM II term.

**Duck decoys**
  USE Decoys (Hunting)

**Duck shooting**
    --[country or state]
  BT  Game bird hunting
  RT  Ducks

**Duckbills**
  USE Platypuses

**Ducks**
    --[country or state]
  BT  Birds
  RT  Duck shooting
    Poultry

**Dueling**
    --[country or state]--[city]
  PN  Search under DUELING GROUNDS for
    images that focus on sites.
  CN  Used in a note under DUELING

---

BT  Broader term          RT  Related term          PN  Public Note
NT  Narrower term         UF  Used for             +  Term has NTs
HN  History Note          CN  Catalogers Note       --[ ]  May subdivide

**Dueling (cont.)**
> GROUNDS.
BT Manners & customs
RT Dueling grounds
> Fencing
> Martial arts

**Dueling grounds**
> --[country or state]--[city]
PN For images that focus on sites. Search under DUELING for activities.
CN Used in a note under DUELING.
BT Sites
RT Dueling

**Dufay color transparencies**
USE Screen color film transparencies

**Dugout houses**
> --[country or state]--[city]
PN Dwellings wholly or partly constructed in the ground, usually in a bank or slope.
BT Houses
RT Sod buildings
> Stone buildings

**Dumb waiters**
USE Dumbwaiters

**Dumbwaiters**
> --[country or state]--[city]
UF Dumb waiters
BT Conveying systems
RT Elevators

**Dump trucks**
> --[country or state]--[city]
BT Trucks

**Dunce caps**
USE Fools' caps

**Dunes**
> --[country or state]
UF Sand drifts
> Sand dunes
BT Land
RT Beaches
> Deserts

**Dungeons**
> --[country or state]--[city]
BT Interiors
RT Detention facilities
> Prisons

**Dunkard churches**
USE Brethren churches

**Duplexes**
> --[country or state]--[city]
UF Two-family dwellings
BT Houses

**Durbars**
> --[country or state]--[city]
PN Courts held by native Indian princes; festive receptions given by maharajahs.
BT Events
RT Festivals
> Rites & ceremonies

**Dusk**
USE Sunrises & sunsets

**Dust jackets**

**Dust jackets (cont.)**
USE Book jackets

**Dust storms**
> --[country or state]--[city]
PN Includes the event and any resulting damage.
BT Storms
RT Erosion

**Dusting**
USE Sweeping & dusting

**Dutch reformed churches**
USE Reformed churches

**Duties**
USE Tariffs

**Dwarfs**
> --[country or state]--[city]
CN As appropriate, double index under HUMAN CURIOSITIES.
UF Midgets
RT Fictitious characters
> Human curiosities

**Dwellings**
> --[country or state]--[city]
PN Structures designed or used as the living quarters for one or more families. Search under BIRTHPLACES for dwellings that were a place of birth and under ESTATES for grounds and outbuildings associated with dwellings. Search also under the subdivision --STRUCTURES used with names of ethnic, racial, and regional groups, and with classes of persons (Appendix A). Search also under the subdivision --HOMES & HAUNTS used with names of persons (Appendix B).
CN Used in a note under ESTATES and BIRTHPLACES.
UF Cottages
> Estate houses
> Homes
> Mansions
> Residences
> Villas
BT Residential facilities
NT Apartment houses +
> Barracks
> Cave dwellings
> Cliff dwellings
> Condominiums
> Dormitories
> Houseboats +
> Houses +
> Housing +
> Igloos
> Mobile homes
> Officers' quarters
> Tipis
> Wickiups
> Wigwams
RT Backyards
> Birthplaces
> Dollhouses
> Estates

BT Broader term
NT Narrower term
HN History Note

RT Related term
UF Used for
CN Catalogers Note

PN Public Note
+ Term has NTs
--[ ] May subdivide

**Dwellings (cont.)**
      Garages
      Gatehouses
      House buying
      Huts
      Lodging houses
      Private camps
      Pueblos
      Ranches
      Residential streets
      Tents
DWI
  USE Drunk driving
**Dye coupler negatives**
  CN  TGM II term.
  UF  Ektacolor negatives
        Fujicolor negatives
        Kodacolor negatives
Dye coupler photoprints
  USE Dye coupler prints
**Dye coupler prints**
  CN  TGM II term.
  UF  Dye coupler photoprints
        Type C prints
        Type R prints
**Dye coupler transparencies**
  CN  TGM II term.
  UF  Agfacolor transparencies
        Ektachrome transparencies
        Fujichrome transparencies
        Kodachrome transparencies
Dye destruction photoprints
  USE Dye destruction prints
**Dye destruction prints**
  CN  TGM II term.
  UF  Cibachrome prints
        Dye destruction photoprints
        Silver dye bleach prints
Dye diffusion transfer photoprints
  USE Dye diffusion transfer prints
**Dye diffusion transfer prints**
  CN  TGM II term.
  UF  Dye diffusion transfer photoprints
        Kodak instant color prints
        Polaroid instant color prints
Dye transfer photoprints
  USE Dye transfer prints
**Dye transfer prints**
  CN  TGM II term.
  UF  Dye transfer photoprints
        Imbibition process prints
        Pinatypes
**Dyeing**
      --[country or state]--[city]
  UF  Coloring
  RT  Textile industry
Dyelines
  USE Diazo prints
Dykes
  USE Dikes (Engineering)
**Dynamite**
  UF  Sticks of dynamite

**Dynamite (cont.)**
  BT  Explosives
Dynamo rooms
  USE Engine rooms
**Eagles**
      --[country or state]
  CN  Used in a note under PATRIOTISM.
  UF  Bald eagles
        Golden eagles
  BT  Birds of prey
Earnings
  USE Wages
**Earrings**
  BT  Jewelry
**Ears**
  RT  Human body
**Earth**
  UF  World
  BT  Planets
  RT  Voyages around the world
Earth satellites
  USE Artificial satellites
Earthenware
  USE Pottery
**Earthquakes**
      --[country or state]--[city]
  PN  Includes the event and any resulting
        damage.
  BT  Natural phenomena
  RT  Disasters
        Tidal waves
**Easter cards**
  CN  TGM II term.
**Easter eggs**
  BT  Eggs
  RT  Holidays
Eastern Orthodox churches
  USE Orthodox churches
**Eating & drinking**
      --[country or state]--[city]
  CN  Double index, as appropriate, under food
        or beverage being consumed. Used in a note
        under COFFEE, COFFEEHOUSES, and
        TEA.
  UF  Dining
        Drinking
        Meals
  BT  Manners & customs
  NT  Children eating & drinking +
  RT  Banquets
        Barbecues
        Beverages
        Cookery
        Dietary laws
        Dining tables
        Drinking vessels
        Eating & drinking facilities
        Food
        Gluttony
        Picnics
        Railroad dining cars
        Reducing

BT Broader term        RT Related term        PN Public Note
NT Narrower term       UF Used for           + Term has NTs
HN History Note         CN Catalogers Note      --[ ] May subdivide

**Eating & drinking (cont.)**
- Silverware
- Tables
- Tableware
- Toasting

**Eating & drinking facilities**
--[country or state]--[city]
- UF  Drinking facilities
- BT  Commercial facilities
- NT  Bars +
  - Beer halls
  - Coffeehouses
  - Employee eating facilities
  - Restaurants +
- RT  Beverages
  - Breakfast rooms
  - Dining rooms
  - Eating & drinking
  - Food
  - Nightclubs

**Eavesdropping**
- HN  Changed 11/1991 from non-postable term (Use SURVEILLANCE).
- RT  Communication
  - Spying
  - Surveillance

**Eclipses**
- BT  Natural phenomena
- RT  Astronomy
  - Moon

**Ecology**
--[country or state]--[city]
- PN  For the subject of the interrelationship of organisms and their environments and the activities of ecologists.
- UF  Balance of nature
- BT  Science
- RT  Air quality
  - Conservation of natural resources
  - Environmental policy
  - Nature
  - Pollution

**Economic aspects of war**
--[country or state]--[city]
- PN  For economic causes of war, cost of war, and effect of war and preparation for war on industrial and commercial activity. Search also under the subdivision --ECONOMIC & INDUSTRIAL ASPECTS used with the names of wars (Appendix C).
- UF  Cost of war
  - Economics of war
  - War costs
- BT  Economic & social conditions
- NT  Reparations
  - War bonds & funds
  - War claims
  - War profiteering
  - War work
- RT  Business & finance
  - Consumer rationing
  - Defense budgets

**Economic aspects of war (cont.)**
- Defense contracts
- Defense industry
- Sutlers
- Victory gardens
- War
- War relief

**Economic assistance**
- USE Assistance

**Economic concentration**
- USE Big business

**Economic integration**
- USE International economic integration

**Economic policy**
--[country or state]
- UF  Appropriations
  - Budget
  - Federal spending
  - Fiscal policy
  - Five-year plans
  - Spending policy
- BT  Politics & government
- NT  Agricultural price supports
  - Bimetallism
  - Defense budgets
  - Deficit financing
  - Embargoes
  - Free trade & protection +
  - Government ownership
  - Government spending policy +
  - Price regulation
  - Wage-price policy
- RT  Assistance
  - Business & finance
  - Currency question

**Economic union**
- USE International economic integration

**Economic & industrial aspects**
- CN  Used only as a subdivision with names of wars (Appendix C).

**Economic & political systems**
- UF  Government systems
  - Political systems
- NT  Anarchism
  - Apartheid
  - Autonomy +
  - Capitalism
  - Communism
  - Conservatism
  - Democracy
  - Fascism
  - Imperialism
  - International economic integration
  - Liberalism
  - Libertarianism
  - Monarchy
  - National socialism
  - Plutocracy
  - Populism
  - Socialism
  - Technocracy
  - Theocracy

---

| | | |
|---|---|---|
| BT Broader term | RT Related term | PN Public Note |
| NT Narrower term | UF Used for | + Term has NTs |
| HN History Note | CN Catalogers Note | --[ ] May subdivide |

**Economic & political systems (cont.)**
    Totalitarianism
  RT  International organization
    Nationalism
    Politics & government
    Solidarity
**Economic & social conditions**
    --[country or state]--[city]
  CN  This heading is primarily used with
    group-level cataloging to cover the material
    situation or social status of individuals or
    groups.
  UF  Social conditions
  NT  Agricultural productivity
    Business panics
    Cost & standard of living
    Depressions
    Deterioration +
    Economic aspects of war +
    Industrial productivity
    Inflation
    Poverty
    Prices +
    Progress
    Prosperity
    Wealth
  RT  Business & finance
    City & town life
    Country life
    Domestic life
    Gross national product
    Sociological dramas
    Sociology
    Urban growth
**Economics of war**
  USE Economic aspects of war
**Editing**
  USE Journalism
**Editions, Limited**
  USE Limited editions
**Editorial cartoons**
  CN  TGM II term.
**Education**
  PN  Includes activities and structures. Search
    also under the subdivision --EDUCATION
    used with names of ethnic, racial, and
    regional groups, and with classes of persons
    (Appendix A).
  CN  As appropriate, double index the NTs by
    level and by type of education. Double index
    under EDUCATIONAL FACILITIES (or
    NTs) for images that focus on facilities.  Used
    in a note under EDUCATIONAL
    FACILITIES.
  UF  Pedagogy
  NT  Adult education
    Art education
    Business education
    Correspondence schools
    Driver education
    Health education
    Legal education

**Education (cont.)**
    Medical education +
    Military education
    Music education
    Physical education
    Prison education
    Religious education
    School excursions
    Vocational education +
  RT  Busing (School integration)
    Chautauquas
    Church & education
    Educational facilities
    Examinations
    Fables
    Libraries
    Literacy
    Reading
    Scholars
    School overcrowding
    School principals
    School superintendents
    Students
    Teachers
    Teaching methods
**Education of handicapped persons**
  HN  Changed 12/1992 to non-postable term.
    Use HANDICAPPED PERSONS with
    Appendix A subdivision --EDUCATION.
**Educational aspirations**
  USE Student aspirations
**Educational buildings**
  USE Educational facilities
**Educational facilities**
    --[country or state]--[city]
  CN  Used in a note under EDUCATION (and
    NTs).
  HN  Changed 1/1993 from EDUCATIONAL
    BUILDINGS.
  UF  Educational buildings
  BT  Facilities
  NT  Schools +
    Universities & colleges +
  RT  Classrooms
    Education
    Student unions
**Educational organizations**
    --[country or state]--[city]
  PN  Includes activities and structures.
  CN  Double index under ORGANIZATIONS'
    FACILTIES (or NTs)  for images that focus
    on facilities.
  BT  Organizations
  NT  Junior republics
**Efficiency, Agricultural**
  USE Agricultural productivity
**Efficiency, Industrial**
  USE Industrial productivity
**Effigy, Executions in**
  USE Executions in effigy
**Egg & anchor moldings**
  USE Egg & dart moldings

---

BT  Broader term        RT  Related term        PN Public Note
NT  Narrower term      UF  Used for           + Term has NTs
HN History Note        CN Catalogers Note    --[ ] May subdivide

Egg & arrow moldings
  USE Egg & dart moldings
**Egg & dart moldings**
      --[country or state]--[city]
  UF  Dart & egg moldings
      Egg & anchor moldings
      Egg & arrow moldings
      Egg & tongue moldings
  BT  Moldings
Egg & tongue moldings
  USE Egg & dart moldings
**Eggplants**
      --[country or state]--[city]
  BT  Vegetables
**Eggs**
  NT  Easter eggs
  RT  Birds' eggs & nests
      Embryology
Eight-hour movement
  USE Hours of labor
Ektachrome transparencies
  USE Dye coupler transparencies
Ektacolor negatives
  USE Dye coupler negatives
Elderly persons
  USE Aged persons
Election posters
  USE Political posters
Election tickets
  USE Ballots
Electioneering
  USE Political elections
Electioneering by railroad
  USE Whistle-stop campaigning
Elections
  USE Political elections
**Electoral college**
  UF  College, Electoral
      Electoral votes
  BT  Delegations
  RT  Presidential elections
Electoral votes
  USE Electoral college
**Electric automobiles**
      --[nationality]--[country or state]--[city]
  BT  Automobiles
  RT  Electricity
**Electric batteries**
  UF  Batteries, electric
  RT  Electrical apparatus
      Electricity
Electric companies
  USE Public utility companies
**Electric fences**
      --[country or state]--[city]
  BT  Fences
  RT  Barricades
      Electricity
**Electric generators**
      --[country or state]--[city]
  BT  Electrical apparatus
**Electric household appliances industry**

**Electric household appliances industry (cont.)**
      --[country or state]--[city]
  PN  Includes activities and structures.
  CN  Double index under INDUSTRIAL
      FACILITIES (or NTs) for images that focus
      on facilities.
  BT  Industry
  RT  Electrical apparatus industry
      Electronic industry
**Electric lighting**
      --[country or state]--[city]
  PN  For images about electric lighting.
  BT  Lighting
  RT  Electricity
**Electric lines**
      --[country or state]--[city]
  PN  Power lines used for transmission and
      distribution of electricity.
  UF  Power lines
      Power transmission lines
      Transmission lines
  RT  Electricity
      Power plants
      Utility poles
**Electric oscillators**
  UF  Oscillators, Electric
  BT  Machinery
  RT  Electrical apparatus
      Radios
**Electric railroads**
      --[country or state]--[city]
  PN  For street railroads between cities.
  UF  Interurban street railroads
  BT  Railroads
  RT  Electricity
      Model railroads
      Street railroads
**Electric shocks**
      --[country or state]--[city]
  RT  Electricity
      Electrocutions
      Wounds & injuries
**Electric signs**
      --[country or state]--[city]
  UF  Neon signs
  BT  Signs
  RT  Electricity
Electric switchboards
  USE Switchboards
**Electrical apparatus**
  PN  For apparatus that generates electric
      power.
  BT  Machinery
  NT  Electric generators
      Hydroelectric generators
  RT  Electric batteries
      Electric oscillators
      Electrical apparatus industry
      Electricity
**Electrical apparatus industry**
      --[country or state]--[city]
  PN  Includes activities and structures.

BT Broader term          RT Related term          PN Public Note
NT Narrower term         UF Used for              + Term has NTs
HN History Note          CN Catalogers Note       --[ ] May subdivide

**Electrical apparatus industry (cont.)**
- CN    Double index under INDUSTRIAL FACILTIES (or NTs) for images that focus on facilities.
- BT    Industry
- RT    Electric household appliances industry
         Electrical apparatus
         Electronic industry

**Electrical systems drawings**
- CN    TGM II term.
- UF    Drawings, Electrical systems

**Electricians' strikes**
         --[country or state]--[city]
- BT    Strikes

**Electricity**
         --[country or state]--[city]
- RT    Electric automobiles
         Electric batteries
         Electric fences
         Electric lighting
         Electric lines
         Electric railroads
         Electric shocks
         Electric signs
         Electrical apparatus
         Hydroelectric power
         Lightning
         Power shortages
         Public utility companies
         Switchboards
         Telegraph
         Telephones

**Electrocutions**
         --[country or state]--[city]
- RT    Accidents
         Electric shocks
         Executions

**Electron microscopes**
- BT    Microscopes

**Electronic bugging**
- USE Electronic surveillance

**Electronic calculating machines**
- USE Computers

**Electronic images**
- USE Computer graphics
         Transmitted images

**Electronic industry**
         --[country or state]--[city]
- PN    Includes activities and structures.
- CN    Double index under INDUSTRIAL FACILTIES (or NTs) for images that focus on facilities.
- BT    Industry
- RT    Electric household appliances industry
         Electrical apparatus industry

**Electronic music**
- UF    Synthesizer music
- BT    Music

**Electronic surveillance**
         --[country or state]--[city]
- UF    Bugs (Electronic surveillance)
         Electronic bugging

**Electronic surveillance (cont.)**
         Wiretapping
- BT    Surveillance

**Electrostatic photocopies**
- USE Photocopies

**Elementary school students**
- USE School children

**Elementary schools**
- USE Schools

**Elephant hunting**
         --[country]
- BT    Big game hunting
- RT    Elephants

**Elephants**
         --[country or state]
- BT    Animals
- NT    Mammoths
- RT    Elephant hunting
         Ivory

**Elevated highways**
         --[country or state]--[city]
- UF    Overpasses
- BT    Express highways
- RT    Bridges

**Elevated railroads**
         --[country or state]--[city]
- UF    Els
- BT    Railroads
- RT    Street railroads

**Elevations**
- CN    TGM II term.

**Elevators**
- BT    Conveying systems
- RT    Dumbwaiters

**Elevators, Grain**
- USE Grain elevators

**Elk**
         --[country or state]
- UF    Wapiti
- BT    Deer
- RT    Elk hunting
         Moose

**Elk hunting**
         --[country or state]
- BT    Big game hunting
- RT    Elk

**Elliptical rooms**
- USE Oval rooms

**Elms**
         --[country or state]--[city]
- BT    Trees

**Elocution**
- USE Public speaking

**Elopements**
         --[country or state]--[city]
- RT    Marriage
         Weddings

**Els**
- USE Elevated railroads

**Elves**
- BT    Fairies

**Emancipation**

| | | |
|---|---|---|
| BT  Broader term | RT  Related term | PN  Public Note |
| NT  Narrower term | UF  Used for | +  Term has NTs |
| HN  History Note | CN  Catalogers Note | --[ ]  May subdivide |

Emancipation (cont.)
  USE Liberty
Emancipation of women
  USE Women's rights
**Embalming**
        --[country or state]--[city]
  BT  Undertaking
  RT  Mummies
**Embargoes**
        --[nationality]--[country or state]--[city]
  CN  Subdivide by nationality of government
        imposing the embargo.
  BT  Economic policy
  RT  Blockades
        Commerce
**Embassies**
        --[nationality]--[country or state]--[city]
  UF  Chanceries
        Legations
  BT  Government facilities
  RT  International relations
        Official residences
Embattlements
  USE Battlements
**Embezzlement**
        --[country or state]--[city]
  BT  Crimes
**Emblem pictures**
  CN  TGM II term.
  UF  Motto prints
**Emblems**
  CN  TGM II term.
  NT  Fleur-de-lis
        National emblems
  RT  Logos
        Symbols
**Embossed prints**
  CN  TGM II term.
**Embossed works**
  CN  TGM II term.
Embracing
  USE Hugging
**Embroidery**
  BT  Sewing
**Embryology**
  PN  For the subject of embryology in general
        and the activities of embryologists.
  BT  Biology
  RT  Eggs
        Incubators
        Metamorphosis
**Emergency housing**
        --[country or state]--[city]
  UF  Disaster housing
        Wartime housing
  BT  Housing
  RT  Disasters
        Temporary buildings
**Emergency medical services**
        --[country or state]--[city]
  BT  Health care
  RT  Ambulances

Emergency medical services (cont.)
        Disaster relief
        Emergency rooms
        Victims
        Wounds & injuries
Emergency preparedness
  USE Civil defense
        Safety
**Emergency rooms**
        --[country or state]--[city]
  BT  Interiors
  RT  Emergency medical services
        Health care facilities
Emigrants
  USE Immigrants
**Emigration & immigration**
        --[nationality]--[country or state]--[city]
  PN  For the process of resettling in a new
        country, including the administration of the
        emigration/immigration process, the reasons
        why persons leave their native land, their
        transportation and trip to another country,
        their arrival, etc.
  CN  Subdivide by nationality for country of
        origin. Used in a note under IMMIGRANTS
        and IMMIGRATION STATIONS.
  UF  Immigration
        Immigration policy
        International migration
  NT  Repatriation
  RT  Aliens
        Arrivals & departures
        Colonies
        Colonists
        Deportations
        Immigrants
        Immigration stations
        Internal migration
        Naturalization
        Refugees
Emotion
  HN  Changed 5/1992 from postable term (prior
        to 5/1992, EMOTION was NT to MENTAL
        STATES).
  USE Mental states
**Emperors**
        --[country]
  BT  Men
        Rulers
  RT  Empresses
        Kings
Employed mothers
  USE Working mothers
Employee dismissal
  USE Dismissal of employees
**Employee eating facilities**
        --[country or state]--[city]
  UF  Canteens (Employee)
        Factory canteens
        Industrial cafeterias
        Lunchrooms, Employee
  BT  Eating & drinking facilities

---

BT Broader term          RT Related term          PN Public Note
NT Narrower term         UF Used for              + Term has NTs
HN History Note          CN Catalogers Note       --[ ] May subdivide

**Employee eating facilities (cont.)**
  RT  Dining rooms
        Employees
        Restaurants
**Employee fringe benefits**
  UF  Benefits, Employee
        Fringe benefits
  NT  Employee vacations
        Pensions
        Veterans' benefits
  RT  Employees
        Employment
**Employee rights**
        --[country or state]--[city]
  UF  Rights of employees
        Workers' rights
  RT  Civil liberties
        Employees
        Employment
        Labor unions
**Employee vacations**
  UF  Annual leave
        Holidays with pay
        Leave with pay
        Paid vacations
  BT  Employee fringe benefits
        Vacations
**Employees**
        --[country or state]--[city]
  PN  For persons identified as working for
        another, but where the nature of the activity,
        occupation, business or industry is not
        known. Search also under --STAFF used with
        names of persons (Appendix B) and
        --PEOPLE used with names of corporate
        bodies (Appendix D).
  CN  Prefer a specific occupation, activity,
        industry, or business, if known, and/or prefer
        a subdivision.
  UF  Personnel
        Staff
        Workers
  BT  People
  NT  Hotel employees +
        Railroad employees +
  RT  Employee eating facilities
        Employee fringe benefits
        Employee rights
        Employment
        Laborers
        Unemployed
**Employment**
        --[country or state]--[city]
  PN  For the subject of employment in general.
        Search also under headings such as
        BUSINESS ENTERPRISES, INDUSTRY,
        and MINING for images of people working.
        Search also under the subdivision
        --EMPLOYMENT used with names of
        ethnic, racial, and regional groups, and with
        classes of persons (Appendix A). Search
        under CHILD LABOR for employment of

**Employment (cont.)**
        children.
  UF  Jobs
        Labor
        Work
  NT  Child labor
        Civil service
        Home labor +
        Public service employment
  RT  Absenteeism (Labor)
        Age & employment
        Dismissal of employees
        Employee fringe benefits
        Employee rights
        Employees
        Employment agencies
        Employment interviewing
        Hours of labor
        Nepotism
        Occupations
        Paydays
        Resignations
        Retirements
        Unemployed
        Wages
        War work
        Work ethic
        Working mothers
**Employment agencies**
        --[country or state]--[city]
  PN  Includes activities and structures.
  UF  Job placement agencies
  BT  Service industry facilities
  RT  Employment
**Employment interviewing**
        --[country or state]--[city]
  UF  Job interviewing
  RT  Employment
        Interviews
**Empresses**
        --[country]
  BT  Rulers
        Women
  RT  Emperors
        Queens
**Empty market basket**
  BT  Symbols
  RT  Full dinner pail
**Encampments, Indian**
  USE  Indian encampments
**Enclosure walls**
  USE  Curtain walls
**Encyclopedias & dictionaries**
  UF  Cyclopedias
        Dictionaries
  BT  Books
**End of the world**
  PN  Includes Judgment Day, as well as
        preceding events, signs, fulfillments of
        prophecies, etc.
  UF  Judgment Day
        World's end

---

BT  Broader term                    RT  Related term                    PN  Public Note
NT  Narrower term                   UF  Used for                        +  Term has NTs
HN  History Note                    CN  Catalogers Note                 --[ ]  May subdivide

**End of the world (cont.)**
- BT Biblical events
- RT Prophecy

Enemy aliens
- USE Aliens

**Energy policy**
- --[country]
- BT Politics & government

Enforcement of law
- USE Law enforcement

**Engine rooms**
- --[country or state]--[city]
- UF Dynamo rooms
- BT Interiors
- RT Engines

**Engineering**
- --[country or state]--[city]
- PN Search also under the subdivision --ENGINEERING & CONSTRUCTION used with names of wars (Appendix C).
- NT Acoustical engineering
  - Civil engineering +
- RT Construction industry
  - Engineers
  - Measuring

**Engineering drawings**
- CN TGM II term.
- UF Drawings, Engineering

Engineering & construction
- CN Used only as a subdivision with names of wars (Appendix C).

**Engineers**
- BT People
- RT Engineering

Engineers, Railroad
- USE Railroad employees

**Engines**
- UF Motors
  - Turbines
- BT Machinery
- NT Airplane engines
  - Boat engines
  - Caloric engines
  - Gasoline engines
  - Steam engines
- RT Engine rooms

**Engravings**
- CN TGM II term.

Engravings, Wood
- USE Wood engravings

Enlistment
- USE Recruiting & enlistment

Ennui
- USE Boredom

Ensembles, Music
- USE Music ensembles

**Entablatures**
- --[country or state]--[city]
- PN Architecturally-treated walls. In classical architecture, the arrangement of three horizontal members (architrave, frieze, and cornice) above the supporting columns in any

**Entablatures (cont.)**
- of the classical orders.
- BT Architectural elements
- RT Architectural orders
  - Architraves
  - Colonnades
  - Cornices
  - Friezes (Entablature components)
  - Walls

Enterprises, Business
- USE Business enterprises

**Entertainers**
- --[country or state]--[city]
- CN Used in a note under IMPERSONATION.
- UF Performing artists
  - Showmen
- BT People associated with entertainment & sports
- NT Actors
  - Actresses
  - Aerialists
  - Bards
  - Chorus girls
  - Circus performers
  - Clowns
  - Comedians
  - Daredevils
  - Fools & jesters
  - Geishas
  - Magicians
  - Minstrels
  - Opera singers
  - Street entertainers +
  - Strong men
  - Troubadours
- RT Celebrities
  - Dancers
  - Entertainment
  - Female impersonators
  - Imitation
  - Impersonation
  - Musicians
  - Rehearsals

**Entertaining**
- --[country or state]--[city]
- PN For social entertainment.
- BT Manners & customs
- NT Masquerades
  - Parties +
  - Receptions

**Entertainment**
- --[country or state]--[city]
- PN Search also under the subdivision --PERFORMANCES & PORTRAYALS used with names of ethnic, racial, and regional groups, and with classes of persons (Appendix A). Search also under the subdivision --PERFORMANCES used with names of persons (Appendix B).
- NT Acrobatics
  - Circuses & shows +
  - Concerts

---

BT Broader term     RT Related term     PN Public Note
NT Narrower term     UF Used for     + Term has NTs
HN History Note     CN Catalogers Note     --[ ] May subdivide

**Entertainment (cont.)**
      Game shows
      Juggling
      Storytelling +
      Stunt driving
      Stunt flying
      Theatrical productions +
      Trick riding
      Ventriloquism
  RT  Chautauquas
      Dancing
      Entertainers
      Events
      Historical reenactments
      Magic
      Midways
      Motion pictures
      Nightclubs
      Premieres
      Recreation
      Rehearsals
      Stilts
**Entertainment posters**
  USE Performing arts posters
**Entrance halls**
      --[country or state]--[city]
  UF  Foyers
      Vestibules
  BT  Interiors
  RT  Lobbies
      Stairhalls
**Entrances**
  USE Doors & doorways
      Gates
**Entrenchment**
  USE Trench warfare
**Entrepreneurs**
  USE Businessmen
**Envelopes**
  CN  TGM II term.
**Environment & state**
  USE Environmental policy
**Environmental control**
  USE Environmental policy
**Environmental management**
  USE Environmental policy
**Environmental policy**
      --[country or state]
  UF  Environment & state
      Environmental control
      Environmental management
  BT  Politics & government
  RT  Ecology
      Government regulation
**Environmental protection**
  USE Conservation of natural resources
**Envy**
  UF  Jealousy
  BT  Mental states
  RT  Deadly sins
**Ephemera**
  CN  TGM II term.

**Ephemera (cont.)**
  UF  Printed ephemera
**Epidemics**
  USE Communicable diseases
**Episcopal churches**
  USE Anglican churches
**Epistyles**
  USE Architraves
**Equal rights amendments**
      --[country or state]
  BT  Constitutional amendments
  RT  Women's rights
**Equality, Racial**
  USE Racism
**Equality, Sexual**
  USE Sexism
**Equator (in religion, folklore, etc.)**
  USE Shellbacks
**Equipment**
  PN  Search also under the subdivision
      --EQUIPMENT & SUPPLIES used with
      names of wars (Appendix C), and with
      corporate bodies and named events (Appendix
      D).
  CN  TGM II term.
  UF  Household equipment
      Household goods
      Implements
      Tools
  NT  Airplane equipment +
      Anchors
      Appliances +
      Arms & armament +
      Arrows
      Artists' materials +
      Automobile equipment & supplies
      Axes +
      Boilers
      Book ends
      Bows (Archery) +
      Brooms & brushes
      Chisels & mallets
      Churns
      Clotheslines
      Cooking utensils +
      Cradleboards
      Crowbars
      Dashboards
      Dollies (Moving equipment)
      Dressing & grooming equipment +
      Drills (Equipment)
      Fishing & hunting gear +
      Gadgets
      Gardening equipment & supplies
      Gavels
      Hammers
      Handcuffs
      Irons (Pressing)
      Kilns
      Knives
      Ladders
      Light fixtures +

BT Broader term
NT Narrower term
HN History Note

RT Related term
UF Used for
CN Catalogers Note

PN Public Note
+ Term has NTs
--[ ] May subdivide

**Equipment (cont.)**
> Matches
> Optical devices +
> Paravanes
> Photographic apparatus & supplies +
> Prospecting equipment & supplies
> Radiators
> Retorts (Equipment)
> Safes
> Safety equipment +
> Sawhorses
> Saws +
> Scales
> Scientific equipment +
> Scissors & shears
> Seesaws
> Sewing equipment & supplies +
> Ship equipment & rigging
> Shovels
> Spades
> Spinning apparatus
> Sporting goods +
> Steering wheels
> Swings
> Tableware +
> Transistors
> Vices (Equipment)
> Washboards
> Water heaters
> Whips
> Wire
> Wrenches
> Yokes
RT  Agricultural machinery & implements
> Bellows
> Equipment industry
> Fire engines & equipment
> Furnishings
> Hardware
> Lathes
> Looms
> Machinery
> Magical devices
> Maintenance & repair
> Medical equipment & supplies
> Office equipment & supplies
> Plumbing fixtures
> Soda fountains
> Tool & die industry

**Equipment industry**
> --[country or state]--[city]
PN  Includes activities and structures.
CN  Double index under INDUSTRIAL
> FACILITIES  (or NTs) for images that focus
> on facilities.
BT  Industry
NT  Cutlery industry
> Refrigerator industry
> Sewing machine industry
> Stove industry
RT  Equipment
> Office equipment & supplies industry

Equipment & supplies
> CN  Used only as a subdivision with names of
> wars (Appendix C), and with corporate
> bodies and named events (Appendix D).
Eremites
> USE Hermits
**Erosion**
> --[country or state]--[city]
> BT  Natural phenomena
> RT  Building deterioration
> Dust storms
> Erosion protection works
> Geology
> Landslides
> Soil conservation
**Erosion protection works**
> --[country or state]--[city]
> BT  Hydraulic facilities
> NT  Jetties
> Sea walls
> RT  Canals
> Dams
> Dikes (Engineering)
> Erosion
> Flood control
> Pilings (Civil engineering)
**Erotic films**
> UF  Pornographic films
> BT  Motion pictures
**Erotica**
> CN  TGM II term.
**Escapes**
> --[country or state]--[city]
> NT  Prison escapes
> RT  Prisoners
Escarpments
> USE Cliffs
Espionage
> USE Spying
Estate houses
> USE Dwellings
Estate taxes
> USE Inheritance & transfer taxes
**Estates**
> --[country or state]--[city]
> PN  For the grounds and outbuildings on
> estates. Search under DWELLINGS for
> dwellings on estates.
> CN  Used in a note under DWELLINGS.
> UF  Manors
> Villas
> BT  Residential facilities
> RT  Dwellings
> Hunting lodges
> Outbuildings
> Plantations
Estuaries
> USE Bays
> Rivers
> Seas
**Etchings**
> CN  TGM II term.

---

BT  Broader term                         RT  Related term                         PN  Public Note
NT  Narrower term                        UF  Used for                             +  Term has NTs
HN  History Note                         CN  Catalogers Note                      --[ ]  May subdivide

Ether
  USE Anesthesia
**Ethics**
  PN  For the discipline dealing with good and
      bad, and with moral duty and obligation, as
      well as for immoral/moral behavior and
      unethical/ethical practices. Search also under
      the subdivision --ETHICS used with names
      of persons (Appendix B).
  UF  Business ethics
      Morals
  NT  Deception
      Exploitation
      Financial disclosure
      Fraud
      Good & evil
      Honesty
      Hypocrisy
      Moral aspects of war +
      Nepotism
      Revenge
      Temperance
      Vice
      Work ethic
  RT  Animal treatment
      Charity
      Corruption
      Discrimination
      Etiquette
      Free love
      Illegitimacy
      Incompetence
      Interpersonal relations
      Justice
      Mental states
      Muckraking
      Prejudice
      Promises
      Rake's progress
      Reform
      Self-interest
      Treason
      Truth
      Wisdom
**Ethnic groups**
      --[country or state]--[city]
  PN  For races or large groups of people classed
      according to common traits and customs. See
      also Library of Congress Subject Headings
      for names of individual groups.
  BT  People
  RT  Ethnic neighborhoods
      Minorities
      Race discrimination
      Race relations
**Ethnic neighborhoods**
      --[country or state]--[city]
  PN  Quarters of cities in which members of a
      minority racial or cultural group live,
      including those which develop because of
      social, legal, or economic pressure.
  UF  Ghettos

**Ethnic neighborhoods (cont.)**
  BT  Residential facilities
  RT  City & town life
      Ethnic groups
      Slums
**Ethnic stereotypes**
  CN  TGM II term.
  UF  National stereotypes
      Racial stereotypes
      Stereotypes, Ethnic
**Ethnographic photographs**
  CN  TGM II term.
  UF  Anthropological photographs
      Ethnological photographs
Ethnological photographs
  USE Ethnographic photographs
**Etiquette**
      --[country]
  PN  For the subject of good breeding in
      general and actions of good breeding
      observed in social and official life.
  UF  Courtesies
      Manners
      Politeness
  BT  Manners & customs
  NT  Bowing
      Curtsying
      Saluting +
      Shaking hands
  RT  Ethics
      Farewells
      Salutations
Eucharist
  USE Communion
**Evacuations**
      --[country or state]--[city]
  UF  Civilians, Evacuation of
  RT  Civil defense
      Disaster relief
      Disaster victims
      Refugees
      Relocation camps
      Safety
Evangelistic meetings
  USE Revivals
**Evangelists**
  BT  People associated with religion
  RT  Christianity
      Healers
      Preaching
      Religion
      Revivals
      Spiritual leaders
Evaporation of food
  USE Food drying
Evening
  USE Night
      Sunrises & sunsets
**Events**
      --[country or state]--[city]
  NT  Accidents +
      Air shows +

---

BT Broader term                    RT Related term              PN Public Note
NT Narrower term                   UF Used for                  + Term has NTs
HN History Note                    CN Catalogers Note           --[ ] May subdivide

**Events (cont.)**
> Anniversaries +
> Announcements
> Banquets
> Bees (Cooperative gatherings) +
> Biblical events +
> Births
> Book talks
> Boycotts
> Business panics
> Campaigns & battles
> Celebrations +
> Contests +
> Counterrevolutions
> Debates
> Declarations of war
> Demonstrations +
> Document signings
> Durbars
> Exhibitions +
> Fairs
> Festivals +
> Firsts
> Gold rushes
> Interviews
> Land rushes
> Launchings
> Meetings +
> Military parades & ceremonies
> Naval parades & ceremonies
> Parades & processions +
> Paydays
> Pilgrimages
> Political parades & rallies
> Rebellions +
> Reunions
> Revolutions
> Riots +
> Rodeos
> Secondhand sales
> Visits of state
> War +
> War rallies

> RT   Audiences
> > Crowds
> > Discovery & exploration
> > Entertainment
> > Historic sites
> > Manners & customs
> > Spectators

**Evictions**
> --[country or state]--[city]
> RT   Housing
> > Law & legal affairs

Evidence photographs
> USE Forensic photographs

Evil
> USE Good & evil

**Evil eye**
> BT   Supernatural practices
> RT   Witchcraft

Evil spirits, Expulsion of

Evil spirits, Expulsion of (cont.)
> USE Exorcism

**Evolution**
> UF   Darwinism
> > Origin of species
> RT   Biology
> > Civilization
> > Creation

Ewers
> USE Pitchers

Ex libris
> USE Bookplates

**Examinations**
> --[country or state]--[city]
> PN   For the testing of persons. Search under
> > TESTING for the testing of things.
> CN   Used in a note under TESTING.
> UF   Tests
> RT   Education
> > Health care
> > Investigation

**Excavation**
> --[country or state]--[city]
> BT   Civil engineering
> NT   Dredging
> > Quarrying +
> RT   Boring
> > Construction
> > Digging
> > Steam shovels

Excavation sites
> USE Archaeological sites

Excess government property
> USE Surplus government property

Exchange of prisoners
> USE Prisoner exchanges

Exchange (Barter)
> USE Barter

Exchanges
> USE Commodity exchanges
> > Merchants' exchanges
> > Stock exchanges

**Excitement**
> BT   Mental states
> RT   Cheering

Excrement
> USE Feces

Excursions
> USE Sightseers
> > Tourist trade

Execration
> USE Cursing

**Executioners**
> BT   People
> NT   Firing squads
> RT   Executions

**Executions**
> --[country or state]--[city]
> PN   Acts of putting to death.
> UF   Capital punishment
> > Death penalty
> NT   Burning at the stake

---

BT Broader term     RT Related term     PN Public Note
NT Narrower term     UF Used for     + Term has NTs
HN History Note     CN Catalogers Note     --[ ] May subdivide

Executions (cont.)
  Crucifixions
  Decapitations
  Hangings
  Walking the plank
RT Atrocities
  Dead persons
  Dismemberment
  Electrocutions
  Executioners
  Executions in effigy
  Firing squads
  Homicides
  Lynchings
  Punishment & torture
  Sacrifices
  Stoning
  Strangling
**Executions in effigy**
  --[country or state]--[city]
PN Search also under the subdivision
  --PORTRAYALS used with names of
  persons (Appendix B).
UF Burning in effigy
  Effigy, Executions in
RT Executions
Executive departments
  USE Administrative agencies
**Executive power**
  --[country or state]
UF Presidential power
BT Politics & government
  Power (Social sciences)
NT Presidential appointments
RT Presidents
  Vetoes
Executives
  USE Businessmen
  Government officials
Exemptions from taxation
  USE Tax exemptions
Exercise
  USE Physical fitness
Exercises, Military
  USE Military training
Exhaustion
  USE Fatigue
Exhibit posters
  USE Exhibition posters
**Exhibition buildings**
  --[country or state]--[city]
PN For images that focus on structures
  depicted at the time of the exhibition. Search
  also under the subdivision --BUILDINGS
  used with corporate bodies and named events
  (Appendix D). Search under EXHIBITIONS
  for activities and general views.
CN Index exhibition buildings depicted after
  the time of the exhibition under their current
  type.  Used in a note under EXHIBITIONS.
HN Changed 11/1992 from non-postable term
  (Use EXHIBITIONS).

**Exhibition buildings (cont.)**
UF Exposition buildings
  Exposition pavilions
  Fair buildings
  Pavilions, Exposition
BT Exhibition facilities
RT Exhibitions
**Exhibition catalogs**
CN TGM II term.
**Exhibition facilities**
  --[country or state]--[city]
BT Facilities
NT Aquariums
  Exhibition buildings
  Galleries & museums +
  Planetaria
  Zoos
RT Sports & recreation facilities
**Exhibition posters**
CN TGM II term.
UF Art exhibition posters
  Exhibit posters
**Exhibitions**
  --[country or state]--[city]
PN Includes activities and general views.
  Search under EXHIBITION BUILDINGS for
  images that focus on structures. Search also
  under the subdivision --EXHIBITIONS used
  with names of ethnic, racial, and regional
  groups, and with classes of persons
  (Appendix A);  names of persons (Appendix
  B); and names of wars (Appendix C). Search
  also under the subdivision --EXHIBITIONS &
  DISPLAYS used with corporate bodies and
  named events (Appendix D).
CN Used in a note under EXHIBITION
  BUILDINGS.
UF Exhibits
  Expositions
  Fairs, Trade
  Shows
  Trade fairs
BT Events
NT Agricultural exhibits
  Animal shows +
  Art exhibitions
  Book fairs
  Dioramas
  Fashion shows
  Flower shows
RT Centennial celebrations
  Contests
  Exhibition buildings
  Fairs
  Galleries & museums
  Merchandise displays
  Midways
  Showcases
Exhibits
  USE Exhibitions
**Exiles**
  --[nationality]--[country or state]--[city]

BT  Broader term                              RT  Related term                              PN  Public Note
NT  Narrower term                             UF  Used for                                  +  Term has NTs
HN  History Note                              CN  Catalogers Note                           --[ ] May subdivide

**Exiles (cont.)**
PN  Persons banished from their home or country by vested authority as a punitive measure.
UF  Political exiles
BT  People
RT  Aliens
    Deportations
    Punishment & torture
    Refugees
    Repatriation
**Exorcism**
    --[country or state]--[city]
UF  Evil spirits, Expulsion of
    Expulsion of evil spirits
BT  Rites & ceremonies
    Supernatural practices
RT  Demons
    Priests
Exotic works
    USE Novelty works
Expansionism
    USE Imperialism
Expectant mothers
    USE Pregnant women
**Expedition photographs**
CN  TGM II term.
**Expeditions & surveys**
    --[country or state]
BT  Discovery & exploration
Experimental animals
    USE Animal experimentation
**Experiments**
    --[country or state]--[city]
UF  Tests
RT  Animal experimentation
    Dissections
    Investigation
    Science
**Exploded drawings**
CN  TGM II term.
UF  Drawings, Exploded
**Exploitation**
    --[country or state]--[city]
BT  Ethics
Exploration
    USE Discovery & exploration
Exploration (Prospecting)
    USE Prospecting
**Explorers**
    --[nationality]--[country or state]--[city]
UF  Discoverers
BT  People
RT  Discovery & exploration
    Guides & scouts
**Explosions**
    --[country or state]--[city]
PN  Includes the event and any resulting damage.
RT  Bombings
    Disasters
    Explosives

**Explosives**
NT  Bombs
    Dynamite
    Fireworks +
    Mines (Warfare)
    Molotov cocktails
    Powder kegs
    Torpedoes
RT  Arms & armament
    Explosions
Export taxes
    USE Tariffs
Exports
    USE Commerce
Exposed children
    USE Abandoned children
Exposition buildings
    USE Exhibition buildings
Exposition pavilions
    USE Exhibition buildings
Expositions
    USE Exhibitions
**Express highways**
    --[country or state]--[city]
PN  Major high speed, high capacity roads.
UF  Expressways
    Freeways
    Superhighways
BT  Roads
NT  Elevated highways
Expression, Freedom of
    USE Freedom of religion
    Freedom of speech
Expressways
    USE Express highways
Expulsion of evil spirits
    USE Exorcism
Expulsions
    USE Deportations
Exterminating
    USE Pest control
**Extinct animals**
    --[country or state]
UF  Prehistoric animals
BT  Animals
NT  Dinosaurs
    Extinct birds +
    Mammoths
RT  Paleontology
    Wildlife conservation
**Extinct birds**
    --[country or state]
BT  Extinct animals
NT  Dodos
RT  Birds
**Extortion**
    --[country or state]--[city]
UF  Blackmail
BT  Crimes
**Extraterrestrial life**
UF  ALF
    Alien life forms

BT Broader term          RT Related term          PN Public Note
NT Narrower term         UF Used for              + Term has NTs
HN History Note          CN Catalogers Note       --[ ] May subdivide

**Extraterrestrial life (cont.)**
   Aliens (Space)
   Life on other planets
   Space aliens
 RT Cosmology
   Planets
   Supernatural beings
   Unidentified flying objects
**Extravagance**
 UF Over-indulgence
 RT Gluttony
   Miserliness
   Vice
   Wealth
Extra-marital sex
 USE Adultery
Extreme unction
 USE Last rites
Extremes
 USE Curiosities & wonders
Extremism
 USE Radicalism
**Ex-convicts**
 BT People
 RT Prisoners
Ex-military personnel
 USE Veterans
Eye catchers
 USE Architectural follies
**Eye examinations**
   --[country or state]--[city]
 BT Health care
 RT Eyes
**Eye patches**
   --[country or state]--[city]
 RT Clothing & dress
   Eyeglasses
   Eyes
**Eyeglasses**
 UF Spectacles
 BT Medical equipment & supplies
   Optical devices
 RT Eye patches
   Eyes
   Vision disorders
**Eyes**
 RT Eye examinations
   Eye patches
   Eyeglasses
   Human body
   Vision disorders
**Fables**
 BT Literature
 RT Education
   Parables
Fabric design drawings
 USE Textile design drawings
**Fabric shops**
   --[country or state]--[city]
 PN Includes activities and structures.
 UF Piece goods shops
   Yard goods shops

**Fabric shops (cont.)**
 BT Stores & shops
 RT Textile industry
Fabrics
 USE Textiles
**Facades**
   --[country or state]--[city]
 BT Walls
 NT False fronts
 RT Show windows
**Faces**
 UF Countenances
   Facial expressions
 RT Human body
   Mouths
   Noses
   Physiognomy
   Smiling
Facial expressions
 USE Faces
**Facilities**
   --[country or state]--[city]
 PN Something that is built, installed, or
   established to serve a particular purpose;
   often combines structure(s) and developed
   terrain; may include activities.
 NT Agricultural facilities +
   Buildings +
   Commercial facilities +
   Communication facilities +
   Cultural facilities +
   Detention facilities +
   Educational facilities +
   Exhibition facilities +
   Funerary facilities +
   Gardens +
   Government facilities +
   Health & hygiene facilities +
   Hydraulic facilities +
   Industrial facilities +
   Junkyards +
   Landscape architecture facilities +
   Military facilities +
   Monuments & memorials +
   Organizations' facilities +
   Parks +
   Public accommodation facilities +
   Religious facilities +
   Research facilities +
   Residential facilities +
   Settlements +
   Shelters +
   Sites +
   Social & civic facilities +
   Sports & recreation facilities +
   Storage facilities +
   Studios +
   Transportation facilities +
   Walkways +
   Waste disposal facilities +
   Welfare facilities +
 RT Architectural & site components

---

BT  Broader term
NT  Narrower term
HN  History Note

RT  Related term
UF  Used for
CN  Catalogers Note

PN  Public Note
+  Term has NTs
--[ ]  May subdivide

Facilities (cont.)
    Architecture
Facsimile transmission images
    USE Transmitted images
**Facsimiles**
    CN   TGM II term.
**Factories**
    --[country or state]--[city]
    PN   Facilities devoted primarily to
        manufacturing of products or processing of
        materials.  Search under INDUSTRY (or
        NTs) for activities.
    UF   Factory buildings
        Mills (Factories)
    BT   Industrial facilities
    NT   Foundries
        Mills +
        Potteries
        Refineries
        Smelters
        Smokehouses
Factory buildings
    USE Factories
Factory canteens
    USE Employee eating facilities
Factory work
    USE Industry
Fact-finding
    USE Investigation
Faculty
    USE Teachers
**Fads**
    --[country or state]--[city]
    UF   Crazes
    BT   Manners & customs
Fagoting
    USE Fuelwood gathering
Failures
    USE Losers
Fainting
    USE Loss of consciousness
Fair buildings
    USE Exhibition buildings
Fair trade
    USE Free trade & protection
        Reciprocity
**Fairies**
    UF   Brownies
    BT   Supernatural beings
    NT   Elves
    RT   Fairy tales
**Fairs**
    --[country or state]--[city]
    CN   Used in a note under MIDWAYS.
    UF   County fairs
        State fairs
    BT   Events
    RT   Agricultural exhibits
        Amusement parks
        Amusement rides
        Celebrations
        Exhibitions

Fairs (cont.)
    Festivals
    Markets
    Medicine shows
    Midways
Fairs, Trade
    USE Exhibitions
**Fairy tales**
    BT   Literature
    RT   Fairies
Faith healers
    USE Healers
Fakes
    USE Fraud
**Fakirs**
    --[country or state]--[city]
    BT   Dervishes
**Falconry**
    --[country or state]--[city]
    UF   Hawking
    BT   Sports
    RT   Falcons
**Falcons**
    --[country or state]
    BT   Hawks
    RT   Falconry
Fall
    USE Autumn
**Falling**
    UF   Tumbling
    RT   Clumsiness
**False advertising**
    --[country or state]--[city]
    BT   Advertising
    RT   Deception
        Fraud
False ceilings
    USE Suspended ceilings
**False fronts**
    --[country or state]--[city]
    CN   Use for facades extending beyond and
        especially above the dimensions of a building
        with specific purpose of giving a more
        imposing appearance.
    UF   Flying facades
        Screen facades
    BT   Facades
**Fame**
    UF   Celebrity
        Renown
    RT   Celebrities
        Interpersonal relations
**Families**
    --[country or state]--[city]
    PN   Search also under the subdivision
        --FAMILY used with names of persons
        (Appendix B).
    CN   Used in a note under CHILDREN &
        ADULTS.
    UF   Ancestors
        Brothers
        Daughters

BT Broader term        RT Related term        PN Public Note
NT Narrower term      UF Used for          + Term has NTs
HN History Note        CN Catalogers Note    --[ ] May subdivide

**Families (cont.)**
>           Parents
>           Siblings
>           Sisters
>           Sons
>   BT   People
>   NT   Fathers & children
>           Grandparents
>           Mothers & children
>           Spouses +
>   RT   Children & adults
>           Custody of children
>           Domestic life
>           Homecomings
>           Love
>           Marriage
>           Mothers-in-law
>           Stepmothers

**Family**
>   CN   Used only as a subdivision with names of
>           persons (Appendix B).

Family planning
>   USE Population control

Family records, Pictorial
>   USE Family trees

Family registers, Pictorial
>   USE Family trees

**Family trees**
>   CN   TGM II term.
>   UF   Family records, Pictorial
>           Family registers, Pictorial
>           Genealogical tables
>           Pictorial family records

**Famines**
>           --[country or state]--[city]
>   BT   Disasters
>   RT   Food relief
>           Scarcity
>           Starvation

Fan windows
>   USE Fanlights

Fancy goods stores
>   USE Dry goods stores

Fancy riding
>   USE Trick riding

**Fanlights**
>           --[country or state]--[city]
>   PN   Semicircular windows made with radiating
>           sash bars like the ribs of a fan and placed
>           over a door or window.
>   UF   Fan windows
>           Sunburst lights
>   BT   Windows

**Fans**
>   CN   TGM II term.

Fans (Persons)
>   USE Sports spectators

**Fantasy**
>   NT   Hallucinations & illusions +
>   RT   Daydreaming
>           Supernatural
>           Thinking

**Fantasy (cont.)**
>           Wishing

Farewell appearances
>   USE Swan songs

**Farewells**
>           --[country or state]--[city]
>   UF   Adieus
>           Goodbyes
>           Leave-takings
>   BT   Manners & customs
>   NT   Swan songs
>   RT   Arrivals & departures
>           Etiquette
>           Salutations

Farm buildings
>   USE Agricultural facilities

Farm crops
>   USE Farming
>           Plants

Farm equipment
>   USE Agricultural machinery & implements

Farm houses
>   USE Farmhouses

**Farm life**
>           --[country or state]--[city]
>   PN   For home life, leisure, and non-work
>           activities. Search under FARMING for
>           activities.
>   BT   Country life
>   RT   Corn husking
>           Farming
>           Hayrides

Farm machinery
>   USE Agricultural machinery & implements

Farm price supports
>   USE Agricultural price supports

**Farm produce**
>           --[country or state]--[city]
>   UF   Agricultural products
>           Produce
>   RT   Agricultural exhibits
>           Agricultural productivity
>           Agriculture
>           Farmers' markets
>           Food

**Farm relief**
>           --[country or state]--[city]
>   CN   Used in a note under INTERNATIONAL
>           AGRICULTURAL ASSISTANCE.
>   UF   Agricultural assistance, Economic
>   BT   Assistance
>   RT   Agricultural productivity
>           International agricultural assistance

Farm women's markets
>   USE Farmers' markets

Farm workers
>   USE Agricultural laborers

**Farmers**
>           --[country or state]--[city]
>   CN   Subdivide geographically for place farmer
>           resides.
>   BT   People associated with agriculture

---

BT  Broader term                 RT  Related term                     PN  Public Note
NT  Narrower term               UF  Used for                           +  Term has NTs
HN  History Note                 CN  Catalogers Note                 --[ ]  May subdivide

**Farmers (cont.)**
- NT Sharecroppers
- RT Agricultural laborers
  - Farmers' markets
  - Farming
  - Hog calling
  - Peasants

**Farmers' groups**
  - --[country or state]--[city]
- PN Includes activities and structures.
- CN Double index under ORGANIZATIONS' FACILITIES (or NTs) for images that focus on facilities.
- UF Agricultural groups
  - Agricultural societies
  - Grange
- BT Fraternal organizations
- RT 4-H clubs
  - Farmers' markets
  - Farms

**Farmers' markets**
  - --[country or state]--[city]
- UF Farm women's markets
- BT Markets
- RT Farm produce
  - Farmers
  - Farmers' groups

**Farmhouses**
  - --[country or state]--[city]
- UF Farm houses
- BT Houses
- RT Farms

**Farming**
  - --[country or state]--[city]
- PN For work activities on farms. Search under PLANTS and NTs for specific farm crops. Search also under the subdivision --SUBSISTENCE ACTIVITIES used with indigenous people (Appendix A).
- UF Crops
  - Cultivation of soils
  - Farm crops
  - Fertilizing
  - Field work
  - Planting
  - Seeding
  - Sowing
  - Tilling
- BT Agriculture
  - Land use
- NT Crop rotation
  - Dairy farming
  - Truck farming
- RT Crop dusting
  - Farm life
  - Farmers
  - Farms
  - Food industry
  - Harvesting
  - Homesteading
  - Horticulture
  - Meat industry

**Farming (cont.)**
  - Mowing
  - Plowing

**Farms**
  - --[country or state]--[city]
- PN For tracts of land or water devoted to agricultural purposes.
- UF Farmsteads
  - Farmyards
  - Pastures
- BT Agricultural facilities
- NT Collective farms
  - Fish hatcheries
  - Horse farms
  - Orchards +
  - Plantations +
- RT Croplands
  - Farmers' groups
  - Farmhouses
  - Farming
  - Livestock
  - Outbuildings
  - Ranches
  - Scarecrows

**Farmsteads**
  - USE Farms

**Farmworkers**
  - USE Agricultural laborers

**Farmyards**
  - USE Farms

**Faro**
  - USE Gambling

**Fascism**
  - --[country or state]--[city]
- PN For the subject of fascism in general.
- UF Neo-Nazism
- BT Economic & political systems
- RT Dictators
  - National socialism
  - Totalitarianism

**Fashion**
  - USE Clothing & dress

**Fashion design drawings**
- CN TGM II term.

**Fashion models**
  - --[country or state]--[city]
- UF Models, Fashion
- BT People
- RT Artists' models
  - Clothing & dress
  - Fashion shows
  - Mannequins

**Fashion photographs**
- CN TGM II term.

**Fashion plates**
- CN TGM II term.

**Fashion prints**
- CN TGM II term.

**Fashion shows**
  - --[country or state]--[city]
- UF Style shows
- BT Exhibitions

BT Broader term                          RT Related term                          PN Public Note
NT Narrower term                         UF Used for                              + Term has NTs
HN History Note                          CN Catalogers Note                       --[ ] May subdivide

**Fashion shows (cont.)**
  RT   Clothing & dress
       Fashion models
**Fast food restaurants**
       --[country or state]--[city]
  PN   For establishments where already prepared
       or readily prepared food that can be packaged
       for take-out is served; often run as part of
       chains or franchises.
  UF   Hamburger stands
       Quick-serve restaurants
  BT   Restaurants
  NT   Drive-in restaurants
**Fast food stores**
  USE  Convenience stores
**Fasting**
  USE  Fasts
**Fasts**
       --[country or state]--[city]
  UF   Fasting
  BT   Manners & customs
  RT   Rites & ceremonies
       Starvation
**Fathers & children**
       --[country or state]--[city]
  BT   Families
  RT   Children & adults
       Men
**Fatigue**
  UF   Exhaustion
       Tiredness
       Weariness
  RT   Boredom
       Health
**Fatness**
  USE  Obesity
**Fault finding**
  USE  Blaming
**Fauna, Marine**
  USE  Aquatic animals
**Fear**
  UF   Fright
       Terror
  BT   Mental states
  RT   Anxiety
       Cowardice
       Danger
       Hiding
       Horror dramas
       Shaking
**Feasts**
  USE  Banquets
**Feathering & tarring**
  USE  Tarring & feathering
**Feathers**
  UF   Down
  RT   Birds
       Tarring & feathering
**Feces**
  UF   Crap
       Excrement
       Shit

**Federal agencies**
  USE  Administrative agencies
**Federal debt**
  USE  Public debt
**Federal employment**
  USE  Civil service
**Federal spending**
  USE  Economic policy
**Federal subsidies**
  USE  Assistance
**Feed stores**
       --[country or state]--[city]
  PN   Includes activities and structures.
  BT   Stores & shops
**Feeding of animals**
  USE  Animal feeding
**Feeding of pets**
  USE  Animal feeding
**Feelings**
  USE  Mental states
**Feet**
  RT   Footbinding
       Footprints
       Human body
       Kicking
       Shoes
       Winged feet
**Female figure drawings**
  CN   TGM II term.
**Female gays**
  USE  Lesbians
**Female impersonators**
       --[country or state]--[city]
  UF   Drag queens
  RT   Cross dressing
       Entertainers
       Impersonation
**Feminism**
       --[nationality]--[country or state]--[city]
  PN   For the subject of feminism beyond a
       reaction against sexism or advocacy of
       women's rights. For example, consciousness
       raising, women's solidarity, etc.
  RT   Feminists
       Sexism
       Women's rights
**Feminists**
       --[country or state]--[city]
  PN   Search under FEMINISM for the subject
       of feminism in general and the activities of
       feminists.
  CN   Used in a note under FEMINISM.
  BT   People
  NT   Suffragists
  RT   Feminism
**Fencers**
       --[country or state]--[city]
  CN   Geographical subdivision indicates place
       where fencer is based.
  BT   Athletes
**Fences**
       --[country or state]--[city]

---

BT  Broader term          RT  Related term          PN  Public Note
NT  Narrower term         UF  Used for              +   Term has NTs
HN  History Note          CN  Catalogers Note       --[ ] May subdivide

**Fences (cont.)**
  BT  Site elements
  NT  Electric fences
  RT  Barbed wire
        Corrals
        Gates
        Hedges (Plants)
        Railings
        Walls
**Fencing**
        --[country or state]--[city]
  BT  Sports
  NT  Kendo
  RT  Dueling
        Martial arts
Fens
  USE Wetlands
**Ferns**
        --[country or state]--[city]
  BT  Plants
**Ferries**
        --[nationality]--[country or state]--[city]
  BT  Boats
  NT  Railroad ferries
  RT  Marine terminals
**Ferris wheels**
        --[country or state]--[city]
  BT  Amusement rides
Ferrotypes
  USE Tintypes
Ferry terminals
  USE Marine terminals
**Fertilizer industry**
        --[country or state]--[city]
  PN  Includes activities and structures.
  CN  Double index under INDUSTRIAL
        FACILITIES (or NTs)  for images that focus
        on facilities.
  BT  Chemical industry
Fertilizing
  USE Farming
        Gardening
**Festivals**
        --[country or state]--[city]
  BT  Events
  NT  Art festivals
        Motion picture festivals
        Music festivals
        Winter carnivals
  RT  Anniversaries
        Celebrations
        Durbars
        Fairs
        Holidays
        Pageants
**Festive decorations**
        --[country or state]--[city]
  UF  Decorations, Festive
  BT  Decorations
  NT  Christmas decorations
        Christmas stockings
        Christmas trees

**Festive decorations (cont.)**
        Crèches (Nativity scenes)
  RT  Balloons
        Bouquets
        Drapery
        Holly
        Mistletoe
**Festoons**
        --[country or state]--[city]
  PN  A festive decoration of pendant semiloops
        with attachments and loose ends, especially a
        swag of fabric, or representations of such
        decorations.
  UF  Garlands
  BT  Architectural decorations & ornaments
Fetishes
  USE Amulets
        Talismans
Fetters
  USE Shackles
Fiat money
  USE Currency question
Fiberglass industry
  USE Glass fiber industry
**Fibers**
  NT  Cotton
        Flax
        Henequen
        Jute
        Nylon
        Rayon
        Silk
        Wool
  RT  Plants
        Rope industry
        Sewing
        Textile industry
        Textiles
        Thread
        Yarn
Fibrous glass industry
  USE Glass fiber industry
**Fictitious characters**
  UF  Cartoon characters
        Characters, Fictitious
        Comic characters
        Imaginary beings
        Legendary characters
  NT  Superheroes
  RT  Dwarfs
        Giants
        Literature
        Supernatural beings
        Symbols
        Villains
Fiddles
  USE Violins
Fidelity
  USE Allegiance
Field crops
  USE Plants
**Field hockey**

BT  Broader term                    RT  Related term                    PN  Public Note
NT  Narrower term                    UF  Used for                         + Term has NTs
HN  History Note                     CN  Catalogers Note                  --[ ] May subdivide

**Field hockey (cont.)**
    --[country or state]--[city]
  PN  Includes organizations and activities.
  UF  Hockey
  BT  Sports
  RT  Hockey masks
Field hospitals
  USE Medical aspects of war
Field laborers
  USE Agricultural laborers
Field trials
  USE Animal training
        Hunting
Field trips
  USE School excursions
Field work
  USE Farming
Fields
  USE Meadows
Fields (Agriculture)
  USE Croplands
Fields, Oil
  USE Oil wells
        Petroleum industry
**Fig leaf**
  BT  Symbols
  RT  Nudes
**Fig trees**
    --[country or state]--[city]
  BT  Trees
**Fighter pilots**
    --[nationality]--[country or state]--[city]
  UF  Aces (Fighter pilots)
        Air aces
        Aviators
  BT  Military air pilots
  RT  Air pilots
        Air warfare
**Fighter planes**
    --[nationality]--[country or state]--[city]
  BT  Airplanes
  RT  Air warfare
**Fighting**
    --[country or state]--[city]
  PN  For fistfights and other spontaneous fighting. Search under QUARRELING for verbal fighting.
  CN  Used in a note under QUARRELING.
  UF  Fisticuffs
  NT  Children fighting
        Gunfights
  RT  Boxing
        Gladiators
        Kicking
        Oriental hand-to-hand fighting
        Wrestling
**Figure drawings**
  CN  TGM II term.
  UF  Studies, Figure
Figure skaters
  USE Skaters
Figure skating

Figure skating (cont.)
  USE Ice skating
Figureheads
  USE Ship figureheads
**Filibustering**
    --[country or state]--[city]
  UF  Speaking
        Talking
  BT  Communication
        Political strategies
  RT  Public speaking
Fillies
  USE Horses
Filling stations
  USE Automobile service stations
Film audiences
  USE Motion picture audiences
Film festivals
  USE Motion picture festivals
Film industry (Motion pictures)
  USE Motion picture industry
**Film negatives**
  CN  TGM II term.
  UF  Gelatin silver film negatives
        Silver gelatin film negatives
Film posters
  USE Motion picture posters
**Film stills**
  CN  TGM II term.
  UF  Motion picture stills
        Movie stills
        Production stills
        Stills
**Film transparencies**
  CN  TGM II term.
Filmgoers
  USE Motion picture audiences
Films
  USE Motion pictures
Finance
  USE Business & finance
Financial buildings
  USE Financial facilities
**Financial disclosure**
  PN  For the disclosure of personal finances of public officials and of candidates and appointees for public office.
  UF  Disclosure of personal finances
        Sunshine legislation
  BT  Ethics
  RT  Business & finance
        Politics & government
**Financial facilities**
    --[country or state]--[city]
  HN  Changed 1/1993 from FINANCIAL BUILDINGS.
  UF  Financial buildings
  BT  Commercial facilities
  NT  Banks
        Commodity exchanges
        Merchants' exchanges
        Stock exchanges

---

BT Broader term      RT Related term      PN Public Note
NT Narrower term      UF Used for      + Term has NTs
HN History Note      CN Catalogers Note      --[ ] May subdivide

Financial panics
  USE Business panics
Finger rings
  USE Rings
Fingerprinting
  USE Fingerprints
**Fingerprints**
        --[country or state]--[city]
  PN  For fingerprints and the activity of
        fingerprinting.
  UF  Fingerprinting
  RT  Fingers
        Investigation
**Fingers**
  NT  Crossed fingers
        Pointing fingers
  RT  Fingerprints
        Hands
**Finials**
        --[country or state]--[city]
  BT  Architectural elements
  RT  Roofs
Fiords
  USE Fjords
**Fire**
  PN  For the subject of fire in general and
        non-destructive fires. Search under FIRES for
        destructive fires.
  CN  Used in a note under FIRES.
  UF  Burning
  BT  Natural phenomena
  NT  Campfires
  RT  Burning coal veins
        Fireplaces
        Fires
        Fuelwood
        Heat
        Incinerators
        Matches
        Olympic flame
        Smoke
**Fire alarms**
  BT  Safety equipment
  RT  Fire prevention
Fire boats
  USE Fireboats
Fire departments
  USE Fire stations
Fire dogs
  USE Andirons
**Fire engines & equipment**
        --[country or state]--[city]
  PN  For images that focus on fire engines or
        equipment. Search under FIRES for general
        views in which fire engines and equipment
        are in use.
  CN  Used in a note under WATER TOWERS.
  UF  Fire fighting equipment
        Fire trucks
  NT  Fireboats
  RT  Equipment
        Fire extinguishers

**Fire engines & equipment (cont.)**
        Fire hydrants
        Fire prevention
        Fire stations
        Fires
        Vehicles
**Fire escapes**
        --[country or state]--[city]
  BT  Safety equipment
  RT  Fires
        Lifesaving at fires
**Fire extinguishers**
  BT  Safety equipment
  RT  Fire engines & equipment
**Fire fighters**
        --[country or state]--[city]
  UF  Firefighters
        Firemen
  BT  People associated with health & safety
  RT  Fire prevention
        Fires
        Lifesaving at fires
Fire fighting equipment
  USE Fire engines & equipment
Fire houses
  USE Fire stations
**Fire hydrants**
  BT  Site elements
  RT  Fire engines & equipment
**Fire insurance maps**
  CN  TGM II term.
Fire lanes
  USE Firebreaks
**Fire lookout stations**
        --[country or state]--[city]
  UF  Firewatch towers
        Lookout towers, Fire
        Stations, Fire lookout
  BT  Government facilities
        Watch towers
  RT  Fire stations
        Fires
**Fire prevention**
        --[country or state]--[city]
  RT  Fire alarms
        Fire engines & equipment
        Fire fighters
        Firebreaks
        Fires
        Safety
**Fire screens**
  BT  Furniture
  RT  Fireplaces
**Fire stations**
        --[country or state]--[city]
  PN  Search under FIRES for activities.
  UF  Fire departments
        Fire houses
  BT  Government facilities
  RT  Fire engines & equipment
        Fire lookout stations
Fire trucks

Fire trucks (cont.)
  USE Fire engines & equipment
**Firearms**
  PN  For weapons from which missiles, as
      bullets, balls, or shells, are hurled by the
      action of explosives.
  UF  Guns
      Small arms
  BT  Arms & armament
  NT  Handguns
      Machine guns +
      Rifles
  RT  Artillery (Weaponry)
      Bullet holes
      Bullets
      Firearms control
      Firearms industry
      Gunfights
      Gunsmithing
      Shooting
**Firearms control**
      --[country or state]
  UF  Control of guns
      Gun control
      Handgun control
  BT  Law & legal affairs
  RT  Civil liberties
      Firearms
**Firearms industry**
      --[country or state]--[city]
  PN  Includes activities and structures.
  CN  Double index under INDUSTRIAL
      FACILITIES (or NTs)  for images that focus
      on facilities.
  BT  Industry
  RT  Firearms
      Gunsmithing
      Ordnance industry
**Firebird (Mythical bird)**
  BT  Supernatural beings
  RT  Birds
**Fireboats**
      --[nationality]--[country or state]--[city]
  UF  Fire boats
  BT  Boats
      Fire engines & equipment
**Firebreaks**
      --[country or state]--[city]
  PN  A strip of land cleared to stop the spread
      of fire, as in a forest or prairie.
  UF  Fire lanes
  RT  Fire prevention
      Fires
**Firecrackers**
      --[country or state]--[city]
  BT  Fireworks
Firefighters
  USE Fire fighters
Firemen
  USE Fire fighters
**Fireplaces**
      --[country or state]--[city]

Fireplaces (cont.)
  UF  Hearths
  BT  Architectural elements
  RT  Andirons
      Chimneypieces
      Chimneys
      Fire
      Fire screens
      Mantels
Fireproof construction
  USE Fire-resistive construction
**Fires**
      --[country or state]--[city]
  PN  For destructive fires. Includes the event
      and any resulting damage. Search under FIRE
      for the general subject of fire and for
      non-destructive fires.
  CN  Used in a note under FIRE ENGINES &
      EQUIPMENT and FIRE STATIONS.
  UF  Conflagrations
  NT  Forest fires
      Grassland fires
  RT  Book burning
      Burning at the stake
      Disasters
      Fire
      Fire engines & equipment
      Fire escapes
      Fire fighters
      Fire lookout stations
      Fire prevention
      Firebreaks
      Fire-resistive construction
      Lifesaving at fires
      Smoke
Firewatch towers
  USE Fire lookout stations
Firewood
  USE Fuelwood
**Fireworks**
      --[country or state]--[city]
  BT  Explosives
  NT  Firecrackers
  RT  Holidays
**Fire-resistive construction**
      --[country or state]--[city]
  PN  Method of construction that prevents or
      retards the passage of hot gases or flames.
  UF  Fireproof construction
  BT  Construction
  RT  Fires
Firing of employees
  USE Dismissal of employees
**Firing squads**
      --[country or state]--[city]
  BT  Executioners
  RT  Executions
Firms
  USE Business enterprises
**Firs**
  BT  Trees
First ladies

---

BT Broader term
NT Narrower term
HN History Note

RT Related term
UF Used for
CN Catalogers Note

PN Public Note
+ Term has NTs
--[ ] May subdivide

First ladies (cont.)
USE Presidents' spouses
First nights
USE Premieres
**Firsts**
    --[country or state]--[city]
PN  For figurative milestones. Search under
    MILESTONES for milestones that measure
    distance.
CN  Used in a note under MILESTONES.
BT  Events
RT  Curiosities & wonders
    History
    World records
Fiscal policy
USE Economic policy
**Fish**
    --[country or state]
PN  For images of fish. Search under FISHING
    for activities.
UF  Fishes
BT  Aquatic animals
NT  Bass
    Bluefish
    Catfish
    Codfish
    Halibut
    Pickerel
    Pike
    Sailfish
    Salmon
    Shad
    Sharks
    Sunfish
    Swordfish
    Tarpon
    Trout
    Tuna
RT  Fish hatcheries
    Fish ladders
    Fishing
    Seafood stores
    Shellfish
**Fish drying**
    --[country or state]--[city]
UF  Drying of fish
RT  Curing (Preservation)
    Fishing
    Food drying
    Food industry
**Fish hatcheries**
    --[country or state]--[city]
UF  Fisheries
    Hatcheries, Fish
BT  Farms
RT  Fish
    Fishing industry
Fish hawks
USE Ospreys
**Fish ladders**
    --[country or state[--[city]
BT  Site elements

Fish ladders (cont.)
RT  Conservation of natural resources
    Fish
    Streams
Fish stores
USE Seafood stores
Fisheries
USE Fish hatcheries
    Fishing industry
**Fishermen**
    --[country or state]--[city]
PN  For fishermen away from the context of
    their activity. Search under FISHING for
    activities.
CN  Subdivide geographically for place
    fisherman resides.
UF  Sea farers
RT  Sailors
Fishes
USE Fish
**Fishing**
    --[country or state]
PN  For the subject of fishing in general and
    fishing as a local livelihood. Includes
    portraits of fishermen with their catch. Search
    under FISHING INDUSTRY for large-scale
    fishing. Search also under the subdivision
    --SUBSISTENCE ACTIVITIES used with
    indigenous peoples (Appendix A).
CN  Double index under the type of fish. Used
    in a note under FISHERMEN, FISHING &
    HUNTING GEAR, and FISHING
    INDUSTRY.
UF  Angling
    Fly fishing
    Recreational fishing
    Sport fishing
NT  Big game fishing +
    Children fishing
    Fishing industry
    Ice fishing
    Spear fishing
    Sponge fishing
    Surf fishing
RT  Fish
    Fish drying
    Fishing & hunting gear
    Game preserves
    Hunting
    Hunting & fishing clubs
    Vessels
**Fishing industry**
    --[country or state]--[city]
PN  For large-scale fishing. Search under
    FISHING for fishing in general or as a local
    livelihood.
CN  Double index under the fish. Used in a
    note under FISHING. Double index under
    INDUSTRIAL FACILITIES (or NTs) for
    images that focus on facilities.
UF  Fisheries
BT  Fishing

---

**Fishing industry (cont.)**
      Industry
  RT  Fish hatcheries
      Food industry
      Shellfish industry
      Whaling
**Fishing nets**
      --[country or state]--[city]
  UF  Nets, Fish
  BT  Fishing & hunting gear
      Nets
  RT  Fishing weirs
Fishing tackle
  USE Fishing & hunting gear
**Fishing weirs**
      --[country or state]--[city]
  BT  Animal traps
  RT  Fishing nets
**Fishing & hunting gear**
  PN  For images that focus on the equipment.
      Search under FISHING and under HUNTING
      for activities using the equipment.
  UF  Fishing tackle
      Hunting gear
  BT  Equipment
  NT  Animal traps +
      Decoys (Hunting)
      Fishing nets
  RT  Arms & armament
      Fishing
      Hunting
      Sporting goods
Fisticuffs
  USE Fighting
**Fists**
  CN  Used in a note under SYMBOLS.
  UF  Clenched fists
  BT  Hands
Fitness, Physical
  USE Physical fitness
Fittings, Sanitary
  USE Plumbing fixtures
Five & ten cent stores
  USE Variety stores
Five-year plans
  USE Economic policy
Fixtures, Plumbing
  USE Plumbing fixtures
**Fjords**
      --[country or state]
  PN  Narrow deep inlets of the sea between
      cliffs or steep slopes.
  UF  Fiords
  BT  Bays
**Flag bearers**
      --[country or state]--[city]
  UF  Color guards
  BT  People
  RT  Military organizations
Flag poles
  USE Flagpoles
**Flag salutes**

**Flag salutes (cont.)**
      --[country or state]--[city]
  BT  Saluting
  RT  Flags
      Patriotism
      Pledges of allegiance
**Flagpoles**
      --[country or state]--[city]
  UF  Flag poles
  BT  Site elements
  RT  Flags
**Flags**
      --[nationality]
  CN  Used in a note under PATRIOTISM.
  NT  Military standards
      Signal flags
      State flags
  RT  Banners
      Flag salutes
      Flagpoles
**Flamingos**
      --[country or state]
  BT  Birds
Flanking windows
  USE Sidelights
**Flappers**
  CN  Used in a note under CLOTHING &
      DRESS.
  BT  Women
**Flash photographs**
  CN  TGM II term.
**Flat tires**
  BT  Tires
  RT  Traffic accidents
**Flatboats**
      --[country or state]--[city]
  UF  Riverboats
  BT  Boats
Flatirons
  USE Irons (Pressing)
Flats
  USE Apartment houses
      Apartments
**Flattery**
  BT  Communication
  RT  Manners & customs
**Flax**
      --[country or state]--[city]
  UF  Baltic hemp
  BT  Fibers
      Plants
  RT  Linen industry
      Textiles
Flax industry
  USE Linen industry
**Flea markets**
      --[country or state]--[city]
  BT  Markets
  RT  Secondhand sales
**Fleur-de-lis**
  BT  Emblems
Fliers

---

BT  Broader term
NT  Narrower term
HN  History Note

RT  Related term
UF  Used for
CN  Catalogers Note

PN  Public Note
+  Term has NTs
--[ ]  May subdivide

Fliers (cont.)
   USE Fliers (Printed matter)
**Fliers (Printed matter)**
   CN   TGM II term.
   UF   Fliers
        Flyers (Printed matter)
**Flies**
        --[country or state]
   BT   Insects
**Flight crews**
        --[nationality]--[country or state]--[city]
   UF   Air crews
        Aircraft crews
        Aviation personnel
        Flight personnel
   BT   People associated with transportation
   RT   Aeronautics
        Air pilots
        Aircraft
        Astronauts
        Military personnel
Flight personnel
   USE Flight crews
**Flight testing**
        --[country or state]--[city]
   CN   Double index under type of aircraft, as
        appropriate.
   UF   Aircraft testing
        Test flights
   BT   Testing
   RT   Aeronautics
        Aircraft
**Flight training**
        --[country or state]--[city]
   BT   Vocational education
   RT   Aeronautics
**Flights around the world**
   UF   Around-the-world flights
   RT   Aeronautics
Flirtation
   USE Courtship
**Floating batteries**
        --[country or state]--[city]
   UF   Water artillery
   BT   Batteries (Weaponry)
   RT   Armored vessels
        Gunboats
Floating bridges
   USE Pontoon bridges
Floating platforms
   USE Landing floats
**Floats (Parades)**
        --[country or state]--[city]
   BT   Vehicles
   RT   Parades & processions
Floats, Landing
   USE Landing floats
Flogging
   USE Whipping
**Flood control**
        --[country or state]--[city]
   RT   Erosion protection works

**Flood control (cont.)**
        Floods
**Floods**
        --[country or state]--[city]
   PN   Includes the event and any resulting
        damage.
   UF   Inundations
   BT   Natural phenomena
   RT   Bodies of water
        Disasters
        Flood control
        Noah's ark
        Storms
**Floor coverings**
   UF   Carpets
        Rugs
   BT   Furnishings
   RT   Red carpet
        Textiles
**Floor plans**
   CN   TGM II term.
**Floors**
        --[country or state]--[city]
   BT   Architectural elements
   RT   Mosaic pavements
Flophouses
   USE Hotels
        Lodging houses
**Florist shops**
        --[country or state]--[city]
   PN   Includes activities and structures.
   UF   Flower shops
   BT   Stores & shops
   RT   Flowers
**Flour & meal industry**
        --[country or state]--[city]
   PN   Includes activities and structures.
   CN   Double index under INDUSTRIAL
        FACILITIES (or NTs) for images that focus
        on facilities.
   UF   Meal industry
        Milling trade
   BT   Food industry
   RT   Grains
Flower leis
   USE Leis
**Flower pots**
   BT   Plant containers
   RT   Flowers
Flower shops
   USE Florist shops
**Flower shows**
        --[country or state]--[city]
   BT   Exhibitions
   RT   Flowers
**Flowers**
        --[country or state]--[city]
   CN   Used in a note under PEONIES and
        RHODODENDRONS.
   UF   Blossoms
   NT   California poppies
        Carnations

---

BT  Broader term                RT  Related term              PN  Public Note
NT  Narrower term               UF  Used for                  +  Term has NTs
HN  History Note                CN  Catalogers Note           --[ ] May subdivide

**Flowers (cont.)**
- Chrysanthemums
- Daffodils
- Daisies
- Goldenrod
- Lilies
- Morning glories
- Orchids +
- Pansies
- Roses
- Sunflowers
- Tulips
- Violets
- Water lilies
- Wildflowers
- RT   Artificial flowers
- Bouquets
- Dried plant arrangements
- Florist shops
- Flower pots
- Flower shows
- Leis
- Plants

Fluorescent works
  USE Luminous works

**Flutes**
- PN   Includes the activity of playing flutes.
- BT   Wind instruments
- NT   Recorders

Fly fishing
  USE Fishing

Fly swatting
  USE Pest control

Flyers (Printed matter)
  USE Fliers (Printed matter)

Flying facades
  USE False fronts

**Flypaper**
- PN   Paper poisoned or coated with sticky substance for killing flies.
- BT   Animal traps
- RT   Insects
- Pest control

Foals
  USE Horses

**Fog**
- --[country or state]--[city]
- BT   Weather
- RT   Fog control

**Fog control**
- --[country or state]--[city]
- BT   Weather control
- RT   Fog

**Folding doors**
- --[country or state]--[city]
- BT   Doors & doorways

Foliage
  USE Leaves

**Folk dancing**
- --[country or state]--[city]
- PN   Search also under the subdivision
  --DANCE used with names of ethnic, racial,

**Folk dancing (cont.)**
- and regional groups, and classes of persons (Appendix A).
- BT   Dancing
- NT   Square dancing
- RT   Folk music
- Hoedowns (Parties)

**Folk music**
- --[country or state]--[city]
- UF   Traditional music
- BT   Music
- NT   Folk songs
- RT   Folk dancing
- Hoedowns (Parties)

**Folk songs**
- BT   Folk music
- Songs

**Folklorists**
- BT   People associated with education & communication
- RT   Scholars

Follies, Architectural
  USE Architectural follies

**Fonts**
- --[country or state]--[city]
- UF   Baptismal fonts
- BT   Religious architectural elements
- RT   Baptisms
- Churches
- Furnishings

**Food**
- --[country or state]--[city]
- NT   Baked products +
- Beverages +
- Condiments
- Confections +
- Dairy products +
- Fruit +
- Margarine
- Meat +
- Nuts +
- Pancakes & waffles
- Pasta products
- Peanut butter
- Prepared cereals
- Preserves
- Sandwiches
- Spices +
- Sugar
- Vegetables +
- RT   Animals
- Cereal products
- Cookery
- Eating & drinking
- Eating & drinking facilities
- Farm produce
- Food adulteration & inspection
- Food industry
- Foraging
- Nutrition

**Food adulteration & inspection**
- --[country or state]--[city]

| | | |
|---|---|---|
| BT Broader term | RT Related term | PN Public Note |
| NT Narrower term | UF Used for | + Term has NTs |
| HN History Note | CN Catalogers Note | --[ ] May subdivide |

**Food adulteration & inspection (cont.)**
  UF  Adulterations
        Analysis of food
        Food inspection
        Inspection of food
  RT  Consumer protection
        Food
        Health
        Investigation
        Product inspection
        Testing
**Food aid programs**
  USE Food relief
**Food drying**
        --[country or state]--[city]
  UF  Dehydration of food
        Drying of food
        Evaporation of food
  RT  Curing (Preservation)
        Fish drying
        Food industry
        Home food processing
**Food gathering**
  USE Foraging
**Food industry**
        --[country or state]--[city]
  PN  Includes activities and structures.
  CN  Double index under INDUSTRIAL
        FACILITIES (or NTs) for images that focus
        on facilities.
  UF  Canneries
        Canning & preserving
        Food preparation
        Food processing
        Food processing plants
        Processing food
  BT  Industry
  NT  Beverage industry +
        Chewing gum industry
        Chocolate industry
        Cocoa industry
        Dairy products industry
        Dairying
        Flour & meal industry
        Fruit industry +
        Kosher food industry
        Meat industry
        Olive oil industry
        Shellfish industry
        Sugar industry +
        Vinegar industry
  RT  Agriculture
        Farming
        Fish drying
        Fishing industry
        Food
        Food drying
        Grain industry
        Home food processing
        Plantations
        Ranches
**Food inspection**

**Food inspection (cont.)**
  USE Food adulteration & inspection
**Food lines**
  USE Bread & soup lines
**Food preparation**
  USE Cookery
        Food industry
        Home food processing
**Food prices**
        --[country or state]--[city]
  UF  Price of food
  BT  Prices
**Food processing**
  USE Food industry
        Home food processing
**Food processing plants**
  USE Food industry
**Food relief**
        --[country or state]--[city]
  UF  Food aid programs
        Food stamps
  BT  Assistance
  NT  Bread & soup lines
  RT  Disaster relief
        Disaster victims
        Famines
        Starvation
**Food stamps**
  USE Food relief
**Food stands**
  USE Food vendors
**Food storage buildings**
        --[country or state]--[city]
  BT  Agricultural facilities
  NT  Corn cribs
        Grain elevators
        Granaries
        Silos
  RT  Storage facilities
**Food vendors**
        --[country or state]--[city]
  CN  Double index under type of food sold.
  UF  Food stands
        Refreshment stands
  BT  Business enterprises
  RT  Peddlers
        Vending stands
**Fools & jesters**
  UF  Jesters
  BT  Entertainers
  RT  Clowns
        Fools' caps
**Foolscaps (Headgear)**
  USE Fools' caps
**Fools' caps**
  PN  Caps or hoods, usually with bells, worn by
        fools or jesters; also, conical caps for slow or
        lazy students.
  UF  Dunce caps
        Foolscaps (Headgear)
  BT  Hats
  RT  Fools & jesters

---

BT  Broader term     RT  Related term     PN Public Note
NT  Narrower term    UF  Used for       + Term has NTs
HN History Note     CN Catalogers Note    --[ ] May subdivide

**Fools' caps (cont.)**
      School discipline
**Foot bridges**
  USE Pedestrian bridges
**Foot prints**
  USE Footprints
**Foot trails**
  USE Trails & paths
**Foot wear**
  USE Footwear
**Football**
      --[country or state]--[city]
  PN  Includes organizations and activities.
  BT  Sports
  RT  Football players
**Football players**
      --[country or state]--[city]
  CN  Geographical subdivision indicates place
      where team or player is based.
  BT  Athletes
  RT  Football
**Footbinding**
      --[country or state]--[city]
  UF  Foot-binding
  RT  Feet
**Footbridges**
  USE Pedestrian bridges
**Footpaths**
  USE Trails & paths
**Footprints**
  UF  Foot prints
  RT  Animal tracks
      Feet
**Footwear**
  HN  Changed 8/1988 from non-postable term
      (Use SHOES).
  UF  Foot wear
  BT  Clothing & dress
  NT  Boots
      Shoes
  RT  Shoe industry
      Shoe stores
**Foot-binding**
  USE Footbinding
**Fops**
  USE Dandies
**Forage**
  USE Foraging
**Foraging**
      --[nationality]--[country or state]--[city]
  PN  Searching for food or provisions.
  UF  Food gathering
      Forage
      Gathering food
  RT  Confiscations
      Food
      Hunting
      Military life
      Ragpicking
      Searching
**Fords (Stream crossings)**
      --[country or state]

**Fords (Stream crossings) (cont.)**
  PN  Includes the activity of fording.
  UF  Crossings, Low water
      Low water crossings
      River fords
      Stream fords
  RT  Streams
      Transportation
**Forecasting**
      --[country or state]--[city]
  PN  Predicting future events or developments
      by means other than supernatural practices or
      interpretation of omens.
  UF  Forecasts
      Prediction
  RT  Conjectural works
      Visionary architecture
      Warnings
**Forecasts**
  USE Forecasting
**Foreign aid programs**
  USE International economic assistance
**Foreign aid to agriculture**
  USE International agricultural assistance
**Foreign participation in war**
      --[nationality]--[country or state]--[city]
  PN  For participation of foreigners as soldiers
      in wars in which their country is not a primary
      party, e.g., the Lincoln Brigade fighting in the
      Spanish Civil War.
  RT  International relations
      Mercenaries (Soldiers)
      War
**Foreign relations**
  USE International relations
**Foreign trade**
  USE Commerce
**Foreign workers**
  USE Alien laborers
**Foreigners**
  USE Aliens
      Tourist trade
**Forensic photographs**
  CN  TGM II term.
  UF  Crime photographs
      Evidence photographs
      Legal photographs
      Police photographs
      Surveillance photographs
**Forest fires**
      --[country or state]--[city]
  BT  Fires
**Forest reserves**
      --[country or state]
  UF  National forests
  BT  National parks & reserves
**Forestry**
      --[country or state]--[city]
  PN  For the subject of forestry in general and
      the activities of foresters.
  BT  Science
  RT  Agriculture

BT Broader term          RT Related term          PN Public Note
NT Narrower term        UF Used for            + Term has NTs
HN History Note           CN Catalogers Note      --[ ] May subdivide

**Forestry (cont.)**
        Cutover lands
        Forests
        Rangers
**Forests**
        --[country or state]--[city]
UF   Woods
BT   Land
NT   Petrified forests
       Tropical forests
RT   Forestry
       Trees
       Wooding stations
**Forge shops**
        --[country or state]--[city]
PN   Search under FORGING for activities.
UF   Blacksmith shops
       Forges
       Smitheries
       Smithies
BT   Workshops
RT   Forging
       Foundries
**Forgeries**
CN   TGM II term.
UF   Counterfeits
Forges
  USE Forge shops
**Forging**
        --[country or state]--[city]
PN   Forming a metal into a particular shape by
       heating and hammering.
CN   Used in a note under FORGE SHOPS.
BT   Metalworking
NT   Blacksmithing
RT   Forge shops
**Formation photographs**
CN   TGM II term.
Formations, Rock
  USE Rock formations
Formica
  USE Laminated plastics
**Forms**
CN   TGM II term.
**Forts & fortifications**
        --[nationality]--[country or state]--[city]
PN   Fortified places occupied by troops or
       permanent army posts. Includes activities &
       structures.
UF   Citadels
       Defenses
       Ramparts
BT   Military facilities
RT   Barricades
       Batteries (Weaponry)
       Battlements
       Blockhouses
       Bombproof construction
       Castles & palaces
       City walls
       Gun turrets
       Martello towers

**Forts & fortifications (cont.)**
        Military camps
        Moats
        Watch towers
**Fortune telling**
        --[country or state]--[city]
PN   Includes activities and structures.
UF   Crystal ball gazing
       Fortunetelling
       Gazing into a crystal ball
       Palmistry
       Predictions
       Scrying
RT   Astrology
       Crystal balls
       Divination
       Prophecy
       Warnings
**Fortune telling cards**
CN   TGM II term.
Fortunes
  USE Wealth
Fortunetelling
  USE Fortune telling
**Forums**
        --[country or state]--[city]
PN   Roman public squares surrounded by
       monumental buildings.
BT   Sites
RT   Government facilities
       Markets
       Plazas
       Social & civic facilities
**Fossils**
        --[country or state]--[city]
RT   Animals
       Paleontology
       Petrified forests
       Petrified wood
       Plants
**Foster home care**
        --[country or state]--[city]
RT   Asylums
       Children
Foundation stones, Laying of
  USE Cornerstone laying
**Founders' Day commemorations**
        --[country or state]--[city]
PN   Search also under the subdivision
       --COMMEMORATION used with names of
       corporate bodies and named events (Appendix
       D).
BT   Rites & ceremonies
RT   Anniversaries
**Founding**
        --[country or state]--[city]
PN   Forming a metal by melting and pouring in
       a mold; casting.
CN   Used in a note under FOUNDRIES.
BT   Metalworking
RT   Foundries
**Foundries**

---

BT  Broader term
NT  Narrower term
HN  History Note

RT  Related term
UF  Used for
CN  Catalogers Note

PN  Public Note
+  Term has NTs
--[ ]  May subdivide

**Foundries (cont.)**
--[country or state]--[city]
PN For images that focus on facilities. Search under FOUNDING for activities.
CN When appropriate, double index under industry, e.g., STEEL INDUSTRY.
BT Factories
RT Forge shops
  Founding
  Metallurgical industry
  Smelters

**Fountains**
--[country or state]--[city]
BT Hydraulic facilities
RT Ablution fountains
  Landscape architecture facilities

Fountains, Ablution
 USE Ablution fountains
Fourth terms, Presidential
 USE Presidential terms of office
Four-H clubs
 USE 4-H clubs
Fowling
 USE Game bird hunting
Fowls
 USE Poultry

**Fox hunting**
--[country or state]
BT Hunting
RT Foxes

**Foxes**
--[country or state]
BT Animals
RT Fox hunting

**Foxholes**
PN A pit dug for individual cover from enemy fire.
RT Campaigns & battles
  Trench warfare

Foyers
 USE Entrance halls
  Lobbies
Fractur
 USE Fraktur

**Fractures**
UF Bone fractures
RT Bones

**Fraktur**
CN TGM II term.
UF Fractur
Frames (Picture)
 USE Picture frames
Frames (Structures)
 USE Structural frames

**Framing drawings**
CN TGM II term.
UF Drawings, Framing
Franchise
 USE Suffrage

**Frankfurters**
--[country or state]--[city]
UF Hot dogs

**Frankfurters (cont.)**
  Wieners
BT Sausages

**Franking privilege**
UF Penalty mail
BT Postal service rates
Fraternal buildings
 USE Fraternal lodges

**Fraternal lodges**
--[country or state]--[city]
UF Fraternal buildings
  Lodges, Fraternal
BT Organizations' facilities
RT Clubhouses

**Fraternal organizations**
--[country or state]--[city]
PN Includes activities and structures.
CN Double index under ORGANIZATIONS' FACILITIES (or NTs) for images that focus on facilities.
UF Benevolent societies
  Friendly societies
  Masonic organizations
  Secret societies
BT Organizations
NT Farmers' groups
  Fraternities & sororities
RT Charitable organizations
  Clubs
  Patriotic societies

**Fraternities & sororities**
--[country or state]--[city]
PN For fraternal organizations associated with colleges and universities, including their professional fraternities, honor societies, and social societies. Includes activities and structures.
CN Double index under ORGANIZATIONS' FACILITIES (or NTs) for images that focus on facilities.
UF College fraternities
  Sororities
BT Fraternal organizations
RT Initiation rites

**Fraternization**
--[nationality]--[country or state]--[city]
PN To engage in comradely exchange or associate on intimate terms, especially with enemy soldiers or with civilians of an occupied country and often contrary to military orders.
UF Collaboration
BT Interpersonal relations
RT Soldiers
  War

**Fratricides**
--[country or state]--[city]
BT Homicides

**Fraud**
--[country or state]--[city]
CN Used in a note under HUMAN CURIOSITIES.

---

BT Broader term     RT Related term     PN Public Note
NT Narrower term    UF Used for       + Term has NTs
HN History Note     CN Catalogers Note    --[ ] May subdivide

**Fraud (cont.)**
- UF   Fakes
     Hoaxes
     Misrepresentation (Law)
- BT   Ethics
- RT   Counterfeiting
     Deception
     False advertising
     Honesty
     Impersonation
     Quacks

Freaks
- USE Human curiosities
     Monsters

**Freckles**
- RT   Human body

Free clinics
- USE Clinics

Free coinage
- USE Currency question

**Free love**
- UF   Sexual freedom
- RT   Courtship
     Ethics
     Love
     Marriage

Free silver issue
- USE Silver question

Free soil movement
- USE Abolition movement

Free speech
- USE Freedom of speech

**Free trade & protection**
- --[country or state]--[city]
- UF   Fair trade
     Protection of free trade
- BT   Commerce
     Economic policy
- NT   Reciprocity
- RT   Government regulation
     Tariffs

Freebooters
- USE Pirates

Freed slaves
- USE Freedmen

**Freedmen**
- --[country or state]--[city]
- UF   Freed slaves
- BT   People
- RT   Slaves

Freedom
- USE Liberty

Freedom from discrimination
- USE Civil rights

Freedom of expression
- USE Freedom of religion
     Freedom of speech

**Freedom of information**
- --[country or state]
- UF   Information, Freedom of
     Intellectual freedom
     Right to know

**Freedom of information (cont.)**
- BT   Civil liberties
- RT   Censorship

**Freedom of religion**
- --[country or state]
- UF   Expression, Freedom of
     Freedom of expression
     Religious liberty
- BT   Civil liberties
- RT   Conscientious objectors
     Dissenters
     Religion

**Freedom of speech**
- --[country or state]
- UF   Expression, Freedom of
     Free speech
     Freedom of expression
     Intellectual freedom
- BT   Civil liberties
- NT   Freedom of the press
- RT   Censorship
     Dissenters
     Libel & slander
     Sedition

**Freedom of the press**
- --[country or state]
- BT   Freedom of speech
- RT   Press

**Freedom of the seas**
- UF   Closed seas
     Open seas
- BT   Law & legal affairs
- RT   International relations
     Territorial waters

Freeways
- USE Express highways

**Freezers**
- BT   Refrigerators

Freight
- USE Shipping

Freight car hopping
- USE Freighthopping

Freight cars
- USE Railroad freight cars

**Freight handlers' strikes**
- --[country or state]--[city]
- BT   Strikes
- NT   Longshoremen's strikes
- RT   Shipping

Freight handling
- USE Shipping

Freight holds
- USE Cargo holds

Freight planes
- USE Transport planes

Freight ships
- USE Cargo ships

Freight wagons
- USE Carts & wagons

Freighters
- USE Cargo ships

**Freighthopping**

---

BT  Broader term                    RT  Related term                    PN  Public Note
NT  Narrower term                   UF  Used for                        +  Term has NTs
HN  History Note                    CN  Catalogers Note                 --[ ] May subdivide

**Freighthopping (cont.)**
    --[country or state]--[city]
  UF  Freight car hopping
        Hopping, Freight car
        Riding, Freight car
  BT  Travel
  RT  Hitchhiking
        Railroad freight cars
        Stowaways
        Tramps
**French doors**
    --[country or state]--[city]
  UF  Casement doors
        Door windows
        French windows
  BT  Doors & doorways
  RT  Windows
French tissues
  USE Tissue stereographs
French windows
  USE French doors
Frescoes
  USE Murals
Friars
  USE Monks
Friday the 13th
  USE Superstitions
Friend churches
  USE Friends' meeting houses
Friend meeting houses
  USE Friends' meeting houses
Friendliness
  USE Friendship
Friendly societies
  USE Fraternal organizations
**Friendship**
  UF  Affection
        Friendliness
  BT  Interpersonal relations
  RT  Love
**Friends' meeting houses**
    --[country or state]--[city]
  PN  For images that focus on buildings, as
        well as the associated grounds.
  UF  Friend churches
        Friend meeting houses
        Meeting houses, Friend
        Quaker meeting houses
  BT  Protestant churches
**Friezes (Entablature components)**
    --[country or state]--[city]
  PN  For middle horizontal members of
        classical entablatures above the architrave and
        below the cornice. Search under FRIEZES
        (ORNAMENTAL BANDS) for horizontal
        bands decorating architecture, furniture, or
        other objects and containing figures, scenes,
        or ornamental motifs.
  HN  Changed 1/1993 from FRIEZES.
  BT  Architectural elements
  RT  Entablatures
**Friezes (Ornamental bands)**

**Friezes (Ornamental bands) (cont.)**
    --[country or state]--[city]
  PN  For horizontal bands decorating
        architecture, furniture, or other objects and
        containing figures, scenes, or ornamental
        motifs.  Search under FRIEZES
        (ENTABLATURE COMPONENTS) for
        specific parts of classical entablatures.
  HN  Changed 1/1993 from FRIEZES.
  BT  Architectural decorations & ornaments
Fright
  USE Fear
Fringe benefits
  USE Employee fringe benefits
**Frisking**
    --[country or state]--[city]
  UF  Searches & seizures
  BT  Searching
  RT  Law enforcement
**Frogs**
    --[country or state]
  BT  Amphibians
**Frontier & pioneer life**
    --[country or state]--[city]
  UF  Pioneer life
  BT  Country life
  RT  Colonists
        Discovery & exploration
        Fur trade
        Ghost towns
        Packtrains
        Pioneers
        Pony express
        Prospecting
        Trading posts
        Wagon trains
        Westerns
        Westward movement
**Frontispieces**
  CN  TGM II term.
Frontons
  USE Pediments
**Frost**
    --[country or state]--[city]
  BT  Natural phenomena
  RT  Winter
**Fruit**
    --[country or state]--[city]
  PN  For the subject of edible fruit in general
        and images that focus on fruit.
  BT  Food
  NT  Apples
        Bananas
        Berries +
        Cherries
        Citrus fruit +
        Coconuts
        Dates
        Grapes +
        Melons +
        Olives
        Peaches

---

**Fruit (cont.)**
    Pears
    Pineapples
    Plums +
    Pumpkins +
    Tomatoes
    RT    Fruit industry
          Orchards
          Plants
          Preserves
Fruit box labels
    USE Fruit crate labels
**Fruit crate labels**
    CN    TGM II term.
    UF    Crate labels, Fruit
          Fruit box labels
**Fruit industry**
          --[country or state]--[city]
    PN    Includes activities and structures.
    CN    Double index under INDUSTRIAL
          FACILITIES (or NTs) for images that focus
          on facilities. Double index under the fruit.
    BT    Food industry
    NT    Citrus fruit industry
    RT    Fruit
          Orchards
**Fuel**
          --[country or state]--[city]
    NT    Coal +
          Fuelwood
          Gasoline
          Natural gas
          Peat
    RT    Air refueling
          Charcoal
          Fuel prices
          Fuel supply
          Fuel tanks
          Fuel trade
**Fuel prices**
          --[country or state]--[city]
    BT    Prices
    NT    Gasoline prices
    RT    Fuel
**Fuel supply**
    RT    Fuel
          Petroleum industry
**Fuel tanks**
    BT    Containers
    RT    Fuel
          Storage tanks
**Fuel trade**
          --[country or state]--[city]
    PN    Manufacture and trade of fuel. Includes
          activities and structures.
    CN    Double index under INDUSTRIAL
          FACILITIES (or NTs) for images that focus
          on facilities.
    BT    Business enterprises
    RT    Fuel
          Gas industry
          Petroleum industry

Fuel wood
    USE Fuelwood
**Fuelwood**
          --[country or state]--[city]
    PN    For images that focus on segments of
          small trees and branches to be used for fires,
          including woodpiles. Search under
          WOODCUTTING for activities.
    CN    Used in a note under LOGS.
    UF    Firewood
          Fuel wood
          Woodpiles
    BT    Fuel
    RT    Fire
          Fuelwood gathering
          Woodcutting
**Fuelwood gathering**
          --[country or state]--[city]
    UF    Fagoting
          Gathering fuelwood
          Wood gathering
    RT    Fuelwood
**Fugitive slaves**
          --[country or state]--[city]
    UF    Runaway slaves
          Slave fugitives
    BT    Refugees
          Slaves
    RT    Underground railroad system
Fujichrome transparencies
    USE Dye coupler transparencies
Fujicolor negatives
    USE Dye coupler negatives
**Full dinner pail**
    BT    Symbols
    RT    Empty market basket
Fund raisers
    USE Fund raising
**Fund raising**
          --[country or state]--[city]
    PN    Entertainments, events, etc., to raise
          money for persons or causes. Search under
          MEMBERSHIP CAMPAIGNS for the raising
          of money for organizations through
          membership drives.
    UF    Benefits (Fund raising)
          Fund raisers
          Fundraisers
          Money raising
    RT    Christmas seals
          Lotteries
          Membership campaigns
          Money
          Organizations
          Political campaign funds
          War bonds & funds
Fundraisers
    USE Fund raising
Funeral directing
    USE Undertaking
Funeral homes
    USE Morgues & mortuaries

BT  Broader term                    RT  Related term                    PN  Public Note
NT  Narrower term                   UF  Used for                        +   Term has NTs
HN  History Note                    CN  Catalogers Note                 --[ ] May subdivide

**Funeral processions**
  --[country or state]--[city]
  BT   Funeral rites & ceremonies
       Parades & processions
**Funeral rites & ceremonies**
  --[country or state]--[city]
  PN   For rites and ceremonies in memory of
       persons, with the deceased present; also for
       customs associated with mourning. Search
       under MEMORIAL RITES &
       CEREMONIES for rites and ceremonies
       without the presence of the deceased. Search
       also under the subdivision --DEATH &
       BURIAL used with names of persons
       (Appendix B).
  CN   Used in a note under MEMORIAL RITES
       & CEREMONIES.
  UF   Burials
       Mortuary customs
       Mourning customs
       Obsequies
  BT   Rites & ceremonies
  NT   Burials at sea
       Funeral processions
       Lying in state
       Scaffold burial
  RT   Coffins
       Cremation
       Dead persons
       Death
       Gravedigging
       Hearses
       Mass burials
       Memorial rites & ceremonies
       Mummies
       Undertaking
**Funeral urns**
  USE Urns
**Funerary facilities**
  --[country or state]--[city]
  BT   Facilities
  NT   Cemeteries +
       Crematoriums
       Morgues & mortuaries
       Tombs & sepulchral monuments +
**Funicular railroads**
  USE Cable railroads
**Fur coats**
  BT   Coats
       Fur garments
**Fur garments**
  BT   Clothing & dress
  NT   Fur coats
  RT   Fur trade
       Hides & skins
**Fur trade**
  --[country or state]--[city]
  PN   Search under TRADING POSTS for
       images that focus on facilities.
  UF   Furriers
       Trapping
  BT   Commerce

**Fur trade (cont.)**
  RT   Business enterprises
       Frontier & pioneer life
       Fur garments
       Hides & skins
       Hunting
       Trading posts
**Furnaces**
  --[country or state]--[city]
  UF   Blast furnaces
  BT   Mechanical systems components
  RT   Industry
       Kilns
       Metalworking
       Ovens
       Smelters
**Furnishings**
  UF   Household goods
  NT   Andirons
       Confessionals
       Floor coverings
       Furniture +
       Pottery +
       Radios
       Spittoons
       Telephones
       Televisions
  RT   Blankets
       Clocks & watches
       Drapery
       Equipment
       Fonts
       Home furnishings stores
       Interiors
       Ovens
       Plant containers
       Stoves
**Furnishings stores**
  USE Home furnishings stores
**Furniture**
  BT   Furnishings
  NT   Beds
       Bookcases
       Bookstacks
       Buffets (Furniture)
       Built-in furniture
       Chests +
       Children's furniture
       Closets
       Convertible furniture
       Cupboards
       Desks
       Fire screens
       Office furniture
       Outdoor furniture +
       Pews
       Seating furniture +
       Showcases
       Soda fountains
       Storage furniture
       Tables +
       Wicker furniture

BT  Broader term                   RT  Related term                PN Public Note
NT  Narrower term                  UF  Used for                    + Term has NTs
HN  History Note                   CN  Catalogers Note             --[ ] May subdivide

**Furniture (cont.)**
RT   Bathtubs & showers
      Blackboards
      Cabinetmaking
      Furniture industry
      Furniture stores
      Hammocks
      Mirrors
      Pigeonholes
      Pulpits
      Screens
      Shelving
      Upholstery
**Furniture industry**
      --[country or state]--[city]
PN   Includes activities and structures.
CN   Double index under INDUSTRIAL
      FACILITIES (or NTs) for images that focus
      on facilities.
BT   Industry
NT   Billiard table industry
RT   Furniture
**Furniture stores**
      --[country or state]--[city]
PN   Includes activities and structures.
BT   Stores & shops
RT   Appliance stores
      Furniture
      Home furnishings stores
Furriers
   USE Fur trade
**Futures markets**
      --[country or state]--[city]
PN   For activities and structures.
Futuristic architecture
   USE Visionary architecture
**Gables**
      --[country or state]--[city]
BT   Architectural elements
NT   Crow-stepped gables
RT   Pediments
      Roofs
**Gadgets**
PN   Small mechanical or electronic devices
      with a practical use but often thought of as
      novelties.
BT   Equipment
**Galaxies**
RT   Astronomy
      Celestial bodies
**Galleries (Rooms & spaces)**
      --[country or state]--[city]
PN   Platforms projecting from interior walls to
      provide additional accommodation.
UF   Khories
BT   Interiors
RT   Balconies
**Galleries & museums**
      --[country or state]--[city]
PN   Includes activities, structures, and objects
      displayed.
CN   Double index under type of object

**Galleries & museums (cont.)**
      displayed, for images that focus on objects.
UF   Museums
BT   Exhibition facilities
NT   Naval museums
RT   Commercial art galleries
      Cultural facilities
      Dioramas
      Exhibitions
Galleries, Shooting
   USE Shooting galleries
**Galleys (Ship kitchens)**
CN   Double index under type of vessel.
BT   Kitchens
RT   Vessels
**Gambling**
      --[country or state]--[city]
PN   Betting of money or valuables on, and
      often participating in, games of chance or
      skill.
UF   Betting
      Craps
      Dice
      Faro
      Gaming
BT   Games
NT   Children gambling
      Lotteries
RT   Bingo
      Card games
      Casinos
      Crimes
      Slot machines
      Wagers
**Gambrel roofs**
      --[country or state]--[city]
PN   Roofs with lower part sloping more
      steeply than upper.
BT   Roofs
**Game bird hunting**
      --[country or state]
UF   Bird hunting
      Fowling
BT   Hunting
NT   Duck shooting
      Goose shooting
      Pheasant shooting
      Prairie hen shooting
      Quail shooting
RT   Birds
      Decoys (Hunting)
**Game boards**
UF   Gameboards
**Game cards**
CN   TGM II term.
**Game industry**
      --[country or state]--[city]
PN   Includes activities and structures.
CN   Double index under INDUSTRIAL
      FACILITIES (or NTs) for images that focus
      on facilities.
BT   Industry

BT  Broader term           RT  Related term           PN Public Note
NT  Narrower term         UF  Used for               + Term has NTs
HN  History Note           CN Catalogers Note      --[ ] May subdivide

**Game industry (cont.)**
  RT   Games
       Toy industry
Game keepers
  USE Gamekeepers
**Game pieces**
  CN   TGM II term.
  UF   Pieces, Game
       Playing pieces
**Game preserves**
       --[country or state]--[city]
  BT   Sites
  RT   Fishing
       Hunting
       Rangers
       Wildlife conservation
Game rooms
  USE Recreation rooms
**Game shows**
  UF   Quiz shows
  BT   Entertainment
  RT   Games
       Radio broadcasting
       Television broadcasting
**Game & game birds**
       --[country or state]
  BT   Animals
  RT   Birds
       Gamekeepers
       Hunting
Gameboards
  USE Game boards
**Gamekeepers**
       --[country or state]--[city]
  UF   Game keepers
       Warreners
  BT   People
  RT   Game & game birds
       Rangers
**Games**
       --[country or state]--[city]
  BT   Recreation
  NT   Billiards +
       Bingo
       Blind man's bluff
       Board games +
       Bobbing for apples
       Card games +
       Croquet
       Darts
       Gambling +
       Hopscotch
       Pin-the-tail-on-the-donkey
       Ring-around-a-rosy
       Shuffleboard
       Tug of war
  RT   Children playing
       Game industry
       Game shows
       Penny arcades
       Physical education
       Sack racing

**Games (cont.)**
       Sports
       Three-legged racing
Gaming
  USE Gambling
**Gangs**
       --[country or state]--[city]
  UF   Boys' gangs
       Street gangs
       Youth gangs
  BT   Organizations
  RT   Children
       Criminals
       Juvenile delinquents
       Organized crime
Gangsters
  USE Criminals
Gaols
  USE Jails
Gaps
  USE Passes (Landforms)
Garage sales
  USE Secondhand sales
**Garages**
       --[country or state]--[city]
  BT   Transportation facilities
  NT   Parking garages
  RT   Automobiles
       Dwellings
       Parking
       Parking lots
       Residential facilities
       Storage facilities
Garages, Commercial
  USE Automobile service stations
Garbage
  USE Refuse
**Garbage collecting**
       --[country or state]--[city]
  BT   Refuse disposal
  RT   Garbage collectors' strikes
**Garbage collectors' strikes**
       --[country or state]--[city]
  BT   Strikes
  RT   Garbage collecting
Garbage dumps
  USE Refuse disposal
Garden farming
  USE Truck farming
Garden houses
  USE Garden structures
Garden lattices
  USE Trellises
**Garden parties**
       --[country or state]--[city]
  BT   Parties
Garden rhubarb
  USE Rhubarb
**Garden rooms**
       --[country or state]--[city]
  UF   Conservatories, Home
  BT   Interiors

---

BT  Broader term                    RT  Related term                    PN  Public Note
NT  Narrower term                   UF  Used for                        +  Term has NTs
HN  History Note                    CN  Catalogers Note                 --[ ] May subdivide

**Garden rooms (cont.)**
RT   Greenhouses
Sunspaces
**Garden structures**
--[country or state]--[city]
UF   Garden houses
NT   Teahouses
Garden walks
USE Trails & paths
**Garden walls**
--[country or state]--[city]
BT   Site elements
RT   Gardens
Landscape architecture facilities
Walls
**Gardening**
--[country or state]--[city]
UF   Fertilizing
Landscape gardening
Planting
Seeding
Sowing
BT   Horticulture
RT   Gardening equipment & supplies
Gardens
Mowing
Pruning
Raking (Sweeping)
Tree planting ceremonies
**Gardening equipment & supplies**
UF   Gardening tools
BT   Equipment
RT   Gardening
Gardening tools
USE Gardening equipment & supplies
**Gardens**
--[country or state]--[city]
BT   Facilities
NT   Botanical gardens
Japanese gardens
Roof gardens
Victory gardens
RT   Backyards
Garden walls
Gardening
Greenhouses
Landscape architecture facilities
Orchards
Parks
Plant containers
Plants
Scarecrows
Topiary work
Gardens, Zoological
USE Zoos
**Gargoyles**
--[country or state]--[city]
BT   Architectural elements
RT   Roofs
Garlands
USE Festoons
Wreaths

Garment workers' strikes
USE Clothing industry strikes
Garments
USE Clothing & dress
**Garrets**
USE Attics
Gas
USE Gasoline
Gas companies
USE Public utility companies
**Gas industry**
--[country or state]--[city]
PN   Includes activities and structures.
CN   Double index under INDUSTRIAL
FACILITIES (or NTs)  for images that focus
on facilities where gas is manufactured.
UF   Gas manufacture
Gas works
Natural gas industry
BT   Industry
RT   Fuel trade
Petroleum industry
Gas light fixtures
USE Gaslight fixtures
Gas manufacture
USE Gas industry
**Gas masks**
BT   Masks
RT   Gas warfare
Poisons
Gas stations
USE Automobile service stations
**Gas street lamps**
--[country or state]--[city]
BT   Street lights
RT   Gaslight fixtures
Gas-lighting
**Gas warfare**
--[country or state]--[city]
UF   Poison gas warfare
BT   Military art & science
RT   Campaigns & battles
Gas masks
Poisons
Tear gas
Gas works
USE Gas industry
**Gaslight fixtures**
UF   Gas light fixtures
BT   Light fixtures
RT   Gas street lamps
Gas-lighting
Natural gas
Gaslight prints
USE Silver gelatin prints
**Gasoline**
--[country or state]--[city]
PN   For the fuel. Search under AUTOMOBILE
SERVICE STATIONS and GASOLINE
PUMPS for gas pumps.
UF   Gas
BT   Fuel

BT  Broader term
NT  Narrower term
HN  History Note

RT  Related term
UF  Used for
CN  Catalogers Note

PN Public Note
+ Term has NTs
--[ ] May subdivide

**Gasoline (cont.)**
RT   Automobile service stations
     Gasoline prices
     Gasoline pumps
     Gasoline taxes
     Pipelines
     Retorts (Equipment)
**Gasoline engines**
UF   Internal combustion engines
     Petroleum engines
BT   Engines
**Gasoline prices**
    --[country or state]--[city]
BT   Fuel prices
RT   Gasoline
**Gasoline pumps**
    --[country or state]--[city]
PN   For gas pumps not associated with service
     stations. Search under AUTOMOBILE
     SERVICE STATIONS for those that are part
     of the station.
BT   Pumps
RT   Automobile service stations
     Gasoline
**Gasoline taxes**
    --[country or state]--[city]
BT   Taxes
RT   Gasoline
Gas, Natural
  USE Natural gas
**Gas-lighting**
    --[country or state]--[city]
PN   For the subject of gas-lighting.
BT   Lighting
RT   Gas street lamps
     Gaslight fixtures
**Gatehouses**
    --[country or state]--[city]
PN   Buildings enclosing or accompanying
     gateways for castles, manor houses, or
     similar buildings of importance.
UF   Gatekeepers' houses
     Lodges (Gatehouses)
BT   Buildings
RT   Dwellings
     Gates
Gatekeepers' houses
  USE Gatehouses
**Gates**
    --[country or state]--[city]
UF   City gates
     Entrances
     Gateways
BT   Site elements
NT   Torii
RT   Doors & doorways
     Fences
     Gatehouses
     Landscape architecture facilities
     Pylons (Gateways)
     Walls
Gateways

**Gateways (cont.)**
  USE Gates
Gathering food
  USE Foraging
Gathering fuelwood
  USE Fuelwood gathering
**Gatling guns**
BT   Machine guns
**Gauchos**
    --[country or state]--[city]
BT   Cowboys
**Gavels**
PN   Mallets used (as by presiding officers or
     auctioneers) for commanding attention or
     confirming actions (as votes or sales).
BT   Equipment
RT   Judicial proceedings
     Meetings
Gay liberation
  USE Gay rights
**Gay men**
    --[country or state]--[city]
UF   Male gays
BT   Gays
     Men
RT   Lesbians
Gay persons
  USE Gays
**Gay rights**
    --[country or state]--[city]
UF   Gay liberation
     Homosexual rights
BT   Civil rights
RT   Gays
**Gays**
    --[country or state]--[city]
CN   Changed 11/1987 from
     HOMOSEXUALS.
UF   Gay persons
     Homosexuals
BT   People
NT   Gay men
     Lesbians
RT   Gay rights
**Gazebos**
    --[country or state]--[city]
UF   Belvederes
BT   Landscape architecture facilities
RT   Bandstands
**Gazelles**
    --[country or state]
BT   Antelopes
Gazing into a crystal ball
  USE Fortune telling
**Geese**
    --[country or state]
BT   Birds
RT   Goose shooting
     Poultry
**Geishas**
    --[country or state]--[city]
BT   Entertainers

---

BT  Broader term                          RT  Related term                          PN  Public Note
NT  Narrower term                         UF  Used for                              +   Term has NTs
HN  History Note                          CN  Catalogers Note                       --[ ] May subdivide

**Geishas (cont.)**
       Women
**Gelatin dry plate negatives**
  USE Dry plate negatives
**Gelatin silver film negatives**
  USE Film negatives
**Gelatin silver prints**
  USE Silver gelatin prints
**Gelatin silver transparencies**
  USE Silver gelatin film transparencies
      Silver gelatin glass transparencies
**Gem photographs**
  CN  TGM II term.
**Gems**
  UF  Jewels
  NT  Diamonds
  RT  Jewelry
      Lapidary work
      Ruby mining
**Gendarmes**
  USE Police
**Gender (Sex)**
  USE Sex
**Genealogical tables**
  USE Family trees
**General stores**
      --[country or state]--[city]
  PN  Includes activities and structures.
  UF  Country stores
  BT  Stores & shops
  RT  Department stores
      Dry goods stores
**Generals**
      --[nationality]--[country or state]--[city]
  BT  Military officers
**Generation gap**
  USE Intergenerational relations
**Genies**
  USE Jinns
**Genii**
  USE Jinns
**Genocide**
      --[country or state]--[city]
  PN  Deliberate and systematic destruction of a
      racial, political, or cultural group.
  BT  Atrocities
  RT  Racism
      Terrorism
**Genre drawings**
  CN  TGM II term.
**Genre paintings**
  CN  TGM II term.
**Genre photographs**
  CN  TGM II term.
**Genre prints**
  CN  TGM II term.
**Genre works**
  CN  TGM II term.
**Geography**
      --[country or state]--[city]
  PN  For the subject of geography in general
      and the activities of geographers.

**Geography (cont.)**
  BT  Science
  RT  Boundaries
      Globes
      Map making
      Milestones
**Geology**
      --[country or state]--[city]
  PN  For the subject of geology in general and
      the activities of geologists.
  BT  Science
  RT  Erosion
      Mineral deposits
      Paleontology
**Geometry**
  PN  For the subject of geometry in general and
      the activities of geometers.
  BT  Mathematics
**George junior republics**
  USE Junior republics
**Germs**
  USE Bacteria
**Gerontology**
  PN  For the subject of gerontology in general
      and the activities of gerontologists.
  RT  Aged persons
      Social science
**Gerrymandering**
      --[country or state]--[city]
  PN  Dividing (a state, country, etc.) into
      election districts or other civil divisions in an
      unnatural or unfair way, especially to give a
      political party an advantage over its
      opponent.
  BT  Political strategies
  RT  Corruption
      Political elections
      Political representation
**Gesture language**
  USE Sign language
**Geysers**
      --[country or state]
  PN  Eruptive springs from which hot water,
      steam, and/or mud are periodically spurted.
  UF  Thermal waters
  BT  Natural phenomena
  RT  Springs
**Ghettos**
  USE Ethnic neighborhoods
**Ghost dance**
      --[country or state]--[city]
  BT  Dancing
      Rites & ceremonies
**Ghost photographs**
  USE Spirit photographs
**Ghost towns**
      --[country or state]--[city]
  PN  Towns, especially boom towns of the
      West, that have been completely abandoned.
  UF  Abandoned towns
      Deserted towns
  BT  Settlements

---

**Ghost towns (cont.)**
- RT  Abandoned buildings
-      Frontier & pioneer life
-      Ruins

**Ghosts**
-      --[country or state]--[city]
- UF  Apparitions
-      Phantoms
-      Shades (Ghosts)
-      Specters
-      Spirits
-      Wraiths
- BT  Supernatural beings
- RT  Haunted houses
-      Seances

**Ghouls**
- UF  Ogres
- BT  Supernatural beings

**Giant sequoias**
-      --[country or state]--[city]
- UF  Sequoias, Giant
-      Sierra redwoods
- BT  Redwoods

**Giants**
- CN  As appropriate, double index under HUMAN CURIOSITIES.
- UF  Ogres
- RT  Fictitious characters
-      Human curiosities

**Gibson girls**
- BT  Women

**Giddiness**
- USE Dizziness

**Gift shops**
-      --[country or state]--[city]
- PN  Includes activities and structures.
- BT  Stores & shops
- RT  Gifts
-      Souvenir shops

**Gifts**
- UF  Donations
-      Presents
- RT  Christmas stockings
-      Gift shops
-      Manners & customs

**Gilding**
- USE Goldwork

**Gilds**
- USE Guilds

**Gin**
- BT  Alcoholic beverages

**Giraffes**
-      --[country or state]
- BT  Animals

**Girders**
-      --[country or state]--[city]
- UF  Beams
- BT  Architectural elements
- RT  Structural frames

**Girdles of chastity**
- USE Chastity belts

**Girls**

**Girls (cont.)**
-      --[country or state]--[city]
- PN  Females, ages 0-16.
- HN  Changed 7/1991 from non-postable term (Use CHILDREN). For earlier cataloging search under CHILDREN.
- BT  Children
- RT  Women

**Give-aways**
- USE Premiums

**Glaciers**
-      --[country or state]
- CN  Used in a note under CLIFFS.
- BT  Ice
-      Land
- RT  Icebergs
-      Mountains

**Gladiators**
- PN  Persons engaged in fights to the death as public entertainment for ancient Romans or persons engaged in public fights or controversies.
- BT  People
- RT  Fighting

**Gladness**
- USE Happiness

**Glamour photographs**
- CN  TGM II term.
- UF  Beefcake photographs
-      Boudoir photographs
-      Cheesecake photographs
-      Pinup photographs

**Glass blowing**
- USE Glassblowing

**Glass bottom boats**
-      --[country or state]--[city]
- BT  Boats

**Glass fiber industry**
-      --[country or state]--[city]
- PN  Includes activities and structures.
- CN  Double index under INDUSTRIAL FACILITIES (or NTs) for images that focus on facilities.
- UF  Fiberglass industry
-      Fibrous glass industry
- BT  Industry

**Glass industry**
-      --[country or state]--[city]
- PN  Includes activities and structures.
- CN  Double index under INDUSTRIAL BUILDINGS for images that focus on buildings.
- BT  Ceramic industries
- RT  Building materials industry
-      Glassware
-      Glassworking

**Glass negatives**
- CN  TGM II term.

**Glass prints**
- USE Clichés-verre

**Glass transparencies**
- CN  TGM II term.

---

| | | |
|---|---|---|
| BT Broader term | RT Related term | PN Public Note |
| NT Narrower term | UF Used for | + Term has NTs |
| HN History Note | CN Catalogers Note | --[ ] May subdivide |

Glass working
  USE Glassworking
**Glassblowing**
      --[country or state]--[city]
  UF   Glass blowing
  BT   Glassworking
Glasshouses
  USE Greenhouses
**Glassware**
  NT   Crystal glass
  RT   Bottles
       Broken glass
       Drinking vessels
       Glass industry
       Tableware
**Glassworking**
      --[country or state]--[city]
  UF   Glass working
  NT   Glassblowing
  RT   Glass industry
       Handicraft
Glass, Broken
  USE Broken glass
Glass, Stained
  USE Stained glass
Gleaning
  USE Harvesting
Glens
  USE Valleys
**Gliders**
      --[nationality]--[country or state]--[city]
  BT   Airplanes
**Gliders (Outdoor furniture)**
  UF   Swing chairs
  BT   Outdoor furniture
**Globes**
  RT   Geography
Gloom (Mental state)
  USE Depression (Mental state)
Gloominess
  USE Pessimism
**Gloves**
  BT   Clothing & dress
**Glue**
  UF   Adhesives
**Gluttony**
  BT   Mental states
  RT   Deadly sins
       Eating & drinking
       Extravagance
**Goat carts**
      --[country or state]--[city]
  PN   Small carts used to convey people,
       especially children.
  BT   Carriages & coaches
  RT   Goats
**Goatherds**
      --[country or state]--[city]
  UF   Herdsmen
  BT   People associated with agriculture
  RT   Goats
**Goats**

**Goats (cont.)**
      --[country or state]
  BT   Animals
  NT   Mountain goats
  RT   Dairying
       Goat carts
       Goatherds
Goblets
  USE Drinking vessels
**Goddesses**
      --[nationality]
  CN   Subdivide by ethnic, national, or regional
       group.
  UF   Deities
  BT   Supernatural beings
**Gods**
      --[nationality]
  CN   Subdivide by ethnic, national, or regional
       group.
  UF   Deities
  BT   Supernatural beings
  NT   Buddhist gods +
       Sea gods
  RT   Idols
       Myths
       Religion
**Gold**
  UF   Gold bullion
  BT   Metals
  RT   Alchemy
       Goldwork
       Money
       Treasure-trove
Gold bullion
  USE Gold
**Gold miners**
      --[country or state]--[city]
  BT   Miners
  RT   Gold mining
**Gold mining**
      --[country or state]--[city]
  CN   Used in a note under HYDRAULIC
       MINING.
  BT   Mining
  RT   Gold miners
       Gold rushes
**Gold rushes**
      --[country or state or territory]
  BT   Events
  RT   Gold mining
       Prospecting
       Prospecting equipment & supplies
Gold work
  USE Goldwork
Golden eagles
  USE Eagles
**Goldenrod**
      --[country or state]--[city]
  BT   Flowers
**Goldwork**
  UF   Gilding
       Gold work

---

BT Broader term              RT Related term              PN Public Note
NT Narrower term             UF Used for                  + Term has NTs
HN History Note              CN Catalogers Note           --[ ] May subdivide

**Goldwork (cont.)**
BT   Metalwork
RT   Gold
**Golf**
--[country or state]--[city]
PN   Includes golf activities, golf courses, and structures.
UF   Golf courses
Links, Golf
BT   Sports
NT   Children golfing
RT   Caddies
Golfers
Sports & recreation facilities
**Golf caddies**
USE Caddies
**Golf courses**
USE Golf
**Golfers**
--[country or state]--[city]
BT   People associated with entertainment & sports
RT   Golf
**Gondolas**
BT   Canal boats
RT   Gondoliers
**Gondoliers**
BT   People associated with transportation
RT   Gondolas
**Good & evil**
UF   Evil
Wickedness
BT   Ethics
RT   Three monkeys (Motif)
Villains
**Goodbyes**
USE Farewells
**Goods transportation**
USE Shipping
**Goodwill**
USE Interpersonal relations
**Goose shooting**
--[country or state]
BT   Game bird hunting
RT   Geese
**Goose stepping**
--[country or state]--[city]
BT   Marching
**Gorges**
USE Canyons
**Gorillas**
--[country or state]
BT   Apes
**Gospel music**
BT   Music
RT   Christianity
Gospel singers
Religion
**Gospel singers**
UF   Gospel vocalists
BT   Singers
RT   Gospel music

**Gospel vocalists**
USE Gospel singers
**Gossip**
USE Conversation
Libel & slander
Rumor
**Gouache drawings**
USE Gouaches
**Gouache paintings**
USE Gouaches
**Gouaches**
CN   TGM II term.
UF   Gouache drawings
Gouache paintings
**Governesses**
UF   Nannies (Children's nurses)
Nurses, Children's
BT   Women
RT   Children
Teachers
**Government**
USE Politics & government
**Government agencies**
USE Administrative agencies
**Government buildings**
USE Government facilities
**Government debt**
USE Public debt
**Government employees**
--[country or state]--[city]
PN   Search also under the subdivision --STAFF used with names of persons (Appendix B).
UF   Public servants
BT   People associated with politics & government
NT   Diplomats +
RT   Civil service
Government officials
Postal service employees
**Government executives**
USE Government officials
**Government facilities**
--[country or state]--[city]
HN   Changed 1/1993 from GOVERNMENT BUILDINGS.
UF   Government buildings
BT   Facilities
NT   Capitols
City & town halls
Courthouses
Customs houses
Embassies
Fire lookout stations
Fire stations
Immigration stations
Mints
Police stations
Post offices
Treasuries
RT   Archives
Forums
Guardhouses

---

BT  Broader term              RT  Related term              PN  Public Note
NT  Narrower term             UF  Used for                  +  Term has NTs
HN  History Note              CN  Catalogers Note            --[ ] May subdivide

Government housing
  USE Housing
Government investigations
  USE Governmental investigations
Government lending
  USE Assistance
**Government officials**
    --[country or state]
  PN  Search also under the subdivision --STAFF
      used with names of PERSONS (Appendix
      B).
  UF  Executives
      Government executives
      Officials, Government
      Public officers
      Public servants
  BT  People associated with politics &
      government
  NT  Cabinet officers +
      Governors
      Judges +
      Legislators
      Municipal officials +
      Presidents
      Vice presidents
  RT  Civil service
      Government employees
      Military officers
      Political patronage
      Politicians
      Politics & government
      Postmasters
      Presidential appointments
      Public service
      Statesmen
**Government ownership**
    --[country or state]
  UF  Nationalization
      Public ownership
      Socialization of industry
      State ownership
  BT  Economic policy
Government paperwork
  USE Paperwork
Government price control
  USE Price regulation
Government property, Surplus
  USE Surplus government property
Government red tape
  USE Red tape
**Government regulation**
    --[country or state]--[city]
  UF  Regulation, Government
  BT  Politics & government
  NT  Consumer rationing
      Price regulation
  RT  Anarchism
      Antitrust law
      Consumer protection
      Environmental policy
      Free trade & protection
      Libertarianism

**Government regulation (cont.)**
      Tariffs
Government relations
  CN  This heading is used only as a subdivision
      with names of indigenous peoples (Appendix
      A).  Search also under the subdivisions
      --POLITICAL ACTIVITY or --CIVIL
      RIGHTS used with the names of ethnic,
      racial, and regional groups, and with classes
      of persons (Appendix A).
**Government reorganization**
    --[country or state]
  UF  Reorganization of government
  BT  Politics & government
  RT  Civil service reform
Government ships
  USE Government vessels
**Government spending policy**
    --[country or state]
  UF  Public spending policy
  BT  Economic policy
  NT  Government spending reductions
  RT  Consumer rationing
      Taxes
**Government spending reductions**
    --[country or state]
  UF  Budget freezes
      Budget reductions
  BT  Government spending policy
Government subsidies
  USE Assistance
Government systems
  USE Economic & political systems
**Government vessels**
    --[nationality]--[country or state]--[city]
  UF  Dreadnoughts
      Government ships
      Naval ships
      State ships
  BT  Vessels
  NT  Landing craft
      Warships +
  RT  Military art & science
**Governmental investigations**
    --[country or state]--[city]
  PN  Investigations initiated by legislative,
      executive, or judicial branches of government
      and usually conducted by ad hoc or
      permanent bodies for the purpose of
      investigating some particular problem of
      public interest.
  UF  Commissions of inquiry
      Congressional investigations
      Government investigations
      Hearings
      Investigations, Governmental
  BT  Investigation
  RT  Committees
      Legislation
      McCarthyism
Government, Resistance to
  USE Civil disobedience

---

BT Broader term          RT Related term          PN Public Note
NT Narrower term         UF Used for              + Term has NTs
HN History Note          CN Catalogers Note       --[ ] May subdivide

**Governors**
  --[state or territory]
  PN  For the subject of the governship in general and for incumbents.
  BT  Government officials
Gowns, Wedding
  USE Wedding costume
Go-carts
  USE Karts (Midget cars)
Go-Karts
  USE Karts (Midget cars)
Grade crossings
  USE Railroad crossings
**Graders (Earthmoving machinery)**
  UF  Grading machinery
      Road graders
  BT  Machinery
  RT  Railroad construction & maintenance
      Road construction
Grading machinery
  USE Graders (Earthmoving machinery)
Graduates
  USE Alumni & alumnae
**Graduation ceremonies**
  --[country or state]--[city]
  UF  Academic processions
      Commencements
  BT  Rites & ceremonies
  RT  Students
**Graffiti**
  --[country or state]--[city]
  BT  Writing systems
  RT  Art
Graft
  USE Corruption
Grain bins
  USE Granaries
**Grain elevators**
  --[country or state]--[city]
  PN  Buildings for elevating, storing, discharging, and sometimes processing grain.
  UF  Country elevators
      Elevators, Grain
  BT  Food storage buildings
  RT  Grain industry
      Grains
      Granaries
**Grain industry**
  --[country or state]--[city]
  PN  Includes activities and structures involved in grain processing and trade.
  CN  Double index under INDUSTRIAL FACILITIES (or NTs) for images that focus on facilities.
  UF  Grain processing plants
      Grain trade
  NT  Rice industry
  RT  Cereal products
      Food industry
      Grain elevators
      Grains
Grain processing plants

Grain processing plants (cont.)
  USE Grain industry
Grain trade
  USE Grain industry
Graineries
  USE Granaries
**Grains**
  --[country or state]--[city]
  BT  Plants
  NT  Barley
      Buckwheat
      Corn +
      Hops
      Millet
      Oats
      Rice
      Rye
      Wheat
  RT  Cereal products
      Flour & meal industry
      Grain elevators
      Grain industry
      Granaries
      Silos
      Threshing
      Winnowing
**Grammar**
  NT  Punctuation +
Gramophones
  USE Phonographs
**Granaries**
  --[country or state]--[city]
  PN  Storehouses or repositories for grain, especially after it has been threshed or husked.
  UF  Grain bins
      Graineries
  BT  Food storage buildings
  RT  Grain elevators
      Grains
**Grand juries**
  BT  Juries
Grandfather clocks
  USE Longcase clocks
Grandfathers
  USE Grandparents
Grandmothers
  USE Grandparents
**Grandparents**
  UF  Grandfathers
      Grandmothers
  BT  Families
  RT  Aged persons
      Men
      Women
**Grandpa's hat**
  PN  Symbol for Benjamin Harrison, whose grandfather, William H. Harrison, was President before him.
  BT  Symbols
  RT  Hats
      Presidents

BT Broader term                    RT Related term                    PN Public Note
NT Narrower term                   UF Used for                        + Term has NTs
HN History Note                    CN Catalogers Note                 --[ ] May subdivide

**Grandstands**
--[country or state]--[city]
PN   A usually roofed stand for spectators at a race course or stadium.
BT   Sports & recreation facilities
RT   Reviewing stands
Spectators
Stadiums
**Grange**
USE Farmers' groups
**Granite quarrying**
--[country or state]--[city]
PN   Includes activities and sites.
BT   Quarrying
**Grants**
USE Assistance
**Grapefruit**
--[country or state]--[city]
BT   Citrus fruit
RT   Grapefruit orchards
**Grapefruit orchards**
--[country or state]--[city]
CN   As appropriate, double index under HARVESTING.
BT   Orchards
RT   Grapefruit
**Grapes**
--[country or state]--[city]
UF   Vineyards
BT   Fruit
NT   Raisins
RT   Wine industry
**Graphic design drawings**
CN   TGM II term.
UF   Commercial art design drawings
Commerical art design drawings
**Graphite drawings**
CN   TGM II term.
**Graphophones**
USE Phonographs
**Grasshoppers**
--[country or state]
BT   Insects
**Grassland**
USE Meadows
**Grassland fires**
--[country or state]--[city]
UF   Prairie fires
BT   Fires
**Gratefulness**
USE Gratitude
**Gratings**
USE Grilles
**Gratitude**
UF   Gratefulness
Thankfulness
BT   Mental states
**Gravedigging**
--[country or state]--[city]
UF   Digging graves
BT   Digging
RT   Cemeteries

**Gravedigging (cont.)**
Funeral rites & ceremonies
**Graves**
--[country or state]--[city]
PN   For excavations in the earth used for burials.  Search under TOMBS & SEPULCHRAL MONUMENTS for constructions over or around burial sites.
CN   Used in a note under TOMBS & SEPULCHRAL MONUMENTS.
RT   Cemeteries
Death
Tombs & sepulchral monuments
**Gravestones**
USE Tombs & sepulchral monuments
**Graveyards**
USE Cemeteries
**Graveyards, Boat**
USE Boat graveyards
**Gravures**
USE Photogravures
Rotogravures
**Gray market**
USE Black market
**Great seals**
USE State seals
**Greed**
USE Avarice
**Greek cross buildings**
--[country or state]--[city]
BT   Buildings distinguished by form
RT   Churches
**Greek Orthodox churches**
USE Orthodox churches
**Greek temples**
--[country or state]--[city]
BT   Temples
**Greenbacks**
BT   Money
**Greenhouses**
--[country or state]--[city]
UF   Conservatories (Greenhouses)
Glasshouses
Hot houses
Hothouses
BT   Horticultural buildings
NT   Palm houses
RT   Garden rooms
Gardens
Landscape architecture facilities
**Greeting cards**
CN   TGM II term.
**Greetings**
USE Salutations
**Grief**
UF   Mourning
Sorrow
BT   Mental states
RT   Depression (Mental state)
Sadness
**Griffins**
PN   Fabulous animals typically having head,

BT  Broader term
NT  Narrower term
HN  History Note

RT  Related term
UF  Used for
CN  Catalogers Note

PN  Public Note
+   Term has NTs
--[ ]  May subdivide

**Griffins (cont.)**
      forepart, and wings like those of an eagle but
      with visible usually erect ears, forelegs like
      the legs of an eagle, and body, hind legs, and
      tail like those of a lion.
  UF  Gryphons
  BT  Supernatural beings

**Grilles**
      --[country or state]--[city]
  PN  Gratings forming openwork barriers,
      screens, or covers (as to doors, windows, or
      other openings).
  UF  Gratings
      Window guards
  BT  Architectural elements
  RT  Doors & doorways
      Ironwork
      Screens
      Security systems
      Windows

**Grinding**
      --[country or state]--[city]
  PN  To pulverize by friction.
  RT  Home food processing

**Grinding wheels**
      --[country or state]--[city]
  UF  Abrasive wheels
      Grindstones
  BT  Machinery

Grindstones
  USE Grinding wheels

Grinning
  USE Smiling

**Grizzly bears**
      --[country or state]
  BT  Bears

**Grocery stores**
      --[country or state]--[city]
  PN  Includes activities and structures.
  UF  Supermarkets
  BT  Stores & shops
  RT  Delicatessens
      Seafood stores

**Grooming**
  PN  Process of making neat or attractive either
      by oneself or by commercial services.
  UF  Personal grooming
      Toilet (Grooming)
  NT  Animal grooming
      Hairdressing +
      Manicuring
      Shaving
  RT  Bathing
      Beauty shops
      Cosmetics & soap
      Dressing tables
      Dressing & grooming equipment
      Hygiene
      Manners & customs
      Perfumes

Grooming equipment
  USE Dressing & grooming equipment

**Grooms (Weddings)**
  PN  For images which focus on persons.
      Search under WEDDINGS for activities.
  UF  Bridegrooms
  RT  Brides
      Wedding costume
      Weddings

**Gross national product**
      --[country]
  UF  National income
  RT  Economic & social conditions
      Wealth

Grottoes
  USE Caves

Ground
  USE Land

**Ground breaking ceremonies**
      --[country or state]--[city]
  UF  Ground breakings
  BT  Dedications
  RT  Building dedications

Ground breakings
  USE Ground breaking ceremonies

Groundhogs
  USE Woodchucks

Group discussion
  USE Discussion

**Group portraits**
  CN  TGM II term.

**Group psychotherapy**
      --[country or state]--[city]
  UF  Therapy, Group
  BT  Psychotherapy

Groups of people
  USE People

**Grouse**
      --[country or state]
  BT  Birds

Growth, Urban
  USE Urban growth

Gryphons
  USE Griffins

**Guardhouses**
      --[country or state]--[city]
  UF  Sentry houses
  BT  Military facilities
  RT  Government facilities
      Guards
      Industrial facilities

**Guards**
      --[country or state]--[city]
  UF  Patrols
      Pickets (Guards)
      Sentinels
      Sentries
  BT  People associated with health & safety
  NT  Private police
  RT  Guardhouses
      Military art & science
      Military personnel
      Watchmen

**Guerrillas**

---

BT  Broader term          RT  Related term          PN  Public Note
NT  Narrower term          UF  Used for             +  Term has NTs
HN  History Note           CN  Catalogers Note      --[ ] May subdivide

**Guerrillas (cont.)**
>--[nationality]--[country or state]--[city]
>PN  Persons who engage in irregular warfare, especially predatory excursions, in wartime. Search also under the subdivision --GUERRILLAS used with names of wars (Appendix C).
>BT  People associated with military activities
>RT  Activists
>     Military art & science
>     National liberation movements
>     Sabotage
>     Soldiers
>     Underground movements
>     War

**Guided missiles**
>USE Rockets

**Guides & scouts**
>--[country or state]--[city]
>PN  Includes those who act as guides or scouts in non-military contexts, e.g. expeditions, exploration, and travel. Search under MILITARY SCOUTS for scouts operating in military contexts.
>UF  Scouts & guides
>BT  People
>RT  Discovery & exploration
>     Explorers
>     Military scouts
>     Travel

**Guildhalls (Municipal buildings)**
>USE City & town halls

**Guilds**
>--[country or state]--[city]
>PN  Medieval associations, as of merchants and tradesmen, formed to protect the interests of their members.
>UF  Gilds
>BT  Labor unions

**Guillotines**
>--[country or state]--[city]
>BT  Machinery
>RT  Decapitations

**Guitars**
>PN  Includes the activity of playing guitars.
>BT  Stringed instruments

**Gulches**
>USE Canyons

**Gulfs**
>USE Bays

**Gullies**
>USE Canyons

**Gulls**
>--[country or state]
>UF  Seagulls
>BT  Birds

**Gum bichromate photoprints**
>USE Gum bichromate prints

**Gum bichromate prints**
>CN  TGM II term.
>UF  Gum bichromate photoprints
>     Gum prints

**Gum prints**
>USE Gum bichromate prints

**Gums & resins**
>UF  Resins
>     Rosin
>RT  Chemical industry
>     Naval stores

**Gum, Chewing**
>USE Chewing gum

**Gun control**
>USE Firearms control

**Gun fights**
>USE Gunfights

**Gun running**
>USE Illegal arms transfers

**Gun turrets**
>--[country or state]--[city]
>PN  Towers or tower-like structures, usually revolving, on which heavy guns are mounted; used on vessels and, sometimes land fortifications.
>UF  Turrets, Gun
>RT  Artillery (Weaponry)
>     Forts & fortifications
>     Turret ships

**Gunboats**
>--[nationality]--[country or state]--[city]
>PN  Armed ships of shallow draft used primarily in rivers and harbors.
>BT  Warships
>RT  Floating batteries

**Gunfighting**
>USE Gunfights

**Gunfights**
>--[country or state]--[city]
>UF  Gun fights
>     Gunfighting
>BT  Fighting
>RT  Firearms
>     Shooting

**Gunning**
>USE Shooting

**Guns**
>USE Artillery (Weaponry)
>     Firearms

**Gunsmithing**
>--[country or state]--[city]
>RT  Firearms
>     Firearms industry
>     Metalworking

**Gutta-percha photograph cases**
>USE Union cases

**Gutters (Roofs)**
>--[country or state]--[city]
>BT  Mechanical systems components
>RT  Leader heads
>     Roofs

**Gymnasiums**
>--[country or state]--[city]
>BT  Sports & recreation facilities
>RT  Locker rooms
>     Sports

---

BT  Broader term                RT  Related term             PN Public Note
NT  Narrower term             UF  Used for                   + Term has NTs
HN  History Note               CN  Catalogers Note          --[ ] May subdivide

**Gymnastics**
--[country or state]--[city]
BT   Sports
RT   Acrobatics
**Gypsum industry**
--[country or state]--[city]
PN   Includes activities and structures.
CN   Double index under INDUSTRIAL
FACILITIES (or NTs) for images that focus
on facilities.
BT   Industry
Gyroplanes
USE Autogiros
**Gyroscopes**
BT   Scientific equipment
Habit, Tobacco
USE Tobacco habit
Haciendas
USE Ranches
Hades
USE Hell
**Hail**
UF   Hailstones
BT   Weather
RT   Storms
Hailstones
USE Hail
Hair dressing
USE Hairdressing
Hair dyes
USE Hair preparations
**Hair preparations**
UF   Hair dyes
RT   Cosmetics & soap
Hairdressing
Hair styles
USE Hairstyles
Hairdos
USE Hairstyles
**Hairdressing**
--[country or state]--[city]
PN   Action or process of washing, cutting,
curling, or arranging hair.
UF   Hair dressing
Hairstyling
BT   Grooming
NT   Barbering
RT   Combs
Hair preparations
Hairstyles
**Hairstyles**
--[country or state]--[city]
UF   Coiffures
Hair styles
Hairdos
NT   Braids (Hairdressing)
RT   Baldness
Beards
Clothing & dress
Hairdressing
Wigs
Hairstyling

Hairstyling (cont.)
USE Hairdressing
**Halftone negatives**
CN   TGM II term.
**Halftone photomechanical prints**
CN   TGM II term.
**Half-timbered buildings**
--[country or state]--[city]
BT   Buildings distinguished by material
**Halibut**
--[country or state]
BT   Fish
Halls of residence
USE Dormitories
Halls (Passageways)
USE Passageways
**Hallucinations & illusions**
UF   Delusions
Illusions
BT   Fantasy
NT   Mirages
RT   Optical illusions
Hallways
USE Passageways
Ham radio
USE Children & radio
Radio broadcasting
Hamburger stands
USE Fast food restaurants
**Hammer & sickle**
UF   Sickle & hammer
BT   Symbols
RT   Communism
**Hammers**
BT   Equipment
Hammers, Steam
USE Steam hammers
**Hammocks**
RT   Furniture
Leisure
Hammocks (Islands)
USE Islands
Hand irons
USE Irons (Pressing)
**Hand lenses**
UF   Lenses, Hand
Loupes
Magnifying glasses
Pocket lenses
BT   Optical devices
RT   Microscopes
**Hand railings**
--[country or state]--[city]
BT   Railings
RT   Stairways
**Handbags**
UF   Pocketbooks (Handbags)
BT   Clothing & dress
RT   Purses
**Handball**
--[country or state]--[city]
BT   Sports

BT  Broader term        RT  Related term        PN Public Note
NT  Narrower term        UF  Used for            + Term has NTs
HN  History Note         CN Catalogers Note      --[ ] May subdivide

**Handbills**
  CN  TGM II term.
**Handcars**
  USE Railroad handcars
**Handcuffs**
  BT  Equipment
      Physical restraints
  RT  Law enforcement
Handgun control
  USE Firearms control
**Handguns**
  PN  For firearms that are held and fired with
      one hand.
  UF  Pistols
      Revolvers
  BT  Firearms
**Handicapped persons**
      --[country or state]--[city]
  PN  This heading may be further subdivided by
      the subdivisions used for classes of persons
      (Appendix A).
  CN  As appropriate, subdivide by the
      subdivisions used for classes of persons
      (Appendix A).
  UF  Crippled persons
      Disabled persons
      Invalids
      Physically handicapped persons
  BT  People
  NT  Amputees
      Blind persons
      Deaf persons
      Disabled veterans
      Mentally ill persons
      Paraplegics
  RT  Birth defects
      Orthopedic braces
      Shut-ins
      Sick persons
      Wheelchairs
**Handicraft**
      --[country or state]--[city]
  PN  Activities requiring skill with the hands.
      Search also under the subdivision --ARTS &
      CRAFTS used with the names of ethnic,
      racial, and regional groups, and with classes
      of persons (Appendix A).
  UF  Crafts (Handicraft)
  NT  Basket making
      Cabinetmaking
      Carving +
      Jewelry making
      Lapidary work
      Modeling (Sculpture)
      Quilting
      Weaving
  RT  Bookbinding
      Glassworking
      Hobbyists
      Metalworking
      Potteries
      Saddlery

**Handicraft (cont.)**
      Sewing
**Handkerchiefs**
  BT  Clothing & dress
**Hands**
  NT  Fists
  RT  Fingers
      Human body
      Shaking hands
Hand-and-foot fighting, Oriental
  USE Oriental hand-to-hand fighting
Hand-to-hand fighting, Oriental
  USE Oriental hand-to-hand fighting
**Hangars**
      --[country or state]--[city]
  UF  Airplane hangars
  BT  Transportation facilities
  RT  Aircraft
      Airports
**Hangings**
      --[country or state]--[city]
  BT  Executions
  RT  Nooses
**Hangovers**
      --[country or state]--[city]
  RT  Alcoholic beverages
      Intoxication
Hansom cabs
  USE Carriages & coaches
**Happiness**
  UF  Gladness
  BT  Mental states
  RT  Optimism
      Sadness
Harassment, Sexual
  USE Sexual harassment
**Harbors**
      --[country or state]--[city]
  PN  Small bays or other sheltered parts of a
      considerable body of water, usually protected
      either naturally or artificially, for mooring
      vessels.
  UF  Ports
      Seaports
  BT  Bodies of water
  RT  Bays
      Jetties
      Marine terminals
      Piers & wharves
      Ships
      Tugboats
      Waterfronts
**Hardoy chairs**
  UF  Butterfly chairs
  BT  Chairs
**Hardware**
  PN  Ware (as fittings, trimmings, cutlery,
      tools, utensils, or parts of machines) made of
      metal.
  UF  Ironmongery
  BT  Metalwork
  NT  Bolts & nuts

BT Broader term          RT Related term          PN Public Note
NT Narrower term         UF Used for              + Term has NTs
HN History Note          CN Catalogers Note       --[ ] May subdivide

**Hardware (cont.)**
>Counterbalances
>Hinges
>Key plates
>Keys (Hardware)
>Locks (Hardware)
>Tacks
- RT Equipment
>Hardware stores

**Hardware stores**
>--[country or state]--[city]
- PN Includes activities and structures.
- BT Stores & shops
- RT Appliance stores
>Hardware

**Harems**
>--[country or state]--[city]
- RT Polygamy
>Women

Hares
>USE Rabbits

Harmonicas
>USE Mouth organs

Harness making
>USE Saddlery

**Harness racing**
>--[country or state]--[city]
- BT Horse racing

**Harps**
- PN Includes the activity of playing harps.
- BT Stringed instruments
- RT Bards

**Harpsichords**
- PN Includes the activity of playing harpsichords.
- UF Cembalos
>Clavicembalos
>Spinets
>Virginals
- BT Keyboard instruments
>Stringed instruments
- RT Pianos

Harvesters
>USE Harvesting machinery

**Harvesting**
>--[country or state]--[city]
- CN As appropriate, double index under crop harvested and/or context in which the harvesting occurs (e.g., ORCHARDS). Used in a note under PLANTATIONS (and NTs) and ORCHARDS (and NTs).
- UF Crop picking
>Gleaning
>Picking crops
>Reaping
- NT Threshing
- RT Farming
>Harvesting machinery
>Mowing
>Tapping

**Harvesting machinery**
- UF Harvesters

**Harvesting machinery (cont.)**
>Reapers
- BT Agricultural machinery & implements
- NT Combines (Agricultural machinery)
>Mowing machines
>Threshing machines
- RT Harvesting

**Hat industry**
>--[country or state]--[city]
- PN Includes activities and structures.
- CN Double index under the type of hat. Double index under INDUSTRIAL FACILITIES (or NTs) for images that focus on facilities.
- BT Clothing industry
- RT Hats

Hatcheries, Fish
>USE Fish hatcheries

Hatchets
>USE Axes

**Hate mail**
- BT Correspondence

**Hats**
- UF Caps
- BT Clothing & dress
- NT Bonnets
>Fools' caps
>Helmets
>Panama hats
>Straw hats
>Turbans
- RT Grandpa's hat
>Hat industry
>Liberty cap
>Millinery

Haulovers
>USE Portages

**Haunted houses**
>--[country or state]--[city]
- BT Houses
- RT Ghosts

Hawking
>USE Falconry

**Hawks**
- CN Used in a note under SYMBOLS.
- BT Birds of prey
- NT Falcons

**Hay**
>--[country or state]--[city]
- BT Plants
- NT Haystacks
- RT Hayrides

Hay mowers
>USE Mowing machines

Hay rides
>USE Hayrides

Hay stacks
>USE Haystacks

**Hayrides**
>--[country or state]--[city]
- UF Hay rides
- BT Recreation

---

BT Broader term
NT Narrower term
HN History Note

RT Related term
UF Used for
CN Catalogers Note

PN Public Note
+ Term has NTs
--[ ] May subdivide

**Hayrides (cont.)**
  RT   Farm life
       Hay
**Haystacks**
       --[country or state]--[city]
  UF   Hay stacks
       Stacks, Hay
  BT   Hay
Hazard
  USE Danger
Head shots
  USE Publicity photographs
Headlands
  USE Capes (Coasts)
Headmasters
  USE School principals
Headquarters, Military
  USE Military headquarters
**Heads of state**
       --[country]
  BT   People associated with politics &
       government
  NT   Presidents
       Prime ministers
  RT   Politics & government
       Rulers
       Statesmen
Heads, Conductor
  USE Leader heads
Heads, Leader
  USE Leader heads
Heads, Rainwater
  USE Leader heads
**Healers**
       --[country or state]--[city]
  PN   Persons who engage in the practice of
       treating illness or relieving suffering by
       calling for divine help or by asserting that the
       mind or spirit can control the body.
  UF   Faith healers
       Mental healers
       Psychic healers
       Spiritual healers
  BT   People associated with health & safety
  RT   Evangelists
       Healing
       Health care
       Religion
       Shamans
**Healing**
       --[country or state]--[city]
  PN   For practices directed at curing or
       restoring to health and for the process of
       getting well. Search under HEALERS for
       images that focus on persons rather than
       activities. Search under HEALTH CARE for
       activities or systems for maintaining or
       improving health.
  CN   Used in a note under HEALTH CARE.
  UF   Cures
       Curing (Healing)
  NT   Phlebotomy

**Healing (cont.)**
  RT   Diseases
       Healers
       Health care
       Medicines
       Shamans
       Sick persons
       Therapy
       Wounds & injuries
**Health**
       --[country or state]--[city]
  PN   For the state of optimal physical and
       mental well-being, free of pain or disease.
       Search under HEALTH CARE for activities
       or systems directed at maintaining or
       improving health. Search under HYGIENE
       for personal body care and cleanliness. Search
       also under the subdivision --HEALTH &
       WELFARE used with names of ethnic,
       racial, and regional groups, and with classes
       of persons (Appendix A). Search also under
       the subdivision --HEALTH used with names
       of persons (Appendix B).
  UF   Personal health
       Wellness
  RT   Coughing
       Diseases
       Fatigue
       Food adulteration & inspection
       Health care
       Hygiene
       Loss of consciousness
       Nausea
       Nutrition
       Obesity
       Pain
       Physical fitness
       Safety
       Sanitation
       Sneezing
**Health care**
       --[country or state]--[city]
  PN   Activities or systems directed at
       maintaining or improving health. Search
       under HEALING for specific curing practices
       and for the process of getting well.
  CN   Used in a note under HEALING.
  UF   Medical care
  NT   Acupuncture +
       Dental hygiene
       Emergency medical services
       Eye examinations
       Nursing
       Preventive medicine
       Quarantines
       Vaccinations
  RT   Abortions
       Druggists
       Examinations
       Healers
       Healing
       Health

BT  Broader term                    RT  Related term                    PN  Public Note
NT  Narrower term                   UF  Used for                        +   Term has NTs
HN  History Note                    CN  Catalogers Note                 --[ ] May subdivide

**Health care (cont.)**
    Health care facilities
    Health education
    Institutional care
    Medicaid
    Medicare
    Medicine
    Midwives
    Opticians' shops
    Physicians
    Quacks
    Sick persons
    Therapeutic baths
    Therapy
**Health care facilities**
    --[country or state]--[city]
UF  Medical buildings
BT  Health & hygiene facilities
NT  Clinics
    Hospital ships
    Hospital trains
    Hospitals +
    Infirmaries
    Mental institutions
    Mobile health units
    Nursing homes
    Rest homes +
    Sanatoriums
    Sick bays
RT  Ambulances
    Dental offices
    Emergency rooms
    Health care
    Medical offices
**Health education**
    --[country or state]--[city]
BT  Education
RT  Health care
**Health resorts**
    --[country or state]--[city]
PN  Includes activities and structures.
UF  Spas
    Watering places
BT  Health & hygiene facilities
RT  Resorts
    Sanatoriums
    Springs
    Therapeutic baths
Health units, Mobile
  USE Mobile health units
**Health & hygiene facilities**
    --[country or state]--[city]
UF  Hygiene facilities
BT  Facilities
NT  Health care facilities +
    Health resorts
    Privies
    Public baths
    Public comfort stations
    Therapeutic baths +
Health & welfare
  CN  Used only as a subdivision with names of

Health & welfare (cont.)
    ethnic, racial, and regional groups, and with
    classes of persons (Appendix A).
**Hearing aids**
BT  Medical equipment & supplies
RT  Deaf persons
    Sounds
Hearings
  USE Governmental investigations
    Judicial proceedings
**Hearses**
    --[country or state]--[city]
BT  Vehicles
RT  Automobiles
    Carriages & coaches
    Funeral rites & ceremonies
Hearths
  USE Fireplaces
**Hearts**
RT  Human body
**Heat**
    --[country or state]--[city]
UF  Hot weather
BT  Natural phenomena
RT  Cold
    Fire
    Ovens
    Perspiration
    Temperature
    Thermometers
Heaters
  USE Radiators
Heaters, Water
  USE Water heaters
**Heating & ventilation industry**
    --[country or state]--[city]
CN  Double index under INDUSTRIAL
    FACILITIES (or NTs) for images that focus
    on facilities.
BT  Industry
NT  Air conditioning industry
RT  Radiators
Heating, ventilating, & air conditioning drawings
  USE HVAC drawings
Heating, ventilation, and air conditioning systems
  USE HVAC systems
**Heaven**
UF  Afterlife
RT  Angels
    Death
    Hell
**Hedges (Plants)**
    --[country or state]--[city]
BT  Plants
RT  Fences
    Shrubs
    Trees
Heifers
  USE Cattle
Heirs
  USE Inheritance & sucession
**Helicopters**

---

**Helicopters (cont.)**
    --[nationality]--[country or state]--[city]
  BT  Aircraft
  RT  Airplanes
**Heliographs (Apparatus)**
  PN  Signalling apparatus that reflects sunlight
      with a movable mirror to flash coded
      messages.
  UF  Heliotropes (Apparatus)
  BT  Communication devices
Heliotropes (Apparatus)
  USE Heliographs (Apparatus)
Heliotypes
  USE Collotypes
**Hell**
  UF  Hades
  RT  Demons
      Heaven
Hellos
  USE Salutations
**Helmets**
  PN  For various protective head coverings
      usually made of a hard material to resist
      impact.
  BT  Hats
  RT  Armor
**Hemp**
    --[country or state]--[city]
  BT  Plants
  NT  Manila hemp
Hen houses
  USE Poultry houses
**Henequen**
  UF  Mexican sisal
      Sisal, Mexican
  BT  Fibers
  RT  Agaves
      Henequen industry
**Henequen industry**
    --[country or state]--[city]
  CN  Double index under INDUSTRIAL
      FACILITIES (or NTs) for images that focus
      on facilities.
  BT  Industry
  RT  Henequen
Heraldic bookplates
  USE Armorial bookplates
**Heralds**
  BT  Messengers
  RT  Announcements
Herbs, Medicinal
  USE Medicinal plants
**Herding**
    --[country or state]
  NT  Cattle herding
      Horse herding
  RT  Animals
Herdsmen
  USE Goatherds
      Shepherds
**Hermits**
    --[country or state]--[city]

**Hermits (cont.)**
  UF  Anchorites
      Eremites
      Recluses
  BT  People
**Herms**
    --[country or state]--[city]
  PN  Rectangular post, usually of stone and
      tapering downward, surmounted by bust of
      Hermes or other divinity, or by a human
      head.
  BT  Sculpture
**Heroes**
    --[country or state]--[city]
  BT  People
  NT  Superheroes
  RT  Courage
      Literature
      Saints
**Herons**
    --[country or state]
  BT  Birds
**Hexagonal buildings**
    --[country or state]--[city]
  UF  Six-sided buildings
  BT  Buildings distinguished by form
**Hibernation**
  RT  Animals
      Sleeping
      Winter
**Hibiscus**
  BT  Shrubs
**Hidden image works**
  CN  TGM II term.
Hidden property
  USE Caches
      Treasure-trove
**Hides & skins**
  UF  Animal skins
      Pelts
      Skins
  RT  Animals
      Curing (Preservation)
      Fur garments
      Fur trade
      Hunting trophies
      Leather industry
      Tanning
      Taxidermy
      Tipis
      Wigwams
**Hiding**
  UF  Taking cover
  RT  Fear
      Searching
**Hieroglyphics**
  UF  Pictographs
      Picture writing
  BT  Writing systems
  RT  Rock art
High blood pressure
  USE Hypertension

---

BT Broader term              RT Related term              PN Public Note
NT Narrower term           UF Used for                   + Term has NTs
HN History Note             CN Catalogers Note         --[ ] May subdivide

High rise apartment buildings
  USE Apartment houses
High school students
  USE Students
High society
  USE Upper class
High wire performers
  USE Aerialists
Highwaymen
  USE Criminals
Highways
  USE Roads
**Hiking**
        --[country or state]--[city]
  UF  Tramping
  NT  Mountaineering
  RT  Recreation
        Snowshoeing
        Sports
        Walking
**Hills**
        --[country or state]--[city]
  UF  Hummocks
        Knolls
  BT  Land
  RT  Buttes
        Mountains
**Hindu temples**
        --[country or state]--[city]
  BT  Temples
**Hinges**
  BT  Hardware
**Hip roofs**
        --[country or state]--[city]
  UF  Hipped roofs
        Italian roofs
  BT  Roofs
Hipped roofs
  USE Hip roofs
**Hippies**
  UF  Nonconformists
  BT  People
  RT  Bohemians
        Manners & customs
Hippodromes
  USE Stadiums
**Hippopotamuses**
        --[country or state]
  BT  Animals
**Historic buildings**
        --[country or state]--[city]
  PN  Buildings generally or formally recognized
        as historically significant for their
        associations, materials, methods of
        construction, or other factors.
  BT  Buildings
  RT  Historic sites
**Historic sites**
        --[country or state]--[city]
  PN  Search also under the subdivision
        --HISTORIC SITES used with names of wars
        (Appendix C).

Historic sites (cont.)
  BT  Sites
  NT  Archaeological sites
        Battlefields
        Birthplaces
  RT  Events
        Historic buildings
        Historical markers
        Monuments & memorials
        Shrines
**Historic trees**
        --[country or state]--[city]
  BT  Trees
**Historical dramas**
  PN  For images representing dramatic
        productions or scenes (theatrical, film, radio,
        or television) of historical events or with
        historical settings that emphasize the
        dramatic.  Search under HISTORICAL
        REENACTMENTS for enactments of
        specific historical events, such as battles, etc.
  RT  Historical reenactments
        Motion pictures
        Radio broadcasting
        Television broadcasting
        Theatrical productions
**Historical markers**
        --[country or state]--[city]
  CN  As appropriate, double index under
        subject of the marker.
  UF  Markers, Historical
  BT  Site elements
  RT  Historic sites
        Monuments & memorials
        Signs
**Historical pageants**
        --[country or state]--[city]
  PN  Elaborate, usually open-air, exhibitions or
        spectacles that are marked by colorful
        costumes and scenery, and consist of a series
        of tableaux as representations of important
        events in the history of a community.
  BT  Historical reenactments
        Pageants
**Historical reenactments**
        --[country or state]--[city]
  PN  For images representing enactments of
        specific historical events, such as battles, etc.
        Search under HISTORICAL DRAMAS for
        images representing dramatic productions or
        scenes (theatrical, film, radio, or television)
        of historical events or with historical settings
        that emphasize the dramatic.  Search also
        under the subdivision --PERFORMANCES &
        PORTRAYALS used with ethnic, racial, and
        regional groups, and with classes of persons
        (Appendix A).
  UF  Battle reenactments
        Reenactments, Historical
  BT  Theatrical productions
  NT  Historical pageants
  RT  Anniversaries

---

BT  Broader term                    RT  Related term                    PN  Public Note
NT  Narrower term                   UF  Used for                        +   Term has NTs
HN  History Note                    CN  Catalogers Note                 --[ ] May subdivide

**Historical reenactments (cont.)**
    Commemoration
    Entertainment
    Historical dramas
    Recreation
**Historical societies**
    --[country or state]--[city]
  PN  Includes activities and structures.
  CN  Double index under ORGANIZATIONS'
      FACILITIES (or NTs) for images that focus
      on facilities.
  BT  Organizations
Historical studies
  USE Conjectural works
**History**
    --[country or state]--[city]
  PN  For the subject of history in general and
      the activities of historians. Search also under
      the subdivision --HISTORY used with names
      of ethnic, racial, and regional groups, and
      with classes of persons (Appendix A).
  CN  Prefer the subdivision.
  RT  Centennial celebrations
      Civilization
      Firsts
**Hitchhiking**
    --[country or state]--[city]
  BT  Travel
  RT  Freighthopping
**Hitching posts**
    --[country or state]--[city]
  PN  Fixed posts to which horses can be
      fastened.
  UF  Posts, Hitching
      Tethering posts
  BT  Site elements
Hives, Bee
  USE Beehives
Hoaxes
  USE Fraud
**Hobby horses**
  UF  Rocking horses
  BT  Toys
  RT  Horses
**Hobbyists**
    --[country or state]--[city]
  PN  For people identified as hobbyists,
      including those engaged in hobbies or
      displaying the results of their work.
  BT  People
  RT  Collectors
      Handicraft
      Recreation
Hoboes
  USE Tramps
Hockey
  USE Field hockey
      Ice hockey
**Hockey masks**
  BT  Masks
      Sporting goods
  RT  Field hockey

**Hockey masks (cont.)**
    Ice hockey
**Hoedowns (Parties)**
    --[country or state]--[city]
  BT  Dance parties
  RT  Folk dancing
      Folk music
**Hog calling**
    --[country or state]--[city]
  BT  Communication
  RT  Farmers
      Swine
Hogs
  USE Swine
**Hoisting machinery**
  UF  Cranes
      Derricks
      Lifts
      Tackles
      Winches
      Windlasses
  BT  Machinery
  RT  Chains
      Pulleys
Holds, Cargo
  USE Cargo holds
Holdups
  USE Robberies
**Hold-to-light works**
  CN  TGM II term.
**Holes**
  UF  Cavities
      Pits (Holes)
  NT  Bullet holes
      Manholes
  RT  Ruts
**Holidays**
    --[country or state]--[city]
  BT  Manners & customs
  RT  Anniversaries
      Caroling
      Celebrations
      Christmas decorations
      Easter eggs
      Festivals
      Fireworks
      Letters to Santa Claus
      May poles
      Vacations
Holidays with pay
  USE Employee vacations
Hollows
  USE Valleys
**Holly**
    --[country or state]--[city]
  BT  Shrubs
  RT  Festive decorations
**Holograms**
  CN  TGM II term.
  UF  Laser photographs
      Three-dimensional photographs
Holy cards

---

BT Broader term      RT Related term      PN Public Note
NT Narrower term      UF Used for      + Term has NTs
HN History Note      CN Catalogers Note      --[ ] May subdivide

Holy cards (cont.)
  USE Devotional images
Holy Communion
  USE Communion
Holy places
  USE Shrines
Home appliances
  USE Appliances
Home births
  USE Births
Home buying
  USE House buying
Home decoration
  USE Interior decoration
**Home economics**
      --[country or state]--[city]
  PN  For theory and instruction about how to
      run the home, including budgeting and the
      proper performance of household tasks.
      Search under HOUSEWORK for the work
      involved in housekeeping.
  CN  Used in a note under HOUSEWORK.
  RT  Cookery
      Domestic life
      Home food processing
      Housewives
      Housework
      Servants
**Home food processing**
      --[country or state]--[city]
  PN  For all processing that takes place to
      convert raw food for later consumption.
  UF  Canning & preserving
      Food preparation
      Food processing
      Processing food
  BT  Cookery
  NT  Butter making
  RT  Country life
      Curing (Preservation)
      Food drying
      Food industry
      Grinding
      Home economics
      Preserves
      Smokehouses
      Victory gardens
**Home furnishings stores**
      --[country or state]--[city]
  PN  Includes structures and activities.
  UF  Furnishings stores
      House furnishings stores
  BT  Stores & shops
  RT  Appliance stores
      Furnishings
      Furniture stores
**Home labor**
      --[country or state]--[city]
  PN  For the production of goods in urban
      homes for an outside employer.
  UF  Home work
      Homework (Labor)

Home labor (cont.)
  BT  Employment
  NT  Sweating system
  RT  Business enterprises
      Industry
Home libraries
  USE Libraries (Rooms)
Home life
  USE Domestic life
Home rule
  USE Autonomy
Home rule for cities
  USE Municipal home rule
Home work
  USE Home labor
**Homecomings**
      --[country or state]--[city]
  PN  For occasions when people return to their
      families or homeland after a long absence.
      Search under REUNIONS for the coming
      together of people to mark a former or
      ongoing association.
  CN  Used in a note under REUNIONS.
  BT  Arrivals & departures
  RT  Families
      Repatriation
      Reunions
**Homeless persons**
      --[country or state]--[city]
  BT  People
  NT  Tramps
  RT  Poor persons
Homemakers
  USE Housewives
Homers (Birds)
  USE Homing pigeons
Homes
  USE Dwellings
Homes (Institutions)
  USE Asylums
      Nursing homes
      Rest homes
Homes & haunts
  CN  Used only as a subdivision with names of
      persons (Appendix B).
**Homesickness**
  BT  Mental states
  RT  Nostalgia
**Homesteading**
      --[country or state]--[city]
  BT  Real estate development
  RT  Farming
      Squatters
      Westward movement
Homework (Labor)
  USE Home labor
**Homicides**
      --[country or state]--[city]
  UF  Killings
      Manslaughter
      Murders
  BT  Crimes

---

BT  Broad term                    RT  Related term              PN Public Note
NT  Narrower term                 UF  Used for                  +  Term has NTs
HN  History Note                  CN  Catalogers Note           --[ ] May subdivide

**Homicides (cont.)**
- NT Assassinations
  - Crimes of passion
  - Fratricides
  - Lynchings
  - Suicides
- RT Death
  - Executions
  - Strangling

**Homing pigeons**
- --[country or state]
- UF Carrier pigeons
  - Homers (Birds)
  - Racing pigeons
- BT Pigeons

Homosexual rights
- USE Gay rights

Homosexuals
- USE Gays

**Honesty**
- UF Dishonesty
  - Lying
  - Truthfulness
- BT Ethics
- RT Deception
  - Fraud
  - Truth

**Honeycombs**
- RT Beehives
  - Bees

**Honeymoons**
- --[country or state]--[city]
- UF Trips
- RT Travel
  - Weddings

Honeysuckle ornaments
- USE Anthemia

**Hookworm disease**
- --[country or state]--[city]
- BT Communicable diseases

**Hoover wagons**
- --[country or state]--[city]
- BT Carts & wagons

Hopefulness
- USE Optimism

Hopelessness
- USE Despair

Hopper cars
- USE Railroad freight cars

Hopping, Freight car
- USE Freighthopping

**Hops**
- --[country or state]--[city]
- BT Grains
- RT Brewing industry

**Hopscotch**
- BT Games
- RT Jumping

Hornets
- USE Wasps

Horns
- USE Horns (Communication devices)

**Horns (cont.)**
- Wind instruments

Horns of plenty
- USE Cornucopias

**Horns (Communication devices)**
- UF Horns
- BT Communication devices
- RT Wind instruments

**Horror dramas**
- PN For images representing dramatic productions or scenes (theatrical, film, radio, or television) which intend to frighten or terrify the audience.
- RT Danger
  - Fear
  - Motion pictures
  - Radio broadcasting
  - Television broadcasting
  - Theatrical productions

**Horse artillery**
- BT Artillery (Weaponry)
- RT Cavalry

**Horse farms**
- --[country or state]--[city]
- UF Stud farms
- BT Farms
- RT Horses

**Horse herding**
- --[country or state]
- BT Herding
- RT Horses

**Horse racing**
- --[country or state]--[city]
- CN Used in a note under RACE HORSES.
- BT Racing
- NT Chariot racing
  - Harness racing
  - Steeplechases
- RT Horseback riding
  - Jockeys
  - Race horses

**Horse railroads**
- --[country or state]--[city]
- UF Horse-drawn railroads
- BT Street railroads
- RT Horses

Horse shoeing
- USE Blacksmithing

Horse show jumping
- USE Jumping (Horsemanship)

**Horse shows**
- --[country or state]--[city]
- BT Animal shows
- RT Show horses
  - Show jumping

**Horse teams**
- --[country or state]--[city]
- BT Animal teams
- RT Horses

Horse troughs
- USE Watering troughs

**Horseback riding**

---

**Horseback riding (cont.)**
    --[country or state]--[city]
    BT   Riding
    NT   Bareback riding
         Children riding horses
         Jumping (Horsemanship) +
    RT   Horse racing
         Horses
         Mounted police
         Polo
**Horses**
    --[country or state]--[city]
    UF   Colts
         Fillies
         Foals
         Mares
         Stallions
    BT   Animals
    NT   Broncos
         Ponies
         Race horses
         Show horses
    RT   Cavalry
         Corrals
         Hobby horses
         Horse farms
         Horse herding
         Horse railroads
         Horse teams
         Horseback riding
         Jumping (Horsemanship)
         Mules
         Pony express
         Rodeos
         Saddlery
         Saddles
         Show jumping
         Stables
         Trojan horses
**Horseshoe pitching**
    --[country or state]--[city]
    BT   Quoits
    RT   Horseshoes
Horseshoeing
    USE Blacksmithing
**Horseshoes**
    RT   Blacksmithing
         Horseshoe pitching
Horse-drawn railroads
    USE Horse railroads
**Horticultural buildings**
    --[country or state]--[city]
    BT   Agricultural facilities
    NT   Greenhouses +
         Nurseries (Horticulture)
    RT   Horticulture
**Horticulture**
    --[country or state]--[city]
    PN   For the subject of the cultivation of
         gardens or orchards, the art of growing fruit,
         vegetables, and ornamental plants, and the
         activities of horticulturalists.

**Horticulture (cont.)**
    BT   Agriculture
    NT   Gardening
         Hydroponics
         Pruning
    RT   Farming
         Horticultural buildings
         Plants
**Hosiery**
    UF   Socks
         Stockings
    BT   Clothing & dress
    RT   Christmas stockings
         Lingerie
**Hosiery industry**
    --[country or state]--[city]
    CN   Double index under INDUSTRIAL
         FACILITIES (or NTs) for images that focus
         on facilities.
    BT   Clothing industry
    RT   Knitting
**Hospital ships**
    --[nationality]--[country or state]--[city]
    BT   Health care facilities
         Ships
         Vehicles
    RT   Hospitals
Hospital supplies
    USE Medical equipment & supplies
**Hospital trains**
    --[country or state]--[city]
    BT   Health care facilities
         Vehicles
    RT   Hospitals
Hospital units
    USE Hospital wards
**Hospital wards**
    --[country or state]--[city]
    UF   Hospital units
         Wards, Hospitals
    BT   Interiors
    RT   Hospitals
**Hospitals**
    --[country or state]--[city]
    PN   Includes activities and structures.
    BT   Health care facilities
    NT   Maternity hospitals
         Prison hospitals
         Veterinary hospitals
    RT   Hospital ships
         Hospital trains
         Hospital wards
         Infirmaries
         Morgues & mortuaries
         Nurseries
         Operating rooms
         Sanatoriums
Hospitals, Field
    USE Medical aspects of war
Hostage exchanges
    USE Prisoner exchanges
Hostels

---

BT Broader term            RT Related term         PN Public Note
NT Narrower term           UF Used for             + Term has NTs
HN History Note            CN Catalogers Note       --[ ] May subdivide

Hostels (cont.)
USE Tourist camps & hostels
Hostilities
USE War
Hot air balloons
USE Balloons (Aircraft)
Hot dogs
USE Frankfurters
Hot houses
USE Greenhouses
Hot lines
USE Hotlines (Communication)
**Hot peppers**
--[country or state]--[city]
BT Peppers
Hot springs
USE Springs
Hot water heaters
USE Water heaters
Hot weather
USE Heat
**Hotel employees**
--[country or state]--[city]
CN Used in a note under HOTELS.
BT Employees
NT Hotel porters
RT Hotels
**Hotel porters**
--[country or state]--[city]
HN Changed 10/1989 from non-postable term
(Use PORTERS).
BT Hotel employees
Porters
RT Luggage
**Hotels**
--[country or state]--[city]
PN Includes structures and activities. Search
under HOTEL EMPLOYEES for images
where the focus is on employees. Search
under RESORTS for resort complexes.
CN Used in a note under HOTEL
EMPLOYEES and RESORTS.
HN Changed 11/1993 from HOTELS &
TAVERNS.
UF Flophouses
Tourist courts
BT Public accommodation facilities
NT Motels
RT Bars
Casinos
Hotel employees
Lodges
Lodging houses
Resorts
Restaurants
Suites
Hothouses
USE Greenhouses
**Hotlines (Communication)**
UF Hot lines
BT Communication devices
RT Telephones

Hot-air engines
USE Caloric engines
Houdahs
USE Howdahs
**Hourglasses**
RT Clocks & watches
**Hours of labor**
--[country or state]--[city]
UF Eight-hour movement
Hours of work
Labor, Hours of
Nine-hour movement
Sunday labor
Working hours
RT Absenteeism (Labor)
Employment
Hours of work
USE Hours of labor
House boats
USE Houseboats
**House buying**
--[country or state]--[city]
UF Home buying
House hunting
RT Dwellings
Real estate business
House decoration
USE Interior decoration
House drainage
USE Sewerage
House furnishings stores
USE Home furnishings stores
House hunting
USE House buying
House moving
USE Moving of structures
House work
USE Housework
**Houseboats**
--[nationality]--[country or state]--[city]
UF House boats
BT Boats
Dwellings
NT Shantyboats
RT Houses
Household equipment
USE Equipment
Household goods
USE Equipment
Furnishings
**Household soap**
PN Soap used in household cleaning tasks.
UF Detergent, Household
Soap
RT Cleaning
Laundry
Housekeeping
USE Housework
Housemaids
USE Servants
Women domestics
**Houses**

BT Broader term                          RT Related term                          PN Public Note
NT Narrower term                         UF Used for                              + Term has NTs
HN History Note                          CN Catalogers Note                       --[ ] May subdivide

**Houses (cont.)**
       --[country or state]--[city]
  BT   Dwellings
  NT   Bungalows
       Cabins +
       Castles & palaces
       Chalets
       Dugout houses
       Duplexes
       Farmhouses
       Haunted houses
       Lodges +
       Model houses
       Official residences
       Religious dwellings +
       Row houses
       Speculative houses
       Stilt houses
       Tree houses
  RT   Apartment houses
       Houseboats
       Housing
**Houses of prostitution**
  USE Brothels
**Houses, Bird**
  USE Birdhouses
**Houses, Pigeon**
  USE Dovecotes
**Houses, Pump**
  USE Pumping stations
**Housewives**
       --[country or state]--[city]
  UF   Homemakers
  BT   Women
  RT   Home economics
       Housework
**Housework**
       --[country or state]--[city]
  PN   For work involved in housekeeping.
       Search under HOME ECONOMICS for
       theory and instruction about how to run the
       home.
  CN   Used in a note under HOME
       ECONOMICS.
  UF   House work
       Housekeeping
  NT   Children doing housework
  RT   Cleaning
       Cookery
       Domestic life
       Home economics
       Housewives
       Laundry
       Servants
       Sewing
**Housing**
       --[country or state]--[city]
  PN   For dwellings provided for people.
  UF   Government housing
       Housing projects
       Low cost housing
       Low income housing

**Housing (cont.)**
       Public housing
       Wartime housing
       Welfare housing
  BT   Dwellings
  NT   Emergency housing
       Housing developments
       Labor housing +
       Servants' quarters
       Slave quarters
       Work camps
  RT   City planning
       Evictions
       Houses
       Landlord & tenant
       Shelters
       Slums
**Housing developments**
       --[country or state]--[city]
  PN   Groups of individual dwellings or
       apartment houses typically of similar design
       that are usually built and sold or leased by
       one management.
  UF   Apartment complexes
       Developments, Housing
  BT   Housing
  RT   Land subdivision
       Real estate development
       Speculative houses
       Suburban life
**Housing projects**
  USE Housing
**Howdahs**
       --[country or state]--[city]
  PN   Seats or covered pavilions on the back of
       an elephant or camel.
  UF   Houdahs
  BT   Vehicles
  RT   Carriages & coaches
**Howitzers**
  BT   Cannons
**Hucksters**
  USE Peddlers
**Hugging**
  UF   Embracing
  BT   Manners & customs
**Hula dancing**
       --[country or state]--[city]
  BT   Dancing
**Human body**
  UF   Body, Human
  RT   Arms (Anatomy)
       Back (Anatomy)
       Bertillon system
       Blood
       Breasts
       Buttocks
       Cardiovascular system
       Ears
       Eyes
       Faces
       Feet

BT Broader term                              RT Related term                              PN Public Note
NT Narrower term                          UF Used for                                  + Term has NTs
HN History Note                           CN Catalogers Note                           --[ ] May subdivide

**Human body (cont.)**
> Freckles
> Hands
> Hearts
> Human locomotion
> Legs
> Mannequins
> Mouths
> Noses
> Nudes
> Obesity
> Physiognomy
> Scalps
> Shrunken heads
> Strong men
> Tattoos
> Teeth
> Tongues

**Human curiosities**
PN For real persons who are being represented as curiosities or freaks, which may be caused by birth defects or accidents or faked. Search under MONSTERS for animals of strange or terrifying shape.
CN As appropriate, double index under FRAUD. Used in a note under ALBINOS, DWARFS, GIANTS, MONSTERS, and SIAMESE TWINS.
UF Abnormalities
> Freaks
> Malformations
BT People
RT Albinos
> Amusement parks
> Birth defects
> Circuses & shows
> Curiosities & wonders
> Dwarfs
> Giants
> Metamorphosis
> Midways
> Monsters
> Siamese twins

**Human life cycle**
UF Life cycle, Human
> Stages of life
RT Aged persons
> Births
> Children
> Creation
> Death
> Middle age
> Youth

**Human locomotion**
BT Locomotion
RT Human body
Human relations
> USE Interpersonal relations
Human rights
> USE Civil liberties
Human understanding
> USE Interpersonal relations

Humane societies
> USE Animal welfare organizations
**Hummingbirds**
> --[country or state]
BT Birds
Hummocks
> USE Hills
> Islands
**Humorous pictures**
CN TGM II term.
UF Comic pictures
Hunger
> USE Starvation
**Hunting**
> --[country or state]
PN Includes portraits of hunters and their quarry. Search also under the subdivision --SUBSISTENCE ACTIVITIES used with ethnic, racial, and regional groups, and with classes of persons (Appendix A).
CN Used in a note under FISHING & HUNTING GEAR, SHOOTING, and SLAUGHTERING.
UF Field trials
> Trapping
NT Alligator hunting
> Big game hunting +
> Bison hunting
> Coyote hunting
> Deer hunting +
> Fox hunting
> Game bird hunting +
> Kangaroo hunting
> Lynx hunting
> Muskox hunting
> Opossum hunting
> Peccary hunting
> Poaching
> Puma hunting
> Rabbit hunting
> Raccoon hunting
> Whaling
> Wolf hunting
RT Animal tracks
> Dead animals
> Fishing
> Fishing & hunting gear
> Foraging
> Fur trade
> Game preserves
> Game & game birds
> Hunting accidents
> Hunting dogs
> Hunting lodges
> Hunting trophies
> Hunting & fishing clubs
> Searching
> Shooting
> Sports
**Hunting accidents**
> --[country or state]--[city]
BT Accidents

| | | |
|---|---|---|
| BT Broader term | RT Related term | PN Public Note |
| NT Narrower term | UF Used for | + Term has NTs |
| HN History Note | CN Catalogers Note | --[ ] May subdivide |

**Hunting accidents (cont.)**
RT  Hunting
**Hunting dogs**
--[country or state]
UF  Bird dogs
BT  Dogs
RT  Hunting
Hunting gear
USE Fishing & hunting gear
**Hunting lodges**
--[country or state]--[city]
BT  Outbuildings
Sports & recreation facilities
RT  Estates
Hunting
**Hunting trophies**
RT  Dead animals
Hides & skins
Hunting
Taxidermy
**Hunting & fishing clubs**
--[country or state]--[city]
PN  Includes activities and structures.
CN  Double index under ORGANIZATIONS'
FACILITIES (or NTs) for images that focus
on facilities.
BT  Clubs
RT  Fishing
Hunting
**Hurdle racing**
--[country or state]--[city]
BT  Running races
Hurdy-gurdy players
USE Organ grinders
**Hurricanes**
--[country or state]--[city]
PN  Includes the event and any resulting
damage.
CN  Used in a note under STORMS.
BT  Storms
RT  Cyclones
Tornadoes
Typhoons
Husbands
USE Spouses
Husking bees
USE Corn husking
**Huts**
--[country or state]--[city]
PN  Simple shelters often roughly built using
available raw materials. Often temporary in
nature.
UF  Shacks
Shanties
BT  Shelters
RT  Dwellings
Military facilities
Residential facilities
Thatched roofs
**HVAC drawings**
CN  TGM II term.
UF  Air conditioning, heating & ventilating

**HVAC drawings (cont.)**
drawings
Heating, ventilating, & air conditioning
drawings
Ventilating, air conditioning & heating
drawings
**HVAC systems**
--[country or state]--[city]
UF  Heating, ventilation, and air conditioning
systems
BT  Mechanical systems
RT  Air conditioners
Temperature
Hyalotypes
USE Albumen transparencies
Hydraulic construction works
USE Hydraulic facilities
**Hydraulic facilities**
--[country or state]--[city]
HN  Changed 1/1993 from HYDRAULIC
CONSTRUCTION WORKS (NT WATER
DISTRIBUTION STRUCTURES was
deleted).
UF  Hydraulic construction works
Water distribution structures
BT  Facilities
NT  Aqueducts
Canals
Culverts
Dams
Dikes (Engineering)
Erosion protection works +
Fountains
Levees
Millraces
Pumping stations
Reservoirs
Sewers
Spillways
Water tanks
Water towers
Waterworks
Wells +
RT  Bodies of water
Water power
Water supply
Water use
**Hydraulic mining**
--[country or state]--[city]
PN  Includes activities and sites.
CN  Double index under GOLD MINING or
other kinds of mining, as appropriate.
UF  Placer mining
BT  Mining
**Hydroelectric generators**
--[country or state]--[city]
BT  Electrical apparatus
RT  Hydroelectric power
Power plants
**Hydroelectric power**
--[country or state]--[city]
BT  Water power

BT  Broader term
NT  Narrower term
HN  History Note

RT  Related term
UF  Used for
CN  Catalogers Note

PN  Public Note
+  Term has NTs
--[ ] May subdivide

**Hydroelectric power (cont.)**
  RT   Dams
        Electricity
        Hydroelectric generators
        Power plants
**Hydrofoil boats**
  USE Hydroplanes
**Hydrogen bombs**
  USE Nuclear weapons
**Hydroplanes**
        --[nationality]--[country or state]--[city]
  PN   Boats that skim over the surface of the
        water but do not become airborne.
  UF   Hydrofoil boats
  BT   Motorboats
**Hydroponics**
        --[country or state]--[city]
  BT   Horticulture
**Hyenas**
        --[country or state]
  BT   Animals
**Hygiene**
        --[country or state]--[city]
  PN   For personal body care and cleanliness.
  NT   Dental hygiene
  RT   Bathing
        Grooming
        Health
        Medicine
        Preventive medicine
        Sanitation
**Hygiene facilities**
  USE Health & hygiene facilities
**Hypertension**
        --[country or state]--[city]
  UF   Blood pressure, High
        High blood pressure
        Vascular hypertension
  BT   Diseases
  RT   Stress
**Hypnotism**
  UF   Autosuggestion
  RT   Magic
        Mental states
**Hypocrisy**
  BT   Ethics
**Hypodermic needles**
  UF   Needles, Hypodermic
  BT   Medical equipment & supplies
**H-bombs**
  USE Nuclear weapons
**Ibis**
        --[country or state]
  BT   Birds
**Ice**
        --[country or state]--[city]
  UF   Ice crystals
  BT   Natural phenomena
  NT   Glaciers
        Ice floes
        Icebergs
        Icicles

**Ice (cont.)**
  RT   Cold
        Ice buckets
        Ice crossings
        Ice industry
        Ice sculpture
        Icehouses
        Snow
        Winter
**Ice boats**
  USE Iceboats
**Ice bridges**
  USE Ice crossings
**Ice buckets**
  BT   Containers
  RT   Ice
        Pails
**Ice castles**
  USE Ice sculpture
**Ice cream & ices**
  UF   Ices
  BT   Dairy products
  RT   Soda fountains
**Ice crossings**
        --[country or state]--[city]
  UF   Ice bridges
  NT   Railroad ice crossings
  RT   Ice
**Ice crystals**
  USE Ice
**Ice cutting**
  USE Ice industry
**Ice fishing**
        --[country or state]
  BT   Fishing
**Ice floes**
        --[country or state]--[city]
  BT   Ice
  RT   Icebergs
**Ice hockey**
        --[country or state]--[city]
  PN   Includes organizations and activities.
  UF   Hockey
  BT   Sports
  RT   Hockey masks
**Ice houses**
  USE Icehouses
**Ice industry**
        --[country or state]--[city]
  PN   Includes activities and structures.
  CN   Double index under INDUSTRIAL
        FACILITIES (or NTs) for images that focus
        on facilities.
  UF   Ice cutting
  BT   Industry
  RT   Ice
        Icehouses
**Ice palaces**
  USE Ice sculpture
**Ice rinks**
  USE Skating rinks
**Ice sculpture**

---

BT  Broader term          RT  Related term          PN Public Note
NT  Narrower term        UF  Used for             + Term has NTs
HN  History Note          CN Catalogers Note      --[ ] May subdivide

**Ice sculpture (cont.)**
    --[country or state]--[city]
  UF  Ice castles
      Ice palaces
  BT  Sculpture
  RT  Ice
      Snowmen
Ice skaters
  USE Skaters
**Ice skating**
    --[country or state]--[city]
  UF  Figure skating
  BT  Skating
  NT  Speed skating
  RT  Ice skating rinks
**Ice skating rinks**
    --[country or state]--[city]
  BT  Skating rinks
  RT  Ice skating
**Icebergs**
  PN  Huge, floating masses of ice, detached
      from glaciers.
  BT  Ice
  RT  Glaciers
      Ice floes
**Iceboats**
    --[nationality]--[country or state]--[city]
  PN  Includes images that focus on people and
      activity.
  UF  Ice boats
  BT  Boats
  RT  Sailboats
Iceboxes
  USE Refrigerators
**Icehouses**
    --[country or state]--[city]
  PN  Buildings in which ice is made or stored.
  UF  Ice houses
  BT  Storage facilities
  RT  Ice
      Ice industry
      Outbuildings
Ices
  USE Ice cream & ices
**Ice-breaking vessels**
    --[nationality]--[country or state]--[city]
  BT  Vessels
**Icicles**
    --[country or state]--[city]
  BT  Ice
**Icons**
  UF  Ikons
  BT  Religious articles
Idealistic architecture
  USE Visionary architecture
Identification keys
  USE Keys (Legends)
**Identification photographs**
  CN  TGM II terms.
  UF  Mug shots
**Idols**
    --[nationality]

**Idols (cont.)**
  RT  Gods
      Religion
**Igloos**
    --[country or state]
  PN  Dome shaped houses built of blocks of
      snow.
  UF  Snow houses
      Snowhouses
  BT  Dwellings
Ignominy
  USE Disgrace
**Ignorance (Knowledge)**
  BT  Mental states
Ikons
  USE Icons
Ill persons
  USE Sick persons
**Illegal aliens**
    --[nationality]--[country or state]--[city]
  UF  Undocumented aliens
  BT  Aliens
**Illegal arms transfers**
  UF  Arms smuggling
      Arms trafficking
      Gun running
  BT  Crimes
  RT  Arms & armament
**Illegitimacy**
  UF  Bastardy
  RT  Births
      Ethics
Illiteracy
  USE Literacy
Illnesses
  USE Diseases
Illumination
  USE Lighting
**Illuminations**
  CN  TGM II term.
Illusionists
  USE Magicians
Illusions
  USE Hallucinations & illusions
Illusions, Optical
  USE Optical illusions
Illustrated covers
  USE Covers (Illustration)
Illustrated envelopes
  USE Pictorial envelopes
Illustrated letter paper
  USE Letterheads
      Pictorial lettersheets
**Illustrations**
  CN  TGM II term.
Imaginary beings
  USE Fictitious characters
      Supernatural beings
Imaginary views
  USE Conjectural works
Imbibition process prints
  USE Dye transfer prints

---

BT Broader term        RT Related term        PN Public Note
NT Narrower term       UF Used for          + Term has NTs
HN History Note        CN Catalogers Note    --[ ] May subdivide

**Imitation**
UF  Mimicry
RT  Entertainers
    Impersonation
    Teaching methods
Immersions, Baptismal
USE Baptisms
**Immigrants**
    --[nationality]--[country or state]--[city]
PN  Persons who leave their native land and
    settle in another country in order to become
    permanent residents or citizens. For
    emigrants as well as immigrants.
CN  Subdivide geographically by country in
    which the immigrants have settled. As
    appropriate, double index under the name of
    the ethnic, racial, or regional group,
    subdivided by country in which they have
    settled.
UF  Emigrants
BT  People
RT  Aliens
    Emigration & immigration
Immigration
USE Emigration & immigration
Immigration policy
USE Emigration & immigration
**Immigration stations**
    --[country or state]--[city]
PN  Search under EMIGRATION &
    IMMIGRATION for activities.
BT  Government facilities
RT  Emigration & immigration
Immunities, Congressional
USE Congressional privileges & immunities
Impaired vision
USE Vision disorders
Impassiveness
USE Apathy
**Impeachments**
    --[country or state]
PN  Search also under the subdivision
    --IMPEACHMENT used with names of
    persons (Appendix B).
RT  Crimes
    Law & legal affairs
**Imperial card photographs**
CN  TGM II term.
**Imperialism**
    --[nationality]--[country or state]--[city]
PN  For the subject of imperialism in general.
UF  Colonialism
    Expansionism
BT  Economic & political systems
    International relations
RT  Chauvinism & jingoism
    Nationalism
    White man's burden
**Impersonation**
    --[country or state]--[city]
PN  For the activity of pretending to be
    another person or type of person. Search also

**Impersonation (cont.)**
    under ENTERTAINERS (and NTs) for
    portraits in costume. Search also under the
    subdivision --PERFORMANCES &
    PORTRAYALS used with ethnic, racial, and
    regional groups, and with classes of persons
    (Appendix A). Search also under the
    subdivisions --PERFORMANCES and
    --PORTRAYALS used with names of
    persons (Appendix B).
NT  Cross dressing
RT  Commemoration
    Deception
    Entertainers
    Female impersonators
    Fraud
    Imitation
    Theatrical productions
Implements
USE Equipment
Import taxes
USE Tariffs
Imports
USE Commerce
Imprecation
USE Cursing
**Inaugurations**
    --[country or state]--[city]
PN  Search also under the subdivision
    --INAUGURATION used with names of
    persons (Appendix B).
BT  Rites & ceremonies
NT  Presidential inaugurations
RT  Oaths
Inaugurations, Presidential
USE Presidential inaugurations
**Incense**
RT  Rites & ceremonies
**Incinerators**
    --[country or state]--[city]
BT  Waste disposal facilities
RT  Fire
**Inclined planes**
    --[country or state]--[city]
PN  Inclined tracks on which vehicles such as
    trains, boats, and cars, are raised or lowered
    from one level to another.
UF  Planes, Inclined
    Ramps
BT  Machinery
**Inclined railroads**
    --[country or state]--[city]
PN  Used only if the railroad is described as
    being inclined.
BT  Railroads
RT  Cable railroads
    Mountain railroads
**Income taxes**
BT  Taxes
Incomes policy
USE Wage-price policy
**Incompetence**

---

BT Broader term              RT Related term          PN Public Note
NT Narrower term             UF Used for              + Term has NTs
HN History Note              CN Catalogers Note       --[ ] May subdivide

**Incompetence (cont.)**
  RT   Ethics
**Incubators**
  BT   Medical equipment & supplies
  RT   Embryology
Independence
  USE Autonomy
**Indian encampments**
       --[country or state]--[city]
  PN   Search also under --STRUCTURES used
       with names of ethnic, racial, and regional
       groups (Appendix A).
  UF   Encampments, Indian
  BT   Settlements
  RT   Camps
       Indian reservations
**Indian reservations**
       --[country or state]--[city]
  UF   Reservations, Indian
  BT   Settlements
  RT   Indian encampments
**Indians of Central America**
       --[country or state]--[city]
  PN   See also Library of Congress Subject
       Headings for names of individual tribes.
  CN   Although it is a proper name, this Library
       of Congress Subject Headings term is
       included in TGM I for ready reference. As
       appropriate, subdivide by subdivisions used
       with names of ethnic, racial, and regional
       groups, and with classes of persons
       (Appendix A).
  UF   Central American Indians
**Indians of North America**
       --[country or state]--[city]
  PN   See also Library of Congress Subject
       Headings for names of individual tribes.
  CN   Although it is a proper name, this Library
       of Congress Subject Headings term is
       included in TGM I for ready reference. As
       appropriate, subdivide by subdivisions used
       with names of ethnic, racial, and regional
       groups, and with classes of persons
       (Appendix A).
  UF   Native Americans
       North American Indians
**Indians of South America**
  PN   See also Library of Congress Subject
       Headings for names of individual tribes.
  CN   Although it is a proper name, this Library
       of Congress Subject Headings term is
       included in TGM I for ready reference. As
       appropriate, subdivide by subdivisions used
       with names of ethnic, racial, and regional
       groups, and with classes of persons
       (Appendix A).
  UF   South American Indians
Indifference
  USE Apathy
**Indigenous peoples**
       --[country or state]
  PN   This heading may be further subdivided by

**Indigenous peoples (cont.)**
       the subdivisions used for classes of persons
       (Appendix A). See also Library of Congress
       Subject Headings for names of specific
       groups.
  CN   Use only when specific ethnic or racial
       group name is not known. As appropriate,
       subdivide by the subdivisions used for classes
       of persons (Appendix A).
  UF   Aborigines
       Native peoples
       Tribes
  BT   People
Indignation
  USE Anger
**Individuality**
  RT   Conformity
       Dissenters
       Interpersonal relations
Indoor baseball
  USE Softball
Indoor baseball players
  USE Softball players
**Industrial arbitration**
       --[country or state]--[city]
  UF   Arbitration of industrial disputes
       Industrial mediation
       Labor arbitration
       Mediation of industrial disputes
  RT   Labor unions
       Strikes
Industrial buildings
  USE Industrial facilities
Industrial cafeterias
  USE Employee eating facilities
**Industrial design drawings**
  CN   TGM II term.
Industrial development
  USE Industrialization
**Industrial facilities**
       --[country or state]--[city]
  PN   Search under INDUSTRY (or NTs) for
       activities.
  CN   Used in a note under INDUSTRY (and
       NTs).
  HN   Changed 1/1993 from INDUSTRIAL
       BUILDINGS.
  UF   Industrial buildings
  BT   Facilities
  NT   Factories +
       Power plants +
       Workshops +
  RT   Guardhouses
       Smokestacks
       Stockrooms
       Studios
       Warehouses
Industrial mediation
  USE Industrial arbitration
**Industrial productivity**
       --[country or state]--[city]
  UF   Efficiency, Industrial

---

| BT Broader term | RT Related term | PN Public Note |
| NT Narrower term | UF Used for | + Term has NTs |
| HN History Note | CN Catalogers Note | --[ ] May subdivide |

**Industrial productivity (cont.)**
  Productivity, Industrial
  BT  Economic & social conditions
  RT  Industry
**Industrial trusts**
  --[country or state]--[city]
  PN  Combinations of firms or corporations
      formed by legal agreement, especially ones
      that reduce or threaten to reduce competition.
  UF  Trusts, Industrial
  BT  Big business
  RT  Antitrust law
      Monopolies
**Industrialization**
  --[country or state]--[city]
  UF  Industrial development
**Industry**
  --[country or state]--[city]
  PN  Manufacture, trade, and the processing of
      materials and products. Includes activities and
      structures. Search also under the subdivision
      --INDUSTRIES used with names of
      indigenous peoples (Appendix A).
  CN  Double index under INDUSTRIAL
      FACILITIES (or NTs) for images that focus
      on FACILITIES. Used in a note under
      INDUSTRIAL FACILITIES.
  UF  Factory work
      Manufacturing
  NT  Artificial flower industry
      Barbed wire industry
      Belt industry
      Boiler industry
      Bottle industry
      Box industry
      Broom & brush industry
      Building materials industry +
      Cable industry
      Can industry
      Ceramic industries +
      Chemical industry +
      Chicken industry
      Clock & watch industry
      Clothing industry +
      Coke industry
      Construction industry
      Cosmetics industry
      Defense industry +
      Electric household appliances industry
      Electrical apparatus industry
      Electronic industry
      Equipment industry +
      Firearms industry
      Fishing industry
      Food industry +
      Furniture industry +
      Game industry
      Gas industry
      Glass fiber industry
      Gypsum industry
      Heating & ventilation industry +
      Henequen industry

**Industry (cont.)**
      Ice industry
      Leather industry
      Lumber industry
      Machinery industry
      Match industry
      Metallurgical industry +
      Musical instrument industry
      Office equipment & supplies industry
      Optical industry
      Ore industry
      Paper industry +
      Parachute industry
      Petroleum industry
      Phonograph industry
      Photography industry +
      Pin industry
      Pipe industry
      Plastics industry
      Radio industry
      Rope industry
      Rubber industry
      Salt industry
      Sound recording industry
      Sporting goods industry
      Starch industry
      Straw industries
      Telecommunications industry +
      Telephone supplies industry
      Television industry
      Textile industry +
      Tire industry
      Tobacco industry +
      Tobacco pipe industry
      Tool & die industry
      Toy industry
      Transportation industry +
      Tube industry
      Twine industry
      Varnishing industry
      Wallpaper industry
  RT  Assembly-line methods
      Business enterprises
      Candlemaking
      Furnaces
      Home labor
      Industrial productivity
      Mining
      Occupations
      Quarrying
      Warehouses
**Inebriety**
  USE Intoxication
**Inequality, Racial**
  USE Racism
**Inequality, Sexual**
  USE Sexism
**Infantile paralysis**
  USE Poliomyelitis
**Infantry**
  --[nationality]--[country or state]--[city]
  BT  Armies

BT  Broader term                RT  Related term                PN Public Note
NT  Narrower term                UF  Used for                    + Term has NTs
HN  History Note                 CN Catalogers Note               --[ ] May subdivide

Infantry landing craft
  USE Landing craft
**Infants**
          --[country or state]--[city]
  UF  Babies
         Papooses
  BT  Children
  RT  Baby carriages
         Breast feeding
         Cradleboards
         Maternity hospitals
Infectious diseases
  USE Communicable diseases
Infidelity, Marital
  USE Adultery
**Infirmaries**
          --[country or state]--[city]
  PN  For health care units which provide
         uncomplicated medical and nursing care for
         residents or members of an institution or
         other facility.
  CN  Double index under name of institution
         sudivided by --FACILITIES.
  BT  Health care facilities
  RT  Clinics
         Hospitals
         Sick bays
Inflatable structures
  USE Air-supported structures
**Inflation**
          --[country or state]--[city]
  BT  Economic & social conditions
  RT  Cost & standard of living
         Price regulation
Information, Freedom of
  USE Freedom of information
**Informers**
          --[country or state]--[city]
  UF  Police informers
         Stool pigeons
  BT  People
  RT  Criminal investigations
         Spying
**Infrared photographs**
  CN  TGM II term.
Ingots, Copper
  USE Copper ingots
**Inheritance & sucession**
  UF  Bequests
         Heirs
  BT  Law & legal affairs
  RT  Death
         Wills
**Inheritance & transfer taxes**
          --[country or state]--[city]
  UF  Death duties
         Estate taxes
         Transfer taxes
  BT  Taxes
  RT  Death
Initial letters
  USE Initials

**Initials**
  UF  Initial letters
         Letters, Initial
  BT  Alphabets (Writing systems)
**Initiation rites**
          --[country or state]--[city]
  PN  For the rites, ceremonies, and associated
         ordeals and instructions, with which one is
         made a member of or gains particular status in
         a sect or society; includes ceremonies in
         which a youth is formally invested with adult
         status.
  BT  Rites & ceremonies
  RT  Fraternities & sororities
         Youth
Initiatives & referendums
  USE Referendums
Injuries
  USE Wounds & injuries
**Ink drawings**
  CN  TGM II term.
Ink stands
  USE Inkstands
**Inkless intaglio prints**
  CN  TGM II term.
  UF  Blind embossed prints
**Inkstands**
  UF  Ink stands
  BT  Writing materials
Inlets
  USE Bays
Inns
  USE Taverns (Inns)
Inoculations
  USE Vaccinations
Inquiry, Military courts of
  USE Courts martial & courts of inquiry
Insane hospitals
  USE Mental institutions
Insane people
  USE Mentally ill persons
**Inscriptions**
  CN  TGM II term.
Insect bites
  USE Bites & stings
Insecticides
  USE Pest control
**Insects**
          --[country or state]
  UF  Bugs
  BT  Animals
  NT  Ants
         Bedbugs
         Bees
         Butterflies
         Caterpillars
         Dragonflies
         Flies
         Grasshoppers
         Mosquitos
         Spiders
         Termites

---

BT Broader term                    RT Related term                    PN Public Note
NT Narrower term                   UF Used for                        + Term has NTs
HN History Note                    CN Catalogers Note                 --[ ] May subdivide

**Insects (cont.)**
　　　　Wasps
　RT　Bites & stings
　　　Flypaper
　　　Pest control
　　　Plant parasites
Insert cards
　USE Advertising cards
Inspection of food
　USE Food adulteration & inspection
Inspections, Customs
　USE Customs inspections
Inspections, Military
　USE Military inspections
**Instant camera photographs**
　CN　TGM II term.
　UF　Polaroid instant photographs
**Institutional care**
　　　--[country or state]--[city]
　PN　Includes activities and structures. Search
　　　also under the subdivision --HEALTH &
　　　WELFARE used with names of ethnic,
　　　racial, and regional groups, and with classes
　　　of persons (Appendix A).
　RT　Asylums
　　　Health care
　　　Nursing homes
　　　Rest homes
Institutions, International
　USE International organizations
Instructors
　USE Teachers
Instrument panels
　USE Dashboards
Instruments, Musical
　USE Musical instruments
**Insulating paper industry**
　　　--[country or state]--[city]
　PN　Includes activities and structures.
　CN　Double index under INDUSTRIAL
　　　FACILITIES (or NTs) for images that focus
　　　on facilities.
　BT　Paper industry
**Insurance**
　BT　Contracts
　NT　Social security
　RT　Accidents
　　　Business & finance
　　　Insurance companies
　　　Medicaid
　　　Medicare
**Insurance certificates**
　CN　TGM II term.
**Insurance companies**
　　　--[country or state]--[city]
　PN　Includes activities and structures.
　CN　Double index under type of building for
　　　images that focus on buildings.
　BT　Business enterprises
　RT　Insurance
Insurgents
　USE Rebels

Insurrections
　USE Rebellions
**Intaglio prints**
　CN　TGM II term.
Intellectual freedom
　USE Censorship
　　　Freedom of information
　　　Freedom of speech
Intemperance
　USE Temperance
Interaction, Social
　USE Interpersonal relations
**Intercommunication systems**
　UF　Intercoms
　BT　Communication devices
　RT　Building systems
　　　Public address systems
Intercoms
　USE Intercommunication systems
Intercourse, Sexual
　USE Sex
Intercultural relations
　USE Cultural relations
Interdependence of nations
　USE International organization
**Intergenerational relations**
　UF　Generation gap
　BT　Interpersonal relations
　RT　Children & adults
Interior courtyards
　USE Atriums
**Interior decoration**
　UF　Decoration, Interior
　　　Home decoration
　　　House decoration
　RT　Decorations
　　　Interior decoration firms
　　　Interiors
**Interior decoration firms**
　　　--[country or state]--[city]
　PN　Includes activities and structures.
　UF　Interior design firms
　BT　Business enterprises
　RT　Interior decoration
　　　Interiors
**Interior design drawings**
　CN　TGM II term.
Interior design firms
　USE Interior decoration firms
**Interiors**
　　　--[country or state]--[city]
　BT　Rooms & spaces
　NT　Alcoves
　　　Apartments
　　　Apses
　　　Attics
　　　Ballrooms
　　　Banquet halls
　　　Barrooms
　　　Basements
　　　Bathrooms
　　　Bedrooms

BT Broader term　　　　　　RT Related term　　　　　　PN Public Note
NT Narrower term　　　　　　UF Used for　　　　　　　　+ Term has NTs
HN History Note　　　　　　　CN Catalogers Note　　　　　--[ ] May subdivide

**Interiors (cont.)**
  Boudoirs
  Breakfast rooms
  Cargo holds
  Ceremonial rooms +
  Chapels
  Circular rooms
  Classrooms
  Concourses
  Conference rooms
  Courtrooms
  Crew quarters
  Dens
  Dining rooms +
  Drawing rooms
  Dungeons
  Emergency rooms
  Engine rooms
  Entrance halls
  Galleries (Rooms & spaces)
  Garden rooms
  Hospital wards
  Kitchens +
  Laundries (Rooms & spaces)
  Libraries (Rooms)
  Living rooms
  Lobbies
  Locker rooms
  Lounges
  Mezzanines
  Music rooms
  Newsrooms
  Nurseries
  Offices
  Operating rooms
  Organ lofts
  Oval rooms
  Pantries
  Parlors
  Passenger quarters +
  Reading rooms
  Recreation rooms +
  Sacristies
  Salons (Social spaces)
  Scriptoria
  Showrooms
  Smoking rooms
  Stairhalls
  Stockrooms
  Studies (Rooms)
  Suites
  Vaults (Strong rooms)
  Waiting rooms
  RT  Furnishings
  Interior decoration
  Interior decoration firms
  Rotundas
  Vaults (Architecture)
  Walls
**Internal combustion engines**
  USE Gasoline engines
**Internal migration**

**Internal migration (cont.)**
  --[country or state]
  PN  Process of moving within a country.
  UF  Migration, Internal
  RT  Arrivals & departures
      Emigration & immigration
      Migrant laborers
      Refugees
**International agreements**
  USE Treaties
**International agricultural assistance**
  --[nationality]--[country or state]--[city]
  PN  International aid to agriculture given to
      underdeveloped areas in the form of technical
      assistance. Search under FARM RELIEF for
      economic assistance to agriculture.
  UF  Agricultural assistance, International
      Foreign aid to agriculture
  BT  Assistance
  RT  Agricultural productivity
      Farm relief
**International communication**
  PN  Systems of global mass communication.
  UF  World communication
  BT  Communication
**International competition**
  RT  Commerce
**International economic assistance**
  --[nationality]--[country or state]--[city]
  PN  For international aid given in the form of
      technical assistance, loans, or relief grants.
  CN  Subdivide by nationality of people giving
      assistance and subdivide geographically by
      country receiving assistance.
  UF  Foreign aid programs
  BT  Assistance
**International economic integration**
  UF  Common markets
      Economic integration
      Economic union
  BT  Economic & political systems
      International relations
**International migration**
  USE Emigration & immigration
**International organization**
  PN  For the theories and efforts leading toward
      world-wide or regional political organization
      of nations.
  UF  Interdependence of nations
      World government
  RT  Cooperation
      Economic & political systems
      International organizations
      International relations
      International security
      Peace
**International organizations**
  PN  Includes governmental and
      nongovernmental bodies, whether established
      on a permanent or temporary basis, where the
      focus is on the international character of the
      body.

---

BT Broader term
NT Narrower term
HN History Note

RT Related term
UF Used for
CN Catalogers Note

PN Public Note
+ Term has NTs
--[ ] May subdivide

**International organizations (cont.)**
  CN   Includes members, activities, and
         structures. Double index under
         ORGANIZATIONS' FACILITIES (or NTs)
         for images that focus on facilities.
  UF   Institutions, International
  BT   Organizations
  NT   International police
  RT   Assistance
         Cooperation
         International organization
**International police**
         --[nationality]--[country or state]--[city]
  PN   United Nations and non-United Nations
         armed forces which assist in maintaining
         peace between warring factions.
  UF   Peacekeeping forces
  BT   International organizations
  RT   International relations
         International security
         Intervention (International law)
         Law enforcement
**International relations**
         --[country or state]
  CN   Subdivide by countries involved in
         relationship.  May use multiple headings to
         reflect all the countries involved, e.g.
         INTERNATIONAL RELATIONS--CHINA;
         INTERNATIONAL
         RELATIONS--FRANCE.
  UF   Diplomacy
         Foreign relations
  BT   Politics & government
  NT   Arms control
         Détente
         Imperialism
         International economic integration
         International security
         Intervention (International law)
         Neutrality
         War allies
  RT   Annexations
         Cultural relations
         Diplomats
         Embassies
         Foreign participation in war
         Freedom of the seas
         International organization
         International police
         Interpersonal relations
         National security
         Nationalism
         Peace conferences
         Peace negotiations
         Solidarity
         Tariffs
         Territorial waters
         Treaties
**International security**
  PN   Policies by associations of nations to
         maintain international peace by collective
         action against violators of the peace by

**International security (cont.)**
         aggressors.
  UF   Collective security
         Security, International
  BT   International relations
  RT   Arms control
         International organization
         International police
         Intervention (International law)
         Peace
**Internment camps**
  USE  Concentration camps
         Relocation camps
**Interpersonal relations**
         --[country or state]--[city]
  PN   Includes relations among individuals and
         groups of people. Search also under the
         subdivision --SOCIAL LIFE used with names
         of ethnic, racial, and regional groups, and
         with classes of persons (Appendix A); with
         names of persons (Appendix B);  and with
         corporate bodies and named events (Appendix
         D).
  UF   Brotherly love
         Goodwill
         Human relations
         Human understanding
         Interaction, Social
         Personal relations
         Relations, Interpersonal
         Social behavior
  NT   Adultery
         Blaming
         Charity
         Courtship +
         Fraternization
         Friendship
         Intergenerational relations
         Jewish-Arab relations
         Landlord & tenant
         Marriage +
         Quarreling
         Race relations +
         Relations between the sexes
  RT   Communication
         Competition (Psychology)
         Conformity
         Cooperation
         Cultural relations
         Ethics
         Fame
         Individuality
         International relations
         Law & legal affairs
         Mental states
         Passing the buck
         People
         Popularity
         Power (Social sciences)
         Sex
         Sociology
         Spouses

BT  Broader term                          RT  Related term                          PN Public Note
NT  Narrower term                         UF  Used for                              + Term has NTs
HN History Note                           CN Catalogers Note                        --[ ] May subdivide

**Interplanetary voyages**
  BT   Space flight
**Interracial marriage**
  USE Miscegenation
**Interrogation**
  USE Questioning
**Interrogation points**
  USE Question marks
**Interurban street railroads**
  USE Electric railroads
**Intervention (International law)**
        --[nationality]--[country or state]
  PN   For governmental interference in the
        political affairs of another country.
  UF   Military intervention
        Nonintervention
  BT   International relations
  RT   International police
        International security
        Military occupations
        Neutrality
**Interviewing**
  USE Interviews
**Interviews**
        --[country or state]--[city]
  UF   Interviewing
  BT   Communication
        Events
  RT   Conversation
        Employment interviewing
        Investigation
        Journalism
        Questioning
**Intimate feminine apparel**
  USE Lingerie
**Intoxication**
  PN   For images of drunk persons.
  CN   Used in a note under ALCOHOLISM.
  UF   Drunkenness
        Inebriety
  RT   Alcoholic beverages
        Alcoholism
        Drunk driving
        Hangovers
        Temperance
**Intrenchments**
  USE Trench warfare
**Introductions (Greetings)**
  USE Salutations
**Inundations**
  USE Floods
**Invalids**
  USE Handicapped persons
        Shut-ins
        Sick persons
**Invasions**
  USE Campaigns & battles
**Inventions**
  UF   Discoveries
  RT   Creation
        Inventors
        Patents

**Inventors**
  UF   Discoverers
  BT   People
  RT   Inventions
**Investigation**
        --[country or state]--[city]
  PN   For the process or acts of systematic
        research or searching inquiry.
  UF   Detection
        Fact-finding
        Sleuthing
        Snooping
  NT   Courts martial & courts of inquiry
        Criminal investigations
        Governmental investigations
  RT   Bertillon system
        Customs inspections
        Detectives
        Discovery & exploration
        Examinations
        Experiments
        Fingerprints
        Food adulteration & inspection
        Interviews
        Questioning
**Investigations, Governmental**
  USE Governmental investigations
**Investigations, Military**
  USE Courts martial & courts of inquiry
**Investment**
  USE Saving & investment
**Investment houses**
  USE Speculative houses
**Invitations**
  CN   TGM II term.
  RT   Announcements
**Ionic order**
        --[country or state]--[city]
  BT   Architectural orders
**Ionizing radiation**
  UF   Radiation, Ionizing
  RT   Radioactivity
        Radiography
**IOUs**
  USE Debt
**Iron industry**
        --[country or state]--[city]
  PN   Includes activities and structures.
  CN   Double index under INDUSTRIAL
        FACILITIES (or NTs) for images that focus
        on facilities.
  BT   Metallurgical industry
  RT   Iron mining
        Steel industry
**Iron lungs**
  BT   Medical equipment & supplies
  RT   Poliomyelitis
**Iron miners**
        --[country or state]--[city]
  BT   Miners
  RT   Iron mining
**Iron mining**

BT Broader term            RT Related term            PN Public Note
NT Narrower term           UF Used for                + Term has NTs
HN History Note            CN Catalogers Note          --[ ] May subdivide

**Iron mining (cont.)**
  --[country or state]--[city]
  PN  Includes activities and sites.
  CN  Used in a note under IRON MINERS.
  BT  Mining
  RT  Iron industry
      Iron miners
Iron photographs
  USE Tintypes
Iron work
  USE Ironwork
Ironclads
  USE Armored vessels
Ironing
  USE Laundry
Ironmongery
  USE Hardware
**Irons (Pressing)**
  UF  Box irons
      Flatirons
      Hand irons
      Pressing irons
      Sadirons
  BT  Equipment
  RT  Appliances
      Laundry
**Ironwork**
  --[country or state]--[city]
  UF  Iron work
      Wrought-iron work
  BT  Metalwork
  NT  Cast ironwork
  RT  Grilles
      Railings
Iron-clad vessels
  USE Armored vessels
Iron-on transfers
  USE Transfer sheets
**Irrigation**
  --[country or state]--[city]
  BT  Reclamation of land
      Water use
  RT  Agriculture
**Islands**
  --[country or state]
  UF  Archipelagoes
      Atolls
      Hammocks (Islands)
      Hummocks
      Keys (Islands)
  BT  Land
Isolation
  USE Solitude
Isolationism
  USE Neutrality
**Isometric projections**
  CN  TGM II term.
**Isthmuses**
  BT  Land
Italian roofs
  USE Hip roofs
**Ivory**

**Ivory (cont.)**
  RT  Elephants
      Ivory carving
      Tusks
**Ivory carving**
  --[country or state]--[city]
  BT  Carving
  RT  Ivory
Ivory tusks
  USE Tusks
Jackets
  USE Coats
Jackets, Book
  USE Book jackets
Jackets, Record
  USE Album covers
Jackrabbits
  USE Rabbits
**Jack-in-the-boxes**
  BT  Toys
**Jack-o-lanterns**
  BT  Pumpkins
  RT  Lanterns
**Jade art objects**
  UF  Jades
  BT  Art objects
Jades
  USE Jade art objects
Jai alai
  USE Pelota (Game)
**Jails**
  --[country or state]--[city]
  UF  Gaols
  BT  Detention facilities
  RT  Cages
      Prisons
Jams
  USE Preserves
**Jangadas**
  --[country or state]--[city]
  PN  A catamaran-like sailing raft made of
      balsa logs, used off the coast of northeast
      Brazil.
  BT  Rafts
Japanese fencing
  USE Kendo
Japanese flowering cherry trees
  USE Cherry trees
**Japanese gardens**
  --[country or state]--[city]
  PN  For gardens in Japanese style outside of
      Japan.
  BT  Gardens
Japanese wrestling
  USE Sumo
Japanning industry
  USE Varnishing industry
Jargon
  USE Slang
**Jazz**
  HN  Changed 1/1993 from JAZZ MUSIC.
  UF  Jazz music

---

BT Broader term                    RT Related term                    PN Public Note
NT Narrower term                   UF Used for                        + Term has NTs
HN History Note                    CN Catalogers Note                 --[ ] May subdivide

Jazz (cont.)
BT   Music
RT   Jazz singers
Jazz music
USE Jazz
**Jazz singers**
UF   Jazz vocalists
BT   Singers
RT   Jazz
Singing
Jazz vocalists
USE Jazz singers
Jealousy
USE Envy
**Jeep automobiles**
--[nationality]--[country or state]--[city]
UF   Army jeeps
Willys jeeps
BT   Vehicles
RT   Automobiles
Military vehicles
Tractors
Trucks
Jellies
USE Preserves
Jelly fishes
USE Jellyfishes
**Jellyfishes**
--[country or state]--[city]
UF   Jelly fishes
BT   Aquatic animals
Jesters
USE Fools & jesters
**Jetties**
--[country or state]--[city]
UF   Breakwaters
BT   Erosion protection works
RT   Harbors
Piers & wharves
**Jewelry**
UF   Jewels
BT   Clothing & dress
NT   Earrings
Necklaces
Rings
RT   Amulets
Art objects
Clocks & watches
Cloisonné
Crowns
Gems
Jewelry stores
Lapidary work
**Jewelry making**
--[country or state]--[city]
BT   Handicraft
**Jewelry stores**
--[country or state]--[city]
PN   Includes activities and structures.
BT   Stores & shops
RT   Jewelry
Jewels

Jewels (cont.)
USE Gems
Jewelry
**Jewish-Arab relations**
UF   Arab-Jewish relations
Palestine problem
BT   Interpersonal relations
RT   Zionism
Jim Crow
USE Segregation
Jingoism
USE Chauvinism & jingoism
**Jinns**
UF   Genies
Genii
BT   Supernatural beings
Jinrikishas
USE Rickshaws
**Jitterbug dancing**
--[country or state]--[city]
UF   Jitterbugging
BT   Dancing
Jitterbugging
USE Jitterbug dancing
Jiu-jitsu
USE Oriental hand-to-hand fighting
Job interviewing
USE Employment interviewing
Job placement agencies
USE Employment agencies
Job training
USE Vocational education
Jobless people
USE Unemployed
Jobs
USE Employment
Occupations
**Jockeys**
--[country or state]--[city]
BT   Athletes
RT   Horse racing
Jogging
USE Running
**Joinery**
--[country or state]--[city]
PN   For construction of articles by joining
pieces of wood and for the results of that
activity.
RT   Cabinetmaking
Carpentry
Woodworking
Jokes, Practical
USE Practical jokes
**Joking**
NT   Practical jokes
Jongleurs
USE Juggling
Minstrels
Troubadours
Jonquils
USE Daffodils
**Joshua trees**

---

BT Broader term
NT Narrower term
HN History Note

RT Related term
UF Used for
CN Catalogers Note

PN Public Note
+ Term has NTs
--[ ] May subdivide

**Joshua trees (cont.)**
    --[country or state]--[city]
BT    Trees
**Journalism**
    --[country or state]--[city]
UF    Editing
BT    Communication
NT    Muckraking
    Photojournalism
    Yellow journalism
RT    Interviews
    Journalists
    Newsrooms
    Press
    Press conferences
**Journalists**
    --[nationality]--[country or state]--[city]
BT    People associated with education &
    communication
NT    Photojournalists
    Reporters
    War correspondents
RT    Journalism
    Newspapers
Journeys
USE    Discovery & exploration
    Pilgrimages
    Travel
**Jousting**
BT    Tournaments
RT    Knights
Jubilees
USE    Anniversaries
**Judges**
    --[country or state]--[city]
CN    Subdivide as appropriate to indicate
    national, state, or municipal jurisdiction.
UF    Justices
    Magistrates
BT    Government officials
NT    Supreme Court justices
RT    Judicial proceedings
    Lawyers
Judgment Day
USE    End of the world
**Judicial proceedings**
    --[country or state]--[city]
PN    Search also under the subdivision
    --TRIALS, LITIGATION, ETC. used with
    names of persons (Appendix B).
UF    Chanceries
    Courts
    Hearings
    Trials
    Tribunals
BT    Law & legal affairs
    Meetings
NT    Courts martial & courts of inquiry
    War crime trials
    Witchcraft trials
RT    Actions & defenses
    Courthouses

**Judicial proceedings (cont.)**
    Courtrooms
    Gavels
    Judges
    Juries
    Vigilance committees
Judo
USE    Oriental hand-to-hand fighting
**Juggling**
    --[country or state]--[city]
UF    Jongleurs
    Legerdemain
    Sleights of hand
BT    Entertainment
RT    Circuses & shows
Jugs
USE    Pitchers
Jujitsu
USE    Oriental hand-to-hand fighting
Juke joints
USE    Bars
**Jukeboxes**
BT    Coin operated machines
    Phonographs
Jumble sales
USE    Secondhand sales
**Jumping**
    --[country or state]--[city]
BT    Locomotion
NT    Children jumping
RT    Hopscotch
    Rope skipping
Jumping rope
USE    Rope skipping
**Jumping (Horsemanship)**
    --[country or state]--[city]
UF    Horse show jumping
BT    Horseback riding
NT    Show jumping
RT    Horses
    Sports
Jungles
USE    Tropical forests
**Junior republics**
    --[country or state]--[city]
PN    Includes activities and structures.
CN    Double index under ORGANIZATIONS'
    FACILITIES (or NTs) for images that focus
    on facilities.
UF    George junior republics
BT    Educational organizations
RT    Reformatories
Junk mail
USE    Advertising mail
**Junks**
    --[nationality]--[country or state]--[city]
UF    Chinese junks
BT    Boats
**Junkyards**
    --[country or state]--[city]
UF    Scrapyards
BT    Facilities

---

BT  Broader term          RT  Related term          PN  Public Note
NT  Narrower term         UF  Used for              +  Term has NTs
HN  History Note          CN  Catalogers Note       --[ ] May subdivide

**Junkyards (cont.)**
NT   Boat graveyards
RT   Ragpicking
    Refuse
    Refuse disposal
    Salvage
Juntas, Military
  USE Military regimes
**Juries**
     --[country or state]--[city]
UF   Jury
BT   People
NT   Grand juries
RT   Committees
    Judicial proceedings
Jury
  USE Juries
**Justice**
NT   Social justice
RT   Ethics
    Law & legal affairs
**Justice facilities**
     --[country or state]--[city]
NT   Police stations
RT   Detention facilities
Justices
  USE Judges
Justices (U.S. Supreme Court)
  USE Supreme Court justices
Jut windows
  USE Bay windows
**Jute**
     --[country or state]--[city]
BT   Fibers
    Plants
RT   Rope industry
Juvenile art
  USE Children's art
**Juvenile delinquents**
     --[country or state]--[city]
UF   Delinquents
BT   Children
RT   Criminals
    Gangs
    Reformatories
**Juvenilia**
CN   TGM II term.
UF   Artists' early works
**Kallitypes**
CN   TGM II term.
UF   Brownprints
    Callitypes
**Kangaroo hunting**
     --[country or state]
BT   Big game hunting
    Hunting
RT   Kangaroos
**Kangaroos**
     --[country or state]
BT   Animals
RT   Kangaroo hunting
**Kankles**

**Kankles (cont.)**
BT   Stringed instruments
Karate
  USE Oriental hand-to-hand fighting
**Karts (Midget cars)**
     --[country or state]--[city]
UF   Go-carts
    Go-Karts
BT   Vehicles
Kayaks
  USE Canoes
**Kazoos**
PN   Includes the activity of playing kazoos.
BT   Musical instruments
RT   Wind instruments
**Keelboats**
     --[country or state]--[city]
BT   Boats
**Keepsakes**
CN   TGM II term.
UF   Souvenirs
RT   Souvenir shops
**Kendo**
     --[country or state]--[city]
UF   Japanese fencing
BT   Fencing
**Kennels**
     --[country or state]--[city]
UF   Doghouses
BT   Animal housing
RT   Dogs
    Pets
**Kettles**
PN   Metallic vessels for boiling liquid.
BT   Cooking utensils
Key blocks
  USE Keystones
**Key plates**
BT   Hardware
RT   Keys (Hardware)
**Keyboard instruments**
PN   Includes the activity of playing keyboard
    instruments.
BT   Musical instruments
NT   Accordions
    Calliopes
    Harpsichords
    Organs
    Pianos +
Keyhole surrounds
  USE Keyholes
**Keyholes**
UF   Door fittings
    Keyhole surrounds
RT   Locks (Hardware)
**Keys (Hardware)**
BT   Hardware
RT   Key plates
    Locks (Hardware)
Keys (Identification)
  USE Keys (Legends)
Keys (Islands)

---

BT Broader term          RT Related term          PN Public Note
NT Narrower term         UF Used for              + Term has NTs
HN History Note          CN Catalogers Note       --[ ] May subdivide

Keys (Islands) (cont.)
  USE Islands
**Keys (Legends)**
  CN   TGM II term.
  UF   Identification keys
       Keys (Identification)
       Legends (Identification)
       Legends (Keys)
**Keystones**
       --[country or state]--[city]
  PN   The wedge-shaped piece at the crown of
       an arch, especially such a piece inserted last
       and locking the other pieces in place.
  UF   Key blocks
       Mensoles
  BT   Voussoirs
**Khories**
  USE Galleries (Rooms & spaces)
**Kicking**
  UF   Booting
  RT   Feet
       Fighting
       Punishment & torture
**Kidnappings**
       --[country or state]--[city]
  UF   Abductions
  BT   Crimes
**Killings**
  USE Homicides
**Kilns**
       --[country or state]--[city]
  BT   Equipment
  RT   Brick industry
       Furnaces
       Ovens
       Potteries
       Pottery industry
**Kilts**
  BT   Clothing & dress
**Kindergartens**
       --[country or state]--[city]
  BT   Schools
**Kinetographs**
  USE Motion picture devices
**Kinetoscopes**
  USE Motion picture devices
**Kingfishers**
       --[country or state]
  BT   Birds
**Kings**
       --[country]
  BT   Men
       Rulers
  RT   Emperors
**Kiosks**
       --[country or state]--[city]
  PN   For small light structures with one or more
       open sides, especially as a newsstand or
       telephone booth. Also for free-standing
       columns on which announcements of
       concerts, plays, etc., are glued.
  RT   Landscape pavilions

Kiosks (cont.)
       Newspaper vendors
**Kissing**
  BT   Manners & customs
  NT   Children kissing
  RT   Courtship
       Love
**Kitchen cabinets**
  USE Cupboards
**Kitchen dressers**
  USE Cupboards
**Kitchen utensils**
  USE Cooking utensils
**Kitchens**
       --[country or state]--[city]
  BT   Interiors
  NT   Galleys (Ship kitchens)
       Street kitchens
  RT   Chuckwagons
       Cookery
       Pantries
**Kitchens, Street**
  USE Street kitchens
**Kites**
  RT   Aircraft
       Children flying kites
       Toys
**Kittens**
  USE Cats
**Kivas**
       --[country or state]--[city]
  PN   Pueblo ceremonial structure that is usually
       round and partly underground.
  BT   Religious facilities
  RT   Pueblos
       Social & civic facilities
**Knighting**
       --[country]
  PN   For images in which knighthood is
       conferred.
  BT   Rites & ceremonies
  RT   Knights
**Knights**
       --[nationality]--[country or state]--[city]
  BT   Nobility
  RT   Armor
       Chivalry
       Jousting
       Knighting
       Tournaments
**Knitting**
       --[country or state]--[city]
  BT   Sewing
  RT   Hosiery industry
       Yarn
**Knives**
  BT   Equipment
  RT   Arms & armament
       Cutlery industry
       Silverware
       Tableware
**Knolls**

---

BT  Broader term                    RT  Related term                    PN  Public Note
NT  Narrower term                   UF  Used for                        +   Term has NTs
HN  History Note                    CN  Catalogers Note                 --[ ] May subdivide

Knolls (cont.)
  USE Hills
Knowledge, Tree of
  USE Tree of knowledge
Kodachrome transparencies
  USE Dye coupler transparencies
Kodacolor negatives
  USE Dye coupler negatives
**Kodak card photographs**
  CN  TGM II term.
Kodak instant color prints
  USE Dye diffusion transfer prints
**Kosher food industry**
       --[country or state]--[city]
  PN  Includes activities and structures.
  CN  Double index under INDUSTRIAL
      FACILITIES (and NTs) for images that focus
      on facilities.
  BT  Food industry
  RT  Dietary laws
      Meat industry
Kriegsspiel
  USE War games
Kung fu
  USE Oriental hand-to-hand fighting
**Labels**
  CN  TGM II term.
Labor
  USE Employment
Labor arbitration
  USE Industrial arbitration
**Labor housing**
       --[country or state]--[city]
  UF  Workers' housing
  BT  Housing
  NT  Construction camps
  RT  Tenement houses
      Work camps
**Labor leaders**
       --[country or state]--[city]
  PN  For labor union officials and other
      individuals involved in organizing labor
      unions or promoting the interests of the
      working class.
  UF  Labor union officials
      Leaders, Labor
  BT  People
  RT  Labor unions
Labor organizations
  USE Labor unions
Labor union officials
  USE Labor leaders
**Labor unions**
       --[country or state]--[city]
  PN  Includes activities and structures.
  CN  Double index under ORGANIZATIONS'
      FACILITIES (or NTs) for images that focus
      on facilities.
  UF  Labor organizations
      Trade unions
      Unions, Labor
  BT  Organizations

**Labor unions (cont.)**
  NT  Agricultural laborers' unions
      Automobile industry unions
      Bricklayers' unions
      Carpenters' unions
      Chorus girls' unions
      Clothing industry unions
      Guilds
      Longshoremen's unions
      Miners' unions
      Musicians' unions
      Printers' unions
      Railroad employees' unions
      Textile industry unions
      Tobacco industry unions
  RT  Employee rights
      Industrial arbitration
      Labor leaders
      Pickets
      Strikes
**Laboratories**
       --[country or state]--[city]
  UF  Labs
  BT  Research facilities
  RT  Science
Laboratory animals
  USE Animal experimentation
**Laboratory schools**
       --[country or state]--[city]
  PN  Includes activities and structures.
  UF  Campus schools
      Demonstration schools
      Model schools
  BT  Schools
  RT  Universities & colleges
**Laborers**
       --[country or state]--[city]
  PN  Includes persons who engage in general or
      unspecified physical labor.
  UF  Blue collar workers
  BT  People associated with manual labor
  NT  Agricultural laborers +
      Alien laborers
      Child laborers
      Contract laborers
      Migrant laborers +
      Prison laborers +
      Woodcutters
  RT  Employees
      Poor persons
      Strikes
      Working class
Laboring classes
  HN  Changed 8/1992 from postable term.
  USE Working class
Labor, Hours of
  USE Hours of labor
Labs
  USE Laboratories
Labyrinths
  USE Mazes
**Lace making**

---

BT  Broader term
NT  Narrower term
HN  History Note

RT  Related term
UF  Used for
CN  Catalogers Note

PN  Public Note
+  Term has NTs
--[ ]  May subdivide

Lace making (cont.)
  UF   Tatting
  BT   Sewing
Lacquering industry
  USE Varnishing industry
Lacrosse
       --[country or state]--[city]
  PN   Includes organizations and activities.
  BT   Sports
Ladders
  UF   Stepladders
  BT   Equipment
Lady's slippers
  BT   Orchids
Lagoons
  USE Lakes & ponds
Lake steamers
  USE Steamboats
Lakefronts
  USE Waterfronts
Lakes & ponds
       --[country or state]--[city]
  UF   Lagoons
       Ponds
       Pools
  BT   Bodies of water
  NT   Lily ponds
       Water holes
  RT   Reservoirs
       Water slides
Lambertypes
  USE Carbon prints
Lambs
  USE Sheep
Laminated plastics
  UF   Formica
       Plastic laminates
  BT   Plastics
  RT   Building materials
Lamp posts
  USE Lampposts
Lamp stores
  USE Light fixture stores
Lampposts
       --[country or state]--[city]
  PN   Posts usually supporting outdoor lamps or
       lanterns.
  UF   Lamp posts
       Light poles
  BT   Site elements
  RT   Light fixtures
       Lighting
Lamps
  BT   Light fixtures
Lancers
       --[nationality]--[country or state]--[city]
  PN   For persons who fight with a spear or
       spear-like weapon, often while mounted on
       horseback. Includes activities.
  BT   People
  RT   Campaigns & battles
       Cavalry

Lancers (cont.)
       Spears
Land
  UF   Ground
       Landforms
       Soil
  NT   Arroyos
       Beaches
       Buttes
       Capes (Coasts)
       Caves
       Cliffs
       Craters
       Croplands
       Cutover lands
       Deltas
       Deserts
       Dunes
       Forests +
       Glaciers
       Hills
       Islands
       Isthmuses
       Meadows
       Mesas
       Mountains
       Oases
       Passes (Landforms)
       Peninsulas
       Plains
       Prairies
       Reefs
       Rock formations
       Sandbars
       Valleys +
       Volcanoes +
       Waterfronts +
       Wetlands
  RT   Bodies of water
       Land tenure
       Land use
       Mud
       Nature
       Soil conservation
Land clearing
  USE Clearing of land
Land development
  USE Real estate development
Land management
  USE Land use
Land mines
  USE Mines (Warfare)
Land reclamation
  USE Reclamation of land
Land rushes
       --[country or state]--[city]
  BT   Events
  RT   Real estate development
       Westward movement
Land subdivision
       --[country or state]--[city]
  PN   Includes process of dividing tracts of land

---

BT  Broader term                    RT  Related term                    PN  Public Note
NT  Narrower term                   UF  Used for                        +  Term has NTs
HN  History Note                    CN  Catalogers Note                 --[ ] May subdivide

**Land subdivision (cont.)**
    into lots for purposes of sale as well as the
    resulting lots.
  UF  Subdivision of land
      Subdivisions (Land)
  BT  Real estate business
  RT  City planning
      Housing developments
      Land use
      Real estate development
Land surveying
  USE Surveying
**Land tenure**
    --[country or state]--[city]
  PN  Rights or terms relating to ownership or
      occupation of land.
  UF  Tenure of land
  RT  Land
      Land use
      Law & legal affairs
      Right of property
**Land use**
    --[country or state]--[city]
  UF  Land management
      Management of land
      Use of land
      Utilization of land
  NT  Farming +
      Real estate development +
      Reclamation of land +
      Terraces (Land use)
  RT  City planning
      Conservation of natural resources
      Croplands
      Land
      Land subdivision
      Land tenure
Landforms
  USE Land
Landing barges
  USE Landing craft
**Landing craft**
    --[nationality]--[country or state]--[city]
  PN  Search also under the subdivision
      --AMPHIBIOUS OPERATIONS used with
      the names of wars (Appendix C).
  UF  Infantry landing craft
      Landing barges
      Landing ships
      Tank landing ships
  BT  Government vessels
  RT  Amphibious vehicles
**Landing floats**
    --[country or state]--[city]
  UF  Floating platforms
      Floats, Landing
      Platforms, Floating
      Swimming floats
  RT  Piers & wharves
      Swimming
Landing ships
  USE Landing craft

Landing vehicles, Tracked
  USE Tracked landing vehicles
Landings
  USE Piers & wharves
Landings (Arrivals)
  USE Arrivals & departures
**Landlord & tenant**
    --[country or state]--[city]
  UF  Landlord-tenant relations
      Tenancy
      Tenant & landlord
  BT  Interpersonal relations
  RT  Housing
      Real estate business
Landlord-tenant relations
  USE Landlord & tenant
**Landscape architecture drawings**
  CN  TGM II term.
  UF  Drawings, Landscape architecture
      Planting drawings
**Landscape architecture facilities**
    --[country or state]--[city]
  HN  Changed 1/1993 from LANDSCAPE
      FACILITIES.
  UF  Landscape facilities
  BT  Facilities
  NT  Arbors (Bowers) +
      Architectural follies
      Gazebos
      Landscape pavilions
  RT  Fountains
      Garden walls
      Gardens
      Gates
      Greenhouses
      Mazes
      Parks
      Rustic work
      Stepping stones
      Stone walls
      Yard ornaments
**Landscape drawings**
  CN  TGM II term.
Landscape facilities
  USE Landscape architecture facilities
Landscape gardening
  USE Gardening
**Landscape paintings**
  CN  TGM II term.
**Landscape pavilions**
    --[country or state]--[city]
  CN  Light, sometimes ornamental structures in
      a garden or a park.
  HN  Changed 1/1993 from PAVILIONS.
  UF  Pavilions, Landscape
      Tent structures
  BT  Landscape architecture facilities
  RT  Canopies
      Kiosks
      Temporary buildings
      Tents
**Landscape photographs**

---

BT Broader term               RT Related term               PN Public Note
NT Narrower term           UF Used for                  + Term has NTs
HN History Note              CN Catalogers Note         --[ ] May subdivide

**Landscape photographs (cont.)**
CN  TGM II term.
**Landscape prints**
CN  TGM II term.
**Landscapes**
CN  TGM II term.
UF  Topographic views
**Landslides**
--[country or state]--[city]
PN  Includes the event and any resulting damage.
UF  Mud slides
BT  Natural phenomena
NT  Avalanches
RT  Disasters
Erosion
Mountains
Lanes, Bowling
USE Bowling alleys
Lanes, Lovers'
USE Lovers' lanes
**Lantern making**
RT  Lanterns
**Lantern slides**
CN  TGM II term.
UF  Magic lantern slides
**Lanterns**
PN  For portable lighting that consists of a protective enclosure with transparent openings and often supporting frames or carrying handles.
NT  Chinese lanterns
RT  Jack-o-lanterns
Lantern making
Light fixtures
**Lanterns (Architecture)**
--[country or state]--[city]
PN  Windowed superstructures crowning a roof or dome, often serving to give light or air to the space below.
BT  Architectural elements
RT  Lighting
Roofs
Steeples
Windows
**Lapidary work**
--[country or state]--[city]
PN  Cutting, carving, or polishing precious stones.
BT  Handicraft
RT  Gems
Jewelry
Largest
USE Curiosities & wonders
Lasciviousness
USE Lust
Laser photographs
USE Holograms
Lassoing
USE Roping
**Last rites**
--[country or state]--[city]

**Last rites (cont.)**
UF  Extreme unction
Last sacraments
BT  Rites & ceremonies
RT  Deathbeds
Last sacraments
USE Last rites
Last words
USE Deathbeds
Latchmakers
USE Locksmiths
**Lathes**
RT  Equipment
Machinery
**Laths**
PN  Narrow, thin strips of wood or metal, used in making a supporting structure for plaster, shingles, slates, or tiles.
UF  Plaster laths
Wall laths
BT  Building materials
**Latin cross buildings**
--[country or state]--[city]
UF  Cruciform (Latin) buildings
BT  Buildings distinguished by form
RT  Churches
Latrines
USE Privies
Lattices, Garden
USE Trellises
**Laughter**
RT  Mental states
**Launches**
--[nationality]--[country or state]--[city]
BT  Motorboats
**Launchings**
--[country or state]--[city]
BT  Events
RT  Boat & ship industry
Naval yards & naval stations
Vessels
Laundries (Commercial establishments)
USE Cleaning establishments
**Laundries (Rooms & spaces)**
--[country or state]--[city]
PN  For non-commercial structures and spaces. Search under CLEANING ESTABLISHMENTS for commercial activities and structures.
UF  Laundry rooms
BT  Interiors
RT  Laundry
**Laundry**
--[country or state]--[city]
PN  For domestic and non-commercial activities, e.g., washing and ironing. Includes laundry work in institutions such as hospitals. Search under CLEANING ESTABLISHMENTS for activities in commercial laundries.
UF  Clothes washing
Ironing

BT Broader term          RT Related term          PN Public Note
NT Narrower term         UF Used for               + Term has NTs
HN History Note           CN Catalogers Note        --[ ] May subdivide

**Laundry (cont.)**
     Pressing
     Washing
  RT  Cleaning establishments
     Clotheslines
     Clothing & dress
     Domestic life
     Household soap
     Housework
     Irons (Pressing)
     Laundries (Rooms & spaces)
     Wash tubs
     Washboards
     Washing machines
Laundry rooms
  USE Laundries (Rooms & spaces)
**Laundry workers' strikes**
     --[country or state]--[city]
  BT  Strikes
  RT  Cleaning establishments
**Laurels**
     --[country or state]--[city]
  RT  Shrubs
     Trees
Lava rock
  USE Volcanic rock
Lavatories
  USE Bathrooms
**Law enforcement**
     --[country or state]--[city]
  PN  Includes law enforcement at the
     international level. Search also under the
     subdivision --CAPTURE &
     IMPRISONMENT used with names of
     ethnic, racial, and regional groups and classes
     of persons (Appendix A) and with names of
     persons (Appendix B).
  UF  Arrests
     Enforcement of law
  BT  Law & legal affairs
  RT  Bailiffs
     Crimes
     Frisking
     Handcuffs
     International police
     Law enforcement training
     Nightsticks
     Police
     Police raids
     Security systems
     Surveillance
     Vigilance committees
Law enforcement officers
  USE Bailiffs
     Police
**Law enforcement training**
     --[country or state]--[city]
  UF  Police training
  BT  Vocational education
  RT  Law enforcement
     Police
**Law offices**

**Law offices (cont.)**
     --[country or state]--[city]
  BT  Service industry facilities
  RT  Law & legal affairs
     Lawyers
     Offices
Law schools
  USE Legal education
**Law & legal affairs**
     --[country or state]--[city]
  UF  Legal affairs
  NT  Actions & defenses
     Amnesty
     Annexations
     Antitrust law
     Community property
     Constitutional amendments +
     Constitutions
     Consumer protection
     Contracts +
     Copyright
     Custody of children
     Deportations
     Divorce
     Firearms control
     Freedom of the seas
     Inheritance & sucession
     Judicial proceedings +
     Law enforcement
     Laws +
     Legislation
     Marriage +
     Naturalization
     Parole
     Patents
     Petroleum leases
     Referendums
     Right to asylum
     Tax exemptions
     Taxes +
     Treaties +
     Treaty violations
     Vetoes
     Wills
  RT  Congressional privileges & immunities
     Evictions
     Impeachments
     Interpersonal relations
     Justice
     Land tenure
     Law offices
     Lawyers
     Legal aid
     Legal education
     Liberty
     Politics & government
     Questioning
Lawn objects
  USE Yard ornaments
**Laws**
     --[country or state]--[city]
  BT  Law & legal affairs

---

BT Broader term               RT Related term               PN Public Note
NT Narrower term          UF Used for                   + Term has NTs
HN History Note             CN Catalogers Note          --[ ] May subdivide

**Laws (cont.)**
 NT  Blue laws
     Prohibition
     Traffic regulations
 RT  Legislation
     Minimum wages
Lawsuits
 USE Actions & defenses
**Lawyers**
     --[country or state]--[city]
 UF  Attorneys
     Solicitors
 BT  People
 RT  Judges
     Law offices
     Law & legal affairs
Layoffs
 USE Dismissal of employees
**Laziness**
 UF  Sloth
 BT  Mental states
 RT  Deadly sins
**Lead industry**
     --[country or state]--[city]
 PN  Includes activities and structures.
 CN  Double index under INDUSTRIAL
     FACILITIES (or NTs) for images that focus
     on facilities.
 BT  Metallurgical industry
Lead lights
 USE Leaded glass windows
**Lead mining**
     --[country or state]--[city]
 PN  Includes activities and sites.
 BT  Mining
**Leaded glass windows**
     --[country or state]--[city]
 UF  Lead lights
     Leaded windows
 BT  Windows
Leaded windows
 USE Leaded glass windows
**Leader heads**
     --[country or state]--[city]
 UF  Conductor heads
     Heads, Conductor
     Heads, Leader
     Heads, Rainwater
     Rainwater heads
 BT  Mechanical systems components
 RT  Downspouts
     Gutters (Roofs)
**Leadership**
 NT  Military leadership
 RT  Sociology
Leaders, Labor
 USE Labor leaders
Leaders, Military
 USE Military officers
**Leaflets**
 CN  TGM II term.
 UF  Booklets

**Leaflets (cont.)**
     Brochures
Lean tos
 USE Lean-tos
**Lean-tos**
     --[country or state]--[city]
 PN  Shack or shed with a single pitched roof
     with higher end abutting a wall or larger
     building.
 UF  Lean tos
 BT  Buildings distinguished by form
 RT  Outbuildings
     Shelters
**Leap years**
 BT  Time
Leases, Oil
 USE Petroleum leases
**Leather goods stores**
     --[country or state]--[city]
 PN  Includes activities and structures.
 BT  Stores & shops
 RT  Leather industry
**Leather industry**
     --[country or state]--[city]
 PN  Includes activities and structures.
 CN  Double index under INDUSTRIAL
     FACILITIES (or NTs) for images that focus
     on facilities.
 UF  Tanneries
 BT  Industry
 RT  Bookbinding
     Hides & skins
     Leather goods stores
     Saddlery
     Shoe industry
     Tanning
**Leather photographs**
 CN  TGM II term.
 UF  Collodion positive photographs
Leave with pay
 USE Employee vacations
**Leaves**
 UF  Foliage
 RT  Acanthi
     Plants
     Raking (Sweeping)
     Skeleton leaf arrangements
Leave-takings
 USE Arrivals & departures
     Farewells
Lechery
 USE Lust
Lecturing
 USE Public speaking
**Lederhosen**
     --[country or state]--[city]
 BT  Trousers
Leeching
 USE Phlebotomy
Legal affairs
 USE Law & legal affairs
**Legal aid**

---

BT  Broader term              RT  Related term              PN  Public Note
NT  Narrower term             UF  Used for                  +   Term has NTs
HN  History Note              CN  Catalogers Note           --[ ] May subdivide

**Legal aid (cont.)**
    --[country or state]--[city]
  BT  Assistance
  RT  Civil rights
      Law & legal affairs
**Legal education**
    --[country or state]--[city]
  PN  Includes activities and structures.
  CN  Double index under EDUCATIONAL
      FACILITIES (or NTs) for images that focus
      on facilities.
  UF  Law schools
  BT  Education
  RT  Law & legal affairs
Legal petitions
  USE Petitions
Legal photographs
  USE Forensic photographs
Legations
  USE Embassies
Legendary characters
  USE Fictitious characters
**Legends**
  BT  Literature
Legends (Identification)
  USE Keys (Legends)
Legends (Keys)
  USE Keys (Legends)
Legerdemain
  USE Juggling
      Magic
**Legislation**
    --[country or state]--[city]
  UF  Bills (Legislation)
  BT  Law & legal affairs
  RT  Governmental investigations
      Laws
      Legislative bodies
      Legislators
      Lobbying
      Referendums
      Resolutions
      Tax reform
      Vetoes
**Legislative bodies**
    --[country or state]--[city]
  CN  Subdivide geographically for the
      jurisdiction of the legislative body.
  UF  Assemblies
      Congresses
      Parliaments
  BT  Organizations
  RT  Legislation
      Legislators
      Politics & government
      Presidents & the Congress
Legislative resolutions
  USE Resolutions
**Legislators**
    --[country or state]
  PN  Members of a legislative body.
  CN  Subdivide geographically for the

**Legislators (cont.)**
    jurisdiction of the body to which the
    legislator belongs (e.g., national, state, etc.).
  UF  Congressmen
      Senators
  BT  Government officials
  RT  Capitol pages
      Congressional privileges & immunities
      Legislation
      Legislative bodies
      Legislators' spouses
**Legislators' spouses**
    --[country or state]
  CN  Subdivide geographically for the
      jurisdiction of the body to which the
      legislator belongs (e.g., national, state, etc.).
  UF  Congressional spouses
      Legislators' wives
      Senators' spouses
  BT  Spouses
  RT  Legislators
Legislators' wives
  USE Legislators' spouses
**Legs**
  RT  Human body
**Leis**
  UF  Flower leis
  RT  Clothing & dress
      Decorations
      Flowers
**Leisure**
    --[country or state]--[city]
  UF  Relaxation
      Rest
  RT  Hammocks
      Manners & customs
      Recreation
      Resorts
      Rest stops
      Retirements
      Sabbaths
      Tourist trade
      Vacations
**Lemons**
    --[country or state]--[city]
  BT  Citrus fruit
Leninism
  USE Communism
Lenses, Hand
  USE Hand lenses
**Lenticular photographs**
  CN  TGM II term.
  UF  Three-dimensional photographs
**Leopards**
    --[country or state]
  BT  Animals
**Leprosy**
    --[country or state]--[city]
  BT  Communicable diseases
**Lesbians**
    --[country or state]--[city]
  UF  Female gays

---

BT Broader term          RT Related term          PN Public Note
NT Narrower term        UF Used for             + Term has NTs
HN History Note          CN Catalogers Note      --[ ] May subdivide

**Lesbians (cont.)**
  BT  Gays
       Women
  RT  Gay men
**Letter carriers**
      --[country or state]--[city]
  UF  Mailmen
  BT  Postal service employees
**Letter pictures**
  CN  TGM II term.
  UF  Calligrams
Letter sheets
  USE Letterheads
**Letterheads**
  CN  TGM II term.
  UF  Illustrated letter paper
       Letter sheets
**Letterpress works**
  CN  TGM II term.
Letters
  USE Correspondence
Letters of the alphabet
  USE Alphabets (Writing systems)
**Letters to Santa Claus**
  BT  Correspondence
  RT  Children reading & writing
       Holidays
       Writing
Lettersheets, Pictorial
  USE Pictorial lettersheets
Letters, Initial
  USE Initials
Letters, Love
  USE Love letters
**Lettuce**
      --[country or state]--[city]
  BT  Vegetables
**Levees**
      --[country or state]--[city]
  PN  Natural or manmade embankments
       flanking rivers or streams.
  BT  Hydraulic facilities
  RT  Dikes (Engineering)
       Piers & wharves
**Levitation**
      --[country or state]--[city]
  BT  Supernatural practices
  RT  Magic
**Libel & slander**
  UF  Calumny
       Defamation
       Gossip
       Slander
  RT  Crimes
       Freedom of speech
**Liberalism**
      --[country or state]--[city]
  BT  Economic & political systems
  RT  Mental states
Liberation movements, National
  USE National liberation movements
**Libertarianism**

**Libertarianism (cont.)**
      --[country or state]--[city]
  BT  Economic & political systems
  RT  Anarchism
       Government regulation
       Liberty
**Liberty**
  UF  Emancipation
       Freedom
  NT  Civil liberties +
  RT  Law & legal affairs
       Libertarianism
       Liberty bell
       Liberty cap
       Liberty tree
**Liberty bell**
  BT  Symbols
  RT  Bells
       Liberty
**Liberty cap**
  PN  Soft, close-fitting, visorless cap, adopted
       by the French and American Revolutionists
       as a symbol of liberty.
  BT  Symbols
  RT  Hats
       Liberty
Liberty loans
  USE War bonds & funds
**Liberty tree**
  UF  Tree of liberty
  BT  Symbols
  RT  Liberty
       Trees
**Librarians**
  BT  People associated with education &
       communication
  RT  Libraries
**Libraries**
      --[country or state]--[city]
  PN  Includes activities and structures.
  BT  Cultural facilities
  NT  Private libraries
  RT  Archives
       Athenaeums
       Book talks
       Bookmobiles
       Books
       Bookstacks
       Education
       Librarians
       Libraries (Rooms)
       Reading rooms
**Libraries (Rooms)**
      --[country or state]--[city]
  UF  Home libraries
  BT  Interiors
  RT  Dens
       Libraries
       Studies (Rooms)
Libraries, Private
  USE Private libraries
**License plates**

---

BT Broader term           RT Related term           PN Public Note
NT Narrower term         UF Used for             + Term has NTs
HN History Note          CN Catalogers Note      --[ ] May subdivide

**License plates (cont.)**
--[country or state]
UF   Automobile license plates
Automobile tags
RT   Automobile equipment & supplies
Recording & registration
Vehicles
Licentiousness
USE Lust
Life boats
USE Lifeboats
Life cycle, Human
USE Human life cycle
Life guards
USE Lifeguards
Life on other planets
USE Extraterrestrial life
**Life preservers**
BT   Safety equipment
RT   Lifesaving
Life saving
USE Lifesaving
**Lifeboats**
--[nationality]--[country or state]--[city]
UF   Life boats
BT   Boats
RT   Longboats
Marine accidents
Rowboats
**Lifeguards**
--[country or state]--[city]
UF   Life guards
BT   People associated with health & safety
RT   Lifesaving
**Lifesaving**
--[country or state]--[city]
PN   For activities involved in saving or
protecting lives, especially those of drowning
persons and shipwrecked persons.
UF   Life saving
BT   Rescue work
NT   Artificial respiration
Lifesaving at fires
RT   Drowning
Life preservers
Lifeguards
Lifesaving stations
Marine accidents
Safety
**Lifesaving at fires**
--[country or state]--[city]
BT   Lifesaving
RT   Fire escapes
Fire fighters
Fires
**Lifesaving stations**
--[country or state]--[city]
RT   Lifesaving
Life, Tree of
USE Tree of life
Lift bridges
USE Drawbridges

**Lift bridges (cont.)**
Vertical lift bridges
**Lifting & carrying**
--[country or state]--[city]
UF   Carrying & lifting
BT   Locomotion
NT   Weight lifting
RT   Portages
Porters
Shipping
Yokes
Lifts
USE Hoisting machinery
Lift-ground aquatints
USE Sugar-lift aquatints
Lift-ground engravings
USE Sugar-lift aquatints
**Light**
--[country or state]--[city]
UF   Sunlight
BT   Natural phenomena
RT   Lighting
Moonlight
Shadows
Sun
**Light bulbs**
--[country or state]--[city]
UF   Bulbs, Light
RT   Light fixtures
Lighting
**Light courts**
--[country or state]--[city]
PN   Courts or recesses which provide light or
ventilation to windows along walls.
BT   Architectural elements
RT   Lighting
**Light fixture stores**
--[country or state]--[city]
PN   Includes activities and structures.
UF   Lamp stores
Lighting fixture stores
BT   Appliance stores
RT   Light fixtures
**Light fixtures**
BT   Equipment
NT   Candelabras
Chandeliers
Gaslight fixtures
Lamps
Sconces
RT   Appliances
Lampposts
Lanterns
Light bulbs
Light fixture stores
Lighting
Searchlights
Street lights
Torches
Light poles
USE Lampposts
Light ships

---

BT  Broader term
NT  Narrower term
HN  History Note

RT  Related term
UF  Used for
CN  Catalogers Note

PN  Public Note
+   Term has NTs
--[ ] May subdivide

Light ships (cont.)
  USE Lightships
Lightheadedness
  USE Dizziness
**Lighthouse keepers**
        --[country or state]--[city]
  BT   People associated with health & safety
  RT   Lighthouses
**Lighthouses**
        --[country or state]--[city]
  BT   Transportation facilities
  RT   Beacons
       Communication facilities
       Lighthouse keepers
       Lightships
       Navigation
**Lighting**
        --[country or state]--[city]
  PN   For the subject of lighting.
  UF   Illumination
  NT   Cove lighting
       Electric lighting
       Gas-lighting
  RT   Building systems
       Candles
       Lampposts
       Lanterns (Architecture)
       Light
       Light bulbs
       Light courts
       Light fixtures
       Night
       Stage lighting
       Street lights
       War blackouts
Lighting fixture stores
  USE Light fixture stores
Lighting, Stage
  USE Stage lighting
**Lightning**
  UF   Thunderbolts
  BT   Natural phenomena
  RT   Electricity
       Lightning strikes
       Storms
**Lightning strikes**
        --[country or state]--[city]
  PN   Includes the event and any resulting
       damage.
  RT   Disasters
       Lightning
**Lightships**
        --[nationality]--[country or state]--[city]
  PN   Ships moored in places dangerous to
       navigation and equipped with warning lights.
  UF   Light ships
  BT   Ships
  RT   Lighthouses
**Lilacs**
        --[country or state]--[city]
  BT   Shrubs
**Lilies**

Lilies (cont.)
        --[country or state]--[city]
  UF   Calla
  BT   Flowers
Lily pads
  USE Water lilies
**Lily ponds**
        --[country or state]--[city]
  UF   Water lily ponds
  BT   Lakes & ponds
  RT   Water lilies
Limbs
  USE Tree limbs
**Limes**
        --[country or state]--[city]
  BT   Citrus fruit
**Limestone quarrying**
        --[country or state]--[city]
  PN   Includes activities and sites.
  BT   Quarrying
  NT   Marble quarrying
**Limited editions**
  CN   TGM II term.
  UF   Editions, Limited
**Limousines**
        --[nationality]--[country or state]--[city]
  BT   Automobiles
Line block prints
  USE Line photomechanical prints
**Line photomechanical prints**
  CN   TGM II term.
  UF   Line block prints
       Process line engravings
Linen closets
  USE Closets
**Linen industry**
        --[country or state]--[city]
  PN   Includes activities and structures.
  CN   Double index under INDUSTRIAL
       FACILITIES (or NTs) for images that focus
       on facilities.
  UF   Flax industry
  BT   Textile industry
  RT   Flax
Linen labels
  USE Textile labels
Liners
  USE Ocean liners
Lines
  USE Queues
**Lingerie**
  UF   Intimate feminine apparel
       Women's underwear
  BT   Underwear
  NT   Corsets
  RT   Hosiery
       Sleepwear
Links, Golf
  USE Golf
**Linocuts**
  CN   TGM II term.
  UF   Linoleum cut prints

---

**Linoleum blocks**
CN  TGM II term.
Linoleum cut prints
USE Linocuts
**Lintels**
--[country or state]--[city]
PN  Horizontal architectural members spanning and usually carrying the load above an opening.
UF  Breast beams
BT  Architectural elements
RT  Doors & doorways
Tympana
Windows
**Lion hunting**
--[country or state]
BT  Big game hunting
RT  Lions
**Lions**
--[country or state]
BT  Animals
RT  Lion hunting
Liquor
USE Alcoholic beverages
Liquor industry
USE Distilling industries
Liquor problem
USE Alcoholism
Liquor stills
USE Stills (Distilleries)
**Liquor stores**
--[country or state]--[city]
PN  Includes activities and structures.
BT  Stores & shops
RT  Alcoholic beverages
**Literacy**
--[country or state]--[city]
UF  Illiteracy
RT  Education
Reading
Writing
Literary critics
USE Critics
**Literature**
UF  Stories
Tales
NT  Fables
Fairy tales
Legends
Myths
Nursery rhymes
Parables
Poetry
Tall tales
RT  Authors
Fictitious characters
Heroes
Plays on words
Proverbs
Storytelling
Lithographic stones
USE Printing stones

**Lithographs**
CN  TGM II term.
**Lithotints**
CN  TGM II term.
Litigation
USE Actions & defenses
Litter (Trash)
USE Refuse
**Litters**
PN  Stretchers, usually of canvas stretched on a frame, for carrying disabled or dead persons.
UF  Stretchers
BT  Medical equipment & supplies
Liturgical objects
USE Religious articles
Livery stables
USE Stables
**Livestock**
--[country or state]
PN  Farm animals raised for use and profit.
BT  Animals
NT  Cattle +
RT  Agriculture
Animal auctions
Farms
Meat industry
Living pictures
USE Tableaux
**Living rooms**
--[country or state]--[city]
UF  Sitting rooms
BT  Interiors
RT  Boudoirs
Dens
Parlors
Living standard
USE Cost & standard of living
**Lizards**
--[country or state]
BT  Reptiles
**Llamas**
--[country or state]
BT  Animals
**Loading docks**
--[country or state]--[city]
UF  Docks, Loading
BT  Transportation facilities
RT  Shipping
Warehouses
Loan sharking
USE Usury
**Lobbies**
--[country or state]--[city]
PN  For large halls serving as foyers or anterooms in public buildings.
UF  Foyers
BT  Interiors
RT  Entrance halls
Parlors
Passageways
**Lobby cards**
CN  TGM II term.

BT  Broader term
NT  Narrower term
HN  History Note

RT  Related term
UF  Used for
CN  Catalogers Note

PN  Public Note
+  Term has NTs
--[ ]  May subdivide

**Lobbying**
    --[country or state]--[city]
  BT  Political participation
  RT  Activists
       Legislation
       Special interests
**Lobsters**
    --[country or state]
  BT  Shellfish
Local transit
  USE Mass transit
**Locker rooms**
    --[country or state]--[city]
  UF  Changing rooms
  BT  Interiors
  RT  Athletic clubs
       Gymnasiums
Locking devices
  USE Locks (Hardware)
Lockouts
  USE Strikes
Locks (Canals)
  USE Locks (Hydraulic engineering)
**Locks (Hardware)**
  UF  Locking devices
       Padlocks
  BT  Hardware
  RT  Keyholes
       Keys (Hardware)
       Locksmiths
       Safes
       Vaults (Strong rooms)
**Locks (Hydraulic engineering)**
    --[country or state]--[city]
  UF  Locks (Canals)
  BT  Architectural elements
  RT  Canals
**Locksmiths**
  UF  Latchmakers
  BT  People associated with manual labor
  RT  Locks (Hardware)
**Locomotion**
  PN  For the subject of locomotion in general.
  UF  Motion
       Movement
  NT  Animal locomotion
       Chasing
       Climbing +
       Crawling & creeping
       Cycling +
       Dancing +
       Human locomotion
       Jumping +
       Lifting & carrying +
       Marching +
       Pacing
       Running
       Spin (Aerodynamics)
       Walking +
  RT  Biomechanics
       Clumsiness
       Pulling

Locomotives
  USE Railroad locomotives
**Lodges**
    --[country or state]--[city]
  PN  Small houses in parks, forests, or
       domains; temporary habitations.
  BT  Houses
  NT  Ski lodges
  RT  Camps
       Hotels
       Shelters
Lodges (Gatehouses)
  USE Gatehouses
Lodges, Fraternal
  USE Fraternal lodges
Lodges, ski
  USE Ski lodges
**Lodging houses**
    --[country or state]--[city]
  PN  Houses in which sleeping
       accommodations are provided.
  UF  Boarding houses
       Flophouses
       Rooming houses
  BT  Public accommodation facilities
  RT  Dwellings
       Hotels
       Tourist camps & hostels
Lofts, Organ
  USE Organ lofts
**Log buildings**
    --[country or state]--[city]
  BT  Wooden buildings
  NT  Log cabins
**Log cabins**
    --[country or state]--[city]
  BT  Cabins
       Log buildings
Logged-off lands
  USE Cutover lands
**Loggias**
    --[country or state]--[city]
  PN  For roofed galleries open on one or more
       sides, sometimes pillared, especially at an
       upper story overlooking an open court; may
       also be separate structures, usually in a
       garden.
  BT  Rooms & spaces
  RT  Arcades (Architectural components)
       Balconies
       Porches
Logging
  USE Lumber industry
**Logos**
  UF  Logotypes
  RT  Advertisements
       Advertising
       Emblems
       Publicity
       Signs
       Symbols
Logotypes

---

BT  Broader term                    RT  Related term                    PN Public Note
NT  Narrower term                   UF  Used for                        + Term has NTs
HN History Note                     CN  Catalogers Note                 --[ ] May subdivide

Logotypes (cont.)
USE Logos

**Logs**
PN   For images that focus on bulky and long
     segments of tree trunks ready for cutting.
     Search under FUELWOOD for pieces of
     smaller trunks and branches to be used for
     fires. Search under WOODCUTTING for
     activities.
CN   As appropriate, double index under
     LUMBER INDUSTRY. Used in a note under
     LUMBER INDUSTRY.
UF   Timber
RT   Lumber industry
     Trees
     Woodcutting

**Longboats**
     --[nationality]--[country or state]--[city]
BT   Boats
RT   Lifeboats
     Rowboats

**Longcase clocks**
UF   Grandfather clocks
     Tall clocks
RT   Clocks & watches

**Longevity**
RT   Aged persons
     Biology

**Longshoremen**
     --[country or state]--[city]
UF   Dock hands
     Stevedores
BT   People associated with manual labor
RT   Longshoremen's strikes
     Longshoremen's unions
     Shipping

**Longshoremen's strikes**
     --[country or state]--[city]
BT   Freight handlers' strikes
RT   Longshoremen
     Longshoremen's unions

**Longshoremen's unions**
     --[country or state]--[city]
BT   Labor unions
RT   Longshoremen
     Longshoremen's strikes

Looking glasses
USE Mirrors

Lookout towers
USE Watch towers

Lookout towers, Fire
USE Fire lookout stations

**Looms**
PN   Frames or machines for interlacing at
     right angles two or more sets of threads or
     yarns to form a cloth.
RT   Equipment
     Textile machinery
     Weaving

**Loons**
     --[country or state]
BT   Birds

Loot
USE Caches
    Treasure-trove

Looting
USE Robberies
    War destruction & pillage

Lord's Day
USE Sabbaths

Lord's Supper
USE Communion

**Losers**
UF   Failures
BT   People

**Loss of consciousness**
UF   Consciousness, Loss of
     Fainting
     Unconsciousness
BT   Mental states
RT   Health

Loss of hope
USE Despair

**Lotteries**
     --[country or state]--[city]
BT   Gambling
RT   Fund raising

**Lottery tickets**
CN   TGM II term.
UF   Tickets, Lottery

Lounge cars
USE Railroad lounge cars

**Lounges**
     --[country or state]--[city]
BT   Interiors

Loupes
USE Hand lenses

**Love**
HN   Changed 11/1992 from non-postable term
     (Use COURTSHIP & LOVE or FREE
     LOVE).
BT   Mental states
RT   Couples
     Courtship
     Cupids
     Families
     Free love
     Friendship
     Kissing
     Love letters
     Marriage
     Romances

**Love letters**
UF   Letters, Love
BT   Correspondence
RT   Courtship
     Love

Lovemaking
USE Sex

**Lovers' lanes**
     --[country or state]--[city]
UF   Lanes, Lovers'
RT   Courtship
     Roads

---

BT  Broader term                          RT  Related term                          PN  Public Note
NT  Narrower term                         UF  Used for                              +  Term has NTs
HN  History Note                          CN  Catalogers Note                       --[ ]  May subdivide

Lovers' lanes (cont.)
    Walkways
Low cost housing
  USE Housing
Low income housing
  USE Housing
Low water crossings
  USE Fords (Stream crossings)
Loyalty, Political
  USE Allegiance
**Luggage**
  UF  Baggage
      Trunks
      Valises
  RT  Hotel porters
**Lumber industry**
      --[country or state]--[city]
  PN  Includes activities and structures.
  CN  As appropriate, double index under
      WOODCUTTING. Double index under
      INDUSTRIAL FACILITIES (or NTs) for
      images that focus on facilities. Used in a note
      under LOGS and MILLS.
  UF  Logging
      Timber industry
  BT  Industry
  RT  Building materials industry
      Crosscut saws
      Cutover lands
      Logs
      Paper industry
      Skid roads
      Trees
      Woodcutting
      Wooding stations
**Luminous works**
  CN  TGM II term.
  UF  Black light works
      Fluorescent works
Lunatic asylums
  USE Mental institutions
Lunchrooms
  USE Cafeterias
      Restaurants
Lunchrooms, Employee
  USE Employee eating facilities
**Lunettes**
      --[country or state]--[city]
  PN  Surfaces at the upper part of a wall partly
      surrounded by a vault which the wall
      intersects, often filled by a window, by
      several windows, or by mural painting.
  BT  Windows
**Lust**
  UF  Lasciviousness
      Lechery
      Licentiousness
      Sexual lust
  BT  Mental states
  RT  Adultery
      Deadly sins
      Rake's progress

Lust (cont.)
      Sex
**Lutes**
  PN  Includes the activity of playing lutes.
  BT  Stringed instruments
**Lutheran churches**
      --[country or state]--[city]
  PN  For images that focus on buildings, as
      well as the associated grounds.
  BT  Protestant churches
LVTs (Amphibian tractors)
  USE Tracked landing vehicles
Lying
  USE Honesty
**Lying in state**
      --[country or state]--[city]
  PN  Search also under the subdivision
      --DEATH & BURIAL used with names of
      persons (Appendix B).
  UF  State funerals
  BT  Funeral rites & ceremonies
  RT  Coffins
Lying tales
  USE Tall tales
Lying-in hospitals
  USE Maternity hospitals
**Lynchings**
      --[country or state]--[city]
  PN  Killings by mob action without legal
      sanction.
  BT  Homicides
  RT  Executions
      Vigilance committees
**Lynx**
      --[country or state]
  BT  Animals
  RT  Lynx hunting
**Lynx hunting**
      --[country or state]
  BT  Hunting
  RT  Lynx
**Machine guns**
  BT  Firearms
  NT  Gatling guns
Machine sewing
  USE Sewing machines
**Machine shops**
      --[country or state]--[city]
  BT  Workshops
**Machinery**
  NT  Air compressors
      Bulldozers
      Coin counting machines
      Coin operated machines +
      Cotton gins
      Drilling & boring machinery
      Electric oscillators
      Electrical apparatus +
      Engines +
      Graders (Earthmoving machinery)
      Grinding wheels
      Guillotines

---

BT Broader term         RT Related term         PN Public Note
NT Narrower term        UF Used for              + Term has NTs
HN History Note          CN Catalogers Note      --[ ] May subdivide

## Machinery (cont.)

Hoisting machinery
Inclined planes
Pile drivers
Presses +
Pulleys
Pumps +
Road rollers
Robots
Spinning machinery
Steam hammers
Steam shovels
Switchboards +
Textile machinery
Treadmills
Waterwheels
Wind tunnels
RT    Agricultural machinery & implements
Ball bearings
Bellows
Equipment
Lathes
Machinery industry
Mechanical systems
Tractors
Vehicles

## Machinery industry

--[country or state]--[city]
PN    Manufacture and trade of machinery.
Includes activities and structures.
CN    Double index under INDUSTRIAL
FACILITIES (or NTs) for images that focus
on facilities.
BT    Industry
RT    Machinery
Tool & die industry

Machines, Coin operated
USE Coin operated machines

## Machismo

PN    A strong sense of masculine pride; an
exaggerated awareness and assertion of
masculinity.
RT    Men
Mental states
Sexism

## Macrophotographs

CN    TGM II term.

Madness
USE Mentally ill persons

## Magazine covers

CN    TGM II term.
UF    Covers, Magazine
Periodical covers

Magazine illustrations
USE Periodical illustrations

Magazine posters
USE Book & magazine posters

Magazine vendors
USE Newspaper vendors

Magazines
USE Periodicals

## Magazines (Military buildings)

## Magazines (Military buildings) (cont.)

--[nationality]--[country or state]--[city]
PN    For buildings in which ammunition and
explosives are kept at military installations.
UF    Ammunition depots
Ammunition magazines
Powder magazines
BT    Military facilities
RT    Ammunition
Ammunition dumps
Military depots

## Magic

--[country or state]--[city]
PN    Use of spells, charms, etc., believed to
have supernatural power to produce or
prevent a particular result considered
unobtainable by natural means, as well as the
type of entertainment in which a performer
does tricks or so-called magic or conjuring.
UF    Conjuring
Legerdemain
Necromancy
Prestidigitation
Sleights of hand
Sorcery
Spells
Wizardry
NT    Card tricks
Snake charming
RT    Alchemy
Amulets
Crystal balls
Entertainment
Hypnotism
Levitation
Magicians
Shamans
Supernatural practices
Talismans
Telepathy
Wishing wells
Witchcraft
Wizards

Magic lantern slides
USE Lantern slides

Magic posters
USE Theatrical posters

## Magical devices

BT    Supernatural
NT    Amulets
Divining rods
Ouija boards
Talismans
Wishing wells
RT    Equipment
Supernatural practices

## Magicians

UF    Conjurers
Illusionists
BT    Entertainers
RT    Magic
Wizards

---

BT  Broader term
NT  Narrower term
HN  History Note

RT  Related term
UF  Used for
CN  Catalogers Note

PN  Public Note
+  Term has NTs
--[ ]  May subdivide

Magistrates
    USE Judges
**Magnets**
    BT   Scientific equipment
Magnifying glasses
    USE Hand lenses
**Magnolias**
        --[country or state]--[city]
    BT   Trees
**Magpies**
        --[country or state]
    BT   Birds
Magueys
    USE Agaves
**Mah jong**
    BT   Board games
**Mahogany trees**
        --[country or state]--[city]
    BT   Trees
Maidens
    USE Single women
Maids
    USE Servants
Mail
    USE Correspondence
Mail boats
    USE Mail steamers
Mail planes
    USE Transport planes
Mail service
    USE Postal service
**Mail steamers**
        --[nationality]--[country or state]--[city]
    UF   Mail boats
         Packet ships
    BT   Vessels
    RT   Postal service
**Mail trucks**
        --[country or state]--[city]
    BT   Trucks
    RT   Postal service
**Mailboxes**
        --[country or state]--[city]
    BT   Containers
    RT   Postal service
Mailing cards
    USE Postcards
Mailmen
    USE Letter carriers
**Mail-order businesses**
        --[country or state]--[city]
    PN   Includes activities and structures.
    UF   Catalog order businesses
    BT   Business enterprises
    RT   Postal service
**Maintenance & repair**
        --[country or state]--[city]
    UF   Repair
    NT   Vehicle maintenance & repair
    RT   Construction
         Equipment
         Mechanics (Persons)

**Maintenance & repair (cont.)**
         Railroad construction & maintenance
Majorettes, Drum
    USE Drum majorettes
Majors, Drum
    USE Drum majors
Makeup (Cosmetics)
    USE Cosmetics & soap
Maladies
    USE Diseases
**Malaria**
        --[country or state]--[city]
    UF   Ague
    BT   Communicable diseases
Male chauvinism
    USE Sexism
**Male figure drawings**
    CN   TGM II term.
Male gays
    USE Gay men
Malediction
    USE Cursing
Males
    USE Men
Malformations
    USE Birth defects
         Human curiosities
Mallets
    USE Chisels & mallets
Malls
    USE Parks
Malnutrition
    USE Nutrition
Maltreated persons
    USE Abused children
         Abused women
Mammary glands
    USE Breasts
**Mammoth plates**
    CN   TGM II term.
**Mammoths**
        --[country or state]
    UF   Woolly mammoths
    BT   Elephants
         Extinct animals
Manacles
    USE Shackles
Management of land
    USE Land use
**Mandolins**
    PN   Includes the activity of playing
         mandolins.
    BT   Stringed instruments
Maneuvers, Military
    USE Military maneuvers
Manger scenes (Crèches)
    USE Crèches (Nativity scenes)
**Mangrove plants**
        --[country or state]--[city]
    UF   Mangroves
    BT   Plants
Mangroves

---

BT Broader term                     RT Related term                     PN Public Note
NT Narrower term                    UF Used for                         + Term has NTs
HN History Note                     CN Catalogers Note                  --[ ] May subdivide

Mangroves (cont.)
USE Mangrove plants
**Manhole covers**
--[country or state]--[city]
RT Manholes
Public utility companies
Streets
**Manholes**
--[country or state]--[city]
BT Holes
RT Manhole covers
Public utility companies
Sewers
Streets
**Manicuring**
--[country or state]--[city]
BT Grooming
Manière criblée prints
USE Dotted prints
**Manila hemp**
UF Abaca
BT Hemp
**Mannequins**
RT Clothing industry
Clothing stores
Fashion models
Human body
Manners
USE Etiquette
**Manners & customs**
--[country or state]--[city]
PN Search also under the subdivision
--SOCIAL LIFE used with names of ethnic,
racial and regional groups, and with classes
of persons (Appendix A), with names of
persons (Appendix B), and with corporate
bodies and named events (Appendix D).
Search also under the subdivision --SOCIAL
ASPECTS used with names of wars
(Appendix C).
CN Prefer the subdivisions.
UF Customs
Social life & customs
Traditions
NT Bees (Cooperative gatherings) +
Chivalry
City & town life
Country life +
Courtship +
Domestic life
Dueling
Eating & drinking +
Entertaining +
Etiquette +
Fads
Farewells +
Fasts
Holidays
Hugging
Kissing +
Marriage +
Mumming

Manners & customs (cont.)
New Year resolutions
Receiving lines
Rites & ceremonies +
Sabbaths
Salutations
Smoking +
Swearing
Toasting
Visiting
RT Body-marking
Bohemians
Burping
Cannibalism
Contests
Debutantes
Events
Flattery
Gifts
Grooming
Hippies
Leisure
Mental states
Military life
Recreation
Red carpet
Superstitions
Manors
USE Estates
**Mansard roofs**
--[country or state]--[city]
PN Roof having two slopes on all sides with
the lower slope steeper than the upper one.
BT Roofs
Manses
USE Religious dwellings
Mansions
USE Dwellings
Manslaughter
USE Homicides
Mantelpieces
USE Chimneypieces
**Mantels**
--[country or state]--[city]
PN Beams, stones, or arches serving as lintels
to support the masonry above fireplaces.
CN Changed 10/1988 from non-postable term
(Use FIREPLACES).
BT Architectural elements
RT Chimneypieces
Fireplaces
Manufacturers
USE Businessmen
**Manufacturers' catalogs**
CN TGM II term.
Manufacturing
USE Industry
Manuscript repositories
USE Archives
Maoism
USE Communism
**Map making**

---

BT Broader term                     RT Related term                     PN Public Note
NT Narrower term                    UF Used for                         + Term has NTs
HN History Note                     CN Catalogers Note                  --[ ] May subdivide

**Map making (cont.)**
    --[country or state]--[city]
  UF  Cartography
  RT  Geography
**Maple sugar industry**
    --[country or state]--[city]
  PN  Includes activities and structures.
  CN  Double index under INDUSTRIAL
      FACILITIES (or NTs) for images that focus
      on facilities.
  BT  Sugar industry
  RT  Maples
      Sugar maple tapping
**Maples**
    --[country or state]--[city]
  BT  Trees
  RT  Maple sugar industry
**Maps**
  CN  TGM II term.
**Marathon running**
    --[country or state]--[city]
  UF  Distance running
  BT  Marathons
**Marathons**
    --[country or state]--[city]
  BT  Contests
  NT  Dance marathons
      Marathon running
  RT  Sports
**Marble**
  BT  Minerals
  RT  Marble quarrying
      Stone cutting
Marble playing
  USE Children playing with marbles
**Marble quarrying**
    --[country or state]--[city]
  PN  Includes activities and sites.
  BT  Limestone quarrying
  RT  Marble
Marble works
  USE Monument builders
Marches, Political
  USE Demonstrations
      Political parades & rallies
**Marching**
    --[country or state]--[city]
  BT  Locomotion
  NT  Goose stepping
  RT  Military art & science
**Marching bands**
  BT  Bands
Mares
  USE Horses
**Margarine**
  UF  Artificial butter
      Oleomargarine
  BT  Food
  RT  Butter
Margin lights
  USE Sidelights
Marihuana

Marihuana (cont.)
  USE Marijuana
**Marijuana**
  UF  Marihuana
  BT  Narcotics
**Marine accidents**
    --[country or state]--[city]
  BT  Accidents
  NT  Ship accidents
      Steamboat accidents
  RT  Drowning victims
      Lifeboats
      Lifesaving
      Naval warfare
      Salvage
      Shipwrecks
      Vessels
Marine animals
  USE Aquatic animals
Marine architecture drawings
  USE Naval architecture drawings
**Marine drawings**
  CN  TGM II term.
  UF  Waterscape drawings
Marine life
  USE Aquatic animals
**Marine paintings**
  CN  TGM II term.
  UF  Waterscape paintings
**Marine photographs**
  CN  TGM II term.
  UF  Waterscape photographs
**Marine prints**
  CN  TGM II term.
  UF  Maritime prints
      Waterscape prints
**Marine terminals**
    --[country or state]--[city]
  PN  Includes both freight and passenger
      terminals.
  UF  Ferry terminals
      Port terminals
      Terminals (Stations)
  BT  Transportation facilities
  RT  Ferries
      Harbors
      Piers & wharves
      Shipping
      Vessels
Mariners
  USE Sailors
**Marines**
    --[nationality]--[country or state]--[city]
  BT  Military organizations
      Military personnel
**Marines (Visual works)**
  CN  TGM II term.
  UF  Waterscapes
Marionettes
  USE Puppets
Marital infidelity
  USE Adultery

---

Maritime museums
  USE Naval museums
Maritime prints
  USE Marine prints
**Marker works**
  CN  TGM II term.
Markers, Historical
  USE Historical markers
Market gardening
  USE Truck farming
Marketing cooperatives
  USE Cooperatives
Marketplaces
  USE Markets
**Markets**
        --[country or state]--[city]
  PN  Includes both indoor and outdoor markets
      where many buyers and sellers are brought
      into contact.
  CN  As appropriate, double index under the
      product sold.
  UF  Marketplaces
      Street markets
  BT  Mercantile facilities
  NT  Bazaars
      Farmers' markets
      Flea markets
  RT  City & town life
      Fairs
      Forums
      Peddlers
      Plazas
      Vending stands
Markings
  USE Marks
**Marks**
  CN  TGM II term.
  UF  Markings
Marksmanship
  USE Sharpshooting
Marmalades
  USE Preserves
**Marmots**
        --[country or state]
  BT  Rodents
  NT  Woodchucks
**Marquees**
        --[country or state]--[city]
  PN  Permanent canopy, usually of metal and
      glass projecting over the entrance to a
      building; on theaters it may display the name
      of current feature.
  UF  Marquises
  BT  Roofs
  RT  Canopies
Marquises
  USE Marquees
**Marriage**
        --[country or state]--[city]
  PN  Search also under the subdivision
      --MARRIAGE used with names of persons
      (Appendix B).

**Marriage (cont.)**
  UF  Matrimony
  BT  Interpersonal relations
      Law & legal affairs
      Manners & customs
  NT  Bigamy
      Polygamy
  RT  Adultery
      Bachelors
      Community property
      Courtship
      Divorce
      Elopements
      Families
      Free love
      Love
      Miscegenation
      Mothers-in-law
      Single women
      Spouses
      Weddings
      Widowers
      Widows
**Marriage certificates**
  CN  TGM II term.
**Marriage proposals**
  UF  Proposals of marriage
  BT  Courtship
Marshes
  USE Wetlands
**Martello towers**
        --[nationality]--[country or state]--[city]
  PN  Circular masonry forts or blockhouses.
  BT  Military facilities
  RT  Blockhouses
      Forts & fortifications
      Towers
**Martial arts**
        --[country or state]--[city]
  PN  Group of diverse activities that have
      evolved from ancient fighting skills
      developed in Asian countries.
  RT  Archery
      Boxing
      Dueling
      Fencing
      Oriental hand-to-hand fighting
      Self-defense
      Wrestling
Marxism
  USE Communism
**Mascots**
  PN  Persons, animals, or objects adopted by a
      group as a symbolic figure, especially to bring
      them good luck.
  RT  Animals
      Symbols
**Masks**
  PN  Search also under the subdivision
      --DEATH MASK used with names of
      persons (Appendix B).
  BT  Clothing & dress

---

BT  Broader term                    RT  Related term                  PN Public Note
NT  Narrower term                   UF  Used for                      +  Term has NTs
HN  History Note                    CN  Catalogers Note               --[ ] May subdivide

**Masks (cont.)**
  NT  Gas masks
        Hockey masks
        Oxygen masks
  RT  Costumes
        Masquerades
        Rites & ceremonies
**Masonic organizations**
  USE Fraternal organizations
**Masonry**
        --[country or state]--[city]
  PN  Construction activity with materials such
        as stone, brick, concrete block, and tile.
  UF  Stone masonry
        Stonemasonry
  NT  Bricklaying
  RT  Construction
        Quoins
        Rustication
        Stone cutting
        Stone walls
        Stonework
**Masquerades**
        --[country or state]--[city]
  UF  Costume balls
  BT  Entertaining
  RT  Costumes
        Masks
        Mumming
        Parties
**Mass burials**
        --[country or state]--[city]
  UF  Common graves
  RT  Funeral rites & ceremonies
**Mass transit**
        --[country or state]--[city]
  UF  Local transit
        Public transportation
        Rapid transit
        Transit systems
        Urban transportation
  BT  Transportation
  RT  Buses
        Street railroads
        Subways
**Massacres**
        --[country or state]--[city]
  BT  Atrocities
  RT  Campaigns & battles
        Death
**Massage**
  RT  Masseurs
        Physical therapy
**Masseurs**
        --[country or state]--[city]
  BT  People
  RT  Massage
        Physical therapy
**Mass, Catholic**
  USE Religious services
**Masters of ships**
  USE Ship captains

**Matadors**
  USE Bullfighters
**Match industry**
        --[country or state]--[city]
  PN  Includes activities and structures.
  CN  Double index under INDUSTRIAL
        FACILITIES (or NTs) for images that focus
        on facilities.
  BT  Industry
  RT  Matches
**Matchcovers**
  CN  TGM II term.
**Matches**
  BT  Equipment
  RT  Fire
        Match industry
        Smoking
**Materials handling**
  USE Shipping
**Maternity hospitals**
        --[country or state]--[city]
  UF  Lying-in hospitals
        Obstetric hospitals
  BT  Hospitals
  RT  Births
        Infants
        Midwives
        Pregnant women
**Math**
  USE Mathematics
**Mathematics**
  PN  For the subject of mathematics in general
        and the activities of mathematicians.
  UF  Arithmetic
        Math
  NT  Geometry
**Matrimony**
  USE Marriage
**Mausoleums**
  USE Tombs & sepulchral monuments
**Maxims**
  USE Proverbs
**May poles**
        --[country or state]--[city]
  RT  Dancing
        Holidays
        Rites & ceremonies
**Mayoral elections**
  USE Political elections
**Mayors**
        --[country or state]--[city]
  PN  For the subject of the office in general and
        for incumbents.
  BT  Municipal officials
**Mazes**
        --[country or state]--[city]
  UF  Labyrinths
  RT  Landscape architecture facilities
        Puzzles
**McCarthyism**
  PN  A mid-20th century political attitude
        characterized chiefly by opposition to

BT Broader term        RT Related term        PN Public Note
NT Narrower term       UF Used for          + Term has NTs
HN History Note        CN Catalogers Note    --[ ] May subdivide

**McCarthyism (cont.)**
elements held to be subversive and by the use of tactics involving personal attacks on individuals by means of widely publicized indiscriminate allegations.
- RT   Anti-communism
-      Communism
-      Governmental investigations
-      Political strategies

**Meadows**
-      --[country or state]
- UF   Fields
-      Grassland
- BT   Land
- RT   Croplands

Meal industry
USE Flour & meal industry

Meals
USE Eating & drinking

**Measles**
- BT   Communicable diseases

**Measured drawings**
- CN   TGM II term.
- UF   Drawings, Measured
-      Survey drawings

Measurement
USE Measuring

Measures
USE Weights & measures

**Measuring**
-      --[country or state]--[city]
- UF   Measurement
-      Mensuration
- RT   Engineering
-      Weights & measures

**Meat**
- BT   Food
- NT   Pork
-      Sausages +
- RT   Meat cutting
-      Slaughtering

**Meat cutting**
-      --[country or state]--[city]
- UF   Meatcutting
- RT   Butcher shops
-      Meat
-      Meat industry
-      Slaughtering

**Meat industry**
-      --[country or state]--[city]
- PN   Includes activities and structures.
- CN   Double index under INDUSTRIAL FACILITIES (or NTs) for images that focus on facilities. Used in a note under SLAUGHTERING.
- UF   Cattle markets
- BT   Food industry
- RT   Butcher shops
-      Farming
-      Kosher food industry
-      Livestock
-      Meat cutting

**Meat industry (cont.)**
-      Meat industry strikes
-      Ranches
-      Slaughtering
-      Stockyards

**Meat industry strikes**
-      --[country or state]--[city]
- BT   Strikes
- RT   Meat industry

Meatcutting
USE Meat cutting

Mechanical computers
USE Calculators

**Mechanical drawings**
- CN   TGM II term.
- UF   Drawings, Mechanical
-      Technical drawings

**Mechanical systems**
-      --[country or state]--[city]
- BT   Building systems
- NT   HVAC systems
-      Plumbing systems
- RT   Machinery
-      Mechanical systems components

**Mechanical systems components**
-      --[country or state]--[city]
- BT   Building systems
- NT   Downspouts
-      Furnaces
-      Gutters (Roofs)
-      Leader heads
-      Plumbing fixtures +
-      Septic tanks
- RT   Mechanical systems

**Mechanical systems drawings**
- CN   TGM II term.
- UF   Drawings, Mechanical systems

**Mechanical toys**
- UF   Wind-up toys
- BT   Toys

**Mechanical works**
- CN   TGM II term.
- UF   Movable works

**Mechanics (Persons)**
-      --[country or state]--[city]
- UF   Auto mechanics
-      Automobile mechanics
-      Aviation mechanics (Persons)
-      Car mechanics
-      Truck mechanics
- BT   People associated with manual labor
- RT   Maintenance & repair

Mechanics, Aviation (Science)
USE Aviation mechanics (Science)

Medallions
USE Medals

**Medallions (Ornament areas)**
- PN   An ornamental plaque (usually oval or square) on which is represented an object in relief, such as a figure, head, flower, etc. applied to a wall frieze, or other architectural member.

---

BT Broader term        RT Related term        PN Public Note
NT Narrower term      UF Used for          + Term has NTs
HN History Note        CN Catalogers Note    --[ ] May subdivide

**Medallions (Ornament areas) (cont.)**
BT    Architectural decorations & ornaments
**Medals**
PN    Pieces of metal often resembling coins and
        having a stamped design that is issued to
        commemorate a person or event or awarded
        for excellence or achievement. Includes the
        ceremonies during which a medal is given.
UF    Medallions
RT    Awards
        Badges
        Military art & science
        Military decorations
        Rites & ceremonies
**Mediation of industrial disputes**
USE  Industrial arbitration
**Medicaid**
        --[country or state]--[city]
BT    Domestic economic assistance
RT    Health care
        Insurance
        Medicare
        Pensions
**Medical aspects of war**
        --[country or state]--[city]
PN    For relief and medical care of casualties.
        Search under WAR CASUALTIES for
        images that focus on dead and wounded
        persons. Search also under the subdivision
        --MEDICAL ASPECTS used with names of
        wars (Appendix C).
UF    Convalescent camps
        Convalescents
        Field hospitals
        Hospitals, Field
BT    Medicine
RT    Military medicine
        Sick persons
        War
        War casualties
**Medical buildings**
USE  Health care facilities
**Medical care**
USE  Health care
**Medical colleges**
USE  Medical education
**Medical drawings**
USE  Medical illustrations
**Medical education**
        --[country or state]--[city]
PN    Includes activities and structures.
CN    Double index under EDUCATIONAL
        FACILITIES (or NTs) for images that focus
        on facilities.
UF    Medical colleges
        Medical schools
BT    Education
NT    Dental education
RT    Medicine
**Medical equipment & supplies**
PN    Search also under the subdivision
        --EQUIPMENT & SUPPLIES used with

**Medical equipment & supplies (cont.)**
        names of wars (Appendix C).
HN    Changed 5/1989 from MEDICAL
        EQUIPMENT.
UF    Hospital supplies
NT    Artificial limbs
        Dental equipment & supplies
        Eyeglasses
        Hearing aids
        Hypodermic needles
        Incubators
        Iron lungs
        Litters
        Orthopedic braces
        Splints (Surgery)
        Wheelchairs
RT    Equipment
        Medicine
        Oxygen masks
**Medical illustrations**
CN    TGM II term.
UF    Drawings, Medical
        Medical drawings
**Medical offices**
        --[country or state]--[city]
UF    Doctors' offices
        Doctors' surgeries
        Physicians' offices
BT    Service industry facilities
RT    Dental offices
        Health care facilities
        Nurses
        Offices
        Physicians
**Medical schools**
USE  Medical education
**Medicare**
BT    Domestic economic assistance
RT    Aged persons
        Health care
        Insurance
        Medicaid
        Pensions
**Medicinal plants**
        --[country or state]--[city]
UF    Herbs, Medicinal
BT    Plants
**Medicine**
        --[country or state]--[city]
BT    Science
NT    Dentistry
        Medical aspects of war
        Military medicine
        Preventive medicine
        Psychiatry
        Surgery
        Veterinary medicine
RT    Birth control
        Blood donations
        Caduceus
        Health care
        Hygiene

BT  Broader term                          RT  Related term                    PN  Public Note
NT  Narrower term                        UF  Used for                          +  Term has NTs
HN  History Note                          CN  Catalogers Note                 --[ ]  May subdivide

**Medicine (cont.)**
       Medical education
       Medical equipment & supplies
       Medicines
**Medicine men**
  USE Shamans
**Medicine shows**
       --[country or state]--[city]
  PN  Travelling shows using entertainers to
       attract crowds among which remedies and
       secret nostrums are sold.
  UF  Drug trade
  BT  Circuses & shows
  RT  Fairs
       Patent medicines
       Peddlers
       Quacks
**Medicines**
  UF  Drugs
       Remedies
  NT  Patent medicines +
       Penicillin
       Pills
       Quinine
       Veterinary drugs
  RT  Anesthesia
       Druggists
       Drugstores
       Healing
       Medicine
       Narcotics
       Pharmaceutical industry
       Poisons
       Vaccinations
**Meditation**
       --[country or state]--[city]
  PN  For the act or process of meditating.
  UF  Mental prayer
  BT  Mental states
  RT  Prayer
**Meeting houses, Friend**
  USE Friends' meeting houses
**Meeting rooms**
  USE Conference rooms
**Meetings**
       --[country or state]--[city]
  PN  For planned gatherings. Search also under
       the subdivision --MEETINGS used with
       names of ethnic, racial, and regional groups,
       and with classes of persons (Appendix A),
       and with corporate bodies and named events
       (Appendix D).
  UF  Conferences
       Congresses
       Conventions (Congresses)
       Symposiums
       Teach-ins
  BT  Events
  NT  Auctions +
       Chautauquas
       Constitutional conventions
       Judicial proceedings +

**Meetings (cont.)**
       Peace conferences
       Political conventions
       Press conferences
       Religious meetings +
       Seances
       Town meetings
  RT  Conference rooms
       Delegations
       Demonstrations
       Discussion
       Gavels
       Peace negotiations
       Public speaking
       Resolutions
**Megalethoscope photoprints**
  USE Megalethoscope prints
**Megalethoscope prints**
  CN  TGM II term.
  UF  Megalethoscope photoprints
**Megaphones**
  UF  Speaking trumpets
  BT  Communication devices
  RT  Public address systems
**Melainotypes**
  USE Tintypes
**Melancholy**
  USE Depression (Mental state)
**Melodramas**
  PN  For images representing dramatic
       productions or scenes (theatrical, film, radio,
       or television) which feature passive
       protagonists who are victimized by situations
       related to society, family, or sexuality,
       frequently characterized by extreme emotion.
  RT  Motion pictures
       Radio broadcasting
       Television broadcasting
       Theatrical productions
**Melons**
       --[country or state]--[city]
  BT  Fruit
  NT  Cantaloupes
       Watermelons
  RT  Pumpkins
**Membership campaigns**
       --[country or state]--[city]
  PN  Search also under the subdivision
       --RECRUITING & ENLISTMENT used with
       corporate bodies and named events (Appendix
       D).
  CN  Used in a note under RECRUITING &
       ENLISTMENT.
  UF  Campaigns, Membership
       Drives, Membership
       Membership drives
  RT  Fund raising
       Organizations
**Membership cards**
  CN  TGM II term.
**Membership certificates**
  CN  TGM II term.

---

BT  Broader term               RT  Related term               PN Public Note
NT  Narrower term             UF  Used for                    + Term has NTs
HN History Note               CN Catalogers Note         --[ ] May subdivide

Membership drives
  USE Membership campaigns
**Memorabilia**
  CN   TGM II term.
  UF   Souvenirs
**Memorial arches**
       --[country or state]--[city]
  UF   Triumphal arches
  BT   Monuments & memorials
  RT   Arches
**Memorial rites & ceremonies**
       --[country or state]--[city]
  PN   For rites and ceremonies in memory of
       individuals or groups, without the presence of
       the deceased. Search under FUNERAL
       RITES & CEREMONIES for rites and
       ceremonies in the presence of the deceased.
       Search also under the subdivision
       --COMMEMORATION used with ethnic,
       racial, and regional groups and with classes
       of persons (Appendix A); with names of
       persons (Appendix B); and with names of
       wars (Appendix C).
  CN   Used in a note under FUNERAL RITES &
       CEREMONIES.
  UF   Memorial services
       Mourning customs
       Services, Memorial
  BT   Rites & ceremonies
  RT   Commemoration
       Funeral rites & ceremonies
Memorial services
  USE Memorial rites & ceremonies
**Memorial works**
  CN   TGM II term.
  UF   Mourning works
Memorials
  USE Monuments & memorials
Memory
  USE Reminiscing
**Men**
       --[country or state]--[city]
  PN   This heading may be further subdivided by
       the subdivisions used for classes of persons
       (Appendix A).
  CN   As appropriate, subdivide by the
       subdivisions used for classes of persons
       (Appendix A).
  UF   Males
  BT   People
  NT   Bachelors
       Cowboys +
       Dandies
       Emperors
       Gay men
       Kings
       Monks
       Princes
       Shepherds
       Strong men
       Waiters
       Widowers

**Men (cont.)**
  RT   Actors
       Boys
       Children & adults
       Fathers & children
       Grandparents
       Machismo
       Spouses
Men in women's clothing
  USE Cross dressing
**Mennonite churches**
       --[country or state]--[city]
  PN   For images that focus on buildings, as
       well as the associated grounds.
  BT   Protestant churches
Mensoles
  USE Keystones
Mensuration
  USE Measuring
Mental healers
  USE Healers
Mental health
  CN   Used only as a subdivision under names
       of persons (Appendix B).
Mental health care
  USE Psychiatry
**Mental institutions**
       --[country or state]--[city]
  PN   For images that focus on buildings. Search
       under MENTALLY ILL PERSONS for
       activities.
  UF   Insane hospitals
       Lunatic asylums
       Psychiatric hospitals
  BT   Health care facilities
  RT   Asylums
       Mentally ill persons
       Psychiatry
Mental prayer
  USE Meditation
**Mental states**
  UF   Affective states
       Attitudes
       Emotion
       Feelings
       Moods
       Passions
       Psychological states
       States of mind
  NT   Adoration
       Allegiance
       Anger
       Anxiety
       Apathy +
       Avarice
       Boredom
       Competition (Psychology)
       Contentment
       Courage
       Cowardice
       Depression (Mental state)
       Despair

---

BT Broader term                     RT Related term                     PN Public Note
NT Narrower term                    UF Used for                         + Term has NTs
HN History Note                     CN Catalogers Note                  --[ ] May subdivide

**Mental states (cont.)**
>> Disgrace
>> Distress
>> Dreaming
>> Envy
>> Excitement
>> Fear
>> Gluttony
>> Gratitude
>> Grief
>> Happiness
>> Homesickness
>> Ignorance (Knowledge)
>> Laziness
>> Loss of consciousness
>> Love
>> Lust
>> Meditation
>> Miserliness
>> Nostalgia
>> Obliviousness
>> Obstinacy
>> Optimism
>> Patriotism
>> Pessimism +
>> Prejudice +
>> Pride
>> Sadness
>> Sleeping +
>> Snobbishness
>> Stress
>> Surprise
>> Suspicion
>> Thinking
>> Waking
>> Wishing
>> Worry
> RT Blindness
>> Crying
>> Dizziness
>> Ethics
>> Hypnotism
>> Interpersonal relations
>> Laughter
>> Liberalism
>> Machismo
>> Manners & customs
>> Nationalism
>> Psychiatry
>> Regionalism
>> Rejuvenation
>> Sectionalism (United States)
>> Smiling

**Mentally ill persons**
>> --[country or state]--[city]
> PN Search also under the subdivision
>> --MENTAL HEALTH used with names of
>> persons (Appendix B).
> CN Used in a note under MENTAL
>> INSTITUTIONS.
> UF Insane people
>> Madness

**Mentally ill persons (cont.)**
> BT Handicapped persons
> RT Mental institutions

**Menus**
> CN TGM II term.
> UF Bills of fare

**Mercantile facilities**
>> --[country or state]--[city]
> BT Commercial facilities
> NT Arcades (Shopping facilities)
>> Automobile dealerships
>> Commercial art galleries
>> Markets +
>> Shopping centers
>> Stores & shops +
>> Vending stands
> RT Merchandise displays
>> Selling
>> Shopping
>> Show windows
>> Showrooms
>> Studios
>> Window displays

**Mercenaries (Soldiers)**
>> --[nationality]--[country or state]--[city]
> UF Mercenary troops
>> Substitute soldiers
> BT Soldiers
> RT Foreign participation in war

Mercenary troops
> USE Mercenaries (Soldiers)

**Merchandise displays**
>> --[country or state]--[city]
> PN Search also under the subdivisions
>> --EXHIBITIONS & DISPLAYS and
>> --PRODUCTS used with corporate bodies and
>> named events (Appendix D).
> UF Displays of merchandise
>> Product displays
> NT Window displays
> RT Business enterprises
>> Exhibitions
>> Mercantile facilities
>> Showcases
>> Showrooms

**Merchandise exchanges**
>> --[country or state]--[city]
> UF Returns (Merchandise)
>> Sales exchanges
> RT Selling
>> Shopping

Merchandising
> USE Selling

Merchant seamen
> USE Sailors

**Merchants**
>> --[country or state]--[city]
> PN Traders, especially ones in the wholesale
>> trade who deal with foreign countries.
> BT Businessmen
> RT Selling

**Merchants' exchanges**

---

**Merchants' exchanges (cont.)**
 --[country or state]--[city]
 PN Includes activities and structures.
 UF Exchanges
 BT Financial facilities
 RT Commodity exchanges
 Stock exchanges
**Mercury mining**
 --[country or state]
 PN Includes activities and sites.
 UF Quicksilver mining
 BT Mining
Merit system
 USE Civil service
**Mermaids**
 BT Supernatural beings
**Merry-go-rounds**
 --[country or state]--[city]
 UF Carousels
 BT Amusement rides
**Mesas**
 --[country or state]
 BT Land
 RT Mountains
**Mess halls**
 --[country or state]--[city]
 BT Dining rooms
 RT Military cookery
 Military facilities
**Messengers**
 --[country or state]--[city]
 PN Double index as appropriate with vehicle
 used.
 BT People associated with education &
 communication
 NT Heralds
 RT Communication
 Delivery boys
**Metal cuts**
 CN TGM II term.
Metal work
 USE Metalwork
**Metallurgical industry**
 --[country or state]--[city]
 PN Includes activities and structures.
 CN Double index under INDUSTRIAL
 FACILITIES (or NTs) for images that focus
 on facilities.
 BT Industry
 NT Aluminum industry
 Brass industry
 Bronze industry
 Copper industry
 Iron industry
 Lead industry
 Steel industry
 RT Foundries
 Metals
 Ore industry
 Smelters
**Metalpoint drawings**
 CN TGM II term.

**Metals**
 NT Aluminum
 Gold
 Silver
 Steel
 RT Metallurgical industry
 Metalwork
 Ore industry
**Metalwork**
 --[country or state]--[city]
 PN Search under METALWORKING for the
 activity of metalworking.
 UF Metal work
 NT Goldwork
 Hardware +
 Ironwork +
 Silverwork
 RT Metals
 Metalworking
 Weather vanes
**Metalworking**
 --[country or state]--[city]
 PN Process of shaping things out of metal.
 CN Used in a note under METALWORK.
 NT Forging +
 Founding
 Tinsmithing
 RT Furnaces
 Gunsmithing
 Handicraft
 Metalwork
 Riveting
 Welding
**Metamorphic pictures**
 CN TGM II term.
 UF Reversible head prints
 Transformation pictures
**Metamorphosis**
 UF Transformations
 Transmutations
 RT Embryology
 Human curiosities
 Supernatural
**Methodist churches**
 --[country or state]--[city]
 PN For images that focus on buildings, as
 well as the associated grounds.
 BT Protestant churches
Metoposcopy
 USE Physiognomy
Metric measures
 USE Weights & measures
Metro stations
 USE Subway stations
Mexican sisal
 USE Henequen
**Mezzanines**
 --[country or state]--[city]
 PN Low-ceilinged stories between the two
 main stories of a building, especially
 intermediate or fractional stories that project
 in the form of a balcony over the ground

BT Broader term          RT Related term          PN Public Note
NT Narrower term         UF Used for              + Term has NTs
HN History Note          CN Catalogers Note       --[ ] May subdivide

**Mezzanines (cont.)**
    story.
  BT  Interiors
**Mezzotints**
  CN  TGM II term.
MIA's
  USE Missing in action
**Mica mining**
    --[country or state]--[city]
  PN  Includes activities and sites.
  BT  Mining
**Mice**
    --[country or state]
  BT  Rodents
  RT  Mousetraps
Microbes
  USE Bacteria
**Microfiches**
  CN  TGM II term.
**Microfilms**
  CN  TGM II term.
**Microforms**
  CN  TGM II term.
**Microopaques**
  CN  TGM II term.
  UF  Microprints
    Opaque microcopies
**Microorganisms**
  UF  Radiolaria
    Unicellular organisms
  RT  Bacteria
**Microphotographs**
  CN  TGM II term.
Microprints
  USE Microopaques
**Microscopes**
  BT  Optical devices
    Scientific equipment
  NT  Electron microscopes
  RT  Hand lenses
**Middle age**
    --[country or state]--[city]
  UF  Midlife
  RT  Aged persons
    Human life cycle
    Youth
**Middle class**
    --[country or state]--[city]
  HN  Changed 11/1993 from MIDDLE
    CLASSES.
  UF  Bourgeoisie
    Middle classes
  BT  Social classes
Middle classes
  USE Middle class
Midgets
  USE Dwarfs
Midlife
  USE Middle age
**Midways**
    --[country or state]--[city]
  PN  A central avenue at a fair or exposition,

**Midways (cont.)**
    for exhibition of curiosities, fantastic
    amusements, concessions, etc.
  CN  As appropriate, double index under FAIRS
    or EXHIBITIONS.
  UF  Side shows
  RT  Circuses & shows
    Entertainment
    Exhibitions
    Fairs
    Human curiosities
**Midwives**
    --[country or state]--[city]
  BT  People associated with health & safety
  RT  Births
    Health care
    Maternity hospitals
    Nurses
**Migrant agricultural laborers**
    --[nationality]--[country or state]--[city]
  BT  Agricultural laborers
    Migrant laborers
**Migrant laborers**
    --[nationality]--[country or state]--[city]
  PN  For laborers who regularly migrate within
    the same country for work. Search under
    ALIEN LABORERS for those who seek work
    outside their own country.
  CN  Used in a note under ALIEN
    LABORERS.
  UF  Migratory workers
    Transient laborers
  BT  Laborers
  NT  Migrant agricultural laborers
  RT  Internal migration
Migration, Internal
  USE Internal migration
Migratory workers
  USE Migrant laborers
**Mihrabs**
    --[country or state]--[city]
  PN  Niches or chambers in mosques indicating
    the direction of Mecca and usually containing
    a copy of the Koran. Sometimes only a slab.
  BT  Religious architectural elements
  RT  Mosques
    Niches
**Milestones**
    --[country or state]--[city]
  PN  For stones that serve as mileposts. Search
    under FIRSTS for figurative milestones.
  CN  Used in a note under FIRSTS.
  RT  Geography
    Roads
    Streets
    Weights & measures
Militants
  USE Activists
**Militarism**
    --[country]
  PN  Subordination of the civil ideals or
    policies of a government to the military;

---

BT  Broader term
NT  Narrower term
HN  History Note

RT  Related term
UF  Used for
CN  Catalogers Note

PN  Public Note
+  Term has NTs
--[ ]  May subdivide

**Militarism (cont.)**
    policy of aggressive military preparedness.
  BT  Politics & government
  RT  Arms control
      Chauvinism & jingoism
      Military art & science
      Pacifism

**Military air pilots**
    --[nationality]--[country or state]--[city]
  UF  Pilots, Military
  BT  Air pilots
      Military personnel
  NT  Fighter pilots
  RT  Air bases

**Military air shows**
    --[country or state]--[city]
  UF  Air tattoos
      Tattoos, Air
  BT  Air shows
  RT  Air bases
      Military parades & ceremonies

**Military art & science**
  PN  Search also under the subdivision
      --MILITARY TACTICS used with names of
      wars (Appendix C). Search also under other
      terms beginning with MILITARY.
  UF  Military science
      Naval art & science
      Warfare
  NT  Air warfare +
      Blockades
      Bombardment
      Camouflage (Military science)
      Gas warfare
      Military intelligence
      Military maneuvers +
      Military mobilizations
      Military policy
      Military reconnaissance
      Mine warfare
      Naval warfare +
      Night warfare
      Ordnance testing +
      Trench warfare
      Troop movements
      Winter warfare
  RT  Armored vehicles
      Arms & armament
      Barricades
      Batteries (Weaponry)
      Campaigns & battles
      Courts martial & courts of inquiry
      Defense budgets
      Government vessels
      Guards
      Guerrillas
      Marching
      Medals
      Militarism
      Military education
      Military facilities
      Military leadership

**Military art & science (cont.)**
      Military life
      Military organizations
      Military parades & ceremonies
      Military personnel
      Parachuting
      Quaker guns
      Spying
      War

**Military assistance**
    --[nationality]--[country or state]--[city]
  CN  Subdivide by nationality of people giving
      assistance. Subdivide geographically by
      country receiving assistance.
  BT  Assistance
  RT  War

**Military bands**
  BT  Bands

Military bases
  USE  Military facilities

**Military camps**
    --[nationality]--[country or state]--[city]
  PN  For images that focus on sites and
      facilities. Search under MILITARY LIFE for
      activities.
  UF  Camps, Military
  BT  Military facilities
  RT  Camps
      Forts & fortifications
      Sutlers
      Tents

Military ceremonies
  USE  Military parades & ceremonies

Military colleges
  USE  Military education

**Military cookery**
    --[country or state]--[city]
  BT  Cookery
  RT  Mess halls

Military courtesy
  USE  Saluting

**Military decorations**
    --[country or state]--[city]
  PN  Includes the ceremonies during which
      military decorations are given.
  HN  Changed 1/1990 from non-postable term.
      For earlier cataloging, search under
      MEDALS.
  UF  Decorations, Military
  RT  Awards
      Medals
      Military parades & ceremonies
      Rites & ceremonies

**Military demobilizations**
    --[country or state]--[city]
  PN  Search also under the subdivision
      --MILITARY DEMOBILIZATIONS used
      with names of wars (Appendix C).
  UF  Demobilizations
  RT  Military discharges
      Military mobilizations
      Peace

---

BT Broader term      RT Related term      PN Public Note
NT Narrower term      UF Used for      + Term has NTs
HN History Note      CN Catalogers Note      --[ ] May subdivide

## Military demobilizations (cont.)
Recruiting & enlistment
Troop movements

## Military depots
--[country or state]--[city]
PN   Places for the storage of military supplies and the reception and forwarding of military replacements.
UF   Depots, Military
Naval depots
BT   Military facilities
RT   Armories
Magazines (Military buildings)
Military exchanges
Storage facilities

## Military deserters
--[nationality]--[country or state]--[city]
UF   AWOL
Deserters, Military
BT   Military personnel
RT   Criminals

## Military discharges
--[country or state]--[city]
UF   Discharges, Military
Dishonorable discharges
Mustering out
RT   Military demobilizations
Military service
Recruiting & enlistment

## Military education
--[country or state]--[city]
PN   Includes activities (classroom and teaching situations) and structures. Search under MILITARY TRAINING for physical activities.
CN   As appropriate, double index under level of education. Double index under EDUCATIONAL FACILITIES  for images that focus on facilities.
UF   Army schools
Military colleges
Military schools
BT   Education
RT   Cadets
Military art & science
Military training

## Military exchanges
--[country or state]--[city]
PN   Includes activities and structures.
HN   Prior to 11/1992 the term POST EXCHANGES was used.
UF   Base exchanges
Commissaries, Military
Post exchanges
BT   Stores & shops
RT   Business enterprises
Military depots
Military facilities
Sutlers

Military exercises
USE Military training

## Military facilities

## Military facilities (cont.)
--[nationality]--[country or state]--[city]
PN   Search also under the subdivision --MILITARY FACILITIES used with names of wars (Appendix C).
UF   Military bases
Military installations
Military stations
BT   Facilities
NT   Air bases
Armories
Barracks
Blockhouses
Drill halls
Forts & fortifications
Guardhouses
Magazines (Military buildings)
Martello towers
Military camps
Military depots
Military headquarters
Military reservations
Naval yards & naval stations
Officers' quarters
RT   Huts
Mess halls
Military art & science
Military exchanges
Naval museums

Military flags
USE Military standards

## Military headquarters
--[nationality]--[country or state]--[city]
UF   Headquarters, Military
BT   Military facilities

## Military inspections
--[country or state]--[city]
UF   Inspections, Military
Troop inspections
RT   Military parades & ceremonies
Military training
Naval parades & ceremonies

Military installations
USE Military facilities

## Military intelligence
--[country or state]--[city]
BT   Military art & science
RT   Covert operations
Spying

Military intervention
USE Intervention (International law)

## Military leadership
UF   Command of troops
BT   Leadership
RT   Military art & science

## Military life
--[nationality]--[country or state]--[city]
PN   Includes all aspects of military life, e.g., training, reviews, camp life, etc. Search also under the subdivision --MILITARY LIFE used with names of wars (Appendix C).
CN   Used in a note under MILITARY

---

BT   Broader term
NT   Narrower term
HN   History Note

RT   Related term
UF   Used for
CN   Catalogers Note

PN   Public Note
+    Term has NTs
--[ ]   May subdivide

**Military life (cont.)**
> CAMPS.
> UF  Camp life
>     Soldiers' life
> RT  Foraging
>     Manners & customs
>     Military art & science
>     USO clubs

**Military maneuvers**
> --[country or state]--[city]
> UF  Maneuvers, Military
> BT  Military art & science
> NT  War games
> RT  Military training

**Military medicine**
> PN  Search also under the subdivision
>     --MEDICAL ASPECTS used with names of
>     wars (Appendix C).
> HN  Changed 10/1989 from non-postable term
>     (Use MEDICAL ASPECTS OF WAR).
> BT  Medicine
> RT  Medical aspects of war

**Military mobilizations**
> --[country or state]--[city]
> PN  Search also under the subdivision
>     --MILITARY MOBILIZATIONS used with
>     names of wars (Appendix C).
> UF  Mobilizations of armed forces
> BT  Military art & science
> RT  Military demobilizations
>     Recruiting & enlistment
>     Troop movements

**Military occupations**
> --[nationality]--[country or state]--[city]
> CN  Subdivide by nationality of the invading
>     country.
> UF  Occupations, Military
>     Occupied territories
> RT  Annexations
>     Intervention (International law)
>     War

**Military officers**
> --[nationality]--[country or state]--[city]
> CN  Subdivide by nationality only when in
>     another country.
> UF  Leaders, Military
>     Officers, Military
> BT  Military personnel
> NT  Admirals
>     Generals
> RT  Government officials

**Military organizations**
> --[nationality]
> UF  Armed forces
> BT  Organizations
> NT  Air forces
>     Armies +
>     Marines
>     Militias
>     Navies
>     Scottish regiments
>     Zouaves

**Military organizations (cont.)**
> RT  Flag bearers
>     Military art & science
>     Military personnel
>     Military regimes
>     Military service
>     National security
>     Recruiting & enlistment

**Military parades & ceremonies**
> --[country or state]--[city]
> PN  Parades, rites, and ceremonies for, by, and
>     of the military.
> CN  Used in a note under NAVAL PARADES
>     & CEREMONIES.
> UF  Military ceremonies
>     Reviews, Military
>     Troop reviews
> BT  Events
> RT  Military air shows
>     Military art & science
>     Military decorations
>     Military inspections
>     Naval parades & ceremonies
>     Parades & processions
>     Rites & ceremonies

**Military personnel**
> --[nationality]--[country or state]--[city]
> PN  Search also under the subdivision
>     --MILITARY SERVICE used with names of
>     ethnic, racial, and regional groups, and with
>     classes of persons (Appendix A), and with
>     names of persons (Appendix B). Search also
>     under the subdivision --MILITARY
>     PERSONNEL used with names of wars
>     (Appendix C) and the subdivision --PEOPLE
>     used with corporate bodies and named events
>     (Appendix D).
> BT  People associated with military activities
> NT  Marines
>     Military air pilots +
>     Military deserters
>     Military officers +
>     Military police
>     Military scouts
>     Missing in action
>     Ski troops
>     Soldiers +
> RT  Flight crews
>     Guards
>     Military art & science
>     Military organizations
>     Military uniforms
>     Sailors
>     Veterans

**Military police**
> --[nationality]--[country or state]--[city]
> BT  Military personnel
>     Police

**Military policy**
> --[country]
> PN  For military, naval, and general defense
>     policy.

---

BT  Broader term                    RT  Related term                  PN  Public Note
NT  Narrower term                   UF  Used for                      +  Term has NTs
HN  History Note                    CN  Catalogers Note               --[ ]  May subdivide

**Military policy (cont.)**
  UF  Arms policy
      Defense policy
      War machine
  BT  Military art & science
      Politics & government
  RT  Defense budgets
      Defense industry
      National security
      Rearmament
      War
**Military reconnaissance**
      --[nationality]--[country or state]--[city]
  CN  Subdivide by nationality of those
      conducting the reconnaissance.
  UF  Reconnaissance, Military
  BT  Military art & science
  RT  Military scouts
      Spying
**Military regimes**
      --[country]
  UF  Juntas, Military
  BT  Politics & government
  RT  Dictators
      Military organizations
**Military reservations**
      --[nationality]--[country or state]--[city]
  UF  Reservations, Military
  BT  Military facilities
**Military retreats**
      --[nationality]--[country or state]--[city]
  PN  Search also under the subdivision
      --MILITARY RETREATS used with names
      of wars (Appendix C).
  UF  Retreats, Military
  RT  Surrenders
      War
Military schools
  USE Military education
Military science
  USE Military art & science
**Military scouts**
      --[nationality]--[country or state]--[city]
  UF  Scouts, Military
  BT  Military personnel
  RT  Guides & scouts
      Military reconnaissance
**Military service**
      --[country or state]--[city]
  PN  Search also under the subdivision
      --MILITARY SERVICE used with names of
      ethnic, racial, and regional groups, and with
      classes of persons (Appendix A), and with
      names of persons (Appendix B).
  NT  Draft
  RT  Military discharges
      Military organizations
      Recruiting & enlistment
**Military standards**
      --[nationality]
  UF  Battle flags
      Military flags

**Military standards (cont.)**
  BT  Flags
Military stations
  USE Military facilities
Military students
  USE Cadets
Military surplus stores
  USE Army-Navy stores
Military tactics
  CN  Used only as a subdivision with names of
      wars (Appendix C).
**Military training**
      --[country or state]--[city]
  PN  For physical activities. Search under
      MILITARY EDUCATION for classroom and
      teaching situations.
  CN  Used in a note under MILITARY
      EDUCATION.
  UF  Drills, Military
      Exercises, Military
      Military exercises
      Training, Military
  RT  Cadets
      Military education
      Military inspections
      Military maneuvers
**Military uniforms**
      --[nationality]
  BT  Uniforms
  RT  Military personnel
**Military vehicles**
      --[nationality]--[country or state]--[city]
  PN  Search also under AIRCRAFT or
      VESSELS and their NTs for specific types of
      vehicles used in a military context.
  BT  Vehicles
  NT  Tanks (Military science)
      Tracked landing vehicles
  RT  Amphibious vehicles
      Armored vehicles
      Jeep automobiles
**Militias**
      --[country or state]
  CN  Subdivide geographically by the country
      or state from which the militia comes.
  UF  National guards & reserves
  BT  Military organizations
**Milk**
  BT  Dairy products
Milk cans
  USE Cans
Milk industry
  USE Dairying
**Milking**
      --[country or state]--[city]
  PN  For the milking of cows and other animals
      away from the context of dairy farming.
      Search under DAIRY FARMING for the
      milking of dairy cattle.
  CN  Used in a note under DAIRY FARMING.
  UF  Cow milking
  RT  Animals

---

BT  Broader term
NT  Narrower term
HN  History Note

RT  Related term
UF  Used for
CN  Catalogers Note

PN  Public Note
+   Term has NTs
--[ ] May subdivide

**Milking (cont.)**
    Dairy farming
**Millet**
    --[country or state]--[city]
  BT  Grains
**Millinery**
  UF  Millinery stores
  RT  Clothing stores
      Hats
Millinery stores
  USE Millinery
Milling trade
  USE Flour & meal industry
**Millraces**
    --[country or state]--[city]
  PN  Canals in which water flows to and from
      mill wheels.
  BT  Hydraulic facilities
  RT  Canals
      Mills
      Waterwheels
**Mills**
    --[country or state]--[city]
  PN  A facility devoted to processing of
      materials, e.g. grain to flour, trees to lumber.
  HN  Before 11/1993, used for mills outside of
      an industrial context.
  BT  Factories
  NT  Windmills
  RT  Millraces
Mills (Factories)
  USE Factories
**Millwork**
    --[country or state]--[city]
  PN  Woodwork (e.g., doors, sashes, trim) that
      has been machined at a planing mill.
  BT  Woodwork
  RT  Doors & doorways
      Windows
Mimbers
  USE Pulpits
**Mimetic buildings**
    --[country or state]--[city]
  UF  California crazy
      Roadside architecture
      Zoomorphic buildings
  BT  Buildings distinguished by form
  RT  Architectural follies
Mimicry
  USE Imitation
**Minarets**
    --[country or state]--[city]
  BT  Religious facilities
  RT  Mosques
      Towers
Minbars
  USE Pulpits
Mind reading
  USE Telepathy
Mindreading
  USE Telepathy
**Mine accidents**

**Mine accidents (cont.)**
    --[country or state]--[city]
  BT  Accidents
  RT  Mine rescue work
      Mining
**Mine railroads**
    --[country or state]--[city]
  CN  Double index under type of mining.
  BT  Railroads
  RT  Mining
**Mine rescue work**
    --[country or state]--[city]
  BT  Rescue work
  RT  Mine accidents
**Mine warfare**
    --[country or state]--[city]
  BT  Military art & science
  RT  Campaigns & battles
      Mines (Warfare)
      Paravanes
      Torpedo boats
**Mineral deposits**
    --[country or state]--[city]
  RT  Geology
      Minerals
      Mining
Mineral springs
  USE Springs
**Mineral waters**
  BT  Beverages
  RT  Minerals
      Springs
**Minerals**
    --[country or state]--[city]
  NT  Coal +
      Crystals
      Marble
      Quartz
  RT  Mineral deposits
      Mineral waters
      Mining
      Ore industry
      Petroleum industry
      Rocks
      Salt industry
      Stone quarrying
**Miners**
    --[country or state]--[city]
  BT  People associated with manual labor
  NT  Clay miners
      Coal miners
      Copper miners
      Diamond miners
      Gold miners
      Iron miners
  RT  Miners' unions
      Mining
Miners' equipment & supplies
  USE Prospecting equipment & supplies
**Miners' strikes**
    --[country or state]--[city]
  BT  Strikes

---

BT Broader term          RT Related term          PN Public Note
NT Narrower term        UF Used for             + Term has NTs
HN History Note          CN Catalogers Note      --[ ] May subdivide

**Miners' strikes (cont.)**
  RT  Miners' unions
      Mining
**Miners' unions**
      --[country or state]--[city]
  BT  Labor unions
  RT  Miners
      Miners' strikes
      Mining
**Mines**
  USE Mining
**Mines (Warfare)**
  HN  Changed 4/1988 from non-postable term.
  UF  Land mines
      Submarine mines
  BT  Arms & armament
      Explosives
  RT  Mine warfare
      Paravanes
**Miniature golf**
      --[country or state]--[city]
**Miniature houses**
  USE Dollhouses
**Miniature railroads**
      --[country or state]--[city]
  PN  Small trains on which people can ride.
  CN  Used in a note under MODEL
      RAILROADS.
  BT  Narrow-gage railroads
  RT  Amusement parks
      Model railroads
**Miniature works**
  CN  TGM II term.
**Miniatures**
  USE Miniatures (Paintings)
**Miniatures (Illuminations)**
  CN  TGM II term.
**Miniatures (Paintings)**
  CN  TGM II term.
  UF  Miniatures
      Portrait miniatures
**Minimum wages**
      --[country or state]--[city]
  BT  Wages
  RT  Laws
**Mining**
      --[country or state]--[city]
  PN  Includes activities and sites where mining
      is taking place. Search also under the
      subdivision --INDUSTRIES used with names
      of indigenous peoples (Appendix A).
  CN  Used in a note under EMPLOYMENT.
  UF  Mines
  NT  Asbestos mining
      Clay mining
      Coal mining
      Copper mining
      Diamond mining
      Gold mining
      Hydraulic mining
      Iron mining
      Lead mining

**Mining (cont.)**
      Mercury mining
      Mica mining
      Nickel mining
      Phosphate mining
      Quartz mining
      Ruby mining
      Salt mining
      Silver mining
      Strip mining
      Tin mining
      Zinc mining
  RT  Industry
      Mine accidents
      Mine railroads
      Mineral deposits
      Minerals
      Miners
      Miners' strikes
      Miners' unions
      Prospecting
      Prospecting equipment & supplies
      Quarrying
**Miniskirts**
  BT  Clothing & dress
**Ministers of the gospel**
  USE Clergy
**Ministers (Diplomatic agents)**
  USE Diplomats
**Minorities**
      --[country or state]--[city]
  PN  For the subject of the condition,
      protection, rights, etc., of racial, religious, and
      other minorities.
  UF  Minority groups
  RT  Aliens
      Busing (School integration)
      Civil rights
      Ethnic groups
      National liberation movements
      People
      Race relations
      Religious groups
      Segregation
**Minority groups**
  USE Minorities
**Minstrel posters**
  USE Theatrical posters
**Minstrel shows**
      --[country or state]--[city]
  PN  Performances of melodies, jokes, and
      impersonations focused on black people,
      often by whites wearing blackface.
  UF  Blackface entertainment
  BT  Musical revues & comedies
**Minstrels**
  PN  Medieval musical entertainers.
  UF  Jongleurs
  BT  Entertainers
      Musicians
  RT  Bards
      Poets

BT Broader term      RT Related term      PN Public Note
NT Narrower term     UF Used for        + Term has NTs
HN History Note       CN Catalogers Note   --[ ] May subdivide

**Minstrels (cont.)**
    Singers
    Troubadours
**Mints**
    --[country or state]--[city]
  PN  Includes activities and structures.
  BT  Government facilities
  RT  Money
**Minuets**
    --[country or state]--[city]
  BT  Dancing
**Miracles**
    --[country or state]--[city]
  BT  Supernatural practices
  RT  Religion
**Mirages**
  BT  Hallucinations & illusions
  RT  Reflections
**Mirrors**
  UF  Looking glasses
  RT  Architectural elements
    Furniture
    Reflections
Misbehaving children
  USE Children misbehaving
**Miscegenation**
  PN  Marriages between persons of different
     races, especially between whites and blacks,
     resulting in a mixture of races.
  UF  Interracial marriage
    Racial crossing
  BT  Race relations
  RT  Marriage
**Miserliness**
  UF  Stinginess
  BT  Mental states
  RT  Avarice
    Extravagance
    Misers
    Wealth
**Misers**
    --[country or state]--[city]
  BT  People
  RT  Miserliness
Misery
  USE Distress
Misrepresentation (Law)
  USE Fraud
Missiles, Guided
  USE Rockets
**Missing in action**
  UF  MIA's
    Servicemen missing in action
  BT  Military personnel
  RT  Prisoners of war
    War
**Mission churches**
    --[country or state]--[city]
  BT  Churches
    Protestant churches
  RT  Missions
**Missionaries**

**Missionaries (cont.)**
    --[nationality]--[country or state]--[city]
  BT  People associated with religion
  RT  Christianity
    Clergy
    Missions
    Religion
    Spiritual leaders
**Missions**
    --[country or state]--[city]
  BT  Religious communities
  RT  Mission churches
    Missionaries
**Mistletoe**
  BT  Shrubs
  RT  Festive decorations
**Mistrust**
  USE Suspicion
**Mixed media**
  CN  TGM II term.
  UF  Multiple processes
Mizrachs
  USE Mizriha'ot
**Mizriha'ot**
  CN  TGM II term.
  UF  Mizrachs
**Moats**
    --[country or state]--[city]
  PN  Deep, wide trenches usually filled with
     water, found around the ramparts of fortified
     places such as castles.
  BT  Architectural elements
  RT  Castles & palaces
    Channels
    Forts & fortifications
**Mobile health units**
    --[country or state]--[city]
  CN  Double index under the type of health
     service being provided, e.g., radiography, eye
     examinations.
  UF  Health units, Mobile
  BT  Health care facilities
    Vehicles
  RT  Ambulances
    Clinics
**Mobile homes**
  UF  Trailers
  BT  Dwellings
Mobilizations of armed forces
  USE Military mobilizations
Mobs
  USE Crowds
**Model airplanes**
  BT  Model vehicles
  RT  Airplanes
    Toys
**Model cars**
  BT  Model vehicles
  RT  Automobiles
    Toys
**Model houses**
    --[country or state]--[city]

---

BT Broader term            RT Related term            PN Public Note
NT Narrower term          UF Used for                + Term has NTs
HN History Note           CN Catalogers Note        --[ ] May subdivide

**Model houses (cont.)**
- PN   Full-scale representations of houses planned to be constructed. Search under ARCHITECTURAL MODELS for miniature representations of structures made for the purpose of showing the result of architectural construction plans.
- CN   Used in a note under ARCHITECTURAL MODELS and BUILDING MODELS.
- UF   Demonstration houses
  - Prototype houses
- BT   Houses
- RT   Construction industry
  - Models
  - Real estate business

**Model railroads**
- PN   Search under MINIATURE RAILROADS for small trains that people can ride.
- BT   Models
- RT   Electric railroads
  - Miniature railroads
  - Model vehicles
  - Narrow-gage railroads
  - Toys

Model schools
- USE Laboratory schools

**Model ships**
- BT   Model vehicles
- NT   Ship models in bottles
- RT   Children sailing boats
  - Ships
  - Toys

**Model vehicles**
- BT   Models
- NT   Model airplanes
  - Model cars
  - Model ships +
- RT   Model railroads
  - Vehicles

**Modeling (Sculpture)**
- --[country or state]--[city]
- CN   Used in a note under SCULPTURE.
- UF   Clay modeling
  - Molding (Clay, plaster, etc.)
  - Sculpting
  - Sculpturing
- BT   Art
  - Handicraft
- RT   Children sculpting
  - Sculpture

**Models**
- HN   Changed 5/1989 from non-postable term (Use ARCHITECTURAL MODELS, etc.).
- NT   Architectural models
  - Building models +
  - Model railroads
  - Model vehicles +
- RT   Model houses

Models, Artists'
- USE Artists' models

Models, Fashion
- USE Fashion models

**Modern dancing**
- --[country or state]--[city]
- BT   Dancing

Modification of weather
- USE Weather control

**Molded plywood**
- BT   Plywood

Molding (Clay, plaster, etc.)
- USE Modeling (Sculpture)

**Moldings**
- --[country or state]--[city]
- UF   Mouldings
- BT   Architectural elements
- NT   Bead & reel moldings
  - Egg & dart moldings
- RT   Cornices
  - Paneling

**Moles (Animals)**
- --[country or state]
- BT   Animals

**Molotov cocktails**
- PN   Crude hand grenades made of a bottle filled with flammable liquid.
- BT   Explosives

Monad (Symbol)
- USE Yin Yang (Symbol)

Monarchs
- USE Rulers

**Monarchy**
- --[country]
- PN   For the subject of monarchy in general. Search under RULERS for images that focus on real persons.
- BT   Economic & political systems
- RT   Democracy
  - Rulers

**Monasteries**
- --[country or state]--[city]
- UF   Cloisters
- BT   Religious communities
- NT   Wats
- RT   Abbeys
  - Convents
  - Monks
  - Religious orders
  - Scriptoria

Monastic orders
- USE Religious orders

Monetary assistance
- USE Assistance

Monetary question
- USE Currency question

**Money**
- --[country]
- CN   TGM II term.
- UF   Currency
  - Paper money
- NT   Coins
  - Greenbacks
  - Political campaign funds
- RT   Barter
  - Business & finance

---

**Money (cont.)**
        Cash registers
        Children & money
        Children's allowances
        Counterfeiting
        Currency question
        Fund raising
        Gold
        Mints
        Pensions
        Silver
        Treasure-trove
        Treasuries
        Wages
        Wealth
**Money crises**
  USE Business panics
**Money lending**
  USE Usury
**Money raising**
  USE Fund raising
**Mongooses**
      --[country or state]
  BT  Animals
**Monitors (Warships)**
  USE Turret ships
**Monkey wrenches**
  USE Wrenches
**Monkeys**
      --[country or state]
  BT  Animals
  NT  Baboons
  RT  Three monkeys  (Motif)
**Monks**
      --[country or state]--[city]
  UF  Friars
  BT  Men
      People associated with religion
  RT  Christianity
      Monasteries
      Nuns
      Religion
      Religious orders
**Monochromatic works**
  CN  TGM II term.
**Monograms**
  CN  TGM II term.
**Monopolies**
  BT  Big business
  RT  Industrial trusts
**Monorail railroads**
      --[country or state]--[city]
  UF  Single-rail railroads
  BT  Railroads
**Monotype prints**
  USE Monotypes
**Monotypes**
  CN  TGM II term.
  UF  Monotype prints
**Monsters**
  PN  For animals of strange or terrifying shape.
      Search under HUMAN CURIOSITIES for

**Monsters (cont.)**
      real persons being represented as freaks.
  CN  Used in a note under HUMAN
      CURIOSITIES.
  UF  Freaks
  BT  Supernatural beings
  NT  Sea monsters
  RT  Animals
      Human curiosities
**Monstrances**
  PN  Religious vessels holding consecrated
      Host or sacred relic.
  UF  Ostensoriums
  BT  Religious articles
**Montages**
  CN  TGM II term.
**Months**
  BT  Time
  RT  Seasons
**Monument builders**
      --[country or state]--[city]
  PN  Includes activities and structures.
  UF  Marble works
  BT  Business enterprises
  RT  Tombs & sepulchral monuments
**Monuments**
  CN  Used only as a subdivision with names of
      persons (Appendix B) and with names of
      wars (Appendix C).
**Monuments & memorials**
      --[country or state]--[city]
  PN  Structures erected to commemorate
      persons, events, or causes. Search also under
      the subdivision --COMMEMORATION used
      with ethnic, racial, and regional groups, and
      with classes of persons (Appendix A), and
      with corporate bodies and named events
      (Appendix D). Search also under the
      subdivision --MONUMENTS used with
      names of persons (Appendix B) and with
      names of wars (Appendix C).
  UF  Memorials
  BT  Facilities
  NT  Memorial arches
      Obelisks
      Sphinxes
  RT  Cairns
      Historic sites
      Historical markers
      Pagodas
      Plaques
      Sculpture
      Tombs & sepulchral monuments
**Moods**
  USE Mental states
**Moon**
  BT  Celestial bodies
  RT  Eclipses
**Moonlight**
  BT  Natural phenomena
  RT  Light
      Night

BT  Broader term                RT  Related term              PN  Public Note
NT  Narrower term           UF  Used for                    +  Term has NTs
HN  History Note              CN  Catalogers Note         --[ ] May subdivide

Moonshine stills
  USE Stills (Distilleries)
Moor baths
  USE Mud baths
**Mooring**
     --[country or state]--[city]
  PN  Making fast vessels or aircraft by means
      of chains, lines, anchors, or other devices.
  UF  Anchorage
      Berthing
  RT  Aircraft
      Anchors
      Navigation
      Piers & wharves
      Vessels
**Moose**
  BT  Deer
  RT  Elk
      Moose hunting
**Moose hunting**
     --[country or state]
  BT  Deer hunting
  RT  Moose
**Moral aspects of war**
     --[country or state]--[city]
  PN  Search also under the subdivision
      --MORAL & ETHICAL ASPECTS used with
      names of wars (Appendix C).
  BT  Ethics
  NT  War crimes
  RT  Conscientious objectors
      Draft resisters
      Pacifism
      Religious aspects of war
      War
Moral & ethical aspects
  CN  Used only as a subdivision with names of
      wars (Appendix C).
Morals
  USE Ethics
Moratoriums
  USE Strikes
**Moravian churches**
     --[country or state]--[city]
  PN  For images that focus on buildings, as
      well as the associated grounds.
  BT  Protestant churches
**Morgues & mortuaries**
     --[country or state]--[city]
  PN  Search under UNDERTAKING for
      activities.
  UF  Funeral homes
      Mortuaries
      Undertaking establishments
  BT  Funerary facilities
  RT  Crematoriums
      Hospitals
      Undertaking
**Mormon churches**
     --[country or state]--[city]
  PN  For images that focus on buildings, as
      well as the associated grounds.

**Mormon churches (cont.)**
  UF  Temples, Mormon
  BT  Churches
**Morning glories**
     --[country or state]--[city]
  BT  Flowers
**Mortars (Ordnance)**
  PN  Cannons with a tube short in relation to
      their caliber, used to throw projectiles with
      low muzzle velocities at high angles. Also,
      any of various contrivances for throwing
      pyrotechnic bombs.
  BT  Artillery (Weaponry)
**Mortgages**
  BT  Contracts
  RT  Business & finance
Mortuaries
  USE Morgues & mortuaries
Mortuary customs
  USE Funeral rites & ceremonies
Mortuary practice
  USE Undertaking
**Mosaic pavements**
     --[country or state]--[city]
  UF  Pavements, Mosaic
  BT  Mosaics
  RT  Floors
**Mosaics**
     --[country or state]--[city]
  NT  Mosaic pavements
  RT  Murals
      Tiles
**Mosques**
     --[country or state]--[city]
  PN  For images that focus on buildings, as
      well as the associated grounds.
  BT  Religious facilities
  RT  Churches
      Mihrabs
      Minarets
**Mosquitos**
     --[country or state]
  BT  Insects
Moss, Spanish
  USE Spanish moss
**Motels**
     --[country or state]--[city]
  PN  Establishments which provide lodging and
      parking and in which the rooms are usually
      accessible from an outdoor parking area.
  UF  Auto courts
      Motor courts
      Motor lodges
      Tourist courts
  BT  Hotels
      Public accommodation facilities
  RT  Tourist camps & hostels
**Mothers**
  BT  Women
  NT  Mothers-in-law
      Stepmothers
      Unmarried mothers

BT Broader term          RT Related term          PN Public Note
NT Narrower term          UF Used for          + Term has NTs
HN History Note          CN Catalogers Note          --[ ] May subdivide

## Mothers (cont.)
Working mothers
RT  Mothers & children
Pregnant women

## Mothers & children
--[country or state]--[city]
BT  Families
RT  Breast feeding
Children & adults
Mothers

Mothers, Employed
USE Working mothers

Mothers, Working
USE Working mothers

## Mothers-in-law
--[country or state]--[city]
BT  Mothers
RT  Families
Marriage

Motifs, Architectural
USE Architectural decorations & ornaments

Motion
USE Locomotion

## Motion picture audiences
--[country or state]--[city]
UF  Film audiences
Filmgoers
Moviegoers
BT  Audiences
RT  Motion pictures

## Motion picture cameras
UF  Movie cameras
BT  Motion picture devices
RT  Cinematography

## Motion picture devices
PN  Devices for making or viewing motion pictures.
UF  Kinetographs
Kinetoscopes
Mutographs
Mutoscopes
Phantoscopes
Projectors, Motion picture
Tachyscopes
Vitascopes
BT  Photographic apparatus & supplies
NT  Motion picture cameras
RT  Motion pictures

## Motion picture festivals
--[country or state]--[city]
UF  Film festivals
BT  Festivals

## Motion picture industry
--[country or state]--[city]
PN  Includes activities and structures.
UF  Film industry (Motion pictures)
BT  Business enterprises
RT  Actors
Actresses
Motion pictures

Motion picture photography
USE Cinematography

## Motion picture posters
CN  TGM II term.
UF  Film posters
Movie posters

## Motion picture premieres
--[country or state]--[city]
BT  Premieres
RT  Motion pictures

Motion picture stills
USE Film stills

## Motion picture theaters
--[country or state]--[city]
UF  Movie theaters
BT  Theaters
NT  Drive-in theaters
RT  Motion pictures

## Motion pictures
UF  Cinema
Films
Movies
Moving pictures
BT  Audiovisual materials
NT  Erotic films
RT  Action & adventure dramas
Comedies
Entertainment
Historical dramas
Horror dramas
Melodramas
Motion picture audiences
Motion picture devices
Motion picture industry
Motion picture premieres
Motion picture theaters
Romances
Sociological dramas
Westerns

## Motion study photographs
CN  TGM II term.
UF  Chronophotographs
Multiple flash photographs
Pulsed-light photographs
Stroboscopic photographs
Time-lapse photographs

Motor courts
USE Motels

Motor lodges
USE Motels

Motor vehicles, Amphibious
USE Amphibious vehicles

Motorboat engines
USE Boat engines

## Motorboats
--[nationality]--[country or state]--[city]
UF  Power boats
BT  Boats
NT  Hydroplanes
Launches

## Motorcycles
--[nationality]--[country or state]--[city]
BT  Vehicles
RT  Bicycles & tricycles

---

BT  Broader term
NT  Narrower term
HN  History Note

RT  Related term
UF  Used for
CN  Catalogers Note

PN  Public Note
+  Term has NTs
--[ ]  May subdivide

Motors
  USE Engines
Motto prints
  USE Emblem pictures
Mouldings
  USE Moldings
Mountain climbing
  USE Mountaineering
**Mountain goat hunting**
      --[country or state]
  BT  Big game hunting
  RT  Mountain goats
**Mountain goats**
      --[country or state]
  BT  Goats
  RT  Mountain goat hunting
Mountain lions
  USE Pumas
Mountain passes
  USE Passes (Landforms)
**Mountain railroads**
      --[country or state]--[city]
  PN  Railroads employing devices, such as
      cables, central rails, racks and pinions, to hold
      the cars on a steep mountain track.
  UF  Cog railroads
      Rack railroads
  BT  Railroads
  RT  Cable railroads
      Inclined railroads
**Mountain sheep**
      --[country or state]
  UF  Barbary sheep
      Bighorn sheep
      Dall sheep
  BT  Sheep
  RT  Mountain sheep hunting
**Mountain sheep hunting**
      --[country or state]
  BT  Big game hunting
  RT  Mountain sheep
**Mountaineering**
      --[country or state]--[city]
  UF  Mountain climbing
  BT  Climbing
      Hiking
  RT  Mountains
**Mountains**
      --[country or state]
  CN  Used in a note under CLIFFS.
  UF  Ridges
  BT  Land
  RT  Avalanches
      Buttes
      Cliffs
      Glaciers
      Hills
      Landslides
      Mesas
      Mountaineering
      Passes (Landforms)
      Volcanoes

**Mounted police**
      --[country or state]--[city]
  BT  Police
  RT  Horseback riding
Mourning
  USE Grief
Mourning customs
  USE Funeral rites & ceremonies
       Memorial rites & ceremonies
Mourning works
  USE Memorial works
**Mousetraps**
  BT  Animal traps
  RT  Mice
      Rodent control
**Mouth organs**
  PN  Includes the activity of playing mouth
      organs.
  UF  Harmonicas
  BT  Wind instruments
**Mouths**
  RT  Faces
      Human body
      Smiling
Movable bridges
  USE Drawbridges
      Swing bridges
      Vertical lift bridges
Movable works
  USE Mechanical works
Movement
  USE Locomotion
Movers
  USE Moving & storage trade
Movie cameras
  USE Motion picture cameras
Movie posters
  USE Motion picture posters
Movie stars
  USE Actors
      Actresses
Movie stills
  USE Film stills
Movie theaters
  USE Motion picture theaters
Moviegoers
  USE Motion picture audiences
Movies
  USE Motion pictures
Moving chairs
  USE Wheelchairs
      Wheeled chairs
Moving of buildings, bridges, etc.
  USE Moving of structures
**Moving of structures**
      --[country or state]--[city]
  UF  House moving
      Moving of buildings, bridges, etc.
  RT  Bridges
      Buildings
      Moving & storage trade
      Shipping

---

BT  Broader term           RT  Related term           PN Public Note
NT  Narrower term         UF  Used for           + Term has NTs
HN History Note          CN Catalogers Note      --[ ] May subdivide

Moving pictures
  USE Motion pictures
**Moving & storage trade**
      --[country or state]--[city]
  PN  Includes activities and structures.
  CN  For images that focus on structures,
      double index under the type of structure.
  UF  Movers
      Storage & moving trade
  BT  Business enterprises
  RT  Dollies (Moving equipment)
      Moving of structures
      Shipping
      Storage facilities
**Mowing**
      --[country or state]--[city]
  RT  Clearing of land
      Farming
      Gardening
      Harvesting
      Mowing machines
**Mowing machines**
  UF  Hay mowers
  BT  Harvesting machinery
  RT  Mowing
**Muckraking**
  PN  Searching for and either charging or
      exposing (in newspapers, etc.) corruption by
      public officials, businessmen, etc.
  BT  Journalism
  RT  Corruption
      Ethics
      Reform
**Mud**
      --[country or state]--[city]
  RT  Children playing in mud
      Land
**Mud baths**
      --[country or state]--[city]
  UF  Moor baths
  BT  Therapeutic baths
Mud slides
  USE Landslides
**Mud volcanoes**
      --[country or state]
  BT  Volcanoes
Mug shots
  USE Identification photographs
Muggings
  USE Robberies
Mugs
  USE Drinking vessels
**Mulberry trees**
      --[country or state]--[city]
  BT  Trees
**Mules**
      --[country or state]--[city]
  BT  Animals
  RT  Donkeys
      Horses
Multiple births
  USE Quadruplets

Multiple births (cont.)
      Quintuplets
      Triplets
      Twins
Multiple flash photographs
  USE Motion study photographs
Multiple marriage
  USE Bigamy
      Polygamy
Multiple processes
  USE Mixed media
**Mummies**
  BT  Dead persons
  RT  Embalming
      Funeral rites & ceremonies
**Mumming**
      --[country or state]--[city]
  BT  Manners & customs
  RT  Costumes
      Masquerades
      Pantomimes
**Municipal home rule**
      --[country or state]--[city]
  UF  Home rule for cities
  BT  Autonomy
**Municipal officials**
      --[country or state]--[city]
  UF  City officials
      Town officials
  BT  Government officials
  NT  City council members
      Mayors
**Municipal services**
      --[country or state]--[city]
  UF  Public services
  BT  Politics & government
  RT  City planning
Munitions industry
  USE Ordnance industry
**Murals**
      --[country or state]--[city]
  UF  Frescoes
  BT  Art
  RT  Cave drawings
      Mosaics
Murders
  USE Homicides
Muscle men
  USE Strong men
Museums
  USE Galleries & museums
**Mushroom clouds**
      --[country or state]--[city]
  RT  Nuclear weapons
**Mushrooms**
      --[country or state]--[city]
  BT  Plants
**Music**
      --[country or state]--[city]
  PN  Search also under the subdivision
      --MUSIC used with names of ethnic, racial,
      and regional groups, and with classes of

---

BT  Broader term              RT  Related term           PN  Public Note
NT  Narrower term             UF  Used for               +   Term has NTs
HN  History Note              CN  Catalogers Note        --[ ] May subdivide

**Music (cont.)**
       persons (Appendix A). Search also under the
       subdivision --SONGS & MUSIC used with
       names of wars (Appendix C).
  BT  Sounds
  NT  Blues music
       Electronic music
       Folk music +
       Gospel music
       Jazz
       Musical notation
       Singing +
       Songs +
  RT  Burlesque shows
       Concerts
       Dancing
       Music education
       Music festivals
       Music publishing industry
       Music rooms
       Music stores
       Musical instruments
       Musical revues & comedies
       Musicians
       Theatrical productions

**Music education**
       --[country or state]--[city]
  PN  Includes activities and structures.
  CN  Double index under EDUCATIONAL
       FACILITIES (or NTs) for images that focus
       on facilities.
  UF  Conservatories, Musical
       Music lessons
       Music schools
  BT  Education
  RT  Music

**Music ensembles**
       --[country or state]--[city]
  UF  Ensembles, Music
  NT  Bands +
       Barbershop quartets
       Choirs (Music)
       Orchestras
  RT  Conductors
       Musical instruments
       Musicians

**Music festivals**
       --[country or state]--[city]
  BT  Festivals
  RT  Concerts
       Music

**Music halls**
       --[country or state]--[city]
  PN  Auditoriums for musical, variety, or
       theatrical productions.
  BT  Concert halls
  RT  Burlesque shows
       Nightclubs
       Theaters

Music lessons
  USE Music education

Music posters

Music posters (cont.)
  USE Concert posters

**Music publishing industry**
       --[country or state]--[city]
  PN  Includes activities and structures.
  UF  Sheet music publishing industry
  BT  Publishing industry
  RT  Music

**Music rooms**
       --[country or state]--[city]
  BT  Interiors
  RT  Music

Music schools
  USE Music education

Music sheet covers
  USE Sheet music covers

**Music stores**
       --[country or state]--[city]
  PN  Includes activities and structures.
  BT  Stores & shops
  RT  Music
       Musical instruments
       Sound recording stores

**Music title pages**
  CN  TGM II term.

Musical comedies
  USE Musical revues & comedies

**Musical instrument cases**
  BT  Containers
  RT  Musical instruments
       Musicians

**Musical instrument industry**
       --[country or state]--[city]
  PN  Includes activities and structures.
  CN  Double index under INDUSTRIAL
       FACILITIES (or NTs) for images that focus
       on facilities.
  BT  Industry
  RT  Musical instruments

**Musical instruments**
       --[country or state]--[city]
  PN  Includes the activity of playing
       instruments. Search also under the
       subdivision --PERFORMANCES used with
       names of persons (Appendix B).
  UF  Instruments, Musical
  NT  Children playing musical instruments
       Kazoos
       Keyboard instruments +
       Percussion instruments +
       Stringed instruments +
       Wind instruments +
  RT  Concerts
       Music
       Music ensembles
       Music stores
       Musical instrument cases
       Musical instrument industry
       Musicians

**Musical notation**
  UF  Notes, Musical
  BT  Music

---

BT  Broader term       RT  Related term       PN  Public Note
NT  Narrower term      UF  Used for         +  Term has NTs
HN  History Note       CN  Catalogers Note    --[ ] May subdivide

Musical play posters
  USE Theatrical posters
**Musical revues & comedies**
     --[country or state]--[city]
  UF  Comedies, Musical
      Musical comedies
  BT  Theatrical productions
  NT  Minstrel shows
  RT  Chorus girls
      Comedies
      Music
      Vaudeville shows
**Musicians**
     --[country or state]--[city]
  PN  For musicians away from the context of
      their activity; includes portraits with
      instruments.
  CN  As appropriate, double index under the
      instrument.
  BT  People associated with entertainment &
      sports
  NT  Composers
      Conductors
      Minstrels
      Singers +
      Street musicians +
  RT  Entertainers
      Music
      Music ensembles
      Musical instrument cases
      Musical instruments
      Musicians' unions
**Musicians' unions**
     --[country or state]--[city]
  BT  Labor unions
  RT  Musicians
**Musk deer**
  BT  Deer
Musk ox
  USE Muskox
Musk ox hunting
  USE Muskox hunting
Musk oxen
  USE Muskox
Muskets
  USE Rifles
**Muskox**
     --[country or state]
  HN  Changed 11/1992 from Musk ox.
  UF  Musk ox
      Musk oxen
  BT  Animals
  RT  Muskox hunting
**Muskox hunting**
     --[country or state]
  HN  Changed 11/1992 from Musk ox hunting.
  UF  Musk ox hunting
  BT  Hunting
  RT  Muskox
Mustering out
  USE Military discharges
**Mutinies**

Mutinies (cont.)
     --[country or state]--[city]
  BT  Rebellions
  RT  Ships
Mutographs
  USE Motion picture devices
Mutoscopes
  USE Motion picture devices
Mythical creatures
  USE Supernatural beings
     Unicorns
**Myths**
  PN  Search also under the subdivision
      --SPIRITUAL LIFE used with ethnic, racial,
      and regional groups, and with classes of
      persons (Appendix A).
  BT  Literature
  RT  Gods
      Supernatural
**Nail industry**
     --[country or state]--[city]
  PN  Includes activities and structures.
  CN  Double index under INDUSTRIAL
      FACILITIES (or NTs) for images that focus
      on facilities.
  BT  Building materials industry
Naked persons
  USE Nudes
**Names**
  PN  For the subject of people's names.
  RT  People
Nannies (Children's nurses)
  USE Governesses
Narcissus
  USE Daffodils
Narcotic habit
  USE Drug abuse
**Narcotics**
  UF  Drugs
      Opiates
  NT  Marijuana
      Opium
  RT  Drug abuse
      Medicines
      Smoking
      Water pipes (Smoking)
**Narrow-gage railroads**
     --[country or state]--[city]
  BT  Railroads
  NT  Miniature railroads
  RT  Model railroads
National anthems
  USE National songs
National costumes
  USE Costumes
National debt
  USE Public debt
National defense
  HN  Changed 12/1992 from postable term.
  USE National security
**National emblems**
     --[country]

---

BT Broader term            RT Related term            PN Public Note
NT Narrower term          UF Used for                + Term has NTs
HN History Note             CN Catalogers Note        --[ ] May subdivide

**National emblems (cont.)**
- BT  Emblems

National forests
- USE Forest reserves

National guards & reserves
- USE Militias

National income
- USE Gross national product

**National liberation movements**
- --[country or state]--[city]
- PN  For minority or other groups in armed rebellion against a colonial government, or against a national government charged with corruption or foreign domination. In general, this heading is applicable only to the post-World War II period.
- UF  Liberation movements, National
- BT  Rebellions
- RT  Autonomy
- Colonies
- Guerrillas
- Minorities

**National parks & reserves**
- --[country or state]
- BT  Parks
- NT  Forest reserves
- RT  Rangers
- State parks & reserves
- Wildlife conservation

**National security**
- --[country or state]
- PN  Policies and preparations for securing a country against foreign aggression and for protecting sensitive information about national affairs.
- UF  Defense, National
- National defense
- Security, National
- NT  Civil defense +
- RT  Censorship
- Defense budgets
- International relations
- Military organizations
- Military policy
- Preparedness
- Spying

**National socialism**
- PN  For the subject of national socialism in general. Search under NATIONAL SOCIALISTS for images that focus on real persons.
- CN  Used in a note under NATIONAL SOCIALISTS.
- UF  Nazism
- BT  Economic & political systems
- RT  Fascism
- National socialists
- Socialism
- Swastika
- Totalitarianism

**National socialists**
- --[country or state]--[city]

**National socialists (cont.)**
- PN  For images that focus on real persons. Search under NATIONAL SOCIALISM for the subject of national socialism in general.
- CN  Used in a note under NATIONAL SOCIALISM.
- UF  Nazis
- BT  People associated with politics & government
- RT  National socialism

**National songs**
- --[country or state]
- CN  Used in a note under PATRIOTISM.
- UF  Anthems, National
- National anthems
- BT  Songs
- RT  Patriotism

National stereotypes
- USE Ethnic stereotypes

**Nationalism**
- --[country or state]--[city]
- PN  Sense of national consciousness exalting one nation above all others and placing primary emphasis on promotion of its culture and interests as opposed to those of other nations or supernational groups.
- CN  Use when the subject of the image(s) is nationalism, not when nationalistic sentiment is merely being expressed.
- RT  Chauvinism & jingoism
- Economic & political systems
- Imperialism
- International relations
- Mental states
- Patriotism
- Political pageantry
- Regionalism
- Sectionalism (United States)

Nationalization
- USE Government ownership

Native Americans
- USE Indians of North America

Native peoples
- USE Indigenous peoples

Nativity scenes (Crèches)
- USE Crèches (Nativity scenes)

Natural bridges
- USE Rock formations

Natural disasters
- PN  Search under appropriate NTs to NATURAL PHENOMENA.

**Natural gas**
- --[country or state]--[city]
- UF  Gas, Natural
- BT  Fuel
- RT  Gaslight fixtures

Natural gas industry
- USE Gas industry

**Natural phenomena**
- --[country or state]--[city]
- CN  Used in a note under NATURAL DISASTERS.

BT  Broader term
NT  Narrower term
HN  History Note

RT  Related term
UF  Used for
CN  Catalogers Note

PN  Public Note
+  Term has NTs
--[ ] May subdivide

**Natural phenomena (cont.)**
- UF  Phenomena, Natural
- NT  Air
  - Auroras
  - Clouds
  - Earthquakes
  - Eclipses
  - Erosion
  - Fire +
  - Floods
  - Frost
  - Geysers
  - Heat
  - Ice +
  - Landslides +
  - Light
  - Lightning
  - Moonlight
  - Night
  - Rainbows
  - Reflections
  - Seasons +
  - Shadows
  - Stalactites & stalagmites
  - Sunrises & sunsets
  - Temperature
  - Tidal waves
  - Tide pools
  - Volcanic eruptions
  - Waterspouts
  - Weather +
  - Whirlpools
- RT  Nature

Natural philosophy
- USE Physics

Natural resource conservation
- USE Conservation of natural resources

**Naturalization**
- --[country]
- BT  Law & legal affairs
- RT  Citizenship
  - Emigration & immigration

**Nature**
- PN  For the subject of nature in general.
- RT  Animals
  - Bodies of water
  - Ecology
  - Land
  - Natural phenomena
  - Plants

**Nausea**
- RT  Health
  - Sick persons

Navajo sandpaintings
- USE Sandpaintings

**Naval architecture drawings**
- CN  TGM II term.
- UF  Drawings, Naval architecture
  - Marine architecture drawings

Naval art & science
- USE Military art & science

Naval bases

Naval bases (cont.)
- USE Naval yards & naval stations

Naval battles
- USE Naval warfare

Naval depots
- USE Military depots

**Naval museums**
- --[country or state]--[city]
- UF  Maritime museums
- BT  Galleries & museums
- RT  Military facilities

Naval operations
- CN  Used only as a subdivision with names of wars (Appendix C).

**Naval parades & ceremonies**
- --[country or state]--[city]
- PN  For civilian or military parades on water. Search under MILITARY PARADES & CEREMONIES for land parades sponsored by the navy.
- UF  Naval reviews
  - Reviews, Military
  - Water parades
- BT  Events
- RT  Military inspections
  - Military parades & ceremonies
  - Parades & processions
  - Rites & ceremonies
  - Vessels

**Naval prints**
- CN  TGM II term.

Naval reviews
- USE Naval parades & ceremonies

Naval ships
- USE Government vessels

Naval stations
- USE Naval yards & naval stations

Naval stores
- RT  Gums & resins
  - Naval yards & naval stations

**Naval warfare**
- --[country or state]
- PN  Search also under the subdivision --NAVAL OPERATIONS used with names of wars (Appendix C).
- CN  Used in a note under SHIPWRECKS.
- UF  Naval battles
- BT  Military art & science
- NT  Submarine warfare
- RT  Campaigns & battles
  - Marine accidents
  - Scuttling of warships
  - Shipwrecks
  - Torpedoes
  - Warships

**Naval yards & naval stations**
- --[nationality]--[country or state]--[city]
- UF  Boatyards
  - Dockyards
  - Dry docks
  - Naval bases
  - Naval stations

---

BT  Broader term
NT  Narrower term
HN  History Note

RT  Related term
UF  Used for
CN  Catalogers Note

PN  Public Note
+ Term has NTs
--[ ] May subdivide

**Naval yards & naval stations (cont.)**
        Navy yards
        Shipyards
  BT   Military facilities
  RT   Boat & ship industry
        Launchings
        Naval stores
**Navies**
        --[nationality]--[country or state]--[city]
  BT   Military organizations
  RT   Sailors
**Navigation**
  BT   Science
  RT   Aeronautics
        Air traffic control
        Aircraft
        Alidades
        Beacons
        Buoys
        Compasses
        Lighthouses
        Mooring
        Oceanography
        Radar
        Sextants
        Signal flags
        Vessels
Navy yards
  USE Naval yards & naval stations
Nazis
  USE National socialists
Nazism
  USE National socialism
Necessaries
  USE Privies
**Necklaces**
  BT   Jewelry
Necks (Coasts)
  USE Capes (Coasts)
**Neckties**
  UF   Cravats
        Ties (Neckwear)
  BT   Clothing & dress
  RT   Neckwear industry
**Neckwear industry**
        --[country or state]--[city]
  PN   Includes activities and structures.
  CN   Double index under INDUSTRIAL
        FACILITIES (or NTs)  for images that focus
        on facilities.
  UF   Tie industry
  BT   Clothing industry
  RT   Neckties
Necromancy
  USE Magic
Needles, Hypodermic
  USE Hypodermic needles
Negative photoprints
  USE Negative prints
**Negative prints**
  CN   TGM II term.
  UF   Negative photoprints

**Negatives**
  CN   TGM II term.
  UF   Photonegatives
Negroes
  USE Afro-Americans
        Blacks
**Neighbors**
  BT   People
Neon signs
  USE Electric signs
Neo-conservatism
  USE Conservatism
Neo-Nazism
  USE Fascism
**Nepotism**
  BT   Ethics
  RT   Employment
        Political patronage
Nestlings
  USE Birds
        Birds' eggs & nests
Nests
  USE Birds' eggs & nests
**Nets**
  NT   Butterfly nets
        Fishing nets
Nets, Butterfly
  USE Butterfly nets
Nets, Fish
  USE Fishing nets
**Neutrality**
        --[country or state]--[city]
  UF   Isolationism
  BT   International relations
  RT   Intervention (International law)
        War
New Left
  USE Radicalism
New Right
  USE Conservatism
**New Year cards**
  CN   TGM II term.
**New Year resolutions**
  UF   Resolutions, New Year
  BT   Manners & customs
Newel posts
  USE Newels
**Newels**
        --[country or state]--[city]
  UF   Newel posts
        Posts, Newel
  BT   Architectural elements
  RT   Stairways
News dealers
  USE Newspaper vendors
News photographers
  USE Photojournalists
News photography
  USE Photojournalism
News vendors
  USE Newspaper vendors
Newsboys

---

BT  Broader term
NT  Narrower term
HN  History Note

RT  Related term
UF  Used for
CN  Catalogers Note

PN  Public Note
+  Term has NTs
--[ ]  May subdivide

Newsboys (cont.)
USE Newspaper carriers
Newscarriers' addresses
USE Carriers' addresses
Newsmen's presents
USE Carriers' addresses
**Newspaper carriers**
--[country or state]--[city]
UF Newsboys
Paper carriers
BT Children
RT Delivery boys
Newspaper vendors
Newspapers
Newspaper clippings
USE Clippings
Newspaper illustrations
USE Periodical illustrations
**Newspaper industry**
--[country or state]--[city]
PN Includes activities and structures.
BT Publishing industry
RT Newspapers
Newsrooms
Newspaper posters
USE Book & magazine posters
Newspaper reporters
USE Reporters
**Newspaper vendors**
--[country or state]--[city]
UF Magazine vendors
News dealers
News vendors
Newsstands
BT Peddlers
RT Kiosks
Newspaper carriers
Newspapers
**Newspapers**
--[country or state]--[city]
CN Subdivide geographically by place where
newspaper is published.
BT Periodicals
RT Journalists
Newspaper carriers
Newspaper industry
Newspaper vendors
**Newsrooms**
--[country or state]--[city]
BT Interiors
RT Broadcasting
Journalism
Newspaper industry
Offices
Newsstands
USE Newspaper vendors
**Niches**
--[country or state]--[city]
BT Architectural elements
RT Mihrabs
Walls
**Nickel mining**

Nickel mining (cont.)
--[country or state]--[city]
BT Mining
**Niello printing plates**
CN TGM II term.
**Night**
--[country or state]--[city]
CN Use when the subject of an image is night
or when it is desirable to indicate the time of
day shown in the image.
UF Evening
BT Natural phenomena
RT Lighting
Moonlight
Night clubs
USE Nightclubs
**Night photographs**
CN TGM II term.
**Night warfare**
--[country or state]--[city]
BT Military art & science
RT Campaigns & battles
Night watchmen
USE Watchmen
Nightclothes
USE Sleepwear
**Nightclubs**
--[country or state]--[city]
PN A place of entertainment open at night,
usually serving food and liquor, having a
floorshow, and providing music and space for
dancing.
UF Cabarets
Night clubs
BT Sports & recreation facilities
RT Bars
Beer halls
Discotheques
Eating & drinking facilities
Entertainment
Music halls
Restaurants
Nightgowns
USE Sleepwear
Nightmares
USE Dreaming
Nightshirts
USE Sleepwear
**Nightsticks**
UF Billy clubs
Police clubs (Weapons)
BT Arms & armament
RT Law enforcement
Police
Riot control
Watchmen
Nine-hour movement
USE Hours of labor
**Nitrate negatives**
CN TGM II term.
UF Cellulose nitrate negatives
Nitrocellulose negatives

BT Broader term
NT Narrower term
HN History Note

RT Related term
UF Used for
CN Catalogers Note

PN Public Note
+ Term has NTs
--[ ] May subdivide

**Nitrates**
  BT  Chemicals
Nitrocellulose negatives
  USE Nitrate negatives
**Noah's ark**
  BT  Ships
  RT  Biblical events
      Floods
**Nobel prizes**
  BT  Awards
**Nobility**
      --[country]
  BT  Upper class
  NT  Knights
      Peerage
  RT  Rulers
**Noise pollution**
      --[country or state]--[city]
  BT  Pollution
  RT  Sounds
Noises
  USE Sounds
Nominations, Political
  USE Political elections
Nominations, Presidential
  USE Presidential appointments
Nonconformists
  USE Bohemians
      Dissenters
      Hippies
Noncooperation
  USE Civil disobedience
Nonintervention
  USE Intervention (International law)
Nonviolent noncooperation
  USE Passive resistance
Nooks
  USE Alcoves
**Nooses**
  RT  Hangings
      Ropes
Normal schools
  USE Teachers' colleges
North American Indians
  USE Indians of North America
North & South relations
  USE Sectionalism (United States)
Northern lights
  USE Auroras
Northlight roofs
  USE Sawtooth roofs
**Noses**
  RT  Faces
      Human body
**Nostalgia**
  BT  Mental states
  RT  Homesickness
Notches
  USE Passes (Landforms)
Notes, Musical
  USE Musical notation
**Novelty works**

**Novelty works (cont.)**
  CN  TGM II term.
  UF  Exotic works
Now & then comparisons
  USE Then & now comparisons
**Nuclear power**
      --[country or state]--[city]
  HN  Changed 12/1988 from non-postable term
      (Use ATOMIC POWER).
  UF  Atomic power
  RT  Particle accelerators
      Radioactive wastes
      Radioactivity
**Nuclear power plants**
      --[country or state]--[city]
  PN  Includes reactors.
  HN  Term changed (12/1988) from NUCLEAR
      REACTORS.
  UF  Nuclear reactors
  BT  Power plants
Nuclear reactors
  USE Nuclear power plants
Nuclear wastes
  USE Radioactive wastes
**Nuclear weapons**
  UF  Atomic bombs
      Atomic weapons
      A-bombs
      Hydrogen bombs
      H-bombs
      Thermonuclear weapons
  BT  Arms & armament
  RT  Bombings
      Bombs
      Mushroom clouds
      Nuclear weapons testing
      Nuclear weapons victims
      Radioactivity
**Nuclear weapons testing**
      --[nationality]--[country or state]--[city]
  BT  Ordnance testing
  RT  Nuclear weapons
**Nuclear weapons victims**
      --[country or state]--[city]
  UF  Atomic bombing victims
  BT  Victims
  RT  Nuclear weapons
      War casualties
**Nudes**
  UF  Naked persons
  BT  People
  RT  Fig leaf
      Human body
Nunneries
  USE Convents
**Nuns**
      --[nationality]--[country or state]--[city]
  BT  People associated with religion
      Women
  RT  Christianity
      Convents
      Monks

---

BT  Broader term
NT  Narrower term
HN  History Note

RT  Related term
UF  Used for
CN  Catalogers Note

PN  Public Note
+   Term has NTs
--[ ] May subdivide

**Nuns (cont.)**
>        Religion
>        Religious orders

**Nurseries**
>        --[country or state]--[city]
>  UF   Children's rooms
>  BT   Interiors
>  RT   Children
>        Hospitals
>        Playrooms

**Nurseries (Horticulture)**
>        --[country or state]--[city]
>  BT   Horticultural buildings

**Nursery rhymes**
>  BT   Literature

**Nurses**
>        --[country or state]--[city]
>  BT   People associated with health & safety
>  RT   Medical offices
>        Midwives
>        Nursing
>        Physicians

Nurses, Children's
>  USE Governesses

**Nursing**
>        --[country or state]--[city]
>  BT   Health care
>  RT   Nurses

**Nursing homes**
>        --[country or state]--[city]
>  PN   Privately operated establishments where
>        maintenance and personal or nursing care are
>        provided for persons (as the aged or
>        chronically ill) who are unable to care for
>        themselves. Includes activities and structures.
>  UF   Convalescent homes
>        Homes (Institutions)
>        Old age homes
>  BT   Health care facilities
>  RT   Institutional care
>        Rest homes
>        Shut-ins

Nursing (Infant feeding)
>  USE Breast feeding

**Nutrition**
>        --[country or state]--[city]
>  UF   Malnutrition
>  RT   Food
>        Health
>        Obesity
>        Starvation
>        Vitamins

**Nuts**
>  BT   Food
>  NT   Chestnuts
>        Walnuts
>  RT   Acorn decorations
>        Peanuts
>        Plants

Nuts (Hardware)
>  USE Bolts & nuts

**Nylon**

**Nylon (cont.)**
>  BT   Fibers
>        Textiles
>  RT   Rayon

**Oaks**
>        --[country or state]--[city]
>  BT   Trees

Oarsmen
>  USE Rowers

**Oases**
>        --[country or state]
>  BT   Land
>  RT   Bodies of water
>        Deserts
>        Water holes

**Oaths**
>        --[country or state]--[city]
>  PN   For judicial or official oaths, including
>        ceremonies. Search under SWEARING for
>        profane language.
>  CN   Used in a note under SWEARING.
>  UF   Swearing in
>        Taking oath
>        Vows
>  BT   Rites & ceremonies
>  RT   Inaugurations
>        Pledges of allegiance
>        Promises
>        Weddings

**Oats**
>        --[country or state]--[city]
>  BT   Grains

**Obelisks**
>        --[country or state]--[city]
>  BT   Monuments & memorials
>  RT   Columns

**Obesity**
>  UF   Adiposity
>        Corpulence
>        Fatness
>        Overweight
>  RT   Health
>        Human body
>        Nutrition
>        Reducing

Objects, Art
>  USE Art objects

Objects, Religious
>  USE Religious articles

**Obliviousness**
>  BT   Mental states
>  RT   Apathy

Obsequies
>  USE Funeral rites & ceremonies

**Observation towers**
>        --[country or state]--[city]
>  BT   Towers

Observatories
>  USE Astronomical observatories

Obstetric hospitals
>  USE Maternity hospitals

**Obstinacy**

---

BT Broader term          RT Related term          PN Public Note
NT Narrower term         UF Used for              + Term has NTs
HN History Note          CN Catalogers Note       --[ ] May subdivide

**Obstinacy (cont.)**
UF   Stubbornness
BT   Mental states
**Occupations**
PN   For the general subject of types of paid
     employment. Search under EMPLOYMENT
     for the general subject of working for pay and
     under NTs to PEOPLE for persons in various
     occupations. Search also under the
     subdivision --EMPLOYMENT used with
     names of ethnic, racial, and regional groups,
     and with classes of persons (Appendix A).
UF   Careers
     Jobs
     Professions
     Trades
RT   Business enterprises
     Employment
     Industry
     People
     Vocational education
**Occupations, Military**
USE Military occupations
**Occupied territories**
USE Military occupations
**Ocean cables**
USE Submarine cables
**Ocean life**
USE Aquatic animals
**Ocean liners**
     --[nationality]--[country or state]--[city]
UF   Liners
BT   Ships
**Ocean travel**
UF   Cruises
     Sea travel
BT   Travel
RT   Ships
**Oceanography**
     --[country or state]--[city]
PN   For the study of the ocean and its
     phenomena and the activities of
     oceanographers.
BT   Science
NT   Sounding
RT   Navigation
     Seas
**Oceans**
PN   For the Atlantic, Pacific, Indian, Arctic,
     and Antarctic oceans.
BT   Seas
**Octagonal buildings**
     --[country or state]--[city]
BT   Buildings distinguished by form
**Octopuses**
     --[country or state]
UF   Devilfish
BT   Aquatic animals
**Oddities**
USE Curiosities & wonders
**Oeil-de-boeuf windows**
USE Bull's eye windows

**Offenders**
USE Criminals
**Office buildings**
     --[country or state]--[city]
CN   As appropriate, double index under the
     type of business.
BT   Buildings
RT   Commercial facilities
     Offices
**Office employees**
USE Office workers
**Office equipment & supplies**
HN   Changed 4/1988 from OFFICE
     EQUIPMENT.
UF   Business machines
     Office machines
     Office supplies
NT   Calculators
     Cash registers
     Computers
     Copying machines
     Dictating machines
     Paper clips
     Rubber stamps
     Typewriters +
RT   Equipment
     Office equipment & supplies industry
     Offices
**Office equipment & supplies industry**
     --[country or state]--[city]
PN   Includes activities and structures.
CN   Double index under INDUSTRIAL
     FACILITIES (or NTs) for images that focus
     on facilities.
HN   Changed 4/1988 from OFFICE
     EQUIPMENT INDUSTRY.
BT   Industry
RT   Equipment industry
     Office equipment & supplies
     Paper industry
**Office furniture**
BT   Furniture
RT   Offices
**Office machines**
USE Office equipment & supplies
**Office supplies**
USE Office equipment & supplies
**Office workers**
     --[country or state]--[city]
UF   Clerical workers
     Office employees
     Secretaries
     Typists
BT   People
RT   Offices
     Typewriting
**Officers, Military**
USE Military officers
**Officers' quarters**
     --[nationality]--[country or state]--[city]
UF   Quarters, Military
     Wardrooms

---

**Officers' quarters (cont.)**
  BT  Dwellings
       Military facilities
  RT  Barracks
       Crew quarters
**Offices**
       --[country or state]--[city]
  BT  Interiors
  RT  Architects' offices
       Business enterprises
       Law offices
       Medical offices
       Newsrooms
       Office buildings
       Office equipment & supplies
       Office furniture
       Office workers
       Studies (Rooms)
       Telegraph offices
Offices, Ticket
  USE Ticket offices
**Official residences**
       --[country or state]--[city]
  BT  Houses
  RT  Castles & palaces
       Embassies
Official visits
  USE Visits of state
Officials, Government
  USE Government officials
**Offset lithographs**
  CN  TGM II term.
**Offset photomechanical prints**
  CN  TGM II term.
Ogres
  USE Ghouls
       Giants
Oil fields
  USE Oil wells
       Petroleum industry
Oil industry
  USE Petroleum industry
**Oil paintings**
  CN TGM II term.
**Oil spills**
       --[country or state]--[city]
  BT  Pollution
  RT  Petroleum industry
       Water pollution
Oil tankers
  USE Tankers
**Oil wells**
       --[country or state]--[city]
  UF  Fields, Oil
       Oil fields
       Wells, Oil
  RT  Petroleum industry
Old age homes
  USE Nursing homes
       Rest homes
Old maids
  USE Single women

Older persons
  USE Aged persons
**Oleographs**
  CN  TGM II term.
Oleomargarine
  USE Margarine
**Olive oil industry**
       --[country or state]--[city]
  PN  Includes activities and structures.
  CN  Double index under INDUSTRIAL
       FACILITIES (or NTs) for images that focus
       on facilities.
  BT  Food industry
  RT  Olives
**Olive trees**
       --[country or state]--[city]
  BT  Trees
  RT  Olives
**Olives**
       --[country or state]--[city]
  BT  Fruit
  RT  Olive oil industry
       Olive trees
**Olympic flame**
  BT  Symbols
  RT  Fire
       Torches
Omnibuses
  USE Buses
One-armed bandits
  USE Slot machines
**One-room schools**
       --[country or state]--[city]
  UF  One-teacher schools
  BT  Schools
  RT  Rural schools
One-teacher schools
  USE One-room schools
**One-way streets**
       --[country or state]--[city]
  BT  Streets
**Onion domes**
       --[country or state]--[city]
  BT  Domes
**Onions**
       --[country or state]--[city]
  BT  Vegetables
**Opalotypes**
  CN  TGM II term.
Opaque microcopies
  USE Microopaques
Open seas
  USE Freedom of the seas
Openings
  USE Premieres
**Open-air schools**
       --[country or state]--[city]
  UF  Outdoor schools
  BT  Schools
**Open-air theaters**
       --[country or state]--[city]
  UF  Outdoor theaters

---

BT Broader term                 RT Related term              PN Public Note
NT Narrower term                UF Used for                  + Term has NTs
HN History Note                 CN Catalogers Note           --[ ] May subdivide

**Open-air theaters (cont.)**
  BT   Theaters
  NT   Amphitheaters
  RT   Open-air theatrical productions
**Open-air theatrical productions**
       --[country or state]--[city]
  UF   Outdoor theatrical productions
  BT   Theatrical productions
  RT   Open-air theaters
       Pageants
**Open-pit mining**
  USE Strip mining
**Opera houses**
       --[country or state]--[city]
  BT   Concert halls
  RT   Operas & operettas
       Theaters
**Opera posters**
  USE Theatrical posters
**Opera singers**
  BT   Entertainers
       Singers
  RT   Actors
       Actresses
       Operas & operettas
**Operas & operettas**
       --[country or state]--[city]
  UF   Operettas
  BT   Theatrical productions
  RT   Opera houses
       Opera singers
       Singing
**Operating rooms**
       --[country or state]--[city]
  BT   Interiors
  RT   Hospitals
       Surgery
**Operations, Covert**
  USE Covert operations
**Operettas**
  USE Operas & operettas
**Opiates**
  USE Narcotics
**Opinion polls**
  USE Public opinion polls
**Opinion, Public**
  USE Public opinion
**Opium**
  HN   Changed 11/1992 from non-postable term
       (Use NARCOTICS).
  BT   Narcotics
**Opossum hunting**
       --[country or state]
  BT   Hunting
  RT   Opossums
**Opossums**
       --[country or state]
  UF   Possums
  BT   Animals
  RT   Opossum hunting
**Opposition (Political science)**
       --[country or state]

**Opposition (Political science) (cont.)**
  PN   For organized political resistance to the
       government in power. Search under
       PROTEST MOVEMENTS for opposition
       regarding particular issues.
  CN   Used in a note under PROTEST
       MOVEMENTS.
  UF   Political opposition
       Resistance movements
  BT   Politics & government
  RT   Dissenters
       Protest movements
       Rebellions
       Revolutions
       Underground movements
**Optical devices**
  BT   Equipment
  NT   Binoculars
       Eyeglasses
       Hand lenses
       Microscopes +
       Telescopes +
  RT   Optical industry
       Opticians' shops
       Scientific equipment
**Optical illusions**
  UF   Illusions, Optical
  RT   Hallucinations & illusions
**Optical industry**
       --[country or state]--[city]
  PN   Includes activities and structures.
  CN   Double index under INDUSTRIAL
       FACILITIES (or NTs) for images that focus
       on facilities.
  BT   Industry
  RT   Optical devices
       Optical industry strikes
       Opticians' shops
**Optical industry strikes**
       --[country or state]--[city]
  BT   Strikes
  RT   Optical industry
**Opticianry**
  USE Opticians' shops
**Opticians' shops**
       --[country or state]--[city]
  PN   Includes activities and structures.
  UF   Opticianry
  BT   Stores & shops
  RT   Health care
       Optical devices
       Optical industry
**Optimism**
  UF   Hopefulness
  BT   Mental states
  RT   Despair
       Happiness
       Pessimism
**Oral tobacco**
  USE Smokeless tobacco
**Orange orchards**
       --[country or state]--[city]

BT  Broader term               RT  Related term          PN Public Note
NT  Narrower term              UF  Used for              +  Term has NTs
HN History Note                CN Catalogers Note        --[ ] May subdivide

**Orange orchards (cont.)**
  CN  As appropriate, double index under
        HARVESTING.
  BT  Orchards
  RT  Citrus fruit industry
        Orange trees
        Oranges
**Orange trees**
        --[country or state]--[city]
  BT  Trees
  RT  Orange orchards
        Oranges
**Oranges**
        --[country or state]--[city]
  BT  Citrus fruit
  RT  Orange orchards
        Orange trees
Oratories
  USE Chapels
Oratory
  USE Public speaking
Orbiting vehicles
  USE Artificial satellites
**Orchards**
        --[country or state]--[city]
  CN  As appropriate, double index under
        HARVESTING.
  BT  Farms
  NT  Apple orchards
        Cherry orchards
        Date orchards
        Grapefruit orchards
        Orange orchards
        Peach orchards
  RT  Fruit
        Fruit industry
        Gardens
        Plantations
        Sugar maple tapping
        Trees
**Orchestras**
  BT  Music ensembles
  RT  Concerts
**Orchids**
        --[country or state]--[city]
  BT  Flowers
  NT  Lady's slippers
Orders, Architectural
  USE Architectural orders
Ordnance
  USE Arms & armament
**Ordnance industry**
        --[country or state]--[city]
  PN  Manufacture of military supplies including
        weapons, ammunition, combat vehicles, and
        maintenance tools and equipment. Includes
        activities and structures.
  CN  Double index under INDUSTRIAL
        FACILITIES (or NTs) for images that focus
        on facilities.
  UF  Arms production
        Munitions industry

**Ordnance industry (cont.)**
        Powder works
  BT  Defense industry
  NT  Armored vehicle industry
  RT  Armories
        Arms & armament
        Firearms industry
        Ordnance testing
**Ordnance testing**
        --[nationality]--[country or state]--[city]
  UF  Testing, Weapons
        Weapons tests
  BT  Military art & science
        Testing
  NT  Nuclear weapons testing
  RT  Bombings
        Ordnance industry
**Ore industry**
        --[country or state]--[city]
  PN  Includes activities and structures.
  CN  Double index under INDUSTRIAL
        FACILITIES (or NTs) for images that focus
        on facilities.
  BT  Industry
  RT  Coal
        Metallurgical industry
        Metals
        Minerals
Organ chamber
  USE Organ lofts
**Organ grinders**
        --[country or state]--[city]
  UF  Barrel organ players
        Hurdy-gurdy players
  BT  Street musicians
**Organ lofts**
        --[country or state]--[city]
  PN  Galleries or lofts in which an organ is
        located, often found in churches.
  UF  Lofts, Organ
        Organ chamber
  BT  Interiors
  RT  Churches
        Organs
**Organizations**
        --[country or state]--[city]
  PN  Includes members, activities, and
        structures.  Search also under the subdivision
        --ORGANIZATIONS used with names of
        ethnic, racial, and regional groups and with
        classes of persons (Appendix A).
  CN  Double index under ORGANIZATIONS'
        FACILITIES (or NTs) for images that focus
        on facilities and under field of endeavor or
        category of persons who make up the
        membership.
  UF  Agencies
        Associations
        Societies
  NT  Administrative agencies
        Animal welfare organizations
        Bible societies

---

BT  Broader term                    RT  Related term                    PN  Public Note
NT  Narrower term                   UF  Used for                        +   Term has NTs
HN  History Note                    CN  Catalogers Note                 --[ ] May subdivide

**Organizations (cont.)**
        Charitable organizations
        Clubs +
        Commercial organizations +
        Committees
        Cults
        Educational organizations +
        Fraternal organizations +
        Gangs
        Historical societies
        International organizations +
        Labor unions +
        Legislative bodies
        Military organizations +
        Patriotic societies
        Political organizations +
        Public service organizations
        Religious groups +
        Secret service
        Student organizations
        Veterans' organizations
        Vigilance committees
        War prisoners' organizations
        Youth organizations +
    RT  Fund raising
        Membership campaigns
        Organizations' facilities
        Organized crime
Organizations' buildings
    USE Organizations' facilities
**Organizations' facilities**
        --[country or state]--[city]
    CN  Double index under type of organization.
        Used in a note under ORGANIZATIONS
        (and NTs).
    HN  Changed 1/1993 from
        ORGANIZATIONS' BUILDINGS.
    UF  Organizations' buildings
    BT  Facilities
    NT  Clubhouses
        Fraternal lodges
    RT  Organizations
Organized camps
    USE Camps
**Organized crime**
        --[country or state]--[city]
    UF  Crime syndicates
    RT  Crimes
        Criminals
        Gangs
        Organizations
**Organs**
    PN  Includes the activity of playing organs.
    BT  Keyboard instruments
    RT  Organ lofts
Oriel windows
    USE Bay windows
Oriental bazaars
    HN  Changed 1/1993 from a postable term.
    USE Bazaars
**Oriental hand-to-hand fighting**
        --[country or state]--[city]

**Oriental hand-to-hand fighting (cont.)**
    UF  Hand-and-foot fighting, Oriental
        Hand-to-hand fighting, Oriental
        Jiu-jitsu
        Judo
        Jujitsu
        Karate
        Kung fu
        Shaolin martial arts
        Tae kwon do
    NT  Sumo
    RT  Fighting
        Martial arts
        Self-defense
        Sports
Orientation centers
    USE Visitors' centers
Origin of species
    USE Evolution
Origins
    USE Creation
Ornaments
    USE Decorations
Ornaments, Architectural
    USE Architectural decorations & ornaments
Orphan asylums
    USE Orphanages
**Orphanages**
        --[country or state]--[city]
    PN  An institution for the care of orphans.
    UF  Orphan asylums
    BT  Welfare facilities
    RT  Orphans
**Orphans**
        --[country or state]--[city]
    CN  Used in a note under ORPHANAGES.
    BT  Children
    RT  Abandoned children
        Orphanages
**Orthodox churches**
        --[country or state]--[city]
    PN  For images that focus on buildings, as
        well as the associated grounds.
    UF  Eastern Orthodox churches
        Greek Orthodox churches
        Russian Orthodox churches
    BT  Churches
**Orthopedic braces**
    UF  Braces
    BT  Medical equipment & supplies
    RT  Handicapped persons
Oscillators, Electric
    USE Electric oscillators
**Ospreys**
        --[country or state]
    UF  Fish hawks
    BT  Birds of prey
Ostensoriums
    USE Monstrances
**Ostriches**
        --[country or state]
    BT  Birds

---

BT  Broader term                    RT  Related term                    PN  Public Note
NT  Narrower term                   UF  Used for                        +   Term has NTs
HN  History Note                    CN  Catalogers Note                 --[ ] May subdivide

**Otters**
    --[country or state]
    BT   Animals
    NT   Sea otters
**Ouija boards**
    BT   Magical devices
**Outbuildings**
    --[country or state]--[city]
    UF   Dependencies (Buildings)
    BT   Buildings
    NT   Hunting lodges
    RT   Backyards
         Estates
         Farms
         Icehouses
         Lean-tos
         Plantations
         Privies
         Ranches
         Smokehouses
         Springhouses
**Outdoor cookery**
    --[country or state]--[city]
    UF   Camp cookery
    BT   Cookery
    RT   Barbecues
         Campfires
         Chuckwagons
         Picnics
**Outdoor furniture**
    BT   Furniture
    NT   Gliders (Outdoor furniture)
    RT   Rustic work
**Outdoor religious services**
    --[country or state]--[city]
    BT   Religious services
    RT   Camp meetings
Outdoor schools
    USE Open-air schools
Outdoor theaters
    USE Open-air theaters
Outdoor theatrical productions
    USE Open-air theatrical productions
Outhouses
    USE Privies
Outlaws
    USE Criminals
**Outrigger canoes**
    --[country or state]--[city]
    UF   Outriggers
    BT   Canoes
Outriggers
    USE Outrigger canoes
Out-of-work people
    USE Unemployed
**Oval rooms**
    --[country or state]--[city]
    UF   Elliptical rooms
    BT   Interiors
**Ovens**
    BT   Architectural elements
    RT   Appliances

**Ovens (cont.)**
         Baking
         Furnaces
         Furnishings
         Heat
         Kilns
         Stoves
Overcoats
    USE Coats
Overland mail service
    USE Stagecoaches
Overlooks, Scenic
    USE Scenic overlooks
Overpasses
    USE Elevated highways
Overpopulation
    USE Population control
Overweight
    USE Obesity
Over-indulgence
    USE Extravagance
**Owls**
    --[country or state]
    BT   Birds of prey
**Ownership marks**
    CN   TGM II term.
**Ox teams**
    --[country or state]--[city]
    UF   Oxen
    BT   Animal teams
    RT   Carts & wagons
         Cattle
Oxen
    USE Cattle
         Ox teams
Oxen, Wild
    USE Buffaloes
Oxeye windows
    USE Bull's eye windows
**Oxygen masks**
    PN   Masks covering the mouth and nose and
         used mainly for inhaling oxygen from a
         bottle, tank, or other source of supply.
    BT   Masks
    RT   Medical equipment & supplies
         Skin diving
**Oystering**
    --[country or state]--[city]
    RT   Oysters
         Shellfish industry
**Oysters**
    --[country or state]
    BT   Shellfish
    RT   Oystering
         Pearl fishing
Ozalids
    USE Diazo prints
Ozobrome photoprints
    USE Carbro prints
**Pacifism**
    --[country or state]
    PN   Opposition to violence as a means of

---

BT  Broader term                RT  Related term              PN Public Note
NT  Narrower term               UF  Used for                  + Term has NTs
HN History Note                 CN Catalogers Note            --[ ] May subdivide

**Pacifism (cont.)**
      settling disputes. Search under PROTEST
      MOVEMENTS for opposition to particular
      conflicts.
  CN  Used in a note under PROTEST
      MOVEMENTS.
  UF  Anti-war
  RT  Militarism
      Moral aspects of war
      Pacifists
      Peace
      Religious aspects of war

**Pacifists**
      --[country or state]--[city]
  PN  Search under PACIFISM for the subject
      of pacifism in general and the activities of
      pacifists.
  BT  People
  RT  Activists
      Conscientious objectors
      Pacifism

**Pacing**
  BT  Locomotion

**Pack animals**
      --[country or state]--[city]
  PN  Search under PACKTRAINS for strings
      of pack animals.
  CN  Double index under type of animal.
  UF  Packhorses
      Supply horses
  BT  Animals
  RT  Animal teams
      Packtrains

Pack trains
  USE Packtrains

Packages
  USE Packaging

**Packaging**
  CN  TGM II term.
  UF  Packages
      Wrappers
      Wrapping materials
      Wrappings

Packet ships
  USE Mail steamers

Packhorses
  USE Pack animals
      Packtrains

Packing & shipping
  USE Shipping

**Packtrains**
      --[country or state]--[city]
  PN  Strings of animals for transporting
      supplies and equipment.
  CN  Used in a note under PACK ANIMALS.
  UF  Pack trains
      Packhorses
      Supply horses
  BT  Animal teams
  RT  Animals
      Caravans
      Frontier & pioneer life

**Packtrains (cont.)**
      Pack animals
      Transportation

Pacts
  USE Treaties

Paddle wheel steamers
  USE Side wheelers
      Stern wheelers

Paddy fields
  USE Rice paddies

Padlocks
  USE Locks (Hardware)

**Pageants**
      --[country or state]--[city]
  BT  Theatrical productions
  NT  Historical pageants
  RT  Celebrations
      Festivals
      Open-air theatrical productions
      Parades & processions
      Political pageantry
      Rites & ceremonies
      Tableaux

Pages, Congressional
  USE Capitol pages

**Pagodas**
      --[country or state]--[city]
  PN  Tower-like storied structures, usually
      temples or memorials, common in India,
      China, Indochina, and Japan.
  BT  Religious facilities
  RT  Monuments & memorials
      Temples
      Towers

Paid vacations
  USE Employee vacations

**Pails**
  UF  Buckets
  BT  Containers
  RT  Ice buckets

**Pain**
  PN  Search under DISTRESS for mental pain.
  CN  Used in a note under DISTRESS.
  UF  Aches
      Agony
      Suffering
  NT  Toothaches
  RT  Acupuncture
      Distress
      Health
      Sick persons
      Wounds & injuries

**Paint industry**
      --[country or state]--[city]
  PN  Includes activities and structures.
  CN  Double index under INDUSTRIAL
      FACILITIES (or NTs) for images that focus
      on facilities.
  BT  Chemical industry
  RT  Paints & varnishes

**Painting**
      --[country or state]--[city]

---

BT Broader term          RT Related term          PN Public Note
NT Narrower term        UF Used for            + Term has NTs
HN History Note          CN Catalogers Note     --[ ] May subdivide

**Painting (cont.)**
   PN  Includes painting both as a trade and an
          artistic endeavor.
   BT  Art
   RT  Children drawing & painting
          Paints & varnishes
Painting auctions
   USE Art auctions
**Paintings**
   CN  TGM II term.
   NT  Screen paintings
**Paints & varnishes**
   UF  Varnishes
   RT  Paint industry
          Painting
          Varnishing industry
Pajamas
   USE Sleepwear
Palaces
   USE Castles & palaces
Palanquins
   USE Sedan chairs
Paleobiology
   USE Paleontology
**Paleontology**
          --[country or state]--[city]
   PN  For the subject of paleontology in general
          and the activities of paleontologists.
   UF  Paleobiology
   BT  Science
   RT  Botany
          Extinct animals
          Fossils
          Geology
          Zoology
Palestine problem
   USE Jewish-Arab relations
**Palettes**
   BT  Artists' materials
Palisades
   USE Cliffs
**Palladian windows**
          --[country or state]--[city]
   PN  Large windows characteristic of neoclassic
          styles, divided by columns or piers
          resembling pilasters, into three lights, the
          middle one of which is usually wider than the
          others, and is sometimes arched.
   HN  Changed 1/1993 from non-postable term
          (Use VENETIAN WINDOWS).
   UF  Diocletian windows
          Tripartite windows
          Venetian windows
   BT  Windows
Palladiotypes
   USE Palladium prints
Palladium photoprints
   USE Palladium prints
**Palladium prints**
   CN  TGM II term.
   UF  Palladiotypes
          Palladium photoprints

Palm fronds
   USE Palms
**Palm houses**
          --[country or state]--[city]
   PN  Greenhouses for growing palms.
   BT  Greenhouses
   RT  Palms
Palm trees
   USE Palms
Palmistry
   USE Fortune telling
**Palms**
          --[country or state]--[city]
   PN  Includes palm trees, leaves, and branches.
   UF  Coconut palms
          Date palms
          Palm fronds
          Palm trees
   BT  Trees
   NT  Rattan palms
   RT  Coconut plantations
          Coconuts
          Date orchards
          Dates
          Palm houses
Pamphlet illustrations
   USE Book illustrations
**Pamphlets**
   CN  TGM II term.
   UF  Booklets
Pan pipes
   USE Panpipes
**Panama hats**
   BT  Hats
   RT  Straw hats
**Pancakes & waffles**
          --[country or state]--[city]
   UF  Battercakes
   BT  Food
**Pandas**
          --[country or state]
   BT  Animals
Pandean pipes
   USE Panpipes
**Panel card photographs**
   CN  TGM II term.
Panel discussions
   USE Discussion
**Paneling**
          --[country or state]--[city]
   PN  Decorative coverings for interior walls or
          ceilings usually consisting of wood panels
          and often framing.
   RT  Ceilings
          Coffers (Ceilings)
          Moldings
          Walls
Panoramic maps
   USE Bird's-eye view prints
**Panoramic photographs**
   CN  TGM II term.
   UF  Cirkut camera photographs

---

BT Broader term          RT Related term          PN Public Note
NT Narrower term        UF Used for           + Term has NTs
HN History Note          CN Catalogers Note     --[ ] May subdivide

**Panoramic views**
- CN   TGM II term.
- UF   Balloon views
  - Views, Panoramic

**Panpipes**
- PN   Includes the activity of playing panpipes.
- UF   Pan pipes
  - Pandean pipes
  - Syrinx (Musical instrument)
- BT   Wind instruments
- RT   Pipes (Musical instruments)

**Pansies**
- --[country or state]--[city]
- BT   Flowers

**Panthers**
- --[country or state]
- BT   Animals
- RT   Pumas

**Pantins**
- CN   TGM II term.

**Pantomimes**
- --[country or state]--[city]
- RT   Mumming
  - Theatrical productions

**Pantries**
- --[country or state]--[city]
- BT   Interiors
- RT   Kitchens

Pantry dressers
- USE Cupboards

Papacy
- USE Popes

Paper box industry
- USE Box industry

Paper carriers
- USE Newspaper carriers

**Paper clips**
- UF   Clips, Paper
- BT   Office equipment & supplies

**Paper cutouts**
- CN   TGM II term.
- UF   Cut paper works
  - Papercuts
  - Scherenschnitte
  - Scissorcraft

**Paper dolls**
- CN   TGM II term.

**Paper industry**
- --[country or state]--[city]
- PN   Includes activities and structures.
- CN   Double index under INDUSTRIAL FACILITIES (or NTs) for images that focus on facilities.
- BT   Industry
- NT   Insulating paper industry
- RT   Lumber industry
  - Office equipment & supplies industry
  - Wallpaper industry

Paper money
- USE Money

**Paper negatives**
- CN   TGM II term.

Paper toys
- USE Toys

Papercuts
- USE Paper cutouts

**Paperwork**
- UF   Bureaucratic paperwork
  - Government paperwork
- RT   Documents
  - Recording & registration
  - Red tape

Papooses
- USE Infants

**Parables**
- BT   Literature
- RT   Fables

**Parachute industry**
- --[country or state]--[city]
- PN   Includes activities and structures.
- CN   Double index under INDUSTRIAL FACILITIES (or NTs) for images that focus on facilities.
- BT   Industry
- RT   Parachuting

**Parachuting**
- --[country or state]--[city]
- UF   Skydiving
- RT   Airplanes
  - Military art & science
  - Parachute industry
  - Parachutists
  - Sports

**Parachutists**
- --[country or state]--[city]
- UF   Skydivers
- BT   People
- RT   Parachuting

**Parades & processions**
- --[country or state]--[city]
- UF   Processions
- BT   Events
- NT   Circus parades
  - Funeral processions
  - Religious processions
  - Ticker tape parades
- RT   Baton twirling
  - Celebrations
  - Drum majorettes
  - Drum majoring
  - Drum majors
  - Floats (Parades)
  - Military parades & ceremonies
  - Naval parades & ceremonies
  - Pageants
  - Political parades & rallies
  - Reviewing stands

**Parapets**
- --[country or state]--[city]
- PN   Low walls or similar barriers to protect the edge of a platform, roof, or bridge.
- BT   Architectural elements
- RT   Battlements
  - Coping

BT Broader term          RT Related term          PN Public Note
NT Narrower term         UF Used for              + Term has NTs
HN History Note          CN Catalogers Note       --[ ] May subdivide

**Parapets (cont.)**
    Walls
**Paraplegics**
    --[country or state]--[city]
  BT  Handicapped persons
Parasols
  USE Umbrellas
**Paravanes**
  PN  Devices for severing moorings from
       underwater mines.
  BT  Equipment
  RT  Mine warfare
       Mines (Warfare)
Parents
  USE Families
**Parish houses**
    --[country or state]--[city]
  PN  Buildings belonging to churches that serve
       as residences of clergymen, as well as for
       business, social, or extension activities.
  BT  Religious dwellings
  RT  Churches
**Parking**
    --[country or state]--[city]
  RT  Automobile driving
       Garages
       Parking garages
       Parking lots
       Vehicles
**Parking garages**
    --[country or state]--[city]
  BT  Garages
  RT  Commercial facilities
       Parking
       Parking lots
       Storage facilities
**Parking lots**
    --[country or state]--[city]
  BT  Transportation facilities
  RT  Garages
       Parking
       Parking garages
       Vehicles
Parking tickets
  USE Ticketing
**Parks**
    --[country or state]--[city]
  UF  Malls
  BT  Facilities
  NT  National parks & reserves +
       State parks & reserves
  RT  Gardens
       Landscape architecture facilities
       Sports & recreation facilities
       Zoos
Parks, Amusement
  USE Amusement parks
Parliament buildings
  USE Capitols
**Parliamentary practice**
  UF  Rules of order
  BT  Politics & government

**Parliamentary practice (cont.)**
  NT  Two-thirds rule
Parliaments
  USE Legislative bodies
Parlor cars
  USE Railroad lounge cars
**Parlors**
    --[country or state]--[city]
  PN  For rooms in hotels, clubs, or the like,
       reserved for guests who desire a greater
       degree of privacy than the public rooms
       provide, and for rooms in private homes
       reserved for the entertainment of visitors.
  UF  Sitting rooms
  BT  Interiors
  RT  Drawing rooms
       Living rooms
       Lobbies
       Reception rooms
       Salons (Social spaces)
Parlors, Billiard
  USE Billiard parlors
Parochial schools
  USE Religious education
**Parole**
    --[country or state]--[city]
  UF  Ticket of leave
  BT  Law & legal affairs
  RT  Prisoners
**Parrots**
    --[country or state]
  BT  Birds
  NT  Cockatoos
Parsonages
  USE Religious dwellings
Participation, Political
  USE Political participation
**Particle accelerators**
    --[country or state]--[city]
  UF  Accelerators, Particle
       Atom smashers
  BT  Scientific equipment
  RT  Nuclear power
**Parties**
    --[country or state]--[city]
  BT  Entertaining
  NT  Balls (Parties)
       Birthday parties
       Children's parties +
       Dance parties +
       Garden parties
       Tea parties +
  RT  Celebrations
       Masquerades
Parties, Political
  USE Political parties
**Partitions**
  RT  Walls
**Partridges**
    --[country or state]
  BT  Birds
  RT  Quails

---

BT Broader term                RT Related term                PN Public Note
NT Narrower term              UF Used for                    + Term has NTs
HN History Note                CN Catalogers Note        --[ ] May subdivide

Party platforms
  USE Political platforms
**Passageways**
      --[country or state]--[city]
  UF  Aisles
      Corridors
      Halls (Passageways)
      Hallways
  BT  Rooms & spaces
  RT  Concourses
      Doors & doorways
      Lobbies
      Stairhalls
      Walkways
Passenger cars
  USE Railroad passenger cars
**Passenger quarters**
  CN  Double index under the type of vehicle.
  BT  Interiors
  NT  Staterooms
      Steerage
  RT  Passengers
      Vehicles
**Passengers**
      --[country or state]--[city]
  PN  For images that focus on travellers by
      some conveyance, e.g., boats, railroads, etc.
      Search under SIGHTSEERS or TOURISTS
      for passengers who are clearly sightseeing
      and under COMMUTERS for persons who
      travel regularly between one place and
      another.
  CN  Double index under type of vehicle. Used
      in a note under COMMUTERS.
  BT  People associated with transportation
  RT  Commuters
      Passenger quarters
      Sightseers
      Stowaways
      Tourists
      Travel
      Vehicles
**Passes (Landforms)**
      --[country or state]
  UF  Gaps
      Mountain passes
      Notches
      Water gaps
  BT  Land
  RT  Mountains
**Passing the buck**
  UF  Buck passing
  RT  Interpersonal relations
Passions
  USE Mental states
**Passive resistance**
      --[country or state]--[city]
  UF  Nonviolent noncooperation
      Resistance, Passive
      Satyagraha
  BT  Civil disobedience
**Pasta products**

Pasta products (cont.)
  BT  Food
**Pastel drawings**
  CN  TGM II term.
**Pastel paintings**
  CN  TGM II term.
Pastures
  USE Farms
**Patent drawings**
  CN  TGM II term.
  UF  Drawings, Patent
**Patent medicines**
  UF  Proprietary medicines
  BT  Medicines
  NT  Anthelmintics
  RT  Bitters
      Medicine shows
      Quacks
      Sarsaparilla
**Patents**
  UF  Discoveries
  BT  Law & legal affairs
  RT  Inventions
Paths
  USE Trails & paths
Patients
  USE Sick persons
**Patios**
      --[country or state]--[city]
  PN  Courtyards, especially an inner court, open
      to the sky; usually adjoins a dwelling.
  BT  Rooms & spaces
  RT  Courtyards
      Terraces
**Patriarchs**
      --[country or state]--[city]
  PN  For the position within an ecclesiastical
      hierarchy.
  BT  Clergy
**Patriotic envelopes**
  CN  TGM II term.
  UF  Civil war envelopes
      Covers, Patriotic
**Patriotic societies**
      --[country or state]--[city]
  PN  Includes activities and structures.
  CN  Double index under ORGANIZATIONS'
      FACILITIES (or NTs) for images that focus
      on facilities.
  BT  Organizations
  RT  Clubs
      Fraternal organizations
**Patriotism**
      --[country or state]--[city]
  PN  Search also under subjects often associated
      with patriotic feeling, e.g., EAGLES,
      FLAGS, NATIONAL SONGS, etc.
  CN  Use when the subject of the image is
      patriotism, not when patriotism is merely
      being expressed.
  BT  Mental states
  RT  Allegiance

---

BT Broader term          RT Related term          PN Public Note
NT Narrower term        UF Used for             + Term has NTs
HN History Note         CN Catalogers Note    --[ ] May subdivide

**Patriotism (cont.)**
> Chauvinism & jingoism
> Flag salutes
> National songs
> Nationalism
> Political pageantry

Patrol work
> USE Police surveillance

Patrols
> USE Guards

Patronage, Political
> USE Political patronage

**Pattern books**
> CN   TGM II term.

**Pattern sheets**
> CN   TGM II term.

Paupers
> USE Poor persons

Pavements, Mosaic
> USE Mosaic pavements

**Pavilions**
> PN   A detached or semidetached structure used for entertainment or for special activities.
> BT   Sports & recreation facilities

**Pavilions (Building divisions)**
> --[country or state]--[city]
> PN   On a facade, a prominent portion usually central or terminal, identified by projections, height, and special roof forms.
> BT   Building divisions

Pavilions, Exposition
> USE Exhibition buildings

Pavilions, Landscape
> USE Landscape pavilions

Pawnbroking
> USE Pawnshops

**Pawnshops**
> --[country or state]--[city]
> PN   Includes activities and structures.
> UF   Pawnbroking
> BT   Stores & shops
> RT   Debt
> Secondhand sales
> Usury

Pay
> USE Wages

**Paydays**
> --[country or state]--[city]
> BT   Events
> RT   Employment
> Wages

**Paying bills**
> UF   Bill paying
> BT   Business & finance
> RT   Debt

Payments
> USE Wages

**Peace**
> PN   Search also under the subdivision --PEACE used with names of wars (Appendix C).
> CN   Used in a note under SYMBOLS.

**Peace (cont.)**
> UF   Anti-war
> RT   Armistices
> Arms control
> Calumets
> International organization
> International security
> Military demobilizations
> Pacifism
> Peace conferences
> Peace negotiations
> Peace signs
> War

**Peace conferences**
> --[country or state]--[city]
> PN   For meetings on the subject of peace in general. Search under PEACE NEGOTIATIONS for diplomatic negotiations during hostilities.
> CN   Used in a note under PEACE NEGOTIATIONS.
> BT   Meetings
> RT   International relations
> Peace

**Peace negotiations**
> --[country or state]--[city]
> PN   For diplomatic negotiations during hostilities. Search under PEACE CONFERENCES for meetings on the subject of peace in general. Search also under the subdivision --PEACE used with names of wars (Appendix C).
> CN   Used in a note under PEACE CONFERENCES.
> UF   Peace talks
> BT   Communication
> RT   Armistices
> International relations
> Meetings
> Peace
> Peace treaties
> War

Peace pipes
> USE Calumets

**Peace signs**
> UF   Peace symbol
> V sign
> BT   Symbols
> RT   Peace
> Victory sign

Peace symbol
> USE Peace signs

Peace talks
> USE Peace negotiations

**Peace treaties**
> PN   Search also under the subdivision --PEACE used with names of wars (Appendix C).
> CN   As appropriate, double index under the subdivision --PEACE used with names of wars (Appendix C).
> BT   Treaties

---

BT Broader term
NT Narrower term
HN History Note

RT Related term
UF Used for
CN Catalogers Note

PN Public Note
+ Term has NTs
--[ ] May subdivide

**Peace treaties (cont.)**
  RT   Peace negotiations
**Peacekeeping forces**
  USE International police
**Peach orchards**
       --[country or state]--[city]
  CN   As appropriate, double index under
       HARVESTING.
  BT   Orchards
  RT   Peach trees
       Peaches
**Peach trees**
       --[country or state]--[city]
  BT   Trees
  RT   Peach orchards
       Peaches
**Peaches**
       --[country or state]--[city]
  BT   Fruit
  RT   Peach orchards
       Peach trees
**Peacocks**
       --[country or state]
  PN   Male peafowl distinguished by crest of
       upright plumules and by greatly elongated
       tail covers mostly tipped with ocellated spots.
  BT   Peafowl
**Peafowl**
       --[country or state]
  BT   Birds
  NT   Peacocks
**Peanut butter**
  BT   Food
  RT   Peanuts
**Peanuts**
       --[country or state]--[city]
  BT   Vegetables
  RT   Nuts
       Peanut butter
**Pear trees**
       --[country or state]--[city]
  BT   Trees
  RT   Pears
**Pearl fishing**
  RT   Diving
       Oysters
**Pears**
       --[country or state]--[city]
  BT   Fruit
  RT   Pear trees
**Peas**
       --[country or state]--[city]
  BT   Vegetables
**Peasant rebellions**
       --[country or state]--[city]
  BT   Rebellions
  RT   Peasants
**Peasants**
       --[country or state]--[city]
  BT   People associated with agriculture
  RT   Agricultural laborers
       Farmers

**Peasants (cont.)**
       Peasant rebellions
       Poor persons
**Peat**
       --[country or state]--[city]
  BT   Fuel
**Peccaries**
       --[country or state]
  BT   Animals
  RT   Peccary hunting
**Peccary hunting**
       --[country or state]
  BT   Hunting
  RT   Peccaries
**Pedagogy**
  USE Education
       Teaching methods
**Peddlers**
       --[nationality]--[country or state]--[city]
  UF   Criers
       Door-to-door selling
       Hucksters
       Street vendors
       Vendors, Street
  BT   People associated with commercial
       activities
  NT   Newspaper vendors
  RT   Canvassing
       City & town life
       Food vendors
       Markets
       Medicine shows
       Selling
       Vending stands
**Pedestals**
       --[country or state]--[city]
  RT   Columns
**Pedestrian bridges**
       --[country or state]--[city]
  UF   Foot bridges
       Footbridges
  BT   Bridges
  RT   Pedestrians
       Pile bridges
       Pontoon bridges
**Pedestrians**
       --[country or state]--[city]
  BT   People
  RT   Pedestrian bridges
       Streets
       Walking
       Walkways
**Pedicabs**
  USE Wheeled chairs
**Pediments**
       --[country or state]--[city]
  PN   In classical architecture, the triangular end
       or gable of a low-pitched roof, sometimes
       filled with sculpture.
  UF   Frontons
  BT   Architectural elements
  RT   Gables

**Pediments (cont.)**
>       Tympana
>       Walls

Peep show prints
>   USE Vues d'optique

**Peerage**
>   UF  Baronage
>   BT  Nobility

**Pelicans**
>       --[country or state]
>   BT  Birds

**Pelota (Game)**
>       --[country or state]--[city]
>   PN  Includes organizations and activities.
>   UF  Jai alai
>   BT  Sports

Pelts
>   USE Hides & skins

**Pen works**
>   CN  TGM II term.

Penalty mail
>   USE Franking privilege

**Pencil works**
>   CN  TGM II term.

**Pencils**
>   BT  Writing materials

**Penguins**
>       --[country or state]
>   BT  Birds

**Penicillin**
>   BT  Medicines

**Peninsulas**
>       --[country or state]
>   BT  Land
>   RT  Capes (Coasts)

Penitentiaries
>   USE Prisons

**Penny arcades**
>       --[country or state]--[city]
>   UF  Arcades, Penny
>   BT  Sports & recreation facilities
>   RT  Boardwalks
>       Games
>       Pinball machines

**Pens**
>   BT  Writing materials

**Pensions**
>   UF  Retirement pensions
>   BT  Employee fringe benefits
>   RT  Aged persons
>       Medicaid
>       Medicare
>       Money
>       Retirements
>       Social security

**Penstocks**
>       --[country or state]--[city]
>   PN  Conduits or pipes for conducting water.
>   UF  Conduits, Water
>       Pipes, Water
>       Water conduits
>       Water pipes

**Penstocks (cont.)**
>   BT  Site elements

**Penthouses**
>       --[country or state]--[city]
>   PN  Structures or dwellings built on roofs.
>   BT  Building divisions
>   RT  Apartment houses
>       Apartments
>       Roofs

**Peonies**
>       --[country or state]--[city]
>   BT  Shrubs

**People**
>   PN  Search also under the subdivision
>       --PEOPLE used with corporate bodies and
>       named events (Appendix D).
>   UF  Groups of people
>   NT  Aged persons
>       Aliens +
>       Apprentices
>       Architects
>       Artists +
>       Audiences +
>       Bailiffs
>       Black sheep
>       Bohemians
>       Cave dwellers
>       Celebrities
>       Children +
>       Children & adults
>       Civil rights leaders
>       Collectors +
>       Colonists
>       Conscientious objectors
>       Cooks
>       Couples
>       Criminals +
>       Critics
>       Crowds
>       Dancers +
>       Dead persons +
>       Delegations +
>       Dissenters
>       Employees +
>       Engineers
>       Ethnic groups
>       Executioners +
>       Exiles
>       Explorers
>       Ex-convicts
>       Families +
>       Fashion models
>       Feminists +
>       Flag bearers
>       Freedmen
>       Gamekeepers
>       Gays +
>       Gladiators
>       Guides & scouts
>       Handicapped persons +
>       Hermits
>       Heroes +

---

BT Broader term                    RT Related term                    PN Public Note
NT Narrower term                   UF Used for                        + Term has NTs
HN History Note                    CN Catalogers Note                 --[ ] May subdivide

People (cont.)
    Hippies
    Hobbyists
    Homeless persons +
    Human curiosities
    Immigrants
    Indigenous peoples
    Informers
    Inventors
    Juries +
    Labor leaders
    Lancers
    Lawyers
    Losers
    Masseurs
    Men +
    Misers
    Neighbors
    Nudes
    Office workers
    Pacifists
    Parachutists
    Pedestrians
    People associated with agriculture +
    People associated with commercial activities +
    People associated with education & communication +
    People associated with entertainment & sports +
    People associated with health & safety +
    People associated with manual labor +
    People associated with military activities +
    People associated with politics & government +
    People associated with religion +
    People associated with transportation +
    Philanthropists
    Photographers +
    Pioneers
    Poor persons +
    Postal service employees +
    Prisoners +
    Pundits
    Quadruplets
    Quintuplets
    Refugees +
    Restaurant workers
    Scapegoats
    Scientists
    Servants
    Shellbacks
    Shoemakers
    Sightseers
    Slaves +
    Social classes +
    Socialites
    Soda jerks
    Spectators +
    Squatters
    Stewards
    Swimmers

People (cont.)
    Tailors
    Tourists
    Unemployed
    Victims +
    Villains
    War casualties
    Women +
    Young adults
RT  Interpersonal relations
    Minorities
    Names
    Occupations
    Phrenology
    Physiognomy
    Straw man

**People associated with agriculture**
CN  This heading is not used for indexing.
BT  People
NT  Farmers +
    Goatherds
    Peasants
    Plantation owners
    Shepherdesses
    Shepherds

**People associated with commercial activities**
CN  This heading is not used for indexing.
BT  People
NT  Art dealers
    Bankers
    Businessmen +
    Consumers
    Peddlers +
    Sutlers

**People associated with education & communication**
CN  This heading is not used for indexing.
BT  People
NT  Alumni & alumnae
    Authors +
    College administrators
    Folklorists
    Journalists +
    Librarians
    Messengers +
    Philosophers
    Printers
    Publishers
    Scholars +
    School principals
    School superintendents
    Scribes
    Students
    Teachers
    Telephone operators
    Town criers

**People associated with entertainment & sports**
CN  This heading is not used for indexing.
BT  People
NT  Acrobats
    Athletes +
    Baseball managers
    Bullfighters

BT  Broader term        RT  Related term        PN  Public Note
NT  Narrower term      UF  Used for          +  Term has NTs
HN  History Note       CN  Catalogers Note    --[ ]  May subdivide

**People associated with entertainment & sports (cont.)**
        Entertainers +
        Golfers
        Musicians +
        Referees
        Skaters
        Tennis players
        Theatrical producers & directors

**People associated with health & safety**
  CN  This heading is not used for indexing.
  BT  People
  NT  Druggists
        Fire fighters
        Guards +
        Healers
        Lifeguards
        Lighthouse keepers
        Midwives
        Nurses
        Physicians
        Police +
        Quacks
        Rangers
        Ratcatchers
        Sick persons +
        Watchmen

**People associated with manual labor**
  CN  This heading is not used for indexing.
  BT  People
  NT  Armorers
        Blacksmiths
        Caddies
        Carpenters
        Chimney sweeps
        Laborers +
        Locksmiths
        Longshoremen
        Mechanics (Persons)
        Miners +
        Porters +
        Seamstresses
        Shoe shiners
        Steeplejacks
        Textile mill workers
        Water carriers

**People associated with military activities**
  CN  This heading is not used for indexing.
  BT  People
        People associated with politics & government
  NT  Cadets
        Guerrillas
        Military personnel +
        Warriors

**People associated with politics & government**
  CN  This heading is not used for indexing.
  BT  People
  NT  Abolitionists
        Activists +
        Anarchists
        Communists
        Government employees +
        Government officials +

**People associated with politics & government (cont.)**
        Heads of state +
        National socialists
        People associated with military activities +
        Politicians
        Rulers +
        Socialists
        Statesmen

**People associated with religion**
  CN  This heading is not used for indexing.
  BT  People
  NT  Ceremonial dancers
        Clergy +
        Dervishes +
        Evangelists
        Missionaries
        Monks
        Nuns
        Saints
        Spiritual leaders
        Swamis

**People associated with transportation**
  CN  This heading is not used for indexing.
  BT  People
  NT  Air pilots +
        Astronauts
        Chauffeurs
        Coach drivers
        Commuters
        Flight crews
        Gondoliers
        Passengers
        Railroad employees +
        Sailors +
        Stowaways
        Taxicab drivers

**Pepper (Spice)**
  BT  Spices

**Peppers**
        --[country or state]--[city]
  UF  Bell peppers
        Sweet peppers
  BT  Vegetables
  NT  Hot peppers

Perambulators
  USE Baby carriages

**Percussion instruments**
  PN  Includes the activity of playing percussion
        instruments.
  BT  Musical instruments
  NT  Bells +
        Bones (Musical instrument)
        Drums +
        Rattles

Perforated card systems
  USE Punched card systems

Performances
  CN  Used only as a subdivision with names of
        persons (Appendix B).

Performances & portrayals
  CN  Used only as a subdivision with names of
        ethnic, racial, and regional groups, and with

---

BT Broader term        RT Related term        PN Public Note
NT Narrower term       UF Used for          + Term has NTs
HN History Note         CN Catalogers Note     --[ ] May subdivide

Performances & portrayals (cont.)
       classes of persons (Appendix A).
**Performances, Theatrical**
  USE Theatrical productions
Performing artists
  USE Entertainers
**Performing arts posters**
  CN  TGM II term.
  UF  Entertainment posters
**Perfume stores**
       --[country or state]--[city]
  BT  Stores & shops
  RT  Perfumes
**Perfumes**
  BT  Cosmetics & soap
  RT  Grooming
       Perfume stores
**Pergolas**
       --[country or state]--[city]
  UF  Pergulas
  BT  Arbors (Bowers)
Pergulas
  USE Pergolas
Peril
  USE Danger
Periodical covers
  USE Magazine covers
**Periodical illustrations**
  CN  TGM II term.
  UF  Magazine illustrations
       Newspaper illustrations
Periodical posters
  USE Book & magazine posters
**Periodicals**
  CN  TGM II term.
  UF  Magazines
  NT  Newspapers
  RT  Publishing industry
**Peristyles**
       --[country or state]--[city]
  PN  Uninterrupted rows of columns around a
       usually round building or courtyard.
  BT  Colonnades
**Perpetual calendars**
  CN  TGM II term.
Personal grooming
  USE Grooming
Personal health
  USE Health
Personal relations
  USE Interpersonal relations
Personnel
  USE Employees
**Perspective projections**
  CN  TGM II term.
**Perspiration**
  UF  Sweat
  RT  Anxiety
       Heat
       Physical fitness
       Sweatbaths
Perukes

Perukes (cont.)
  USE Wigs
**Pessimism**
  UF  Gloominess
  BT  Mental states
  NT  Cynicism
  RT  Optimism
**Pest control**
       --[country or state]--[city]
  UF  Control of pests
       Exterminating
       Fly swatting
       Insecticides
       Pesticides
       Swatting insects
  NT  Biological pest control
       Crop dusting
       Rodent control +
  RT  Biology
       Flypaper
       Insects
       Poisons
       Scarecrows
Pesticides
  USE Pest control
Pestilences
  USE Communicable diseases
Pet feeding
  USE Animal feeding
Pet foods
  USE Pet supplies
**Pet shops**
       --[country or state]--[city]
  PN  Includes activities and structures.
  BT  Stores & shops
  RT  Pet supplies
       Pets
**Pet supplies**
       --[country or state]--[city]
  UF  Pet foods
  RT  Pet shops
       Pets
Petitioning
  USE Petitions
**Petitions**
       --[nationality]--[country or state]--[city]
  PN  Includes activities involved in petitioning.
  UF  Legal petitions
       Petitioning
  RT  Activists
       Document signings
       Documents
       Political participation
       Protest movements
       Solidarity
**Petrified forests**
       --[country or state]
  BT  Forests
  RT  Fossils
       Petrified wood
**Petrified wood**
  RT  Fossils

---

BT Broader term
NT Narrower term
HN History Note

RT Related term
UF Used for
CN Catalogers Note

PN Public Note
+ Term has NTs
--[ ] May subdivide

**Petrified wood (cont.)**
      Petrified forests
**Petroglyphs**
  USE Rock art
**Petroleum engines**
  USE Gasoline engines
**Petroleum fields**
  USE Petroleum industry
**Petroleum industry**
      --[country or state]--[city]
  PN  For activities and structures.
  CN  Double index under INDUSTRIAL
      FACILITIES (or NTs)  for images that focus
      on facilities.
  UF  Fields, Oil
      Oil fields
      Oil industry
      Petroleum fields
  BT  Industry
  RT  Boring
      Fuel supply
      Fuel trade
      Gas industry
      Minerals
      Oil spills
      Oil wells
      Petroleum leases
      Pipelines
      Tankers
**Petroleum leases**
      --[country or state]--[city]
  UF  Leases, Oil
  BT  Law & legal affairs
  RT  Petroleum industry
**Pets**
  PN  Search also under the subdivision
      --ANIMALS & PETS used with names of
      persons (Appendix B).
  BT  Animals
  RT  Birdcages
      Children & animals
      Kennels
      Pet shops
      Pet supplies
**Pews**
      --[country or state]--[city]
  BT  Furniture
  RT  Benches
      Churches
      Religious architectural elements
**Phantom leaf arrangements**
  USE Skeleton leaf arrangements
**Phantoms**
  USE Ghosts
**Phantoscopes**
  USE Motion picture devices
**Pharmaceutical industry**
      --[country or state]--[city]
  PN  Includes activities and structures.
  CN  Double index under INDUSTRIAL
      FACILITIES (or NTs) for images that focus
      on facilities.

**Pharmaceutical industry (cont.)**
  UF  Drug trade
  BT  Chemical industry
  RT  Druggists
      Medicines
**Pharmacies**
  USE Drugstores
**Pharmacists**
  USE Druggists
**Pheasant shooting**
      --[country or state]
  BT  Game bird hunting
  RT  Pheasants
**Pheasants**
      --[country or state]
  BT  Birds
  RT  Pheasant shooting
**Phenomena, Natural**
  USE Natural phenomena
**Philanthropists**
  UF  Altruists
  BT  People
  RT  Philanthropy
**Philanthropy**
      --[country or state]--[city]
  PN  Benevolence in support of a cause, event,
      or individual's or organization's activities.
  RT  Assistance
      Charitable organizations
      Charity
      Philanthropists
**Philosophers**
  BT  People associated with education &
      communication
**Phlebotomy**
      --[country or state]--[city]
  PN  For letting of blood in treatment of
      disease.
  UF  Bleeding (Therapy)
      Blood letting
      Bloodletting
      Leeching
  BT  Healing
  RT  Blood
      Blood donations
**Phoenix (Mythical bird)**
  BT  Supernatural beings
  RT  Birds
**Phone books**
  USE Telephone directories
**Phones**
  USE Telephones
**Phonetic alphabets**
  BT  Alphabets (Writing systems)
**Phonograph industry**
      --[country or state]--[city]
  PN  Includes activities and structures.
  CN  Double index under INDUSTRIAL
      FACILITIES (or NTs)  for images that focus
      on facilities.
  BT  Industry
  RT  Phonographs

---

BT Broader term              RT Related term              PN Public Note
NT Narrower term           UF Used for                 + Term has NTs
HN History Note            CN Catalogers Note         --[ ] May subdivide

Phonograph records
  USE Sound recordings
Phonograph stores
  USE Sound recording stores
**Phonographs**
  UF  Gramophones
      Graphophones
      Record players
  BT  Communication devices
  NT  Jukeboxes
  RT  Phonograph industry
      Sound recordings
**Phosphate industry**
      --[country or state]--[city]
  PN  Includes activities and structures.
  CN  Double index under INDUSTRIAL
      FACILITIES (or NTs) for images that focus
      on facilities.
  BT  Chemical industry
  RT  Phosphate mining
**Phosphate mining**
      --[country or state]--[city]
  PN  Includes activities and sites.
  BT  Mining
  RT  Phosphate industry
Photoceramics
  USE Ceramic photographs
**Photochrom prints**
  CN  TGM II term.
  UF  Äac prints
**Photocopies**
  CN  TGM II term.
  UF  Electrostatic photocopies
      Xerographs
**Photoengravings**
  CN  TGM II term.
Photoglypties
  USE Woodburytypes
**Photograms**
  CN  TGM II term.
  UF  Rayographs
      Schadographs
      Vortographs
**Photograph albums**
  CN  TGM II term.
**Photograph cases**
  CN  TGM II term.
  UF  Cased photographs
**Photographers**
      --[country or state]--[city]
  BT  People
  NT  Photojournalists
  RT  Artists
      Photographic studios
      Photography
**Photographic apparatus & supplies**
  UF  Photographic supplies
  BT  Equipment
  NT  Cameras
      Motion picture devices +
      Spectrographs
  RT  Photography

**Photographic apparatus & supplies (cont.)**
      Photography industry
      Photography stores
      Portable darkrooms
**Photographic postcards**
  CN  TGM II term.
**Photographic prints**
  CN  TGM II term.
  UF  Black-and-white prints
      Chloride prints
      Photoprints
**Photographic studios**
      --[country or state]--[city]
  PN  Includes activities and structures.
  BT  Studios
  RT  Artists' studios
      Photographers
      Photography
      Photography industry
      Photography stores
      Portable darkrooms
Photographic supplies
  USE Photographic apparatus & supplies
**Photographs**
  CN  TGM II term.
**Photography**
      --[country or state]--[city]
  PN  For the subject of photography in general
      and the activities of photographers.
  NT  Cinematography
      Photojournalism
      Underwater photography
  RT  Art exhibitions
      Camera clubs
      Photographers
      Photographic apparatus & supplies
      Photographic studios
      Photography industry
      Radiography
Photography clubs
  USE Camera clubs
**Photography industry**
      --[country or state]--[city]
  PN  Includes activities and structures.
  CN  Double index under INDUSTRIAL
      FACILITIES (or NTs) for images that focus
      on facilities.
  BT  Industry
  NT  Stereograph industry
  RT  Photographic apparatus & supplies
      Photographic studios
      Photography
**Photography stores**
      --[country or state]--[city]
  PN  Includes activities and structures.
  BT  Stores & shops
  RT  Photographic apparatus & supplies
      Photographic studios
**Photogravures**
  CN  TGM II term.
  UF  Gravures
**Photojournalism**

---

BT Broader term          RT Related term          PN Public Note
NT Narrower term        UF Used for             + Term has NTs
HN History Note          CN Catalogers Note      --[ ] May subdivide

**Photojournalism (cont.)**
--[country or state]--[city]
PN  For the subject of photojournalism in
general and the activities of photojournalists.
UF  News photography
Press photography
BT  Journalism
Photography
RT  Photojournalists
**Photojournalists**
--[nationality]--[country or state]--[city]
UF  News photographers
Press photographers
BT  Journalists
Photographers
RT  Photojournalism
**Photolithographs**
CN  TGM II term.
**Photomechanical prints**
CN  TGM II term.
UF  Process prints
**Photomicrographs**
CN  TGM II term.
**Photomontages**
CN  TGM II term.
UF  Composite prints
Photonegatives
USE  Negatives
Photoprints
USE  Photographic prints
Photostats
USE  Stats
Phototransparencies
USE  Transparencies
Phragmites
USE  Reeds (Plants)
**Phrenology**
RT  People
Physiognomy
Skulls
Physical characteristics
CN  Used only as a subdivision with names of
ethnic, racial, and regional groups, and with
classes of persons (Appendix A).
**Physical education**
--[country or state]--[city]
BT  Education
RT  Calisthenics
Coaching (Athletics)
Games
Physical fitness
Sports
**Physical fitness**
--[country or state]--[city]
UF  Exercise
Fitness, Physical
NT  Children exercising
RT  Calisthenics
Health
Perspiration
Physical education
Reducing

**Physical fitness (cont.)**
Sports
Treadmills
**Physical restraints**
--[country or state]--[city]
UF  Bondage
Restraints, Physical
NT  Handcuffs
RT  Punishment devices
Ropes
Physical surveillance
USE  Police surveillance
**Physical therapy**
--[country or state]--[city]
BT  Therapy
RT  Massage
Masseurs
Therapeutic baths
Physical trauma
USE  Wounds & injuries
Physically handicapped persons
USE  Handicapped persons
**Physicians**
--[country or state]--[city]
UF  Doctors
BT  People associated with health & safety
RT  Children playing doctors
Health care
Medical offices
Nurses
Quacks
Physicians' offices
USE  Medical offices
**Physics**
--[country or state]--[city]
PN  For the subject of physics in general and
the activities of physicists.
UF  Natural philosophy
BT  Science
NT  Biomechanics
**Physiognomy**
--[country or state]
UF  Metoposcopy
RT  Faces
Human body
People
Phrenology
Physiognotrace works
USE  Physionotrace works
Physiognotraces
USE  Physionotraces
**Physionotrace works**
CN  TGM II term.
UF  Physiognotrace works
**Physionotraces**
PN  A device invented in the late 18th century
for making tracings.
UF  Physiognotraces
**Pianos**
PN  Includes the activity of playing pianos.
BT  Keyboard instruments
Stringed instruments

---

BT  Broader term
NT  Narrower term
HN  History Note

RT  Related term
UF  Used for
CN  Catalogers Note

PN  Public Note
+  Term has NTs
--[ ]  May subdivide

**Pianos (cont.)**
  NT   Player pianos
  RT   Harpsichords
Piazzas
  USE Plazas
        Porches
**Pickerel**
        --[country or state]
  BT   Fish
**Pickets**
        --[country or state]--[city]
  PN   For persons posted, usually with signs, at
        places of business in an effort to discourage
        access by employees or patrons.
  BT   Activists
  RT   Demonstrations
        Labor unions
Pickets (Guards)
  USE Guards
Picking crops
  USE Harvesting
Picnic areas
  USE Picnic grounds
**Picnic grounds**
        --[country or state]--[city]
  UF   Picnic areas
  BT   Sports & recreation facilities
  RT   Picnics
**Picnics**
        --[country or state]--[city]
  BT   Recreation
  RT   Eating & drinking
        Outdoor cookery
        Picnic grounds
Pictographs
  USE Cave drawings
        Hieroglyphics
        Rock art
**Pictorial envelopes**
  CN   TGM II term.
  UF   Covers, Illustrated
        Illustrated envelopes
Pictorial family records
  USE Family trees
Pictorial letter sheets
  USE Pictorial lettersheets
**Pictorial lettersheets**
  CN   TGM II term.
  UF   Illustrated letter paper
        Lettersheets, Pictorial
        Pictorial letter sheets
**Picture frames**
  UF   Frames (Picture)
**Picture puzzles**
  CN   TGM II term.
Picture writing
  USE Hieroglyphics
**Pictures**
  CN   TGM II term.
Pie plants
  USE Rhubarb
Piece goods shops

Piece goods shops (cont.)
  USE Fabric shops
Pieces, Game
  USE Game pieces
Pieplants
  USE Rhubarb
**Pier & wharf failures**
        --[country or state]--[city]
  UF   Collapse of piers & wharves
        Wharf failures
  BT   Disasters
  RT   Bridge failures
        Piers & wharves
**Piers & wharves**
        --[country or state]--[city]
  UF   Boat landings
        Docks
        Landings
        Quays
        Wharves
  BT   Transportation facilities
  RT   Amusement piers
        Harbors
        Jetties
        Landing floats
        Levees
        Marine terminals
        Mooring
        Pier & wharf failures
        Shipping
        Vessels
        Waterfronts
**Pies**
  UF   Tarts (Pies)
  BT   Baked products
Pig ironwork
  USE Cast ironwork
Pigeon holes
  USE Pigeonholes
Pigeon houses
  USE Dovecotes
**Pigeonholes**
  PN   Small open compartments (as in desks or
        cabinets) for keeping letters or documents.
  UF   Pigeon holes
  RT   Furniture
**Pigeons**
        --[country or state]
  UF   Squabs
  BT   Birds
  NT   Doves
        Homing pigeons
Piggy banks
  USE Coin banks
Pigs
  USE Swine
Pigtails
  USE Braids (Hairdressing)
**Pike**
        --[country or state]
  BT   Fish
**Pilasters**

---

BT  Broader term          RT  Related term          PN  Public Note
NT  Narrower term         UF  Used for              +   Term has NTs
HN  History Note          CN  Catalogers Note       --[ ] May subdivide

Pilasters (cont.)
--[country or state]--[city]
PN Upright architectural elements that are rectangular in plan and structurally piers but treated as a columns.
BT Architectural elements
RT Columns

Pile bridges
--[country or state]--[city]
BT Bridges
RT Pedestrian bridges

Pile drivers
BT Machinery
RT Pilings (Civil engineering)

Pilgrimages
--[country or state]--[city]
UF Journeys
BT Events
RT Religion
Shrines

Pilings (Civil engineering)
--[country or state]--[city]
BT Site elements
RT Civil engineering
Erosion protection works
Pile drivers

Pillage
USE War destruction & pillage

Pillar stones
USE Cornerstones

Pillars
USE Columns

Pillars, Rock
USE Rock formations

Pillories
--[country or state]--[city]
PN Devices for publicly punishing offenders consisting of a wooden frame with holes in which the head and hands can be locked.
BT Punishment devices
RT Stocks (Punishment)

Pillow fighting
USE Children pillow fighting

Pills
BT Medicines
RT Vitamins

Pilot boats
--[country or state]--[city]
BT Boats

Pilots (Aeronautics)
USE Air pilots

Pilots, Military
USE Military air pilots

Pilots' strikes
USE Airline industry strikes

Pin boys
--[country or state]--[city]
BT Children
RT Pinsetting

Pin industry
--[country or state]--[city]
PN Includes activities and structures.

Pin industry (cont.)
CN Double index under INDUSTRIAL FACILITIES (or NTs) for images that focus on facilities.
BT Industry
RT Pins & needles

Pin setting
USE Pinsetting

Pinatypes
USE Dye transfer prints

Pinball machines
--[country or state]--[city]
BT Coin operated machines
RT Penny arcades

Pine trees
USE Pines

Pineapple plantations
--[country or state]--[city]
PN Includes activities and structures.
CN As appropriate, double index under HARVESTING.
BT Plantations
RT Pineapples

Pineapples
--[country or state]--[city]
BT Fruit
RT Pineapple plantations

Pines
--[country or state]--[city]
UF Pine trees
BT Trees

Ping pong
USE Table tennis

Pinhole camera photographs
CN TGM II term.

Pins & needles
BT Sewing equipment & supplies
RT Pin industry

Pinsetting
--[country or state]--[city]
UF Pin setting
Pinspotting
RT Bowling
Bowling alleys
Pin boys

Pinspotting
USE Pinsetting

Pinup photographs
USE Glamour photographs

Pin-the-tail-on-the-donkey
BT Games
RT Donkeys

Pioneer life
USE Frontier & pioneer life

Pioneers
--[country or state]--[city]
UF Settlers
BT People
RT Frontier & pioneer life
Westward movement

Pipe industry
--[country or state]--[city]

BT Broader term      RT Related term      PN Public Note
NT Narrower term     UF Used for          + Term has NTs
HN History Note      CN Catalogers Note   --[ ] May subdivide

**Pipe industry (cont.)**
CN   Double index under INDUSTRIAL
     FACILITIES (or NTs) for images that focus
     on facilities.
BT   Industry
RT   Pipelines
Pipe lines
USE Pipelines
**Pipelines**
     --[country or state]--[city]
PN   Lines of pipe with pumping machinery and
     apparatus for conveying liquids, especially
     petroleum.
UF   Pipe lines
RT   Gasoline
     Petroleum industry
     Pipe industry
**Pipes**
PN   A long tube or hollow body for conducting
     substances or for structural purposes.
NT   Tobacco pipes +
     Water pipes (Smoking)
RT   Downspouts
**Pipes (Musical instruments)**
BT   Wind instruments
RT   Panpipes
Pipes, Water
USE Penstocks
**Pirates**
HN   Changed 10/1988 from PIRACY.
UF   Barbary corsairs
     Buccaneers
     Corsairs
     Freebooters
BT   Criminals
     Sailors
Pistols
USE Handguns
**Pitchers**
PN   A container for holding and pouring
     liquids that usually has a lip or spout and a
     handle.
UF   Ewers
     Jugs
BT   Containers
RT   Beverages
     Tableware
     Urns
**Pitchforks**
BT   Agricultural machinery & implements
Pits (Holes)
USE Holes
Pivot bridges
USE Swing bridges
Placards
USE Posters
Placer mining
USE Hydraulic mining
**Plague**
     --[country or state]--[city]
UF   Bubonic plague
BT   Communicable diseases

**Plague (cont.)**
RT   Rats
**Plains**
     --[country or state]
BT   Land
Planes, Inclined
USE Inclined planes
**Planetaria**
     --[country or state]--[city]
BT   Exhibition facilities
RT   Astronomical observatories
**Planets**
BT   Celestial bodies
NT   Earth
RT   Extraterrestrial life
**Plank buildings**
     --[country or state]--[city]
BT   Wooden buildings
**Plank roads**
     --[country or state]
BT   Roads
Planks, Party
USE Political platforms
Planned parenthood
USE Population control
**Planning drawings**
CN   TGM II term.
UF   City planning drawings
     Drawings, Planning
     Urban planning drawings
Planning, City
USE City planning
**Planographic prints**
CN   TGM II term.
**Plans**
CN   TGM II term.
**Plant containers**
UF   Planters (Containers)
BT   Containers
NT   Flower pots
RT   Furnishings
     Gardens
     Window boxes
**Plant parasites**
     --[country or state]--[city]
RT   Biological pest control
     Insects
     Plants
Plant tapping
USE Tapping
**Plantation owners**
     --[country or state]--[city]
BT   People associated with agriculture
RT   Plantations
**Plantations**
     --[country or state]--[city]
PN   Includes activities and structures.
CN   As appropriate, double index under
     activity, e.g., HARVESTING. Used in a note
     under PLOWING.
BT   Farms
NT   Agave plantations

BT  Broader term          RT  Related term          PN  Public Note
NT  Narrower term         UF  Used for              +   Term has NTs
HN  History Note          CN  Catalogers Note       --[ ] May subdivide

**Plantations (cont.)**
       Banana plantations
       Coconut plantations
       Coffee plantations
       Cotton plantations
       Pineapple plantations
       Rice plantations +
       Rubber plantations
       Sugar plantations
       Tea plantations
       Tobacco plantations
  RT  Estates
       Food industry
       Orchards
       Outbuildings
       Plantation owners
**Planters (Containers)**
  USE Plant containers
**Planting**
  USE Farming
       Gardening
**Planting drawings**
  USE Landscape architecture drawings
**Plants**
       --[country or state]--[city]
  CN  Used in a note under FARMING.
  UF  Crops
       Farm crops
       Field crops
  NT  Agaves
       Alfalfa
       Artichokes
       Bamboo
       Banana plants
       Bittersweet
       Cactus
       Coffee plants
       Ferns
       Flax
       Grains +
       Hay +
       Hedges (Plants)
       Hemp +
       Jute
       Mangrove plants
       Medicinal plants
       Mushrooms
       Poi
       Reeds (Plants)
       Rhubarb
       Rubber plants
       Seeds
       Shamrocks
       Shrubs +
       Spanish moss
       Sugarcane
       Sweet clover
       Tobacco
       Trees +
       Vines
       Weeds +
  RT  Botany

**Plants (cont.)**
       Cotton
       Dried plant arrangements
       Fibers
       Flowers
       Fossils
       Fruit
       Gardens
       Horticulture
       Leaves
       Nature
       Nuts
       Plant parasites
       Spices
       Tapping
       Vegetables
**Plaques**
       --[country or state]--[city]
  PN  Inscribed, usually metal tablets placed (as
       on a building or post) to identify a site or
       commemorate an individual or event.
  UF  Building plaques
       Tablets
  BT  Signs
  RT  Monuments & memorials
**Plaster laths**
  USE Laths
**Plaster work**
  USE Plasterwork
**Plasterwork**
       --[country or state]--[city]
  UF  Decorative plasterwork
       Plaster work
       Stuccowork
**Plastic laminates**
  USE Laminated plastics
**Plastic printing plates**
  CN  TGM II term.
**Plastics**
  NT  Laminated plastics
  RT  Plastics industry
**Plastics industry**
       --[country or state]--[city]
  PN  Includes activities and structures.
  CN  Double index under INDUSTRIAL
       FACILITIES (or NTs) for images that focus
       on facilities.
  BT  Industry
  RT  Plastics
**Plastos**
  CN  TGM II term.
**Plates, Printing**
  USE Printing plates
**Platforms, Floating**
  USE Landing floats
**Platforms, Political**
  USE Political platforms
**Platforms, Speakers'**
  USE Podiums
**Platinotypes**
  USE Platinum prints
**Platinum photoprints**

BT  Broader term
NT  Narrower term
HN  History Note

RT  Related term
UF  Used for
CN  Catalogers Note

PN  Public Note
+  Term has NTs
--[ ] May subdivide

Platinum photoprints (cont.)
 USE Platinum prints
**Platinum prints**
 CN TGM II term.
 UF Platinotypes
  Platinum photoprints
**Plats**
 CN TGM II term.
**Platypuses**
  --[country or state]
 UF Duckbills
 BT Animals
Play
 USE Children playing
**Playbills**
 CN TGM II term.
**Player pianos**
 PN Includes the activity of playing player
  pianos.
 BT Pianos
Playground ball
 USE Softball
**Playgrounds**
  --[country or state]--[city]
 BT Sports & recreation facilities
 RT Athletic fields
  Children playing outdoors
  School recesses
  Seesaws
  Sliding boards
  Swings
**Playing cards**
 CN TGM II term.
 RT Card games
  Card tricks
Playing pieces
 USE Game pieces
**Playrooms**
  --[country or state]--[city]
 UF Children's rooms
  Rumpus rooms
 BT Recreation rooms
 RT Nurseries
Plays
 HN Changed 12/1992 from a postable term.
 USE Theatrical productions
**Plays on words**
 UF Word plays
 RT Literature
Playthings
 USE Toys
Playwrights
 USE Dramatists
**Plazas**
  --[country or state]--[city]
 PN Open places in towns; public squares.
 UF Piazzas
  Public squares
  Squares, Public
  Town squares
 BT Sites
 RT Forums

Plazas (cont.)
  Markets
  Streets
**Pleading (Begging)**
 UF Begging (Pleading)
 BT Communication
**Pledges of allegiance**
  --[country or state]--[city]
 BT Rites & ceremonies
 RT Allegiance
  Flag salutes
  Oaths
  Promises
Plot plans
 USE Site plans
Ploughs
 USE Plows
**Plowing**
  --[country or state]--[city]
 CN As appropriate, double index under
  context in which activity occurs (e.g.,
  PLANTATIONS).
 RT Farming
  Raking (Sweeping)
**Plows**
 UF Ploughs
 BT Agricultural machinery & implements
**Plum trees**
  --[country or state]--[city]
 BT Trees
 RT Plums
**Plumbing fixtures**
  --[country or state]--[city]
 UF Fittings, Sanitary
  Fixtures, Plumbing
  Sanitary fittings
 BT Mechanical systems components
 NT Bathtubs & showers
  Toilets
 RT Equipment
  Plumbing industry
  Plumbing stores
  Plumbing systems
**Plumbing industry**
  --[country or state]--[city]
 PN Includes activities and structures.
 BT Business enterprises
 RT Construction industry
  Plumbing fixtures
  Plumbing stores
**Plumbing stores**
  --[country or state]--[city]
 PN Includes activities and structures.
 BT Stores & shops
 RT Plumbing fixtures
  Plumbing industry
**Plumbing systems**
  --[country or state]--[city]
 PN Systems within buildings that supply
  water to the occupants and carry off liquid or
  liquid-suspended wastes.
 BT Mechanical systems

---

BT Broader term
NT Narrower term
HN History Note

RT Related term
UF Used for
CN Catalogers Note

PN Public Note
+ Term has NTs
--[ ] May subdivide

**Plumbing systems (cont.)**
  RT   Plumbing fixtures
       Sanitation
       Waste disposal facilities
       Water heaters
       Water pumps
**Plums**
       --[country or state]--[city]
  BT   Fruit
  NT   Prunes
  RT   Plum trees
Plundering
  USE  Robberies
       War destruction & pillage
**Plutocracy**
       --[country]
  PN   For the subject of plutocracy in general.
  BT   Economic & political systems
  RT   Upper class
       Wealth
**Plywood**
  NT   Molded plywood
Pneumatic conveying
  USE  Pneumatic tubes
Pneumatic tube transportation
  USE  Pneumatic tubes
**Pneumatic tubes**
  HN   Changed 1/1993 from PNEUMATIC
       TUBE TRANSPORTATION.
  UF   Pneumatic conveying
       Pneumatic tube transportation
  BT   Conveying systems
  RT   Communication devices
       Transportation
**Poaching**
       --[country or state]--[city]
  PN   Taking or killing game or fish by illegal
       methods.
  BT   Crimes
       Hunting
**Pochoir prints**
  CN   TGM II term.
Pocket battleships
  USE  Battleships
Pocket lenses
  USE  Hand lenses
Pocketbooks (Handbags)
  USE  Handbags
**Podiums**
       --[country or state]--[city]
  PN   Raised platforms in halls and large rooms.
  UF   Dais
       Platforms, Speakers'
       Speakers' platforms
  RT   Public speaking
Poems
  USE  Poetry
**Poetry**
  UF   Poems
  BT   Literature
  RT   Poets
**Poets**

**Poets (cont.)**
       --[country or state]--[city]
  BT   Authors
  RT   Bards
       Minstrels
       Poetry
**Poi**
       --[country or state]--[city]
  BT   Plants
**Pointing fingers**
  BT   Fingers
Pointing the finger
  USE  Blaming
Points (Coasts)
  USE  Capes (Coasts)
Poison gas warfare
  USE  Gas warfare
**Poisons**
  UF   Toxic substances
  NT   Snake venom
  RT   Gas masks
       Gas warfare
       Medicines
       Pest control
Poke bonnets
  USE  Bonnets
**Polar bears**
       --[country or state]
  BT   Bears
Polaroid instant color prints
  USE  Dye diffusion transfer prints
Polaroid instant photographs
  USE  Instant camera photographs
Poles, Utility
  USE  Utility poles
Pole-vaulting
  USE  Vaulting
**Police**
       --[country or state]--[city]
  PN   Includes policemen, mixed groups of
       policemen and policewomen, as well as
       police departments and occasions when
       gender is not specified.
  CN   Used in a note under POLICE
       STATIONS.
  UF   Gendarmes
       Law enforcement officers
       Police departments
  BT   People associated with health & safety
  NT   Military police
       Mounted police
       Policewomen
       Traffic police
  RT   Bailiffs
       Detectives
       Law enforcement
       Law enforcement training
       Nightsticks
       Police shootings
       Police surveillance
       Private police
       Riot control

---

BT  Broader term            RT  Related term            PN  Public Note
NT  Narrower term           UF  Used for                +   Term has NTs
HN  History Note            CN  Catalogers Note         --[ ] May subdivide

**Police (cont.)**
      Secret service
      Watchmen
Police clubs (Weapons)
  USE Nightsticks
Police departments
  USE Police
      Police stations
Police informers
  USE Informers
Police photographs
  USE Forensic photographs
**Police raids**
      --[country or state]--[city]
  UF  Searches & seizures
  RT  Confiscations
      Law enforcement
      Searching
**Police shootings**
      --[country or state]--[city]
  PN  For shootings by police.
  UF  Shootings, Police
  RT  Police
      Shooting
**Police stations**
      --[country or state]--[city]
  PN  For images that focus on buildings. Search
      under POLICE for activities.
  UF  Police departments
  BT  Government facilities
      Justice facilities
**Police surveillance**
      --[country or state]--[city]
  UF  Patrol work
      Physical surveillance
  BT  Surveillance
  RT  Police
Police training
  USE Law enforcement training
**Policewomen**
      --[country or state]--[city]
  BT  Police
      Women
Police, Private
  USE Private police
Polio
  USE Poliomyelitis
**Poliomyelitis**
      --[country or state]--[city]
  UF  Infantile paralysis
      Polio
  BT  Communicable diseases
  RT  Iron lungs
Politeness
  USE Etiquette
Political action
  USE Political participation
Political activists
  USE Activists
Political activity
  CN  Used only as a subdivision with ethnic,
      racial, and regional groups, and with classes

Political activity (cont.)
      of persons (Appendix A).
Political amnesty
  USE Amnesty
**Political campaign funds**
      --[country or state]--[city]
  UF  Campaign funds
  BT  Money
  RT  Fund raising
      Political elections
Political candidates
  USE Political elections
**Political cartoons**
  CN  TGM II term.
**Political conventions**
      --[country or state]--[city]
  BT  Meetings
      Political participation
  RT  Political elections
      Political parties
      Political platforms
Political corruption
  USE Corruption
**Political elections**
      --[country or state]--[city]
  CN  Double index under the name of the
      candidate or the political party, as
      appropriate.
  UF  Campaigns, Political
      Candidates, Political
      Canvassing, Political
      Electioneering
      Elections
      Mayoral elections
      Nominations, Political
      Political candidates
      Primary elections
  BT  Political participation
  NT  Presidential elections
  RT  Apportionment
      Gerrymandering
      Political campaign funds
      Political conventions
      Political platforms
      Political representation
      Referendums
      Slogans
      Vote counting
      Voting
      Whistle-stop campaigning
Political exiles
  USE Exiles
**Political issues**
      --[country or state]--[city]
  PN  For political issues in general. Search also
      under headings for specific issues.
  BT  Politics & government
  RT  Political platforms
Political life
  PN  This heading is used only as a standard
      subdivision with names of ethnic, racial, and
      regional groups (Appendix A) and with broad

Political life (cont.)
> categories of people (Appendix B).
CN   Used in a note under POLITICAL
> PARTICIPATION and POLITICS &
> GOVERNMENT.

Political loyalty
> USE  Allegiance

Political murders
> USE  Assassinations

Political opposition
> USE  Opposition (Political science)

**Political organizations**
> --[country or state]--[city]
CN   Double index under ORGANIZATIONS'
> FACILITIES (or NTs) for images that focus
> on facilities.
BT   Organizations
> Political participation
NT   Political parties +
RT   Activists
> Two-thirds rule

**Political pageantry**
> --[country or state]--[city]
PN   Public celebration of political ideals, the
> power of the state, or particular rulers by
> means of symbolic displays or spectacles.
> Search under POLITICAL PARADES &
> RALLIES for events in support of political
> candidates, parties, or their causes.
CN   Used in a note under POLITICAL
> PARADES & RALLIES.
BT   Celebrations
RT   Nationalism
> Pageants
> Patriotism
> Political parades & rallies

**Political parades & rallies**
> --[country or state]--[city]
PN   For events in support of political
> candidates, political parties, and/or their
> causes. Search under POLITICAL
> PAGEANTRY for public celebration of
> political ideals, the power of the state, or
> particular rulers by means of symbolic
> displays or spectacles.
CN   Double index under the name of the
> candidate or the political party, as
> appropriate. Used in a note under
> POLITICAL PAGEANTRY.
UF   Marches, Political
> Rallies, Political
BT   Events
> Political participation
RT   Parades & processions
> Political pageantry
> War rallies

**Political participation**
> --[country or state]--[city]
PN   Search also under the subdivision
> --POLITICAL ACTIVITY used with names
> of ethnic, racial, and regional groups, and
> with classes of persons (Appendix A).

Political participation (cont.)
UF   Citizen participation
> Participation, Political
> Political action
BT   Politics & government
NT   Lobbying
> Political conventions
> Political elections +
> Political organizations +
> Political parades & rallies
> Voting
RT   Activists
> Black power
> Civil rights leaders
> Debates
> Petitions
> Protest movements
> Radicalism
> Student movements

**Political parties**
> --[country or state]--[city]
CN   Double index under ORGANIZATIONS'
> FACILITIES (or NTs) for images that focus
> on facilities.
UF   Parties, Political
BT   Political organizations
NT   Third parties
RT   Political conventions
> Political platforms
> Political purges

**Political patronage**
> --[country or state]--[city]
UF   Patronage, Political
> Pork barreling
> Spoils system
BT   Political strategies
RT   Congressional privileges & immunities
> Government officials
> Nepotism
> Special interests

**Political platforms**
> --[country or state]
UF   Party platforms
> Planks, Party
> Platforms, Political
RT   Political conventions
> Political elections
> Political issues
> Political parties
> Political strategies

**Political posters**
CN   TGM II term.
UF   Campaign posters
> Election posters
> Propaganda posters

**Political prisoners**
> --[country or state]--[city]
BT   Prisoners
RT   Activists
> Civil disobedience
> Concentration camps

**Political purges**

---

BT  Broader term              RT  Related term              PN  Public Note
NT  Narrower term             UF  Used for                  +  Term has NTs
HN  History Note              CN  Catalogers Note           --[ ] May subdivide

**Political purges (cont.)**
    --[country or state]--[city]
  UF  Purges, Political
  BT  Politics & government
  RT  Political parties
Political refugees
  USE Refugees
**Political representation**
    --[country or state]--[city]
  UF  Representation, Political
  BT  Politics & government
  RT  Apportionment
      Delegations
      Democracy
      Gerrymandering
      Political elections
Political scandals
  USE Corruption
**Political strategies**
    --[country or state]--[city]
  PN  Techniques for guiding or influencing
      government or political organization policy.
  UF  Political tactics
      Strategies, Political
      Tactics, Political
  BT  Politics & government
  NT  Filibustering
      Gerrymandering
      Political patronage
  RT  McCarthyism
      Political platforms
Political systems
  USE Economic & political systems
Political tactics
  USE Political strategies
Political violence
  USE Assassinations
      Civil disobedience
      Terrorism
**Politicians**
    --[country or state]--[city]
  PN  For persons actively engaged in politics as
      managed by parties; often, persons primarily
      interested in political offices or the profits
      from them as a source of private gain.
  BT  People associated with politics &
      government
  RT  Government officials
      Politics & government
**Politics & government**
    --[country or state]--[city]
  PN  For the conduct of and participation in
      government in the broadest sense. Search also
      under the subdivision --POLITICAL
      ACTIVITY used with names of ethnic,
      racial, and regional groups, and with classes
      of persons (Appendix A).
  CN  Subdivide geographically by jurisdiction,
      e.g., national, state, or city levels of politics
      and government.
  UF  Government
  NT  Apportionment

**Politics & government (cont.)**
    Church & state
    Citizenship
    Civil service
    County government
    Economic policy +
    Energy policy
    Environmental policy
    Executive power +
    Government regulation +
    Government reorganization
    International relations +
    Militarism
    Military policy
    Military regimes
    Municipal services
    Opposition (Political science)
    Parliamentary practice +
    Political issues
    Political participation +
    Political purges
    Political representation
    Political strategies +
    Progressivism (United States politics)
    Special interests
    State rights
    Statehood
    Town meetings
  RT  Censorship
    Economic & political systems
    Financial disclosure
    Government officials
    Heads of state
    Law & legal affairs
    Legislative bodies
    Politicians
    Power (Social sciences)
    Presidents & the Congress
    Propaganda
    Red tape
    Rulers
    Ship of state
    Solidarity
    Tenure of office
**Poll taxes**
    --[country or state]--[city]
  BT  Taxes
  RT  Voting
Pollination, Artificial
  USE Artificial pollination
Polls
  USE Public opinion polls
**Pollution**
    --[country or state]--[city]
  NT  Air pollution
    Noise pollution
    Oil spills
    Water pollution
  RT  Air quality
    Ecology
    Radioactive wastes
    Refuse

---

BT Broader term      RT Related term      PN Public Note
NT Narrower term      UF Used for      + Term has NTs
HN History Note      CN Catalogers Note      --[ ] May subdivide

**Pollution (cont.)**
    Sanitation
**Polo**
    --[country or state]--[city]
  BT  Sports
  RT  Horseback riding
Polychromy, Architecture
  USE Color in architecture
**Polyester negatives**
  CN  TGM II term.
**Polygamy**
    --[country or state]--[city]
  PN  Practice of having more than one spouse.
      Search under BIGAMY for multiple marriage
      as a criminal offense.
  CN  Used in a note under BIGAMY.
  UF  Multiple marriage
  BT  Marriage
  RT  Bigamy
      Harems
**Polymer paintings**
  CN  TGM II term.
Pond lilies
  USE Water lilies
Pondering
  USE Thinking
Ponds
  USE Lakes & ponds
**Ponies**
  BT  Horses
  RT  Pony carts
**Pontoon bridges**
    --[country or state]--[city]
  UF  Floating bridges
  BT  Bridges
  RT  Pedestrian bridges
**Pony carts**
    --[country or state]--[city]
  PN  Small carts used to convey people,
      especially children.
  BT  Carriages & coaches
  RT  Ponies
**Pony express**
    --[country or state]--[city]
  BT  Postal service
  RT  Frontier & pioneer life
      Horses
Pool
  USE Billiards
Pool halls
  USE Billiard parlors
Pool houses
  USE Bathhouses
Pool parlors
  USE Billiard parlors
Poolrooms
  USE Billiard parlors
Pools
  USE Lakes & ponds
      Swimming pools
Poor farms
  USE Almshouses

**Poor persons**
    --[country or state]--[city]
  UF  Paupers
  BT  People
  NT  Beggars
  RT  Almshouses
      Assistance
      Charity
      Homeless persons
      Laborers
      Peasants
      Poverty
      Ragpicking
      Tenement houses
      Unemployed
Poorhouses
  USE Almshouses
**Popcorn**
    --[country or state]--[city]
  BT  Corn
**Popes**
  PN  For the papacy or for images of popes.
  UF  Papacy
  BT  Bishops
      Rulers
Poppies, California
  USE California poppies
**Popularity**
  RT  Interpersonal relations
**Population control**
    --[country or state]--[city]
  UF  Family planning
      Overpopulation
      Planned parenthood
  RT  Birth control
Population surveys
  USE Census
**Populism**
    --[country or state]--[city]
  BT  Economic & political systems
**Porcelain**
  UF  China
  BT  Pottery
Porcelain photographs
  USE Ceramic photographs
**Porches**
    --[country or state]--[city]
  PN  Covered entrances to buildings, usually
      with a separate roof.
  UF  Piazzas
      Verandas
  BT  Rooms & spaces
  NT  Sleeping porches
  RT  Balconies
      Loggias
      Porte cocheres
      Porticoes (Porches)
Porches, Sun
  USE Sunspaces
**Porcupines**
    --[country or state]
  BT  Rodents

---

BT  Broader term
NT  Narrower term
HN  History Note

RT  Related term
UF  Used for
CN  Catalogers Note

PN  Public Note
+  Term has NTs
--[ ] May subdivide

**Pork**
  BT   Meat
  RT   Swine
Pork barreling
  USE Political patronage
Pornographic films
  USE Erotic films
Port terminals
  USE Marine terminals
**Portable buildings**
        --[country or state]--[city]
  BT   Buildings
  RT   Air-supported structures
        Tents
        Vending stands
**Portable darkrooms**
  UF   Darkrooms, Portable
  RT   Carts & wagons
        Photographic apparatus & supplies
        Photographic studios
        Tents
**Portages**
        --[country or state]
  PN   Carrying of boats, goods, etc., overland
        between navigable waters; also, the routes
        over which they are carried.
  UF   Carries
        Haulovers
  RT   Boats
        Lifting & carrying
        Porters
        Rivers
        Roads
        Shipping
        Trails & paths
        Transportation
Portals
  USE Doors & doorways
**Porte cocheres**
        --[country or state]--[city]
  PN   Roofs projecting at entrances to buildings,
        providing shelter to those getting in and out
        of vehicles; also, carriage entrances leading
        into courtyards.
  HN   Changed 8/1988 from non-postable term
        (Use PORCHES).
  BT   Rooms & spaces
  RT   Porches
**Porters**
        --[country or state]--[city]
  BT   People associated with manual labor
  NT   Hotel porters
        Railroad porters
  RT   Lifting & carrying
        Portages
        Shipping
**Portfolios**
  CN   TGM II term.
Porticoes (Covered walks)
  USE Covered walks
**Porticoes (Porches)**
        --[country or state]--[city]

Porticoes (Porches) (cont.)
  PN   Covered entrances or galleries for
        buildings of certain scale and importance,
        usually associated with classical and
        neoclassical architecture.
  CN   Changed 8/1988 from non-postable term
        (use PORCHES).
  BT   Rooms & spaces
  RT   Porches
**Portrait drawings**
  CN   TGM II term.
Portrait miniatures
  USE Miniatures (Paintings)
**Portrait paintings**
  CN   TGM II term.
**Portrait photographs**
  CN   TGM II term.
  UF   Studio portraits
**Portrait prints**
  CN   TGM II term.
**Portraits**
  CN   TGM II term.
Portrayals
  CN   Used only as a subdivision with names of
        persons (Appendix B).
Ports
  USE Harbors
Possums
  USE Opossums
Post cards
  USE Postcards
Post exchanges
  USE Military exchanges
**Post offices**
        --[country or state]--[city]
  PN   For images that focus on facilities. Search
        under POSTAL SERVICE for activities.
  BT   Government facilities
  RT   Postal service
Postage
  USE Postal service rates
**Postage stamps**
  CN   TGM II term.
  UF   Stamps, Postage
  RT   Christmas seals
**Postal cards**
  CN   TGM II term.
Postal delivery
  USE Postal service
**Postal service**
        --[country or state]--[city]
  CN   Used in a note under POST OFFICES.
  UF   Mail service
        Postal delivery
  NT   Air mail service
        Pony express
        Railroad mail service
  RT   Correspondence
        Mail steamers
        Mail trucks
        Mailboxes
        Mail-order businesses

BT Broader term          RT Related term          PN Public Note
NT Narrower term          UF Used for              + Term has NTs
HN History Note           CN Catalogers Note       --[ ] May subdivide

**Postal service (cont.)**
       Post offices
       Postal service employees
       Postal service rates
       Stagecoaches
**Postal service employees**
       --[country or state]--[city]
  BT  People
  NT  Letter carriers
       Postmasters
  RT  Government employees
       Postal service
**Postal service rates**
       --[country]
  UF  Postage
  NT  Franking privilege
  RT  Postal service
       Prices
**Postal stationery**
  CN  TGM II term.
**Postal telegraph**
  USE Telegraph
**Postcards**
  CN  TGM II term.
  UF  Mailing cards
       Post cards
**Posters**
  CN  TGM II term.
  UF  Placards
**Postitives, Color separation**
  USE Color separation positives
**Postives, Color separation**
  USE Color separation positives
**Postmasters**
       --[country or state]--[city]
  BT  Postal service employees
  RT  Government officials
**Posts, Hitching**
  USE Hitching posts
**Posts, Newel**
  USE Newels
**Potatoes**
       --[country or state]--[city]
  BT  Vegetables
**Potteries**
       --[country or state]--[city]
  PN  For potteries where wares are made for
       private or commercial purposes but not
       mass-produced. Includes activities and
       structures. Search under POTTERY
       INDUSTRY for large-scale operations.
  CN  Used in a note under POTTERY
       INDUSTRY.
  BT  Factories
  RT  Artists' studios
       Handicraft
       Kilns
       Pottery
       Pottery industry
**Pottery**
       --[country or state]--[city]
  UF  Ceramics

**Pottery (cont.)**
       Crockery
       Earthenware
  BT  Furnishings
  NT  Porcelain
  RT  Cloisonné
       Potteries
       Pottery industry
       Tableware
       Tiles
       Urns
       Vases
**Pottery industry**
       --[country or state]--[city]
  PN  For large-scale operations. Includes
       activities and structures. Search under
       POTTERIES for private or small-scale
       commercial activities.
  CN  Double index under INDUSTRIAL
       FACILITIES (or NTs)  for images that focus
       on facilities. Used in a note under
       POTTERIES.
  BT  Clay industries
  RT  Ceramic industries
       Kilns
       Potteries
       Pottery
**Poultry**
       --[country or state]--[city]
  UF  Fowls
  BT  Birds
  NT  Chickens +
  RT  Ducks
       Geese
       Poultry houses
       Turkeys
**Poultry houses**
       --[country or state]--[city]
  UF  Chicken coops
       Chicken houses
       Hen houses
  BT  Animal housing
  RT  Poultry
**Pounds (Animal)**
  USE Animal shelters
**Poupée prints**
  USE A la poupée prints
**Poverty**
       --[country or state]--[city]
  PN  For the subject of the economic condition
       of the poor. Search under POOR PERSONS
       when the focus is on people.
  BT  Economic & social conditions
  RT  Cost & standard of living
       Depressions
       Poor persons
       Wealth
**Powder kegs**
  BT  Containers
       Explosives
  RT  Arms & armament
**Powder magazines**

---

BT Broader term           RT Related term           PN Public Note
NT Narrower term        UF Used for           + Term has NTs
HN History Note         CN Catalogers Note     --[ ] May subdivide

Powder magazines (cont.)
  USE Magazines (Military buildings)
Powder works
  USE Ordnance industry
Power boats
  USE Motorboats
Power lines
  USE Electric lines
**Power plants**
      --[country or state]--[city]
  BT  Industrial facilities
  NT  Nuclear power plants
  RT  Dams
      Electric lines
      Hydroelectric generators
      Hydroelectric power
      Public utility companies
**Power shortages**
      --[country or state]--[city]
  RT  Electricity
      Scarcity
Power transmission lines
  USE Electric lines
**Power (Social sciences)**
      --[country or state]--[city]
  NT  Black power
      Coalition (Social sciences)
      Executive power +
  RT  Ceremonial maces
      Interpersonal relations
      Politics & government
      Sociology
POW's
  USE Prisoners of war
**Practical jokes**
  UF  Jokes, Practical
  BT  Joking
  RT  Children misbehaving
Prairie chickens
  USE Prairie hens
**Prairie dogs**
      --[country or state]
  BT  Rodents
Prairie fires
  USE Grassland fires
**Prairie hen shooting**
      --[country or state]
  BT  Game bird hunting
  RT  Prairie hens
**Prairie hens**
      --[country or state]
  UF  Prairie chickens
      Whitebelly
  BT  Birds
  RT  Prairie hen shooting
**Prairies**
      --[country or state]
  BT  Land
**Prayer**
  PN  The act of praying.
  NT  Children praying
  RT  Cursing

**Prayer (cont.)**
      Meditation
      Religion
Prayer meetings
  USE Religious services
**Preaching**
      --[country or state]--[city]
  PN  For the activity of making a religious
      address. Search also under the subdivision
      --PUBLIC APPEARANCES used with
      names of persons (Appendix B).
  BT  Public speaking
  RT  Baptisms
      Benedictions
      Communion
      Evangelists
      Religious services
      Sabbaths
Precipices
  USE Cliffs
Predellas
  USE Altarpieces
Prediction
  USE Forecasting
Predictions
  USE Divination
      Fortune telling
      Prophecy
      Warnings
**Prefabricated buildings**
      --[country or state]--[city]
  BT  Buildings
**Pregnancy**
  NT  Teenage pregnancy
  RT  Abortions
      Births
      Pregnant women
      Sex
Pregnant schoolgirls
  USE Teenage pregnancy
**Pregnant women**
  UF  Expectant mothers
  BT  Women
  RT  Maternity hospitals
      Mothers
      Pregnancy
Prehistoric animals
  USE Extinct animals
**Prejudice**
  PN  For the subject of prejudiced attitudes.
      Search under DISCRIMINATION for images
      relating to acts of discrimination.
  CN  Used in a note under
      DISCRIMINATION.
  UF  Antipathy
      Bias (Psychology)
      Bigotry
  BT  Mental states
  NT  Racism +
      Sexism
  RT  Bloody shirt
      Discrimination

---

BT  Broader term                    RT  Related term                    PN  Public Note
NT  Narrower term                   UF  Used for                         +  Term has NTs
HN  History Note                    CN  Catalogers Note                 --[ ] May subdivide

**Prejudice (cont.)**
> Ethics
> Stereotyping
> White man's burden

**Premieres**
> --[country or state]--[city]
> UF  First nights
>      Openings
> NT  Motion picture premieres
> RT  Entertainment

Premiers
> USE Prime ministers

Premium stores
> USE Coupon stores

**Premiums**
> CN  TGM II term.
> UF  Give-aways
> RT  Coupon stores

Preparatory schools
> USE Schools

**Prepared cereals**
> --[country or state]--[city]
> UF  Breakfast cereals
> BT  Cereal products
>      Food

**Preparedness**
> --[country or state]--[city]
> UF  Readiness
> NT  Civil defense +
> RT  National security

**Presbyterian churches**
> --[country or state]--[city]
> PN  For images that focus on buildings, as
>      well as the associated grounds.
> BT  Protestant churches

**Presentation albums**
> CN  TGM II term.

**Presentation drawings**
> CN  TGM II term.
> UF  Display drawings
>      Drawings, Presentation

Presents
> USE Gifts

Preservation of wildlife
> USE Wildlife conservation

**Preserves**
> --[country or state]--[city]
> UF  Jams
>      Jellies
>      Marmalades
> BT  Food
> RT  Fruit
>      Home food processing

**Presidential appointments**
> --[country]
> UF  Appointments, Presidential
>      Nominations, Presidential
> BT  Executive power
> RT  Government officials
>      Presidents

Presidential candidates
> USE Presidential elections

**Presidential elections**
> --[country or state]--[city]
> PN  Includes primaries, as well as candidates
>      who fail to be nominated at party
>      conventions.
> UF  Candidates, Presidential
>      Presidential candidates
>      Presidential primaries
> BT  Political elections
> RT  Electoral college
>      Presidents
>      Vice presidents

**Presidential inaugurations**
> --[country or state]--[city]
> PN  Search also under the subdivision
>      --INAUGURATION used with names of
>      persons (Appendix B).
> UF  Inaugurations, Presidential
> BT  Inaugurations
> RT  Presidents

Presidential power
> USE Executive power

Presidential primaries
> USE Presidential elections

**Presidential seal**
> --[country]
> BT  Seals
> RT  Presidents

**Presidential terms of office**
> --[country]
> UF  Fourth terms, Presidential
>      Third terms, Presidential
> BT  Tenure of office
> RT  Presidents

**Presidents**
> --[country]
> PN  For the office of the president or for
>      incumbents.
> BT  Government officials
>      Heads of state
> RT  Executive power
>      Grandpa's hat
>      Presidential appointments
>      Presidential elections
>      Presidential inaugurations
>      Presidential seal
>      Presidential terms of office
>      Presidents & the Congress
>      Presidents' spouses

**Presidents & the Congress**
> UF  Congress & presidents
> RT  Legislative bodies
>      Politics & government
>      Presidents

**Presidents' spouses**
> --[country]
> PN  For presidents' spouses in general or for
>      those whose spouses are incumbent
>      presidents.
> HN  Changed 10/1992 from PRESIDENTS'
>      WIVES.
> UF  First ladies

---

BT  Broader term        RT  Related term        PN  Public Note
NT  Narrower term        UF  Used for        +  Term has NTs
HN  History Note        CN  Catalogers Note        --[ ] May subdivide

**Presidents' spouses (cont.)**
            Presidents' wives
    BT    Spouses
    RT    Presidents
Presidents' wives
    HN    Changed 10/1992 to non-postable term.
    USE Presidents' spouses
**Press**
            --[country or state]
    RT    Communication
            Freedom of the press
            Journalism
            Press conferences
            Public opinion
Press clippings
    USE Clippings
**Press conferences**
            --[country or state]--[city]
    UF    Conferences, Press
    BT    Communication
            Meetings
    RT    Journalism
            Press
            Public speaking
            Publicity
Press photographers
    USE Photojournalists
Press photography
    USE Photojournalism
**Presses**
    PN    For presses which cut, shape, stamp, or
            compress.
    CN    Double index under the activity.
    BT    Machinery
    NT    Printing presses
Pressing
    USE Laundry
Pressing irons
    USE Irons (Pressing)
Pressure groups
    USE Special interests
Prestidigitation
    USE Magic
**Pretzels**
            --[country or state]--[city]
    BT    Baked products
**Preventive medicine**
            --[country or state]--[city]
    UF    Disease prevention
    BT    Health care
            Medicine
    RT    Amulets
            Hygiene
            Quarantines
Prey, Birds of
    USE Birds of prey
**Price lists**
    CN    TGM II term.
Price of food
    USE Food prices
**Price regulation**
            --[country or state]--[city]

**Price regulation (cont.)**
    UF    Government price control
    BT    Economic policy
            Government regulation
    RT    Agricultural price supports
            Black market
            Inflation
            Prices
            Wage-price policy
**Prices**
            --[country or state]--[city]
    BT    Economic & social conditions
    NT    Food prices
            Fuel prices +
    RT    Cost & standard of living
            Postal service rates
            Price regulation
            Wages
Price-wage policy
    USE Wage-price policy
**Pride**
    UF    Vanity
    BT    Mental states
    RT    Bragging
            Deadly sins
            Snobbishness
**Priests**
            --[country or state]--[city]
    BT    Clergy
    NT    Shamans
    RT    Exorcism
Primary elections
    USE Political elections
Primary school students
    USE School children
**Prime ministers**
            --[country]
    UF    Premiers
    BT    Cabinet officers
            Heads of state
Primuline process prints
    USE Diazo prints
**Princes**
            --[country]
    BT    Men
            Rulers
**Princesses**
            --[country]
    BT    Rulers
            Women
Principals, School
    USE School principals
Printed ephemera
    USE Ephemera
**Printers**
    BT    People associated with education &
            communication
    RT    Printers' unions
            Printing
            Printing industry
**Printers' unions**
            --[country or state]--[city]

---

**Printers' unions (cont.)**
- BT  Labor unions
- RT  Printers
  - Printing industry

**Printing**
- --[country or state]--[city]
- PN  For the act of impressing or otherwise reproducing text, design, or images onto a surface. Search under PRINTMAKING for printing as an artistic endeavor.
- NT  Textile printing
- RT  Printers
  - Printing industry
  - Printmaking
  - Typesetting

**Printing blocks**
- CN  TGM II term.
- UF  Blocks, Printing

**Printing industry**
- --[country or state]--[city]
- PN  Includes activities and structures.
- BT  Business enterprises
- RT  Printers
  - Printers' unions
  - Printing
  - Printing presses
  - Publishing industry
  - Typesetting

**Printing plates**
- CN  TGM II term.
- UF  Plates, Printing

**Printing presses**
- BT  Presses
- RT  Printing industry
  - Publishing industry
  - Typesetting

**Printing stones**
- CN  TGM II term.
- UF  Lithographic stones
  - Stones, Printing

Printing-out paper photographs, Silver
- USE Silver printing-out paper photographs

**Printmaking**
- --[country or state]--[city]
- PN  For printing as an artistic endeavor. Search under PRINTING for the act of impressing or otherwise reproducing text, design, or image onto a surface.
- BT  Art
- RT  Printing

**Printmaking equipment**
- CN  TGM II term.

**Prints**
- CN  TGM II term.

**Prison education**
- --[country or state]--[city]
- BT  Education
- RT  Prisoners
  - Reformatories

**Prison escapes**
- --[country or state]--[city]
- BT  Escapes

**Prison escapes (cont.)**
- RT  Prisons

Prison facilities
- USE Prisons

**Prison hospitals**
- --[country or state]--[city]
- BT  Hospitals
- RT  Detention facilities

**Prison hulks**
- --[nationality]--[country or state]--[city]
- BT  Ships
- RT  Prisons
  - Slave ships

**Prison laborers**
- --[country or state]--[city]
- UF  Convict laborers
- BT  Laborers
  - Prisoners
- NT  Chain gangs

**Prison reform**
- --[country or state]--[city]
- BT  Reform

**Prison riots**
- --[country or state]--[city]
- BT  Riots
- RT  Prisoners

Prison stripes
- USE Prison uniforms

**Prison uniforms**
- --[country or state]--[city]
- UF  Prison stripes
- BT  Uniforms
- RT  Prisoners

**Prisoner exchanges**
- --[country or state]--[city]
- PN  For exchanges of all types of prisoners, including prisoners of war and hostages.
- UF  Exchange of prisoners
  - Hostage exchanges
  - Trade of prisoners
- RT  Prisoners

**Prisoners**
- --[country or state]--[city]
- PN  Search also under the subdivision --CAPTURE & IMPRISONMENT used with names of ethnic, racial, and regional groups, and with classes of persons (Appendix A), and with names of persons (Appendix B). Search also under the subdivision --PRISONERS used with names of wars (Appendix C).
- UF  Convicts
- BT  People
- NT  Captives
  - Political prisoners
  - Prison laborers +
  - Prisoners of war
- RT  Ball & chain
  - Criminals
  - Escapes
  - Ex-convicts
  - Parole

BT  Broader term                RT  Related term              PN  Public Note
NT  Narrower term               UF  Used for                  +   Term has NTs
HN  History Note                CN  Catalogers Note           --[ ] May subdivide

**Prisoners (cont.)**
     Prison education
     Prison riots
     Prison uniforms
     Prisoner exchanges
     Prisons
     Punishment devices
     Punishment & torture
     Relocation camps

**Prisoners of war**
     --[nationality]--[country or state]--[city]
PN   Search also under the subdivision
     --PRISONERS used with names of wars
     (Appendix C).
CN   Subdivide by the nationality of the
     prisoners.
UF   POW's
BT   Prisoners
RT   Concentration camps
     Missing in action
     War
     War prisoners' organizations

**Prisons**
     --[country or state]--[city]
HN   Changed 1/1993 from PRISON
     FACILITIES.
UF   Correctional facilities
     Penitentiaries
     Prison facilities
BT   Detention facilities
RT   Dungeons
     Jails
     Prison escapes
     Prison hulks
     Prisoners
     Reformatories

**Private camps**
     --[country or state]--[city]
PN   For retreats, complexes of cabins,
     boathouses, etc., for families and friends.
     Includes activities and sites.
CN   Used in a note under CAMPS.
BT   Camps
RT   Dwellings
     Religious retreats

**Private detectives**
     USE Detectives

**Private eyes**
     USE Detectives

**Private libraries**
     --[country or state]--[city]
PN   For large, privately owned libraries,
     whether established for use by the public or
     by members only. Search under LIBRARIES
     (ROOMS) for libraries in homes,
HN   Usage changed 1/1993; formerly used for
     libraries in homes rather than large, privately
     owned but publicly used libraries.
UF   Libraries, Private
BT   Libraries
RT   Studies (Rooms)

**Private police**

**Private police (cont.)**
     --[country or state]--[city]
UF   Company police
     Police, Private
BT   Guards
RT   Police

Private property rights
     USE Right of property

Private railroad cars
     USE Railroad private cars

**Privies**
     --[country or state]--[city]
UF   Latrines
     Necessaries
     Outhouses
BT   Health & hygiene facilities
RT   Bathrooms
     Outbuildings
     Public comfort stations
     Toilets

Privileges, Congressional
     USE Congressional privileges & immunities

Prizefighting
     USE Boxing

Prizes
     USE Awards

Process line engravings
     USE Line photomechanical prints

Process prints
     USE Photomechanical prints

Processing food
     USE Food industry
         Home food processing

Processions
     USE Parades & processions

Proclamations
     USE Announcements

Produce
     USE Farm produce

Produce exchanges
     USE Commodity exchanges

Producers, Theatrical
     USE Theatrical producers & directors

Product displays
     USE Merchandise displays

**Product inspection**
     --[country or state]--[city]
UF   Quality control
RT   Food adulteration & inspection
     Testing

Production drawings
     USE Design drawings
         Diagrams

Production stills
     USE Film stills

Productions, Theatrical
     USE Theatrical productions

Production-line methods
     USE Assembly-line methods

Productivity, Agricultural
     USE Agricultural productivity

Productivity, Industrial

BT Broader term        RT Related term        PN Public Note
NT Narrower term      UF Used for          + Term has NTs
HN History Note        CN Catalogers Note      --[ ] May subdivide

Productivity, Industrial (cont.)
  USE Industrial productivity
Products
  CN  Used only as a subdivision with corporate
      bodies and named events (Appendix D).
Profanity
  USE Swearing
Professions
  USE Occupations
Professors
  USE Teachers
Profiteering, War
  USE War profiteering
Programs
  CN  TGM II term.
Progress
  BT  Economic & social conditions
  RT  Deterioration
      Progressivism (United States politics)
Progress photographs
  CN  TGM II term.
  UF  Construction progress photographs
Progressive proofs
  CN  TGM II term.
  UF  Successive proofs
Progressivism (United States politics)
  PN  For the subject of the principles and
      beliefs of progressives.
  BT  Politics & government
  RT  Progress
      Reform
Prohibition
      --[country or state]--[city]
  PN  Legal prevention of the manufacture,
      transportation, and sale of alcoholic
      beverages.
  UF  Bootlegging
      Contraband trade
      Rumrunning
  BT  Laws
  RT  Alcoholic beverages
      Blue laws
      Speakeasies
      Stills (Distilleries)
      Temperance
Projections
  CN  TGM II term.
Projectors, Motion picture
  USE Motion picture devices
Proletariat
  USE Working class
Promenade card photographs
  CN  TGM II term.
Promenades
  USE Walkways
Promises
  RT  Ethics
      Oaths
      Pledges of allegiance
Promotional photographs
  USE Publicity photographs
Proofs

Proofs (cont.)
  CN  TGM II term.
Proofs before letters
  CN  TGM II term.
  UF  Avant des lettres prints
Propaganda
      --[nationality]
  PN  Search also under the subdivision
      --COMMUNICATIONS used with names of
      wars (Appendix C).
  BT  Communication
  RT  Politics & government
      Public opinion
      Publicity
      Rumor
      Slogans
Propaganda posters
  USE Political posters
Propellers, Airplane
  USE Airplane propellers
Property damage
  USE Accidents
      Disasters
      Sabotage
      Vandalism
      War damage
      War destruction & pillage
Property rights
  USE Right of property
Prophecy
  PN  Inspired declarations of divine will and
      purpose.
  UF  Predictions
  BT  Supernatural practices
  RT  Astrology
      Divination
      End of the world
      Fortune telling
      Prophets
      Warnings
Prophets
  RT  Prophecy
      Religion
Proposals of marriage
  USE Marriage proposals
Proposed works
  CN  TGM II term.
Proprietary medicines
  USE Patent medicines
Props, Stage
  USE Stage props
Props, Studio
  USE Studio props
Prospecting
      --[country or state]
  PN  Exploring areas for mineral deposits.
  UF  Exploration (Prospecting)
  RT  Discovery & exploration
      Frontier & pioneer life
      Gold rushes
      Mining
      Prospecting equipment & supplies

BT Broader term          RT Related term          PN Public Note
NT Narrower term         UF Used for              + Term has NTs
HN History Note          CN Catalogers Note       --[ ] May subdivide

**Prospecting equipment & supplies**
UF   Miners' equipment & supplies
BT   Equipment
RT   Gold rushes
        Mining
        Prospecting
**Prosperity**
        --[country or state]--[city]
PN   Condition of being successful and
        thriving, especially economic well-being.
BT   Economic & social conditions
RT   Cornucopias
        Depressions
        Wealth
Prosthetics
USE   Artificial limbs
**Prostitution**
        --[country or state]--[city]
RT   Brothels
        Crimes
        Sex
Protection of animals
USE   Animal treatment
        Wildlife conservation
Protection of free trade
USE   Free trade & protection
**Protest movements**
        --[country or state]--[city]
PN   For opposition in regard to particular
        political or social issues. Search under
        PACIFISM for opposition to violence. Search
        under OPPOSITION (POLITICAL
        SCIENCE) for organized political resistance
        to the government in power.
CN   Used in a note under PACIFISM and
        OPPOSITION (POLITICAL SCIENCE).
UF   Anti-war movements
        Public protest
NT   Abolition movement
RT   Activists
        Civil disobedience
        Civil rights leaders
        Demonstrations
        Opposition (Political science)
        Petitions
        Political participation
        Rebellions
        Student movements
        Underground movements
**Protest posters**
CN   TGM II term.
UF   Revolutionary posters
**Protest works**
CN   TGM II term.
**Protestant churches**
        --[country or state]--[city]
PN   For images that focus on buildings, as
        well as the associated grounds.
BT   Churches
NT   Baptist churches
        Brethren churches
        Christian Science churches

**Protestant churches (cont.)**
        Congregational churches
        Friends' meeting houses
        Lutheran churches
        Mennonite churches
        Methodist churches
        Mission churches
        Moravian churches
        Presbyterian churches
        Reformed churches
        Unitarian Universalist churches
Protesters
USE   Activists
Protests
USE   Demonstrations
Prototype houses
USE   Model houses
**Proverbs**
UF   Adages
        Aphorisms
        Maxims
RT   Literature
**Prunes**
        --[country or state]--[city]
BT   Plums
**Pruning**
        --[country or state]--[city]
BT   Horticulture
RT   Gardening
        Topiary work
Psychiatric hospitals
USE   Mental institutions
**Psychiatry**
        --[country or state]--[city]
PN   For the subject of psychiatry in general
        and the activities of psychiatrists.
UF   Mental health care
BT   Medicine
RT   Mental institutions
        Mental states
        Psychotherapy
Psychic healers
USE   Healers
Psychological states
USE   Mental states
**Psychotherapy**
        --[country or state]--[city]
PN   For the subject of psychotherapy in
        general and the activities of psychotherapists.
BT   Therapy
NT   Group psychotherapy
RT   Psychiatry
        Shock therapy
PT boats
USE   Torpedo boats
**Public accommodation facilities**
        --[country or state]--[city]
BT   Facilities
NT   Caravansaries
        Hotels +
        Lodging houses
        Motels

---

BT   Broader term
NT   Narrower term
HN   History Note

RT   Related term
UF   Used for
CN   Catalogers Note

PN   Public Note
+   Term has NTs
--[ ]   May subdivide

**Public accommodation facilities (cont.)**
       Taverns (Inns)
       Tourist camps & hostels
  RT  Residential facilities
       Resorts
**Public address systems**
  BT  Communication devices
  RT  Building systems
       Intercommunication systems
       Megaphones
**Public affairs radio programs**
  RT  Radio broadcasting
**Public affairs television programs**
  UF  Television programs, Public service
  RT  Television broadcasting
Public appearances
  CN  Used only as a subdivision with names of
       persons (Appendix B).
**Public baths**
       --[country or state]--[city]
  PN  Public buildings for bathing. Includes
       activities and structures. Search under
       BATHHOUSES for public facilities
       containing dressing rooms.
  CN  Used in a note under BATHHOUSES.
  UF  Bathing houses
  BT  Health & hygiene facilities
  RT  Bathhouses
       Bathing
**Public comfort stations**
       --[country or state]--[city]
  UF  Comfort stations
       Convenience stations
  BT  Health & hygiene facilities
  RT  Bathrooms
       Privies
       Toilets
**Public debt**
       --[country or state]--[city]
  UF  Federal debt
       Government debt
       National debt
  BT  Debt
  RT  Deficit financing
       War bonds & funds
Public demonstrations
  USE Demonstrations
Public houses
  USE Bars
       Taverns (Inns)
Public housing
  USE Housing
Public officers
  USE Government officials
**Public opinion**
       --[country or state]--[city]
  UF  Opinion, Public
  BT  Communication
  RT  Press
       Propaganda
       Public opinion polls
       Publicity

**Public opinion (cont.)**
       Rumor
       Stereotyping
**Public opinion polls**
       --[country or state]--[city]
  UF  Opinion polls
       Polls
  RT  Public opinion
Public ownership
  USE Government ownership
Public protest
  USE Demonstrations
       Protest movements
Public relations
  CN  Used only as a subdivision with corporate
       bodies and named events (Appendix D).
Public servants
  USE Government employees
       Government officials
**Public service**
       --[country or state]--[city]
  UF  Service, Public
  NT  Community service +
  RT  Charitable organizations
       Civil service
       Government officials
       Public spiritedness
**Public service employment**
       --[country or state]--[city]
  PN  For the subject of public sector
       employment as a counter-cyclical policy
       measure intended to provide jobs for the
       unemployed as well as to provide economic
       assistance to distressed areas and state and
       local governments. Search under CIVIL
       SERVICE for government employment in
       general.
  HN  Changed 4/1989 from non-postable term
       (Use WORK RELIEF).
  UF  Work relief
  BT  Domestic economic assistance
       Employment
  RT  Civil service
**Public service organizations**
       --[country or state]--[city]
  PN  Includes activities and structures.
  CN  Double index under ORGANIZATIONS'
       FACILITIES (or NTs) for images that focus
       on facilities.
  UF  Social welfare organizations
  BT  Organizations
  RT  Assistance
Public services
  USE Municipal services
**Public speaking**
       --[country or state]--[city]
  PN  Search also under the subdivision
       --PUBLIC APPEARANCES used with
       names of persons (Appendix B).
  UF  Addresses
       Elocution
       Lecturing

---

BT Broader term      RT Related term      PN Public Note
NT Narrower term     UF Used for       + Term has NTs
HN History Note       CN Catalogers Note    --[ ] May subdivide

**Public speaking (cont.)**
         Oratory
         Soap box oratory
         Speaking
         Speechmaking
         Talking
         Talks
  BT  Communication
  NT  Book talks
         Preaching
  RT  Debates
         Discussion
         Filibustering
         Meetings
         Podiums
         Press conferences
         Speechwriting
         Toasting
         Whistle-stop campaigning
**Public spending policy**
  USE Government spending policy
**Public spiritedness**
  RT  Public service
**Public squares**
  USE Plazas
**Public transportation**
  USE Mass transit
**Public utility companies**
         --[country or state]--[city]
  PN  Includes activities and structures.
  UF  Electric companies
         Gas companies
         Utility companies, Public
         Water companies
  BT  Business enterprises
  RT  Electricity
         Manhole covers
         Manholes
         Power plants
         Water supply
**Public welfare**
  USE Assistance
**Publicity**
  PN  Acts or devices designed to attract public attention or support. Search also under the subdivision --PUBLIC RELATIONS used with names of corporate bodies and named events (Appendix D).
  BT  Communication
  RT  Advertisements
         Advertising
         Logos
         Press conferences
         Propaganda
         Public opinion
         Slogans
**Publicity photographs**
  CN  TGM II term.
  UF  Head shots
         Promotional photographs
         Publicity stills
**Publicity stills**

**Publicity stills (cont.)**
  USE Publicity photographs
**Publishers**
  BT  People associated with education & communication
  RT  Publishing industry
**Publishing industry**
         --[country or state]--[city]
  PN  Includes activities and structures.
  UF  Book trade
  BT  Business enterprises
  NT  Music publishing industry
         Newspaper industry
  RT  Bible societies
         Book fairs
         Books
         Bookselling
         Periodicals
         Printing industry
         Printing presses
         Publishers
**Pubs**
  USE Bars
         Taverns (Inns)
**Pueblos**
         --[country or state]--[city]
  PN  Multistory, multiroom complex dwellings, often built on mesas or cliffs, common among Hopi, Pueblo, and other Native American cultures of the southwestern United States.
  BT  Settlements
  RT  Adobe buildings
         Dwellings
         Kivas
         Stone buildings
**Pulleys**
  BT  Machinery
  RT  Hoisting machinery
**Pulling**
         --[country or state]--[city]
  UF  Dragging
         Tugging
  RT  Locomotion
         Tug of war
**Pullman cars**
  USE Railroad passenger cars
**Pullman porters**
  USE Railroad porters
**Pulpits**
         --[country or state]--[city]
  UF  Mimbers
         Minbars
  BT  Religious architectural elements
  RT  Altars
         Furniture
**Pulsed-light photographs**
  USE Motion study photographs
**Puma hunting**
         --[country or state]
  BT  Big game hunting
         Hunting

BT  Broader term      RT  Related term      PN Public Note
NT  Narrower term    UF  Used for       + Term has NTs
HN History Note     CN Catalogers Note  --[ ] May subdivide

**Puma hunting (cont.)**
RT    Pumas
**Pumas**
           --[country or state]
UF    Cougars
          Mountain lions
BT    Animals
RT    Panthers
          Puma hunting
Pump houses
USE Pumping stations
**Pumping stations**
           --[country or state]--[city]
UF    Houses, Pump
          Pump houses
          Water pumping stations
BT    Hydraulic facilities
RT    Pumps
          Water pumps
          Waterworks
**Pumpkins**
           --[country or state]--[city]
BT    Fruit
NT    Jack-o-lanterns
RT    Melons
**Pumps**
BT    Machinery
NT    Air pumps
          Gasoline pumps
          Water pumps
RT    Pumping stations
**Punched card systems**
UF    Perforated card systems
          Punch-card systems
RT    Calculators
Punch-card systems
USE Punched card systems
**Punctuation**
BT    Grammar
NT    Dollar signs
          Question marks
**Pundits**
PN    Scholars or learned people, especially
          those who give opinions in an authoritative
          manner.
BT    People
RT    Critics
          Religion
          Scholars
**Punishment devices**
           --[country or state]--[city]
UF    Corporal punishment devices
          Torture devices
NT    Pillories
          Shackles
          Stocks (Punishment)
RT    Criminals
          Physical restraints
          Prisoners
          Punishment & torture
          Whips
Punishment of children

Punishment of children (cont.)
USE Child discipline
**Punishment & torture**
           --[country or state]--[city]
PN    Search also under ABUSED WOMEN and
          ABUSED CHILDREN for punishment &
          torture of members of these groups. Search
          also under the subdivision --PUNISHMENT &
          TORTURE used with names of ethnic, racial,
          and regional groups, and with classes of
          persons (Appendix A).
UF    Disciplinary action
          Torture
NT    Atrocities +
          Beating +
          Tarring & feathering
RT    Child discipline
          Criminals
          Dismemberment
          Executions
          Exiles
          Kicking
          Prisoners
          Punishment devices
          Stoning
          Strangling
          Vigilance committees
          Violence
**Puns**
CN    TGM II term.
**Puppet shows**
           --[country or state]--[city]
BT    Theatrical productions
RT    Puppets
**Puppets**
PN    For puppets not being used in puppet
          shows.
UF    Marionettes
BT    Toys
RT    Puppet shows
Puppies
USE Dogs
Purges, Political
USE Political purges
**Purses**
UF    Change purses
          Coin purses
BT    Clothing & dress
RT    Handbags
Pursuing
USE Chasing
**Push ball**
           --[country or state]--[city]
BT    Sports
**Puzzles**
CN    TGM II term.
NT    Crossword puzzles
RT    Mazes
**Pylons (Bridges)**
           --[country or state]--[city]
HN    Changed 1/1993 from PYLONS.
BT    Architectural elements

BT  Broader term                    RT  Related term                    PN Public Note
NT  Narrower term                  UF  Used for                          + Term has NTs
HN History Note                     CN Catalogers Note              --[ ] May subdivide

**Pylons (Bridges) (cont.)**
RT   Bridges
**Pylons (Gateways)**
--[country or state]--[city]
HN   Changed 1/1993 from PYLONS.
RT   Gates
**Pyramids**
--[country or state]--[city]
BT   Tombs & sepulchral monuments
**Quacks**
--[country or state]--[city]
PN   Persons who pretend to have medical
skills.
UF   Charlatans
BT   People associated with health & safety
RT   Fraud
Health care
Medicine shows
Patent medicines
Physicians
**Quadrangles (Courtyards)**
--[country or state]--[city]
PN   Square or oblong courtyards enclosed on
all sides by buildings.
UF   Quads
BT   Rooms & spaces
RT   Courtyards
**Quadruplets**
UF   Births, Multiple
Multiple births
BT   People
Quads
USE Quadrangles (Courtyards)
Quail hunting
USE Quail shooting
**Quail shooting**
--[country or state]
UF   Quail hunting
BT   Game bird hunting
RT   Quails
**Quails**
--[country or state]
BT   Birds
NT   Bobwhites
RT   Partridges
Quail shooting
**Quaker guns**
PN   Dummy pieces of artillery, usually of
wood (from the Quaker doctrine of
nonresistance).
RT   Artillery (Weaponry)
Military art & science
Quaker meeting houses
USE Friends' meeting houses
Quaking
USE Shaking
Quality control
USE Product inspection
**Quarantines**
--[country or state]--[city]
PN   Includes images related to the activity of
quarantining and the places where

**Quarantines (cont.)**
quarantined persons are kept.
BT   Health care
RT   Communicable diseases
Preventive medicine
Sanatoriums
**Quarreling**
--[country or state]--[city]
PN   Search under FIGHTING for physical
fighting.
CN   Used in a note under FIGHTING.
UF   Arguments
BT   Interpersonal relations
RT   Anger
Blaming
Quarries
USE Quarrying
**Quarrying**
--[country or state]--[city]
PN   Extraction of stone, marble, slate, etc., from
quarries. Includes activities and sites.
UF   Quarries
Rock quarrying
BT   Excavation
NT   Granite quarrying
Limestone quarrying +
Sandstone quarrying
Slate quarrying
Stone quarrying
RT   Industry
Mining
Quarters, Military
USE Barracks
Officers' quarters
Quartets, Barbershop
USE Barbershop quartets
**Quartz**
--[country or state]--[city]
UF   Rock crystal
BT   Minerals
RT   Crystals
Quartz mining
**Quartz mining**
--[country or state]--[city]
PN   Includes activities and sites.
BT   Mining
RT   Quartz
**Quatrefoils**
--[country or state]--[city]
PN   Conventionalized representations of a
flower with four petals or a leaf with four
leaflets; figures enclosed by four joined foils,
specifically, a four-lobed foliation in Gothic
tracery.
BT   Architectural decorations & ornaments
Quays
USE Piers & wharves
**Queens**
--[country]
BT   Rulers
Women
RT   Empresses

---

BT  Broader term                    RT  Related term                    PN  Public Note
NT  Narrower term                   UF  Used for                       +  Term has NTs
HN  History Note                    CN  Catalogers Note                --[ ] May subdivide

**Question marks**
　　UF　Interrogation points
　　BT　Punctuation
**Questioning**
　　　　--[country or state]--[city]
　　UF　Interrogation
　　BT　Communication
　　RT　Interviews
　　　　Investigation
　　　　Law & legal affairs
**Queues**
　　　　--[country or state]--[city]
　　PN　Lines, especially of persons or vehicles.
　　UF　Lines
　　NT　Bread & soup lines
　　　　Receiving lines
　　RT　Crowds
Quicksilver mining
　　USE Mercury mining
Quick-serve restaurants
　　USE Fast food restaurants
**Quilting**
　　　　--[country or state]--[city]
　　BT　Handicraft
　　RT　Quilting bees
　　　　Quilts
　　　　Sewing
**Quilting bees**
　　　　--[country or state]--[city]
　　UF　Quilting parties
　　BT　Bees (Cooperative gatherings)
　　RT　Quilting
　　　　Quilts
Quilting parties
　　USE Quilting bees
**Quilts**
　　RT　Quilting
　　　　Quilting bees
　　　　Textiles
**Quinine**
　　BT　Medicines
Quints
　　USE Quintuplets
**Quintuplets**
　　UF　Births, Multiple
　　　　Multiple births
　　　　Quints
　　BT　People
Quits
　　USE Resignations
Quivering
　　USE Shaking
Quiz shows
　　USE Game shows
**Quoins**
　　　　--[country or state]--[city]
　　UF　Coigns
　　　　Coillons
　　　　Coins (Wall components)
　　　　Coyns
　　　　Cunes
　　BT　Architectural elements

**Quoins (cont.)**
　　RT　Masonry
　　　　Walls
**Quoits**
　　　　--[country or state]--[city]
　　BT　Sports
　　NT　Horseshoe pitching
Quotations
　　CN　Used only as a subdivision with names of persons (Appendix B).
**Rabbis**
　　　　--[country or state]--[city]
　　BT　Clergy
**Rabbit hunting**
　　　　--[country or state]
　　BT　Hunting
　　RT　Rabbits
**Rabbits**
　　　　--[country or state]
　　UF　Hares
　　　　Jackrabbits
　　BT　Rodents
　　RT　Rabbit hunting
**Rabies**
　　　　--[country or state]--[city]
　　BT　Communicable diseases
**Raccoon hunting**
　　　　--[country or state]
　　BT　Hunting
　　RT　Raccoons
**Raccoons**
　　　　--[country or state]
　　UF　Coons
　　BT　Animals
　　RT　Raccoon hunting
Race cars
　　USE Racing automobiles
**Race discrimination**
　　　　--[country or state]--[city]
　　PN　For overt discriminatory behavior directed against racial or ethnic groups. Search under RACE RELATIONS for relations among races in general and under RACISM for the subject of racist attitudes.
　　CN　Used in a note under RACE RELATIONS and RACISM.
　　BT　Discrimination
　　RT　Ethnic groups
　　　　Race relations
　　　　Racism
　　　　Segregation
　　　　White man's burden
**Race horses**
　　PN　For race horses away from the context of racing. Search under HORSE RACING for activities.
　　BT　Horses
　　RT　Horse racing
**Race relations**
　　　　--[country or state]--[city]
　　PN　For relations among races in general. Search under RACE DISCRIMINATION for

BT Broader term　　　　　RT Related term　　　　　PN Public Note
NT Narrower term　　　　　UF Used for　　　　　　　+ Term has NTs
HN History Note　　　　　　CN Catalogers Note　　　　--[ ] May subdivide

**Race relations (cont.)**
      overt discriminatory behavior directed
      against racial or ethnic groups and under
      RACISM for the subject of racist attitudes.
  CN  Used in a note under RACE
      DISCRIMINATION and RACISM.
  BT  Interpersonal relations
  NT  Miscegenation
  RT  Apartheid
      Busing (School integration)
      Ethnic groups
      Minorities
      Race discrimination
      Race riots
      Racism
      Segregation

**Race riots**
      --[country or state]--[city]
  BT  Riots
  RT  Race relations
      Racism

Race tracks
  USE Racetracks

Race walking
  USE Walking races

Races
  USE Racing

**Racetracks**
      --[country or state]--[city]
  PN  For images that focus on physical
      facilities. Search under RACING for
      activities.
  CN  Double index under the type of racing.
  UF  Race tracks
  BT  Sports & recreation facilities
  RT  Racing

Racewalking
  USE Walking races

Racial crossing
  USE Miscegenation

Racial equality
  USE Racism

Racial inequality
  USE Racism

Racial stereotypes
  USE Ethnic stereotypes

**Racing**
      --[country or state]--[city]
  CN  Used in a note under RACETRACKS.
  UF  Races
  BT  Sports
  NT  Airplane racing
      Automobile racing
      Balloon racing
      Bicycle racing
      Horse racing +
      Regattas +
      Relay racing
      Running races +
      Sack racing
      Speed skating
      Steamboat racing

**Racing (cont.)**
      Three-legged racing
      Walking races
  RT  Racetracks

**Racing automobiles**
      --[nationality]--[country or state]--[city]
  PN  For racing automobiles away from the
      context of racing. Search under
      AUTOMOBILE RACING for activities.
  UF  Race cars
      Racing cars
  BT  Automobiles
  RT  Automobile racing
      Coaster cars

Racing cars
  USE Racing automobiles

Racing pigeons
  USE Homing pigeons

**Racing shells**
      --[nationality]--[country or state]--[city]
  UF  Shells, Racing
  BT  Boats
  RT  Rowers
      Rowing
      Rowing races

**Racism**
      --[country or state]--[city]
  PN  For the subject of racist and anti-racist
      attitudes. Search under RACE
      DISCRIMINATION for overt discriminatory
      behavior directed against racial or ethnic
      groups and under RACE RELATIONS for
      relations among races in general.
  CN  Used in a note under RACE
      DISCRIMINATION and RACE
      RELATIONS.
  UF  Equality, Racial
      Inequality, Racial
      Racial equality
      Racial inequality
  BT  Prejudice
  NT  Antisemitism
  RT  Genocide
      Race discrimination
      Race relations
      Race riots

Rack railroads
  USE Mountain railroads

**Radar**
      --[country or state]--[city]
  BT  Scientific equipment
  RT  Navigation

Radiation, Ionizing
  USE Ionizing radiation

**Radiators**
  UF  Heaters
  BT  Equipment
  RT  Heating & ventilation industry

**Radicalism**
      --[country or state]--[city]
  PN  For the subject of radicalism in general.
  UF  Extremism

---

BT Broader term            RT Related term           PN Public Note
NT Narrower term          UF Used for              + Term has NTs
HN History Note           CN Catalogers Note      --[ ] May subdivide

**Radicalism (cont.)**
  New Left
  RT  Political participation
**Radio broadcasting**
  --[country or state]--[city]
  UF  Amateur radio
  Ham radio
  BT  Broadcasting
  RT  Action & adventure dramas
  Children & radio
  Comedies
  Game shows
  Historical dramas
  Horror dramas
  Melodramas
  Public affairs radio programs
  Radio stations
  Radios
  Romances
  Sociological dramas
  Westerns
Radio broadcasting stations
  USE Radio stations
**Radio industry**
  --[country or state]--[city]
  PN  Manufacture and trade of radios. Includes
  activities and structures.
  CN  Double index under INDUSTRIAL
  FACILITIES (or NTs)  for images that focus
  on facilities.
  BT  Industry
  RT  Radios
**Radio photographs**
  CN  TGM II term.
**Radio stations**
  --[country or state]--[city]
  UF  Radio broadcasting stations
  BT  Communication facilities
  RT  Radio broadcasting
Radio & children
  USE Children & radio
Radioactive waste
  USE Radioactive wastes
**Radioactive wastes**
  --[country or state]--[city]
  UF  Nuclear wastes
  Radioactive waste
  Radwastes
  Wastes, Radioactive
  RT  Nuclear power
  Pollution
  Radioactivity
  Refuse disposal
**Radioactivity**
  --[country or state]--[city]
  RT  Ionizing radiation
  Nuclear power
  Nuclear weapons
  Radioactive wastes
**Radiographs**
  CN  TGM II term.
  UF  X-ray photographs

**Radiography**
  UF  Skiagraphy
  X-ray photography
  RT  Ionizing radiation
  Photography
Radiolaria
  USE Microorganisms
**Radiophones**
  PN  Transmitting or receiving sets for
  radiotelephony.
  UF  Radiotelephones
  Telephones, Wireless
  Wireless telephones
  BT  Communication devices
  RT  Telephones
**Radios**
  BT  Communication devices
  Furnishings
  RT  Children & radio
  Electric oscillators
  Radio broadcasting
  Radio industry
  Transistors
Radiotelephones
  USE Radiophones
**Radishes**
  --[country or state]--[city]
  BT  Vegetables
Radwastes
  USE Radioactive wastes
**Rafters**
  --[country or state]--[city]
  BT  Architectural elements
  RT  Roofs
Rafting
  USE Rafts
**Rafts**
  --[nationality]--[country or state]--[city]
  UF  Rafting
  BT  Boats
  NT  Jangadas
Rag picking
  USE Ragpicking
**Ragpicking**
  --[country or state]--[city]
  PN  Picking up rags and refuse (as from
  garbage cans or public dumps) as a means of
  livelihood.
  UF  Rag picking
  RT  Foraging
  Junkyards
  Poor persons
  Recycling
  Refuse disposal
Rail transportation
  USE Railroads
**Railings**
  --[country or state]--[city]
  BT  Architectural elements
  NT  Hand railings
  RT  Balustrades
  Fences

BT  Broader term                                    RT  Related term                                    PN  Public Note
NT  Narrower term                                   UF  Used for                                         +  Term has NTs
HN  History Note                                    CN  Catalogers Note                                  --[ ] May subdivide

**Railings (cont.)**
Ironwork
**Railroad accidents**
--[country or state]--[city]
UF  Derailments
BT  Accidents
NT  Street railroad accidents +
RT  Railroads
**Railroad artillery**
BT  Artillery (Weaponry)
RT  Railroads
**Railroad bridges**
--[country or state]--[city]
UF  Railroad viaducts
BT  Bridges
RT  Railroad tracks
Railroads
**Railroad cabooses**
--[nationality]--[country or state]--[city]
PN  For images that focus on the exterior or interior of cabooses.
UF  Cabooses
BT  Railroad cars
Railroad campaigning
USE Whistle-stop campaigning
**Railroad car industry**
--[country or state]--[city]
PN  Includes activities and structures.
CN  Double index under INDUSTRIAL FACILITIES (or NTs) for images that focus on facilities.
BT  Transportation industry
RT  Railroad cars
Railroads
**Railroad cars**
--[nationality]--[country or state]--[city]
PN  For images that focus on the exterior and interior of railroad cars. Search under RAILROADS for general views of trains.
BT  Vehicles
NT  Armored trains
Railroad cabooses
Railroad freight cars +
Railroad handcars
Railroad passenger cars +
RT  Railroad car industry
Railroad locomotives
Railroads
**Railroad companies**
--[country or state]--[city]
PN  For companies operating passenger or freight lines. Includes activities and structures.
CN  Used in a note under RAILROADS.
BT  Business enterprises
RT  Railroads
**Railroad construction workers**
BT  Railroad employees
RT  Construction
Railroad construction & maintenance
**Railroad construction & maintenance**
--[country or state]--[city]

**Railroad construction & maintenance (cont.)**
UF  Railroad maintenance
Railroad repair
RT  Construction
Graders (Earthmoving machinery)
Maintenance & repair
Railroad construction workers
Railroad cuts
Railroad shops & yards
Railroads
**Railroad crossings**
--[country or state]--[city]
UF  Crossings, Railroad
Grade crossings
BT  Railroad tracks
**Railroad cuts**
--[country or state]--[city]
RT  Railroad construction & maintenance
Railroad tracks
Railroad depots
USE Railroad stations
**Railroad dining cars**
--[nationality]--[country or state]--[city]
PN  For images that focus on the exterior or interior of dining cars.
UF  Diners (Railroad cars)
Dining cars
BT  Railroad passenger cars
RT  Eating & drinking
**Railroad employees**
UF  Conductors, Railroad
Engineers, Railroad
BT  Employees
People associated with transportation
NT  Railroad construction workers
RT  Railroad employees' unions
Railroad strikes
Railroads
**Railroad employees' unions**
--[country or state]--[city]
UF  Railroad unions
BT  Labor unions
RT  Railroad employees
Railroad strikes
Railroads
**Railroad facilities**
--[country or state]--[city]
BT  Transportation facilities
NT  Railroad roundhouses
Railroad shops & yards
Railroad signal towers
Railroad stations
Street railroad facilities +
RT  Railroads
**Railroad ferries**
--[nationality]--[country or state]--[city]
BT  Ferries
RT  Railroads
**Railroad freight cars**
--[nationality]--[country or state]--[city]
PN  For images that focus on the exterior or interior of freight cars.

---

**Railroad freight cars (cont.)**
   UF  Box cars
        Freight cars
        Hopper cars
   BT  Railroad cars
   NT  Railroad refrigerator cars
        Railroad section cars
        Railroad tank cars
   RT  Freighthopping
        Shipping

**Railroad handcars**
        --[nationality]--[country or state]--[city]
   UF  Handcars
   BT  Railroad cars

Railroad ice bridges
   USE Railroad ice crossings

**Railroad ice crossings**
        --[country or state]--[city]
   UF  Railroad ice bridges
   BT  Ice crossings
   RT  Railroad tracks

**Railroad locomotive industry**
        --[country or state]--[city]
   PN  Includes activities and structures.
   CN  Double index under INDUSTRIAL
        FACILITIES (or NTs) for images that focus
        on facilities.
   BT  Transportation industry
   RT  Railroad locomotives

**Railroad locomotives**
        --[nationality]--[country or state]--[city]
   PN  For images that focus on the exterior or
        interior of locomotives.
   UF  Locomotives
        Streamliners
   BT  Vehicles
   NT  Railroad snowplow locomotives
   RT  Railroad cars
        Railroad locomotive industry
        Railroads

**Railroad lounge cars**
        --[nationality]--[country or state]--[city]
   PN  For images that focus on the exterior or
        interior of lounge cars.
   UF  Lounge cars
        Parlor cars
   BT  Railroad passenger cars

**Railroad mail service**
        --[country or state]--[city]
   BT  Postal service
   RT  Railroads

Railroad maintenance
   USE Railroad construction & maintenance

**Railroad observation cars**
        --[nationality]--[country or state]--[city]
   PN  For images that focus on the exterior or
        interior of observation cars.
   BT  Railroad passenger cars

**Railroad passenger cars**
        --[nationality]--[country or state]--[city]
   PN  For images that focus on the exterior or
        interior of passenger cars.

**Railroad passenger cars (cont.)**
   UF  Passenger cars
        Pullman cars
   BT  Railroad cars
   NT  Railroad dining cars
        Railroad lounge cars
        Railroad observation cars
        Railroad private cars
        Railroad sleeping cars
        Railroad smoking cars

Railroad platforms
   USE Railroad stations

**Railroad porters**
        --[country or state]--[city]
   UF  Pullman porters
        Red caps
        Redcaps
   BT  Porters
   RT  Railroads

**Railroad private cars**
        --[nationality]--[country or state]--[city]
   PN  For images that focus on the exterior or
        interior of private cars.
   UF  Private railroad cars
   BT  Railroad passenger cars
   RT  Staterooms

**Railroad refrigerator cars**
        --[nationality]--[country or state]--[city]
   PN  For images that focus on the exterior or
        interior of refrigerator cars.
   UF  Refrigerator cars
   BT  Railroad freight cars

Railroad repair
   USE Railroad construction & maintenance
        Railroad shops & yards

Railroad reservation counters
   USE Railroad stations

**Railroad roundhouses**
        --[country or state]--[city]
   PN  A circular building for housing and
        repairing locomotives.
   UF  Roundhouses
   BT  Railroad facilities

**Railroad section cars**
        --[nationality]--[country or state]--[city]
   PN  For images that focus on the exterior or
        interior of section cars.
   UF  Section cars
   BT  Railroad freight cars

**Railroad shops & yards**
        --[country or state]--[city]
   UF  Railroad repair
        Railroad yards
   BT  Railroad facilities
   RT  Railroad construction & maintenance

Railroad shunting
   USE Railroad switching

**Railroad sidings**
        --[country or state]--[city]
   UF  Sidings, Railroad
   BT  Railroad tracks

**Railroad signal towers**

---

BT  Broader term           RT  Related term           PN Public Note
NT  Narrower term        UF  Used for             + Term has NTs
HN  History Note         CN  Catalogers Note     --[ ] May subdivide

**Railroad signal towers (cont.)**
    --[country or state]--[city]
- BT  Railroad facilities
-     Signal towers
- RT  Railroad signals

**Railroad signals**
    --[country or state]--[city]
- BT  Signal lights
- RT  Railroad signal towers
-     Railroad switching
-     Railroad tracks

**Railroad sleeping cars**
    --[nationality]--[country or state]--[city]
- PN  For images that focus on the exterior or interior of sleeping cars.
- UF  Sleeping cars
- BT  Railroad passenger cars
- RT  Staterooms

**Railroad smoking cars**
    --[nationality]--[country or state]--[city]
- PN  For images that focus on the exterior or interior of smoking cars.
- UF  Smoking cars
- BT  Railroad passenger cars
- RT  Smoking

**Railroad snowplow locomotives**
    --[nationality]--[country or state]--[city]
- UF  Snowplow locomotives
- BT  Railroad locomotives
- RT  Snow removal

**Railroad stations**
    --[country or state]--[city]
- UF  Depots
-     Railroad depots
-     Railroad platforms
-     Railroad reservation counters
-     Railroad ticket counters
-     Sheds, Train
-     Stations, Railroad
-     Terminals (Stations)
-     Train sheds
- BT  Railroad facilities

**Railroad strikes**
    --[country or state]--[city]
- BT  Strikes
- RT  Railroad employees
-     Railroad employees' unions
-     Railroads

**Railroad switching**
    --[country or state]--[city]
- UF  Railroad shunting
-     Switching, Railroad
- RT  Railroad signals
-     Railroad tracks

**Railroad tank cars**
    --[nationality]--[country or state]--[city]
- UF  Tank cars
- BT  Railroad freight cars

Railroad ticket counters
  USE Railroad stations

**Railroad tracks**
    --[country or state]--[city]

**Railroad tracks (cont.)**
- CN  Used in a note under RAILROAD CONSTRUCTION & MAINTENANCE.
- NT  Railroad crossings
-     Railroad sidings
-     Street railroad tracks
- RT  Railroad bridges
-     Railroad cuts
-     Railroad ice crossings
-     Railroad signals
-     Railroad switching
-     Railroads

Railroad unions
  USE Railroad employees' unions

Railroad viaducts
  USE Railroad bridges

Railroad yards
  USE Railroad shops & yards

**Railroads**
    --[country or state]--[city]
- PN  For the subject of railroads and general views of trains. Search under RAILROAD COMPANIES for organizations that operate railroads.
- CN  Used in a note under RAILROAD CARS.
- UF  Rail transportation
-     Railways
-     Trains
- BT  Transportation
- NT  Cable railroads +
-     Electric railroads
-     Elevated railroads
-     Inclined railroads
-     Mine railroads
-     Monorail railroads
-     Mountain railroads
-     Narrow-gage railroads +
-     Street railroads +
- RT  Railroad accidents
-     Railroad artillery
-     Railroad bridges
-     Railroad car industry
-     Railroad cars
-     Railroad companies
-     Railroad construction & maintenance
-     Railroad employees
-     Railroad employees' unions
-     Railroad facilities
-     Railroad ferries
-     Railroad locomotives
-     Railroad mail service
-     Railroad porters
-     Railroad strikes
-     Railroad tracks
-     Tunnels
-     Whistle-stop campaigning

Railways
  USE Railroads

**Rain**
    --[country or state]--[city]
- UF  Rainfall
- BT  Weather

---

BT Broader term      RT Related term      PN Public Note
NT Narrower term      UF Used for      + Term has NTs
HN History Note      CN Catalogers Note      --[ ] May subdivide

Rain (cont.)
 RT   Droughts
      Rain making
      Storms
      Umbrellas
Rain making
      --[country or state]--[city]
 UF   Cloud seeding
 BT   Weather control
 RT   Rain
Rainbows
 BT   Natural phenomena
Rainfall
 USE Rain
Rainwater heads
 USE Leader heads
Rainwater pipes
 USE Downspouts
Raising of children
 USE Child rearing
Raisins
      --[country or state]--[city]
 BT   Grapes
Rake's progress
 RT   Deterioration
      Ethics
      Lust
Raking (Sweeping)
      --[country or state]--[city]
 RT   Gardening
      Leaves
      Plowing
      Sweeping & dusting
Rallies, Political
 USE Political parades & rallies
Rallies, War
 USE War rallies
Ramparts
 USE Barricades
      Forts & fortifications
Ramps
 USE Inclined planes
Rams
 USE Sheep
Rams, Battering
 USE Battering rams
Ranch houses
 USE Ranches
Ranches
      --[country or state]--[city]
 PN   Includes activities and structures.
 UF   Haciendas
      Ranch houses
 BT   Agricultural facilities
 NT   Cattle ranches
      Sheep ranches
 RT   Animals
      Cowboys
      Cowgirls
      Dwellings
      Farms
      Food industry

Ranches (cont.)
      Meat industry
      Outbuildings
Rangers
      --[country or state]--[city]
 PN   Persons responsible for ranging over a
      region for its protection.
 BT   People associated with health & safety
 RT   Forestry
      Game preserves
      Gamekeepers
      National parks & reserves
      State parks & reserves
Ranges
 USE Stoves
Rapes
      --[country or state]--[city]
 BT   Crimes
 RT   Sex
Rapid transit
 USE Mass transit
Rapids
      --[country or state]--[city]
 RT   Rivers
      Shooting rapids
Rapids shooting
 USE Shooting rapids
Raspberries
      --[country or state]--[city]
 BT   Berries
Ratcatchers
 UF   Ratter
 BT   People associated with health & safety
 RT   Ratcatching
      Rats
Ratcatching
      --[country or state]--[city]
 BT   Rodent control
 RT   Ratcatchers
      Rats
Rationing, Consumer
 USE Consumer rationing
Rats
      --[country or state]
 BT   Rodents
 RT   Plague
      Ratcatchers
      Ratcatching
Rattan furniture
 USE Wicker furniture
Rattan palms
      --[country or state]--[city]
 BT   Palms
Ratter
 USE Ratcatchers
Rattles
 BT   Percussion instruments
 RT   Toys
Ravens
      --[country or state]
 BT   Birds
Ravines

---

BT  Broader term                  RT  Related term              PN Public Note
NT  Narrower term                 UF  Used for                  + Term has NTs
HN  History Note                  CN  Catalogers Note           --[ ] May subdivide

Ravines (cont.)
    USE Canyons
Rayographs
    USE Photograms
**Rayon**
    UF   Silk, Artificial
    BT   Fibers
    RT   Nylon
**Razor blades**
    BT   Shaving equipment
RC paper prints
    USE Resin-coated paper prints
Reactionism
    USE Conservatism
Readiness
    USE Preparedness
**Reading**
    --[country or state]--[city]
    RT   Book clubs
         Book talks
         Children reading & writing
         Education
         Literacy
         Reading rooms
**Reading rooms**
    --[country or state]--[city]
    BT   Interiors
    RT   Libraries
         Reading
**Real estate business**
    --[country or state]--[city]
    PN   Includes activities.
    BT   Business enterprises
    NT   Land subdivision
    RT   House buying
         Landlord & tenant
         Model houses
         Real estate development
**Real estate development**
    --[country or state]--[city]
    UF   Land development
    BT   Land use
    NT   Homesteading
    RT   Business enterprises
         Clearing of land
         Construction industry
         Housing developments
         Land rushes
         Land subdivision
         Real estate business
         Speculative houses
**Ream wrappers**
    CN   TGM II term.
Reapers
    USE Harvesting machinery
Reaping
    USE Harvesting
Reapportionment
    USE Apportionment
Rearing of children
    USE Child rearing
**Rearmament**

**Rearmament (cont.)**
    --[nationality]
    RT   Arms control
         Arms & armament
         Military policy
**Rebellions**
    --[country or state]--[city]
    PN   Open resistance to, or defiance of,
         authority by an organized group of people.
         Search under REBELS for images that focus
         on real persons.
    UF   Insurrections
         Resistance movements
         Uprisings
    BT   Events
    NT   Mutinies
         National liberation movements
         Peasant rebellions
         Slave rebellions
    RT   Activists
         Civil wars
         Crimes
         Opposition (Political science)
         Protest movements
         Rebels
         Revolutions
**Rebels**
    --[country or state]--[city]
    PN   Those who engage in open defiance of
         authority.
    CN   Used in a note under REBELLIONS.
    UF   Insurgents
    BT   Activists
    RT   Dissenters
         Rebellions
         Revolutionaries
**Rebuses**
    CN   TGM II term.
Recalling
    USE Reminiscing
**Receiving lines**
    --[country or state]--[city]
    BT   Manners & customs
         Queues
    RT   Receptions
**Reception rooms**
    --[country or state]--[city]
    UF   Throne rooms
    BT   Ceremonial rooms
    RT   Drawing rooms
         Parlors
         Receptions
         Waiting rooms
**Receptions**
    --[country or state]--[city]
    BT   Entertaining
    RT   Receiving lines
         Reception rooms
         Rites & ceremonies
Recesses
    USE School recesses
Recesses (Architecture)

---

BT  Broader term          RT  Related term          PN Public Note
NT  Narrower term        UF  Used for              + Term has NTs
HN History Note          CN Catalogers Note      --[ ] May subdivide

Recesses (Architecture) (cont.)
    USE Alcoves
**Reciprocity**
    UF   Fair trade
    BT   Free trade & protection
    RT   Tariffs
Reckless driving
    USE Traffic accidents
**Reclamation of land**
        --[country or state]--[city]
    PN   Bringing wild, waste, or marshy land into
          a condition for cultivation or other use.
          Search under CLEARING OF LAND for
          removal of timber and bushes from land.
    CN   Used in a note under CLEARING OF
          LAND.
    UF   Land reclamation
    BT   Civil engineering
          Land use
    NT   Clearing of land
          Irrigation
    RT   Dikes (Engineering)
          Wetlands
Recluses
    USE Hermits
Reconnaissance, Military
    USE Military reconnaissance
Reconstruction
    USE Remodeling
**Reconstructions**
    CN   TGM II term.
    UF   Re-creations
Record covers
    USE Album covers
Record industry
    USE Sound recording industry
Record jackets
    USE Album covers
Record keeping
    USE Recording & registration
Record players
    USE Phonographs
Record repositories
    USE Archives
Record stores
    USE Sound recording stores
Recorded sound
    USE Sound recording
**Recorders**
    PN   Includes the activity of playing recorders.
    BT   Flutes
Recording industry
    USE Sound recording industry
**Recording & registration**
        --[country or state]--[city]
    UF   Record keeping
          Registration
    RT   Archives
          Documents
          License plates
          Paperwork
          Registers

**Recording & registration (cont.)**
          Voter registration
Records (Information)
    USE Documents
Records, World
    USE World records
Recovery vehicles
    USE Wreckers (Vehicles)
**Recreation**
        --[country or state]--[city]
    PN   Search also under the subdivision
          --SOCIAL LIFE used with names of ethnic,
          racial, and regional groups and with classes
          of persons (Appendix A), with names of
          persons (Appendix B), and with corporate
          bodies and named events (Appendix D).
          Search also under the subdivision --SPORTS
          used with names of ethnic, racial, and
          regional groups and with classes of persons
          (Appendix A), and with corporate bodies and
          named events (Appendix D).
    NT   Children playing +
          Games +
          Hayrides
          Picnics
          School recesses
    RT   Automobile driving
          Camping
          Dancing
          Entertainment
          Hiking
          Historical reenactments
          Hobbyists
          Leisure
          Manners & customs
          Recreation rooms
          School excursions
          Sports
          Vacations
          Walking
Recreation facilities
    USE Sports & recreation facilities
Recreation piers
    USE Amusement piers
**Recreation rooms**
        --[country or state]--[city]
    UF   Game rooms
    BT   Interiors
    NT   Billiard rooms
          Playrooms
    RT   Recreation
          Sports & recreation facilities
Recreational fishing
    USE Fishing
Recreations (Conjectural works)
    USE Conjectural works
**Recruiting & enlistment**
        --[country or state]--[city]
    PN   For military recruiting and enlistment.
          Search under MEMBERSHIP CAMPAIGNS
          for other types of recruitment. Search also
          under the subdivision --RECRUITING &

---

**Recruiting & enlistment (cont.)**
> ENLISTMENT used with names of wars (Appendix C), and with corporate bodies and named events (Appendix D).
- UF  Enlistment
- RT  Military demobilizations
       Military discharges
       Military mobilizations
       Military organizations
       Military service
       War rallies

**Rectories (Buildings)**
- USE Religious dwellings

**Recycled buildings**
- USE Recycled structures

**Recycled structures**
> --[country or state]--[city]
- UF  Adaptive reuse
       Converted structures
       Recycled buildings
       Rehabilitated structures
- BT  Buildings
- RT  Architectural follies
       Conservation & restoration
       Remodeling

**Recycling**
> --[country or state]--[city]
- UF  Waste recycling
- BT  Conservation of natural resources
- RT  Ragpicking
       Refuse disposal
       Salvage
       Scrap drives

**Red caps**
- USE Railroad porters

**Red carpet**
- PN  Symbol of greetings or receptions marked by ceremonial courtesy.
- BT  Symbols
- RT  Floor coverings
       Manners & customs

**Red tape**
- PN  Symbol of bureaucratic procedure, especially as characterized by mechanical adherence to regulations, needless duplication of records, and compilation of an excessive amount of extraneous information.
- UF  Bureaucratic red tape
       Government red tape
- BT  Symbols
- RT  Paperwork
       Politics & government

**Redcaps**
- USE Railroad porters

**Reducing**
- UF  Dieting
       Weight control
- RT  Eating & drinking
       Obesity
       Physical fitness

**Redwood trees**
- USE Redwoods

**Redwoods**
> --[country or state]--[city]
- UF  Redwood trees
       Sequoias
- BT  Trees
- NT  Giant sequoias

**Reeds (Plants)**
> --[country or state]--[city]
- UF  Phragmites
- BT  Plants

**Reefs**
> --[country or state]--[city]
- UF  Barrier reefs
- BT  Land
- RT  Seas

**Reel & bead moldings**
- USE Bead & reel moldings

**Reenactments**
- USE Theatrical productions

**Reenactments, Historical**
- USE Historical reenactments

**Refereeing**
- USE Sports officiating

**Referees**
- UF  Sports officials
- BT  People associated with entertainment & sports
- RT  Sports
       Sports officiating

**Referendums**
> --[country or state]--[city]
- PN  Practice of referring measures passed upon or proposed by legislative bodies to the electorate for approval or rejection.
- UF  Initiatives & referendums
- BT  Law & legal affairs
- RT  Democracy
       Legislation
       Political elections

**Refineries**
> --[country or state]--[city]
- CN  Double index for the type of industry with which the refinery is associated.
- BT  Factories

**Reflections**
- PN  For images reflected by a surface such as water or a mirror.
- BT  Natural phenomena
- RT  Bodies of water
       Mirages
       Mirrors

**Reform**
> --[country or state]--[city]
- NT  Civil service reform
       Dress reform
       Prison reform
       Tax reform
- RT  Ethics
       Muckraking
       Progressivism (United States politics)

**Reform schools**
- USE Reformatories

---

BT  Broader term                    RT  Related term                    PN  Public Note
NT  Narrower term                    UF  Used for                         +  Term has NTs
HN  History Note                     CN  Catalogers Note                  --[ ]  May subdivide

**Reformatories**
--[country or state]--[city]
PN   Includes activities and structures.
UF   Correctional facilities
    Reform schools
BT   Detention facilities
    Schools
RT   Junior republics
    Juvenile delinquents
    Prison education
    Prisons
    Vocational education

**Reformed churches**
--[country or state]--[city]
PN   For images that focus on buildings, as
    well as the associated grounds.
UF   Dutch reformed churches
BT   Protestant churches

Refreshment stands
USE Food vendors

Refrigerator cars
USE Railroad refrigerator cars

**Refrigerator industry**
--[country or state]--[city]
CN   Double index under INDUSTRIAL
    FACILITIES (or NTs) for images that focus
    on facilities.
BT   Equipment industry
RT   Refrigerators

**Refrigerators**
UF   Iceboxes
BT   Appliances
NT   Freezers
RT   Refrigerator industry

**Refugee camps**
--[country or state]--[city]
UF   Displaced persons camps
    Resettlement camps
BT   Welfare facilities
RT   Refugees

**Refugees**
--[nationality]--[country or state]--[city]
PN   Persons fleeing to a foreign country or
    power to escape danger or persecution. Search
    under DISASTER VICTIMS for refugees
    from disasters. Search also under the
    subdivision --REFUGEES used with names
    of wars (Appendix C).
UF   Boat people
    Displaced persons
    Political refugees
BT   People
NT   Fugitive slaves
RT   Aliens
    Emigration & immigration
    Evacuations
    Exiles
    Internal migration
    Refugee camps
    Repatriation
    Right to asylum
    Victims

**Refuse**
--[country or state]--[city]
UF   City dumps
    Garbage
    Litter (Trash)
    Rubbish
    Trash
RT   Junkyards
    Pollution
    Refuse disposal
    Waste disposal facilities

**Refuse disposal**
--[country or state]--[city]
PN   Includes activities and disposal sites.
UF   City dumps
    Disposal of refuse
    Garbage dumps
    Waste disposal sites
BT   Cleaning
    Sanitation
NT   Ash disposal
    Garbage collecting
RT   Junkyards
    Radioactive wastes
    Ragpicking
    Recycling
    Refuse
    Sewerage
    Urban beautification
    Waste disposal facilities

**Regattas**
--[country or state]--[city]
PN   Rowing, speedboat, or sailing races, or
    organized series of such races.
UF   Boat racing
BT   Racing
NT   Rowing races
    Sailboat racing
    Yacht racing
RT   Boats
    Rowing

**Regionalism**
--[country or state]
PN   Consciousness of and loyalty to a distinct
    region with a homogeneous population.
RT   Mental states
    Nationalism
    Sectionalism (United States)

**Register marks**
CN   TGM II term.
UF   Registration marks

**Registers**
UF   Rosters
RT   Books
    Recording & registration

Registration
USE Recording & registration

Registration marks
USE Register marks

Regulation, Government
USE Government regulation

Regulatory agencies

---

BT Broader term          RT Related term          PN Public Note
NT Narrower term         UF Used for              + Term has NTs
HN History Note          CN Catalogers Note       --[ ] May subdivide

Regulatory agencies (cont.)
   USE Administrative agencies
Rehabilitated structures
   USE Recycled structures
**Rehearsals**
        --[country or state]--[city]
   RT  Auditions
       Entertainers
       Entertainment
**Reindeer**
   BT  Deer
**Reinforced concrete construction**
        --[country or state]--[city]
   BT  Construction
   RT  Concrete
**Rejuvenation**
   RT  Aged persons
       Mental states
       Youth
**Relations between the sexes**
        --[country or state]--[city]
   UF  Sexes, Relations between the
   BT  Interpersonal relations
   RT  Courtship
       Cross dressing
       Sexism
       Sexual harassment
Relations, Interpersonal
   USE Interpersonal relations
Relaxation
   USE Leisure
**Relay racing**
        --[country or state]--[city]
   BT  Racing
   RT  Running races
       Track athletics
**Relief printed etchings**
   CN  TGM II term.
**Relief prints**
   CN  TGM II term.
   UF  Block prints
**Relief ships**
        --[nationality]--[country or state]--[city]
   BT  Ships
   RT  Disaster relief
Relief (Aid)
   USE Assistance
**Religion**
   NT  Christianity
       Voodooism
   RT  Angels
       Church & education
       Church & state
       Clergy
       Confession
       Dietary laws
       Evangelists
       Freedom of religion
       Gods
       Gospel music
       Healers
       Idols

**Religion (cont.)**
       Miracles
       Missionaries
       Monks
       Nuns
       Pilgrimages
       Prayer
       Prophets
       Pundits
       Religious articles
       Religious aspects of war
       Religious books
       Religious education
       Religious facilities
       Religious groups
       Religious meetings
       Religious orders
       Religious processions
       Religious retreats
       Rites & ceremonies
       Saints
       Sandpaintings
       Secularism
       Shamans
       Spiritual leaders
       Stations of the Cross
       Supernatural
       Talmudists
       Theocracy
**Religious architectural elements**
        --[country or state]--[city]
   BT  Architectural elements
   NT  Ablution fountains
       Altarpieces
       Altars
       Confessionals
       Fonts
       Mihrabs
       Pulpits
   RT  Pews
       Religious articles
       Religious facilities
Religious art objects
   USE Religious articles
**Religious articles**
   UF  Devotional objects
       Liturgical objects
       Objects, Religious
       Religious art objects
       Religious goods
   NT  Icons
       Monstrances
       Tabernacles
   RT  Art objects
       Buddhas
       Chalices
       Religion
       Religious architectural elements
       Shrines
**Religious aspects of war**
        --[country or state]--[city]
   PN  Search also under the subdivision

---

BT Broader term          RT Related term          PN Public Note
NT Narrower term         UF Used for               + Term has NTs
HN History Note           CN Catalogers Note       --[ ] May subdivide

**Religious aspects of war (cont.)**
> --RELIGIOUS ASPECTS used with names
> of wars (Appendix C).
>  RT  Moral aspects of war
>       Pacifism
>       Religion
>       War

**Religious books**
> --[country or state]--[city]
>  BT  Books
>  NT  Bibles
>  RT  Religion

Religious buildings
> USE Religious facilities

**Religious calendars**
>  CN  TGM II term.

Religious celebrations
> USE Religious processions
>       Rites & ceremonies

**Religious communities**
> --[country or state]--[city]
>  UF  Communities, Religious
>  BT  Religious facilities
>  NT  Convents
>       Missions
>       Monasteries +
>  RT  Collective settlements
>       Religious orders
>       Religious retreats

**Religious dwellings**
> --[country or state]--[city]
>  UF  Deaneries (Buildings)
>       Manses
>       Parsonages
>       Rectories (Buildings)
>       Vicarages (Buildings)
>  BT  Houses
>  NT  Parish houses
>  RT  Religious facilities

**Religious education**
> --[country or state]--[city]
>  PN  Includes activities and structures.
>  CN  Double index under EDUCATIONAL
>       FACILITIES (or NTs) for images that focus
>       on facilities.
>  UF  Denominational schools
>       Parochial schools
>  BT  Education
>  RT  Church schools
>       Religion
>       Swamis
>       Theological seminaries

**Religious facilities**
> --[country or state]--[city]
>  HN  Changed 2/1993 from RELIGIOUS
>       BUILDINGS.
>  UF  Religious buildings
>  BT  Facilities
>  NT  Abbeys
>       Churches +
>       Kivas
>       Minarets

**Religious facilities (cont.)**
>       Mosques
>       Pagodas
>       Religious communities +
>       Shrines
>       Synagogues
>       Temples +
>  RT  Church schools
>       Religion
>       Religious architectural elements
>       Religious dwellings
>       Religious services

Religious goods
> USE Religious articles

**Religious groups**
> --[country or state]--[city]
>  UF  Religious sects
>       Sects
>  BT  Organizations
>  NT  Religious orders
>  RT  Cults
>       Minorities
>       Religion
>       Religious retreats
>       Zionism

Religious liberty
> USE Freedom of religion

**Religious meetings**
> --[country or state]--[city]
>  PN  For religious rallies and meetings of
>       religious organizations.
>  BT  Meetings
>  NT  Religious services +
>       Revivals
>  RT  Auto-da-fé sermons
>       Religion
>       Religious retreats

**Religious orders**
> --[country or state]--[city]
>  PN  For groups of persons living according to a
>       common religious discipline.
>  UF  Monastic orders
>  BT  Religious groups
>  RT  Clergy
>       Convents
>       Monasteries
>       Monks
>       Nuns
>       Religion
>       Religious communities

Religious pictures
> USE Devotional images

**Religious processions**
> --[country or state]--[city]
>  UF  Religious celebrations
>  BT  Parades & processions
>  RT  Religion
>       Rites & ceremonies

**Religious retreats**
> --[country or state]--[city]
>  PN  Withdrawal by members of a religious
>       group for purposes of prayer, meditation,

---

BT  Broader term          RT  Related term          PN Public Note
NT  Narrower term          UF  Used for              + Term has NTs
HN History Note            CN  Catalogers Note       --[ ] May subdivide

**Religious retreats (cont.)**
    study, and instruction under a director.
    Includes activities and structures.
  CN  Double index under type of structure for
    images that focus on structures.
  UF  Retreats, Religious
  RT  Private camps
    Religion
    Religious communities
    Religious groups
    Religious meetings
**Religious sects**
  USE Religious groups
**Religious services**
    --[country or state]--[city]
  UF  Church services
    Mass, Catholic
    Prayer meetings
    Services, Religious
  BT  Religious meetings
    Rites & ceremonies
  NT  Camp meetings
    Outdoor religious services
  RT  Baptisms
    Benedictions
    Choirboys
    Choirs (Music)
    Clergy
    Communion
    Preaching
    Religious facilities
    Sabbaths
**Relocation camps**
    --[country or state]--[city]
  UF  Camps, Internment
    Internment camps
  BT  Detention facilities
  RT  Concentration camps
    Evacuations
    Prisoners
    Settlements
**Remarques**
  CN  TGM II term.
**Remedies**
  USE Medicines
**Reminiscing**
  UF  Memory
    Recalling
  RT  Conversation
    Storytelling
    Thinking
**Remodeling**
    --[country or state]--[city]
  PN  For situations in which an existing
    structure or its features are clearly being
    restructured or converted.
  UF  Reconstruction
  RT  Conservation & restoration
    Construction
    Recycled structures
**Removals**
  USE Deportations

**Remuneration**
  USE Wages
**Renderings**
  CN  TGM II term.
Renown
  USE Fame
Reorganization of government
  USE Government reorganization
Repair
  USE Maintenance & repair
**Reparations**
    --[nationality]--[country]
  PN  Compensation, either in money or in
    materials, commodities, equipment, etc.,
    payable by a nation for damages and loss
    sustained as a result of aggression.
  CN  Subdivide by nationality of country paying
    reparations; subdivide geographically by
    country receiving reparations.
  UF  Compensation for war damage
    War compensations
    War damage compensation
  BT  Economic aspects of war
  RT  War claims
**Repatriation**
    --[country or state]
  CN  Subdivide geographically by place to
    which people are returning.
  BT  Emigration & immigration
  RT  Aliens
    Citizenship
    Exiles
    Homecomings
    Refugees
**Reporters**
    --[nationality]--[country or state]--[city]
  UF  Correspondents
    Newspaper reporters
  BT  Journalists
  RT  Broadcasting
Repositories
  USE Archives
Representation, Political
  USE Political representation
Reproaching
  USE Blaming
Reproduction of sound
  USE Sound recording
**Reproductions**
  CN  TGM II term.
  UF  Copies
**Reproductive prints**
  CN  TGM II term.
**Reptiles**
    --[country or state]
  BT  Animals
  NT  Alligators
    Crocodiles
    Dinosaurs
    Lizards
    Snakes
    Turtles

BT Broader term        RT Related term        PN Public Note
NT Narrower term      UF Used for        + Term has NTs
HN History Note        CN Catalogers Note    --[ ] May subdivide

**Reredos**
USE Altarpieces

**Rescue work**
--[nationality]--[country or state]--[city]
PN  For the subject of rescue work in general and images that focus on the operations of rescue workers in accidents or disasters. Search under RESCUES for activities in freeing persons or animals from confinement, danger, and evil.
CN  Subdivide by nationality of those conducting the rescue. Used in a note under RESCUES.
NT  Lifesaving +
Mine rescue work
Search & rescue operations
RT  Accidents
Disaster relief
Disaster victims
Disasters
Rescues
Victims

**Rescues**
--[country or state]--[city]
PN  For activities involved in freeing persons or animals from confinement, danger, and evil. Search under RESCUE WORK for the subject of rescue work in general and images that focus on the operations of rescue workers in accidents or disasters.
CN  Used in a note under RESCUE WORK.
RT  Danger
Rescue work

**Research facilities**
--[country or state]--[city]
BT  Facilities
NT  Astronomical observatories
Laboratories

Reservations, Indian
USE Indian reservations

Reservations, Military
USE Military reservations

Reserves, State
USE State parks & reserves

**Reservoirs**
--[country or state]--[city]
BT  Hydraulic facilities
RT  Dams
Lakes & ponds
Waterworks

Resettlement camps
USE Refugee camps

Residence halls
USE Dormitories

Residences
USE Dwellings

**Residential facilities**
--[country or state]--[city]
BT  Facilities
NT  Dwellings +
Estates
Ethnic neighborhoods

**Residential facilities (cont.)**
Slums
RT  Carriage houses
Garages
Huts
Public accommodation facilities
Settlements

**Residential streets**
--[country or state]--[city]
PN  For views of streets in residential areas. Search under DWELLINGS for images that focus on buildings.
BT  Streets
RT  Dwellings

Resignation from office
CN  Used only as a subdivision with names of persons (Appendix B).

**Resignations**
PN  Search also under the subdivisions --RESIGNATION FROM OFFICE and --ABDICATION used with names of persons (Appendix B).
UF  Quits
Terminations of employment
RT  Dismissal of employees
Employment
Retirements

Resins
USE Gums & resins

Resin-coated paper photoprints
USE Resin-coated paper prints

**Resin-coated paper prints**
CN  TGM II term.
UF  RC paper prints
Resin-coated paper photoprints

Resistance movements
USE Opposition (Political science)
Rebellions
Underground movements

Resistance to government
USE Civil disobedience

Resistance, Passive
USE Passive resistance

**Resolutions**
PN  Formal expressions of opinion, will, or intent by an official body or assembled group.
UF  Legislative resolutions
RT  Legislation
Meetings

Resolutions, New Year
USE New Year resolutions

Resort cottages
USE Cabins

**Resorts**
--[country or state]--[city]
PN  Includes activities and structures.
CN  Double index under HOTELS for images that focus on buildings. Used in a note under HOTELS.
BT  Sports & recreation facilities
RT  Beaches

BT Broader term      RT Related term      PN Public Note
NT Narrower term      UF Used for      + Term has NTs
HN History Note      CN Catalogers Note      --[ ] May subdivide

**Resorts (cont.)**
        Cabins
        Casinos
        Health resorts
        Hotels
        Leisure
        Public accommodation facilities
        Tourist camps & hostels

Rest
  USE Leisure
        Sleeping

Rest areas
  USE Rest stops

**Rest homes**
        --[country or state]--[city]
  PN  Establishments that provide housing and general care for the aged or convalescents.
  UF  Convalescent homes
        Homes (Institutions)
        Old age homes
        Sheltered care homes
  BT  Health care facilities
  NT  Soldiers' homes
  RT  Aged persons
        Institutional care
        Nursing homes
        Shut-ins

**Rest stops**
        --[country or state]--[city]
  PN  For pauses in journeys and the sites where such pauses occur; includes activities and structures.
  UF  Rest areas
        Roadside rest areas
  BT  Transportation facilities
  RT  Leisure
        Travel

**Restaurant workers**
        --[country or state]--[city]
  BT  People
  RT  Cooks
        Restaurants
        Soda jerks
        Waiters
        Waitresses

**Restaurants**
        --[country or state]--[city]
  PN  Includes activities and structures.
  UF  Lunchrooms
        Tea rooms
  BT  Eating & drinking facilities
  NT  Automats
        Cafes
        Cafeterias
        Diners (Restaurants)
        Fast food restaurants +
        Snack bars
  RT  Bars
        Beer halls
        Canteens (Wartime, emergency, etc.)
        Delicatessens
        Employee eating facilities

**Restaurants (cont.)**
        Hotels
        Nightclubs
        Restaurant workers
        Soda fountains
        Taverns (Inns)
        Waiters
        Waitresses

Restoration
  USE Conservation & restoration

Restraints, Physical
  USE Physical restraints

**Restrikes**
  CN  TGM II term.

Restrooms
  USE Bathrooms

Rest, Days of
  USE Sabbaths

Retables
  USE Altarpieces

Retail stores
  USE Stores & shops

**Retail trade strikes**
        --[country or state]--[city]
  UF  Clerks' strikes
  BT  Strikes

**Retaining walls**
        --[country or state]--[city]
  BT  Walls

Retirement pensions
  USE Pensions

**Retirements**
        --[country or state]--[city]
  RT  Age & employment
        Aged persons
        Employment
        Leisure
        Pensions
        Resignations

**Retorts (Equipment)**
  BT  Equipment
  RT  Distilling industries
        Gasoline
        Stills (Distilleries)

Retreats, Military
  USE Military retreats

Retreats, Religious
  USE Religious retreats

Returns (Merchandise)
  USE Merchandise exchanges

**Reunions**
        --[country or state]--[city]
  PN  For the coming together of people to mark a former or ongoing association. Search under HOMECOMINGS for occasions when people return to their families or homeland after a long absence. Search also under COMMEMORATION used with names of wars (Appendix C).
  CN  Used in a note under HOMECOMINGS.
  HN  Changed 5/91 from non-postable term. For earlier cataloging, search under

---

BT Broader term
NT Narrower term
HN History Note

RT Related term
UF Used for
CN Catalogers Note

PN Public Note
+ Term has NTs
--[ ] May subdivide

**Reunions (cont.)**
    ANNIVERSARIES or CELEBRATIONS.
  BT   Events
  RT   Anniversaries
       Celebrations
       Commemoration
       Homecomings
**Revenge**
  UF   Vengeance
  BT   Ethics
Revenue stamps
  USE Tax stamps
Reversible head prints
  USE Metamorphic pictures
**Reviewing stands**
    --[country or state]--[city]
  PN   A seating area, sometimes covered, from
       which officials view parades and processions.
  RT   Grandstands
       Parades & processions
Reviews, Military
  USE Military parades & ceremonies
       Naval parades & ceremonies
**Revivals**
    --[country or state]--[city]
  PN   Includes activities and sites.
  UF   Evangelistic meetings
  BT   Religious meetings
  RT   Camp meetings
       Evangelists
**Revolutionaries**
    --[country or state]--[city]
  PN   For those who advocate fundamental
       change in political, economic, and/or social
       structures, often associated with overthrow of
       established government.
  CN   Used in a note under REVOLUTIONS.
  HN   Prior to 5/1992 the term
       REVOLUTIONISTS was used.
  UF   Revolutionists
  BT   Activists
  RT   Rebels
       Revolutions
Revolutionary posters
  USE Protest posters
Revolutionists
  USE Revolutionaries
**Revolutions**
    --[country or state]--[city]
  PN   For sudden, fundamental change in
       political, economic, or social structures, often
       associated with overthrow of established
       government. Search under
       REVOLUTIONARIES for images that focus
       on real persons.
  BT   Events
  RT   Civil wars
       Counterrevolutions
       Opposition (Political science)
       Rebellions
       Revolutionaries
       Terrorism

**Revolutions (cont.)**
    War
Revolvers
  USE Handguns
Revolving cupolas (Warships)
  USE Turret ships
**Revolving doors**
    --[country or state]--[city]
  BT   Doors & doorways
Reward posters
  USE Wanted posters
Rewards
  USE Awards
**Rewards of merit**
  CN   TGM II term.
  UF   Awards of merit
Rewards & prizes
  USE Awards
Re-creations
  USE Reconstructions
**Rhinoceroses**
    --[country or state]
  BT   Animals
**Rhododendrons**
  CN   Double index under FLOWERS when the
       flowers are cut.
  BT   Shrubs
  NT   Azaleas
**Rhubarb**
    --[country or state]--[city]
  UF   Garden rhubarb
       Pie plants
       Pieplants
  BT   Plants
Rhyolite
  USE Volcanic rock
Ribbon badges
  USE Badges
Ribbon-cutting ceremonies
  USE Dedications
**Rice**
    --[country or state]--[city]
  BT   Grains
  RT   Rice industry
       Rice plantations
**Rice industry**
    --[country or state]--[city]
  PN   Includes activities and structures.
  CN   Double index under INDUSTRIAL
       FACILITIES (or NTs) for images that focus
       on facilities.
  UF   Rice trade
  BT   Grain industry
  RT   Rice
       Rice plantations
**Rice paddies**
    --[country or state]--[city]
  PN   For images that focus on rice fields.
  UF   Paddy fields
  BT   Rice plantations
**Rice plantations**
    --[country or state]--[city]

BT Broader term           RT Related term           PN Public Note
NT Narrower term         UF Used for               + Term has NTs
HN History Note           CN Catalogers Note       --[ ] May subdivide

**Rice plantations (cont.)**
- PN Includes activities and structures.
- CN As appropriate, double index under HARVESTING.
- BT Plantations
- NT Rice paddies
- RT Rice
- Rice industry

Rice trade
- USE Rice industry

Riches
- USE Wealth

Ricking
- USE Bundling (Packing)

**Rickshaws**
- --[nationality]--[country or state]--[city]
- UF Jinrikishas
- BT Wheeled chairs

Rides, Amusement
- USE Amusement rides

Ridges
- USE Mountains

**Riding**
- --[country or state]--[city]
- CN As appropriate, double index under animal being ridden.
- NT Horseback riding +
- Trick riding
- RT Sports
- Transportation

Riding rapids
- USE Shooting rapids

Riding, Freight car
- USE Freighthopping

**Rifle ranges**
- UF Target ranges
- BT Sites
- RT Shooting
- Targets (Sports)

**Rifles**
- PN For firearms that are fired from the shoulder.
- UF Carbines
- Muskets
- Shotguns
- Shoulder arms
- BT Firearms
- RT Bayonets

Rigging
- USE Ship equipment & rigging

**Right of property**
- --[country or state]--[city]
- UF Private property rights
- Property rights
- BT Civil liberties
- RT Land tenure

**Right to asylum**
- --[country or state]--[city]
- UF Asylum, Right to
- BT Law & legal affairs
- RT Refugees

Right to know

Right to know (cont.)
- USE Freedom of information

Rights of employees
- USE Employee rights

Rights of states
- USE State rights

Rights, Civil
- USE Civil rights

**Rings**
- UF Finger rings
- BT Jewelry

**Ring-around-a-rosy**
- BT Games
- RT Singing

Rinks
- USE Skating rinks

**Riot control**
- --[country or state]--[city]
- PN Civil or military actions or involvement to prevent, contain, or suppress group acts of violence or civil disorders.
- UF Riot prevention
- RT Nightsticks
- Police
- Riots

Riot prevention
- USE Riot control

**Riots**
- --[country or state]--[city]
- PN Search also under the subdivision --RIOTS & DEMONSTRATIONS used with corporate bodies and named events (Appendix D).
- UF Civil disorders
- BT Events
- NT Prison riots
- Race riots
- RT Demonstrations
- Riot control
- Violence

Riots & demonstrations
- CN Used only as a subdivision with corporate bodies and named events (Appendix D).

**Rites & ceremonies**
- --[country or state]--[city]
- PN Search also under the subdivision --SPIRITUAL LIFE used with names of ethnic, racial, and regional groups, and with classes of persons (Appendix A). Search also under the subdivision --RITES & CEREMONIES used with corporate bodies and named events (Appendix D).
- UF Ceremonies
- Religious celebrations
- Worship
- BT Manners & customs
- NT Auto-da-fé sermons
- Baptisms
- Benedictions
- Communion
- Confirmations
- Coronations
- Dedications +

---

Rites & ceremonies (cont.)
>> Exorcism
>> Founders' Day commemorations
>> Funeral rites & ceremonies +
>> Ghost dance
>> Graduation ceremonies
>> Inaugurations +
>> Initiation rites
>> Knighting
>> Last rites
>> Memorial rites & ceremonies
>> Oaths
>> Pledges of allegiance
>> Religious services +
>> Sacrifices
>> Snake dance
>> Tea ceremonies
>> Toppings out
>> Tree planting ceremonies
>> Weddings +
> RT Ablution fountains
>> Adoration
>> Awards
>> Celebrations
>> Ceremonial dancers
>> Crowds
>> Dancing
>> Durbars
>> Fasts
>> Incense
>> Masks
>> May poles
>> Medals
>> Military decorations
>> Military parades & ceremonies
>> Naval parades & ceremonies
>> Pageants
>> Receptions
>> Religion
>> Religious processions
>> Sandpaintings
>> Spiritual leaders
>> Stations of the Cross
>> Sweatbaths

Rivalry
> USE Competition (Psychology)

River channels
> USE Channels

River deltas
> USE Deltas

River fords
> USE Fords (Stream crossings)

River valleys
> USE Valleys

Riverboats
> USE Barges
>> Flatboats
>> Steamboats
>> Stern wheelers

Riverfronts
> USE Waterfronts

**Rivers**

Rivers (cont.)
>> --[country or state]--[city]
> UF Estuaries
> BT Streams
> RT Deltas
>> Portages
>> Rapids
>> Valleys

**Riveting**
>> --[country or state]--[city]
> RT Metalworking

Road accidents
> USE Traffic accidents

**Road construction**
>> --[country or state]--[city]
> BT Civil engineering
>> Construction
> RT Bridge construction
>> Graders (Earthmoving machinery)
>> Road rollers
>> Roads

Road graders
> USE Graders (Earthmoving machinery)

**Road rollers**
> UF Steamrollers
> BT Machinery
> RT Road construction

Road signs
> USE Traffic signs & signals

**Roads**
>> --[country or state]
> PN For thoroughfares outside of cities, towns, and villages. Search under STREETS for thoroughfares in cities, towns, and villages.
> CN Used in a note under STREETS.
> UF Highways
>> Thoroughfares
> BT Transportation facilities
> NT Causeways
>> Corduroy roads
>> Crossroads
>> Driveways
>> Express highways +
>> Plank roads
>> Roman roads
>> Skid roads
>> Toll roads
> RT Lovers' lanes
>> Milestones
>> Portages
>> Road construction
>> Ruts
>> Street cleaning
>> Streets
>> Trails & paths
>> Tunnels

Roadside architecture
> USE Mimetic buildings

Roadside rest areas
> USE Rest stops

Roadside stands
> USE Vending stands

---

BT Broader term
NT Narrower term
HN History Note

RT Related term
UF Used for
CN Catalogers Note

PN Public Note
+ Term has NTs
--[ ] May subdivide

**Robberies**

--[country or state]--[city]
- UF Burglaries
  Holdups
  Looting
  Muggings
  Plundering
  Stealing
  Thefts
- BT Crimes
- NT Art thefts
- RT Children stealing

Robbers
  USE Criminals

**Robins**

--[country or state]
- BT Birds

**Robots**
- UF Automatons
- BT Machinery
- RT Computers

Rock and roll posters
  USE Rock posters

**Rock art**

--[country or state]--[city]
- PN Engraved or painted designs on natural
  rock surfaces. Search also under subdivisions
  --ARTS & CRAFTS,
  --COMMUNICATION, and --SPIRITUAL
  LIFE used with names of ethnic, racial, and
  regional groups, and with classes of persons
  (Appendix A).
- UF Petroglyphs
  Pictographs
- BT Art
- RT Cave drawings
  Hieroglyphics

Rock bands
  USE Rock groups

Rock cairns
  USE Cairns

Rock crystal
  USE Quartz

Rock fences
  USE Stone walls

**Rock formations**

--[country or state]--[city]
- UF Arches, Rock
  Bridges, Natural
  Formations, Rock
  Natural bridges
  Pillars, Rock
- BT Land
- RT Boulders
  Caves
  Rocks
  Volcanic rock

**Rock groups**

--[nationality]--[country or state]--[city]
- UF Rock bands
  Rock & roll bands
- BT Bands

**Rock posters**
- CN TGM II term.
- UF Rock and roll posters

Rock quarrying
  USE Quarrying

Rock throwing
  USE Stoning

Rock & roll bands
  USE Rock groups

**Rock & roll dancing**

--[country or state]--[city]
- BT Dancing

Rocket flight
  USE Space flight

**Rockets**

--[nationality]
- PN Includes powered and guided missiles.
- UF Guided missiles
  Missiles, Guided
- RT Aircraft
  Artillery (Weaponry)
  Space flight

**Rocking chairs**
- BT Chairs

Rocking horses
  USE Hobby horses

**Rocks**

--[country or state]--[city]
- NT Volcanic rock
- RT Minerals
  Rock formations
  Stone cutting
  Stone quarrying
  Stonework

**Rodent control**

--[country or state]--[city]
- BT Pest control
- NT Ratcatching
- RT Mousetraps
  Rodents

**Rodents**

--[country or state]
- BT Animals
- NT Beavers
  Marmots +
  Mice
  Porcupines
  Prairie dogs
  Rabbits
  Rats
  Squirrels
- RT Rodent control

**Rodeos**

--[country or state]--[city]
- BT Events
  Sports
- RT Broncos
  Cattle
  Circuses & shows
  Cowboys
  Cowgirls
  Horses

BT Broader term            RT Related term            PN Public Note
NT Narrower term           UF Used for                + Term has NTs
HN History Note            CN Catalogers Note          --[ ] May subdivide

**Rodeos (cont.)**
      Trick riding
Roller chairs
  USE Wheeled chairs
**Roller coasters**
      --[country or state]--[city]
  BT  Amusement rides
**Roller skating**
      --[country or state]--[city]
  UF  Roller-skating
  BT  Skating
      Sports
  RT  Skaters
Roller-skating
  USE Roller skating
Rolling papers
  USE Cigarette papers
Rolls
  USE Scrolls
**Roman roads**
      --[country]--[city]
  BT  Roads
**Roman temples**
      --[country or state]--[city]
  BT  Temples
**Romances**
  PN  For images representing dramatic
      productions or scenes (theatrical, film, radio,
      or television) which focus on the love or
      courting relationship of couples.
  RT  Couples
      Courtship
      Love
      Motion pictures
      Radio broadcasting
      Television broadcasting
      Theatrical productions
Roof collapses
  USE Building failures
**Roof gardens**
      --[country or state]--[city]
  UF  Rooftop gardens
  BT  Gardens
  RT  Roofs
**Roof trusses**
      --[country or state]--[city]
  BT  Trusses
  RT  Roofs
**Roofing tiles**
  BT  Tiles
  RT  Roofs
**Roofs**
      --[country or state]--[city]
  BT  Architectural elements
  NT  Canopies
      Cantilevered roofs
      Gambrel roofs
      Hip roofs
      Mansard roofs
      Marquees
      Sawtooth roofs
      Thatched roofs

**Roofs (cont.)**
  RT  Balustrades
      Cupolas
      Domes
      Dormers
      Downspouts
      Finials
      Gables
      Gargoyles
      Gutters (Roofs)
      Lanterns (Architecture)
      Penthouses
      Rafters
      Roof gardens
      Roof trusses
      Roofing tiles
      Skylights
      Spires
      Terraces
      Vaults (Architecture)
Rooftop gardens
  USE Roof gardens
**Rookeries**
      --[country or state]--[city]
  PN  Breeding grounds or colonies of mammals
      or birds.
  UF  Breeding grounds
  RT  Animals
Rooming houses
  USE Lodging houses
Rooms
  USE Rooms & spaces
**Rooms & spaces**
      --[country or state]--[city]
  UF  Rooms
      Spaces
  BT  Building divisions
  NT  Atriums
      Balconies
      Courtyards
      Decks (Rooms & spaces)
      Interiors +
      Loggias
      Passageways
      Patios
      Porches +
      Porte cocheres
      Porticoes (Porches)
      Quadrangles (Courtyards)
      Stages (Platforms)
      Sunspaces
**Roosters**
  BT  Chickens
**Rope industry**
      --[country or state]--[city]
  PN  Includes activities and structures.
  CN  Double index under INDUSTRIAL
      FACILITIES (or NTs) for images that focus
      on facilities.
  UF  Ropemaking industry
  BT  Industry
  RT  Fibers

---

BT Broader term          RT Related term          PN Public Note
NT Narrower term        UF Used for            + Term has NTs
HN History Note          CN Catalogers Note      --[ ] May subdivide

**Rope industry (cont.)**
        Jute
        Ropes
        Twine industry
**Rope skipping**
        --[country or state]--[city]
  UF  Jumping rope
        Skipping rope
  RT  Children playing
        Jumping
        Ropes
Ropemaking industry
  USE Rope industry
**Ropes**
  RT  Nooses
        Physical restraints
        Rope industry
        Rope skipping
        Roping
        Ship equipment & rigging
        Tug of war
        Twine
**Roping**
  PN  Binding, fastening, or tieing with rope or
        cord; capturing by means of rope.
  UF  Lassoing
  RT  Ropes
**Roses**
        --[country or state]--[city]
  BT  Flowers
**Rosettes**
        --[country or state]--[city]
  PN  Ornamental disks consisting of leafage or
        a floral design resembling a rose, usually in
        relief.
  BT  Architectural decorations & ornaments
Rosin
  USE Gums & resins
Rosters
  USE Registers
Rostrums
  USE Stages (Platforms)
Rotation of crops
  USE Crop rotation
**Rotogravures**
  CN  TGM II term.
  UF  Gravures
**Rotundas**
        --[country or state]--[city]
  PN  For round buildings, especially ones
        covered by domes; also, large round rooms
        and large central areas (as in hotels).
  RT  Circular buildings
        Circular rooms
        Domes
        Interiors
Round buildings
  USE Circular buildings
**Round dancing**
        --[country or state]--[city]
  BT  Dancing
Round rooms

Round rooms (cont.)
  USE Circular rooms
**Roundels**
        --[country or state]--[city]
  PN  Circular panels usually sculptured or
        otherwise decorated, set as decorative
        elements in an architectural context. For
        similarly shaped and decorated motifs in
        two-dimensional media, use MEDALLIONS
        (ORNAMENT AREAS).
  BT  Architectural elements
Roundhouses
  USE Railroad roundhouses
Round-ups
  USE Cattle herding
**Row houses**
        --[country or state]--[city]
  UF  Rowhouses
        Town houses (Attached houses)
        Townhouses (Attached houses)
  BT  Houses
**Rowboats**
        --[nationality]--[country or state]--[city]
  BT  Boats
  RT  Lifeboats
        Longboats
        Rowing
        Rowing races
**Rowers**
        --[country or state]--[city]
  CN  Geographical subdivision indicates place
        where team or rower is based.
  UF  Oarsmen
  BT  Athletes
  RT  Racing shells
        Rowing
        Rowing races
Rowhouses
  USE Row houses
**Rowing**
        --[country or state]--[city]
  PN  For activity of rowing where vessel is not
        a rowboat, or where vessel is not visible.
        Search under TEAM ROWING for crew or
        team rowing and under ROWING RACES
        for races or regattas involving rowing. Search
        under ROWERS for rowers not engaged in
        the activity.
  UF  Sculling
  BT  Sports
  NT  Team rowing
  RT  Racing shells
        Regattas
        Rowboats
        Rowers
**Rowing races**
        --[country or state]--[city]
  HN  Changed 3/1989 from non-postable term
        (use REGATTAS).
  UF  Sculling
  BT  Regattas
  RT  Racing shells

---

BT Broader term                  RT Related term                  PN Public Note
NT Narrower term               UF Used for                     + Term has NTs
HN History Note                 CN Catalogers Note              --[ ] May subdivide

**Rowing races (cont.)**
>    Rowboats
>    Rowers
>    Team rowing

Royal visits
>    USE Visits of state

Royalty
>    USE Rulers

**Rubber industry**
>    --[country or state]--[city]
- PN Includes activities and structures.
- CN Double index under INDUSTRIAL
   FACILITIES (or NTs) for images that focus
   on facilities.
- BT Industry
- RT Artificial rubber industry
   Rubber plantations
   Tire industry

**Rubber plantations**
>    --[country or state]--[city]
- PN Includes activities and structures.
- CN As appropriate, double index under
   HARVESTING.
- BT Plantations
- RT Rubber industry
   Rubber plants

**Rubber plants**
>    --[country or state]--[city]
- BT Plants
- RT Rubber plantations

**Rubber stamps**
- UF Stamps, Rubber
- BT Office equipment & supplies

**Rubbings**
- CN TGM II term.

Rubbish
>    USE Refuse

**Ruby mining**
>    --[country or state]--[city]
- PN Includes activities and sites.
- BT Mining
- RT Gems

**Rugby**
>    --[country or state]--[city]
- PN Includes organizations and activities.
- BT Sports

Rugs
>    USE Floor coverings

**Ruins**
>    --[country or state]--[city]
- PN For remains of structures not of ancient
   times that have been destroyed or are in a
   state of great disrepair or decay. Search under
   ARCHAEOLOGICAL SITES for ancient
   structures still largely intact, remains of
   ancient structures, and any active
   excavations. Search under ABANDONED
   BUILDINGS for vacant, possibly dilapidated
   buildings. Search under DISASTERS or WAR
   DAMAGE for structures ruined by particular
   events.
- CN Used in a note under ABANDONED

**Ruins (cont.)**
>    BUILDINGS and ARCHAEOLOGICAL
>    SITES.
- BT Sites
- RT Abandoned buildings
   Antiquities
   Archaeological sites
   Ghost towns

**Rulers**
>    --[country]
- UF Monarchs
   Royalty
   Sovereigns
- BT People associated with politics &
   government
- NT Dictators
   Emperors
   Empresses
   Kings
   Popes
   Princes
   Princesses
   Queens
   Sultans
   Tribal chiefs
- RT Coronations
   Crowns
   Heads of state
   Monarchy
   Nobility
   Politics & government
   Thrones

Rules of order
>    USE Parliamentary practice

Rule, Two-thirds
>    USE Two-thirds rule

**Rumor**
- UF Gossip
- RT Propaganda
   Public opinion

Rumpus rooms
>    USE Playrooms

Rumrunning
>    USE Prohibition

Runaway slaves
>    USE Fugitive slaves

**Runes**
- BT Writing systems

**Runners (Sports)**
>    --[country or state]--[city]
- BT Athletes
- RT Running
   Running races

**Running**
>    --[country or state]--[city]
- UF Jogging
- BT Locomotion
- RT Chasing
   Runners (Sports)
   Running races

**Running races**
>    --[country or state]--[city]

---

BT Broader term     RT Related term     PN Public Note
NT Narrower term     UF Used for     + Term has NTs
HN History Note     CN Catalogers Note     --[ ] May subdivide

**Running races (cont.)**
- BT Racing
  - Track athletics
- NT Hurdle racing
- RT Relay racing
  - Runners (Sports)
  - Running
  - Sack racing
  - Three-legged racing

Running rapids
- USE Shooting rapids

**Runways (Aeronautics)**
- --[country or state]--[city]
- BT Transportation facilities
- RT Airports

Rural life
- USE Country life

**Rural schools**
- --[country or state]--[city]
- PN Includes activities and structures.
- BT Schools
- RT One-room schools

**Rural women**
- --[country or state]--[city]
- BT Women

Russian Orthodox churches
- USE Orthodox churches

**Rustic work**
- --[country or state]--[city]
- PN Summerhouses or furniture for outdoor use made of rough limbs of trees.
- RT Landscape architecture facilities
  - Outdoor furniture
  - Woodworking

**Rustication**
- --[country or state]--[city]
- PN Surface pattern giving the effect of large blocks with deep, wide joints.
- RT Masonry
  - Stone cutting

**Ruts**
- --[country or state]--[city]
- RT Holes
  - Roads

**Rye**
- --[country or state]--[city]
- BT Grains

Sabattier effect photographs
- USE Solarization photographs

**Sabbaths**
- --[country or state]--[city]
- PN For Saturday or Sunday observance and activities on the day of rest.
- UF Days of rest
  - Lord's Day
  - Rest, Days of
  - Seventh-Day observance
  - Sundays
  - Worship days
- BT Manners & customs
- RT Leisure
  - Preaching

**Sabbaths (cont.)**
- Religious services

**Sabotage**
- --[country or state]--[city]
- PN For malicious waste or destruction of an employer's property by workers, as during labor troubles; and for destructive actions by civilians or enemy agents within a country, designed to impede the armed forces.
- UF Damage to property
  - Destruction of property
  - Property damage
- BT Crimes
- RT Guerrillas
  - Spying
  - Strikes
  - Terrorism
  - War destruction & pillage

**Sack racing**
- --[country or state]--[city]
- BT Racing
- RT Games
  - Running races

Sacks
- USE Bags

Sacrament of the Altar
- USE Communion

**Sacrifices**
- --[country or state]--[city]
- UF Burnt offerings
- BT Rites & ceremonies
- RT Executions

**Sacristies**
- --[country or state]--[city]
- PN Rooms in churches where vessels and vestments are kept.
- BT Interiors
- RT Churches

Saddle making
- USE Saddlery

**Saddlery**
- --[country or state]--[city]
- UF Harness making
  - Saddle making
- RT Handicraft
  - Horses
  - Leather industry
  - Saddles

**Saddles**
- RT Horses
  - Saddlery

Sadirons
- USE Irons (Pressing)

**Sadness**
- UF Dejection
  - Despondency
  - Sorrow
  - Unhappiness
- BT Mental states
- RT Depression (Mental state)
  - Distress
  - Grief

BT Broader term      RT Related term      PN Public Note
NT Narrower term      UF Used for      + Term has NTs
HN History Note      CN Catalogers Note      --[ ] May subdivide

Sadness (cont.)
      Happiness
Safaris
      --[country]
  BT  Travel
  RT  Big game hunting
Safes
  UF  Depositories
  BT  Equipment
  RT  Banks
      Locks (Hardware)
      Vaults (Strong rooms)
Safety
  UF  Emergency preparedness
  RT  Accidents
      Air traffic control
      Automobile inspections
      Children & safety
      Danger
      Evacuations
      Fire prevention
      Health
      Lifesaving
      Safety equipment
      School safety patrols
      Self-defense
Safety equipment
  BT  Equipment
  NT  Fire alarms
      Fire escapes
      Fire extinguishers
      Life preservers
  RT  Safety
      Security systems
Safety film negatives
  CN  TGM II term.
Sailboat racing
      --[country or state]--[city]
  HN  Changed 3/1989 from non-postable term
      (Use REGATTAS).
  BT  Regattas
  RT  Sailboats
Sailboats
      --[nationality]--[country or state]--[city]
  UF  Sailing
  BT  Boats
  RT  Children sailing boats
      Iceboats
      Sailboat racing
      Yachts
Sailfish
      --[country or state]
  BT  Fish
Sailing
  USE Sailboats
Sailing cards
  CN  TGM II term.
  UF  Ship cards
Sailing ships
      --[nationality]--[country or state]--[city]
  BT  Ships
  NT  Clipper ships

Sailing ships (cont.)
      Slave ships
      Viking ships
Sailors
      --[nationality]--[country or state]--[city]
  PN  For personnel of all types of vessels.
      Double index under the service for military
      personnel.
  HN  Changed 9/94 from SEAMEN.
  UF  Crews
      Mariners
      Merchant seamen
      Seamen
  BT  People associated with transportation
  NT  Pirates
      Ship captains
  RT  Fishermen
      Military personnel
      Navies
      Shellbacks
      Vessels
Saints
  BT  People associated with religion
  RT  Christianity
      Heroes
      Religion
      Shrines
Salaries
  USE Wages
Salary policy
  USE Wage-price policy
Sales catalogs
  CN  TGM I term.
  UF  Commercial catalogs
Sales exchanges
  USE Merchandise exchanges
Salesmanship
  USE Selling
Sales, Secondhand
  USE Secondhand sales
Salmon
      --[country or state]
  BT  Fish
Salons (Social spaces)
      --[country or state]--[city]
  UF  Saloons (Social spaces)
  BT  Interiors
  RT  Parlors
Salons, Beauty
  USE Beauty shops
Saloons
  USE Bars
Saloons (Social spaces)
  USE Salons (Social spaces)
Salt industry
      --[country or state]--[city]
  PN  Includes activities and structures.
  CN  Double index under INDUSTRIAL
      FACILITIES (or NTs) for images that focus
      on facilities.
  BT  Industry
  RT  Minerals

---

BT  Broader term        RT  Related term        PN Public Note
NT  Narrower term      UF  Used for           + Term has NTs
HN History Note        CN Catalogers Note      --[ ] May subdivide

**Salt industry (cont.)**
Salt mining
**Salt mining**
--[country or state]--[city]
PN   Includes activities and sites.
BT   Mining
RT   Salt industry
Salt prints
USE Salted paper prints
Salted paper photoprints
USE Salted paper prints
**Salted paper prints**
CN   TGM II term.
UF   Salt prints
Salted paper photoprints
**Salutations**
--[country or state]--[city]
UF   Greetings
Hellos
Introductions (Greetings)
BT   Manners & customs
RT   Arrivals & departures
Etiquette
Farewells
**Saluting**
--[country or state]--[city]
UF   Military courtesy
BT   Etiquette
NT   Flag salutes
**Salvage**
--[country or state]--[city]
PN   Saving or securing property, as well as
property saved.
UF   Scrap
RT   Junkyards
Marine accidents
Recycling
Scrap drives
Shipwrecks
Samisens
USE Shamisens
**Samovars**
BT   Containers
Tableware
RT   Tea
Teapots
**Sampans**
--[country or state]--[city]
BT   Boats
**Sample books**
CN   TGM II term.
UF   Specimen books
**Samples**
CN   TGM II term.
**Sanatoriums**
--[country or state]--[city]
PN   Establishments for the treatment of the
sick, especially if suffering from chronic
disease, e.g., alcoholism, tuberculosis,
requiring protracted care. Includes activities
and structures.
UF   Sanitariums

**Sanatoriums (cont.)**
BT   Health care facilities
RT   Health resorts
Hospitals
Quarantines
Sand drifts
USE Dunes
Sand dunes
USE Dunes
Sand paintings
USE Sandpaintings
**Sand sculpture**
BT   Sculpture
RT   Beaches
**Sandbars**
--[country or state]--[city]
UF   Bars (Sand)
BT   Land
RT   Seas
Streams
**Sandpaintings**
--[country or state]--[city]
PN   Search also under the subdivision --ARTS
& CRAFTS used with names of ethnic,
racial, and regional groups and with classes
of persons (Appendix A).
UF   Dry paintings
Navajo sandpaintings
Sand paintings
RT   Art
Religion
Rites & ceremonies
**Sandpipers**
--[country or state]
BT   Birds
**Sandstone quarrying**
--[country or state]--[city]
BT   Quarrying
**Sandwich boards**
PN   Two boards, usually hinged, designed to
be hung from the shoulders for advertising
purposes.
BT   Advertisements
Signs
**Sandwiches**
--[country or state]--[city]
BT   Food
RT   Bread
Sanitariums
USE Sanatoriums
Sanitary fittings
USE Plumbing fixtures
**Sanitation**
--[country or state]--[city]
NT   Refuse disposal +
Sewerage
RT   Health
Hygiene
Plumbing systems
Pollution
Ventilation
**Sarcophagi**

---

BT  Broader term                    RT  Related term                    PN Public Note
NT  Narrower term                   UF  Used for                        + Term has NTs
HN  History Note                    CN  Catalogers Note                 --[ ] May subdivide

**Sarcophagi (cont.)**
    --[country or state]--[city]
  PN  Stone coffins, often ornamented with
       sculpture and usually placed in a church,
       tomb, or vault.
  BT  Coffins
  RT  Tombs & sepulchral monuments
**Sardine cans**
  BT  Cans
**Sarsaparilla**
  BT  Carbonated beverages
  RT  Patent medicines
**Sash windows**
    --[country or state]--[city]
  BT  Windows
Satan
  USE Demons
Satellite vehicles
  USE Artificial satellites
**Satires**
  CN  TGM II term.
Satyagraha
  USE Passive resistance
**Sausages**
    --[country or state]--[city]
  BT  Meat
  NT  Frankfurters
**Saving & investment**
    --[country or state]--[city]
  UF  Investment
  BT  Business & finance
  RT  Bonds (Financial records)
       Wealth
Sawbucks
  USE Sawhorses
**Sawhorses**
  UF  Sawbucks
  BT  Equipment
  RT  Saws
       Woodcutting
Sawing wood
  USE Woodcutting
**Saws**
  BT  Equipment
  NT  Crosscut saws
  RT  Sawhorses
Sawtooth monitors
  USE Sawtooth roofs
**Sawtooth roofs**
    --[country or state]--[city]
  PN  Roofs that have parallel roof surfaces of
       triangular section with a profile resembling
       teeth in a saw.
  UF  Northlight roofs
       Sawtooth monitors
  BT  Roofs
**Saxophones**
  PN  Includes the activity of playing
       saxophones.
  BT  Wind instruments
**Scaffold burial**
    --[country or state]--[city]

**Scaffold burial (cont.)**
  PN  Search also under the subdivision
       --SPIRITUAL LIFE used with names of
       ethnic, racial, and regional groups, and with
       classes of persons (Appendix A).
  BT  Funeral rites & ceremonies
  RT  Tombs & sepulchral monuments
Scalds
  USE Burns & scalds
**Scales**
  BT  Equipment
  RT  Weights & measures
**Scalps**
  RT  Baldness
       Human body
Scandals, Political
  USE Corruption
**Scapegoats**
  BT  People
       Symbols
  RT  Blaming
**Scarcity**
    --[country or state]--[city]
  PN  For the general subject of shortages.
       Search under ASSISTANCE for efforts to
       ameliorate scarcity.
  CN  Double index under the material which is
       scarce.
  UF  Shortages
  RT  Assistance
       Consumer rationing
       Droughts
       Famines
       Power shortages
**Scarecrows**
    --[country or state]--[city]
  RT  Farms
       Gardens
       Pest control
**Scenic overlooks**
    --[country or state]--[city]
  UF  Overlooks, Scenic
       Scenic turnouts
       Turnouts, Scenic
  BT  Sites
Scenic turnouts
  USE Scenic overlooks
Schadographs
  USE Photograms
Schedules
  USE Schedules (Time plans)
**Schedules (Architectural records)**
  CN  TGM II term.
  UF  Schedules (Contract documents)
Schedules (Contract documents)
  USE Schedules (Architectural records)
**Schedules (Time plans)**
  CN  TGM II term.
  UF  Schedules
Scherenschnitte
  USE Paper cutouts
**Scholars**

---

BT  Broader term          RT  Related term          PN  Public Note
NT  Narrower term         UF  Used for               +   Term has NTs
HN  History Note          CN  Catalogers Note        --[ ] May subdivide

**Scholars (cont.)**
- BT   People associated with education & communication
- NT   Talmudists
- RT   Education
       Folklorists
       Pundits
       Teachers

School administrators
- USE School superintendents

School busing (Integration)
- USE Busing (School integration)

**School children**
- --[country or state]--[city]
- PN   For students below high school age depicted in the context of school activities.
- UF   Elementary school students
       Primary school students
- BT   Children
- RT   Classrooms
       School recesses
       Schools
       Students

School classrooms
- USE Classrooms

**School discipline**
- --[country or state]--[city]
- BT   Child discipline
- RT   Fools' caps
       Schools

**School excursions**
- --[country or state]--[city]
- UF   Field trips
- BT   Education
- RT   Recreation
       Schools
       Travel

**School meals**
- --[country or state]--[city]
- RT   Cafeterias
       Children eating & drinking
       Schools

**School overcrowding**
- --[country or state]--[city]
- RT   Classrooms
       Education

**School principals**
- --[country or state]--[city]
- UF   Headmasters
       Principals, School
- BT   People associated with education & communication
- RT   Education
       Schools
       Teachers

**School recesses**
- --[country or state]--[city]
- UF   Recesses
- BT   Recreation
- RT   Children playing
       Playgrounds
       School children

**School recesses (cont.)**
       Schools

**School safety patrols**
- --[country or state]--[city]
- RT   Safety
       Schools

**School superintendents**
- --[country or state]--[city]
- UF   School administrators
       Superintendents, School
- BT   People associated with education & communication
- RT   Education
       Schools

Schoolchildren
- USE Children

Schoolrooms
- USE Classrooms

**Schools**
- --[country or state]--[city]
- PN   Includes elementary and secondary educational facilities.  May include activities.
- HN   Usage changed 1/1993 to emphasize facilities aspect, rather than  level of education.
- UF   Elementary schools
       Preparatory schools
       Secondary schools
- BT   Educational facilities
- NT   Church schools +
       Kindergartens
       Laboratory schools
       One-room schools
       Open-air schools
       Reformatories
       Rural schools
- RT   Busing (School integration)
       Children
       School children
       School discipline
       School excursions
       School meals
       School principals
       School recesses
       School safety patrols
       School superintendents
       Students

**Sciagraphic projections**
- CN   TGM II term.
- UF   Shades & shadows

**Science**
- --[country or state]
- NT   Archaeology
       Aviation mechanics (Science)
       Biology +
       Chemistry
       Ecology
       Forestry
       Geography
       Geology
       Medicine +
       Navigation

| BT Broader term | RT Related term | PN Public Note |
| NT Narrower term | UF Used for | + Term has NTs |
| HN History Note | CN Catalogers Note | --[ ] May subdivide |

**Science (cont.)**
        Oceanography +
        Paleontology
        Physics +
        Social science +
  RT  Animal experimentation
      Experiments
      Laboratories
      Scientists
      Testing
**Scientific equipment**
        --[country or state]--[city]
  BT  Equipment
  NT  Barometers
      Bathyspheres
      Compasses
      Gyroscopes
      Magnets
      Microscopes +
      Particle accelerators
      Radar
      Sextants
      Spectrographs
      Surveying equipment
      Telescopes +
      Thermometers
  RT  Optical devices
      Weights & measures
**Scientific illustrations**
  CN  TGM II term.
  UF  Technical drawings
**Scientists**
        --[nationality]--[country or state]--[city]
  BT  People
  RT  Science
Scissorcraft
  USE Paper cutouts
**Scissors & shears**
  UF  Shears
  BT  Equipment
**Sconces**
  BT  Light fixtures
  RT  Candles
**Scottish regiments**
        --[country or state]--[city]
  BT  Military organizations
  RT  Soldiers
Scouts & guides
  USE Guides & scouts
Scouts, Military
  USE Military scouts
Scrap
  USE Salvage
**Scrap drives**
        --[country or state]--[city]
  UF  Campaigns, Scrap
      Drives, Scrap
  BT  Community service
  RT  Recycling
      Salvage
      War
      War work

**Scrapbooks**
  CN  TGM II term.
Scraperboard drawings
  USE Scratchboard drawings
**Scraps**
  CN  TGM II term.
Scrapyards
  USE Junkyards
**Scratchboard drawings**
  CN  TGM II term.
  UF  Scraperboard drawings
**Screen color film transparencies**
  CN  TGM II term.
  UF  Color screen transparencies
      Dufay color transparencies
**Screen color glass transparencies**
  CN  TGM II term.
  UF  Color screen transparencies
Screen facades
  USE False fronts
**Screen paintings**
  BT  Paintings
  RT  Screens
**Screen prints**
  CN  TGM II term.
  UF  Serigraphs
      Silk screen prints
      Silkscreen prints
**Screens**
        --[country or state]--[city]
  RT  Architectural elements
      Furniture
      Grilles
      Screen paintings
**Scribes**
  UF  Writers
  BT  People associated with education &
      communication
  RT  Writing
**Scrip**
  CN  TGM II term.
**Scriptoria**
        --[country or state]--[city]
  UF  Copying rooms
      Writing rooms
  BT  Interiors
  RT  Monasteries
Scripture cards
  USE Bible cards
**Scrolls**
  CN  TGM II term.
  UF  Rolls
Scrying
  USE Fortune telling
Scuba diving
  USE Skin diving
Sculling
  USE Rowing
      Rowing races
Sculling, Team
  USE Team rowing
Sculpting

---

BT Broader term        RT Related term        PN Public Note
NT Narrower term       UF Used for           + Term has NTs
HN History Note          CN Catalogers Note     --[ ] May subdivide

Sculpting (cont.)
  USE Carving
      Modeling (Sculpture)
      Stone carving
**Sculpture**
      --[country or state]--[city]
  PN  Primarily for representations of figures in
      the round, sculptured or modeled out of some
      solid substance, such as wood, stone, marble,
      or wax. Includes statues and indoor and
      outdoor sculpture of all kinds. Search under
      MODELING (SCULPTURE), STONE
      CARVING and WOOD CARVING for
      activities. Search also under the subdivision
      --STATUES used with names of persons
      (Appendix B).
  CN  When a sculpture and a structure of which
      it is an integral part are depicted, double index
      under the appropriate heading; e.g.
      MONUMENTS & MEMORIALS.
  UF  Carvings
      Statues
  BT  Art
  NT  Architectural sculpture +
      Bas-reliefs
      Herms
      Ice sculpture
      Sand sculpture
      Wax figures
      Wood carvings +
  RT  Buddhas
      Carving
      Modeling (Sculpture)
      Monuments & memorials
      Stone carving
Sculpturing
  USE Carving
      Modeling (Sculpture)
      Stone carving
**Scuttling of warships**
      --[nationality]--[country or state]--[city]
  CN  Subdivide by nationality of those doing
      the scuttling.
  RT  Naval warfare
      Warships
**Scythes**
  BT  Agricultural machinery & implements
Sea animals
  USE Aquatic animals
Sea captains
  USE Ship captains
Sea farers
  USE Fishermen
Sea food stores
  USE Seafood stores
**Sea gods**
  BT  Gods
Sea life
  USE Aquatic animals
**Sea lions**
      --[country or state]
  BT  Seals (Animals)

**Sea monsters**
  UF  Sea serpents
      Serpents
  BT  Monsters
**Sea otters**
      --[country or state]
  BT  Otters
  RT  Aquatic animals
Sea serpents
  USE Sea monsters
Sea travel
  USE Ocean travel
Sea trials
  USE Ship trials
**Sea walls**
      --[country or state]--[city]
  BT  Erosion protection works
  RT  Dikes (Engineering)
      Walls
**Seafood stores**
      --[country or state]--[city]
  PN  Includes activities and structures.
  UF  Fish stores
      Sea food stores
  BT  Stores & shops
  RT  Fish
      Grocery stores
      Shellfish
Seagulls
  USE Gulls
**Seals**
  NT  Presidential seal
      State seals
      Vice presidential seal
**Seals (Animals)**
      --[country or state]
  BT  Animals
  NT  Sea lions
Seamen
  USE Sailors
**Seamstresses**
  BT  People associated with manual labor
  RT  Sewing
      Tailoring
**Seances**
      --[country or state]--[city]
  PN  Spiritualistic meetings to receive spirit
      communications.
  CN  Used in a note under SPIRITUALISM.
  BT  Meetings
      Spiritualism
  RT  Dead persons
      Ghosts
**Seaplanes**
      --[nationality]--[country or state]--[city]
  PN  Airplanes designed to take off from and
      land on the water.
  BT  Airplanes
Seaports
  USE Harbors
**Search & rescue operations**
      --[country or state]

---

BT Broader term          RT Related term          PN Public Note
NT Narrower term        UF Used for             + Term has NTs
HN History Note         CN Catalogers Note     --[ ] May subdivide

**Search & rescue operations (cont.)**
  UF  Air rescue service
       Air-sea rescues
  BT  Rescue work
**Searches & seizures**
  USE Frisking
       Police raids
**Searching**
     --[country or state]--[city]
  NT  Frisking
  RT  Customs inspections
       Foraging
       Hiding
       Hunting
       Police raids
**Searchlights**
     --[country or state]--[city]
  RT  Light fixtures
**Seas**
  UF  Breakers
       Estuaries
       Surf
       Waves, Ocean
  BT  Bodies of water
  NT  Oceans
  RT  Aquatic animals
       Bays
       Oceanography
       Reefs
       Sandbars
       Tidal waves
       Tide pools
**Seascapes**
  CN  TGM II term.
  UF  Waterscapes
**Seashells**
  USE Shells
**Seashores**
  USE Beaches
       Waterfronts
**Seasons**
     --[country or state]--[city]
  BT  Natural phenomena
       Time
  NT  Autumn
       Spring
       Summer
       Winter
  RT  Months
**Seating furniture**
     --[country or state]--[city]
  BT  Furniture
  NT  Benches +
       Chairs +
       Couches
       Sofas
**Seats, Window**
  USE Window seats
**Seclusion**
  USE Solitude
**Secondary schools**
  USE Schools

**Secondhand bookstores**
  UF  Used bookstores
  BT  Bookstores
  RT  Books
       Bookselling
**Secondhand sales**
     --[country or state]--[city]
  UF  Garage sales
       Jumble sales
       Sales, Secondhand
       White elephant sales
       Yard sales
  BT  Events
  RT  Business enterprises
       Flea markets
       Pawnshops
       Shopping
       Thrift shops
**Secret service**
     --[nationality]--[country or state]--[city]
  UF  Service, Secret
  BT  Organizations
  RT  Covert operations
       Police
       Spying
**Secret societies**
  USE Fraternal organizations
**Secretaries**
  USE Office workers
**Section cars**
  USE Railroad section cars
**Sectionalism (United States)**
  UF  North & South relations
  RT  Bloody shirt
       Mental states
       Nationalism
       Regionalism
**Sections**
  CN  TGM II term.
**Sects**
  USE Religious groups
**Secularism**
     --[country or state]--[city]
  RT  Church & state
       Religion
**Security engravings**
  USE Bank note vignettes
**Security measures**
  USE Security systems
**Security systems**
     --[country or state]--[city]
  UF  Burglar alarms
       Security measures
  RT  Crimes
       Grilles
       Law enforcement
       Safety equipment
**Security, International**
  USE International security
**Security, National**
  USE National security
**Sedan chairs**

---

BT  Broader term
NT  Narrower term
HN  History Note

RT  Related term
UF  Used for
CN  Catalogers Note

PN  Public Note
+  Term has NTs
--[ ]  May subdivide

**Sedan chairs (cont.)**
--[country or state]--[city]
UF  Palanquins
BT  Vehicles
RT  Chairs
**Sedition**
--[country]
BT  Crimes
RT  Freedom of speech
Treason
**Seed trade**
--[country or state]--[city]
RT  Seeds
Seeding
USE Farming
Gardening
**Seeds**
BT  Plants
RT  Seed trade
Seeps
USE Springs
**Seesaws**
--[country or state]--[city]
UF  Teeter-totters
BT  Equipment
RT  Playgrounds
**Segregation**
--[country or state]--[city]
UF  Desegregation
Jim Crow
BT  Discrimination
RT  Apartheid
Busing (School integration)
Civil rights
Minorities
Race discrimination
Race relations
Seizures
USE Confiscations
Selective service
USE Draft
Selfishness
USE Self-interest
**Self-defense**
RT  Crimes
Martial arts
Oriental hand-to-hand fighting
Safety
Self-government
USE Autonomy
Democracy
**Self-interest**
UF  Selfishness
RT  Ethics
**Self-portraits**
CN  TGM II term.
Self-service restaurants
USE Cafeterias
**Selling**
--[country or state]--[city]
UF  Merchandising
Salesmanship

**Selling (cont.)**
BT  Commerce
NT  Canvassing
RT  Mercantile facilities
Merchandise exchanges
Merchants
Peddlers
Shopping
Seminaries, Theological
USE Theological seminaries
Senators
USE Legislators
Senators' spouses
USE Legislators' spouses
Senior citizens
USE Aged persons
**Sentiment cards**
CN  TGM II term.
Sentinels
USE Guards
Sentries
USE Guards
Sentry houses
USE Guardhouses
Separate development (Race relations)
USE Apartheid
Separation negatives
USE Color separation negatives
Separation positives, Color
USE Color separation positives
Separation transparencies, Color
USE Color separation positives
**Septic tanks**
--[country or state]--[city]
UF  Tanks, Septic
BT  Containers
Mechanical systems components
RT  Sewerage
Waste disposal facilities
Sepulchral monuments
USE Tombs & sepulchral monuments
Sepulchral urns
USE Urns
Sequoias
USE Redwoods
Sequoias, Giant
USE Giant sequoias
Seraphim
USE Angels
Serigraphs
USE Screen prints
Serpents
USE Sea monsters
Snakes
**Servants**
--[country or state]--[city]
UF  Domestics
Housemaids
Maids
BT  People
RT  Home economics
Housework

---

BT Broader term      RT Related term      PN Public Note
NT Narrower term      UF Used for      + Term has NTs
HN History Note      CN Catalogers Note      --[ ] May subdivide

Servants (cont.)
  Servants' quarters
  Women domestics
**Servants' quarters**
  --[country or state]--[city]
  BT   Housing
  RT   Servants
**Service industry facilities**
  --[country or state]--[city]
  BT   Commercial facilities
  NT   Advertising agencies
       Architects' offices
       Barbershops
       Beauty shops
       Brothels
       Car washes
       Cleaning establishments
       Dental offices
       Employment agencies
       Law offices
       Medical offices
       Tattoo parlors
Service stations
  USE Automobile service stations
Servicemen missing in action
  USE Missing in action
Services, Memorial
  USE Memorial rites & ceremonies
Services, Religious
  USE Religious services
Service, Community
  USE Community service
Service, Public
  USE Public service
Service, Secret
  USE Secret service
**Set design drawings**
  CN   TGM II term.
Set props
  USE Stage props
**Settlements**
  --[country or state]--[city]
  BT   Facilities
  NT   Artist colonies
       Cities & towns
       Collective settlements
       Ghost towns
       Indian encampments
       Indian reservations
       Pueblos
       Villages
  RT   Concentration camps
       Relocation camps
       Residential facilities
Settlers
  USE Pioneers
Seven deadly sins
  USE Deadly sins
Seventh-Day observance
  USE Sabbaths
Sewage disposal
  USE Sewerage

**Sewerage**
  --[country or state]--[city]
  PN   Removal and disposal of sewage and
       surface water by sewers.
  UF   Disposal of waste
       Drainage
       House drainage
       Sewage disposal
       Waste disposal
  BT   Sanitation
  RT   Refuse disposal
       Septic tanks
       Sewers
       Waste disposal facilities
**Sewers**
  --[country or state]--[city]
  BT   Hydraulic facilities
  RT   Manholes
       Sewerage
       Waste disposal facilities
       Waterworks
**Sewing**
  --[country or state]--[city]
  UF   Dressmaking
  NT   Children sewing
       Crocheting
       Embroidery
       Knitting
       Lace making
  RT   Clothing industry
       Fibers
       Handicraft
       Housework
       Quilting
       Seamstresses
       Sewing equipment & supplies
       Sewing machines
       Tailoring
**Sewing equipment & supplies**
  BT   Equipment
  NT   Pins & needles
       Sewing machines
  RT   Sewing
**Sewing machine industry**
  --[country or state]--[city]
  PN   Includes activities and structures.
  CN   Double index under INDUSTRIAL
       FACILITIES (or NTs) for images that focus
       on facilities.
  BT   Equipment industry
  RT   Sewing machines
**Sewing machines**
  PN   Includes sewing activities.
  UF   Machine sewing
  BT   Sewing equipment & supplies
  RT   Appliances
       Sewing
       Sewing machine industry
**Sex**
  --[country or state]--[city]
  UF   Gender (Sex)
       Intercourse, Sexual

---

BT  Broader term                    RT  Related term                    PN Public Note
NT  Narrower term                   UF  Used for                        + Term has NTs
HN  History Note                    CN  Catalogers Note                 --[ ] May subdivide

Sex (cont.)
        Lovemaking
        Sexual behavior
        Sexuality
    RT  Interpersonal relations
        Lust
        Pregnancy
        Prostitution
        Rapes
        Sexual harassment
        Sexually transmitted diseases
Sexes, Relations between the
    USE Relations between the sexes
**Sexism**
        --[country or state]--[city]
    PN  For the subject of sexist attitudes.
    UF  Chauvinism, Male
        Equality, Sexual
        Inequality, Sexual
        Male chauvinism
        Sexual equality
        Sexual inequality
    BT  Prejudice
    RT  Feminism
        Machismo
        Relations between the sexes
        Sexual harassment
        Sociology
        Women's rights
**Sextants**
    BT  Scientific equipment
    RT  Astronomy
        Navigation
Sexual behavior
    USE Sex
Sexual equality
    USE Sexism
Sexual freedom
    USE Free love
**Sexual harassment**
        --[country or state]--[city]
    UF  Harassment, Sexual
    BT  Discrimination
    RT  Crimes
        Relations between the sexes
        Sex
        Sexism
        Voyeurism
        Women
        Women's rights
Sexual inequality
    USE Sexism
Sexual lust
    USE Lust
Sexuality
    USE Sex
**Sexually transmitted diseases**
        --[country or state]--[city]
    UF  STD (Diseases)
        VD (Diseases)
        Venereal diseases
    BT  Communicable diseases

**Sexually transmitted diseases (cont.)**
    RT  Sex
**Shackles**
    UF  Chains (Shackles)
        Fetters
        Manacles
    BT  Punishment devices
    RT  Ball & chain
        Chains
Shacks
    USE Huts
**Shad**
        --[country or state]
    BT  Fish
Shades (Ghosts)
    USE Ghosts
Shades & shadows
    USE Sciagraphic projections
**Shadows**
        --[country or state]--[city]
    BT  Natural phenomena
    RT  Light
**Shaking**
    UF  Quaking
        Quivering
        Trembling
    RT  Anger
        Fear
**Shaking hands**
    BT  Etiquette
    RT  Hands
**Shamans**
        --[country or state]--[city]
    PN  Priests who use magic for the purpose of
        curing the sick, divining the hidden, and
        controlling events.
    UF  Medicine men
        Witch doctors
    BT  Priests
    RT  Healers
        Healing
        Magic
        Religion
        Supernatural practices
Shame
    USE Disgrace
**Shamisens**
    PN  Includes the activity of playing shamisens.
    UF  Samisens
    BT  Stringed instruments
**Shamrocks**
        --[country or state]--[city]
    BT  Plants
Shanties
    USE Huts
**Shantyboats**
        --[country or state]--[city]
    PN  Small, crude houseboats.
    BT  Houseboats
Shaolin martial arts
    USE Oriental hand-to-hand fighting
**Sharecroppers**

---

BT Broader term          RT Related term          PN Public Note
NT Narrower term         UF Used for              + Term has NTs
HN History Note          CN Catalogers Note       --[ ] May subdivide

**Sharecroppers (cont.)**
>    --[country or state]--[city]
BT   Farmers
**Shark fishing**
>    --[country or state]
BT   Big game fishing
RT   Sharks
**Sharks**
>    --[country or state]
BT   Fish
RT   Shark fishing
**Sharpshooting**
>    --[country or state]--[city]
UF   Marksmanship
BT   Shooting
**Shaving**
BT   Grooming
RT   Barbering
>    Shaving equipment
**Shaving equipment**
BT   Dressing & grooming equipment
NT   Razor blades
RT   Shaving
Shearing sheep
USE Sheep shearing
Shears
USE Scissors & shears
**Shed dormers**
>    --[country or state]--[city]
BT   Dormers
**Sheds**
>    --[country or state]--[city]
BT   Storage facilities
NT   Drying sheds
>    Wagon sheds
Sheds, Drying
USE Drying sheds
Sheds, Train
USE Railroad stations
Sheds, Wagon
USE Wagon sheds
**Sheep**
>    --[country or state]
UF   Lambs
>    Rams
BT   Animals
NT   Mountain sheep
RT   Sheep ranches
>    Sheep shearing
>    Shepherdesses
>    Shepherds
**Sheep ranches**
>    --[country or state]--[city]
UF   Sheep stations
BT   Ranches
RT   Sheep
**Sheep shearing**
>    --[country or state]--[city]
UF   Shearing sheep
RT   Sheep
>    Wool
Sheep stations

Sheep stations (cont.)
USE Sheep ranches
Sheep, Black
USE Black sheep
**Sheet music covers**
CN   TGM II term.
UF   Music sheet covers
Sheet music publishing industry
USE Music publishing industry
**Shellbacks**
PN   Persons who have crossed the equator and
>    been initiated in the traditional ceremony.
UF   Baptism, Sailors'
>    Equator (in religion, folklore, etc.)
BT   People
RT   Sailors
**Shellfish**
>    --[country or state]
BT   Aquatic animals
NT   Clams
>    Crabs
>    Lobsters
>    Oysters
RT   Fish
>    Seafood stores
>    Shellfish industry
>    Shells
**Shellfish industry**
>    --[country or state]--[city]
PN   Includes activities and structures.
CN   Double index under the shellfish. Double
>    index under INDUSTRIAL FACILITIES (or
>    NTs) for images that focus on facilities.
BT   Food industry
RT   Fishing industry
>    Oystering
>    Shellfish
**Shells**
UF   Seashells
RT   Aquatic animals
>    Shellfish
Shells, Racing
USE Racing shells
Sheltered care homes
USE Rest homes
**Shelters**
>    --[country or state]--[city]
PN   Structures that cover or provide protection
>    from the elements.
BT   Facilities
NT   Air raid shelters
>    Huts
>    Snowsheds
>    Tents +
RT   Bathhouses
>    Housing
>    Lean-tos
>    Lodges
>    Tree houses
**Shelving**
>    --[country or state]--[city]
NT   Bookcases

---

BT  Broader term          RT  Related term          PN Public Note
NT  Narrower term         UF  Used for              + Term has NTs
HN History Note           CN Catalogers Note        --[ ] May subdivide

**Shelving (cont.)**
- RT   Furniture

**Shepherdesses**
- --[country or state]--[city]
- BT   People associated with agriculture
-       Women
- RT   Sheep

**Shepherds**
- --[country or state]--[city]
- UF   Herdsmen
- BT   Men
-       People associated with agriculture
- RT   Sheep

**Shields**
- BT   Armor

**Ship accidents**
- --[country or state]--[city]
- BT   Marine accidents

**Ship captains**
- --[nationality]--[country or state]--[city]
- PN   For masters and commanders of all types of vessels.
- HN   Changed 3/1989 from SHIPMASTERS.
- UF   Captains, Ship
-       Masters of ships
-       Sea captains
-       Shipmasters
-       Ships' captains
- BT   Sailors
- RT   Admirals
-       Ships

**Ship cards**
- USE Sailing cards

**Ship engines**
- USE Boat engines

**Ship equipment & rigging**
- UF   Rigging
- BT   Equipment
- RT   Anchors
-       Ropes

**Ship figureheads**
- UF   Figureheads
- BT   Wood carvings

**Ship models in bottles**
- UF   Bottled ships
- BT   Model ships
- RT   Bottles

**Ship of state**
- BT   Symbols
- RT   Politics & government
-       Ships

**Ship trials**
- --[country or state]--[city]
- UF   Sea trials
-       Trials of vessels
- BT   Testing
- RT   Ships

**Shipbuilding**
- USE Boat & ship industry

**Shipmasters**
- USE Ship captains

**Shipping**

**Shipping (cont.)**
- --[country or state]--[city]
- PN   For activities involved in the packing, dispatch, and unloading of goods and commodities.
- CN   As appropriate, double index under the mode of transportation and under specific goods, commodities, or industry.
- UF   Cargo
-       Cargo handling
-       Freight
-       Freight handling
-       Goods transportation
-       Materials handling
-       Packing & shipping
-       Trucking
- RT   Barges
-       Bundling (Packing)
-       Cargo ships
-       Carts & wagons
-       Commerce
-       Crates
-       Freight handlers' strikes
-       Lifting & carrying
-       Loading docks
-       Longshoremen
-       Marine terminals
-       Moving of structures
-       Moving & storage trade
-       Piers & wharves
-       Portages
-       Porters
-       Railroad freight cars
-       Tankers
-       Transport planes
-       Transportation

**Ships**
- --[nationality]--[country or state]--[city]
- PN   Includes steamships that are ocean-going vessels. Search under STEAMBOATS for steamships that are used on inland or coastal waters.
- UF   Steamships
- BT   Vessels
- NT   Cargo ships +
-       Hospital ships
-       Lightships
-       Noah's ark
-       Ocean liners
-       Prison hulks
-       Relief ships
-       Sailing ships +
-       Submarines
-       Warships +
- RT   Blockade running
-       Boats
-       Harbors
-       Model ships
-       Mutinies
-       Ocean travel
-       Ship captains
-       Ship of state

**Ships (cont.)**
>        Ship trials
>        Yachts

**Ships' captains**
>   USE Ship captains

**Shipwrecks**
>        --[country or state]--[city]
>   PN   For the destruction or loss of a ship and
>        the remains of destroyed or sunken vessels.
>        Search under NAVAL WARFARE for
>        vessels damaged as a result of war.
>   UF   Wrecks
>   BT   Disasters
>   RT   Castaways
>        Marine accidents
>        Naval warfare
>        Salvage
>        Vessels

**Shipyards**
>   USE Boat & ship industry
>        Naval yards & naval stations

**Shit**
>   USE Feces

**Shock therapy**
>        --[country or state]--[city]
>   UF   Therapy, Shock
>   BT   Therapy
>   RT   Psychotherapy

**Shoe industry**
>        --[country or state]--[city]
>   PN   Includes all kinds of footwear. Includes
>        activities and structures. Search under
>        SHOEMAKING for small businesses.
>   CN   Double index under INDUSTRIAL
>        FACILITIES (or NTs) for images that focus
>        on facilities. Used in a note under
>        SHOEMAKING.
>   UF   Boot industry
>   BT   Clothing industry
>   RT   Footwear
>        Leather industry
>        Shoe industry strikes
>        Shoemaking

**Shoe industry strikes**
>        --[country or state]--[city]
>   BT   Strikes
>   RT   Shoe industry

**Shoe making**
>   USE Shoemaking

**Shoe shiners**
>        --[country or state]--[city]
>   UF   Bootblacks
>   BT   People associated with manual labor
>   RT   Shoe shining

**Shoe shining**
>        --[country or state]--[city]
>   UF   Shoeshining
>   RT   Business enterprises
>        Shoe shiners
>        Shoes

**Shoe stores**
>        --[country or state]--[city]

**Shoe stores (cont.)**
>   PN   Includes activities and structures.
>   BT   Clothing stores
>   RT   Footwear

**Shoemakers**
>   UF   Cobblers
>   BT   People
>   RT   Shoemaking

**Shoemaking**
>        --[country or state]--[city]
>   CN   Used in a note under SHOE INDUSTRY.
>   UF   Boot making
>        Shoe making
>   RT   Shoe industry
>        Shoemakers
>        Shoes

**Shoes**
>   PN   Footwear made of leather or similar
>        material, reaching about to the ankle and
>        having a heel of variable height.
>   BT   Footwear
>   RT   Feet
>        Shoe shining
>        Shoemaking

**Shoeshining**
>   USE Shoe shining

**Shoestring industry**
>        --[country or state]--[city]
>   PN   Includes activities and structures.
>   CN   Double index under INDUSTRIAL
>        FACILITIES (or NTs) for images that focus
>        on facilities.
>   BT   Clothing industry

**Shooting**
>        --[country or state]--[city]
>   PN   Search under HUNTING for shooting
>        game.
>   UF   Gunning
>   NT   Archery
>        Sharpshooting
>   RT   Bullet holes
>        Firearms
>        Gunfights
>        Hunting
>        Police shootings
>        Rifle ranges
>        Shooting galleries
>        Sports
>        Targets (Sports)

**Shooting galleries**
>        --[country or state]--[city]
>   PN   For indoor ranges or covered structures
>        equipped with targets for practice or
>        competition with firearms.
>   UF   Galleries, Shooting
>   BT   Sports & recreation facilities
>   RT   Shooting

**Shooting rapids**
>        --[country or state]--[city]
>   UF   Rapids shooting
>        Riding rapids
>        Running rapids

---

BT  Broader term                 RT  Related term              PN  Public Note
NT  Narrower term                UF  Used for                  +  Term has NTs
HN  History Note                 CN  Catalogers Note           --[ ] May subdivide

**Shooting rapids (cont.)**
  BT  Aquatic sports
  RT  Canoes
      Rapids
      Streams
Shootings, Police
  USE Police shootings
Shop windows
  USE Show windows
      Window displays
**Shopping**
      --[country or state]--[city]
  PN  For the activities of shoppers.
  CN  Double index under the type of business,
      if known.
  UF  Window shopping
  RT  Commercial streets
      Mercantile facilities
      Merchandise exchanges
      Secondhand sales
      Selling
      Showrooms
      Window displays
Shopping arcades
  USE Arcades (Shopping facilities)
**Shopping centers**
      --[country or state]--[city]
  BT  Mercantile facilities
  RT  Arcades (Shopping facilities)
Shops
  USE Stores & shops
Shorefronts
  USE Waterfronts
Shorelines
  USE Waterfronts
Shortages
  USE Scarcity
**Shot putting**
      --[country or state]--[city]
  BT  Track athletics
**Shotgun weddings**
      --[country or state]--[city]
  BT  Weddings
Shotguns
  USE Rifles
Shoulder arms
  USE Rifles
**Shovels**
  BT  Equipment
  RT  Digging
      Steam shovels
Show cases
  USE Showcases
**Show horses**
      --[country or state]--[city]
  BT  Horses
  RT  Horse shows
**Show jumping**
      --[country or state]--[city]
  BT  Jumping (Horsemanship)
  RT  Horse shows
      Horses

Show rooms
  USE Showrooms
**Show tents**
      --[country or state]--[city]
  UF  Big top
  BT  Tents
  RT  Circuses & shows
**Show windows**
      --[country or state]--[city]
  PN  For images that focus on windows as a
      part of mercantile facilities rather than their
      displays. Search under WINDOW
      DISPLAYS for window dressings and
      displays.
  CN  Used in a note under WINDOW
      DISPLAYS.
  HN  Changed 11/1989 from non-postable term
      (Use WINDOW DISPLAYS).
  UF  Display windows
      Shop windows
      Store windows
  BT  Windows
  RT  Facades
      Mercantile facilities
      Showcases
      Window displays
**Showcases**
  UF  Cases, Display
      Cases, Show
      Display cases
      Show cases
  BT  Furniture
  RT  Exhibitions
      Merchandise displays
      Show windows
      Showrooms
Showers
  USE Bathtubs & showers
Showmen
  USE Entertainers
**Showrooms**
      --[country or state]--[city]
  PN  Rooms where merchandise is exposed for
      sale or where samples are displayed.
  UF  Display rooms
      Show rooms
  BT  Interiors
  RT  Mercantile facilities
      Merchandise displays
      Shopping
      Showcases
      Window displays
Shows
  USE Circuses & shows
      Exhibitions
      Theatrical productions
**Shrines**
      --[country or state]--[city]
  PN  For structures or sites serving as places of
      religious veneration or pilgrimage, often
      consecrated or devoted to a person or deity.
      Search under TOMBS & SEPULCHRAL

BT  Broader term                      RT  Related term                      PN  Public Note
NT  Narrower term                     UF  Used for                          +  Term has NTs
HN  History Note                      CN  Catalogers Note                   --[ ]  May subdivide

**Shrines (cont.)**
> MONUMENTS for tombs of those considered
> holy or of hallowed memory. Search also
> under the subdivision --SHRINES used with
> names of persons (Appendix B).
- UF   Holy places
- BT   Religious facilities
- RT   Historic sites
  - Pilgrimages
  - Religious articles
  - Saints

**Shrubs**
> --[country or state]--[city]
- UF   Bushes
- BT   Plants
- NT   Hibiscus
  - Holly
  - Lilacs
  - Mistletoe
  - Peonies
  - Rhododendrons +
- RT   Hedges (Plants)
  - Laurels
  - Topiary work
  - Willows

**Shrunken heads**
- RT   Cannibalism
  - Human body

**Shuffleboard**
- BT   Games

**Shutters**
> --[country or state]--[city]
- BT   Architectural elements
- RT   Windows

**Shut-ins**
- PN   Invalids confined to home, room, or bed.
- UF   Invalids
- RT   Handicapped persons
  - Nursing homes
  - Rest homes
  - Sick persons

**Siamese twins**
- CN   As appropriate, double index under
  HUMAN CURIOSITIES.
- BT   Twins
- RT   Human curiosities

**Siblings**
- USE Families

**Sick bays**
- PN   Section in vessels, especially a war vessel
  or transport, used as a dispensary and
  hospital.
- CN   Double index under type of vessel.
- BT   Health care facilities
- RT   Infirmaries
  - Vessels

**Sick children**
- BT   Children
  - Sick persons

**Sick persons**
- PN   Persons affected with unspecified diseases
  or ill health; also, persons awaiting or under

**Sick persons (cont.)**
> medical treatment. Search under DISEASES
> and NTs for specific illnesses. Search also
> under the subdivisions --HEALTH used with
> names of persons (Appendix B) and
> --HEALTH & WELFARE used with names
> of ethnic, racial, and regional groups and with
> classes of persons (Appendix A).
- CN   Used in a note under DISEASES.
- UF   Convalescents
  - Ill persons
  - Invalids
  - Patients
- BT   People associated with health & safety
- NT   Sick children
- RT   Diseases
  - Handicapped persons
  - Healing
  - Health care
  - Medical aspects of war
  - Nausea
  - Pain
  - Shut-ins
  - Wounds & injuries

**Sickle cell anemia**
> --[country or state]--[city]
- BT   Diseases

**Sickle & hammer**
- USE Hammer & sickle

**Sickness**
- USE Diseases

**Side shows**
- USE Amusement parks
  - Circuses & shows
  - Midways

**Side wheelers**
> --[nationality]--[country or state]--[city]
- UF   Paddle wheel steamers
- BT   Steamboats
- RT   Stern wheelers

**Sideboards**
- USE Buffets (Furniture)

**Sidelights**
> --[country or state]--[city]
- PN   Narrow windows flanking doors or larger
  windows.
- UF   Flanking windows
  - Margin lights
  - Winglights
- BT   Windows

**Sidewalks**
> --[country or state]--[city]
- BT   Walkways
- NT   Wooden sidewalks
- RT   Streets

**Sidings, Railroad**
- USE Railroad sidings

**Siding, Bevel**
- USE Clapboard siding

**Siding, Clapboard**
- USE Clapboard siding

**Sierra redwoods**

---

BT Broader term      RT Related term      PN Public Note
NT Narrower term      UF Used for      + Term has NTs
HN History Note      CN Catalogers Note      --[ ] May subdivide

Sierra redwoods (cont.)
  USE Giant sequoias
Sightseeing
  USE Sightseers
    Tourists
**Sightseers**
    --[country or state]--[city]
  PN  For persons who go about seeing sights of
      interest on their own. Search under
      TOURISTS for persons who are on organized
      tours.
  CN  Used in a note under PASSENGERS and
      TOURISTS.
  UF  Excursions
      Sightseeing
  BT  People
  RT  Passengers
      Tourists
      Travel
**Sign language**
  UF  Gesture language
  BT  Communication
  RT  Deaf persons
**Signal flags**
  BT  Communication devices
      Flags
  RT  Navigation
**Signal lights**
    --[country or state]--[city]
  BT  Communication devices
  NT  Railroad signals
  RT  Traffic signs & signals
**Signal stations**
    --[country or state]--[city]
  BT  Communication facilities
**Signal towers**
    --[country or state]--[city]
  BT  Communication facilities
  NT  Railroad signal towers
Signing autographs
  USE Autographing
Signing of documents
  USE Document signings
**Signs**
    --[country or state]--[city]
  CN  TGM II term.
  BT  Communication devices
  NT  Banners
      Billboards
      Electric signs
      Plaques
      Sandwich boards
      Traffic signs & signals
  RT  Advertisements
      Historical markers
      Logos
      Symbols
**Silence**
  BT  Communication
  RT  Solitude
**Silhouettes**
  CN  TGM II term.

**Silk**
  BT  Fibers
  RT  Silk industry
**Silk industry**
    --[country or state]--[city]
  PN  Includes activities and structures.
  CN  Double index under INDUSTRIAL
      BUILDINGS for images that focus on
      buildings.
  BT  Textile industry
  RT  Silk
Silk screen prints
  USE Screen prints
Silkscreen prints
  USE Screen prints
Silk, Artificial
  USE Rayon
Silk-cotton trees
  USE Ceibas
**Silos**
    --[country or state]--[city]
  PN  Typically cylindrical structures usually
      sealed when full to exclude air and used for
      storing silage (fodder).
  BT  Food storage buildings
  RT  Grains
**Silver**
  UF  Silver bullion
  BT  Metals
  RT  Money
      Silver mining
      Silver question
      Treasure-trove
Silver bullion
  USE Silver
Silver dye bleach prints
  USE Dye destruction prints
Silver gelatin film negatives
  USE Film negatives
**Silver gelatin film transparencies**
  CN  TGM II term.
  UF  Gelatin silver transparencies
Silver gelatin glass negatives
  USE Dry plate negatives
**Silver gelatin glass transparencies**
  CN  TGM II term.
  UF  Gelatin silver transparencies
Silver gelatin photoprints
  USE Silver gelatin prints
Silver gelatin printing-out paper photoprints
  USE Silver gelatin printing-out paper prints
**Silver gelatin printing-out paper prints**
  CN  TGM II term.
  UF  Silver gelatin printing-out paper
      photoprints
      Studio proof paper prints
**Silver gelatin prints**
  CN  TGM II term.
  UF  Bromide prints
      Chloro-bromide prints
      Gaslight prints
      Gelatin silver prints

---

BT  Broader term
NT  Narrower term
HN  History Note

RT  Related term
UF  Used for
CN  Catalogers Note

PN  Public Note
+   Term has NTs
--[ ] May subdivide

**Silver gelatin prints (cont.)**
Silver gelatin photoprints
**Silver mining**
--[country or state]--[city]
PN  Includes activities and sites.
BT  Mining
RT  Silver
**Silver printing-out paper photographs**
CN  TGM II term.
UF  Printing-out paper photographs, Silver
**Silver question**
PN  For the issue of free coinage of silver in the United States.
UF  Free silver issue
Specie payments
BT  Currency question
RT  Bimetallism
Coins
Silver
Silver services
USE Tableware
**Silverpoint drawings**
CN  TGM II term.
**Silverware**
RT  Cooking utensils
Cutlery industry
Eating & drinking
Knives
Tableware
**Silverwork**
BT  Metalwork
Simulated images
USE Composite photographs
Computer graphics
**Singers**
UF  Choruses
Vocalists
BT  Musicians
NT  Blues singers
Choirboys
Gospel singers
Jazz singers
Opera singers
RT  Bards
Minstrels
Singing
**Singing**
--[country or state]--[city]
PN  Search also under the subdivision --PERFORMANCES used with names of persons (Appendix B).
BT  Music
NT  Caroling
Children singing
RT  Barbershop quartets
Choirs (Music)
Jazz singers
Operas & operettas
Ring-around-a-rosy
Singers
Whistling
**Single women**

**Single women (cont.)**
UF  Maidens
Old maids
Spinsters
BT  Women
NT  Unmarried mothers
Widows
RT  Bachelors
Marriage
Single-rail railroads
USE Monorail railroads
Sins, Deadly
USE Deadly sins
Sisal plants
USE Agaves
Sisal, Mexican
USE Henequen
Sisters
USE Families
**Site elements**
--[country or state]--[city]
BT  Architectural & site components
NT  Bus stops
Fences +
Fire hydrants
Fish ladders
Flagpoles
Garden walls
Gates +
Historical markers
Hitching posts
Lampposts
Penstocks
Pilings (Civil engineering)
Stepping stones
Stone walls
Street lights +
Terraces
Traffic signs & signals
Yard ornaments +
RT  Sites
**Site plans**
CN  TGM II term.
UF  Plot plans
**Sites**
--[country or state]--[city]
BT  Facilities
NT  Backyards
Dueling grounds
Forums
Game preserves
Historic sites +
Plazas
Rifle ranges
Ruins
Scenic overlooks
RT  Site elements
Sitting rooms
USE Living rooms
Parlors
Sit-ins
USE Demonstrations

---

Six-sided buildings
  USE Hexagonal buildings
**Skaters**
  UF  Figure skaters
       Ice skaters
  BT  People associated with entertainment &
       sports
  RT  Roller skating
       Skating
**Skating**
       --[country or state]--[city]
  NT  Ice skating +
       Roller skating
  RT  Skaters
       Skating rinks
       Sports
**Skating rinks**
       --[country or state]--[city]
  UF  Ice rinks
       Rinks
  BT  Sports & recreation facilities
  NT  Ice skating rinks
  RT  Skating
**Skeleton leaf arrangements**
  UF  Phantom leaf arrangements
  BT  Dried plant arrangements
  RT  Leaves
**Skeletons**
  NT  Skulls
  RT  Bones
       Dead animals
       Dead persons
**Sketchbooks**
  CN  TGM II term.
  UF  Sketchpads
**Sketches**
  CN  TGM II term.
Sketchpads
  USE Sketchbooks
**Ski jumping**
       --[country or state]--[city]
  BT  Sports
  RT  Skiing
**Ski lodges**
       --[country or state]--[city]
  UF  Lodges, ski
  BT  Lodges
  RT  Skiing
**Ski troops**
       --[nationality]--[country or state]--[city]
  PN  Troops trained to maneuver and fight on
       skis.
  UF  Troops, Ski
  BT  Military personnel
  RT  Skiing
       Winter warfare
Skiagraphy
  USE Radiography
**Skid roads**
       --[country or state]
  PN  Roads along which logs are dragged to a
       skidway or landing, often over heavy logs

Skid roads (cont.)
       partly sunken at intervals of about five feet.
  BT  Roads
  RT  Lumber industry
**Skiing**
       --[country or state]--[city]
  RT  Ski jumping
       Ski lodges
       Ski troops
       Snow
       Sports
       Water skiing
       Winter warfare
**Skin diving**
       --[country or state]--[city]
  UF  Scuba diving
       Underwater swimming
  RT  Diving
       Diving suits
       Oxygen masks
       Swimming
Skins
  USE Hides & skins
Skipping rope
  USE Rope skipping
Skits
  USE Theatrical productions
Skull & crossbones
  USE Death's head
**Skulls**
  BT  Skeletons
  RT  Death's head
       Phrenology
Skydivers
  USE Parachutists
Skydiving
  USE Parachuting
**Skylights**
       --[country or state]--[city]
  BT  Windows
  RT  Roofs
Skyline views
  USE Cityscapes
**Skyscrapers**
       --[country or state]--[city]
  CN  Assign according to the time period of the
       image (a skyscraper by the standards of the
       1890s may not be a skyscraper today). As
       appropriate, double index under function of
       the building, e.g., OFFICE BUILDINGS.
  BT  Buildings distinguished by form
Slander
  USE Libel & slander
**Slang**
  UF  Argot
       Jargon
  BT  Communication
**Slate quarrying**
       --[country or state]--[city]
  BT  Quarrying
**Slaughtering**
       --[country or state]--[city]

---

BT Broader term           RT Related term           PN Public Note
NT Narrower term         UF Used for              + Term has NTs
HN History Note           CN Catalogers Note      --[ ] May subdivide

**Slaughtering (cont.)**
PN   For killing of domesticated animals in
       non-industrial contexts. Search under MEAT
       INDUSTRY for images of slaughter in
       industrial contexts; search under HUNTING
       for killing of non-domesticated animals.
RT   Meat
       Meat cutting
       Meat industry
Slave auctions
   USE Slave trade
Slave fugitives
   USE Fugitive slaves
Slave markets
   USE Slave trade
**Slave quarters**
       --[country or state]--[city]
BT   Housing
RT   Slaves
**Slave rebellions**
       --[country or state]--[city]
BT   Rebellions
RT   Slaves
**Slave ships**
       --[country or state]--[city]
BT   Sailing ships
RT   Detention facilities
       Prison hulks
       Slaves
**Slave trade**
       --[country or state]--[city]
UF   Slave auctions
       Slave markets
BT   Commerce
RT   Auctions
       Slaves
**Slavery**
       --[country or state]--[city]
PN   For the subject of slavery in general.
       Search under SLAVES for images that focus
       on persons.
CN   Used in a note under SLAVES.
RT   Abolition movement
       Civil rights
       Slaves
       Underground railroad system
**Slaves**
       --[country or state]--[city]
PN   For images that focus on persons. Search
       under SLAVERY for the subject of slavery in
       general.
CN   Used in a note under SLAVERY.
BT   People
NT   Fugitive slaves
RT   Freedmen
       Slave quarters
       Slave rebellions
       Slave ships
       Slave trade
       Slavery
Sledding, Dog
   USE Dogsledding

Sledges
   USE Sleds & sleighs
**Sleds & sleighs**
       --[nationality]--[country or state]--[city]
PN   Includes the activity of sledding and riding
       in sleighs.
UF   Sledges
       Sleighs
BT   Vehicles
NT   Bobsleds
       Toboggans
RT   Animal teams
       Dogsledding
       Snow
       Sports
       Travois
**Sleeping**
UF   Rest
BT   Mental states
NT   Children sleeping
RT   Alarm clocks
       Beds
       Dreaming
       Hibernation
       Somnambulism
       Waking
       Yawning
Sleeping cars
   USE Railroad sleeping cars
**Sleeping porches**
       --[country or state]--[city]
BT   Porches
Sleepwalking
   USE Somnambulism
**Sleepwear**
UF   Nightclothes
       Nightgowns
       Nightshirts
       Pajamas
BT   Clothing & dress
RT   Lingerie
Sleeves, Record
   USE Album covers
Sleighs
   USE Sleds & sleighs
Sleights of hand
   USE Juggling
       Magic
Sleuthing
   USE Investigation
Sleuths
   USE Detectives
**Slides**
CN   TGM II term.
**Sliding boards**
       --[country or state]--[city]
NT   Water slides
RT   Playgrounds
**Slogans**
RT   Advertisements
       Political elections
       Propaganda

---

BT  Broader term                    RT  Related term                    PN  Public Note
NT  Narrower term                   UF  Used for                        +  Term has NTs
HN  History Note                    CN  Catalogers Note                 --[ ] May subdivide

**Slogans (cont.)**
        Publicity
**Slot machines**
        --[country or state]--[city]
  PN  Coin operated gambling machines.
  UF  One-armed bandits
  BT  Coin operated machines
  RT  Casinos
      Gambling
Sloth
  USE Laziness
**Sloths**
        --[country or state]
  BT  Animals
**Slums**
        --[country or state]--[city]
  BT  Residential facilities
  RT  Building deterioration
      City & town life
      Ethnic neighborhoods
      Housing
      Tenement houses
Small arms
  USE Firearms
Smallest
  USE Curiosities & wonders
**Smallpox**
        --[country or state]--[city]
  BT  Communicable diseases
Smelteries
  USE Smelters
**Smelters**
        --[country or state]--[city]
  UF  Smelteries
      Smelting mills
  BT  Factories
  RT  Foundries
      Furnaces
      Metallurgical industry
Smelting mills
  USE Smelters
**Smiling**
  UF  Grinning
  RT  Faces
      Mental states
      Mouths
Smitheries
  USE Forge shops
Smithies
  USE Forge shops
**Smoke**
        --[country or state]--[city]
  RT  Fire
      Fires
      Smoking
Smoke houses
  USE Smokehouses
Smoke shops
  USE Tobacco shops
**Smokehouses**
        --[country or state]--[city]
  UF  Smoke houses

**Smokehouses (cont.)**
  BT  Factories
  RT  Curing (Preservation)
      Home food processing
      Outbuildings
**Smokeless tobacco**
  UF  Chewing tobacco
      Oral tobacco
  BT  Tobacco products
  RT  Spittoons
**Smokestacks**
        --[country or state]--[city]
  BT  Chimneys
  RT  Industrial facilities
Smoke-ins
  USE Demonstrations
**Smoking**
        --[country or state]--[city]
  UF  Tobacco smoking
  BT  Manners & customs
  NT  Children smoking
  RT  Cigarettes
      Cigars
      Matches
      Narcotics
      Railroad smoking cars
      Smoke
      Smoking rooms
      Tobacco habit
      Tobacco pipes
      Water pipes (Smoking)
Smoking cars
  USE Railroad smoking cars
**Smoking rooms**
        --[country or state]--[city]
  BT  Interiors
  RT  Smoking
**Smuggling**
        --[country or state]--[city]
  UF  Contraband trade
  BT  Crimes
  RT  Black market
      Blockade running
**Snack bars**
        --[country or state]--[city]
  BT  Restaurants
**Snails**
        --[country or state]
  BT  Animals
**Snake charming**
        --[country or state]--[city]
  BT  Magic
  RT  Snakes
**Snake dance**
        --[country or state]--[city]
  BT  Dancing
      Rites & ceremonies
  RT  Snakes
**Snake venom**
  BT  Poisons
  RT  Snakes
**Snakes**

---

BT Broader term        RT Related term        PN Public Note
NT Narrower term      UF Used for          + Term has NTs
HN History Note        CN Catalogers Note    --[ ] May subdivide

**Snakes (cont.)**
> --[country or state]
UF    Serpents
BT    Reptiles
RT    Snake charming
      Snake dance
      Snake venom
**Snapshots**
CN    TGM II term.
**Sneezing**
RT    Coughing
      Health
**Snipes**
> --[country or state]
BT    Birds
**Snobbishness**
BT    Mental states
RT    Pride
Snooping
USE    Investigation
**Snow**
> --[country or state]--[city]
BT    Weather
RT    Avalanches
      Blizzards
      Children playing in snow
      Ice
      Skiing
      Sleds & sleighs
      Snow removal
      Snowballs
      Snowmen
      Snowsheds
      Snowshoeing
      Winter
Snow houses
USE    Igloos
**Snow removal**
> --[country or state]--[city]
BT    Cleaning
RT    Railroad snowplow locomotives
      Snow
      Snowsheds
      Street cleaning
Snow sheds
USE    Snowsheds
**Snowballs**
RT    Children playing in snow
      Snow
Snowhouses
USE    Igloos
**Snowmen**
RT    Children playing in snow
      Ice sculpture
      Snow
Snowplow locomotives
USE    Railroad snowplow locomotives
**Snowsheds**
> --[country or state]--[city]
UF    Snow sheds
BT    Shelters
RT    Snow

**Snowsheds (cont.)**
      Snow removal
**Snowshoeing**
> --[country or state]--[city]
BT    Walking
RT    Hiking
      Snow
      Sports
Snowstorms
USE    Blizzards
Soap
USE    Cosmetics & soap
       Household soap
Soap box derby racers
USE    Coaster cars
Soap box oratory
USE    Public speaking
**Soccer**
> --[country or state]--[city]
BT    Sports
Social aspects
CN    Used only as a subdivision with names of
      wars (Appendix C).
Social behavior
USE    Interpersonal relations
**Social classes**
> --[country or state]--[city]
UF    Classes (Social)
BT    People
NT    Middle class
      Upper class +
      Working class
RT    Cost & standard of living
      Sociology
Social conditions
USE    Economic & social conditions
**Social justice**
> --[country or state]--[city]
BT    Justice
RT    Sociological dramas
Social life
CN    Used only as a subdivision with names of
      ethnic, racial, and regional groups, and with
      classes of persons (Appendix A), and names
      of persons (Appendix B).
Social life & customs
USE    Manners & customs
**Social science**
> --[country or state]--[city]
PN    For the subject of social science in general
      and the activities of social scientists.
BT    Science
NT    Anthropology
      Sociology
RT    Gerontology
**Social security**
> --[country]
BT    Insurance
RT    Domestic economic assistance
      Pensions
      Taxes
Social welfare organizations

---

| | | |
|---|---|---|
| BT Broader term | RT Related term | PN Public Note |
| NT Narrower term | UF Used for | + Term has NTs |
| HN History Note | CN Catalogers Note | --[ ] May subdivide |

Social welfare organizations (cont.)
USE Public service organizations

**Social & civic facilities**
--[country or state]--[city]
HN  Changed 1/1993 from
CEREMONIAL-CIVIC BUILDINGS.
UF  Ceremonial-civic buildings
Civic buildings
Convention halls
BT  Facilities
NT  Community centers
Student unions
RT  Auditoriums
Forums
Kivas

**Socialism**
--[country or state]--[city]
PN  For the subject of socialism in general.
BT  Economic & political systems
RT  National socialism
Socialists

**Socialists**
--[country or state]--[city]
PN  Search under SOCIALISM for the subject
of socialism in general and the activities of
socialists.
BT  People associated with politics &
government
RT  Socialism

**Socialites**
--[country or state]--[city]
CN  Use only for images of people identified
as socially prominent.
UF  Society women
BT  People
RT  Celebrities
Clubwomen

Socialization of industry
USE Government ownership

Societies
USE Organizations

Society women
USE Socialites

Society, High
USE Upper class

**Sociological dramas**
PN  For images representing dramatic
productions or scenes (theatrical, film, radio,
or television) which focus on social
conditions and social injustice.
RT  Economic & social conditions
Motion pictures
Radio broadcasting
Social justice
Television broadcasting
Theatrical productions

**Sociology**
PN  For the subject of sociology in general and
the activities of sociologists.
BT  Social science
RT  Economic & social conditions
Interpersonal relations

Sociology (cont.)
Leadership
Power (Social sciences)
Sexism
Social classes
Urban growth

Socks
USE Hosiery

**Sod buildings**
--[country or state]--[city]
BT  Buildings distinguished by material
RT  Dugout houses

**Soda fountains**
--[country or state]--[city]
PN  Equipment and counters for the
preparation and serving of sodas, sundaes,
and ice cream.
BT  Furniture
RT  Drugstores
Equipment
Ice cream & ices
Restaurants
Soda jerks

**Soda industry**
--[country or state]--[city]
PN  Includes activities and structures.
CN  Double index under INDUSTRIAL
FACILITIES (or NTs) for images that focus
on facilities.
BT  Chemical industry

**Soda jerks**
--[country or state]--[city]
BT  People
RT  Restaurant workers
Soda fountains

Soda water
USE Carbonated beverages

**Sofas**
PN  Long, upholstered seating furniture with a
back and two ends, generally used for sitting,
not reclining.
BT  Seating furniture
RT  Couches

Soft drinks
USE Carbonated beverages

**Softball**
--[country or state]--[city]
CN  Used in a note under SOFTBALL
PLAYERS.
UF  Indoor baseball
Playground ball
BT  Sports
RT  Baseball
Softball players

**Softball players**
--[country or state]--[city]
CN  Geographical subdivision indicates place
where team or player is based.
UF  Indoor baseball players
BT  Athletes
RT  Baseball players
Softball

BT  Broader term                    RT  Related term                    PN  Public Note
NT  Narrower term                   UF  Used for                        +  Term has NTs
HN  History Note                    CN  Catalogers Note                 --[ ]  May subdivide

**Soft-ground etchings**
  CN  TGM II term.
Soil
  USE Land
**Soil conservation**
    --[country or state]--[city]
  BT  Conservation of natural resources
  RT  Erosion
      Land
Solariums
  USE Sunspaces
**Solarization photographs**
  CN  TGM II term.
  UF  Sabattier effect photographs
**Soldiers**
    --[nationality]--[country or state]--[city]
  PN  Persons engaged in the military below
      officer's level. For images of soldiers and
      troops in the context of war, search under the
      names of specific wars and relevant topical
      subdivisions such as --MILITARY
      PERSONNEL (Appendix C).
  BT  Military personnel
  NT  Mercenaries (Soldiers)
  RT  Children playing soldiers
      Fraternization
      Guerrillas
      Scottish regiments
      Unknown soldiers
      Warriors
**Soldiers' homes**
    --[country or state]--[city]
  PN  Establishments that provide care and relief
      for military veterans.
  UF  Veterans' homes
  BT  Rest homes
  RT  Veterans
Soldiers' life
  USE Military life
Solicitors
  USE Lawyers
**Solidarity**
    --[country or state]--[city]
  PN  Unity (as of a group or class) that
      produces or is based on community of
      interests, objectives, or standards.
  RT  Allegiance
      Cooperation
      Economic & political systems
      International relations
      Petitions
      Politics & government
**Solitude**
  UF  Isolation
      Seclusion
  RT  Silence
**Somnambulism**
  UF  Sleepwalking
  BT  Walking
  RT  Dreaming
      Sleeping
**Songs**

Songs (cont.)
  PN  Search also under the subdivision
      --SONGS & MUSIC used with names of
      wars (Appendix C).
  BT  Music
  NT  Ballads
      Folk songs
      National songs
**Songs & music**
  CN  Used only as a subdivision with names of
      wars (Appendix C).
Songs, Swan
  USE Swan songs
Sons
  USE Families
Soothsaying
  USE Divination
Sorcerers
  USE Wizards
Sorcery
  USE Magic
Sororities
  USE Fraternities & sororities
Sorrow
  USE Grief
      Sadness
Souks
  USE Bazaars
**Sound recording**
    --[country or state]--[city]
  PN  For activity of recording sound, including
      performers' sound recording sessions.
  UF  Recorded sound
      Reproduction of sound
      Sound reproduction
  BT  Communication
  RT  Broadcasting
      Dictating machines
      Sound recording industry
      Sound recordings
**Sound recording industry**
    --[country or state]--[city]
  PN  Manufacture and trade of sound
      recordings. Includes activities and structures.
  CN  Double index under INDUSTRIAL
      FACILITIES (or NTs) for images that focus
      on facilities.
  UF  Record industry
      Recording industry
  BT  Industry
  RT  Sound recording
      Sound recording stores
      Sound recordings
**Sound recording stores**
    --[country or state]--[city]
  PN  Includes activities and structures.
  UF  Phonograph stores
      Record stores
  BT  Stores & shops
  RT  Music stores
      Sound recording industry
      Sound recordings

BT Broader term      RT Related term      PN Public Note
NT Narrower term      UF Used for      + Term has NTs
HN History Note      CN Catalogers Note      --[ ] May subdivide

Sound recordings
   UF   Discs, Sound
         Disks, Sound
         Phonograph records
   BT   Audiovisual materials
   RT   Phonographs
         Sound recording
         Sound recording industry
         Sound recording stores
         Sounds
Sound reproduction
   USE Sound recording
Sound waves
   UF   Waves, Sound
   RT   Sounds
Sounding
   BT   Oceanography
Sounds
   UF   Noises
   NT   Music +
         Whistling
   RT   Communication
         Hearing aids
         Noise pollution
         Sound recordings
         Sound waves
Sounds (Geomorphology)
   USE Bays
         Channels
Soup lines
   USE Bread & soup lines
South American Indians
   USE Indians of South America
Souvenir albums
   USE Viewbooks
Souvenir booklets
   USE Viewbooks
Souvenir shops
         --[country or state]--[city]
   PN   Includes activities and structures.
   BT   Stores & shops
   RT   Gift shops
         Keepsakes
         Tourist trade
Souvenir viewbooks
   USE Viewbooks
Souvenirs
   USE Keepsakes
         Memorabilia
Sovereigns
   USE Rulers
Sowing
   USE Farming
         Gardening
Soybeans
         --[country or state]--[city]
   BT   Beans
Space aliens
   USE Extraterrestrial life
Space flight
         --[nationality]--[country or state]--[city]
   CN   Subdivide geographically by site in which

Space flight (cont.)
         spacecraft is depicted or, if outside of earth's
         airspace, by destination.
   UF   Rocket flight
         Space travel
   BT   Travel
   NT   Interplanetary voyages
   RT   Aeronautics
         Artificial satellites
         Astronauts
         Rockets
Space photographs
   CN   TGM II term.
   UF   Digital images
Space travel
   USE Space flight
Spaces
   USE Rooms & spaces
Spades
   BT   Equipment
   RT   Digging
Spandrels
         --[nationality]--[country or state]--[city]
   PN   An area roughly triangular in shape,
         included between the extradoses of two
         adjoining arches and a line approximately
         connecting their crowns.
   BT   Architectural elements
Spanish moss
         --[country or state]--[city]
   UF   Moss, Spanish
   BT   Plants
   RT   Trees
Spanking
   BT   Beating
   RT   Children misbehaving
Spanners
   USE Wrenches
Spas
   USE Health resorts
Speakeasies
         --[country or state]--[city]
   PN   Places where alcoholic beverages are
         illegally sold.
   BT   Bars
   RT   Prohibition
Speakeasy cards
   CN   TGM II term.
Speakers' platforms
   USE Podiums
Speaking
   USE Conversation
         Discussion
         Filibustering
         Public speaking
Speaking trumpets
   USE Megaphones
Spear fishing
         --[country or state]
   BT   Fishing
Spears
   BT   Arms & armament

---

BT  Broader term                 RT  Related term               PN Public Note
NT  Narrower term              UF  Used for                     + Term has NTs
HN  History Note               CN  Catalogers Note        --[ ] May subdivide

Spears (cont.)
  RT  Lancers
       Throwing sticks
**Special interests**
       --[country or state]
  PN  Persons or groups seeking to influence
       legislation or government policy to further
       often narrowly defined interests.
  UF  Pressure groups
  BT  Politics & government
  RT  Big business
       Lobbying
       Political patronage
Specialty acts
  USE Circuses & shows
       Theatrical productions
Specie
  USE Coins
Specie payments
  USE Silver question
**Specifications**
  CN  TGM II term.
Specimen books
  USE Sample books
Spectacles
  USE Eyeglasses
**Spectators**
       --[country or state]--[city]
  PN  Groups or assemblies of people looking at
       or witnessing particular events or activities.
  HN  Changed 3/1989 from non-postable term
       (Use CROWDS).
  BT  People
  NT  Sports spectators
  RT  Audiences
       Crowds
       Events
       Grandstands
Specters
  USE Ghosts
**Spectrographs**
  PN  Apparatus for dispersing radiation into a
       spectrum and then photographing or mapping
       the spectrum.
  BT  Photographic apparatus & supplies
       Scientific equipment
**Speculative houses**
       --[country or state]--[city]
  PN  Use for homes built without a particular
       client and in hopes, but with no assurances,
       of sales.
  UF  Investment houses
  BT  Houses
  RT  Housing developments
       Real estate development
Speech correction
  USE Speech therapy
**Speech therapy**
       --[country or state]--[city]
  UF  Speech correction
  BT  Therapy
  RT  Communication

Speech writing
  USE Speechwriting
Speechmaking
  USE Public speaking
**Speechwriting**
       --[country or state]--[city]
  UF  Speech writing
  BT  Writing
  RT  Public speaking
**Speed skating**
       --[country or state]--[city]
  BT  Ice skating
       Racing
**Spelling bees**
       --[country or state]--[city]
  BT  Contests
Spells
  USE Magic
Spelunking
  USE Caves
Spending policy
  USE Economic policy
Spending, Deficit
  USE Deficit financing
Sperm
  USE Spermatozoa
**Spermatozoa**
  UF  Sperm
**Sphinxes**
       --[country or state]--[city]
  BT  Monuments & memorials
**Spices**
  BT  Food
  NT  Pepper (Spice)
  RT  Condiments
       Plants
**Spiders**
       --[country or state]
  BT  Insects
  RT  Cobwebs
Spiderwebs
  USE Cobwebs
**Spillways**
       --[country or state]--[city]
  PN  A passage for surplus water to run over or
       around a dam or other obstruction.
  UF  Wasteways
  BT  Hydraulic facilities
  RT  Dams
**Spin (Aerodynamics)**
  UF  Spinning (Aerodynamics)
  BT  Locomotion
  RT  Aeronautics
**Spinach**
       --[country or state]--[city]
  BT  Vegetables
Spinets
  USE Harpsichords
**Spinning**
       --[country or state]--[city]
  PN  For spinning by hand using a spindle or
       spinning wheel.

BT  Broader term            RT  Related term            PN  Public Note
NT  Narrower term          UF  Used for                + Term has NTs
HN  History Note           CN  Catalogers Note        --[ ] May subdivide

**Spinning (cont.)**
RT   Spinning apparatus
     Spinning machinery

**Spinning apparatus**
PN   For equipment used in hand spinning.
BT   Equipment
RT   Spinning

Spinning jennies
USE Spinning machinery

**Spinning machinery**
PN   For images that focus on spinning using a
     spinning jenny or other machinery.
UF   Spinning jennies
BT   Machinery
RT   Spinning
     Textile industry

Spinning (Aerodynamics)
USE Spin (Aerodynamics)

Spinsters
USE Single women

**Spires**
     --[country or state]--[city]
PN   For tall pyramidal, polygonal, or conical
     structures that rise from towers or roofs.
BT   Architectural elements
RT   Roofs
     Steeples
     Towers

**Spirit photographs**
CN   TGM II term.
UF   Ghost photographs

Spiritism
USE Spiritualism

Spirits
USE Ghosts

Spiritual healers
USE Healers

**Spiritual leaders**
     --[country or state]--[city]
PN   For persons who provide spiritual
     guidance, although they may not occupy a
     formal position in an organized religion.
     Search also under the subdivision
     --SPIRITUAL LIFE used with names of
     ethnic, racial, and regional groups, and with
     classes of persons (Appendix A).
BT   People associated with religion
RT   Clergy
     Evangelists
     Missionaries
     Religion
     Rites & ceremonies
     Swamis

Spiritual life
CN   Used only as a subdivision with names of
     ethnic, racial, and regional groups, and with
     classes of persons (Appendix A).

**Spiritualism**
     --[country or state]--[city]
PN   For the subject of the belief that spirits of
     the dead communicate with the living, usually
     through a medium. Search under SEANCES

**Spiritualism (cont.)**
     for scenes of people meeting to communicate
     with the dead.
UF   Communication with the dead
     Spiritism
BT   Supernatural practices
NT   Seances

**Spittoons**
UF   Cuspidors
BT   Containers
     Furnishings
RT   Smokeless tobacco

Spitz dogs
USE Chow chows (Dogs)

**Splints (Surgery)**
BT   Medical equipment & supplies
RT   Wounds & injuries

Splitting wood
USE Woodcutting

Spoils of war
USE War destruction & pillage

Spoils system
USE Political patronage

**Sponge fishing**
     --[country or state]--[city]
BT   Fishing
RT   Sponges

**Sponges**
     --[country or state]
BT   Aquatic animals
RT   Sponge fishing

Spools of thread
USE Thread

Sport fishing
USE Fishing

Sport posters
USE Sports posters

**Sporting goods**
UF   Athletic equipment
     Sports equipment
BT   Equipment
NT   Hockey masks
     Targets (Sports)
RT   Fishing & hunting gear
     Sporting goods industry
     Sports

**Sporting goods industry**
     --[country or state]--[city]
PN   Manufacture and trade of sporting goods.
     Includes activities and structures.
CN   Double index under INDUSTRIAL
     FACILITIES (or NTs) for images that focus
     on facilities.
BT   Industry
RT   Sporting goods

**Sports**
     --[country or state]--[city]
PN   Search also under the subdivision
     --SPORTS used with names of ethnic, racial,
     and regional groups and with classes of
     persons (Appendix A) , and with corporate
     bodies and named events (Appendix D).

---

BT Broader term                 RT Related term              PN Public Note
NT Narrower term                UF Used for                  + Term has NTs
HN History Note                 CN Catalogers Note           --[ ] May subdivide

**Sports (cont.)**
Search also under the subdivision --SOCIAL
LIFE used with names of persons (Appendix
B).
UF  Competitions
     Sports teams
     Teams, Sports
NT  Aquatic sports +
     Archery
     Badminton
     Baseball +
     Basketball
     Bowling
     Boxing
     Bullfighting
     Cockfighting
     Cricket
     Curling
     Falconry
     Fencing +
     Field hockey
     Football
     Golf +
     Gymnastics
     Handball
     Ice hockey
     Lacrosse
     Pelota (Game)
     Polo
     Push ball
     Quoits +
     Racing +
     Rodeos
     Roller skating
     Rowing +
     Rugby
     Ski jumping
     Soccer
     Softball
     Table tennis +
     Tennis +
     Tournaments +
     Track athletics +
     Volleyball
     Wrestling +
RT  Athletes
     Athletic clubs
     Cheerleading
     Children playing
     Coaching (Athletics)
     Contests
     Cycling
     Games
     Gymnasiums
     Hiking
     Hunting
     Jumping (Horsemanship)
     Marathons
     Oriental hand-to-hand fighting
     Parachuting
     Physical education
     Physical fitness

**Sports (cont.)**
     Recreation
     Referees
     Riding
     Shooting
     Skating
     Skiing
     Sleds & sleighs
     Snowshoeing
     Sporting goods
     Sports officiating
     Sports spectators
     Stadiums
     Victories
     Weight lifting
     Winter carnivals

**Sports cards**
CN  TGM II term.
UF  Bubble gum cards

Sports clubs
  USE Athletic clubs

Sports equipment
  USE Sporting goods

Sports facilities
  USE Sports & recreation facilities

Sports fans
  USE Sports spectators

Sports officials
  USE Referees

**Sports officiating**
     --[country or state]--[city]
UF  Refereeing
     Umpiring
RT  Referees
     Sports

**Sports posters**
CN  TGM II term.
UF  Sport posters

**Sports spectators**
     --[country or state]--[city]
UF  Fans (Persons)
     Sports fans
BT  Spectators
RT  Sports

Sports teams
  USE Athletes
       Sports

**Sports & recreation facilities**
     --[country or state]--[city]
HN  Changed 1/1993 from two separate terms:
     SPORTS FACILITIES and RECREATION
     FACILITIES.
UF  Recreation facilities
     Sports facilities
BT  Facilities
NT  Amusement parks
     Amusement piers
     Amusement rides +
     Athletic fields
     Bathhouses +
     Billiard parlors
     Bowling alleys

---

BT Broader term
NT Narrower term
HN History Note

RT Related term
UF Used for
CN Catalogers Note

PN Public Note
+ Term has NTs
--[ ] May subdivide

**Sports & recreation facilities (cont.)**
- Camps +
- Canteens (Wartime, emergency, etc.)
- Casinos
- Dance halls
- Discotheques
- Grandstands
- Gymnasiums
- Hunting lodges
- Nightclubs
- Pavilions
- Penny arcades
- Picnic grounds
- Playgrounds
- Racetracks
- Resorts
- Shooting galleries
- Skating rinks +
- Stadiums
- Swimming pools
- Tennis courts
- RT  Athletes
  - Boathouses
  - Clubhouses
  - Community centers
  - Exhibition facilities
  - Golf
  - Parks
  - Recreation rooms
  - Student unions

**Spouses**
- --[country or state]--[city]
- UF  Husbands
  - Wives
- BT  Families
- NT  Cabinet officers' spouses
  - Legislators' spouses
  - Presidents' spouses
- RT  Couples
  - Interpersonal relations
  - Marriage
  - Men
  - Women

**Spring**
- --[country or state]--[city]
- BT  Seasons

**Springhouses**
- --[country or state]--[city]
- PN  Buildings enclosing a natural spring; sufficiently cool for use as a storehouse of milk and other dairy products.
- BT  Storage facilities
- RT  Outbuildings

**Springs**
- --[country or state]--[city]
- UF  Hot springs
  - Mineral springs
  - Seeps
  - Thermal springs
- BT  Bodies of water
- RT  Geysers
  - Health resorts

**Springs (cont.)**
- Mineral waters
- Therapeutic baths

**Sputniks**
- USE Artificial satellites

**Spyglasses**
- USE Telescopes

**Spying**
- --[country or state]--[city]
- PN  Search also under the subdivision --COVERT OPERATIONS used with names of wars (Appendix C).
- UF  Espionage
- RT  Covert operations
  - Eavesdropping
  - Informers
  - Military art & science
  - Military intelligence
  - Military reconnaissance
  - National security
  - Sabotage
  - Secret service
  - Surveillance

**Squabs**
- USE Pigeons

**Square dancing**
- --[country or state]--[city]
- BT  Dancing
  - Folk dancing
- RT  Country life

**Squares, Public**
- USE Plazas

**Squatters**
- --[country or state]--[city]
- BT  People
- RT  Homesteading

**Squids**
- --[country or state]
- BT  Aquatic animals

**Squirrels**
- --[country or state]
- BT  Rodents

**Stabilization photoprints**
- USE Stabilization prints

**Stabilization prints**
- CN  TGM II term.
- UF  Stabilization photoprints

**Stables**
- --[country or state]--[city]
- UF  Livery stables
- BT  Animal housing
- RT  Barns
  - Horses

**Stacks, Book**
- USE Bookstacks

**Stacks, Hay**
- USE Haystacks

**Stadia**
- USE Stadiums

**Stadiums**
- --[country or state]--[city]
- PN  Large, often unroofed structure, in which

---

BT  Broader term                    RT  Related term                    PN  Public Note
NT  Narrower term                   UF  Used for                        +  Term has NTs
HN  History Note                    CN  Catalogers Note                 --[ ]  May subdivide

**Stadiums (cont.)**
athletic events are held.
CN  Used in a note under
     AMPHITHEATERS.
UF  Hippodromes
     Stadia
BT  Sports & recreation facilities
RT  Amphitheaters
     Grandstands
     Sports
**Staff**
CN  Used only as a subdivision with names of
     persons (Appendix B).
USE Employees
**Staffs (Sticks)**
UF  Canes
     Sticks
     Walking sticks
NT  Ceremonial maces
RT  Clothing & dress
**Stage lighting**
UF  Lighting, Stage
     Theatrical lighting
RT  Lighting
     Theatrical productions
**Stage props**
UF  Props, Stage
     Set props
RT  Stages (Platforms)
     Theatrical productions
**Stagecoach lines**
USE Stagecoaches
**Stagecoaches**
     --[country or state]--[city]
UF  Overland mail service
     Stagecoach lines
BT  Carriages & coaches
RT  Postal service
**Stages of life**
USE Human life cycle
**Stages (Platforms)**
UF  Rostrums
BT  Rooms & spaces
RT  Auditoriums
     Stage props
     Theaters
**Stained glass**
     --[country or state]--[city]
UF  Glass, Stained
BT  Art
RT  Windows
**Staircases**
USE Stairways
**Stairhalls**
     --[country or state]--[city]
BT  Interiors
RT  Entrance halls
     Passageways
     Stairways
**Stairways**
     --[country or state]--[city]
UF  Staircases

**Stairways (cont.)**
BT  Architectural elements
RT  Hand railings
     Newels
     Stairhalls
**Stalactites & stalagmites**
     --[country or state]
UF  Stalagmites
BT  Natural phenomena
RT  Caves
**Stalagmites**
USE Stalactites & stalagmites
**Stallions**
USE Horses
**Stampedes**
     --[country or state]--[city]
RT  Animal behavior
     Animals
**Stamps, Blind**
USE Blind stamps
**Stamps, Postage**
USE Postage stamps
**Stamps, Rubber**
USE Rubber stamps
**Stamps, Tax**
USE Tax stamps
**Standard of living**
USE Cost & standard of living
**Standardization**
RT  Testing
     Weights & measures
**Stanhopes**
CN  TGM II term.
**Star gazing**
USE Stargazing
**Starch industry**
     --[country or state]--[city]
PN  Includes activities and structures.
CN  Double index under INDUSTRIAL
     FACILITIES (or NTs) for images that focus
     on facilities.
BT  Industry
**Stargazing**
     --[country or state]--[city]
UF  Astronomical observation
     Star gazing
RT  Astrology
     Astronomy
**Starlings**
     --[country or state]
BT  Birds
**Stars**
BT  Celestial bodies
**Starvation**
     --[country or state]--[city]
UF  Hunger
RT  Famines
     Fasts
     Food relief
     Nutrition
**State arms**
USE State seals

---

BT Broader term          RT Related term          PN Public Note
NT Narrower term          UF Used for          + Term has NTs
HN History Note          CN Catalogers Note          --[ ] May subdivide

State fairs
  USE Fairs
**State flags**
      --[state]
  BT   Flags
  RT   State seals
State funerals
  USE Lying in state
State houses
  USE Capitols
State ownership
  USE Government ownership
**State parks & reserves**
      --[country or state]--[city]
  UF   Reserves, State
  BT   Parks
  RT   National parks & reserves
       Rangers
State proofs
  USE Trial proofs
**State rights**
  UF   Rights of states
       States' rights
  BT   Politics & government
  RT   Statehood
**State seals**
      --[state]
  UF   Great seals
       State arms
  BT   Seals
  RT   State flags
State ships
  USE Government vessels
State visits
  USE Visits of state
State & church
  USE Church & state
**Statehood**
      --[state]
  PN   For states of the United States.
  BT   Politics & government
  RT   State rights
Statehouses
  USE Capitols
**Staterooms**
  PN   For private rooms on ships or railroad cars
       designed to accommodate one or more
       persons.
  UF   Cabins, Ship
  BT   Passenger quarters
  RT   Bedrooms
       Railroad private cars
       Railroad sleeping cars
States of mind
  USE Mental states
**Statesmen**
      --[nationality]--[country or state]--[city]
  PN   Persons who engage in conducting the
       business of a government or in shaping its
       policies but do not hold a government post.
  HN   Scope note changed 12/1992.
  BT   People associated with politics &

Statesmen (cont.)
       government
  RT   Government officials
       Heads of state
States' rights
  USE State rights
**Stationery**
  CN   TGM II term.
  RT   Stationery trade
Stationery shops
  USE Stationery trade
**Stationery trade**
      --[country or state]--[city]
  PN   Includes activities and structures.
  CN   Double index under COMMERCIAL
       BUILDINGS or appropriate NT for images
       that focus on buildings.
  UF   Stationery shops
  BT   Business enterprises
  RT   Stationery
**Stations of the Cross**
  RT   Christianity
       Crosses
       Crucifixions
       Religion
       Rites & ceremonies
Stations, Fire lookout
  USE Fire lookout stations
Stations, Railroad
  USE Railroad stations
Stations, Subway
  USE Subway stations
**Stats**
  CN   TGM II term.
  UF   Photostats
Statues
  CN   Used only as a subdivision with names of
       persons (Appendix B).
  USE Sculpture
STD (Diseases)
  USE Sexually transmitted diseases
Stealing
  USE Children stealing
       Robberies
**Steam automobiles**
      --[nationality]--[country or state]--[city]
  BT   Automobiles
**Steam engines**
  BT   Engines
**Steam hammers**
  UF   Hammers, Steam
  BT   Machinery
**Steam shovels**
  UF   Steam-shovels
  BT   Machinery
  RT   Bulldozers
       Digging
       Excavation
       Shovels
**Steam yachts**
      --[nationality]--[country or state]--[city]
  BT   Steamboats

---

BT  Broader term                   RT  Related term                    PN  Public Note
NT  Narrower term                  UF  Used for                        +   Term has NTs
HN  History Note                   CN  Catalogers Note                 --[ ]  May subdivide

**Steam yachts (cont.)**
    Yachts
**Steamboat accidents**
    --[country or state]--[city]
  BT  Marine accidents
  RT  Steamboats
**Steamboat racing**
    --[country or state]--[city]
  UF  Boat racing
  BT  Racing
  RT  Steamboats
**Steamboats**
    --[nationality]--[country or state]--[city]
  UF  Lake steamers
      Riverboats
      Steamships
  BT  Vessels
  NT  Side wheelers
      Steam yachts
      Stern wheelers
  RT  Steamboat accidents
      Steamboat racing
      Whalebacks
Steamrollers
  USE Road rollers
Steamships
  USE Ships
      Steamboats
Steam-shovels
  USE Steam shovels
**Steel**
  BT  Metals
  RT  Steel industry
**Steel industry**
    --[country or state]--[city]
  PN  Includes activities and structures.
  CN  Double index under INDUSTRIAL
      FACILITIES (or NTs) for images that focus
      on facilities. Used in a note under
      FOUNDRIES.
  BT  Metallurgical industry
  RT  Iron industry
      Steel
      Steel industry strikes
**Steel industry strikes**
    --[country or state]--[city]
  BT  Strikes
  RT  Steel industry
**Steeplechases**
    --[country or state]--[city]
  BT  Horse racing
**Steeplejacks**
    --[country or state]--[city]
  BT  People associated with manual labor
  RT  Construction
      Construction industry
**Steeples**
  PN  For towers terminated by spires, includes
      tower, spire, and lantern.
  BT  Architectural elements
  RT  Lanterns (Architecture)
      Spires

**Steeples (cont.)**
    Towers
**Steerage**
  PN  For any section of a passenger vessel
      occupied by passengers paying the lowest
      fares.
  BT  Passenger quarters
  RT  Vessels
Steering gear
  USE Steering wheels
**Steering wheels**
  UF  Steering gear
  BT  Equipment
  RT  Automobile equipment & supplies
Steers
  USE Cattle
**Stencil prints**
  CN  TGM II term.
**Stencils**
  CN  TGM II term.
Step gables
  USE Crow-stepped gables
Stepladders
  USE Ladders
**Stepmothers**
    --[country or state]--[city]
  BT  Mothers
  RT  Families
**Stepping stones**
    --[country or state]--[city]
  PN  Stones on which to step (as in crossing a
      stream).
  BT  Site elements
  RT  Landscape architecture facilities
      Streams
Stereograms
  USE Stereographs
**Stereograph industry**
    --[country or state]--[city]
  PN  Includes activities and structures.
  CN  Double index under INDUSTRIAL
      FACILITIES (or NTs) for images that focus
      on facilities.
  BT  Photography industry
  RT  Stereographs
**Stereographs**
  CN  TGM II term.
  UF  Stereograms
      Stereoscopic views
      Stereoviews
      Three-dimensional photographs
      Viewmaster cards
  RT  Stereograph industry
Stereoscopic views
  USE Stereographs
Stereotypes
  USE Caricatures
Stereotypes, Ethnic
  USE Ethnic stereotypes
**Stereotyping**
    --[country or state]--[city]
  RT  Prejudice

BT Broader term               RT Related term               PN Public Note
NT Narrower term           UF Used for                  + Term has NTs
HN History Note             CN Catalogers Note       --[ ] May subdivide

**Stereotyping (cont.)**
        Public opinion
Stereoviews
  USE Stereographs
**Sterilization**
        --[country or state]--[city]
  BT  Birth control
**Stern wheelers**
        --[nationality]--[country or state]--[city]
  UF  Paddle wheel steamers
        Riverboats
  BT  Steamboats
  RT  Side wheelers
Stevedores
  USE Longshoremen
**Stewards**
  PN  Employees on ships, airplanes, or trains
        who manage the provision of food and attend
        passengers.
  BT  People
  RT  Travel
        Vehicles
        Waiters
**Stickers**
  CN  TGM II term.
Sticks
  USE Staffs (Sticks)
Sticks of dynamite
  USE Dynamite
**Still life drawings**
  CN  TGM II term.
**Still life paintings**
  CN  TGM II term.
**Still life photographs**
  CN  TGM II term.
**Still life prints**
  CN  TGM II term.
**Still lifes**
  CN  TGM II term.
Stills
  USE Film stills
        Television stills
**Stills (Distilleries)**
  PN  For the apparatus used for the distillation
        of alcoholic liquor.
  UF  Bootlegging
        Distillation apparatus
        Liquor stills
        Moonshine stills
  RT  Distilling industries
        Prohibition
        Retorts (Equipment)
**Stilt houses**
        --[country or state]--[city]
  BT  Houses
**Stilts**
  RT  Entertainment
        Transportation
Stinginess
  USE Miserliness
Stings & bites
  USE Bites & stings

**Stipple engravings**
  CN  TGM II term.
  UF  Stipple prints
Stipple prints
  USE Stipple engravings
**Stock cards**
  CN  TGM II term.
**Stock certificates**
  CN  TGM II term.
**Stock exchanges**
        --[country or state]--[city]
  PN  Includes activities and structures.
  UF  Curb markets
        Exchanges
  BT  Financial facilities
  RT  Commodity exchanges
        Merchants' exchanges
        Stock market
        Ticker tape
**Stock market**
  RT  Stock exchanges
Stockings
  USE Hosiery
Stockmen (Animal industry)
  USE Cowboys
**Stockrooms**
        --[country or state]--[city]
  UF  Supply rooms
  BT  Interiors
  RT  Communication facilities
        Industrial facilities
**Stocks (Punishment)**
        --[country or state]--[city]
  PN  Devices for publicly punishing offenders
        consisting of a wooden frame with holes in
        which the feet or feet and hands can be
        locked.
  BT  Punishment devices
  RT  Pillories
**Stockyards**
        --[country or state]--[city]
  UF  Cattle markets
        Cattle pens
  RT  Meat industry
**Stone buildings**
        --[country or state]--[city]
  BT  Buildings distinguished by material
  RT  Dugout houses
        Pueblos
**Stone carving**
        --[country or state]--[city]
  PN  Carving stone to make sculpture or
        architectural elements.
  CN  Used in a note under SCULPTURE.
  UF  Sculpting
        Sculpturing
  BT  Carving
  RT  Sculpture
**Stone cutting**
        --[country or state]--[city]
  PN  Cutting or dressing stone.
  UF  Stone working

---

**Stone cutting (cont.)**
 Stonecutting
 Stoneworking
RT Chisels & mallets
 Marble
 Masonry
 Rocks
 Rustication
 Stonework
**Stone masonry**
 USE Masonry
**Stone quarrying**
 --[country or state]--[city]
PN Includes activities and sites.
BT Quarrying
RT Minerals
 Rocks
**Stone walls**
 --[country or state]--[city]
UF Rock fences
BT Site elements
RT Landscape architecture facilities
 Masonry
 Walls
**Stone working**
 USE Stone cutting
**Stonecutting**
HN Changed 11/1993 from stoneworking.
 USE Stone cutting
**Stonemasonry**
 USE Masonry
**Stones, Printing**
 USE Printing stones
**Stonework**
 --[country or state]--[city]
RT Cairns
 Masonry
 Rocks
 Stone cutting
**Stoneworking**
 USE Stone cutting
**Stoning**
 --[country or state]--[city]
UF Rock throwing
 Throwing stones
RT Executions
 Punishment & torture
**Stool pigeons**
 USE Informers
**Stools**
BT Chairs
**Storage facilities**
 --[country or state]--[city]
BT Facilities
NT Drying sheds
 Icehouses
 Sheds +
 Springhouses
 Storage tanks
 Storehouses
 Warehouses
RT Carriage houses

**Storage facilities (cont.)**
 Food storage buildings
 Garages
 Military depots
 Moving & storage trade
 Parking garages
**Storage furniture**
BT Furniture
**Storage tanks**
 --[country or state]--[city]
PN Stationary storage tanks.
UF Tanks (Storage)
BT Storage facilities
RT Fuel tanks
 Water tanks
**Storage & moving trade**
 USE Moving & storage trade
**Store windows**
 USE Show windows
 Window displays
**Storefronts**
PN Search under COMMERCIAL
 FACILITIES and FACADES for images that
 focus on fronts of stores.
**Storehouses**
 --[country or state]--[city]
BT Storage facilities
RT Warehouses
**Stores & shops**
 --[country or state]--[city]
HN Changed 1/1993 from non-postable term
 (Use BUSINESS ENTERPRISES).
UF Chain stores
 Retail stores
 Shops
BT Mercantile facilities
NT Antique stores
 Appliance stores +
 Army-Navy stores
 Automobile equipment & supplies stores
 Bakeries
 Bicycle shops
 Bookstores +
 Butcher shops
 Christmas decoration stores
 Clothing stores +
 Confectioneries
 Convenience stores
 Cosmetics stores
 Coupon stores
 Dairy stores
 Delicatessens
 Department stores
 Drugstores
 Dry goods stores
 Fabric shops
 Feed stores
 Florist shops
 Furniture stores
 General stores
 Gift shops
 Grocery stores

BT Broader term  RT Related term  PN Public Note
NT Narrower term  UF Used for  + Term has NTs
HN History Note  CN Catalogers Note  --[ ] May subdivide

**Stores & shops (cont.)**
    Hardware stores
    Home furnishings stores
    Jewelry stores
    Leather goods stores
    Liquor stores
    Military exchanges
    Music stores
    Opticians' shops
    Pawnshops
    Perfume stores
    Pet shops
    Photography stores
    Plumbing stores
    Seafood stores
    Sound recording stores
    Souvenir shops
    Tailor shops
    Thrift shops
    Ticket offices
    Tobacco shops
    Trading posts
    Variety stores

**Stories**
  USE Literature

**Storks**
    --[country or state]
  BT  Birds

**Storms**
    --[country or state]--[city]
  PN  Includes the event and any resulting
      damage.
  BT  Weather
  NT  Blizzards
      Cyclones
      Dust storms
      Hurricanes
      Tornadoes
      Typhoons
  RT  Disasters
      Floods
      Hail
      Lightning
      Rain
      Winds

**Storytelling**
    --[country or state]--[city]
  UF  Telling of stories
  BT  Communication
      Entertainment
  NT  Children telling stories
  RT  Literature
      Reminiscing
      Tall tales

**Stove industry**
    --[country or state]--[city]
  PN  Includes activities and structures.
  CN  Double index under INDUSTRIAL
      FACILITIES (or NTs) for images that focus
      on facilities.
  BT  Equipment industry
  RT  Stoves

**Stoves**
  PN  Includes both heating and cooking stoves.
  UF  Camp stoves
      Ranges
  RT  Appliances
      Cookery
      Furnishings
      Ovens
      Stove industry

**Stowaways**
    --[country or state]--[city]
  BT  People associated with transportation
  RT  Freighthopping
      Passengers

**Straits**
  USE Channels

**Strands**
  USE Beaches
      Waterfronts

**Strangling**
    --[country or state]--[city]
  UF  Choking
  RT  Executions
      Homicides
      Punishment & torture
      Violence

**Strategies, Political**
  USE Political strategies

**Straw hats**
  BT  Hats
  RT  Panama hats

**Straw industries**
    --[country or state]--[city]
  PN  Includes activities and structures.
  CN  As appropriate, double index under the
      product. Double index under INDUSTRIAL
      FACILITIES (or NTs) for images that focus
      on facilities.
  BT  Industry

**Straw man**
  PN  A weak or imaginary opposition set up
      only to be easily refuted; or, a person set up to
      serve as a cover for a usually questionable
      transaction.
  RT  People
      Symbols

**Strawberries**
    --[country or state]--[city]
  BT  Berries

**Stream fords**
  USE Fords (Stream crossings)

**Stream valleys**
  USE Valleys

**Streamfronts**
  USE Waterfronts

**Streamliners**
  USE Railroad locomotives

**Streams**
    --[country or state]--[city]
  UF  Brooks
      Creeks
  BT  Bodies of water

BT Broader term      RT Related term      PN Public Note
NT Narrower term     UF Used for       + Term has NTs
HN History Note      CN Catalogers Note    --[ ] May subdivide

**Streams (cont.)**
  NT  Bayous
      Rivers
  RT  Arroyos
      Channels
      Fish ladders
      Fords (Stream crossings)
      Sandbars
      Shooting rapids
      Stepping stones
      Waterfalls
**Street cleaning**
      --[country or state]--[city]
  UF  Street sweeping
  BT  Cleaning
  RT  Roads
      Snow removal
Street cries
  USE Cries
**Street entertainers**
      --[country or state]--[city]
  UF  Buskers
  BT  Entertainers
  NT  Street musicians +
  RT  City & town life
Street gangs
  USE Gangs
**Street kitchens**
  UF  Kitchens, Street
  BT  Kitchens
  RT  Cookery
Street lamps
  USE Street lights
Street life
  USE City & town life
**Street lights**
      --[country or state]--[city]
  UF  Street lamps
      Streetlights
  BT  Site elements
  NT  Gas street lamps
  RT  Light fixtures
      Lighting
      Streets
Street markets
  USE Markets
**Street musicians**
      --[country or state]--[city]
  BT  Musicians
      Street entertainers
  NT  Organ grinders
**Street railroad accidents**
      --[country or state]--[city]
  BT  Railroad accidents
  NT  Subway accidents
  RT  Street railroads
      Traffic accidents
**Street railroad facilities**
      --[country or state]--[city]
  BT  Railroad facilities
  NT  Street railroad stations
      Subway stations

**Street railroad stations**
      --[country or state]--[city]
  UF  Streetcar stations
      Trolley stations
  BT  Street railroad facilities
  RT  Street railroads
**Street railroad strikes**
      --[country or state]--[city]
  BT  Strikes
  RT  Street railroads
**Street railroad tracks**
      --[country or state]--[city]
  BT  Railroad tracks
  RT  Street railroads
**Street railroads**
      --[country or state]--[city]
  PN  For railroads within cities. Search under
      ELECTRIC RAILROADS for street railroads
      between cities and under CABLE
      RAILROADS for street railroads powered by
      cable.
  UF  Streetcars
      Tramways
      Trolleys
  BT  Railroads
  NT  Horse railroads
      Subways
  RT  Cable railroads
      Electric railroads
      Elevated railroads
      Mass transit
      Street railroad accidents
      Street railroad stations
      Street railroad strikes
      Street railroad tracks
      Streets
Street signs
  USE Traffic signs & signals
Street sweeping
  USE Street cleaning
Street traffic regulations
  USE Traffic regulations
Street vendors
  USE Peddlers
Streetcar stations
  USE Street railroad stations
Streetcars
  USE Street railroads
Streetlights
  USE Street lights
**Streets**
      --[country or state]--[city]
  PN  For thoroughfares in cities, towns, and
      villages.  Search under CITY & TOWN LIFE
      for images that focus on activities.  Search
      under ROADS for thoroughfares outside of
      cities, towns, and villages.
  CN  Used in a note under CITY & TOWN
      LIFE and ROADS.
  UF  Avenues
      Thoroughfares
  BT  Transportation facilities

---

BT  Broader term
NT  Narrower term
HN  History Note

RT  Related term
UF  Used for
CN  Catalogers Note

PN  Public Note
+  Term has NTs
--[ ] May subdivide

**Streets (cont.)**
  NT  Alleys
      Cobblestone streets
      Commercial streets
      One-way streets
      Residential streets
  RT  Boardwalks
      Cities & towns
      City & town life
      Driveways
      Manhole covers
      Manholes
      Milestones
      Pedestrians
      Plazas
      Roads
      Sidewalks
      Street lights
      Street railroads
      Traffic congestion
      Vehicles

**Stress**
  UF  Tension
  BT  Mental states
  RT  Anxiety
      Distress
      Hypertension

**Stretchers**
  USE Litters

**Strikes**
      --[country or state]--[city]
  PN  Search also under the subdivision
      --STRIKES used with corporate bodies and
      named events (Appendix D).
  UF  Lockouts
      Moratoriums
      Work stoppages
  BT  Demonstrations
  NT  Airline industry strikes
      Automobile industry strikes
      Barbers' strikes
      Beverage industry strikes
      Boat & ship industry strikes
      Clothing industry strikes
      Defense industry strikes
      Electricians' strikes
      Freight handlers' strikes +
      Garbage collectors' strikes
      Laundry workers' strikes
      Meat industry strikes
      Miners' strikes
      Optical industry strikes
      Railroad strikes
      Retail trade strikes
      Shoe industry strikes
      Steel industry strikes
      Street railroad strikes
      Teachers' strikes
      Textile industry strikes
      Tobacco industry strikes
      Tube industry strikes
  RT  Boycotts

**Strikes, (cont.)**
      Industrial arbitration
      Labor unions
      Laborers
      Sabotage

**Stringcourses**
      --[country or state]--[city]
  PN  Horizontal bands of masonry, narrower
      than other courses, running across a wall.
  UF  Belt courses
      Cordons
      Courses, Belt
  BT  Courses (Wall components)

**Stringed instruments**
  PN  Includes the activity of playing stringed
      instruments.
  BT  Musical instruments
  NT  Balalaikas
      Banjos
      Guitars
      Harps
      Harpsichords
      Kankles
      Lutes
      Mandolins
      Pianos +
      Shamisens
      Ukeleles
      Violins
      Violoncellos

**Strip mining**
      --[country or state]--[city]
  PN  Includes activities and sites.
  CN  Double index under COAL MINING or
      other kinds of mining, as appropriate. Used in
      a note under COAL MINING.
  UF  Open-pit mining
      Surface mining
  BT  Mining

**Stroboscopic photographs**
  USE Motion study photographs

**Strolling**
  USE Walking

**Strong men**
      --[country or state]--[city]
  UF  Bodybuilders
      Muscle men
  BT  Entertainers
      Men
  RT  Human body
      Weight lifting

**Strong rooms (Vaults)**
  USE Vaults (Strong rooms)

**Structural frames**
      --[country or state]--[city]
  UF  Frames (Structures)
  BT  Structural systems
  RT  Girders
      Trusses

**Structural support systems**
  USE Structural systems

**Structural systems**

---

**Structural systems (cont.)**
--[country or state]--[city]
UF  Structural support systems
BT  Architectural elements
NT  Structural frames
RT  Construction

**Structural systems drawings**
CN  TGM II term.
UF  Drawings, Structural systems

Structures
CN  Used only as a subdivision with names of ethnic, racial, and regional groups, and with classes of persons (Appendix A).

Stubbornness
USE Obstinacy

Stuccowork
USE Plasterwork

Stud farms
USE Horse farms

Student activism
USE Student movements

**Student aspirations**
UF  Aspirations, Student
Educational aspirations
RT  Students

Student busing (School integration)
USE Busing (School integration)

Student centers
USE Student unions

**Student movements**
--[country or state]--[city]
UF  Campus disorders
Student activism
Student protest
Student strikes
Student unrest
RT  Demonstrations
Political participation
Protest movements
Students
Universities & colleges

**Student organizations**
--[country or state]--[city]
PN  Includes activities and structures.
CN  Subdivide geographically as appropriate to indicate national, state, or city levels of organization. Double index under ORGANIZATIONS' FACILITIES (or NTs) for images that focus on facilities.
BT  Organizations
RT  Students
Youth organizations

Student protest
USE Student movements

Student strikes
USE Student movements

**Student unions**
--[country or state]--[city]
UF  College unions
Student centers
Unions, Student
University & college unions

**Student unions (cont.)**
BT  Social & civic facilities
RT  Educational facilities
Sports & recreation facilities

Student unrest
USE Student movements

**Student works**
CN  TGM II term.

**Students**
--[nationality]--[country or state]--[city]
PN  For high school and college students. Search under SCHOOLCHILDREN for younger students.
UF  College students
High school students
University students
BT  People associated with education & communication
RT  Alumni & alumnae
Cadets
Classrooms
Education
Graduation ceremonies
School children
Schools
Student aspirations
Student movements
Student organizations
Teachers
Universities & colleges
Young adults

**Studies**
CN  TGM II term.

**Studies (Rooms)**
--[country or state]--[city]
PN  Building or room furnished especially with books and devoted to work, study, or literary pursuits.
BT  Interiors
RT  Libraries (Rooms)
Offices
Private libraries

Studies, Figure
USE Figure drawings

Studio portraits
USE Portrait photographs

Studio proof paper prints
USE Silver gelatin printing-out paper prints

**Studio props**
UF  Backdrops
Props, Studio
RT  Studios

**Studios**
--[country or state]--[city]
HN  Changed 2/1993 from STUDIOS & WORKSHOPS.
BT  Facilities
NT  Artists' studios
Photographic studios
RT  Industrial facilities
Mercantile facilities
Studio props

---

BT  Broader term
NT  Narrower term
HN  History Note

RT  Related term
UF  Used for
CN  Catalogers Note

PN  Public Note
+  Term has NTs
--[ ]  May subdivide

Stunt driving
    --[country or state]--[city]
  BT  Automobile driving
       Entertainment
Stunt flying
    --[country or state]--[city]
  UF  Aerobatics
  BT  Entertainment
  RT  Aeronautics
       Airplanes
       Daredevils
Stunt riding
  USE Trick riding
Stuntmen
  USE Daredevils
Style shows
  USE Fashion shows
Subdivision of land
  USE Land subdivision
Subdivisions (Land)
  USE Land subdivision
Submarine boats
  USE Submarines
Submarine cables
  UF  Cables, Submarine
       Ocean cables
       Undersea cables
  BT  Telecommunication cables
  RT  Telegraph
       Telephones
Submarine drilling
  USE Underwater drilling
Submarine mines
  USE Mines (Warfare)
Submarine photographs
  USE Underwater photographs
Submarine warfare
    --[country or state]
  BT  Naval warfare
  RT  Submarines
       Torpedo boats
Submarines
    --[country or state]--[city]
  UF  Submarine boats
  BT  Ships
  RT  Submarine warfare
       Warships
Subsidies
  USE Assistance
Subsistance activities
  PN  Used only as a subdivision with names of
       indigenous peoples (Appendix A).
Substance abuse
  USE Drug abuse
Substitute soldiers
  USE Mercenaries (Soldiers)
Subterfuge
  USE Deception
Suburban life
    --[country or state]--[city]
  UF  Suburbs
  RT  Housing developments

Suburbs
  USE Suburban life
Subway accidents
    --[country or state]--[city]
  BT  Street railroad accidents
  RT  Subways
Subway stations
    --[country or state]--[city]
  UF  Metro stations
       Stations, Subway
       Underground stations
  BT  Street railroad facilities
  RT  Subways
Subways
    --[country or state]--[city]
  BT  Street railroads
  RT  Mass transit
       Subway accidents
       Subway stations
       Tunnels
Successive proofs
  USE Progressive proofs
Suffering
  USE Distress
       Pain
Suffrage
    --[country or state]--[city]
  UF  Franchise
       Universal suffrage
  BT  Civil liberties
  NT  Women's suffrage
  RT  Voting
Suffragettes
  USE Suffragists
Suffragists
  PN  People who advocate suffrage for women.
  HN  Changed 12/1992 from SUFRAGETTES.
  UF  Suffragettes
  BT  Activists
       Feminists
  RT  Women
Sugar
    --[country or state]--[city]
  UF  Beet sugar
       Cane sugar
       Sweeteners, Natural
  BT  Food
  RT  Beets
       Sugar industry
       Sugarcane
Sugar beets
  USE Beets
Sugar cane
  USE Sugarcane
Sugar cane plantations
  USE Sugar plantations
Sugar industry
    --[country or state]--[city]
  PN  Includes activities and structures.
  CN  Double index under INDUSTRIAL
       FACILITIES (or NTs) for images that focus
       on facilities.

---

BT Broader term            RT Related term            PN Public Note
NT Narrower term          UF Used for                + Term has NTs
HN History Note            CN Catalogers Note        --[ ] May subdivide

**Sugar industry (cont.)**
- BT   Food industry
- NT   Maple sugar industry
- RT   Beets
- Sugar
- Sugar plantations

**Sugar maple tapping**
--[country or state]--[city]
- BT   Tapping
- RT   Maple sugar industry
- Orchards

**Sugar plantations**
--[country or state]--[city]
- PN   Includes activities and structures.
- CN   As appropriate, double index under HARVESTING.
- UF   Sugar cane plantations
- Sugarcane plantations
- BT   Plantations
- RT   Sugar industry
- Sugarcane

**Sugarcane**
--[country or state]--[city]
- UF   Sugar cane
- BT   Plants
- RT   Sugar
- Sugar plantations

Sugarcane plantations
USE   Sugar plantations

**Sugar-lift aquatints**
- CN   TGM II term.
- UF   Lift-ground aquatints
- Lift-ground engravings

**Suicides**
--[country or state]--[city]
- BT   Homicides

**Suites**
--[country or state]--[city]
- PN   Group of rooms designed for occupancy as a unit.
- BT   Interiors
- RT   Hotels

Suits (Law)
USE   Actions & defenses

Sulfuric acid industry
USE   Sulphuric acid industry

**Sulphur industry**
--[country or state]--[city]
- PN   Includes activities and structures.
- CN   Double index under INDUSTRIAL FACILITIES (or NTs) for images that focus on facilities.
- BT   Chemical industry

**Sulphuric acid industry**
--[country or state]--[city]
- PN   Includes activities and structures.
- CN   Double index under INDUSTRIAL FACILITIES (or NTs ) for images that focus on facilities.
- UF   Sulfuric acid industry
- BT   Chemical industry

**Sultans**

**Sultans (cont.)**
--[country]
- BT   Rulers

**Summer**
--[country or state]--[city]
- BT   Seasons

Summer camps
USE   Camps

**Sumo**
--[country or state]--[city]
- UF   Japanese wrestling
- BT   Oriental hand-to-hand fighting
- Wrestling
- RT   Sumo wrestlers

**Sumo wrestlers**
--[country or state]--[city]
- UF   Wrestlers, Sumo
- BT   Wrestlers
- RT   Sumo

**Sun**
- BT   Celestial bodies
- RT   Light
- Sunburns
- Sunrises & sunsets

Sun decks
USE   Decks (Rooms & spaces)

Sun dials
USE   Sundials

Sun fish
USE   Sunfish

Sun parlors
USE   Sunspaces

Sunbonnets
USE   Bonnets

**Sunburns**
- BT   Burns & scalds
- RT   Sun

Sunburst lights
USE   Fanlights

Sunday labor
USE   Hours of labor

Sunday school cards
USE   Bible cards

**Sunday schools**
--[country or state]--[city]
- BT   Church schools

Sundays
USE   Sabbaths

**Sundials**
--[country or state]--[city]
- UF   Sun dials
- RT   Clocks & watches

**Sunfish**
--[country or state]
- UF   Sun fish
- BT   Fish

**Sunflowers**
--[country or state]--[city]
- BT   Flowers

Sunlight
USE   Light

**Sunrises & sunsets**

---

BT  Broader term                    RT  Related term                    PN  Public Note
NT  Narrower term                   UF  Used for                        +   Term has NTs
HN  History Note                    CN  Catalogers Note                 --[ ] May subdivide

**Sunrises & sunsets (cont.)**
  UF  Dawn
       Dusk
       Evening
       Sunsets
       Twilight
  BT  Natural phenomena
  RT  Sun
Sunrooms
  USE Sunspaces
Sunsets
  USE Sunrises & sunsets
Sunshine legislation
  USE Financial disclosure
**Sunspaces**
      --[country or state]--[city]
  PN  Additions to buildings which act as high
       performance heat collectors or provide
       additional solar heated living or recreational
       space.
  UF  Porches, Sun
       Solariums
       Sun parlors
       Sunrooms
  BT  Rooms & spaces
  RT  Decks (Rooms & spaces)
       Garden rooms
**Superheroes**
  PN  People or characters with superhuman
       strength, capabilities or special means of
       communication. Based on comic strips and
       comic book heroes such as Batman,
       Superman, and Tarzan.
  BT  Fictitious characters
       Heroes
  RT  Supernatural beings
Superhighways
  USE Express highways
Superintendents, School
  USE School superintendents
Supermarkets
  USE Grocery stores
**Supernatural**
  NT  Magical devices +
       Supernatural beings +
       Supernatural practices +
  RT  Fantasy
       Metamorphosis
       Myths
       Religion
**Supernatural beings**
  UF  Imaginary beings
       Mythical creatures
  BT  Supernatural
  NT  Angels
       Demons
       Dragons
       Fairies +
       Firebird (Mythical bird)
       Ghosts
       Ghouls
       Goddesses

**Supernatural beings (cont.)**
       Gods +
       Griffins
       Jinns
       Mermaids
       Monsters +
       Phoenix (Mythical bird)
       Unicorns
       Vampires
       Witches
       Wizards
  RT  Extraterrestrial life
       Fictitious characters
       Superheroes
**Supernatural practices**
      --[country or state]--[city]
  BT  Supernatural
  NT  Astrology
       Divination
       Evil eye
       Exorcism
       Levitation
       Miracles
       Prophecy
       Spiritualism +
       Witchcraft
  RT  Cursing
       Magic
       Magical devices
       Shamans
       Superstitions
**Superstitions**
  UF  Delusions
       Friday the 13th
  RT  Cursing
       Manners & customs
       Supernatural practices
Supertankers
  USE Tankers
Supply horses
  USE Pack animals
       Packtrains
Supply rooms
  USE Stockrooms
**Supreme Court justices**
      --[country or state]
  CN  Subdivide geographically as appropriate to
       indicate national or state level.
  UF  Chief justices
       Justices (U.S. Supreme Court)
  BT  Judges
Suqs
  USE Bazaars
Surf
  USE Seas
**Surf fishing**
      --[country or state]
  BT  Fishing
  RT  Beaches
Surf riding
  USE Surfing
Surface mining

---

BT Broader term
NT Narrower term
HN History Note

RT Related term
UF Used for
CN Catalogers Note

PN Public Note
+ Term has NTs
--[ ] May subdivide

Surface mining (cont.)
  USE Strip mining
Surfboard riding
  USE Surfing
**Surfing**
       --[country or state]--[city]
  UF  Surf riding
      Surfboard riding
  BT  Aquatic sports
**Surgery**
       --[country or state]--[city]
  PN  For the subject of surgery in general and
      the activities of surgeons.
  UF  Amputation
  BT  Medicine
  RT  Anesthesia
      Operating rooms
**Surplus commodities**
       --[country or state]--[city]
  UF  Commodities, Surplus
  NT  Surplus government property
  RT  Commerce
**Surplus government property**
       --[country or state]--[city]
  UF  Excess government property
      Government property, Surplus
  BT  Surplus commodities
Surplus stores, Military
  USE Army-Navy stores
**Surprise**
  BT  Mental states
**Surrealism**
  CN  For the subject of surrealism in general,
      not for examples of surrealist art.
  RT  Art
**Surrenders**
       --[nationality]--[country or state]--[city]
  PN  Search also under the subdivision
      --SURRENDERS used with the names of
      wars (Appendix C).
  CN  Subdivide by nationality of country
      surrendering and subdivide geographically by
      place of depiction.
  UF  Capitulations, Military
  RT  Military retreats
      Victories
      War
**Surveillance**
       --[country or state]--[city]
  PN  Search also under the subdivision
      --COVERT OPERATIONS used with the
      names of wars (Appendix C).
  CN  Used in a note under VIGILS.
  HN  Changed 8/1989 from non-postable term
      (Use VIGILS).
  NT  Electronic surveillance
      Police surveillance
  RT  Eavesdropping
      Law enforcement
      Spying
      Vigils
Surveillance photographs

Surveillance photographs (cont.)
  USE Forensic photographs
Survey drawings
  USE Measured drawings
**Surveying**
       --[country or state]--[city]
  UF  Land surveying
  RT  Census
      Civil engineering
      Construction industry
      Surveying equipment
**Surveying equipment**
  UF  Surveying instruments
  BT  Scientific equipment
  RT  Surveying
Surveying instruments
  USE Surveying equipment
**Suspended ceilings**
       --[country or state]--[city]
  UF  Drop ceilings
      False ceilings
  BT  Ceilings
Suspended railroads
  USE Aerial tramways
**Suspension bridges**
       --[country or state]--[city]
  PN  For bridges where the roadway is
      suspended from two or more cables, usually
      passing over towers.
  BT  Bridges
**Suspicion**
  UF  Doubt
      Mistrust
  BT  Mental states
**Sutlers**
       --[country or state]--[city]
  PN  Civilian provisioners to an army, or an
      army post, often with a shop on the post.
  BT  People associated with commercial
      activities
  RT  Business enterprises
      Economic aspects of war
      Military camps
      Military exchanges
**Swallows**
       --[country or state]
  BT  Birds
**Swamis**
  PN  For Hindu ascetics or religious teachers.
  BT  People associated with religion
  RT  Religious education
      Spiritual leaders
      Teachers
Swamps
  USE Wetlands
**Swan songs**
  PN  Farewell appearances or final acts or
      pronouncements.
  UF  Farewell appearances
      Songs, Swan
  BT  Farewells
**Swans**

---

BT  Broader term                 RT  Related term                PN  Public Note
NT  Narrower term                UF  Used for                    +   Term has NTs
HN  History Note                 CN  Catalogers Note             --[ ] May subdivide

**Swans (cont.)**
  --[country or state]
  BT  Birds
**Swastika**
  BT  Symbols
  RT  Crosses
      National socialism
Swatting insects
  USE Pest control
**Swearing**
  PN  For profane language. Search under
      OATHS for judicial or official oaths.
  CN  Used in a note under OATHS.
  UF  Profanity
  BT  Manners & customs
  RT  Anger
Swearing in
  USE Oaths
Sweat
  USE Perspiration
**Sweatbaths**
      --[country or state]--[city]
  PN  For ritual (social and religious) sweatbaths
      as practised by Indians of North America and
      Eskimos.
  BT  Therapeutic baths
  RT  Perspiration
      Rites & ceremonies
**Sweating system**
      --[country or state]--[city]
  PN  Employment of workers at substandard
      wages, hours, and working conditions.
  CN  Double index under the type of work or
      industry.
  UF  Sweatshops
      Tenement work
  BT  Home labor
Sweatshops
  USE Sweating system
**Sweeping & dusting**
      --[country or state]--[city]
  CN  Used in a note under BROOMS &
      BRUSHES.
  UF  Dusting
  BT  Cleaning
  NT  Chimney sweeping
  RT  Brooms & brushes
      Raking (Sweeping)
      Vacuum cleaners
**Sweet clover**
      --[country or state]--[city]
  BT  Plants
Sweet peppers
  USE Peppers
Sweeteners, Natural
  USE Sugar
Sweetmeats
  USE Confections
Sweets
  USE Confections
**Swimmers**
      --[country or state]--[city]

**Swimmers (cont.)**
  PN  For swimmers not engaged in swimming.
      Use SWIMMING for activities.
  BT  People
  RT  Athletes
      Swimming
**Swimming**
      --[country or state]--[city]
  CN  Used in a note under SWIMMERS.
  NT  Children swimming
      Wading
  RT  Aquatic sports
      Bathhouses
      Bathing suits
      Beaches
      Children playing in water
      Diving
      Landing floats
      Skin diving
      Swimmers
      Swimming pools
Swimming floats
  USE Landing floats
**Swimming pools**
      --[country or state]--[city]
  UF  Pools
  BT  Sports & recreation facilities
  RT  Swimming
      Water slides
Swimsuits
  USE Bathing suits
**Swine**
      --[country or state]
  UF  Hogs
      Pigs
  BT  Animals
  NT  Boars
  RT  Hog calling
      Pork
**Swing bridges**
      --[country or state]--[city]
  CN  Used in a note under DRAWBRIDGES.
  UF  Movable bridges
      Pivot bridges
      Turn bridges
  BT  Bridges
Swing chairs
  USE Gliders (Outdoor furniture)
**Swings**
      --[country or state]--[city]
  PN  Seats suspended from above, on which one
      may ride back and forth in an arc for
      recreation; also for single suspended ropes
      and other kinds of swings used for recreation.
      Search under CHILDREN SWINGING for
      the activity.
  CN  Used in a note under CHILDREN
      SWINGING.
  BT  Equipment
  RT  Children swinging
      Playgrounds
Switchboard operators

---

| BT Broader term | RT Related term | PN Public Note |
| NT Narrower term | UF Used for | + Term has NTs |
| HN History Note | CN Catalogers Note | --[ ] May subdivide |

Switchboard operators (cont.)
USE Telephone operators
**Switchboards**
--[country or state]--[city]
UF Electric switchboards
BT Machinery
NT Telephone switchboards
RT Electricity
Switching, Railroad
USE Railroad switching
**Swordfish**
--[country or state]
BT Fish
Swords
USE Daggers & swords
**Symbols**
PN Search also under terms for animals, objects, and other things which may be used as symbols, e.g., FISTS (for power) and HAWKS (for aggression).
CN Do not double index under SYMBOLS to indicate that one term is being used as a symbol of another term. Thus, PEACE and DOVES, not PEACE and DOVES and SYMBOLS.
NT Ball & chain
Black sheep
Bloody shirt
Caduceus
Ceremonial maces
Cornucopias
Crown of thorns
Cupids
Death's head
Dogs of war
Dollar signs
Empty market basket
Fig leaf
Full dinner pail
Grandpa's hat
Hammer & sickle
Liberty bell
Liberty cap
Liberty tree
Olympic flame
Peace signs
Red carpet
Red tape
Scapegoats
Ship of state
Swastika
Tree of knowledge
Tree of life
Unknown soldiers
Victory sign
Yin Yang (Symbol)
RT Emblems
Fictitious characters
Logos
Mascots
Signs
Straw man

Symbols (cont.)
Totem poles
Zodiac
Symbols, Artists
USE Artists' devices
Symbols, Artists'
USE Artists' devices
Symphony halls
USE Concert halls
Symposiums
USE Meetings
**Synagogues**
--[country or state]--[city]
PN For images that focus on buildings, as well as the associated grounds.
UF Temples, Jewish
BT Religious facilities
RT Churches
Tabernacles
Synthesizer music
USE Electronic music
Synthetic rubber industry
USE Artificial rubber industry
Syrinx (Musical instrument)
USE Panpipes
**Tabernacles**
BT Religious articles
RT Churches
Synagogues
Table decorations
USE Table settings & decorations
**Table settings & decorations**
UF Table decorations
RT Decorations
Tableware
**Table tennis**
--[country or state]--[city]
UF Ping pong
BT Sports
NT Children playing table tennis
**Tableaux**
--[country or state]--[city]
PN Representations of scenes by posing persons who remain silent and motionless in appropriate postures.
UF Living pictures
BT Theatrical productions
RT Pageants
**Tables**
BT Furniture
NT Coffee tables
Dining tables
Dressing tables
RT Dining rooms
Eating & drinking
Tables, Coffee
USE Coffee tables
Tables, Dining
USE Dining tables
Tables, Dressing
USE Dressing tables
Tablets

BT Broader term
NT Narrower term
HN History Note

RT Related term
UF Used for
CN Catalogers Note

PN Public Note
+ Term has NTs
--[ ] May subdivide

Tablets (cont.)
  USE Plaques
**Tableware**
  UF   China
       Dishes
       Silver services
  BT   Equipment
  NT   Bowls (Tableware)
       Drinking vessels +
       Samovars
  RT   Cooking utensils
       Cutlery industry
       Eating & drinking
       Glassware
       Knives
       Pitchers
       Pottery
       Silverware
       Table settings & decorations
Tabulation of ballots
  USE Vote counting
Tabulation of votes
  USE Vote counting
Tachyscopes
  USE Motion picture devices
Tackles
  USE Hoisting machinery
**Tacks**
  UF   Carpet tacks
  BT   Hardware
Tactics, Political
  USE Political strategies
Tae kwon do
  USE Oriental hand-to-hand fighting
**Tailor shops**
       --[country or state]--[city]
  PN   Includes activities and structures.
  BT   Stores & shops
  RT   Tailoring
       Tailors
**Tailoring**
       --[country or state]--[city]
  CN   Used in a note under TAILORS.
  UF   Dressmaking
  RT   Clothing industry
       Seamstresses
       Sewing
       Tailor shops
       Tailors
**Tailors**
       --[country or state]--[city]
  PN   For tailors away from the context of their
       work. Search under TAILORING for
       activities.
  BT   People
  RT   Tailor shops
       Tailoring
Taking cover
  USE Hiding
Taking oath
  USE Oaths
Talbotypes

Talbotypes (cont.)
  USE Calotypes
Tales
  USE Literature
**Talismans**
  UF   Charms
       Fetishes
  BT   Magical devices
  RT   Amulets
       Magic
Talking
  USE Conversation
       Discussion
       Filibustering
       Public speaking
Talks
  USE Public speaking
Tall clocks
  USE Longcase clocks
**Tall tales**
  UF   Lying tales
       Tall talk
  BT   Literature
  RT   Storytelling
Tall talk
  USE Tall tales
**Talmudists**
  BT   Scholars
  RT   Religion
**Tambourines**
  BT   Drums
Tank cars
  USE Railroad tank cars
Tank landing ships
  USE Landing craft
Tankards
  USE Drinking vessels
Tanker aircraft
  USE Airtankers
Tanker ships
  USE Tankers
**Tankers**
       --[nationality]--[country or state]--[city]
  UF   Oil tankers
       Supertankers
       Tanker ships
       Tank-vessels
  BT   Cargo ships
  RT   Petroleum industry
       Shipping
**Tanks (Military science)**
       --[nationality]--[country or state]--[city]
  BT   Armored vehicles
       Military vehicles
       Tracklaying vehicles
Tanks (Storage)
  USE Storage tanks
Tanks, Septic
  USE Septic tanks
Tank-vessels
  USE Tankers
Tanneries

BT  Broader term          RT  Related term          PN  Public Note
NT  Narrower term         UF  Used for              +   Term has NTs
HN  History Note          CN  Catalogers Note       --[ ] May subdivide

Tanneries (cont.)
USE Leather industry

**Tanning**
--[country or state]--[city]
PN   Search under LEATHER INDUSTRY for
tanning activities on a large scale.
RT   Hides & skins
Leather industry

**Tap dancing**
--[country or state]--[city]
BT   Dancing

Tap rooms
USE Barrooms

**Tapestries**
BT   Textiles
RT   Tapestry industry

**Tapestry industry**
--[country or state]--[city]
PN   Includes activities and structures.
CN   Double index under INDUSTRIAL
FACILITIES for images that focus on
facilities.
BT   Textile industry
RT   Tapestries

**Tapirs**
--[country or state]
BT   Animals

**Tapping**
--[country or state]--[city]
UF   Plant tapping
Tree tapping
NT   Sugar maple tapping
RT   Harvesting
Plants

Taprooms
USE Barrooms

Target ranges
USE Rifle ranges

**Targets (Sports)**
UF   Bull's-eyes
BT   Sporting goods
RT   Archery
Rifle ranges
Shooting

**Tariffs**
--[country]
UF   Customs duties
Duties
Export taxes
Import taxes
BT   Taxes
RT   Commerce
Customs inspections
Free trade & protection
Government regulation
International relations
Reciprocity

**Tarot cards**
CN   TGM II term.
UF   Tarots

Tarots
USE Tarot cards

**Tarpon**
--[country or state]
BT   Fish

**Tarring & feathering**
--[country or state]--[city]
UF   Feathering & tarring
BT   Punishment & torture
RT   Feathers

Tarts (Pies)
USE Pies

Tatting
USE Lace making

**Tattoo parlors**
--[country or state]--[city]
PN   Includes activities and structures.
BT   Service industry facilities
RT   Tattoos

**Tattoos**
BT   Body-marking
RT   Human body
Tattoo parlors

Tattoos, Air
USE Military air shows

Taverns
USE Bars
Taverns (Inns)

**Taverns (Inns)**
--[country or state]--[city]
PN   Primarily 17th to early 19th century
English and American places for eating,
drinking, and public accomodations. Includes
activities and structures.
HN   Changed 1/1993 from HOTELS &
TAVERNS.
UF   Inns
Public houses
Pubs
Taverns
BT   Public accommodation facilities
RT   Bars
Restaurants

**Tax exemptions**
--[country or state]--[city]
UF   Exemptions from taxation
BT   Law & legal affairs
RT   Taxes

**Tax reform**
--[country or state]--[city]
PN   For the subject of specific legislation for
tax reform. Search under TAXES for the
subject of taxes in general and criticisms of
the tax system.
BT   Reform
RT   Legislation
Taxes

**Tax stamps**
CN   TGM II term.
UF   Revenue stamps
Stamps, Tax

**Taxes**
--[country or state]--[city]
BT   Law & legal affairs

---

**Taxes (cont.)**
  NT  Gasoline taxes
      Income taxes
      Inheritance & transfer taxes
      Poll taxes
      Tariffs
      Tolls
  RT  Government spending policy
      Social security
      Tax exemptions
      Tax reform
Taxi drivers
  USE Taxicab drivers
**Taxicab drivers**
  UF  Cab drivers
      Taxi drivers
  BT  People associated with transportation
  RT  Taxicabs
**Taxicabs**
      --[country or state]--[city]
  UF  Cabs
  BT  Vehicles
  RT  Taxicab drivers
      Wheeled chairs
**Taxidermy**
  RT  Dead animals
      Hides & skins
      Hunting trophies
**Tea**
      --[country or state]--[city]
  PN  Includes the activity of tea drinking.
  CN  Double index under EATING &
      DRINKING for the activity of tea drinking.
  BT  Beverages
  RT  Children's tea parties
      Samovars
      Tea ceremonies
      Tea industry
      Tea parties
      Tea plantations
      Teapots
**Tea ceremonies**
      --[country or state]--[city]
  BT  Rites & ceremonies
  RT  Tea
**Tea industry**
      --[country or state]--[city]
  PN  Includes activities and structures.
  CN  Double index under INDUSTRIAL
      FACILITIES (or NTs) for images that focus
      on facilities.
  BT  Beverage industry
  RT  Tea
      Tea plantations
**Tea parties**
      --[country or state]--[city]
  BT  Parties
  NT  Children's tea parties
  RT  Tea
**Tea plantations**
      --[country or state]--[city]
  PN  Includes activities and structures.

**Tea plantations (cont.)**
  CN  As appropriate, double index under
      HARVESTING.
  BT  Plantations
  RT  Tea
      Tea industry
Tea rooms
  USE Restaurants
Teacher training colleges
  USE Teachers' colleges
**Teachers**
      --[country or state]--[city]
  PN  For teachers at all levels.
  UF  Faculty
      Instructors
      Professors
  BT  People associated with education &
      communication
  RT  Classrooms
      Education
      Governesses
      Scholars
      School principals
      Students
      Swamis
      Teachers' strikes
      Teaching methods
**Teachers' colleges**
      --[country or state]--[city]
  PN  Includes activities and structures.
  UF  Normal schools
      Teacher training colleges
  BT  Universities & colleges
**Teachers' strikes**
      --[country or state]--[city]
  BT  Strikes
  RT  Teachers
**Teaching methods**
      --[country or state]--[city]
  UF  Pedagogy
  RT  Education
      Imitation
      Teachers
Teach-ins
  USE Meetings
**Teahouses**
      --[country or state]--[city]
  PN  Small garden houses used for the Japanese
      tea ceremony.
  BT  Garden structures
**Team rowing**
      --[country or state]--[city]
  UF  Crew rowing
      Crewing
      Sculling, Team
  BT  Rowing
  RT  Rowing races
Teams, Sports
  USE Athletes
      Sports
**Teapots**
  BT  Containers

---

BT  Broader term              RT  Related term              PN  Public Note
NT  Narrower term              UF  Used for                  +  Term has NTs
HN  History Note               CN  Catalogers Note           --[ ] May subdivide

Teapots (cont.)
RT   Coffeepots
     Samovars
     Tea
Tear gas
BT   Chemicals
RT   Arms & armament
     Gas warfare
Tear sheets
CN   TGM II term.
UF   Tearsheets
Tearsheets
USE Tear sheets
Technical drawings
USE Diagrams
     Mechanical drawings
     Scientific illustrations
Technocracy
     --[country]
PN   Management of society by technical
     people.
BT   Economic & political systems
Teddies
USE Teddy bears
Teddy bears
UF   Teddies
BT   Toys
Teenage pregnancy
     --[country or state]--[city]
UF   Adolescent pregnancy
     Pregnant schoolgirls
BT   Pregnancy
RT   Children
Teenagers
USE Children
Teepees
USE Tipis
Teeter-totters
USE Seesaws
Teeth
NT   Tusks
RT   Dental hygiene
     Human body
     Toothaches
Telecommunication cables
     --[country or state]--[city]
UF   Cables, Telecommunication
     Communication cables
BT   Communication devices
NT   Submarine cables
RT   Telecommunication lines
Telecommunication lines
     --[country or state]--[city]
BT   Communication devices
NT   Telegraph lines
     Telephone lines
RT   Telecommunication cables
     Utility poles
Telecommunications industry
     --[country or state]--[city]
CN   Double index under INDUSTRIAL
     FACILITIES (or NTs) for images that focus

Telecommunications industry (cont.)
     on facilities.
BT   Industry
NT   Telegraph industry
     Telephone industry
Telegrams
RT   Correspondence
     Telegraph
Telegraph
     --[country or state]--[city]
UF   Postal telegraph
BT   Communication devices
RT   Electricity
     Submarine cables
     Telegrams
     Telegraph offices
     Teletypewriters
     Ticker tape
Telegraph industry
     --[country or state]--[city]
CN   Double index under INDUSTRIAL
     FACILITIES (or NTs) for images that focus
     on facilities.
BT   Telecommunications industry
RT   Telegraph offices
Telegraph lines
     --[country or state]--[city]
BT   Telecommunication lines
Telegraph offices
     --[country or state]--[city]
BT   Communication facilities
RT   Offices
     Telegraph
     Telegraph industry
Telegraph poles
USE Utility poles
Telegraph & telephone poles
USE Utility poles
Telepathy
PN   Includes both real and theatrical telepathy.
UF   Mind reading
     Mindreading
RT   Magic
Telephone apparatus industry
USE Telephone supplies industry
Telephone booths
     --[country or state]--[city]
BT   Communication facilities
RT   Telephones
Telephone companies
     --[country or state]--[city]
BT   Business enterprises
RT   Telephone industry
     Telephone operators
     Telephones
Telephone directories
UF   Phone books
BT   Books
RT   Telephones
Telephone equipment industry
USE Telephone supplies industry
Telephone industry

BT Broader term                                 RT Related term                              PN Public Note
NT Narrower term                                UF Used for                                  + Term has NTs
HN History Note                                 CN Catalogers Note                           --[ ] May subdivide

**Telephone industry (cont.)**
    --[country or state]--[city]
  CN  Double index under INDUSTRIAL
      FACILITIES (or NTs) for images that focus
      on facilities.
  BT  Telecommunications industry
  RT  Telephone companies
      Telephone operators
**Telephone lines**
    --[country or state]--[city]
  BT  Telecommunication lines
  RT  Telephones
**Telephone operators**
    --[country or state]--[city]
  UF  Switchboard operators
  BT  People associated with education &
      communication
  RT  Telephone companies
      Telephone industry
      Telephone switchboards
      Telephones
Telephone poles
  USE Utility poles
**Telephone supplies industry**
    --[country or state]--[city]
  CN  Double index under INDUSTRIAL
      FACILITIES (or NTs) for images that focus
      on facilities.
  UF  Telephone apparatus industry
      Telephone equipment industry
  BT  Industry
  RT  Telephones
**Telephone switchboards**
    --[country or state]--[city]
  BT  Switchboards
  RT  Telephone operators
      Telephones
**Telephones**
  UF  Phones
  BT  Communication devices
      Furnishings
  RT  Children using telephones
      Electricity
      Hotlines (Communication)
      Radiophones
      Submarine cables
      Telephone booths
      Telephone companies
      Telephone directories
      Telephone lines
      Telephone operators
      Telephone supplies industry
      Telephone switchboards
Telephones, Wireless
  USE Radiophones
**Telescopes**
    --[country or state]--[city]
  UF  Spyglasses
  BT  Optical devices
      Scientific equipment
  NT  Alidades
  RT  Astronomical observatories

**Teletypewriters**
  BT  Typewriters
  RT  Telegraph
**Television broadcasting**
    --[country or state]--[city]
  BT  Broadcasting
  RT  Action & adventure dramas
      Comedies
      Game shows
      Historical dramas
      Horror dramas
      Melodramas
      Public affairs television programs
      Romances
      Sociological dramas
      Televisions
      Westerns
**Television industry**
    --[country or state]--[city]
  PN  Manufacture and trade of televisions.
      Includes activities and structures.
  CN  Double index under INDUSTRIAL
      FACILITIES (or NTs)  for images that focus
      on facilities.
  BT  Industry
  RT  Actors
      Actresses
      Televisions
Television program stills
  USE Television stills
Television programs, Public service
  USE Public affairs television programs
**Television stills**
  CN  TGM II terms.
  UF  Stills
      Television program stills
      TV stills
**Televisions**
  BT  Communication devices
      Furnishings
  RT  Television broadcasting
      Television industry
Telling of stories
  USE Storytelling
**Temper tantrums**
  RT  Crying
**Tempera paintings**
  CN  TGM II term.
**Temperance**
    --[country or state]--[city]
  PN  For the question of moderation of or
      abstinence from the use of intoxicating drink,
      as well as for the temperance movement.
  UF  Abstinence
      Intemperance
  BT  Ethics
  RT  Alcoholism
      Intoxication
      Prohibition
**Temperature**
    --[country or state]--[city]
  BT  Natural phenomena

---

BT  Broader term
NT  Narrower term
HN History Note

RT  Related term
UF  Used for
CN Catalogers Note

PN Public Note
+ Term has NTs
--[ ] May subdivide

**Temperature (cont.)**
- RT   Cold
-      Heat
-      HVAC systems
-      Thermometers

**Temples**
-      --[country or state]--[city]
- BT   Religious facilities
- NT   Buddhist temples
-      Confucian temples
-      Greek temples
-      Hindu temples
-      Roman temples
- RT   Churches
-      Pagodas
-      Torii

Temples, Jewish
- USE Synagogues

Temples, Mormon
- USE Mormon churches

**Temporary buildings**
-      --[country or state]--[city]
- PN   For buildings erected and then dismantled after a stated period of occupancy, or structures erected for a clearly temporary purpose or event.
- BT   Buildings
- RT   Emergency housing
-      Landscape pavilions
-      Tents

Tenancy
- USE Landlord & tenant

Tenant & landlord
- USE Landlord & tenant

**Tenement houses**
-      --[country or state]--[city]
- BT   Apartment houses
- RT   Labor housing
-      Poor persons
-      Slums

Tenement work
- USE Sweating system

**Tennis**
-      --[country or state]--[city]
- BT   Sports
- NT   Children playing tennis
- RT   Tennis courts
-      Tennis players

**Tennis courts**
-      --[country or state]--[city]
- UF   Courts, Tennis
- BT   Sports & recreation facilities
- RT   Tennis

**Tennis players**
-      --[country or state]--[city]
- PN   For tennis players not engaged in the activity of the game. Search under TENNIS for activities.
- BT   People associated with entertainment & sports
- RT   Athletes
-      Tennis

Tension
- USE Stress

Tent structures
- USE Landscape pavilions

**Tents**
-      --[country or state]--[city]
- PN   For tents used by soldiers, campers, nomads, etc.
- BT   Shelters
- NT   Show tents
- RT   Camping
-      Canopies
-      Dwellings
-      Landscape pavilions
-      Military camps
-      Portable buildings
-      Portable darkrooms
-      Temporary buildings
-      Tipis

Tenure of land
- USE Land tenure

**Tenure of office**
-      --[country or state]--[city]
- UF   Terms of office
- NT   Presidential terms of office
- RT   Politics & government

Tepees
- USE Tipis

Tercentennials
- USE Centennial celebrations

Terminals (Stations)
- USE Marine terminals
-      Railroad stations

Terminations of employment
- USE Dismissal of employees
-      Resignations

Terminations of pregnancy
- USE Abortions

**Termites**
-      --[country or state]
- UF   White ants
- BT   Insects

Terms of office
- USE Tenure of office

**Terraces**
-      --[country or state]--[city]
- PN   For flat roofs or open platforms and relatively level paved or planted areas adjoining buildings.
- BT   Site elements
- RT   Patios
-      Roofs

**Terraces (Land use)**
-      --[country or state]--[city]
- PN   For level spaces supported in one or more places by a wall or bank and the practice of shaping the earth into this form.
- BT   Land use

Terrapins
- USE Turtles

**Territorial waters**
-      --[country or state]

---

Territorial waters (cont.)
CN  Subdivide geographically by the country
    claiming jurisdiction.
UF  Three-mile limit
BT  Bodies of water
RT  Freedom of the seas
    International relations
Territory, Annexation of
USE Annexations
Terror
USE Fear
**Terrorism**
      --[nationality]--[country or state]--[city]
CN  Subdivide by nationality of those
    commiting terrorist acts, when operating
    outside their own country.
UF  Political violence
    Violence, Political
BT  Crimes
RT  Activists
    Bombings
    Genocide
    Revolutions
    Sabotage
    Violence
Test flights
USE Flight testing
Test proofs
USE Trial proofs
**Testing**
      --[country or state]--[city]
PN  For the testing of things. Search under
    EXAMINATIONS for the testing of persons.
CN  Used in a note under EXAMINATIONS.
UF  Tests
NT  Flight testing
    Ordnance testing +
    Ship trials
RT  Food adulteration & inspection
    Product inspection
    Science
    Standardization
Testing, Weapons
USE Ordnance testing
Tests
USE Examinations
    Experiments
    Testing
Tethering posts
USE Hitching posts
**Textile art**
BT  Art
RT  Textiles
**Textile design drawings**
CN  TGM II term.
UF  Fabric design drawings
**Textile industry**
      --[country or state]--[city]
PN  For unspecified textiles or more than one
    kind. Search under NTs for the manufacture
    of specific textiles. Includes activities and
    structures.

Textile industry (cont.)
CN  Double index under INDUSTRIAL
    FACILITIES (or NTs) for images that focus
    on facilities.
UF  Doffing
BT  Industry
NT  Cotton industry
    Linen industry
    Silk industry
    Tapestry industry
    Thread industry
    Wool industry
RT  Clothing industry
    Dyeing
    Fabric shops
    Fibers
    Spinning machinery
    Textile industry unions
    Textile machinery
    Textile mill workers
    Textile printing
    Textiles
    Weaving
**Textile industry strikes**
      --[country or state]--[city]
BT  Strikes
RT  Clothing industry strikes
    Textile industry unions
**Textile industry unions**
      --[country or state]--[city]
BT  Labor unions
RT  Clothing industry unions
    Textile industry
    Textile industry strikes
**Textile labels**
CN  TGM II term.
UF  Cloth labels
    Linen labels
**Textile machinery**
BT  Machinery
RT  Looms
    Textile industry
**Textile mill workers**
      --[country or state]--[city]
BT  People associated with manual labor
RT  Textile industry
**Textile printing**
      --[country or state]--[city]
BT  Printing
RT  Textile industry
**Textiles**
UF  Cloth
    Fabrics
NT  Batiks
    Blankets
    Calico
    Drapery
    Nylon
    Tapestries
    Yarn
RT  Fibers
    Flax

BT  Broader term
NT  Narrower term
HN  History Note

RT  Related term
UF  Used for
CN  Catalogers Note

PN  Public Note
+   Term has NTs
--[ ] May subdivide

**Textiles (cont.)**
     Floor coverings
     Quilts
     Textile art
     Textile industry
     Upholstery
     Weaving
**Thankfulness**
  USE Gratitude
**Thatched roofs**
     --[country or state]--[city]
  HN  Changed 1/1993 from THATCHED
       BUILDINGS.
  BT  Roofs
  RT  Huts
**Theater audiences**
     --[country or state]--[city]
  UF  Theatergoers
  BT  Audiences
  RT  Theatrical productions
**Theater costumes**
  USE Costumes
**Theater posters**
  USE Theatrical posters
**Theater programs**
  CN  TGM II term.
**Theatergoers**
  USE Theater audiences
**Theaters**
     --[country or state]--[city]
  PN  For images that focus on facilities. Search
       under THEATRICAL PRODUCTIONS for
       activities.
  CN  Used in a note under THEATRICAL
       PRODUCTIONS.
  BT  Cultural facilities
  NT  Motion picture theaters +
       Open-air theaters +
  RT  Auditoriums
       Music halls
       Opera houses
       Stages (Platforms)
       Theatrical producers & directors
       Theatrical productions
**Theatrical lighting**
  USE Stage lighting
**Theatrical posters**
  CN  TGM II term.
  UF  Burlesque posters
       Magic posters
       Minstrel posters
       Musical play posters
       Opera posters
       Theater posters
       Vaudeville posters
**Theatrical producers & directors**
     --[country or state]--[city]
  UF  Directors, Theatrical
       Producers, Theatrical
  BT  People associated with entertainment &
       sports
  RT  Theaters

**Theatrical producers & directors (cont.)**
     Theatrical productions
**Theatrical productions**
     --[country or state]--[city]
  PN  For theater activities, including plays,
       monologues, etc. Search under THEATERS
       for images that focus on buildings. Search
       also under the subdivision
       --PERFORMANCES & PORTRAYALS used
       with the names of ethnic, racial, and regional
       groups and with classes of persons (Appendix
       A). Search also under the subdivisions
       --PORTRAYALS and --PERFORMANCES
       used with names of persons (Appendix B).
  CN  Used in a note under COSTUMES and
       THEATERS.
  UF  Dramas
       Performances, Theatrical
       Plays
       Productions, Theatrical
       Reenactments
       Shows
       Skits
       Specialty acts
  BT  Entertainment
  NT  Burlesque shows
       Historical reenactments +
       Musical revues & comedies +
       Open-air theatrical productions
       Operas & operettas
       Pageants +
       Puppet shows
       Tableaux
       Vaudeville shows
  RT  Action & adventure dramas
       Actors
       Actresses
       Auditions
       Comedies
       Drama clubs
       Historical dramas
       Horror dramas
       Impersonation
       Melodramas
       Music
       Pantomimes
       Romances
       Sociological dramas
       Stage lighting
       Stage props
       Theater audiences
       Theaters
       Theatrical producers & directors
       Westerns
**Thefts**
  USE Robberies
**Then & now comparisons**
  CN  TGM II term.
  UF  Before & after views
       Comparisons, Then & now
       Now & then comparisons
**Theocracy**

---

BT Broader term        RT Related term        PN Public Note
NT Narrower term      UF Used for           + Term has NTs
HN History Note        CN Catalogers Note    --[ ] May subdivide

**Theocracy (cont.)**
- PN  For the subject of theocracy in general.
- BT  Economic & political systems
- RT  Church & state
  - Religion

**Theological seminaries**
- --[country or state]--[city]
- PN  Includes activities and structures.
- UF  Divinity schools
  - Seminaries, Theological
- BT  Universities & colleges
- RT  Clergy
  - Religious education

**Therapeutic baths**
- --[country or state]--[city]
- PN  Includes activities and sites identified as "therapeutic."
- BT  Health & hygiene facilities
- NT  Mud baths
  - Sweatbaths
- RT  Bathing
  - Health care
  - Health resorts
  - Physical therapy
  - Springs

Therapeutics
- USE Therapy

**Therapy**
- --[country or state]--[city]
- UF  Therapeutics
- NT  Physical therapy
  - Psychotherapy +
  - Shock therapy
  - Speech therapy
- RT  Healing
  - Health care

Therapy, Group
- USE Group psychotherapy

Therapy, Shock
- USE Shock therapy

**Thermal copies**
- CN  TGM II term.

Thermal springs
- USE Springs

Thermal waters
- USE Geysers

**Thermometers**
- --[country or state]--[city]
- BT  Scientific equipment
- RT  Heat
  - Temperature

Thermonuclear weapons
- USE Nuclear weapons

**Thinking**
- UF  Pondering
- BT  Mental states
- RT  Fantasy
  - Reminiscing

**Third parties**
- --[country or state]--[city]
- PN  A major political party operating over a limited period of time in addition to two other

**Third parties (cont.)**
- major parties in a nation or state normally characterized by a two-party system.
- CN  Double index under ORGANIZATIONS' FACILITIES (or NTs) for images that focus on facilities.
- BT  Political parties

Third terms, Presidential
- USE Presidential terms of office

**Thistles**
- --[country or state]--[city]
- BT  Weeds

Thoroughfares
- USE Roads
  - Streets

**Thread**
- UF  Spools of thread
- RT  Fibers
  - Thread industry

**Thread industry**
- --[country or state]--[city]
- PN  Includes activities and structures.
- CN  Double index under INDUSTRIAL FACILITIES (or NTs) for images that focus on facilities.
- BT  Textile industry
- RT  Thread

**Threats**
- PN  Expression of intention to inflict injury or damage.
- RT  Crimes
  - Danger
  - Warnings

Three chalk drawings
- USE A trois crayons drawings

**Three monkeys  (Motif)**
- RT  Good & evil
  - Monkeys

**Three wheel automobiles**
- --[nationality]--[country or state]--[city]
- UF  Three wheeled automobiles
  - Three-wheelers
- BT  Automobiles

Three wheeled automobiles
- USE Three wheel automobiles

Three-color carbro prints
- USE Tricolor carbro prints

Three-dimensional photographs
- USE Holograms
  - Lenticular photographs
  - Stereographs

**Three-legged racing**
- --[country or state]--[city]
- UF  3-legged racing
- BT  Racing
- RT  Games
  - Running races

Three-mile limit
- USE Territorial waters

Three-wheelers
- USE Three wheel automobiles

Threshers

| | | |
|---|---|---|
| BT Broader term | RT Related term | PN Public Note |
| NT Narrower term | UF Used for | + Term has NTs |
| HN History Note | CN Catalogers Note | --[ ] May subdivide |

Threshers (cont.)
  USE Threshing machines
**Threshing**
    --[country or state]--[city]
  BT  Harvesting
  RT  Grains
      Threshing machines
      Winnowing
**Threshing machines**
  UF  Threshers
  BT  Harvesting machinery
  RT  Threshing
**Thrift shops**
    --[country or state]--[city]
  PN  Includes activities and structures.
  BT  Stores & shops
  RT  Charitable organizations
      Secondhand sales
Throne rooms
  USE Reception rooms
**Thrones**
  BT  Chairs
  RT  Rulers
**Throwing sticks**
  BT  Arms & armament
  NT  Boomerangs
  RT  Spears
Throwing stones
  USE Stoning
Thunderbolts
  USE Lightning
**Ticker tape**
  PN  For ticker tape as used for printing stock
      quotations or news. Includes ticker tape
      machines.
  UF  Tickers
  RT  Stock exchanges
      Telegraph
      Ticker tape parades
**Ticker tape parades**
    --[country or state]--[city]
  BT  Parades & processions
  RT  Ticker tape
Tickers
  USE Ticker tape
Ticket of leave
  USE Parole
**Ticket offices**
    --[country or state]--[city]
  PN  Includes activities and structures.
  UF  Offices, Ticket
      Ticket windows
      Windows, Ticket
  BT  Stores & shops
  RT  Tickets
Ticket windows
  USE Ticket offices
**Ticketing**
    --[country or state]--[city]
  UF  Citations, Traffic
      Parking tickets
      Violations, Traffic

Ticketing (cont.)
  RT  Tickets
      Traffic police
      Traffic regulations
**Tickets**
  CN  TGM II term.
  RT  Ticket offices
      Ticketing
Tickets, Lottery
  USE Lottery tickets
Tidal flats
  USE Wetlands
**Tidal waves**
    --[country or state]--[city]
  PN  Includes the event and any resulting
      damage.
  UF  Tsunamis
  BT  Natural phenomena
  RT  Disasters
      Earthquakes
      Seas
      Volcanic eruptions
**Tide pools**
    --[country or state]--[city]
  PN  Pools left by ebbing tides.
  UF  Tidepools
  BT  Bodies of water
      Natural phenomena
  RT  Aquatic animals
      Seas
      Waterfronts
Tidepools
  USE Tide pools
Tie industry
  USE Neckwear industry
Ties (Neckwear)
  USE Neckties
**Tigers**
    --[country or state]
  BT  Animals
Tightrope performers
  USE Aerialists
**Tile industry**
    --[country or state]--[city]
  PN  Includes activities and structures.
  CN  Double index under INDUSTRIAL
      FACILITIES (or NTs) for images that focus
      on facilities.
  BT  Clay industries
  RT  Tiles
**Tiles**
  UF  Tilework
  NT  Roofing tiles
  RT  Building materials
      Mosaics
      Pottery
      Tile industry
Tilework
  USE Tiles
Tilling
  USE Farming
Timber

---

BT  Broader term
NT  Narrower term
HN  History Note

RT  Related term
UF  Used for
CN  Catalogers Note

PN  Public Note
+   Term has NTs
--[ ] May subdivide

Timber (cont.)
USE Logs
Timber industry
USE Lumber industry
Timber wolves
USE Wolves
**Time**
NT Daylight savings
Leap years
Months
Seasons +
RT Clocks & watches
Time travel
Time tables
USE Timetables
**Time travel**
BT Travel
RT Time
**Timetables**
CN TGM II term.
UF Time tables
Time-lapse photographs
USE Motion study photographs
**Tin cups**
BT Containers
RT Beggars
Drinking vessels
**Tin mining**
--[country or state]--[city]
PN Includes activities and sites.
BT Mining
**Tinsmithing**
--[country or state]--[city]
BT Metalworking
**Tintypes**
CN TGM II term.
UF Collodion positive photographs
Ferrotypes
Iron photographs
Melainotypes
**Tipis**
--[country or state]--[city]
PN American Indian conical tents, usually
consisting of skins and used especially by the
Plains people.
UF Teepees
Tepees
BT Dwellings
RT Hides & skins
Tents
**Tiptoeing**
--[country or state]--[city]
BT Walking
**Tire industry**
--[country or state]--[city]
PN Includes activities and structures.
CN Double index under INDUSTRIAL
FACILITIES (or NTs) for images that focus
on facilities.
BT Industry
RT Rubber industry
Tires

**Tire industry (cont.)**
Transportation industry
Tiredness
USE Fatigue
**Tires**
NT Flat tires
RT Tire industry
Vehicles
**Tissue stereographs**
CN TGM II term.
UF French tissues
**Title pages**
CN TGM II term.
**Titmice**
--[country or state]
BT Birds
**Toads**
--[country or state]
BT Amphibians
Toad's-eye views
USE Worm's-eye views
**Toasters**
BT Appliances
RT Cookery
**Toasting**
--[country or state]--[city]
BT Manners & customs
RT Eating & drinking
Public speaking
**Tobacco**
--[country or state]--[city]
BT Plants
RT Tobacco habit
Tobacco industry
Tobacco plantations
Tobacco products
Tobacco addiction
USE Tobacco habit
Tobacco cards
USE Cigarette cards
**Tobacco habit**
--[country or state]--[city]
UF Addiction to tobacco
Habit, Tobacco
Tobacco addiction
RT Drug abuse
Smoking
Tobacco
Tobacco products
**Tobacco industry**
--[country or state]--[city]
PN Includes activities and structures.
CN Double index under INDUSTRIAL
FACILITIES (or NTs) for images that focus
on facilities.
BT Industry
NT Cigar industry
Cigarette industry
RT Tobacco
Tobacco industry unions
Tobacco plantations
Tobacco products

---

**Tobacco industry strikes**
--[country or state]--[city]
BT   Strikes
RT   Tobacco industry unions
**Tobacco industry unions**
--[country or state]--[city]
BT   Labor unions
RT   Tobacco industry
Tobacco industry strikes
**Tobacco package labels**
UF   Tobacco tin tags
**Tobacco pipe industry**
--[country or state]--[city]
PN   Includes activities and structures.
CN   Double index under INDUSTRIAL
FACILITIES (or NTs) for images that focus
on facilities.
BT   Industry
RT   Tobacco pipes
**Tobacco pipes**
BT   Pipes
NT   Calumets
RT   Smoking
Tobacco pipe industry
**Tobacco plantations**
--[country or state]--[city]
PN   Includes activities and structures.
CN   As appropriate, double index under
HARVESTING.
BT   Plantations
RT   Tobacco
Tobacco industry
**Tobacco products**
NT   Cigarettes
Cigars
Smokeless tobacco
RT   Tobacco
Tobacco habit
Tobacco industry
Tobacco shops
**Tobacco shops**
--[country or state]--[city]
PN   Includes activities and structures.
UF   Smoke shops
Tobacconists' shops
BT   Stores & shops
RT   Tobacco products
Tobacco smoking
USE Smoking
Tobacco tin tags
USE Tobacco package labels
Tobacconists' shops
USE Tobacco shops
**Toboggans**
--[country or state]--[city]
PN   Includes the activity of tobogganing.
HN   Changed 7/1989 from non-postable term
(Use SLEDS & SLEIGHS).
BT   Sleds & sleighs
Toilet articles
USE Cosmetics & soap
Dressing & grooming equipment

Toilet (Grooming)
USE Grooming
Toiletries
USE Cosmetics & soap
Dressing & grooming equipment
**Toilets**
--[country or state]--[city]
PN   For the fixtures.
BT   Plumbing fixtures
RT   Bathrooms
Privies
Public comfort stations
**Toll bridges**
--[country or state]--[city]
BT   Bridges
RT   Tolls
**Toll roads**
--[country or state]
UF   Tollways
Turnpike roads
BT   Roads
RT   Tolls
**Tolls**
--[country or state]--[city]
BT   Taxes
RT   Toll bridges
Toll roads
Tollways
USE Toll roads
**Tomahawks**
BT   Axes
**Tomatoes**
--[country or state]--[city]
BT   Fruit
RT   Vegetables
Tomb
CN   Used only as a subdivision with names of
persons (Appendix B).
**Tombs & sepulchral monuments**
--[country or state]--[city]
PN   For constructions over or around burial
sites.  Search under GRAVES for excavations
in the earth.  Search also under the
subdivision --TOMB used with names of
persons (Appendix B).
CN   Used in a note under GRAVES.
UF   Burial vaults
Gravestones
Mausoleums
Sepulchral monuments
Tombstones
Vaults (Sepulchral)
BT   Funerary facilities
NT   Pyramids
RT   Catacombs
Cemeteries
Death
Graves
Monument builders
Monuments & memorials
Sarcophagi
Scaffold burial

BT   Broader term                          RT   Related term                          PN Public Note
NT   Narrower term                         UF   Used for                              + Term has NTs
HN   History Note                          CN   Catalogers Note                       --[ ] May subdivide

**Tombs & sepulchral monuments (cont.)**
    Urns
Tombstones
  USE Tombs & sepulchral monuments
**Tongues**
  RT  Human body
**Tool & die industry**
    --[country or state]--[city]
  PN  Includes activities and structures.
  CN  Double index under INDUSTRIAL
      FACILITIES (or NTs)  for images that focus
      on facilities.
  UF  Die industry
  BT  Industry
  RT  Equipment
      Machinery industry
**Tools**
  USE Equipment
**Toothaches**
  BT  Pain
  RT  Teeth
**Topiary work**
    --[country or state]--[city]
  RT  Gardens
      Pruning
      Shrubs
      Trees
**Topographic maps**
  CN  TGM II term.
Topographic views
  USE Cityscapes
      Landscapes
**Toppings out**
    --[country or state]--[city]
  BT  Rites & ceremonies
  RT  Building construction
      Building dedications
**Torches**
  RT  Light fixtures
      Olympic flame
Toreadors
  USE Bullfighters
Toreros
  USE Bullfighters
**Torii**
    --[country or state]--[city]
  PN  Gateway, or gateways, of light,
      skeletonlike construction, built at the
      approach to a Shinto temple.
  BT  Gates
  RT  Temples
**Tornadoes**
    --[country or state]--[city]
  PN  Includes the event and any resulting
      damage.
  BT  Storms
  RT  Cyclones
      Hurricanes
      Waterspouts
**Torpedo boats**
    --[country or state]--[city]
  UF  PT boats

**Torpedo boats (cont.)**
  BT  Warships
  RT  Mine warfare
      Submarine warfare
      Torpedoes
**Torpedoes**
  BT  Arms & armament
      Explosives
  RT  Naval warfare
      Torpedo boats
**Tortillas**
  BT  Bread
Tortoises
  USE Turtles
Torture
  USE Punishment & torture
Torture devices
  USE Punishment devices
**Totalitarianism**
    --[country or state]--[city]
  BT  Economic & political systems
  RT  Communism
      Dictators
      Fascism
      National socialism
**Totem poles**
    --[country or state]--[city]
  BT  Wood carvings
  RT  Columns
      Symbols
**Toucans**
    --[country or state]
  BT  Birds
Touring
  USE Tourists
Touring, Celebrity
  USE Celebrity touring
Touring, Whistle-stop
  USE Whistle-stop campaigning
Tourism
  USE Tourist trade
**Tourist camps & hostels**
    --[country or state]--[city]
  UF  Hostels
  BT  Public accommodation facilities
  RT  Camping
      Lodging houses
      Motels
      Resorts
      Tourist trade
Tourist courts
  USE Hotels
      Motels
**Tourist trade**
    --[country or state]--[city]
  PN  For the subject of tourism in general.
      Search under TOURISTS for images that
      focus on persons.
  UF  Excursions
      Foreigners
      Tourism
  BT  Commerce

---

BT  Broader term
NT  Narrower term
HN History Note

RT  Related term
UF  Used for
CN Catalogers Note

PN Public Note
+ Term has NTs
--[ ] May subdivide

**Tourist trade (cont.)**
- RT  Leisure
- Souvenir shops
- Tourist camps & hostels
- Tourists
- Travel
- Visitors' centers

**Tourist trade posters**
- USE Travel posters

**Tourists**
- --[country or state]--[city]
- PN  For persons on organized tours. Search under SIGHTSEERS for persons who go about seeing sights of interest on their own.
- CN  Used in a note under PASSENGERS, SIGHTSEERS, and TOURIST TRADE.
- UF  Sightseeing
- Touring
- BT  People
- RT  Passengers
- Sightseers
- Tourist trade
- Travel

**Tournaments**
- --[country or state]--[city]
- PN  For knightly sports in which mounted armored combatants engage one another to exhibit their skill and courage. Search under appropriate NTs to SPORTS for modern tournaments.
- BT  Contests
- Sports
- NT  Jousting
- RT  Knights

**Tow trucks**
- USE Wreckers (Vehicles)

**Towboats**
- USE Tugboats

**Towers**
- --[country or state]--[city]
- BT  Buildings distinguished by form
- NT  Bell towers
- Clock towers
- Observation towers
- Watch towers +
- RT  Architectural elements
- Martello towers
- Minarets
- Pagodas
- Spires
- Steeples
- Water towers

**Towing**
- --[country or state]--[city]
- RT  Transportation
- Tugboats
- Vehicles
- Wreckers (Vehicles)

**Town beautification**
- USE Urban beautification

**Town criers**
- --[country or state]--[city]

**Town criers (cont.)**
- BT  People associated with education & communication
- RT  City & town life
- Communication
- Watchmen

**Town halls**
- USE City & town halls

**Town houses (Attached houses)**
- USE Row houses

**Town life**
- USE City & town life

**Town meetings**
- --[country or state]--[city]
- BT  Meetings
- Politics & government
- RT  City & town life

**Town officials**
- USE Municipal officials

**Town squares**
- USE Plazas

**Townhouses (Attached houses)**
- USE Row houses

**Townscapes**
- USE Cityscapes

**Towpaths**
- USE Trails & paths

**Towtrucks**
- USE Wreckers (Vehicles)

**Toxic substances**
- USE Poisons

**Toy industry**
- --[country or state]--[city]
- PN  Includes activities and structures.
- CN  Double index under INDUSTRIAL FACILITIES (or NTs) for images that focus on facilities.
- BT  Industry
- RT  Game industry
- Toys

**Toys**
- CN  TGM II term.
- UF  Paper toys
- Playthings
- NT  Blocks (Toys)
- Dolls
- Hobby horses
- Jack-in-the-boxes
- Mechanical toys
- Puppets
- Teddy bears
- Yo-yos
- RT  Balloons
- Children playing
- Kites
- Model airplanes
- Model cars
- Model railroads
- Model ships
- Rattles
- Toy industry

**Tracings**

---

BT Broader term     RT Related term     PN Public Note
NT Narrower term     UF Used for     + Term has NTs
HN History Note     CN Catalogers Note     --[ ] May subdivide

**Tracings (cont.)**
   CN  TGM II term.
**Track athletics**
       --[country or state]--[city]
   PN  Various competitive athletic events (as
        running, jumping, and weight throwing)
        performed on a running track and on the
        adjacent field.
   BT  Sports
   NT  Discus throwing
        Running races +
        Shot putting
        Vaulting
   RT  Relay racing
        Walking races
**Tracked landing vehicles**
       --[nationality]--[country or state]--[city]
   UF  Amphibian tractors
        Landing vehicles, Tracked
        LVTs (Amphibian tractors)
        Tractors, Amphibian
   BT  Amphibious vehicles
        Military vehicles
**Tracklaying vehicles**
       --[nationality]--[country or state]--[city]
   PN  For vehicles which use the endless belt
        principle for traction.
   UF  Caterpillar-type machinery
   BT  Vehicles
   NT  Tanks (Military science)
   RT  Bulldozers
        Tractors
Tracks, Animal
   USE Animal tracks
**Tractors**
       --[nationality]--[country or state]--[city]
   BT  Vehicles
   RT  Agricultural machinery & implements
        Bulldozers
        Jeep automobiles
        Machinery
        Tracklaying vehicles
Tractors, Amphibian
   USE Tracked landing vehicles
Trade
   USE Commerce
**Trade cards**
   CN  TGM II term.
   UF  Tradecards
**Trade catalogs**
   CN  TGM II term.
   HN  Changed 3/1989 from non-postable term
        (Use COMMERCIAL CATALOGS).
Trade fairs
   USE Exhibitions
Trade of prisoners
   USE Prisoner exchanges
Trade schools
   USE Vocational education
Trade unions
   USE Labor unions
Tradecards

**Tradecards (cont.)**
   USE Advertising cards
        Business cards
        Trade cards
**Trademarks**
   CN  TGM II term.
Trades
   USE Occupations
Trading cards
   USE Advertising cards
        Collecting cards
**Trading posts**
       --[country or state]--[city]
   CN  Used in a note under FUR TRADE.
   BT  Stores & shops
   RT  Frontier & pioneer life
        Fur trade
Traditional music
   USE Folk music
Traditions
   USE Manners & customs
**Traffic accidents**
       --[country or state]--[city]
   UF  Reckless driving
        Road accidents
   BT  Accidents
   RT  Automobiles
        City & town life
        Flat tires
        Street railroad accidents
        Wreckers (Vehicles)
**Traffic congestion**
       --[country or state]--[city]
   UF  Congestion, Traffic
        Traffic jams
   RT  City & town life
        Streets
        Vehicles
Traffic jams
   USE Traffic congestion
Traffic laws
   USE Traffic regulations
**Traffic police**
       --[country or state]--[city]
   BT  Police
   RT  Ticketing
**Traffic regulations**
       --[country or state]--[city]
   UF  Street traffic regulations
        Traffic laws
   BT  Laws
   RT  Drunk driving
        Ticketing
        Traffic signs & signals
**Traffic signs & signals**
       --[country or state]--[city]
   UF  Road signs
        Street signs
   BT  Signs
        Site elements
   RT  Signal lights
        Traffic regulations

---

BT Broader term        RT Related term        PN Public Note
NT Narrower term       UF Used for          + Term has NTs
HN History Note         CN Catalogers Note    --[ ] May subdivide

Trailers
  USE Mobile homes
**Trails & paths**
      --[country or state]--[city]
  UF  Bridle paths
      Foot trails
      Footpaths
      Garden walks
      Paths
      Towpaths
  BT  Walkways
  RT  Portages
      Roads
      Walking
Train sheds
  USE Railroad stations
**Trained animals**
      --[country or state]
  UF  Animal acts
  BT  Animals
  RT  Animal training
      Circuses & shows
Training of animals
  USE Animal training
Training, Military
  USE Military training
Training, Vocational
  USE Vocational education
Trains
  USE Railroads
Tramping
  USE Hiking
**Tramps**
      --[nationality]--[country or state]--[city]
  UF  Hoboes
      Vagrants
  BT  Homeless persons
  RT  Beggars
      Freighthopping
Tramways
  USE Aerial tramways
      Street railroads
**Transcontinental journeys**
  UF  Cross-country journeys
  BT  Travel
  RT  Voyages around the world
      Westward movement
**Transfer sheets**
  CN  TGM II term.
  UF  Iron-on transfers
Transfer taxes
  USE Inheritance & transfer taxes
Transformation pictures
  USE Metamorphic pictures
Transformations
  USE Metamorphosis
Transient laborers
  USE Migrant laborers
**Transistors**
  BT  Equipment
  RT  Radios
Transit systems

Transit systems (cont.)
  USE Mass transit
Transmission lines
  USE Electric lines
**Transmitted images**
  CN  TGM II term.
  UF  Digital images
      Electronic images
      Facsimile transmission images
Transmutation of metals
  USE Alchemy
Transmutations
  USE Metamorphosis
**Transparencies**
  CN  TGM II term.
  UF  Phototransparencies
**Transport planes**
      --[nationality]--[country or state]--[city]
  UF  Cargo planes
      Freight planes
      Mail planes
  BT  Airplanes
  RT  Shipping
**Transportation**
      --[country or state]--[city]
  PN  Search also under the subdivision
      --TRANSPORTATION used with names of
      indigenous peoples (Appendix A) and with
      names of wars (Appendix C).
  NT  Automobile driving +
      Mass transit
      Railroads +
  RT  Busing (School integration)
      Caravans
      Fords (Stream crossings)
      Packtrains
      Pneumatic tubes
      Portages
      Riding
      Shipping
      Stilts
      Towing
      Transportation facilities
      Transportation industry
      Travel
      Vehicles
**Transportation facilities**
      --[country or state]--[city]
  CN  Used in a note under AIRLINE
      INDUSTRY.
  BT  Facilities
  NT  Airports
      Automobile service stations
      Boathouses
      Bridges +
      Bus terminals
      Carriage houses
      Garages +
      Hangars
      Lighthouses
      Loading docks
      Marine terminals

---

BT Broader term         RT Related term         PN Public Note
NT Narrower term        UF Used for            + Term has NTs
HN History Note          CN Catalogers Note      --[ ] May subdivide

**Transportation facilities (cont.)**
    Parking lots
    Piers & wharves
    Railroad facilities +
    Rest stops
    Roads +
    Runways (Aeronautics)
    Streets +
    Tunnels
  RT  Concourses
    Transportation
    Wagon sheds
**Transportation industry**
    --[country or state]--[city]
  PN  Manufacture and trade of vehicles.
    Includes activities and structures.
  CN  Double index under INDUSTRIAL
    FACILITIES (or NTs)  for images that focus
    on facilities.
  BT  Industry
  NT  Airplane industry
    Armored vehicle industry
    Automobile industry
    Boat & ship industry
    Railroad car industry
    Railroad locomotive industry
    Truck industry
  RT  Tire industry
    Transportation
**Transportation posters**
  USE Travel posters
**Transporter bridges**
    --[country or state]--[city]
  PN  Bridges designed to span navigable
    waterways between low shores and made of a
    high framework from which is suspended a
    car for carrying traffic back and forth.
  UF  Aerial passenger lift bridges
  BT  Bridges
Transvestism
  USE Cross dressing
Trapeze artists
  USE Aerialists
Trapping
  USE Fur trade
    Hunting
Traps, Animal
  USE Animal traps
Trash
  USE Refuse
Trauma, Physical
  USE Wounds & injuries
**Travel**
    --[country or state]--[city]
  PN  For the subject of travel in general. Search
    also under the subdivision --JOURNEYS used
    with names of persons (Appendix B).
  UF  Journeys
    Trips
  NT  Air travel
    Celebrity touring
    Freighthopping

**Travel (cont.)**
    Hitchhiking
    Ocean travel
    Safaris
    Space flight +
    Time travel
    Transcontinental journeys
    Voyages around the world
    Whistle-stop campaigning
  RT  Discovery & exploration
    Guides & scouts
    Honeymoons
    Passengers
    Rest stops
    School excursions
    Sightseers
    Stewards
    Tourist trade
    Tourists
    Transportation
    Visiting
    Visitors' centers
    Visits of state
**Travel posters**
  CN  TGM II term.
  UF  Tourist trade posters
    Transportation posters
**Travel sketches**
  CN  TGM II term.
Traveling salesmanship
  USE Canvassing
**Travois**
    --[country or state]--[city]
  BT  Vehicles
  RT  Sleds & sleighs
**Treadmills**
  BT  Machinery
  RT  Physical fitness
**Treason**
    --[country]
  BT  Crimes
  RT  Ethics
    Sedition
**Treasure-trove**
    --[country or state]--[city]
  PN  Gold or silver in the form of money, plate,
    or bullion which is found hidden and whose
    ownership is not known.
  UF  Hidden property
    Loot
  RT  Caches
    Gold
    Money
    Silver
**Treasuries**
    --[country or state]--[city]
  BT  Government facilities
  RT  Money
**Treaties**
  PN  Search also under the subdivision
    --TREATIES used with names of wars
    (Appendix C).

---

BT  Broader term               RT  Related term               PN  Public Note
NT  Narrower term          UF  Used for                   + Term has NTs
HN  History Note           CN  Catalogers Note        --[ ] May subdivide

**Treaties (cont.)**
- UF  Agreements
  - Alliances
  - Conventions
  - International agreements
  - Pacts
- BT  Law & legal affairs
- NT  Peace treaties
- RT  International relations
  - Treaty violations
  - War allies

**Treaty violations**
- --[country or state]
- BT  Law & legal affairs
- RT  Treaties

**Tree houses**
- --[country or state]--[city]
- BT  Houses
- RT  Shelters
  - Trees

**Tree limbs**
- UF  Branches
  - Limbs
- RT  Trees

**Tree of knowledge**
- UF  Knowledge, Tree of
- BT  Symbols
- RT  Trees

Tree of liberty
- USE Liberty tree

**Tree of life**
- UF  Life, Tree of
- BT  Symbols
- RT  Trees

**Tree planting ceremonies**
- --[country or state]--[city]
- BT  Rites & ceremonies
- RT  Gardening
  - Trees

**Tree stumps**
- --[country or state]--[city]
- RT  Trees

Tree tapping
- USE Tapping

**Trees**
- --[country or state]--[city]
- BT  Plants
- NT  Apple trees
  - Banyan trees
  - Baobab
  - Birches
  - Cacao
  - Ceibas
  - Cherry trees
  - Christmas trees
  - Cypresses
  - Elms
  - Fig trees
  - Firs
  - Historic trees
  - Joshua trees
  - Magnolias

**Trees (cont.)**
- Mahogany trees
- Maples
- Mulberry trees
- Oaks
- Olive trees
- Orange trees
- Palms +
- Peach trees
- Pear trees
- Pines
- Plum trees
- Redwoods +
- Willows
- RT  Cork
  - Forests
  - Hedges (Plants)
  - Laurels
  - Liberty tree
  - Logs
  - Lumber industry
  - Orchards
  - Spanish moss
  - Topiary work
  - Tree houses
  - Tree limbs
  - Tree of knowledge
  - Tree of life
  - Tree planting ceremonies
  - Tree stumps
  - Woodcutting

Treillises
- USE Trellises

**Trellises**
- --[country or state]--[city]
- PN  Frames of latticework used as a screen or as support for climbing plants.
- UF  Garden lattices
  - Lattices, Garden
  - Treillises
- BT  Arbors (Bowers)

Trembling
- USE Shaking

**Trench mouth**
- --[country or state]--[city]
- UF  Vincent's infection
- BT  Communicable diseases
- RT  Dental hygiene

**Trench warfare**
- --[country or state]--[city]
- PN  Search also under the subdivision --TRENCH WARFARE used with names of wars (Appendix C).
- UF  Entrenchment
  - Intrenchments
- BT  Military art & science
- RT  Campaigns & battles
  - Chevaux-de-frise
  - Foxholes

**Trestles**
- --[country or state]--[city]
- PN  For images that focus on the braced

---

BT  Broader term          RT  Related term          PN  Public Note
NT  Narrower term        UF  Used for               +  Term has NTs
HN History Note           CN  Catalogers Note      --[ ] May subdivide

**Trestles (cont.)**
    frameworks of timbers, piles, or steelwork,
    usually of considerable height, for carrying a
    road or railroad over a depression.
  CN  As appropriate, double index under
      BRIDGES.
  RT  Bridges
Triacetate negatives
  USE Acetate negatives
**Trial proofs**
  CN  TGM II term.
  UF  State proofs
      Test proofs
      Working proofs
Trial sketches
  USE Courtroom sketches
Trials
  USE Judicial proceedings
Trials of vessels
  USE Ship trials
Trials, litigation, etc.
  CN  Used only as a subdivision with names of
      persons (Appendix B).
**Tribal chiefs**
    --[country]
  UF  Chiefs, Tribal
  BT  Rulers
Tribal dancers
  USE Ceremonial dancers
Tribes
  USE Indigenous peoples
Tribunals
  USE Judicial proceedings
Tricentennials
  USE Centennial celebrations
Trichrome carbro prints
  USE Tricolor carbro prints
**Trick riding**
    --[country or state]--[city]
  UF  Fancy riding
      Stunt riding
  BT  Entertainment
      Riding
  RT  Bareback riding
      Broncos
      Circuses & shows
      Rodeos
**Tricolor carbro prints**
  CN  TGM II term.
  UF  Three-color carbro prints
      Trichrome carbro prints
Tricycles
  USE Bicycles & tricycles
Tripartite windows
  HN  Term made non-postable, 1/1993, when
      PALLADIAN WINDOWS was made
      postable, and DIOCLETIAN WINDOWS and
      VENETIAN WINDOWS were made
      non-postable.
  USE Palladian windows
**Triplets**
  UF  Births, Multiple

**Triplets (cont.)**
    Multiple births
Trips
  USE Honeymoons
      Travel
      Visits of state
Triumphal arches
  USE Memorial arches
Triumphal celebrations
  USE Victory celebrations
Triumphs
  USE Victories
Trivia
  USE Curiosities & wonders
Trois crayons drawings
  USE A trois crayons drawings
**Trojan horses**
  RT  Horses
Trolley stations
  USE Street railroad stations
Trollies
  USE Street railroads
**Trombones**
  PN  Includes the activity of playing
      trombones.
  BT  Brass instruments
  RT  Bugles
      Cornets
      Trumpets
      Tubas
Troop inspections
  USE Military inspections
**Troop movements**
    --[nationality]--[country or state]--[city]
  PN  Shifting of troops from one location to
      another, as between battles. Search also under
      the subdivisions --AMPHIBIOUS
      OPERATIONS and --CAMPAIGNS &
      BATTLES used with names of wars
      (Appendix C).
  BT  Military art & science
  RT  Armies
      Military demobilizations
      Military mobilizations
Troop reviews
  USE Military parades & ceremonies
Troops, Ski
  USE Ski troops
Trophies
  USE Awards
**Trophies (Architectural ornaments)**
    --[country or state]--[city]
  PN  Architectural ornaments representing
      groups of military weapons.
  BT  Architectural decorations & ornaments
  RT  Arms & armament
**Tropical forests**
    --[country or state]--[city]
  UF  Jungles
  BT  Forests
**Troubadours**
  PN  Medieval musical poets, often of knightly

---

BT  Broader term               RT  Related term               PN  Public Note
NT  Narrower term            UF  Used for                   +  Term has NTs
HN  History Note              CN  Catalogers Note           --[ ]  May subdivide

**Troubadours (cont.)**
    rank.
  UF  Jongleurs
  BT  Entertainers
  RT  Minstrels
Troughs
  USE Watering troughs
**Trousers**
  BT  Clothing & dress
  NT  Lederhosen
**Trout**
    --[country or state]
  BT  Fish
Truces
  USE Armistices
**Truck farming**
    --[country or state]--[city]
  UF  Garden farming
       Market gardening
  BT  Farming
  RT  Vegetables
**Truck industry**
    --[country or state]--[city]
  PN  Manufacture and trade of trucks. Includes
       activities and structures.
  CN  Double index under INDUSTRIAL
       FACILITIES (or NTs) for images that focus
       on facilities.
  BT  Transportation industry
  RT  Automobile industry
       Trucks
Truck mechanics
  USE Mechanics (Persons)
Trucking
  USE Shipping
**Trucks**
    --[nationality]--[country or state]--[city]
  UF  Delivery trucks
  BT  Vehicles
  NT  Dump trucks
       Mail trucks
       Wreckers (Vehicles)
  RT  Jeep automobiles
       Truck industry
**Trumpets**
  PN  Includes the activity of playing trumpets.
  BT  Brass instruments
  RT  Bugles
       Cornets
       Trombones
       Tubas
Trunks
  USE Luggage
**Trusses**
    --[country or state]--[city]
  BT  Architectural elements
  NT  Roof trusses
  RT  Bridges
       Structural frames
Trusts, Industrial
  USE Industrial trusts
**Truth**

**Truth (cont.)**
  PN  A judgement, proposition, or idea that is
       true or accepted as true.
  UF  Truthfulness
  RT  Ethics
       Honesty
Truthfulness
  USE Honesty
       Truth
Tryouts
  USE Auditions
Tsunamis
  USE Tidal waves
**Tubas**
  BT  Brass instruments
  RT  Bugles
       Cornets
       Trombones
       Trumpets
**Tube industry**
    --[country or state]--[city]
  PN  Includes activities and structures.
  CN  Double index under INDUSTRIAL
       FACILITIES (or NTs) for images that focus
       on facilities.
  BT  Industry
**Tube industry strikes**
    --[country or state]--[city]
  BT  Strikes
**Tuberculosis**
    --[country or state]--[city]
  UF  Consumption (Disease)
  BT  Communicable diseases
Tubs, Bath
  USE Bathtubs & showers
**Tug of war**
  BT  Games
  RT  Pulling
       Ropes
**Tugboats**
    --[country or state]--[city]
  UF  Towboats
  BT  Boats
  RT  Harbors
       Towing
Tugging
  USE Pulling
**Tulips**
    --[country or state]--[city]
  BT  Flowers
Tumbling
  USE Falling
**Tuna**
    --[country or state]
  BT  Fish
**Tunnels**
    --[country or state]--[city]
  BT  Transportation facilities
  RT  Railroads
       Roads
       Subways
Tunnels, Wind

---

Tunnels, Wind (cont.)
USE Wind tunnels
**Turbans**
--[country or state]--[city]
BT Hats
Turbines
USE Engines
**Turkeys**
--[country or state]
BT Birds
RT Poultry
Turn bridges
USE Swing bridges
**Turnips**
--[country or state]--[city]
BT Vegetables
Turnouts
USE Carriages & coaches
Turnouts, Scenic
USE Scenic overlooks
Turnpike roads
USE Toll roads
Turnvereine
USE Athletic clubs
**Turpentine industry**
--[country or state]--[city]
PN Includes activities and structures.
CN Double index under INDUSTRIAL
FACILITIES (or NTs) for images that focus
on facilities.
BT Chemical industry
**Turret ships**
--[country or state]--[city]
UF Monitors (Warships)
Revolving cupolas (Warships)
BT Armored vessels
RT Gun turrets
Turrets, Gun
USE Gun turrets
**Turtles**
--[country or state]
UF Terrapins
Tortoises
BT Reptiles
**Tusks**
UF Ivory tusks
BT Teeth
RT Ivory
**Tuxedoes**
BT Clothing & dress
TV stills
USE Television stills
Twilight
USE Sunrises & sunsets
**Twine**
UF Binding twine
RT Ropes
**Twine industry**
--[country or state]--[city]
CN Double index under INDUSTRIAL
FACILITIES (or NTs) for images that focus
on facilities.

Twine industry (cont.)
BT Industry
RT Rope industry
**Twins**
UF Births, Multiple
Multiple births
NT Siamese twins
Two-family dwellings
USE Duplexes
**Two-thirds rule**
UF Rule, Two-thirds
BT Parliamentary practice
RT Political organizations
**Tympana**
--[country or state]--[city]
PN Recessed, usually triangular faces of
pediments within the frame made by the
upper and lower cornices; spaces within
arches and above lintels or subordinate
arches.
UF Tympanums
BT Architectural elements
RT Arches
Lintels
Pediments
Tympanums
USE Tympana
Type C prints
USE Dye coupler prints
Type R prints
USE Dye coupler prints
Type setting
USE Typesetting
**Typesetting**
--[country or state]--[city]
UF Composition (Printing)
Type setting
RT Printing
Printing industry
Printing presses
**Typewriters**
BT Office equipment & supplies
NT Teletypewriters
RT Typewriting
**Typewriting**
--[country or state]--[city]
UF Typing (Writing)
BT Writing
RT Office workers
Typewriters
**Typhoons**
--[country or state]--[city]
PN Includes the event and any resulting
damage.
CN Used in a note under STORMS.
BT Storms
RT Hurricanes
**Typhus fever**
--[country or state]--[city]
BT Communicable diseases
Typing (Writing)
USE Typewriting

---

BT Broader term
NT Narrower term
HN History Note

RT Related term
UF Used for
CN Catalogers Note

PN Public Note
+ Term has NTs
--[ ] May subdivide

Typists
   USE Office workers
Tyrants
   USE Dictators
UFO's
   USE Unidentified flying objects
**Ukeleles**
   PN   Includes the activity of playing ukeleles.
   BT   Stringed instruments
**Umbrellas**
   UF   Parasols
   RT   Clothing & dress
         Rain
Umpiring
   USE Sports officiating
Unconsciousness
   USE Loss of consciousness
**Underground movements**
         --[country or state]--[city]
   PN   Search also under the subdivision
         --UNDERGROUND MOVEMENTS used
         with names of wars (Appendix C).
   UF   Resistance movements
   RT   Guerrillas
         Opposition (Political science)
         Protest movements
         War
**Underground railroad system**
         --[country or state]--[city]
   RT   Abolition movement
         Fugitive slaves
         Slavery
Underground stations
   USE Subway stations
Undersea cables
   USE Submarine cables
**Undertaking**
         --[country or state]--[city]
   CN   Used in a note under MORGUES &
         MORTUARIES.
   UF   Funeral directing
         Mortuary practice
   NT   Embalming
   RT   Cremation
         Crematoriums
         Dead persons
         Funeral rites & ceremonies
         Morgues & mortuaries
Undertaking establishments
   USE Morgues & mortuaries
**Underwater drilling**
         --[country or state]--[city]
   UF   Drilling, Underwater
         Submarine drilling
   BT   Boring
   RT   Dredging
**Underwater photographs**
   CN   TGM II term.
   UF   Submarine photographs
**Underwater photography**
   PN   For the subject of taking photographs
         underwater.

**Underwater photography (cont.)**
   BT   Photography
Underwater swimming
   USE Skin diving
**Underwear**
   BT   Clothing & dress ·
   NT   Lingerie +
   RT   Bloomers
Undocumented aliens
   USE Illegal aliens
**Unemployed**
         --[country or state]--[city]
   UF   Jobless people
         Out-of-work people
   BT   People
   RT   Depressions
         Dismissal of employees
         Employees
         Employment
         Poor persons
Unhappiness
   USE Depression (Mental state)
         Sadness
Unicellular organisms
   USE Microorganisms
**Unicorns**
   UF   Mythical creatures
   BT   Supernatural beings
**Unicycles**
         --[country or state]--[city]
   BT   Vehicles
   RT   Cycling
**Unidentified flying objects**
   UF   UFO's
   RT   Aircraft
         Extraterrestrial life
**Uniforms**
   PN   Includes uniforms for sports and schools.
   BT   Clothing & dress
   NT   Band uniforms
         Military uniforms
         Prison uniforms
**Union cases**
   CN   TGM II term.
   UF   Composition cases
         Gutta-percha photograph cases
Unions, Labor
   USE Labor unions
Unions, Student
   USE Student unions
Unitarian churches
   USE Unitarian Universalist churches
**Unitarian Universalist churches**
         --[country or state]--[city]
   PN   For images that focus on buildings, as
         well as the associated grounds.
   CN   Changed 6/1987 from UNITARIAN
         CHURCHES.
   UF   Unitarian churches
         Universalist churches
   BT   Protestant churches
United Service Organizations clubs

---

BT Broader term          RT Related term          PN Public Note
NT Narrower term        UF Used for            + Term has NTs
HN History Note          CN Catalogers Note     --[ ] May subdivide

United Service Organizations clubs (cont.)
  USE USO clubs
Universal suffrage
  USE Suffrage
Universalist churches
  USE Unitarian Universalist churches
**Universities & colleges**
      --[country or state]--[city]
  HN Usage changed 1/1993 to emphasize
      facilities aspect, rather than level of
      education.
  UF Colleges
  BT Educational facilities
  NT Teachers' colleges
      Theological seminaries
  RT Alumni & alumnae
      College administrators
      Laboratory schools
      Student movements
      Students
University administrators
  USE College administrators
University students
  USE Students
University & college unions
  USE Student unions
**Unknown soldiers**
  CN As appropriate, double index under
      MONUMENTS & MEMORIALS.
  BT Symbols
  RT Soldiers
**Unmarried mothers**
  UF Unwed mothers
  BT Mothers
      Single women
Unwed mothers
  USE Unmarried mothers
**Upholstery**
  RT Furniture
      Textiles
**Upper class**
      --[country or state]--[city]
  HN Changed 1/1993 from UPPER
      CLASSES.
  UF Aristocracy
      High society
      Society, High
      Upper classes
  BT Social classes
  NT Nobility +
  RT Plutocracy
Upper classes
  USE Upper class
Uprisings
  USE Rebellions
**Urban beautification**
      --[country or state]--[city]
  UF Beautification of cities & towns
      City beautification
      Community beautification
      Town beautification
  RT City planning

**Urban beautification (cont.)**
      Refuse disposal
      Urban growth
**Urban growth**
      --[country or state]--[city]
  UF Growth, Urban
  RT City planning
      Economic & social conditions
      Sociology
      Urban beautification
Urban life
  USE City & town life
Urban planning
  USE City planning
Urban planning drawings
  USE Planning drawings
Urban transportation
  USE Mass transit
**Urns**
      --[country or state]--[city]
  PN Vessels of various forms, usually with a
      foot or pedestal and used for holding liquids,
      for ornamental purposes, for preserving ashes
      of the dead after cremation and, anciently, for
      holding lots to be drawn.
  UF Cinerary urns
      Funeral urns
      Sepulchral urns
  BT Containers
  RT Pitchers
      Pottery
      Tombs & sepulchral monuments
      Vases
Use of land
  USE Land use
Used bookstores
  USE Secondhand bookstores
Used car lots
  USE Automobile dealerships
**USO clubs**
      --[country or state]--[city]
  CN Double index under ORGANIZATIONS'
      FACILITIES (or NTs) for images that focus
      on facilities.
  UF United Service Organizations clubs
      U.S.O. clubs
  BT Clubs
  RT Canteens (Wartime, emergency, etc.)
      Military life
      War work
**Usury**
      --[country or state]--[city]
  UF Loan sharking
      Money lending
  BT Business & finance
  RT Credit
      Debt
      Pawnshops
Utility companies, Public
  USE Public utility companies
**Utility poles**
      --[country or state]--[city]

---

**Utility poles (cont.)**
- UF  Poles, Utility
  - Telegraph poles
  - Telegraph & telephone poles
  - Telephone poles
- RT  Electric lines
  - Telecommunication lines

Utilization of land
- USE Land use

Utopian communities
- USE Collective settlements

U.S.O. clubs
- USE USO clubs

V sign
- USE Peace signs
  - Victory sign

Vacant buildings
- USE Abandoned buildings

Vacation Bible schools
- USE Christian vacation schools

**Vacations**
- --[country or state]--[city]
- NT  Employee vacations
- RT  Holidays
  - Leisure
  - Recreation

**Vaccinations**
- --[country or state]--[city]
- UF  Inoculations
- BT  Health care
- RT  Communicable diseases
  - Medicines

**Vacuum cleaners**
- BT  Appliances
- RT  Sweeping & dusting

Vagrants
- USE Tramps

**Valentines**
- CN  TGM II term.

Valises
- USE Luggage

**Valleys**
- --[country or state]
- UF  Glens
  - Hollows
  - River valleys
  - Stream valleys
- BT  Land
- NT  Canyons
- RT  Rivers

**Vampires**
- --[country or state]--[city]
- BT  Supernatural beings

**Vandalism**
- --[country or state]--[city]
- UF  Damage to property
  - Destruction of property
  - Property damage
- BT  Crimes
- RT  Building deterioration

Vandyke photoprints
- USE Vandyke prints

**Vandyke prints**
- CN  TGM II term.
- UF  Vandyke photoprints

Vanes, Weather
- USE Weather vanes

Vanities
- USE Dressing tables

Vanity
- USE Pride

**Variety stores**
- --[country or state]--[city]
- PN  Includes activities and structures.
- UF  Five & ten cent stores
- BT  Stores & shops

Varnishes
- USE Paints & varnishes

**Varnishing industry**
- --[country or state]--[city]
- PN  Includes activities and structures.
- CN  Double index under INDUSTRIAL FACILITIES (or NTs) for images that focus on facilities.
- UF  Japanning industry
  - Lacquering industry
- BT  Industry
- RT  Paints & varnishes

Vascular hypertension
- USE Hypertension

Vascular system
- USE Cardiovascular system

**Vases**
- PN  For vessels, commonly decorative or for flowers.
- RT  Containers
  - Pottery
  - Urns

**Vats**
- BT  Containers

Vaudeville posters
- USE Theatrical posters

**Vaudeville shows**
- --[country or state]--[city]
- PN  Theatrical pieces, usually comic, consisting of dialogue or pantomime, intermingled with light songs and, sometimes, dances.
- BT  Theatrical productions
- RT  Musical revues & comedies

**Vaulting**
- --[country or state]--[city]
- UF  Pole-vaulting
- BT  Track athletics

**Vaults (Architecture)**
- --[country or state]--[city]
- PN  Arched structure, usually of masonry, and usually forming a ceiling or roof.
- BT  Architectural elements
- RT  Ceilings
  - Interiors
  - Roofs

Vaults (Sepulchral)
- USE Tombs & sepulchral monuments

BT  Broader term          RT  Related term          PN  Public Note
NT  Narrower term         UF  Used for               +  Term has NTs
HN  History Note          CN  Catalogers Note        --[ ]  May subdivide

**Vaults (Strong rooms)**
    --[country or state]--[city]
  UF  Strong rooms (Vaults)
  BT  Interiors
  RT  Banks
       Locks (Hardware)
       Safes
**VD (Diseases)**
  USE Sexually transmitted diseases
**Vegetables**
    --[country or state]--[city]
  PN  For the subject of edible vegetables in
       general and images that focus on vegetables.
  BT  Food
  NT  Asparagus
       Beans +
       Beets
       Cabbage
       Carrots
       Cauliflower
       Celery
       Cucumbers
       Eggplants
       Lettuce
       Onions
       Peanuts
       Peas
       Peppers +
       Potatoes
       Radishes
       Spinach
       Turnips
  RT  Plants
       Tomatoes
       Truck farming
**Vehicle maintenance & repair**
    --[country or state]--[city]
  CN  As appropriate, double index under
       AUTOMOBILE SERVICE STATIONS for
       images that focus on service stations.
  UF  Vehicle repair
  BT  Maintenance & repair
  RT  Automobile equipment & supplies stores
       Automobile service stations
       Vehicles
**Vehicle repair**
  USE Vehicle maintenance & repair
**Vehicles**
    --[nationality]--[country or state]--[city]
  CN  Subdivide by nationality only when in
       another country.
  NT  Aircraft +
       Ambulances
       Amphibious vehicles +
       Armored vehicles +
       Artificial satellites
       Automobiles +
       Baby carriages
       Bicycles & tricycles
       Bookmobiles
       Buses +
       Carriages & coaches +

**Vehicles (cont.)**
       Carts & wagons +
       Chariots
       Coaster cars
       Floats (Parades)
       Hearses
       Hospital ships
       Hospital trains
       Howdahs
       Jeep automobiles
       Karts (Midget cars)
       Military vehicles +
       Mobile health units
       Motorcycles
       Railroad cars +
       Railroad locomotives +
       Sedan chairs
       Sleds & sleighs +
       Taxicabs
       Tracklaying vehicles +
       Tractors
       Travois
       Trucks +
       Unicycles
       Vessels +
       Wheelbarrows
       Wheelchairs
       Wheeled chairs +
  RT  Fire engines & equipment
       License plates
       Machinery
       Model vehicles
       Parking
       Parking lots
       Passenger quarters
       Passengers
       Stewards
       Streets
       Tires
       Towing
       Traffic congestion
       Transportation
       Vehicle maintenance & repair
       Wagon trains
       Wheels
**Veils**
    --[country or state]--[city]
  BT  Clothing & dress
**Velocipedes**
  USE Bicycles & tricycles
**Vending machines**
    --[country or state]--[city]
  BT  Coin operated machines
**Vending stands**
    --[country or state]--[city]
  UF  Roadside stands
  BT  Mercantile facilities
  RT  Food vendors
       Markets
       Peddlers
       Portable buildings
**Vendors, Street**

---

BT Broader term      RT Related term      PN Public Note
NT Narrower term    UF Used for       + Term has NTs
HN History Note     CN Catalogers Note   --[ ] May subdivide

Vendors, Street (cont.)
  USE Peddlers
Venereal diseases
  USE Sexually transmitted diseases
Venetian windows
  USE Palladian windows
Vengeance
  USE Revenge
Ventilating, air conditioning & heating drawings
  USE HVAC drawings
**Ventilation**
      --[country or state]--[city]
  RT  Sanitation
**Ventriloquism**
      --[country or state]--[city]
  BT  Entertainment
Verandas
  USE Porches
Vermifuges
  USE Anthelmintics
**Vertical lift bridges**
      --[country or state]--[city]
  CN  Used in a note under DRAWBRIDGES.
  UF  Lift bridges
      Movable bridges
  BT  Bridges
**Vessels**
      --[nationality]--[country or state]--[city]
  UF  Watercraft
  BT  Vehicles
  NT  Boats +
      Government vessels +
      Ice-breaking vessels
      Mail steamers
      Ships +
      Steamboats +
      Yachts +
  RT  Anchors
      Boat graveyards
      Boat & ship companies
      Boat & ship industry
      Crew quarters
      Fishing
      Galleys (Ship kitchens)
      Launchings
      Marine accidents
      Marine terminals
      Mooring
      Naval parades & ceremonies
      Navigation
      Piers & wharves
      Sailors
      Shipwrecks
      Sick bays
      Steerage
Vest camera photographs
  USE Detective camera photographs
Vestibules
  USE Entrance halls
**Veterans**
      --[nationality]
  PN  Search also under the subdivision

Veterans (cont.)
      --VETERANS used with names of wars
      (Appendix C).
  UF  Ex-military personnel
  NT  Disabled veterans
  RT  Military personnel
      Soldiers' homes
      Veterans' benefits
      Veterans' organizations
      Veterans' rights
**Veterans' benefits**
      --[country]
  UF  Benefits, Veterans'
  BT  Employee fringe benefits
  RT  Veterans
      Veterans' rights
Veterans' homes
  USE Soldiers' homes
**Veterans' organizations**
      --[country or state]--[city]
  PN  Includes activities and structures.
  CN  Double index under ORGANIZATIONS'
      FACILITIES (or NTs) for images that focus
      on facilities.
  BT  Organizations
  RT  Veterans
**Veterans' rights**
      --[country]
  BT  Civil rights
  RT  Veterans
      Veterans' benefits
**Veterinary drugs**
  BT  Medicines
  RT  Veterinary hospitals
      Veterinary medicine
**Veterinary hospitals**
      --[country or state]--[city]
  PN  Includes activities and structures.
  UF  Animal hospitals
  BT  Hospitals
  RT  Animals
      Veterinary drugs
      Veterinary medicine
**Veterinary medicine**
      --[country or state]--[city]
  PN  For the subject of veterinary medicine in
      general and the activities of veterinarians.
  BT  Medicine
  RT  Animals
      Veterinary drugs
      Veterinary hospitals
**Vetoes**
  BT  Law & legal affairs
  RT  Executive power
      Legislation
Viaducts
  USE Bridges
Vicarages (Buildings)
  USE Religious dwellings
**Vice**
  BT  Ethics
  RT  Corruption

BT Broader term            RT Related term            PN Public Note
NT Narrower term           UF Used for                + Term has NTs
HN History Note            CN Catalogers Note         --[ ] May subdivide

**Vice (cont.)**
      Crimes
      Deadly sins
      Extravagance
**Vice presidential seal**
      --[country]
  BT  Seals
  RT  Vice presidents
**Vice presidents**
      --[country]
  PN  For the office of the vice president or for
      incumbents.
  BT  Government officials
  RT  Presidential elections
      Vice presidential seal
**Vices (Equipment)**
  BT  Equipment
**Victims**
      --[country or state]--[city]
  BT  People
  NT  Abused children
      Abused women
      Disaster victims
      Drowning victims
      Nuclear weapons victims
  RT  Emergency medical services
      Refugees
      Rescue work
      Wounds & injuries
**Victims of abuse**
  USE  Abused children
      Abused women
**Victoria card photographs**
  CN  TGM II term.
**Victories**
      --[nationality]--[country or state]--[city]
  PN  Successes in any contests or struggles
      involving the defeat of an opponent or the
      overcoming of obstacles.
  CN  Subdivide by nationality of the victors.
  UF  Triumphs
      Winners
      Wins
  RT  Contests
      Sports
      Surrenders
      Victory celebrations
      Victory sign
      World records
**Victory celebrations**
      --[country or state]--[city]
  PN  Search also under the subdivision
      --PEACE used with names of wars (Appendix
      C).
  CN  As appropriate, double index under the
      subdivision --PEACE used with names of
      wars (Appendix C).
  UF  Triumphal celebrations
  BT  Celebrations
  RT  Victories
      War
**Victory gardens**

**Victory gardens (cont.)**
      --[country or state]--[city]
  BT  Gardens
  RT  Economic aspects of war
      Home food processing
**Victory sign**
  UF  V sign
  BT  Symbols
  RT  Peace signs
      Victories
**Video disks**
  USE  Videodiscs
**Videodiscs**
  CN  TGM II term.
  UF  Video disks
**Viewbooks**
  CN  TGM II term.
  UF  Booklets
      Souvenir albums
      Souvenir booklets
      Souvenir viewbooks
      Viewbooks, Souvenir
**Viewbooks, Souvenir**
  USE  Viewbooks
**Viewmaster cards**
  USE  Stereographs
**Views, Aerial**
  USE  Aerial views
**Views, Bird's-eye**
  USE  Bird's-eye views
**Views, City**
  USE  Cityscapes
**Views, Panoramic**
  USE  Panoramic views
**Views, Toad's-eye**
  USE  Worm's-eye views
**Views, Worm's eye**
  USE  Worm's-eye views
**Vigilance committees**
      --[country or state]--[city]
  UF  Vigilantes
  BT  Organizations
  RT  Judicial proceedings
      Law enforcement
      Lynchings
      Punishment & torture
**Vigilantes**
  USE  Vigilance committees
**Vigils**
  PN  Keeping awake at times when sleep is
      customary, or periods of watching. Search
      under SURVEILLANCE for images related to
      law enforcement or criminal investigation.
  UF  Watching
  RT  Surveillance
**Vignettes**
  CN  TGM II term.
**Viking ships**
      --[country or state]--[city]
  BT  Sailing ships
**Village halls**
  USE  City & town halls

---

BT  Broader term
NT  Narrower term
HN  History Note

RT  Related term
UF  Used for
CN  Catalogers Note

PN  Public Note
+  Term has NTs
--[ ]  May subdivide

Village life
  USE Villages
**Villages**
      --[country or state]
  PN  A unit of compact settlement, usually
      larger than a hamlet and smaller than a town,
      and distinguished from a surrounding rural
      area.
  UF  Village life
  BT  Settlements
  RT  Cities & towns
**Villains**
  BT  People
  RT  Fictitious characters
      Good & evil
Villas
  USE Dwellings
      Estates
Vincent's infection
  USE Trench mouth
**Vinegar industry**
      --[country or state]--[city]
  PN  Includes activities and structures.
  CN  Double index under INDUSTRIAL
      FACILITIES (or NTs) for images that focus
      on facilities.
  BT  Food industry
**Vines**
      --[country or state]--[city]
  UF  Climbing plants
  BT  Plants
Vineyards
  USE Grapes
      Wine industry
Violations, Traffic
  USE Ticketing
**Violence**
      --[country or state]--[city]
  RT  Abused children
      Abused women
      Crimes
      Punishment & torture
      Riots
      Strangling
      Terrorism
      War
Violence, Political
  USE Assassinations
      Civil disobedience
      Terrorism
**Violets**
      --[country or state]--[city]
  BT  Flowers
**Violins**
  PN  Includes the activity of playing violins.
  UF  Fiddles
  BT  Stringed instruments
**Violoncellos**
  PN  Includes the activity of playing
      violoncellos.
  UF  Cellos
  BT  Stringed instruments

Virginals
  USE Harpsichords
**Vision disorders**
      --[country or state]--[city]
  UF  Impaired vision
      Visual impairments
  BT  Diseases
  RT  Blindness
      Eyeglasses
      Eyes
**Visionary architecture**
      --[country or state]--[city]
  UF  Futuristic architecture
      Idealistic architecture
  BT  Architecture
  RT  Architectural follies
      Conjectural works
      Forecasting
**Visiting**
  BT  Manners & customs
  RT  Travel
**Visiting cards**
  CN  TGM II term.
  UF  Calling cards
      Cartes de visite (Visiting cards)
**Visitors' centers**
      --[country or state]--[city]
  PN  Includes activities and structures.
  UF  Centers, Visitors'
      Orientation centers
  BT  Cultural facilities
  RT  Tourist trade
      Travel
**Visits of state**
      --[nationality]--[country or state]--[city]
  PN  Search also under the subdivision
      --JOURNEYS used with names of persons
      (Appendix B).
  UF  Official visits
      Royal visits
      State visits
      Trips
  BT  Events
  RT  Travel
Visual impairments
  USE Vision disorders
**Vitamins**
  RT  Nutrition
      Pills
Vitascopes
  USE Motion picture devices
Vocalists
  USE Singers
**Vocational education**
      --[country or state]--[city]
  PN  Includes on-the-job training and other
      activities and structures.
  CN  Double index under EDUCATIONAL
      FACILITIES (or NTs) for images that focus
      on facilities.
  UF  Job training
      Trade schools

---

BT  Broader term            RT  Related term            PN  Public Note
NT  Narrower term           UF  Used for                 +  Term has NTs
HN  History Note            CN  Catalogers Note          --[ ] May subdivide

**Vocational education (cont.)**
Training, Vocational
BT  Education
NT  Flight training
Law enforcement training
RT  Apprentices
Occupations
Reformatories
Volantarism
USE Community service
**Volcanic eruptions**
--[country or state]--[city]
PN  Includes the event and any resulting
damage.
BT  Natural phenomena
RT  Disasters
Tidal waves
Volcanoes
**Volcanic rock**
--[country or state]--[city]
UF  Lava rock
Rhyolite
BT  Rocks
RT  Rock formations
Volcanoes
**Volcanoes**
--[country or state]--[city]
BT  Land
NT  Mud volcanoes
RT  Mountains
Volcanic eruptions
Volcanic rock
**Volleyball**
--[country or state]--[city]
PN  Includes organizations and activities.
BT  Sports
Volunteer work
USE Community service
**Voodooism**
--[country or state]--[city]
BT  Religion
RT  Witchcraft
Vortographs
USE Photograms
**Vote counting**
--[country or state]--[city]
UF  Ballot counting
Ballot tabulation
Counting of votes
Tabulation of ballots
Tabulation of votes
Vote tabulation
RT  Political elections
Voting
Vote tabulation
USE Vote counting
**Voter apathy**
--[country or state]--[city]
BT  Apathy
RT  Voting
**Voter registration**
--[country or state]--[city]

**Voter registration (cont.)**
RT  Recording & registration
Voting
**Voting**
--[country or state]--[city]
BT  Political participation
RT  Political elections
Poll taxes
Suffrage
Vote counting
Voter apathy
Voter registration
**Voussoirs**
--[country or state]--[city]
PN  Stones forming part of an arch;
wedge-shaped, they make the arch
self-supporting.
UF  Arch blocks
BT  Architectural elements
NT  Keystones
RT  Arches
Vows
USE Oaths
**Voyages around the world**
UF  Around the world voyages
Circumnavigation
World travel
BT  Travel
RT  Earth
Transcontinental journeys
**Voyeurism**
--[country or state]--[city]
RT  Sexual harassment
**Vues d'optique**
CN  TGM II term.
UF  Peep show prints
**Vultures**
--[country or state]
UF  Buzzards
BT  Birds
V-support roofs
USE Cantilevered roofs
**Wading**
--[country or state]--[city]
BT  Swimming
RT  Bodies of water
**Wagers**
PN  To make a bet on a final outcome.
UF  Betting
RT  Gambling
**Wages**
--[country or state]--[city]
UF  Compensation for work
Earnings
Pay
Payments
Remuneration
Salaries
NT  Minimum wages
RT  Cost & standard of living
Employment
Money

BT Broader term          RT Related term          PN Public Note
NT Narrower term          UF Used for          + Term has NTs
HN History Note          CN Catalogers Note          --[ ] May subdivide

**Wages (cont.)**
  Paydays
  Prices
  Wage-price policy
**Wage-price policy**
  --[country or state]
  UF  Incomes policy
    Price-wage policy
    Salary policy
  BT  Economic policy
  RT  Price regulation
    Wages
**Wagon sheds**
  --[country or state]--[city]
  UF  Sheds, Wagon
  BT  Sheds
  RT  Carts & wagons
    Transportation facilities
**Wagon trains**
  --[country or state]--[city]
  RT  Covered wagons
    Frontier & pioneer life
    Vehicles
Wagons
  USE Carts & wagons
**Wainscoting**
  --[country or state]--[city]
  PN  The lower part of interior walls when
    specially decorated or faced; also the
    decoration adorning this part of a wall.
  UF  Dadoes (Walls)
  BT  Architectural elements
  RT  Walls
**Waiters**
  --[country or state]--[city]
  BT  Men
  RT  Restaurant workers
    Restaurants
    Stewards
    Waitresses
**Waiting rooms**
  --[country or state]--[city]
  BT  Interiors
  RT  Reception rooms
**Waitresses**
  --[country or state]--[city]
  UF  Cocktail waitresses
  BT  Women
  RT  Restaurant workers
    Restaurants
    Waiters
**Waking**
  UF  Awaking
  BT  Mental states
  RT  Sleeping
**Walking**
  --[country or state]--[city]
  UF  Strolling
  BT  Locomotion
  NT  Children walking
    Snowshoeing
    Somnambulism

**Walking (cont.)**
  Tiptoeing
  RT  Hiking
    Pedestrians
    Recreation
    Trails & paths
    Walking races
    Walkways
**Walking races**
  --[country or state]--[city]
  UF  Race walking
    Racewalking
  BT  Racing
  RT  Track athletics
    Walking
Walking sticks
  USE Staffs (Sticks)
**Walking the plank**
  BT  Executions
**Walkways**
  --[country or state]--[city]
  UF  Promenades
  BT  Facilities
  NT  Boardwalks
    Covered walks
    Sidewalks +
    Trails & paths
  RT  Lovers' lanes
    Passageways
    Pedestrians
    Walking
Wall laths
  USE Laths
**Wallpaper**
  CN  TGM II term.
**Wallpaper industry**
  --[country or state]--[city]
  PN  Includes activities and structures.
  CN  Double index under INDUSTRIAL
    FACILITIES (or NTs) for images that focus
    on facilities.
  BT  Industry
  RT  Paper industry
**Walls**
  --[country or state]--[city]
  PN  Vertical architectural members used to
    define and divide spaces.
  BT  Architectural elements
  NT  Curtain walls
    Facades +
    Retaining walls
  RT  Arcades (Architectural components)
    City walls
    Coping
    Courses (Wall components)
    Courtyards
    Entablatures
    Fences
    Garden walls
    Gates
    Interiors
    Niches

BT Broader term       RT Related term        PN Public Note
NT Narrower term       UF Used for            + Term has NTs
HN History Note        CN Catalogers Note     --[ ] May subdivide

**Walls (cont.)**
> Paneling
> Parapets
> Partitions
> Pediments
> Quoins
> Sea walls
> Stone walls
> Wainscoting

**Walnuts**
> BT Nuts

**Wanted posters**
> CN TGM II term.
> UF Reward posters

Wapiti
> USE Elk

**War**
> --[country or state]--[city]
> PN For the subject of war in general and for wars that cannot be identified by name. Search primarily under names of specific wars and relevant topical subdivisions (Appendix C). The subdivision --WAR is used with names of ethnic, racial and regional groups, and with classes of persons (Appendix A) only when the war cannot be identified.
> CN Prefer the name of the war with relevant topical subdivisions (Appendix C).
> HN Changed 12/1992 to incorporate the concept WARS, which was made non-postable.
> UF Hostilities
> Wars
> BT Events
> NT Civil wars
> RT Campaigns & battles
> Civil defense
> Concentration camps
> Confiscations
> Declarations of war
> Defense industry
> Dogs of war
> Economic aspects of war
> Foreign participation in war
> Fraternization
> Guerrillas
> Medical aspects of war
> Military art & science
> Military assistance
> Military occupations
> Military policy
> Military retreats
> Missing in action
> Moral aspects of war
> Neutrality
> Peace
> Peace negotiations
> Prisoners of war
> Religious aspects of war
> Revolutions
> Scrap drives

**War (cont.)**
> Surrenders
> Underground movements
> Victory celebrations
> Violence
> War allies
> War blackouts
> War casualties
> War correspondents
> War damage
> War destruction & pillage
> War relief

**War allies**
> UF Allies, War
> Axis powers
> BT International relations
> RT Treaties
> War

**War blackouts**
> --[country or state]--[city]
> PN For periods of enforced darkness as a precaution against or practice for air raids.
> RT Aerial bombings
> Civil defense
> Lighting
> War

**War bonds & funds**
> --[country]
> UF Liberty loans
> BT Economic aspects of war
> RT Bonds (Financial records)
> Fund raising
> Public debt

**War casualties**
> --[country or state]--[city]
> PN For images that focus on dead and wounded persons. Search under MEDICAL ASPECTS OF WAR for relief and medical care of casualties. Search also under the subdivision --CASUALTIES or --MEDICAL ASPECTS used with names of wars (Appendix C).
> CN Used in a note under MEDICAL ASPECTS OF WAR.
> UF Casualties, War
> Wounded in war
> BT People
> RT Dead persons
> Disabled veterans
> Medical aspects of war
> Nuclear weapons victims
> War
> Wounds & injuries

**War claims**
> BT Economic aspects of war
> RT Reparations

War compensations
> USE Reparations

**War correspondents**
> --[nationality]--[country or state]--[city]
> PN Search also under the subdivision --COMMUNICATIONS used with names of

BT Broader term
NT Narrower term
HN History Note

RT Related term
UF Used for
CN Catalogers Note

PN Public Note
+ Term has NTs
--[ ] May subdivide

**War correspondents (cont.)**
        wars (Appendix C).
  BT  Journalists
  RT  War
War costs
  USE Economic aspects of war
**War crime trials**
        --[country or state]--[city]
  BT  Judicial proceedings
  RT  War crimes
**War crimes**
        --[nationality]--[country or state]--[city]
  CN  Subdivide by nationality of those
        committing the crimes.
  BT  Moral aspects of war
  RT  Atrocities
        War crime trials
        War destruction & pillage
**War damage**
        --[country or state]--[city]
  PN  For images made to show damage or views
        after the fighting. Search also under the
        subdivision --DESTRUCTION & PILLAGE
        used with names of wars (Appendix C).
  CN  Double index with the name of the war
        and the subdivision --DESTRUCTION &
        PILLAGE (Appendix C). Used in a note
        under RUINS.
  UF  Bomb damage
        Damage to property
        Destruction of property
        Property damage
  RT  Battlefields
        War
        War destruction & pillage
War damage compensation
  USE Reparations
**War destruction & pillage**
        --[country or state]--[city]
  PN  For the general subject of looting and
        destruction of property in the context of war
        as well as specific acts of plundering. Search
        also under the subdivision --DESTRUCTION
        & PILLAGE used with names of wars
        (Appendix C).
  UF  Booty
        Damage to property
        Destruction of property
        Looting
        Pillage
        Plundering
        Property damage
        Spoils of war
  RT  Sabotage
        War
        War crimes
        War damage
War effort
  USE War work
**War games**
        --[country or state]--[city]
  PN  Umpired training maneuvers imitative of

**War games (cont.)**
        war, in which opposed forces engage in attack
        and defense with actual personnel and
        equipment.
  UF  Kriegsspiel
        Wargames
  BT  Military maneuvers
War industry
  USE Defense industry
War machine
  USE Military policy
**War posters**
  CN  TGM II term.
**War prisoners' organizations**
        --[country or state]--[city]
  CN  Double index under ORGANIZATIONS'
        FACILITIES (or NTs) for images that focus
        on facilities.
  BT  Organizations
  RT  Prisoners of war
War production
  USE Defense industry
**War profiteering**
        --[country or state]--[city]
  PN  Making an unreasonable profit by taking
        advantage of a public need in time of war.
  UF  Profiteering, War
  BT  Economic aspects of war
  RT  Commercialism
        Corruption
**War rallies**
        --[country or state]--[city]
  PN  For events intended to rally support for
        war or to spur labor production on behalf of
        war. Search also under the subdivisions
        --ECONOMIC & INDUSTRIAL ASPECTS,
        --EQUIPMENT & SUPPLIES,
        --RECRUITMENT & ENLISTMENT, and
        --SOCIAL ASPECTS used with names of
        wars (Appendix C).
  UF  Rallies, War
  BT  Events
  RT  Defense industry
        Political parades & rallies
        Recruiting & enlistment
        War work
**War relief**
        --[nationality]--[country or state]--[city]
  PN  Official or private aid to civilians during
        wars in the form of money or necessities.
  CN  Subdivide for the nationality of people
        giving relief and subdivide geographically for
        country receiving relief.
  UF  Civilian war relief
  BT  Disaster relief
  RT  Blockade running
        Economic aspects of war
        War
War ships
  USE Warships
War surplus stores
  USE Army-Navy stores

BT  Broader term
NT  Narrower term
HN  History Note

RT  Related term
UF  Used for
CN  Catalogers Note

PN  Public Note
+  Term has NTs
--[ ]  May subdivide

**War work**
--[country or state]--[city]
PN  For civilian work as part of a war effort.
For the effect of war on industrial and
commerical activity search under the
subdivision --ECONOMIC & INDUSTRIAL
ASPECTS or by ethnic, racial, regional
groups, and classes of persons subdivisions
used with names of specific wars (Appendix
C).  The subdivision --WAR used with the
names of ethnic, racial and regional groups,
and with classes of persons (Appendix A) is
used only when the war cannot be identified.
UF  War effort
BT  Economic aspects of war
RT  Employment
Scrap drives
USO clubs
War rallies
Wardrobes
USE Closets
Wardrooms
USE Officers' quarters
Wards, Hospitals
USE Hospital wards
**Warehouses**
--[country or state]--[city]
BT  Storage facilities
RT  Industrial facilities
Industry
Loading docks
Storehouses
Warfare
USE Military art & science
Wargames
USE War games
Warmongering
USE Chauvinism & jingoism
**Warnings**
UF  Predictions
RT  Danger
Forecasting
Fortune telling
Prophecy
Threats
Warreners
USE Gamekeepers
**Warriors**
--[country or state]--[city]
BT  People associated with military activities
RT  Soldiers
Wars
HN  Changed 12/1992 from postable term.
USE War
**Warships**
--[nationality]--[country or state]--[city]
UF  War ships
BT  Government vessels
Ships
NT  Aircraft carriers
Armored vessels +
Battleships

**Warships (cont.)**
Cruisers (Warships)
Gunboats
Torpedo boats
RT  Arms & armament
Naval warfare
Scuttling of warships
Submarines
Wartime housing
USE Emergency housing
Housing
**Wash drawings**
CN  TGM II term.
**Wash tubs**
BT  Containers
RT  Cleaning
Laundry
Washbasins
USE Basins
**Washboards**
BT  Equipment
RT  Cleaning
Laundry
Washing
USE Cleaning
Laundry
Washing dishes
USE Dishwashing
**Washing machines**
BT  Appliances
RT  Laundry
Washrooms
USE Bathrooms
**Wasps**
--[country or state]
UF  Hornets
BT  Insects
RT  Wasps' nests
**Wasps' nests**
--[country or state]--[city]
RT  Beehives
Wasps
Waste disposal
USE Sewerage
**Waste disposal facilities**
--[country or state]--[city]
BT  Facilities
NT  Incinerators
RT  Plumbing systems
Refuse
Refuse disposal
Septic tanks
Sewerage
Sewers
Waste disposal sites
USE Refuse disposal
Waste recycling
USE Recycling
Wastes, Radioactive
USE Radioactive wastes
Wasteways
USE Spillways

BT  Broader term
NT  Narrower term
HN  History Note

RT  Related term
UF  Used for
CN  Catalogers Note

PN  Public Note
+  Term has NTs
--[ ] May subdivide

Watch industry
USE Clock & watch industry
Watch making
USE Clock & watch making
**Watch papers**
CN TGM II term.
**Watch towers**
--[country or state]--[city]
UF Lookout towers
Watchtowers
BT Towers
NT Fire lookout stations
RT Forts & fortifications
Watches
USE Clocks & watches
Watching
USE Vigils
**Watchmen**
--[country or state]--[city]
UF Building guards
Night watchmen
BT People associated with health & safety
RT Guards
Nightsticks
Police
Town criers
Watchtowers
USE Watch towers
**Water**
CN Use for allegorical images of water. For
images of real bodies of water, use BODIES
OF WATER (or NTs).
Water animals
USE Aquatic animals
Water artillery
USE Floating batteries
**Water baseball**
--[country or state]--[city]
BT Baseball
Water bearers
USE Water carriers
**Water buffaloes**
--[country or state]
BT Buffaloes
**Water carriers**
--[country or state]--[city]
PN Persons who carry or transport water for
distribution.
UF Water bearers
BT People associated with manual labor
RT Water supply
Water companies
USE Public utility companies
Water conduits
USE Aqueducts
Penstocks
Water distribution structures
USE Hydraulic facilities
Water gaps
USE Passes (Landforms)
**Water heaters**
UF Heaters, Water

**Water heaters (cont.)**
Hot water heaters
BT Equipment
RT Plumbing systems
**Water holes**
--[country or state]--[city]
BT Lakes & ponds
RT Oases
**Water lilies**
--[country or state]--[city]
UF Lily pads
Pond lilies
BT Flowers
RT Lily ponds
Water lily ponds
USE Lily ponds
Water marks
USE Watermarks
Water paper negatives
USE Calotypes
Water parades
USE Naval parades & ceremonies
Water pipes
USE Penstocks
**Water pipes (Smoking)**
BT Pipes
RT Narcotics
Smoking
**Water pollution**
--[country or state]--[city]
BT Pollution
RT Bodies of water
Oil spills
**Water power**
--[country or state]--[city]
UF Waterpower
NT Hydroelectric power
RT Hydraulic facilities
Waterwheels
Water pumping stations
USE Pumping stations
**Water pumps**
--[country or state]--[city]
BT Pumps
RT Plumbing systems
Pumping stations
Water purification plants
USE Waterworks
**Water skiing**
--[country or state]--[city]
BT Aquatic sports
RT Skiing
**Water slides**
--[country or state]--[city]
BT Sliding boards
RT Amusement rides
Lakes & ponds
Swimming pools
Water sports
USE Aquatic sports
**Water supply**
--[country or state]--[city]

---

BT Broader term
NT Narrower term
HN History Note

RT Related term
UF Used for
CN Catalogers Note

PN Public Note
+ Term has NTs
--[ ] May subdivide

**Water supply (cont.)**
- PN  For the subject of water resources both superficial and underground, primarily for domestic, manufacturing, or agricultural purposes.
- RT  Conservation of natural resources
  - Droughts
  - Hydraulic facilities
  - Public utility companies
  - Water carriers
  - Water use

**Water tanks**
- --[country or state]--[city]
- BT  Hydraulic facilities
- RT  Storage tanks

**Water towers**
- --[country or state]--[city]
- PN  Towers or standpipes serving as a reservoir to deliver water at a required head. Search under FIRE ENGINES & EQUIPMENT for fire apparatus having a vertical pipe which can be extended to various heights, and supplied with water under high pressure.
- BT  Hydraulic facilities
- RT  Towers

**Water use**
- --[country or state]--[city]
- PN  For various uses of water.
- NT  Irrigation
- RT  Conservation of natural resources
  - Hydraulic facilities
  - Water supply

Water wells
  USE Wells
Water wheels
  USE Waterwheels
Water witches
  USE Divining rods
Water works
  USE Waterworks
Watercolor drawings
  USE Watercolors
Watercolor paintings
  USE Watercolors

**Watercolors**
- CN  TGM II term.
- UF  Watercolor drawings
  - Watercolor paintings

Watercraft
  USE Vessels

**Waterfalls**
- --[country or state]--[city]
- UF  Cascades
  - Cataracts
- BT  Bodies of water
- RT  Streams

**Waterfronts**
- --[country of state]--[city]
- PN  For images that focus on land beside water, whether habited or uninhabited.
- UF  Coastlines

**Waterfronts (cont.)**
  - Lakefronts
  - Riverfronts
  - Seashores
  - Shorefronts
  - Shorelines
  - Strands
  - Streamfronts
- BT  Land
- NT  Beaches
- RT  Boardwalks
  - Bodies of water
  - Capes (Coasts)
  - Harbors
  - Piers & wharves
  - Tide pools

Watering places
  USE Health resorts

**Watering troughs**
- --[country or state]--[city]
- UF  Horse troughs
  - Troughs
- BT  Containers
- RT  Animals

**Watermarks**
- CN  TGM II term.
- UF  Water marks

**Watermelons**
- --[country or state]--[city]
- BT  Melons

Waterpower
  USE Water power
Waterscape drawings
  USE Marine drawings
Waterscape paintings
  USE Marine paintings
Waterscape photographs
  USE Marine photographs
Waterscape prints
  USE Marine prints
Waterscapes
  USE Marines (Visual works)
  Seascapes

**Waterspouts**
- --[country or state]--[city]
- BT  Natural phenomena
- RT  Tornadoes

**Waterwheels**
- --[country or state]--[city]
- PN  Any wheel made to rotate by action of water.
- CN  As appropriate, double index under type of industry or activity.
- UF  Water wheels
- BT  Machinery
- RT  Millraces
  - Water power

**Waterworks**
- --[country or state]--[city]
- PN  The system of reservoirs, channels, mains, and pumping and purifying equipment by which a water supply is obtained and

BT Broader term          RT Related term          PN Public Note
NT Narrower term          UF Used for              + Term has NTs
HN History Note           CN Catalogers Note       --[ ] May subdivide

**Waterworks (cont.)**
         distributed (as to a city).
   UF   Water purification plants
        Water works
   BT   Hydraulic facilities
   RT   Pumping stations
        Reservoirs
        Sewers
Water, Bodies of
   USE   Bodies of water
**Wats**
        --[country]--[city]
   BT   Monasteries
   RT   Buddhist temples
Waves, Ocean
   USE   Seas
Waves, Sound
   USE   Sound waves
Waving the bloody shirt
   USE   Bloody shirt
**Wax figures**
   BT   Sculpture
Waxed paper negatives
   USE   Calotypes
**Wealth**
        --[country or state]--[city]
   UF   Distribution of wealth
        Fortunes
        Riches
   BT   Economic & social conditions
   RT   Avarice
        Cost & standard of living
        Extravagance
        Gross national product
        Miserliness
        Money
        Plutocracy
        Poverty
        Prosperity
        Saving & investment
Weapons
   USE   Arms & armament
Weapons tests
   USE   Ordnance testing
Weariness
   USE   Fatigue
**Weasels**
        --[country or state]
   BT   Animals
   RT   Wolverines
**Weather**
        --[country or state]--[city]
   UF   Climate
   BT   Natural phenomena
   NT   Fog
        Hail
        Rain
        Snow
        Storms +
        Winds
   RT   Barometers
        Weather control

**Weather control**
        --[country or state]--[city]
   UF   Artificial weather control
        Modification of weather
   NT   Fog control
        Rain making
   RT   Weather
**Weather vanes**
        --[country or state]--[city]
   UF   Vanes, Weather
        Weathercocks
   BT   Architectural elements
   RT   Metalwork
        Winds
Weatherboard siding
   USE   Clapboard siding
Weathercocks
   USE   Weather vanes
Weathering of buildings
   USE   Building deterioration
**Weaving**
        --[country or state]--[city]
   BT   Handicraft
   RT   Basket making
        Looms
        Textile industry
        Textiles
**Wedding costume**
   UF   Bridal gowns
        Gowns, Wedding
   BT   Clothing & dress
   RT   Brides
        Grooms (Weddings)
        Weddings
**Weddings**
        --[country or state]--[city]
   PN   Search also under the subdivision
        --MARRIAGE used with names of persons
        (Appendix B).
   BT   Rites & ceremonies
   NT   Shotgun weddings
   RT   Brides
        Elopements
        Grooms (Weddings)
        Honeymoons
        Marriage
        Oaths
        Wedding costume
**Weeds**
        --[country or state]--[city]
   BT   Plants
   NT   Thistles
Weeping
   USE   Crying
Weight control
   USE   Reducing
**Weight lifting**
        --[country or state]--[city]
   UF   Bodybuilding
   BT   Lifting & carrying
   RT   Sports
        Strong men

---

**Weights & measures**
--[country or state]--[city]
UF   Measures
      Metric measures
RT   Calculators
      Coin counting machines
      Counterbalances
      Measuring
      Milestones
      Scales
      Scientific equipment
      Standardization

**Welding**
--[country or state]--[city]
PN   Uniting metallic parts by heating and
      allowing the metals to flow together or by
      hammering or compressing with or without
      previous heating.
CN   As appropriate, double index under the
      industry, e.g., AUTOMOBILE INDUSTRY.
RT   Metalworking

Welfare
  USE Assistance

Welfare buildings
  USE Welfare facilities

**Welfare facilities**
--[country or state]--[city]
UF   Welfare buildings
BT   Facilities
NT   Almshouses
      Animal shelters
      Asylums
      Orphanages
      Refugee camps
      Women's shelters
RT   Assistance

Welfare housing
  USE Housing

Wellness
  USE Health

**Wells**
--[country or state]--[city]
UF   Water wells
BT   Hydraulic facilities
NT   Artesian wells
RT   Wishing wells

Wells, Oil
  USE Oil wells

Wells, Wishing
  USE Wishing wells

**Westerns**
PN   For images representing dramatic
      productions or scenes (theatrical, film, radio,
      or television) which have frontier or
      American western settings. Frequently
      features cowboys, Native Americans, or
      pioneers.
RT   Cowboys
      Cowgirls
      Frontier & pioneer life
      Motion pictures
      Radio broadcasting

**Westerns (cont.)**
      Television broadcasting
      Theatrical productions
      Westward movement

Westward expansion
  USE Westward movement

**Westward movement**
PN   For the Westward expansion of the United
      States.
UF   Westward expansion
BT   Discovery & exploration
RT   Frontier & pioneer life
      Homesteading
      Land rushes
      Pioneers
      Transcontinental journeys
      Westerns

**Wet collodion negatives**
CN   TGM II term.
UF   Collodion negatives
      Wet plate negatives

Wet plate negatives
  USE Wet collodion negatives

**Wetlands**
--[country or state]--[city]
UF   Bogs
      Fens
      Marshes
      Swamps
      Tidal flats
BT   Land
RT   Bodies of water
      Reclamation of land

**Whalebacks**
--[nationality]--[country or state]--[city]
BT   Barges
RT   Steamboats

**Whales**
--[country or state]
BT   Aquatic animals
RT   Whaling

**Whaling**
BT   Hunting
RT   Fishing industry
      Whales

Wharf failures
  USE Pier & wharf failures

Wharves
  USE Piers & wharves

**Wheat**
--[country or state]--[city]
BT   Grains

**Wheelbarrows**
BT   Vehicles

**Wheelchairs**
UF   Moving chairs
BT   Medical equipment & supplies
      Vehicles
RT   Chairs
      Handicapped persons
      Wheeled chairs

**Wheeled chairs**

---

| | | |
|---|---|---|
| BT Broader term | RT Related term | PN Public Note |
| NT Narrower term | UF Used for | + Term has NTs |
| HN History Note | CN Catalogers Note | --[ ] May subdivide |

**Wheeled chairs (cont.)**
    --[nationality]--[country or state]--[city]
PN  Chairs for passengers, mounted on two or three wheels, and drawn, pushed, or pedaled by another person.
UF  Bath chairs
    Moving chairs
    Pedicabs
    Roller chairs
BT  Vehicles
NT  Rickshaws
RT  Bicycles & tricycles
    Carriages & coaches
    Chairs
    Taxicabs
    Wheelchairs
**Wheels**
RT  Vehicles
**Whipping**
    --[country or state]--[city]
UF  Flogging
BT  Beating
RT  Whips
**Whips**
BT  Equipment
RT  Punishment devices
    Whipping
**Whirlpools**
    --[country or state]--[city]
BT  Natural phenomena
RT  Bodies of water
Whiskers
    USE Beards
**Whiskey**
BT  Alcoholic beverages
**Whispering**
    --[country or state]--[city]
RT  Conversation
**Whistle-stop campaigning**
    --[country or state]--[city]
PN  Brief personal appearances or speeches, especially by a political candidate usually on the rear platform of a train during the course of a tour.
UF  Campaigning, Whistle-stop
    Electioneering by railroad
    Railroad campaigning
    Touring, Whistle-stop
BT  Travel
RT  Celebrity touring
    Political elections
    Public speaking
    Railroads
**Whistling**
BT  Sounds
RT  Singing
White ants
    USE Termites
White elephant sales
    USE Secondhand sales
**White man's burden**
PN  The supposed duty of white people to

**White man's burden (cont.)**
    manage the affairs of non-white people. Originated (1899) by Rudyard Kipling.
RT  Colonies
    Imperialism
    Prejudice
    Race discrimination
Whitebelly
    USE Prairie hens
Whiteprints
    USE Diazo prints
Whooping cranes
    USE Cranes (Birds)
Whorehouses
    USE Brothels
Wickedness
    USE Good & evil
**Wicker furniture**
UF  Rattan furniture
BT  Furniture
**Wickiups**
    --[country or state]--[city]
PN  Shelters having a usually oval base and a rough frame covered with reed mats, grass, or brushwood. Used by the nomadic Native Americans of the arid regions of the western and southwestern United States.
BT  Dwellings
**Widowers**
BT  Men
RT  Marriage
    Widows
**Widows**
BT  Single women
RT  Marriage
    Widowers
Wieners
    USE Frankfurters
Wife abuse victims
    USE Abused women
**Wigs**
UF  Perukes
RT  Costumes
    Hairstyles
**Wigwams**
    --[country or state]--[city]
PN  Shelters of Native Americans of the Great Lakes region and eastward, having typically an arched framework of poles overlaid with bark, rush mats, or hides.
BT  Dwellings
RT  Hides & skins
Wild oxen
    USE Buffaloes
Wild west show posters
    USE Circus posters
**Wild west shows**
    --[country or state]--[city]
BT  Circuses & shows
RT  Cowboys
    Cowgirls
**Wildflowers**

---

BT  Broader term
NT  Narrower term
HN  History Note

RT  Related term
UF  Used for
CN  Catalogers Note

PN  Public Note
+   Term has NTs
--[ ] May subdivide

**Wildflowers (cont.)**
      --[country or state]--[city]
  BT  Flowers
**Wildlife conservation**
      --[country or state]--[city]
  UF  Preservation of wildlife
      Protection of animals
  BT  Conservation of natural resources
  RT  Animal treatment
      Extinct animals
      Game preserves
      National parks & reserves
**Willows**
      --[country or state]--[city]
  BT  Trees
  RT  Shrubs
**Wills**
  UF  Codicils
  BT  Law & legal affairs
  RT  Death
      Inheritance & sucession
Willys jeeps
  USE Jeep automobiles
Winches
  USE Hoisting machinery
**Wind instruments**
  PN  Includes the activity of playing wind
      instruments.
  UF  Horns
      Woodwind instruments
  BT  Musical instruments
  NT  Accordions
      Bagpipes
      Bassoons
      Brass instruments +
      Flutes +
      Mouth organs
      Panpipes
      Pipes (Musical instruments)
      Saxophones
  RT  Bands
      Horns (Communication devices)
      Kazoos
**Wind tunnels**
  UF  Tunnels, Wind
  BT  Machinery
  RT  Aeronautics
Windlasses
  USE Hoisting machinery
**Windmills**
      --[country or state]--[city]
  BT  Mills
Window benches
  USE Window seats
**Window boxes**
      --[country or state]--[city]
  BT  Architectural elements
  RT  Plant containers
      Windows
**Window cleaning**
      --[country or state]--[city]
  UF  Window washing

**Window cleaning (cont.)**
  BT  Cleaning
  RT  Windows
**Window displays**
      --[nationality]
  PN  For images that focus on window
      dressings and displays. Search under SHOW
      WINDOWS for windows as a part of
      mercantile facilities rather than their displays.
  CN  As appropriate, double index under type
      of store or business. Used in a note under
      SHOW WINDOWS.
  UF  Decorations, Window
      Display windows
      Shop windows
      Store windows
  BT  Merchandise displays
  RT  Advertisements
      Mercantile facilities
      Shopping
      Show windows
      Showrooms
      Windows
Window guards
  USE Grilles
**Window seats**
      --[country or state]--[city]
  PN  Freestanding or built-in benches in the
      recess of a window.
  UF  Benches, Windows
      Seats, Window
      Window benches
  BT  Architectural elements
      Benches
Window shopping
  USE Shopping
Window walls
  USE Curtain walls
Window washing
  USE Window cleaning
**Windows**
      --[country or state]--[city]
  BT  Architectural elements
  NT  Bay windows +
      Bull's eye windows
      Fanlights
      Leaded glass windows
      Lunettes
      Palladian windows
      Sash windows
      Show windows
      Sidelights
      Skylights
  RT  Curtain walls
      Dormers
      French doors
      Grilles
      Lanterns (Architecture)
      Lintels
      Millwork
      Shutters
      Stained glass

---

**Windows (cont.)**
- Window boxes
- Window cleaning
- Window displays

**Windows, Bow**
- USE Bow windows

**Windows, Ticket**
- USE Ticket offices

**Winds**
- --[country or state]--[city]
- BT  Weather
- RT  Storms
- Weather vanes

Wind-up toys
- USE Mechanical toys

**Wine**
- --[country or state]--[city]
- CN  Double index under EATING & DRINKING for the activity of wine drinking.
- BT  Alcoholic beverages
- NT  Champagne (Wine)
- RT  Cider
- Wine cellars
- Wine industry

**Wine cellars**
- RT  Wine

**Wine industry**
- --[country or state]--[city]
- PN  Includes activities and structures.
- UF  Alcoholic beverage industry
- Vineyards
- BT  Beverage industry
- RT  Grapes
- Wine

**Winged feet**
- RT  Feet

Winglights
- USE Sidelights

**Wings (Building divisions)**
- --[country or state]--[city]
- HN  Changed 1/1993 from WINGS (ROOMS & SPACES).
- BT  Building divisions

Wings, Airplane
- USE Airplane wings

Winners
- USE Victories

**Winnowing**
- --[country or state]--[city]
- RT  Grains
- Threshing

Wins
- USE Victories

**Winter**
- --[country or state]--[city]
- BT  Seasons
- RT  Frost
- Hibernation
- Ice
- Snow
- Winter carnivals
- Winter warfare

**Winter carnivals**
- --[country or state]--[city]
- UF  Carnivals, Winter
- BT  Festivals
- RT  Sports
- Winter

**Winter warfare**
- --[country or state]--[city]
- BT  Military art & science
- RT  Ski troops
- Skiing
- Winter

**Wire**
- BT  Equipment

Wire cable industry
- USE Cable industry

**Wire photographs**
- CN  TGM II term.
- UF  Wirephotos

Wireless telephones
- USE Radiophones

Wirephotos
- USE Wire photographs

Wiretapping
- USE Electronic surveillance

**Wisdom**
- RT  Ethics

**Wishing**
- BT  Mental states
- RT  Fantasy
- Wishing wells

**Wishing wells**
- --[country or state]--[city]
- UF  Wells, Wishing
- BT  Magical devices
- RT  Magic
- Wells
- Wishing

Witch doctors
- HN  Changed 1/1993 to non-postable term.
- USE Shamans

**Witchcraft**
- --[country or state]--[city]
- UF  Black art (Witchcraft)
- BT  Supernatural practices
- RT  Amulets
- Evil eye
- Magic
- Voodooism
- Witchcraft trials
- Witches

**Witchcraft trials**
- --[country or state]--[city]
- BT  Judicial proceedings
- RT  Witchcraft

**Witches**
- BT  Supernatural beings
- RT  Witchcraft

Withdrawing rooms
- USE Drawing rooms

Wives
- USE Spouses

BT  Broader term
NT  Narrower term
HN  History Note

RT  Related term
UF  Used for
CN  Catalogers Note

PN  Public Note
+  Term has NTs
--[ ] May subdivide

Wizardry
  USE Magic
**Wizards**
  UF   Sorcerers
  BT   Supernatural beings
  RT   Magic
       Magicians
**Wolf hunting**
      --[country or state]
  BT   Hunting
  RT   Wolves
**Wolverines**
      --[country or state]
  BT   Animals
  RT   Weasels
**Wolves**
      --[country or state]
  UF   Timber wolves
  BT   Animals
  NT   Coyotes
  RT   Wolf hunting
**Women**
      --[country or state]--[city]
  PN   This heading may be further subdivided by
       the subdivisions used for classes of persons
       (Appendix A). Search also under other
       headings beginning with WOMEN or
       WOMEN'S. Search also under the
       subdivision --WOMEN used with names of
       ethnic, racial, and regional groups (Appendix
       A) and with names of wars (Appendix C).
  CN   As appropriate, subdivide by subdivisions
       for classes of persons (Appendix A).
  BT   People
  NT   Abused women
       Actresses
       Ballerinas
       Bathing beauties
       Beauty contestants
       Chorus girls
       Clubwomen
       Cowgirls
       Debutantes
       Empresses
       Flappers
       Geishas
       Gibson girls
       Governesses
       Housewives
       Lesbians
       Mothers +
       Nuns
       Policewomen
       Pregnant women
       Princesses
       Queens
       Rural women
       Shepherdesses
       Single women +
       Waitresses
       Women domestics
  RT   Birth control

**Women (cont.)**
      Children & adults
      Girls
      Grandparents
      Harems
      Sexual harassment
      Spouses
      Suffragists
      Women's rights
**Women domestics**
  UF   Housemaids
  BT   Women
  RT   Servants
Women in men's clothing
  USE Cross dressing
Women's crisis housing
  USE Women's shelters
Women's education
  HN   Changed 1/1993 to non-postable term.
       Use WOMEN with Appendix A subdivision
       --EDUCATION.
Women's liberation
  USE Women's rights
**Women's rights**
      --[country or state]--[city]
  PN   For the constitutional and legal status and
       treatment of women.
  UF   Emancipation of women
       Women's liberation
  BT   Civil rights
  NT   Women's suffrage
  RT   Equal rights amendments
       Feminism
       Sexism
       Sexual harassment
       Women
**Women's shelters**
      --[country or state]--[city]
  UF   Abused women's shelters
       Women's crisis housing
  BT   Welfare facilities
  RT   Abused women
**Women's suffrage**
      --[country or state]--[city]
  BT   Suffrage
       Women's rights
Women's underwear
  USE Lingerie
Wonders
  USE Curiosities & wonders
**Wood blocks**
  CN   TGM II term.
Wood buildings
  USE Wooden buildings
**Wood carving**
      --[country or state]--[city]
  PN   Fashioning or ornamenting objects of
       wood by cutting with a sharp implement held
       in the hand.
  CN   Used in a note under SCULPTURE.
  BT   Carving
  RT   Wood carvings

---

BT Broader term            RT Related term           PN Public Note
NT Narrower term         UF Used for               + Term has NTs
HN History Note           CN Catalogers Note      --[ ] May subdivide

**Wood carving (cont.)**
    Woodworking
**Wood carvings**
  BT  Sculpture
  NT  Cigar store Indians
       Ship figureheads
       Totem poles
  RT  Decoys (Hunting)
       Wood carving
       Woodwork
Wood cuts
  USE Woodcuts
Wood cutting
  USE Woodcutting
**Wood engravings**
  CN  TGM II term.
  UF  Engravings, Wood
       Xylographs
Wood gathering
  USE Fuelwood gathering
Wood work
  USE Woodwork
Wood working
  USE Woodworking
**Woodburytypes**
  CN  TGM II term.
  UF  Photoglypties
**Woodchucks**
      --[country or state]
  UF  Groundhogs
  BT  Marmots
**Woodcocks**
      --[country or state]
  BT  Birds
**Woodcuts**
  CN  TGM II term.
  UF  Wood cuts
**Woodcutters**
  BT  Laborers
  RT  Woodcutting
**Woodcutting**
      --[country or state]--[city]
  PN  For the activity of cutting, splitting,
       chopping, or sawing trees and branches.
  CN  As appropriate, double index under
       LUMBER INDUSTRY. Used in a note under
       FUELWOOD, LOGS, and LUMBER
       INDUSTRY.
  UF  Chopping wood
       Sawing wood
       Splitting wood
       Wood cutting
  RT  Crosscut saws
       Fuelwood
       Logs
       Lumber industry
       Sawhorses
       Trees
       Woodcutters
Wooden box industry
  USE Box industry
**Wooden buildings**

**Wooden buildings (cont.)**
      --[country or state]--[city]
  UF  Wood buildings
  BT  Buildings distinguished by material
  NT  Log buildings +
       Plank buildings
**Wooden sidewalks**
      --[country or state]--[city]
  BT  Sidewalks
**Wooding stations**
      --[country or state]
  PN  Places near a riverbank where cut logs are
       kept before being transported downriver.
  RT  Forests
       Lumber industry
**Woodpeckers**
      --[country or state]
  BT  Birds
Woodpiles
  USE Fuelwood
Woods
  USE Forests
Woodwind instruments
  USE Wind instruments
**Woodwork**
      --[country or state]--[city]
  PN  For work made of wood, especially indoor
       fittings (e.g., moldings or stairways).
  UF  Wood work
  NT  Millwork
  RT  Wood carvings
       Woodworking
**Woodworking**
      --[country or state]--[city]
  PN  The act, process, or occupation of working
       with wood.
  UF  Wood working
  RT  Cabinetmaking
       Carpentry
       Chisels & mallets
       Joinery
       Rustic work
       Wood carving
       Woodwork
Wooing
  USE Courtship
**Wool**
  BT  Fibers
  RT  Sheep shearing
       Wool industry
**Wool industry**
      --[country or state]--[city]
  PN  Includes activities and structures.
  CN  Double index under INDUSTRIAL
       FACILITIES (or NTs) for images that focus
       on facilities.
  BT  Textile industry
  RT  Wool
Woolly mammoths
  USE Mammoths
Word plays
  USE Plays on words

BT Broader term               RT Related term              PN Public Note
NT Narrower term           UF Used for                   + Term has NTs
HN History Note             CN Catalogers Note        --[ ] May subdivide

Work
  USE Employment
**Work camps**
      --[country or state]--[city]
  PN  Includes volunteer camps.
  BT  Housing
  RT  Camps
      Labor housing
**Work ethic**
      --[country or state]--[city]
  PN  A belief in work as a moral good.
  BT  Ethics
  RT  Employment
Work relief
  USE Public service employment
Work stoppages
  USE Strikes
Workers
  USE Employees
Workers' housing
  USE Labor housing
Workers' rights
  USE Employee rights
Workhouses (Poorhouses)
  USE Almshouses
**Working class**
      --[country or state]
  PN  For the class of people who work for
      wages, excluding managers and
      professionals; generally at lower end of
      economic scale.
  UF  Blue collar (Social class)
      Commons (Social order)
      Laboring classes
      Proletariat
  BT  Social classes
  RT  Laborers
**Working dogs**
      --[country or state]--[city]
  BT  Dogs
**Working drawings**
  CN  TGM II term.
  UF  Drawings, Working
Working hours
  USE Hours of labor
**Working mothers**
      --[country or state]--[city]
  UF  Employed mothers
      Mothers, Employed
      Mothers, Working
  BT  Mothers
  RT  Employment
Working proofs
  USE Trial proofs
**Workshops**
      --[country or state]--[city]
  HN  Changed 2/1993 from STUDIOS &
      WORKSHOPS.
  BT  Industrial facilities
  NT  Carpenter shops
      Forge shops
      Machine shops

Work, Absence from
  USE Absenteeism (Labor)
World
  USE Earth
World communication
  USE International communication
World government
  USE International organization
**World records**
      --[country or state]--[city]
  CN  Double index by type of endeavor.
  UF  Records, World
      World's records
  RT  Contests
      Curiosities & wonders
      Firsts
      Victories
World travel
  USE Voyages around the world
World's end
  USE End of the world
World's records
  USE World records
Worm medicines
  USE Anthelmintics
**Worms**
      --[country or state]
  BT  Animals
**Worm's-eye views**
  UF  Toad's-eye views
      Views, Toad's-eye
      Views, Worm's eye
**Worry**
  BT  Mental states
  RT  Anxiety
Worship
  USE Adoration
      Rites & ceremonies
Worship days
  USE Sabbaths
Wounded in war
  USE War casualties
**Wounds & injuries**
      --[country or state]--[city]
  UF  Injuries
      Physical trauma
      Trauma, Physical
  NT  Bites & stings
  RT  Accidents
      Electric shocks
      Emergency medical services
      Healing
      Pain
      Sick persons
      Splints (Surgery)
      Victims
      War casualties
Wraiths
  USE Ghosts
Wrappers
  USE Packaging
Wrapping materials

---

Wrapping materials (cont.)
  USE Packaging
Wrappings
  USE Packaging
Wrath
  USE Anger
**Wreaths**
        --[country or state]--[city]
  UF  Garlands
  BT  Decorations
  RT  Crown of thorns
**Wreckers (Vehicles)**
        --[country or state]--[city]
  UF  Recovery vehicles
      Tow trucks
      Towtrucks
      Wrecking trucks
  BT  Trucks
  RT  Towing
      Traffic accidents
Wrecking
  USE Demolition
Wrecking trucks
  USE Wreckers (Vehicles)
Wrecks
  USE Accidents
      Disasters
      Shipwrecks
**Wrenches**
  UF  Monkey wrenches
      Spanners
  BT  Equipment
**Wrestlers**
        --[country or state]--[city]
  CN  Geographical subdivision indicates place
      where team or wrestler is based.
  BT  Athletes
  NT  Sumo wrestlers
  RT  Wrestling
Wrestlers, Sumo
  USE Sumo wrestlers
**Wrestling**
        --[country or state]--[city]
  BT  Sports
  NT  Sumo
  RT  Fighting
      Martial arts
      Wrestlers
Writers
  USE Authors
      Scribes
**Writing**
        --[country or state]--[city]
  UF  Drafting
  BT  Communication
  NT  Calligraphy
      Speechwriting
      Typewriting
  RT  Autographing
      Children reading & writing
      Document signings
      Letters to Santa Claus

**Writing (cont.)**
      Literacy
      Scribes
      Writing materials
**Writing materials**
  NT  Inkstands
      Pencils
      Pens
  RT  Communication devices
      Desks
      Writing
Writing rooms
  USE Scriptoria
**Writing systems**
  BT  Communication
  NT  Alphabets (Writing systems) +
      Braille
      Cuneiform
      Graffiti
      Hieroglyphics
      Runes
Wrought-iron work
  USE Ironwork
Xerographic art
  USE Copy art
Xerographs
  USE Photocopies
Xylographs
  USE Wood engravings
X-ray photographs
  USE Radiographs
X-ray photography
  USE Radiography
**Yacht clubs**
        --[country or state]--[city]
  PN  Includes activities and structures.
  CN  Double index under ORGANIZATIONS'
      FACILITIES (or NTs) for images that focus
      on facilities.
  BT  Boat clubs
**Yacht racing**
        --[country or state]--[city]
  HN  Changed 3/1989 from non-postable term
      (use REGATTAS).
  BT  Regattas
  RT  Yachts
Yachting
  USE Yachts
**Yachts**
        --[nationality]--[country or state]--[city]
  UF  Yachting
  BT  Vessels
  NT  Steam yachts
  RT  Sailboats
      Ships
      Yacht racing
Yankee clipper cards
  USE Clipper ship cards
Yard goods shops
  USE Fabric shops
**Yard ornaments**
        --[country or state]--[city]

---

BT Broader term                    RT Related term              PN Public Note
NT Narrower term                   UF Used for                  + Term has NTs
HN History Note                    CN Catalogers Note            --[ ] May subdivide

**Yard ornaments (cont.)**
  UF  Lawn objects
  BT  Site elements
  NT  Birdbaths
  RT  Decorations
       Landscape architecture facilities
**Yard sales**
  USE Secondhand sales
**Yarn**
  BT  Textiles
  RT  Crocheting
       Fibers
       Knitting
**Yawning**
  RT  Sleeping
**Yellow fever**
       --[country or state]--[city]
  BT  Communicable diseases
**Yellow journalism**
  BT  Journalism
**Yin Yang (Symbol)**
  UF  Monad (Symbol)
  BT  Symbols
**Yokes**
  PN  Bar or frame used to carry a load, usually
       suspended in two equal portions on opposite
       sides of the body, or used to join draft
       animals.
  BT  Equipment
  RT  Animal teams
       Lifting & carrying
**Young adults**
       --[country or state]--[city]
  PN  For persons in the general age range of
       eighteen to twenty-five years. Search also
       under the subdivision --WOMEN used with
       ethnic, racial, and regional groups and with
       classes of persons (Appendix A). Search also
       under the subdivision --CHILDHOOD AND
       YOUTH used with names of persons
       (Appendix B).
  CN  Used in a note under YOUTH.
  UF  Young persons
  BT  People
  RT  Children
       Students
       Youth
       Youth bands
**Young Men's Christian associations**
       --[country or state]--[city]
  PN  Includes activities and structures.
  CN  Subdivide geographically as appropriate to
       indicate national, state, or city levels of
       organization. Double index under
       ORGANIZATIONS' FACILITIES (or NTs)
       for images that focus on facilities.
  BT  Youth organizations
Young persons
  USE Young adults
**Youth**
       --[country or state]--[city]
  PN  The quality or state of being young. Search

**Youth (cont.)**
       under CHILDREN or YOUNG ADULTS for
       young people. Search also under the
       subdivision --CHILDHOOD & YOUTH used
       with names of persons (Appendix B).
  RT  Age & employment
       Children
       Human life cycle
       Initiation rites
       Middle age
       Rejuvenation
       Young adults
**Youth bands**
       --[country or state]--[city]
  BT  Bands
  RT  Children
       Young adults
Youth gangs
  USE Gangs
**Youth organizations**
       --[country or state]--[city]
  PN  Includes activities and structures.
  CN  Double index under ORGANIZATIONS'
       FACILITIES (or NTs)  for images that focus
       on facilities.
  BT  Organizations
  NT  4-H clubs
       Young Men's Christian associations
  RT  Student organizations
**Yo-yos**
  BT  Toys
**Zebras**
       --[country or state]
  BT  Animals
Zeppelins
  USE Airships
**Zinc mining**
       --[country or state]--[city]
  PN  Includes activities and sites.
  BT  Mining
**Zincographs**
  CN  TGM II term.
**Zionism**
       --[country or state]--[city]
  PN  Theory, plan, or movement for setting up a
       Jewish national or religious community in
       Palestine.
  UF  Zionist movement
  RT  Jewish-Arab relations
       Religious groups
Zionist movement
  USE Zionism
**Zodiac**
  UF  Astrological signs
  RT  Astrology
       Astronomy
       Celestial bodies
       Symbols
Zoological gardens
  USE Zoos
**Zoology**
       --[country or state]--[city]

BT  Broader term                    RT  Related term                  PN  Public Note
NT  Narrower term                  UF  Used for                       +  Term has NTs
HN  History Note                   CN  Catalogers Note               --[ ]  May subdivide

**Zoology (cont.)**
- PN   For the subject of zoology in general and
     the activities of zoologists.
- BT   Biology
- RT   Paleontology

Zoomorphic buildings
  USE   Mimetic buildings

**Zoos**
    --[country or state]--[city]
- UF   Gardens, Zoological
     Zoological gardens
- BT   Exhibition facilities
- RT   Animals
     Aviaries
     Parks

**Zouaves**
    --[country or state]
- PN   For the French infantry unit that wore a
     brillant uniform or any military unit that
     adopted the dress of the Zouaves.
- CN   Subdivide geographically by the country
     or state from which the Zouave unit comes.
- BT   Military organizations

BT Broader term                 RT Related term              PN Public Note
NT Narrower term                UF Used for                  + Term has NTs
HN History Note                 CN Catalogers Note           --[ ] May subdivide

## Subdivisions Used With Names of Ethnic, Racial, and
## Regional Groups, and With Classes of Persons

The Prints and Photographs Division uses this list of subdivisions so that large files under <u>names</u> of ethnic, racial, regional groups, and classes of persons can be sub-arranged by broad topic. As appropriate, catalogers should double index with more specific headings. The proper names for ethnic, racial, and regional groups are taken from *Library of Congress Subject Headings*. When subdivisions listed below are used with such headings, P&P uses the MARC coding of 650 -4 which signifies that the source is not specified. Institutions creating MARC records should check with their networks on how the field should be coded when non-LCSH topical subdivisions are used.

**Classes of Persons** are limited to the following headings:
> **Aged persons**
> **Children**
> **Handicapped persons**
> **Indigenous peoples**
> **Men**
> **Women**

When headings for these classes of persons are subdivided, P&P uses MARC code 650 -7 and "lctgm" in subfield 2.

Headings that can be further subdivided geographically include a facet note [country or state]--[city]. For general information on use of subdivisions, see Introduction, Section III.D.

**--Antiquities & archaeological sites**
> --[country or state]--[city]
> PN    Search also under the corresponding thesaurus terms ANTIQUITIES, ARCHAEOLOGICAL SITES.
> CN    Used in a note under the corresponding thesaurus terms ANTIQUITIES, ARCHAEOLOGICAL SITES.

**--Arts & crafts**
> PN    For images in which the focus is on objects made by members of the group for aesthetic and utilitarian purposes. Includes images about these objects as well as activities associated with making these objects. Search also under the subdivisions --DANCE, --MUSIC, --SOCIAL LIFE, --SPIRITUAL LIFE for activities in which arts & crafts are featured. Search also under the corresponding thesaurus terms ART, HANDICRAFT.
> CN    Used in a note under the corresponding thesaurus terms ART, ARTS & CRAFTS, HANDICRAFT.

---

## --Capture & imprisonment

--[country or state]--[city]

PN      Search also under the subdivision --WAR.  Search also under the corresponding thesaurus terms LAW ENFORCEMENT, PRISONERS.

CN      Used in a note under the corresponding thesaurus terms CAPTURE & IMPRISONMENT, LAW ENFORCEMENT, PRISONERS.

## --Children

--[country or state]--[city]

PN      Includes ages 0 to 16.  Search also under the corresponding thesaurus term CHILDREN.

CN      Double index under specific age group as appropriate.  Not generally used as a subdivision for other "classes of persons" headings.  For example, do not use the headings HANDICAPPED PERSONS--CHILDREN or WOMEN--CHILDREN.  Used in a note under the corresponding thesaurus term CHILDREN.

## --Civil rights

--[country or state]--[city]

PN      Rights having to do with equal opportunity for employment, education, political participation, etc.  Search also under the subdivisions --GOVERNMENT RELATIONS, --POLITICAL ACTIVITY.  Search also under the corresponding thesaurus term CIVIL RIGHTS.

CN      Used in a note under the corresponding thesaurus term CIVIL RIGHTS.

## --Clothing & dress

--[country or state]--[city]

PN      For images that focus on clothing and dress.  Includes adornment, masks, and costumes worn for events.  Search also under the corresponding thesaurus terms CLOTHING & DRESS, COSTUMES.

CN      Used in a note under the corresponding thesaurus term CLOTHING & DRESS, COSTUMES.

## --Commerce

--[country or state]--[city]

PN      Large and small business transactions, including commodity exchanges among members of the group and with other groups.  Search also under corresponding thesaurus term COMMERCE.

CN      Used in a note under the corresponding thesaurus term COMMERCE.

## --Commemoration

--[country or state]--[city]

PN      Includes monuments, memorials, anniversaries, and other celebrations intended to commemorate a category of persons.  Search also under corresponding thesaurus terms ANNIVERSARIES, COMMEMORATION, CELEBRATIONS, MEMORIAL RITES & CEREMONIES, MONUMENTS & MEMORIALS.

CN      Used in note under ANNIVERSARIES, CELEBRATIONS, COMMEMORATION, MEMORIAL RITES & CEREMONIES, MONUMENTS & MEMORIALS.

## --Communication

PN       Includes writing systems and other modes of communication shared among members of the group. Search also under the corresponding thesaurus term COMMUNICATION.

CN       Used in a note under the corresponding thesaurus term COMMUNICATION.

## --Dance

PN       For images in which the focus is on dance.  Search also under the subdivisions --ARTS & CRAFTS, --MUSIC, --SOCIAL LIFE, --SPIRITUAL LIFE.  Search also under corresponding thesaurus terms CEREMONIAL DANCERS, DANCERS, DANCING, FOLK DANCING.

CN       Used in a note under the corresponding thesaurus terms CEREMONIAL DANCERS, DANCE, DANCING, FOLK DANCING.

## --Domestic life

--[country or state]--[city]

PN       Domestic activities and family life; includes activities performed inside and away from the home, e.g., grocery shopping, outdoor laundry, etc. Search also under the corresponding thesaurus term DOMESTIC LIFE.

CN       Used in a note under the corresponding thesaurus term DOMESTIC LIFE.

## --Dwellings

See --Structures

## --Education

--[country or state]--[city]

PN       For all aspects of education, including activities, structures, and extracurricular activities.  Search also under the corresponding thesaurus term EDUCATION.

CN       Used in a note under the corresponding thesaurus term EDUCATION.

## --Employment

--[country or state]--[city]

PN       Work activities or the subject of employment.  For employment of children, search under the corresponding thesaurus term CHILD LABOR.  Search also under the corresponding thesaurus terms EMPLOYMENT, OCCUPATIONS.

CN       Do not subdivide CHILDREN by this subdivision; use CHILD LABOR instead.  Used in a note under the corresponding thesaurus terms EMPLOYMENT, OCCUPATIONS.

## --Escapes

See --Capture & imprisonment

## --Exhibitions

--[country or state]--[city]

PN       Exhibitions about the group or class of people.

CN       Used in a note under the corresponding thesaurus term EXHIBITIONS.

---

## --Government relations

PN    Used only under headings for indigenous peoples for their relations with a state or national government. Search also under the subdivisions --CIVIL RIGHTS, --POLITICAL ACTIVITY. Search also under the corresponding thesaurus term GOVERNMENT RELATIONS.

CN    Prefer the subdivisions --CIVIL RIGHTS, --POLITICAL ACTIVITY, for non-indigenous peoples. Used in a note under corresponding thesaurus term GOVERNMENT RELATIONS.

## --Health & welfare

--[country or state]--[city]

PN    Health conditions and actions taken to improve health and welfare of members of a group or to protect members of the group, including health and institutional care. Search also under the corresponding thesaurus terms DISEASES, HEALTH, HEALTH & WELFARE, INSTITUTIONAL CARE.

CN    Used in a note under the corresponding thesaurus terms DISEASES, HEALTH, HEALTH & WELFARE, INSTITUTIONAL CARE.

## --History

PN    For the subject of a group's development over a span of time. Search also under the corresponding thesaurus term HISTORY.

CN    Used in a note under the corresponding thesaurus term HISTORY.

## --Industries

PN    Search also under the corresponding thesaurus terms INDUSTRY, INDUSTRIES, MINING.

CN    Used in a note under the corresponding thesaurus terms INDUSTRY, INDUSTRIES, MINING.

## --Meetings

--[country or state]--[city]

PN    Search also under the subdivision --ORGANIZATIONS. Search also under the corresponding thesaurus term MEETINGS.

CN    Used in a note under the corresponding thesaurus term MEETINGS.

## --Military service

PN    Participation in modern, officially organized military units. Search also under the corresponding thesaurus terms MILITARY PERSONNEL, MILITARY SERVICE.

CN    Used in a note under the corresponding thesaurus term MILITARY PERSONNEL, MILITARY SERVICE.

## --Music

PN    For images in which the focus is on music of members of the group. Search also under the subdivisions --ARTS & CRAFTS, --DANCE, --SOCIAL LIFE, --SPIRITUAL LIFE. Search also under the corresponding thesaurus term MUSIC.

CN    Used in a note under the corresponding thesaurus term MUSIC.

---

PN  Public note          CN  Catalogers note          HN  History note          --[  ]May subdivide

## --Organizations

--[country or state]--[city]

PN    Search also under the subdivision --MEETINGS. Search also under the corresponding thesaurus terms CLUBS, ORGANIZATIONS.

CN    Used in a note under the corresponding thesaurus terms CLUBS, ORGANIZATIONS.

## --Performances & portrayals

--[country or state]--[city]

PN    For images that focus on performances by, for, or about a group, including portrayals by those who are not really members of the group. Search also under the corresponding thesaurus terms ENTERTAINMENT, HISTORICAL REENACTMENTS, IMPERSONATION, THEATRICAL PRODUCTIONS.

CN    Used in a note under the corresponding thesaurus terms ENTERTAINMENT, HISTORICAL REENACTMENTS, IMPERSONATION, THEATRICAL PRODUCTIONS.

## --Physical characteristics

CN    Used in a note under the corresponding thesaurus term PHYSICAL CHARACTERISTICS.

## --Political activity

--[country or state]--[city]

PN    Actions relating to politics or government, as well as the effect of politics or government on the group or its members. Includes political activity internal to the group as well as activity between the group and an external entity. Search also under the subdivisions --CIVIL RIGHTS, --GOVERNMENT RELATIONS. Search also under corresponding thesaurus terms POLITICAL ACTIVITY, POLITICAL PARTICIPATION, POLITICS & GOVERNMENT.

CN    Used in a note under the corresponding thesaurus terms POLITICAL ACTIVITY, POLITICAL PARTICIPATION, POLITICS & GOVERNMENT.

## --Punishment & torture

--[country or state]--[city]

PN    For punishment and torture of members of the group. Search also under the subdivisions --CIVIL RIGHTS, --WAR. Search also under the corresponding thesaurus term PUNISHMENT & TORTURE.

CN    Used in a note under the corresponding thesaurus term PUNISHMENT & TORTURE.

## --Pursuit

See **--Capture & imprisonment**

---

PN Public note    CN Catalogers note    HN History note    --[ ]May subdivide

## --Social life

        --[country or state]--[city]

        PN      Includes social interactions, customs, and recreational activities.   Search also under the
                subdivisions --ARTS & CRAFTS, --DANCE, --MUSIC, --SPIRITUAL LIFE.  Search also under
                the corresponding thesaurus terms INTERPERSONAL RELATIONS, MANNERS & CUSTOMS,
                RECREATION.

        CN      Used in a note under the corresponding thesaurus terms INTERPERSONAL RELATIONS,
                MANNERS & CUSTOMS, RECREATION.

## --Spiritual life

        --[country or state]--[city]

        PN      Includes religion, mythology, rites, and activities of spiritual significance.  Search also under the
                subdivisions --ARTS & CRAFTS, --DANCE, --MUSIC, --SOCIAL LIFE.  Search also under the
                corresponding thesaurus terms MYTHS, RELIGION, RITES & CEREMONIES.

        CN      Used in a note under thesaurus terms MYTHS, RELIGION, RITES & CEREMONIES.

## --Sports

        --[country or state]--[city]

        PN      Search also under the subdivision --SOCIAL LIFE.  Search also under the corresponding thesaurus
                terms RECREATION, SPORTS.

        CN      Used in a note under the corresponding thesaurus terms RECREATION, SPORTS.

## --Structures

        --[country or state]--[city]

        PN      For built works, including dwellings, walls, aqueducts, roads, etc.  Search also under the
                corresponding thesaurus terms BUILDINGS, DWELLINGS.

        CN      Used in a note under the corresponding thesaurus terms BUILDINGS and DWELLINGS.

        HN      Changed 8/91.   Formerly --STRUCTURES may have been indexed with the subdivision
                --DWELLINGS.

## --Subsistence activities

        PN      Used only with headings for indigenous peoples.  Includes agriculture, hunting, and fishing,
                insofar as the products of the activities are used directly by members of the group rather than for
                commercial purposes.  Search also under the subdivision --EMPLOYMENT.  Search also under
                the corresponding thesaurus term EMPLOYMENT.

        CN      Used in a note under the corresponding thesaurus terms EMPLOYMENT, FARMING, FISHING,
                HUNTING, SUBSISTENCE ACTIVITIES.

## --Transportation

        PN      Includes activities and vehicles.   Search also under the corresponding thesaurus term
                TRANSPORTATION.

        CN      Used in a note under the corresponding thesaurus term TRANSPORTATION.

---

        PN  Public note              CN  Catalogers note              HN History note              --[  ]May subdivide

## --War

PN     Used for the general subject of the conduct of warfare by a people collectively, individuals' civilian involvement in war, or effect of war on members of the group. Used only when the war depicted cannot be identified. Search also under the names of specific wars, subdivided by the name of the ethnic group or class of persons. Search also under the subdivision --MILITARY SERVICE for participation in modern, officially organized military units. Search also under the corresponding thesaurus term WAR.

CN     Prefer [Name of war]--[name of ethnic group/class of persons] when the specific war is known and such headings are authorized. Used in a note under WAR, WAR WORK.

## --Women

--[country or state]--[city]

PN     Includes ages 17 and over. Search also under the corresponding thesaurus terms WOMEN, YOUNG ADULTS.

CN     Double index under specific age group as appropriate. Used in a note under the corresponding thesaurus terms WOMEN, YOUNG ADULTS.

## --Work

See **--Employment**

---

PN  Public note          CN  Catalogers note          HN  History note          --[   ]May subdivide

The Prints and Photographs Division uses this list of subdivisions so that large files under <u>names</u> of persons can be sub-arranged by broad topic. As appropriate, catalogers should double index with more specific headings.

The proper names for people are taken from Library of Congress Name Authority File. When subdivisions listed below are used with such headings, P&P uses the MARC coding of 600 -4 which signifies that the source is not specified. Institutions creating MARC records should check with their networks on how the field should be coded when non-LCSH topical subdivisions are used.

Headings that can be further subdivided geographically include a facet note [country or state]--[city]. For general information on use of subdivisions, see Introduction, Section III.D.


**--Abdication**
> PN    Search also under the subdivisions --IMPEACHMENT, --RESIGNATION FROM OFFICE.
> CN    Used in a note under the corresponding thesaurus term ABDICATION.

**--Animals & pets**
> PN    For pets and other animals associated with a person.  Search also under the corresponding thesaurus terms ANIMALS, PETS.
> CN    Used in a note under the corresponding thesaurus terms ANIMALS, PETS.

**--Anniversaries**
> See **--Commemoration**

**--Assassination**
> --[country or state]--[city]
> PN    Search also under the subdivision --DEATH AND BURIAL.  Search also under the corresponding thesaurus term ASSASSINATIONS.
> CN    Used in a note under the corresponding thesaurus term ASSASSINATIONS.

**--Assassination attempts**
> --[country or state]--[city]
> CN    Used in a note under the corresponding thesaurus term ASSASSINATIONS.

**--Associated objects**
> PN    Includes clothing, furniture, "collectibles," commemorative objects, e.g., medals.  Search also under the subdivision --MONUMENTS.

**--Birthdays**
> See **--Commemoration**

---

PN  Public note          CN  Catalogers note          HN  History note          --[  ]May subdivide

**--Birthplace**
> --[country or state]--[city]
> PN     Search also under the subdivision --HOMES & HAUNTS.  Search also under the corresponding thesaurus term BIRTHPLACES.
> CN     Used in a note under the corresponding thesaurus term BIRTHPLACES.

**--Cabinets**
> See **--Staff**

**--Capture & imprisonment**
> PN     Includes interrogation.  Search under the corresponding thesaurus terms LAW ENFORCEMENT, PRISONERS.
> CN     Prefer the subdivision --CAPTURE & IMPRISONMENT, [date] if a specific date is known.  Used in a note under the corresponding thesaurus terms CAPTURE & IMPRISONMENT, LAW ENFORCEMENT, PRISONERS.

**--Capture & imprisonment, [date]**
> PN     Search also under the corresponding thesaurus terms LAW ENFORCEMENT, PRISONERS.
> CN     Used in a note under the corresponding thesaurus terms LAW ENFORCEMENT, PRISONERS.

**--Childhood & youth**
> CN     Used in a note under the corresponding thesaurus terms CHILDHOOD & YOUTH, YOUNG ADULTS, YOUTH.

**--Clothing**
> See **--Associated objects**

**--Collectibles**
> See **--Associated objects**

**--Commemoration**
> --[country or state]--[city]
> PN     Events and objects in honor or memory of the person.  Search also under the subdivisions --MONUMENTS, --SHRINES, --STATUES, --TOMB.  Search also under the corresponding thesaurus terms ANNIVERSARIES, BIRTHDAYS, CELEBRATIONS, COMMEMORATION, MEMORIAL RITES & CEREMONIES.
> CN     Used in a note under the corresponding thesaurus terms ANNIVERSARIES, BIRTHDAYS, CELEBRATIONS, COMMEMORATION, MEMORIAL RITES & CEREMONIES.

**--Coronation**
> --[country or state]--[city]
> PN     Search also under the subdivision --INAUGURATION.  Search also under the corresponding thesaurus term CORONATIONS.
> CN     Used in a note under the corresponding thesaurus term CORONATIONS.

---

PN  Public note      CN  Catalogers note      HN History note      --[  ]May subdivide

**--Death & burial**
    --[country or state]--[city]
    PN    Search also under the subdivisions --ASSASSINATION, --TOMB.  Search also under the corresponding thesaurus terms DEATH, DEATHBEDS, FUNERAL RITES & CEREMONIES, LYING IN STATE.
    CN    Double index under more specific corresponding thesaurus terms as appropriate, e.g., DEATHBEDS, LYING IN STATE, FUNERAL RITES & CEREMONIES.  Used in a note under the corresponding thesaurus terms DEATH, DEATHBEDS, LYING IN STATE, FUNERAL RITES & CEREMONIES.

**--Death mask**
    PN    Search also under the corresponding thesaurus terms DEATH, DEATH MASKS, MASKS.
    CN    Used in a note under the corresponding thesaurus terms DEATH, DEATH MASKS, MASKS.

**--Escapes**
    See **--Capture & imprisonment**

**--Ethics**
    PN    For works that are about or comment on the person's ethical system, values, or behavior.  Search also under the corresponding thesaurus term ETHICS.
    CN    Used in a note under the corresponding thesaurus term ETHICS.

**--Exhibitions**
    --[country or state]--[city]
    PN    For exhibitions on the life or work of the person.  Search also under the corresponding thesaurus term EXHIBITIONS.
    CN    Used in a note under the corresponding thesaurus term EXHIBITIONS.

**--Family**
    PN    For the person's family or members of his/her family (including wives and husbands). Search also under individual family members' names.  Search also under the subdivision --MARRIAGE for works about or depicting the person's marriage or wedding.  Search also under the corresponding thesaurus term FAMILIES.
    CN    Used in a note under the corresponding thesaurus terms FAMILIES, FAMILY.

**--Funeral**
    See **--Death & burial**

**--Health**
    PN    For the person's state of health, including injuries or diseases suffered.  Search also under the subdivisions --DEATH & BURIAL, --MENTAL HEALTH.  Search also under the corresponding thesaurus terms HEALTH, SICK PERSONS.
    CN    Used in a note under the corresponding thesaurus terms HEALTH, SICK PERSONS.

## --Homes & haunts
### --[country or state]--[city]
PN    For the person's homes or dwellings, favorite places, places s/he habitually frequented, or places associated with him/her in some way. Search also under the subdivision --BIRTHPLACE. Search also under the corresponding thesaurus term DWELLINGS.

CN    Used in a note under the corresponding thesaurus term DWELLINGS.

## --Illnesses
See **--Health**

## --Impeachment
PN    Search also under the subdivisions --ABDICATION, --RESIGNATION FROM OFFICE. Search also under the corresponding thesaurus term IMPEACHMENTS.

CN    Used in a note under the corresponding thesaurus term IMPEACHMENTS.

## --Inauguration
PN    Search also under the subdivision --CORONATION. Search also under the corresponding thesaurus term INAUGURATIONS.

CN    Use if no specific date is known; if specific date is known, use the subdivision --INAUGURATION, [date].

## --Inauguration, [date]
PN    Search also under the subdivision --CORONATION. Search also under the corresponding thesaurus terms INAUGURATIONS, PRESIDENTIAL INAUGURATIONS.

CN    Use if specific date is known; if no specific date is known, use the subdivision --INAUGURATION. Double index under the corresponding thesaurus terms PRESIDENTIAL INAUGURATIONS, as appropriate. Used in a note under the corresponding thesaurus terms INAUGURATIONS, PRESIDENTIAL INAUGURATIONS.

## --Journeys
### --[country or state]--[city]
PN    For voyages and travels undertaken by the person. Search also under the corresponding thesaurus terms TRAVEL, VISITS OF STATE.

CN    Used in a note under the corresponding thesaurus terms JOURNEYS, TRAVEL, VISITS OF STATE. Double index under the corresponding thesaurus term VISITS OF STATE, as appropriate.

## --Last illness
See **--Death & burial**

## --Marriage
PN    For works that are about or depict the person's marriage or wedding ceremony. Search also under the subdivision --FAMILY for images of family members, husbands, and wives. Search also under the corresponding thesaurus terms MARRIAGE, WEDDINGS.

CN    Used in a note under the corresponding thesaurus terms MARRIAGE, WEDDINGS.

---

PN  Public note        CN  Catalogers note        HN  History note        --[  ]May subdivide

--Medals
      See **--Associated objects**

**--Mental health**
      PN      Search also under the subdivision --HEALTH.
      CN      Used in a note under the corresponding thesaurus term MENTAL HEALTH.

**--Military service**
      PN      Search also under the corresponding thesaurus terms MILITARY PERSONNEL, MILITARY SERVICE.
      CN      Used in a note under the corresponding thesaurus terms MILITARY SERVICE, MILITARY PERSONNEL.

**--Monuments**
      --[country or state]--[city]
      PN      Search also under the subdivisions --SHRINES, --STATUES, --TOMB.  Search also under the corresponding thesaurus term MONUMENTS & MEMORIALS.
      CN      Used in a note under the corresponding thesaurus terms MONUMENTS & MEMORIALS.

--Oratory
      See **--Public appearances**

**--Performances**
      PN      For the person's performances, including posed images of persons in costume.  Includes, for example, actors, actresses, and musicians.  Search also under the corresponding thesaurus terms ENTERTAINMENT, MUSICAL INSTRUMENTS, PERFORMANCES, SINGING, THEATRICAL PRODUCTIONS.
      CN      Double index under the occupation, as appropriate, e.g., ACTORS, ACTRESSES, ENTERTAINERS, SINGERS.  Used in a note under the corresponding thesaurus terms ENTERTAINMENT, MUSICAL INSTRUMENTS, PERFORMANCES, SINGING, THEATRICAL PRODUCTIONS.

--Personnel
      See **--Staff**

**--Portrayals**
      --[country or state]--[city]
      PN      For activities involving others impersonating the person or using an effigy or substitute for the person.  Search also under the subdivisions --ASSOCIATED OBJECTS, --DEATH MASK, --PERFORMANCES, --SHRINES, --STATUES.  Search also under the corresponding thesaurus terms EXECUTIONS IN EFFIGY, IMPERSONATION, THEATRICAL PRODUCTIONS.
      CN      Used in a note under the corresponding thesaurus terms EXECUTIONS IN EFFIGY, IMPERSONATION, THEATRICAL PRODUCTIONS.

--Public speaking
      See **--Public appearances**

---

      PN  Public note      CN  Catalogers note      HN History note      --[  ]May subdivide

## --Public appearances
### --[country or state]--[city]
PN    For the attendance of public figures at formal events, such as ceremonies, celebrations, dedications, etc. Includes public speaking. Search also under the subdivision --JOURNEYS. Search also under the corresponding thesaurus term PUBLIC SPEAKING.

CN    Used in a note under the corresponding thesaurus term PUBLIC SPEAKING.

## --Pursuit
See  --Capture & imprisonment

## --Quotations
PN    For works in which a quotation from the person is the predominant focus of the image. Search also under the subdivision --COMMEMORATION.

CN    Used in a note under the corresponding thesaurus term QUOTATIONS.

## --Religion
PN    For the person's religious beliefs and practices. Search also under the corresponding thesaurus term RELIGION.

CN    As appropriate, double index under the name of the religious group to which the person belonged. Used in a note under the corresponding thesaurus term RELIGION.

## --Resignation from office
PN    Search also under the subdivisions --ABDICATION, --IMPEACHMENT.

CN    Used in a note under the corresponding thesaurus terms RESIGNATIONS, RESIGNATIONS FROM OFFICE.

## --Shrines
### --[country or state]--[city]
PN    For structures or places consecrated or devoted to the person and serving as places of religious veneration or pilgrimage. Search also under the subdivisions --MONUMENTS, --STATUES, --TOMB.

CN    Used in a note under the corresponding thesaurus term SHRINES.

## --Social life
### --[country or state]--[city]
PN    Includes social interactions, customs, and recreational activities. Search also under the corresponding thesaurus terms INTERPERSONAL RELATIONS, MANNERS & CUSTOMS, RECREATION, SPORTS.

CN    Prefer the subdivision --PUBLIC APPEARANCES when person is represented as making a formal appearance at an event. Used in a note under the corresponding thesaurus terms INTERPERSONAL RELATIONS, MANNERS & CUSTOMS, RECREATION, SOCIAL LIFE, SPORTS.

---

PN  Public note      CN  Catalogers note      HN History note      --[  ]May subdivide

**--Staff**

PN    For employees, including presidential cabinets.  Search also under the corresponding thesaurus terms GOVERNMENT EMPLOYEES, GOVERNMENT OFFICIALS.

CN    Used in a note under the corresponding thesaurus terms GOVERNMENT OFFICIALS, GOVERNMENT EMPLOYEES, STAFF.

**--Statues**

--[country or state]--[city]

PN    For statues representing the person.  Search also under the subdivisions --MONUMENTS, --SHRINES, --TOMB.

CN    Used in a note under the corresponding thesaurus terms SCULPTURE, STATUES.

**--Tomb**

--[country or state]--[city]

PN    For the person's grave, interred bones, etc.  Search also under the subdivisions --DEATH & BURIAL, --MONUMENTS, --SHRINES, --STATUES.  Search also under the corresponding thesaurus term TOMBS & SEPULCHRAL MONUMENTS.

CN    Used in a note under thesaurus terms TOMBS & SEPULCHRAL MONUMENTS.

**--Trials, litigation, etc.**

--[country or state]--[city]

PN    For proceedings or civil or criminal actions to which the person is a party.  Search also under the subdivision --IMPEACHMENT.  Search also under term JUDICIAL PROCEEDINGS.

CN    Used in a note under the terms JUDICIAL PROCEEDINGS, TRIALS, LITIGATION, ETC.

**--Youth**

See **--Childhood & youth**

---

PN  Public note          CN  Catalogers note          HN History note          --[  ]May subdivide

## Subdivisions Used With Names of Wars

The Prints & Photographs Division uses this list of subdivisions so that large files under <u>names</u> of wars can be sub-arranged by broad topic. As appropriate, catalogers should double index with more specific headings.

The proper names for wars are taken from *Library of Congress Subject Headings*. When subdivisions listed below are used with such headings, P&P uses the MARC coding of 650 -4 or 651 -4. Institutions creating MARC records should check with their networks on how the field should be coded when non-LCSH topical subdivisions are used.

<u>Nationality subdivisions</u>: Includes --**Confederate** and --**Union**, as appropriate. Code all nationality subdivisions in a subfield 'x'.

<u>Geographic subdivisions</u>: Headings that can be further subdivided geographically include a facet note [country or state]--[city]. However, do not use a geographic subdivision with headings for wars entered directly under place names. For the effect of a war on a country as a whole or for participation of a particular country in a world war, see --[**Geographic facet**] below.

For general information on use of subdivisions, see Introduction, Section III.D.

### --Air operations
--[nationality]--[country or state]--[city]

PN    All aspects of aerial combat; includes bombing action and combat flight training. Search also under the subdivisions --CAMPAIGNS & BATTLES for images of ground fighting and other military operations. Search also under the corresponding thesaurus term AIR WARFARE.

CN    Used in a note under AIR OPERATIONS, AIR WARFARE.

### --Aircraft
See --**Transportation**

### --Aftermath
See --**Peace**

### --Amphibious operations
--[nationality]--[country or state]--[city]

PN    Joint operation of land, air, and sea forces to establish troops on shore as developed in World War II. Includes landing operations. Search also under the subdivisions --CAMPAIGNS & BATTLES for images of fighting and other military operations. Search also under the corresponding thesaurus terms LANDING CRAFT, TROOP MOVEMENTS.

CN    Prefer the subdivision --CAMPAIGNS & BATTLES for images of fighting. Used in a note under AMPHIBIOUS OPERATIONS, LANDING CRAFT, TROOP MOVEMENTS.

---

PN Public note        CN Catalogers note        HN History note        --[ ]May subdivide

## --Animals

> --[country or state]--[city]
> PN    Animals as mascots, transport animals, etc., in any civilian or military activity, alive or dead. Search also under the corresponding thesaurus term ANIMALS.
> CN    Used in a note under ANIMALS.

## --Armistices

> --[country or state]--[city]
> PN    Search also under the subdivision --PEACE.  Search also under the corresponding thesaurus term ARMISTICES.
> CN    Used in a note under the corresponding thesaurus term ARMISTICES.

## --Battlefields

> --[country or state]--[city]
> PN    Battle sites after the time of fighting.  Search also under the subdivision --CAMPAIGNS & BATTLES for scenes during battle.  Search also under the corresponding thesaurus term BATTLEFIELDS.
> CN    Used in a note under the corresponding thesaurus term BATTLEFIELDS.

## --Bridges

> See --Transportation

## --Camouflage

> --[country or state]--[city]
> PN    Search also under the corresponding thesaurus term CAMOUFLAGE (MILITARY SCIENCE).
> CN    Used in a note under CAMOUFLAGE (MILITARY SCIENCE).

## --Campaigns & battles

> --[country or state]--[city]
> PN    Combat fighting, troop movements and occupations, and other activities during organized military operations; includes guerrilla warfare and rebellions associated with war.  Search also under the subdivisions --AIR OPERATIONS, --AMPHIBIOUS OPERATIONS, --NAVAL OPERATIONS, --TRENCH WARFARE.  Search also under the corresponding thesaurus terms CAMPAIGNS & BATTLES, TROOP MOVEMENTS.
> CN    Prefer the subdivision --MILITARY TACTICS when the focus is on planning and strategy prior to execution of military operations.  Used in a note under the corresponding thesaurus terms CAMPAIGNS & BATTLES, TROOP MOVEMENTS.

## --Casualties

> --[nationality]--[country or state]--[city]
> PN    Dead and wounded soldiers and civilians. Search also under the subdivision --MEDICAL ASPECTS.  Search also under the corresponding thesaurus term WAR CASUALTIES.
> CN    Used in a note under the corresponding thesaurus term WAR CASUALTIES.

## --Causes

---

PN  Public note          CN  Catalogers note          HN  History note          --[  ]May subdivide

## --Cemeteries
    --[nationality]--[country or state]--[city]
    PN    Search also under the corresponding thesaurus term CEMETERIES.
    CN    Used in a note under the corresponding thesaurus term CEMETERIES.

## --Censorship
    See --Communications

## --Children
    --[nationality]--[country or state]--[city]
    PN    Effect of war on children and the involvement of children in war.  Search also under the subdivision --SOCIAL ASPECTS for effect of war on classes of persons in general.  Search also under the corresponding thesaurus term CHILDREN.
    CN    Use CHILDREN--WAR when the war depicted cannot be identified.  Used in a note under the corresponding thesaurus term CHILDREN.

## --Civil defense
    --[country or state]--[city]
    PN    Includes war blackouts, air raid drills, and other activities associated with protection of civilians from enemy attack.  Search also under the corresponding thesaurus term CIVIL DEFENSE.
    CN    Used in a note under the corresponding thesaurus term CIVIL DEFENSE.

## --Commemoration
    --[country or state]--[city]
    PN    Activities to commemorate a war; includes centennial celebrations, anniversaries, social gatherings, ceremonies, historical reenactments, etc. Search also under the corresponding thesaurus terms ANNIVERSARIES, CELEBRATIONS, COMMEMORATION.
    CN    Prefer the subdivision --VETERANS when the focus is on that group. Used in a note under the corresponding thesaurus terms ANNIVERSARIES, CELEBRATIONS, COMMEMORATION.

## --Communications
    --[country or state]--[city]
    PN    Broadcasting, journalism, censorship, propaganda, and telecommunications activities during a war.  Search also under the subdivision --MILITARY TACTICS for planning and strategy in military operations.  Search also under the corresponding thesaurus terms BROADCASTING, CENSORSHIP, COMMUNICATION, PROPAGANDA.
    CN    Used in a note under the corresponding thesaurus terms BROADCASTING, CENSORSHIP, COMMUNICATION, COMMUNICATIONS, PROPAGANDA.

## --Concentration camps
    See --Detention facilities

## --Confiscations
    See --Destruction & pillage

---

    PN  Public note        CN  Catalogers note        HN History note        --[  ]May subdivide

## --Covert operations

--[nationality]--[country or state]--[city]

PN    Military espionage and sabotage activities. Search also under the subdivision --CAMPAIGNS & BATTLES. Search also under the corresponding thesaurus terms COVERT OPERATIONS, SPYING, SURVEILLANCE.

CN    Used in a note under the corresponding thesaurus terms COVERT OPERATIONS, SPYING, SURVEILLANCE.

## --Defeat

See --Peace

## --Demobilizations

See --Military demobilizations

## --Destruction & pillage

--[nationality of country causing destruction]--[country or state]--[city]

PN    Includes damage to property and confiscated or captured property.  Search also under the corresponding thesaurus terms CONFISCATIONS, DESTRUCTION & PILLAGE, WAR DAMAGE.

CN    Double index under the corresponding thesaurus term WAR DAMAGE if the image shows damage after the fighting is over.  Used in a note under the corresponding thesaurus terms CONFISCATIONS, DESTRUCTION & PILLAGE, WAR DAMAGE, WAR DESTRUCTION & PILLAGE.

## --Detention facilities

--[nationality of country carrying out the detention]--[country or state]--[city]

PN    Prisons, concentration camps, relocation camps. Search also under the subdivision --MILITARY FACILITIES for installations, forts, etc. Search also under the corresponding thesaurus term DETENTION FACILITIES.

CN    Used in a note under the corresponding thesaurus term DETENTION FACILITIES.

## --Economic & industrial aspects

--[country or state]--[city]

PN    Cost of war, war relief, effect of war on industrial and commercial activity, manufacture of war equipment. Includes effect on civilian population such as consumer rationing and black market activities. Search also under the corresponding thesaurus terms ASSISTANCE, ECONOMIC ASPECTS OF WAR, WAR WORK.

CN    Used in a note under the corresponding thesaurus terms ASSISTANCE, ECONOMIC ASPECTS OF WAR, WAR WORK.

## --Engineering & construction

--[country or state]--[city]

PN    Search also under the corresponding thesaurus terms CONSTRUCTION, ENGINEERING.

CN    Used in a note under the corresponding thesaurus terms CONSTRUCTION, ENGINEERING.

---

PN  Public note          CN  Catalogers note          HN  History note          --[  ]May subdivide

--Enlistment
>    See --**Recruiting & enlistment**

--Entrenchments
>    See --**Trench warfare**

--**Equipment & supplies**
>    --[nationality]--[country or state]--[city]
>
>    PN   Military artillery, arms, vehicles, flags, medical supplies, etc.; includes procurement, shipping and transport or shortage of equipment and supplies.   Search also under the corresponding thesaurus terms EQUIPMENT, MEDICAL EQUIPMENT & SUPPLIES.
>
>    CN   Prefer the subdivision --ECONOMIC & INDUSTRIAL ASPECTS when the focus is on manufacture of military equipment and supplies.   Used in a note under the corresponding thesaurus terms EQUIPMENT, MEDICAL EQUIPMENT & SUPPLIES.

--Espionage
>    See --**Covert activities**

--Ethical aspects of war
>    See --**Moral & ethical aspects**

**[Ethnic groups], e.g., Afro-Americans, Japanese Americans, Jews**
>    --[country or state]--[city]
>
>    PN   Effect of war on a particular ethnic group, reaction to war by members of the group, and civilian involvement in war.   Search under the heading for the specific ethnic group as found in *Library of Congress Subject Headings*.
>
>    CN   Use [ETHNIC GROUP]--WAR when the war depicted cannot be identified.   Headings for specific ethnic groups are taken from *Library of Congress Subject Headings*.

--Evacuations
>    See --**Campaigns & battles**

--**Exhibitions**
>    --[country or state]--[city]
>
>    PN   Exhibitions about a war.   Search also under the corresponding thesaurus term EXHIBITIONS.
>    CN   Used in a note under the corresponding thesaurus term EXHIBITIONS.

--Field hospitals
>    See --**Medical aspects**

--Finance
>    See --**Economic & industrial aspects**

--Flags
>    See --**Equipment & supplies**

---

PN  Public note          CN  Catalogers note          HN  History note          --[   ]May subdivide

--Fox holes
>    See --Trench warfare

[Geographic facet]
>    --[country or state]--[city]
>> PN    Effect of war on particular country as a whole or for participation of a particular country in one of the world wars.
>> CN    Use only after wars entered directly under their own names, e.g., World War, 1914-1918--Germany--Frankfurt.

--Guerrillas
>> PN    Images which focus on people.  Search also under the corresponding thesaurus term GUERRILLAS.
>> CN    Used in a note under the corresponding thesaurus term GUERRILLAS.

--Historic sites
>    --[country or state]--[city]
>> PN    Images depicting sites or structures which are associated with a war but not located on battlegrounds. Search also under the subdivisions --BATTLEFIELDS, --MONUMENTS. Search also under the corresponding thesaurus term HISTORIC SITES.
>> CN    Prefer the subdivision --BATTLEFIELDS when the focus is on the site of a named battle.  Prefer the subdivision --MONUMENTS for structures erected to commemorate a particular war event or person.  Used in a note under corresponding thesaurus term HISTORIC SITES.

--Home front
>    See --Social aspects

--Homecoming
>    See --Peace

--Industry
>    See --Economic & industrial aspects

--Invasions
>    See --Campaigns & battles

--Landing operations
>    See --Amphibious operations

---

PN  Public note          CN  Catalogers note          HN  History note          --[  ]May subdivide

## --Medical aspects
--[country or state]--[city]

PN    Relief and medical care for casualties and military medicine in general. Search also under the subdivision --CASUALTIES for images that focus on dead and wounded persons. Search also under the corresponding thesaurus terms MEDICAL ASPECTS OF WAR, MILITARY MEDICINE, WAR CASUALTIES.

CN    Used in a note under the corresponding thesaurus terms MEDICAL ASPECTS OF WAR, MILITARY MEDICINE, WAR CASUALTIES.

## --Military demobilizations
--[country or state]--[city]

PN    Search also under the subdivision --PEACE. Search also under the corresponding thesaurus term MILITARY DEMOBILIZATIONS.

CN    Used in a note under the corresponding thesaurus term MILITARY DEMOBILIZATIONS.

## --Military facilities
--[nationality]--[country or state]--[city]

PN    Military camps, bases, installations, forts, headquarters and associated buildings. Includes field sites and temporary structures. Search also under the subdivision --DETENTION FACILITIES for prisons and concentration camps, etc. Search also under the corresponding thesaurus term MILITARY FACILITIES.

CN    Used in a note under the corresponding thesaurus term MILITARY FACILITIES.

## --Military life
--[nationality]--[country or state]--[city]

PN    Activities associated with a military person's life in a camp-like setting; includes social activities away from camp, leisure activities. Search also under the subdivision --MILITARY PERSONNEL for portraits of individuals and general views of troops. Search also under the corresponding thesaurus term MILITARY LIFE.

CN    Prefer --MILITARY PERSONNEL for portraits and groups. Used in a note under MILITARY LIFE.

## --Military mobilizations
--[country or state]--[city]

PN    Search also under the subdivision --RECRUITING & ENLISTMENT. Search also under the corresponding thesaurus term MILITARY MOBILIZATIONS.

CN    Used in a note under the corresponding thesaurus term MILITARY MOBILIZATIONS.

--Military occupations
     See --Campaigns & battles

---

PN  Public note      CN  Catalogers note      HN  History note      --[  ]May subdivide

## --Military personnel
--[nationality]--[country or state]--[city]

PN     Individuals and groups; includes drills and general views of troops. Search also under the subdivision --MILITARY LIFE for activities associated with a military person's life. Search also under the corresponding thesaurus terms MILITARY PERSONNEL, SOLDIERS.

CN     Used in a note under the corresponding thesaurus terms MILITARY PERSONNEL, SOLDIERS.

## --Military retreats
--[nationality]--[country or state]--[city]

PN     Search also under the corresponding thesaurus term MILITARY RETREATS.

CN     Used in a note under the corresponding thesaurus term MILITARY RETREATS.

## --Military tactics
--[nationality]

PN     Planning and strategy for execution of military operations, includes reconnaissance. Search also under the subdivision --CAMPAIGNS & BATTLES for images of fighting. Search also under the corresponding thesaurus term MILITARY ART & SCIENCE.

CN     Prefer --CAMPAIGNS & BATTLES for images of fighting and other activities during execution of military operations. Used in a note under the corresponding thesaurus term MILITARY ART & SCIENCE, MILITARY TACTICS.

## --Monuments
--[country or state]--[city]

PN     Structures erected to commemorate a war; includes memorials, sculpture, plaques, and monuments to soldiers. Search also under the subdivisions --COMMEMORATION, --HISTORIC SITES. Search also under the corresponding thesaurus term MONUMENTS & MEMORIALS.

CN     Used in a note under the corresponding thesaurus term MONUMENTS & MEMORIALS.

## --Moral & ethical aspects

PN     Moral and ethical questions about war practices, specific events such as war crimes, war atrocities, public protests and demonstrations against war. Search also under the subdivision --RELIGIOUS ASPECTS. Search also under the corresponding thesaurus term MORAL ASPECTS OF WAR.

CN     Used in a note under the corresponding thesaurus term MORAL ASPECTS OF WAR.

--Music

See --Songs & music

## --Naval operations
--[nationality]--[country or state]--[city]

PN     All aspects of naval operations and marine combat; includes training. Search also under the subdivision --CAMPAIGNS & BATTLES for images of ground fighting and other military operations. Search also under the corresponding thesaurus term NAVAL WARFARE.

CN     Used in a note under the corresponding thesaurus term NAVAL WARFARE.

--Partisans
>See --**Guerrillas**

--**Peace**
> --[country or state]--[city]
> PN   For peace negotiations and the ending and aftermath of war, including homecomings, victory celebrations, paying of reparations, etc. Search also under the subdivisions --ARMISTICES, --COMMEMORATION, --MILITARY DEMOBILIZATIONS, --SURRENDERS, --VETERANS. Search also under the corresponding thesaurus terms ARMISTICES, PEACE, PEACE CONFERENCES, PEACE NEGOTIATIONS, PEACE TREATIES, VICTORY CELEBRATIONS.
> CN   Used in a note under the corresponding thesaurus terms ARMISTICES, PEACE, PEACE CONFERENCES, PEACE NEGOTIATIONS, PEACE TREATIES, VICTORY CELEBRATIONS.

--Prison camps
> See --**Detention facilities**

--**Prisoners**
> --[nationality]--[country or state in which prisoners held]--[city]
> PN   The taking of prisoners during wartime, or captured soldiers taken as part of war action, during their captivity. Search also under the corresponding thesaurus terms PRISONERS, PRISONERS OF WAR.
> CN   Used in a note under the corresponding thesaurus terms PRISONERS, PRISONERS OF WAR.

--Provisions
> See --**Equipment & supplies**

--Railroads
> See --**Transportation**

--Relocation camps
> See --**Detention facilities**

--Resistance movements
> See --**Underground movements**

--**Recruiting & enlistment**
> --[country or state]--[city]
> PN   Search also under the subdivision --MILITARY MOBILIZATIONS. Search also under the corresponding thesaurus term RECRUITING & ENLISTMENT.
> CN   Used in a note under the corresponding thesaurus term RECRUITING & ENLISTMENT.

## --Refugees

--[nationality]--[country or state in which taking refuge]--[city]

PN    Search also under the corresponding thesaurus term REFUGEES.

CN    Used in a note under the corresponding thesaurus term REFUGEES.

## --Religious aspects

--[country or state]--[city]

PN    Search also under the subdivisions --MORAL & ETHICAL ASPECTS.  Search also under the corresponding thesaurus term RELIGIOUS ASPECTS OF WAR.

CN    Used in a note under the corresponding thesaurus term RELIGIOUS ASPECTS OF WAR.

## --Repatriation

See --**Refugees**

## --Retreats

See --**Military retreats**

## --Social aspects

--[country or state]--[city]

PN    Social activities and the home front during war; effect of war on social programs and classes of persons, other than women and children.  Search also under the subdivisions --CHILDREN, --VETERANS, --WOMEN for effect of war on members of these groups and civilian involvement of women and children in war.

CN    Prefer the subdivisions --CHILDREN, --VETERANS, --WOMEN when the focus is on members of these groups.

## --Songs & music

PN    Search also under the corresponding thesaurus terms MUSIC, SONGS,

CN    Used in a note under the corresponding thesaurus terms MUSIC, SONGS.

## --Supplies

See --**Equipment & supplies**

## --Surrenders

--[nationality]--[country or state]--[city]

PN    Search also under the subdivision --PRISONERS for capture or surrender of individual soldiers and troops.  Search also under the corresponding thesaurus term SURRENDERS.

CN    Used in a note under the corresponding thesaurus term SURRENDERS.

PN  Public note          CN  Catalogers note          HN History note          --[  ]May subdivide

## --Transportation
  --[country or state]--[city]
  PN    Land, air, or sea transportation; includes activities, vehicles, and structures, such as bridges, canals, railroads.  Search also under the subdivision --EQUIPMENT & SUPPLIES.  Search also under the corresponding thesaurus term TRANSPORTATION.
  CN    Prefer the subdivision --EQUIPMENT & SUPPLIES when the focus is on procurement of military vehicles or aircraft.  Prefer the subdivision --ECONOMIC & INDUSTRIAL ASPECTS when the focus is on manufacture of military vehicles or aircraft.  Used in a note under the corresponding thesaurus term TRANSPORTATION.

## --Treaties
  PN    Search also under the corresponding thesaurus term TREATIES.
  CN    Used in a note under the corresponding thesaurus term TREATIES.

## --Trench warfare
  --[country or state]--[city]
  PN    Includes combat and training activities.  Search also under the subdivision --CAMPAIGNS & BATTLES.  Search also under the corresponding thesaurus term TRENCH WARFARE.
  CN    Used in a note under the corresponding thesaurus term TRENCH WARFARE.

--Troop movements
  See --Campaigns & battles

--Troops
  See --Military personnel

## --Underground movements
  --[country or state]--[city]
  PN    Resistance movements and guerrilla warfare.  Search also under the subdivision --GUERRILLAS for images that focus on people.  Search also under the corresponding thesaurus terms GUERRILLAS, UNDERGROUND MOVEMENTS.
  CN    Used in a note under the corresponding thesaurus term UNDERGROUND MOVEMENTS.

## --Veterans
  --[nationality]--[country or state]--[city]
  PN    Portraits of veterans; effect of war on veterans.  Search also under the subdivision --SOCIAL ASPECTS for effect of war on other classes of persons.  Search also under the corresponding thesaurus term VETERANS.
  CN    Used in a note under the corresponding thesaurus term VETERANS.

--War work
  See --Economic & industrial aspects

---

PN  Public note          CN  Catalogers note          HN  History note          --[  ]May subdivide

**--Women**

--[nationality]--[country or state]--[city]

PN      Civilian involvement of women in war.  Search also under the subdivision --SOCIAL ASPECTS for effect of war on classes of persons in general. Search also under the corresponding thesaurus term WOMEN.

CN      Use WOMEN--WAR when the war depicted cannot be identified.  Used in a note under the corresponding thesaurus term WOMEN.

## Subdivisions Used With Corporate Bodies and Named Events

The Prints and Photographs Division uses this list of subdivisions so that large files under <u>names</u> of corporate bodies and <u>named events</u> can be sub-arranged by broad topic. As appropriate, catalogers should double index with more specific headings.

The proper names for corporate bodies and named events are taken from the Library of Congress Name Authority File and *Library of Congress Subject Headings*. The term "corporate bodies" includes organizations and institutions, commercial enterprises, military services, legislative bodies, educational and medical institutions. Named events include conferences and exhibitions. When subdivisions listed below are used with such headings, P&P uses the MARC coding of 61x -24 or 61x -014. Institutions creating MARC records should check with their networks on how the field should be coded when non-LCSH topical subdivisions are used.

Headings that can be further subdivided geographically include a facet note [country or state] [city]. For general information on the use of subdivisions, see Introduction, Section III.D.


--Anniversaries
　　See --**Commemoration**

--**Buildings**
　　--[country or state]--[city]
　　PN　　Use when emphasis is on structure, particularly when interior details or exteriors are visible. Search also under the subdivision --FACILITIES. Search also under the corresponding thesaurus term BUILDINGS.
　　CN　　Used in a note under the corresponding thesaurus term BUILDINGS.

--Ceremonies
　　See --**Rites & ceremonies**

--**Commemoration**
　　--[country or state]--[city]
　　PN　　For anniversaries, birthdays, centennial celebrations, and other events held in honor or memory of the corporate body, its founding, or other notable event. Search also under the subdivision --MEETINGS. Search also under the thesaurus term ANNIVERSARIES.
　　CN　　Used in a note under the corresponding thesaurus term ANNIVERSARIES.

--Conventions
　　See --**Meetings**

--Demonstrations
　　See --**Riots & demonstrations**

---

PN  Public note　　　　CN  Catalogers note　　　　HN History note　　　　--[  ]May subdivide

**--Disasters**
> --[country or state]--[city]
> PN    For explosions, fires, floods, and other disasters. Search also under the corresponding thesaurus term DISASTERS.
> CN    Used in a note under the corresponding thesaurus term DISASTERS.

**--Displays**
> See **--Exhibitions & displays**

**--Employees**
> See **--People**

**--Equipment & supplies**
> --[country or state]--[city]
> PN    Includes materials used to create the product or service, or used in daily activities of the organization. Search also under the subdivision --PRODUCTS. Search also under corresponding thesaurus term EQUIPMENT.
> CN    Used in a note under the corresponding thesaurus term EQUIPMENT.

**--Exhibitions & displays**
> --[country or state]--[city]
> PN    Search also under the corresponding thesaurus terms EXHIBITIONS, MERCHANDISE DISPLAYS.
> CN    Used in a note under the corresponding thesaurus terms EXHIBITIONS, MERCHANDISE DISPLAYS.

**--Explosions**
> See **--Disasters**

**--Facilities**
> --[country or state]--[city]
> PN    For structures (other than buildings), spaces, furnishings, and services associated with the corporate body or event. Search also under the subdivision --BUILDINGS. Search also under the corresponding thesaurus term FACILITIES.
> CN    Used in a note under the corresponding thesaurus term FACILITIES.

**--Fires**
> See **--Disasters**

**--Inmates**
> See **--People**

**--Interiors**
> See **--Buildings, --Facilities**

---

PN  Public note    CN  Catalogers note    HN History note    --[  ]May subdivide

**--Meetings**
>    --[country or state]--[city]
>    PN     Includes board meetings, annual meetings, and other planned gatherings.  Search also under the subdivision --COMMEMORATION.  Search also under the corresponding thesaurus term MEETINGS.
>    CN     Used in a note under the corresponding thesaurus term MEETINGS.

**--Members**
>    See --**People**

**--Offices**
>    See --**Buildings, --Facilities**

**--Officials & employees**
>    See --**People**

**--Owners**
>    See --**People**

**--People**
>    --[country or state]--[city]
>    PN     For those who make up the organization or institution, including officials, employees, owners, staff, personnel, members, officers and persons in military service, students in educational institutions, and inmates.  Search also under the corresponding thesaurus terms MILITARY PERSONNEL, PEOPLE.
>    CN     Used in a note under the corresponding thesaurus terms MILITARY PERSONNEL, PEOPLE.

**--Personnel**
>    See --**People**

**--Products**
>    --[country or state]--[city]
>    PN     Search also under the subdivision --EQUIPMENT & SUPPLIES.  Search also under the corresponding thesaurus term MERCHANDISE DISPLAYS.
>    CN     Used in a note under the corresponding thesaurus terms MERCHANDISE DISPLAYS, PRODUCTS.

**--Public relations**
>     --[country or state]--[city]
>    PN     For actions or products of the organization or institution intended to promote goodwill toward itself.  Search also under the corresponding thesaurus term PUBLIC RELATIONS.
>    CN     Used in a note under the corresponding thesaurus term PUBLIC RELATIONS.

PN   Public note          CN   Catalogers note          HN   History note          --[   ]May subdivide

## --Recruiting & enlistment

    --[country or state]--[city]

       PN      Includes both military and non-military activities.  Search also under the corresponding thesaurus terms MEMBERSHIP CAMPAIGNS, RECRUITING & ENLISTMENT.

       CN      Used in a note under the corresponding thesaurus terms MEMBERSHIP CAMPAIGNS, RECRUITING & ENLISTMENT.

## --Riots & demonstrations

    --[country or state]--[city]

       PN      Includes all civil disorders.  Search also under the corresponding thesaurus terms DEMONSTRATIONS, RIOTS.

       CN      Used in a note under the corresponding thesaurus terms DEMONSTRATIONS, RIOTS.

## --Rites & ceremonies

    --[country or state]--[city]

       PN      Includes dedications.  Search also under the subdivisions --COMMEMORATION, --SOCIAL LIFE.  Search also under the corresponding thesaurus term RITES & CEREMONIES.

       CN      Used in a note under the corresponding thesaurus term RITES & CEREMONIES.

## --Social life

    --[country or state]--[city]

       PN      Includes social interaction and recreational activities.  Search also under the subdivisions --RITES & CEREMONIES, --SPORTS.  Search also under the corresponding thesaurus terms INTERPERSONAL RELATIONS, MANNERS & CUSTOMS, RECREATION.

       CN      Used in a note under the corresponding thesaurus terms INTERPERSONAL RELATIONS, MANNERS & CUSTOMS, RECREATION.

## --Sports

    --[country or state]--[city]

       PN      Search also under the corresponding thesaurus terms RECREATION, SPORTS.

       CN      Used in a note under the corresponding thesaurus terms RECREATION, SPORTS.

## --Staff

    See --People

## --Strikes

    --[country or state]--[city]

       PN      Search also under the subdivision --RIOTS & DEMONSTRATIONS.  Search also under the corresponding thesaurus term STRIKES.

       CN      Used in a note under the corresponding thesaurus term STRIKES.

## --Students

    See --People

## --Supplies

    See --Equipment & supplies

---

PN  Public note        CN  Catalogers note        HN History note        --[  ]May subdivide

# TGM II:

## Genre and Physical Characteristic Terms

The following code has been assigned to this thesaurus for the MARC format. It must be entered in subfield 2 of fields 655 and 755:

**gmgpc**

# TGM II: TABLE OF CONTENTS

# ACKNOWLEDGMENTS

The reconciliation of vocabulary from many specialized areas of pictorial collections would not have been possible without suggestions from colleagues in libraries, museums, and archives who reviewed the list. We extend thanks to everyone who made comments and are particularly grateful to several individuals who contributed numerous ideas.


**For the first edition (1986):**

Georgia Bumgardner (American Antiquarian Society); Kathleen Collins, Terri Echter, Joyce Nalewajk, Barbara Orbach, Stephen Ostrow, Ford Peatross, Carol Pulin, Bernard Reilly, and Renata Shaw (Library of Congress, Prints and Photographs Division); Lynn Cox (Alabama Archives); Jackie Dooley (University of California, San Diego); Christine Hennessey (National Museum of American Art); David Horvath (University of Louisville); Waverly Lowell and John Maounis (National Maritime Museum); Toni Petersen (Art and Architecture Thesaurus); Sara Shatford and Elaine Svenonius (University of California, Los Angeles); Joe Springer (Goshen College); Amy Stark (Center for Creative Photography); Gerald Stone (Public Archives of Canada); and Larry Viskochil (Chicago Historical Society).

The compilers, Helena Zinkham and Elisabeth Betz Parker, are also grateful for the support of the Association of College and Research Libraries Rare Books and Manuscripts Standards Committee.


**For the second edition:**

Elisabeth Betz Parker, Assistant Chief, Prints & Photographs Division (P&P) provided extensive guidance, advice, and editing. P&P catalogers DeAnna Dare Evans, Marcy Flynn, Jeanne Korda, and Woody Woodis helped prepare new terms and update the introduction and bibliography. A number of contributors provided suggestions and reviewed new terms: Beth Delaney (Albany Institute of History and Art); Jane Greenberg (Schomburg Center for Research in Black Culture, New York Public Library); Christine Hennessey (National Museum of American Art); John Slade (University of Texas at Austin); Laura Stalker (Huntington Library); Diane Vogt-O'Connor (U.S. Dept. of the Interior, National Park Service); Susanne Warren (Art and Architecture Thesaurus); Beverly Brannan, Mary Ison, Carol Johnson, Jacqueline Manapsal, Elena Millie, Barbara Orbach Natanson, Bernard Reilly (P&P); Bonnie Wilson and Nancy Erickson (Minnesota Historical Society). Prasad Nair and Lyn Neal of Project Management, Inc., converted the terms from word processing software into their LEXICO thesaurus software. The Library of Congress Information Technology Services (ITS) and Automation Planning and Liaison Office (APLO) provided technical assistance, and the Cataloging Distribution Service published and marketed the thesaurus.

Participation in the Working Group for Form and Genre Vocabulary, hosted by the Art and Architecture Thesaurus, has resolved variations in terminology that had arisen among our related thesauri and provided a welcome mechanism to prevent conflicts in new terms.


Sarah Rouse, editor, 1994-
Cataloger, Pictorial Collections
Prints and Photographs Division

Helena Zinkham, editor, 1986-1994
Head, Processing Section
Prints and Photographs Division

November 1994

The *Thesaurus for Graphic Materials II: Genre and Physical Characteristic Terms* (*TGM II*) is the second edition of *Descriptive Terms for Graphic Materials: Genre and Physical Characteristic Headings* (1986). This thesaurus was developed by the Library of Congress Prints and Photographs Division, with input from other archival image repositories. The new name reflects its role as a companion to *Thesaurus for Graphic Materials I: Subject Headings* (*TGM I*). The cataloging code for the first edition, *gmgpc*, has been retained.

## I. BACKGROUND

Access to graphic materials in libraries and archival collections frequently has been limited to retrieval by subject content and names of creators. Although catalog records often include information on genre and physical characteristics, researchers have not always had ready access to it. A student of lithography, for example, may be compelled to consult reference books for names of printmakers likely to have produced lithographs, then to search a library's catalog of prints for artists' names, and, finally, examine each catalog record to find those for lithographs. A scholar investigating the cultural impact of photographically illustrated books may be forced to rely on a few published bibliographies, in-house example files, staff memory, and chance discoveries to locate examples of such works. As graphic collections grow and catalog records accumulate, it is clear that additional access points greatly facilitate research related to functional categories, production contexts, and artifactual aspects of graphic materials.[1]

A single list of standard terms from which catalogers and researchers can choose indexing and retrieval vocabulary was needed, along with widely accepted provisions for applying the terms as access points. The first edition of *Descriptive Terms for Graphic Materials: Genre and Physical Characteristic Headings* (GMGPC) appeared in 1986. Before then, the lack of such a list and cataloging guidelines was a problem because of the great variety of media and pictorial types and because of the broad range of users of graphic materials, whose knowledge and experience vary. While an extensive and often informal vocabulary is employed in the descriptive portion of the catalog record, indexing terms should be controlled. Reconciling variant terms by designating a preferred indexing term not only simplifies the cataloger's task but also makes retrieval more efficient. For example, the standard term "dry plate negatives" collocates "silver gelatin glass negatives," "glass plates," and "dry plates." Furthermore, the terms for indexing graphic materials can be used most effectively when presented within the structure of a thesaurus designed to establish relationships and guide users.

While *TGM II* can be used in a variety of cataloging systems, it was created primarily in response to the needs of institutions using the communications format called MAchine-Readable Cataloging (MARC) for their automated catalog records. In 1979, the Independent Research Libraries Association (IRLA) recommended in "Proposals for Establishing Standards for the Cataloguing of Rare Books and Specialized Research Materials in Machine-Readable Form" the addition of two new fields to the MARC format for terms indicating genre and publishing/physical aspects. In 1980, the field 655 was authorized for genre headings and in 1984 field 755 was authorized for physical

---

[1] Helena Zinkham, Patricia D. Cloud, and Hope Mayo, "Providing Access by Form of Material, Genre, and Physical Characteristics: Benefits and Techniques," *American Archivist* 52 (summer 1989): 300-319.

characteristic headings.[2] These fields are now defined for all types of material in the *USMARC Format for Bibliographic Data*.[3]

IRLA asked the Standards Committee of the Rare Books and Manuscripts Section of the Association of College and Research Libraries to develop thesauri appropriate for rare books and special collections. The lack of vocabulary to index book illustrations led the Committee to encourage staff of the Library of Congress Prints and Photographs Division to expand and integrate several of their genre and physical description lists into a thesaurus constructed according to guidelines set out by the American National Standards Institute.[4] The result was *Descriptive Terms for Graphic Materials: Genre and Physical Characteristic Headings* with 513 authorized terms and 290 cross references. When the second edition, *TGM II*, closed for publication in June 1994, it had 600 authorized terms and 448 cross references, a 15% increase in postable terms.

## II. SCOPE AND PURPOSE

In the context of *TGM II*, genre headings denote distinctive categories of material: an established class of pictorial types (PORTRAITS), a vantage point or method of projection (BIRD'S-EYE VIEWS; PERSPECTIVE PROJECTIONS), or intended purpose (ADVERTISEMENTS; COMPETITION DRAWINGS). Some indicate characteristics of an image's creator (STUDENT WORKS) or a publication status or occasion (CENSORED WORKS; NEW YEAR CARDS). Others imply a subject but also designate a method of representation (ABSTRACT WORKS; LANDSCAPES). Terms denoting artistic movements and styles are not included in this definition of genre. Physical characteristic headings designate graphic materials distinguished by production processes or techniques (ALBUMEN PRINTS), production stages or versions (PROOFS; REPRODUCTIONS), instrument employed (PINHOLE CAMERA PHOTOGRAPHS; AIRBRUSH WORKS), markings (WATERMARKS), shape and size (SCROLLS; MINIATURE WORKS), and other physical aspects of graphic materials.

---

[2] The Library of Congress MARC Standards Office has prepared Discussion Paper no. 82 (December 1994) for American Library Association (ALA) Machine-Readable Bibliographic Information Committee (MARBI), weighing the need for the 755 field. The discussion paper is sponsored by the Bibliographic Standards Committee of the Rare Books and Manuscripts Section (RBMS) of the Association of College and Research Libraries Division (ACRL) of ALA and the Subject Analysis Committee (SAC) of the Cataloging and Classification Section of the Association for Library Collections and Technical Services (ALCTS). As a result of the discussion field 755 might be made obsolete.

[3] *USMARC Format for Bibliographic Data*, prepared by Network Development and MARC Standards Office (Washington, D.C., Library of Congress, 1994). Includes guidelines for content designation. New and replacement pages are issued periodically.

[4] American National Standards Institute, Guidelines for Thesaurus Structure, Construction, and Use: Approved June 30, 1980 (New York, 1980), ANSI Z39.19-1980. The new standard, scheduled for publication in 1994, is: National Information Standards Organization, *Guidelines for the Construction, Format, and Management of Monolingual Thesauri* (Bethesda, Md., 1994), NISO Z39.19 1994.

*TGM II* terms are:

▪ applicable to two-dimensional, chiefly pictorial, graphic materials (among them, prints, photographs, drawings, and ephemera) whether they are part of a book, or in a manuscript, graphic, or other collection;
▪ applicable to some non-pictorial and three-dimensional material commonly found in graphic collections, such as visiting cards and photograph cases;
▪ appropriate for materials commonly found in general graphic collections of research libraries and historical societies. (Thus, there are more terms for photographs and historical prints than for fine prints, drawings, and paintings. There are few terms for educational audiovisual materials.)


*TGM II* terms will:

▪ assist research into the development and distribution of a particular genre or technical process;
▪ aid retrieval of information about aspects of graphic materials frequently requested by people who want to understand how a certain technique is performed;
▪ aid selection of materials for exhibitions or class demonstrations;
▪ assist collection preservation, since collections are handled less when the catalog provides more specific access;
▪ help collection management by providing, for example, the information needed to calculate the quantity of glass transparencies held by an institution;
▪ aid cataloging, since pinpointing a process or format may help to date or identify an image;
▪ make cataloging more consistent and encourage specificity by providing standard terminology in a ready reference format;
▪ assist institutions in disseminating information about their collections through database networks or other means.

For example, genre and physical characteristic terms will make it easier for the student of lithography to find examples of lithographs; indeed, the student could narrow the search to lithographic posters printed in Germany between 1900 and 1920. Or, by using these headings, the scholar can rapidly retrieve photographically illustrated books.


## III. SYNTAX AND STRUCTURE

In accordance with thesaurus construction standards, terms usually represent single concepts and are plural nouns with phrases in natural language order. English words follow American spelling practice. The draft NISO thesaurus standard suggests that all homographs receive a qualifier to distinguish those words that have the same spelling and different meanings.

    <u>Example:</u>        CARTOONS (COMMENTARY)
                       CARTOONS (WORKING DRAWINGS)

Thus, the second edition includes qualifiers; most were chosen by consensus in the Working Group on Form and Genre Vocabulary (WGFGV).[5]  More qualifiers are likely to be added as the WGFGV completes its review of terms.

The thesaurus structure is intended to help both catalogers and researchers select the term(s) most appropriate for indexing and retrieval.  Terms appear in alphabetical order and are listed in word-by-word filing sequence.  Scope notes (here called "public notes") define the terms in the context of the thesaurus.  Associations between terms are indicated by the convention of broader, narrower, related, and "used for" relationships.  Terms listed under a heading also appear in the alphabetical filing sequence with the reciprocal relationship noted.  For example, the term EPHEMERA has LABELS listed as a narrower term, and the term LABELS has EPHEMERA listed as its broader term.

The difference between genres and physical characteristics may be unclear, for example, with terms like BROADSIDES, in which purpose is closely identified with one physical manifestation.  In order to simplify the assignment of MARC field tags, each term entry includes a cataloger's note suggesting the appropriate MARC field.  Each institution may, however, choose its own field assignments; some may prefer to use only the form-genre field (655) for the entire vocabulary.[6]

Notes and relationships:

PN: **Public note** - defines the scope of a term.

CN: **Cataloger's note** - guides indexers in selecting a term; for thesaurus maintenance, records other notes in which the term appears.

HN: **History note** - accounts for earlier ways in which a term appeared in the list, in particular terms that formerly appeared as non-preferred (UF) terms; also, prompts the catalog user to search under earlier forms of headings, in case headings in a catalog have not been updated to the current forms.

>        Example:        Gem photographs: HN: Changed 5/89.  Formerly, Gem photographs may have been
>                        indexed as Miniature works.

UF: **Used for** - indicates a non-preferred term, such as an alternative spelling, inverted form, or synonym; helps define a term's meaning.

BT: **Broader term** - indicates the more general class to which a term belongs; everything that is true of a term is also true of its broader term.

NT: **Narrower term** - indicates a more specific term or member of a class.

---

[5] In 1992, AAT director Toni Petersen and RBMS chair Laura Stalker received a Council on Library Resources grant to identify and resolve as many conflicting terms as possible through a Working Group on Form and Genre Vocabulary (WGFGV).  Many thesauri were being constructed simultaneously in the 1980s.  Despite efforts to use the same terminology, the resolution of conflicts was not always possible.  The WGFGV participants represent: AAT, *TGM II*, *Guidelines on Subject Access to Individual Works of Fiction, Drama, Etc. (GSA)*, LCSH, *Medical Subject Headings (MeSH)*, and RBMS.  The reports of the 1992 and 1993 meetings are available from the AAT; the review work is expected to conclude in 1995.

[6] The drawbacks that have developed from having two fields are discussed in Jackie Dooley and Helena Zinkham, "The Object as 'Subject': Providing Access to Genres, Forms of Material, and Physical Characteristics," in *Beyond the Book: Extending MARC for Subject Access* (Boston: G.K. Hall, 1990), 43-80.

**RT: Related term** - brings to the catalog user's attention terms that are associated because of overlapping meanings or part-whole relationships.

**USE:** leads from a non-preferred, unauthorized form of a term to the term as used.

**+** : indicates that one or more narrower (i.e., more specific) terms will be found under this term's own entry. Appears only with NT terms, not RT terms.

The **public note** provides definitions for about 90% of the terms. The undefined terms are chiefly fine art or printmaking terms that can be found in commonly available dictionaries. The definitions have an American bias, particularly in the dates of popular usage and sizes that are cited. Most definitions have been modified to reflect their application within the context of this thesaurus; none should be considered too rigidly. The experimental techniques and subtle variations in many graphic processes preclude complete precision. The definitions are usually derived from several sources listed in the bibliography. Those based chiefly on one source mention the source, e.g., [AAT] for *Art and Architecture Thesaurus*.

While this thesaurus does not require facets to subdivide headings, such information may be added to a term to indicate where the cataloged material was made, when, and whether it is in color. General guidelines for sub-divisions, as well as examples, are given in section V.6 of this introduction.

The Classed Display and Hierarchical Display, which appeared in the first edition, have been discontinued. They were not used enough to warrant their updating.


## IV. TERM SELECTION AND FORMULATION

*TGM II* is designed to provide terms for access to categories of media and formats rather than to enumerate terms for indexing every conceivable aspect of graphic materials. It is not an exhaustive glossary. The degree of term specificity is meant to permit reasonably direct searches to locate the most commonly requested examples of graphic materials. Some terms for relatively rare material have been included, when such materials are commonly requested and hard to locate.

The need for access to categories of material outweighed the desire for access to very specific types that require great technical expertise, considerable analysis, or elaborate tests in order for the cataloger to assign a term. The identification of some processes may, in fact, depend entirely on the presence of manufacturers' labels, captions, imprints, or accompanying information. However, retrieval of some formats and physical types that are difficult to recognize cannot be neglected. For example, while it may be excessive to analyze every photographic print for indexing by a specific photographic process, terms have been included for processes that are fairly readily identified and that could help meet the demand for study examples.

The variety of material found in graphic collections prompted some modification of ambiguous informal terminology. For example, in a purely photographic collection, the words "prints" and "negatives" may suffice. In a mixed collection or in a database of records for a variety of material, however, "prints" is better reserved for engravings and related media, while "photographic prints" refers without confusion to photographs. Such formal vocabulary is necessary for indexing purposes, even though the notes in the catalog record continue to be expressed in informal language.[7]

---

[7] Use of the terms "photoprints" and "photonegatives" from the first edition has been supplanted by the widely used terms "photographic prints" (and its narrower terms, for example, "silver gelatin prints") and "negatives." This change was made in response to requests from many thesaurus users, despite the possible problems in searching a database for "prints"

Based on experience gained since the first edition, terms have been added to specify graphic material content and distinguish it from textual genres. This has been done because so much pictorial material is found in catalogs for mixed or textual collections.

> Examples:          PICTORIAL ENVELOPES (instead of just Envelopes)
>                    PRINTMAKING EQUIPMENT (instead of just Equipment)

Graphic designs and their finished products (e.g., BOOK JACKETS) are in the category of materials in which pictorial content is implicit in the term, so the word "Pictorial" is not part of the phrase; the design work may also be indexed with GRAPHIC DESIGN DRAWINGS. Different manifestations of an object type are also brought together under the same term; all possible physical forms of a genre are not given special terms. Thus, PLAYING CARDS includes both the cut and uncut sheets. With ARCHITECTURAL DRAWINGS, which may be hand-drawn, photographic, or printed, separate headings such as BLUEPRINTS are used to convey the physical characteristics.

As in the first edition of this thesaurus, certain types of vocabulary have been excluded. Terms that describe art movements or styles as well as those requiring subjective judgment, such as documentary photographs, pictorialism, propaganda, and primitive paintings, are beyond the scope of *TGM II*.

Terms that combine broad subject categories and forms have, however, begun to be included, thus providing more direct access to well-established categories of material that catalog users are likely to request, e.g., BASEBALL CARDS and BOTANICAL ILLUSTRATIONS. The fullest example is under POSTERS. (For example, instead of searching a database for the topical term DANCE and the form term POSTERS, now one can search for DANCE POSTERS.) The phrases reflect typical categories for filing posters, listing them in auction catalogs, or writing about them in books. The phrases also draw together posters which may have many different subject headings that cannot be easily retrieved together, e.g., WAR POSTERS indexed under the names of many different wars; POLITICAL POSTERS indexed under presidential elections, protest movements, and other subjects.

The new edition also includes a few historic trade name processes that are more recognizable than more generic expressions of the material. Examples include AUTOCHROMES (instead of Screen color glass transparencies) and PHOTOCHROM PRINTS (instead of Photomechanical prints--Color). To provide access to the numerous trade names not included here, the names may be stated elsewhere in the catalog record. Other terms often used in the descriptive portion of the catalog record have also been excluded because they do not seem practical as access points. Among these are: contact prints, copper engravings, die-cut lithographs, glossy prints, and half-length portraits.

The complex formulation of a string of words to express a description such as "pen, pencil, ink, and graphite drawing with blue wash on laid paper" cannot be accomplished within the structure of *TGM II* with its emphasis on basic categories and simple subdivisions. Separate terms were, therefore, established to designate application instruments (e.g., PENCIL WORKS). Terms that describe the primary and secondary support material were largely excluded in favor of medium designations. Since, however, the primary support may sometimes be the only distinctive feature of a photograph, terms for support were coupled with general photographic terms (e.g., CERAMIC PHOTOGRAPHS, FILM NEGATIVES). For institutions employing the MARC format, codes in the 007 field provide access to primary and secondary support materials, such as paper, glass, and wood. Information about the support material and application instrument may also appear in the physical description or note area of the catalog record.

Several genre terms (e.g., ABSTRACT WORKS, ALLEGORIES, CITYSCAPES, GENRE WORKS, LANDSCAPES, PORTRAITS, STILL LIFES) were combined with general physical characteristic terms (DRAWINGS, PAINTINGS, PHOTOGRAPHS, PRINTS) in order to provide a means for dividing up large files of catalog records indexed by a general term. For

---

(in the sense of engravings and lithographs) and retrieving instead photographic "prints."

example, an extensive file of portraits may be broken into categories for PORTRAIT DRAWINGS, PORTRAIT PAINTINGS, PORTRAIT PHOTOGRAPHS, and PORTRAIT PRINTS.

*TGM II* is not a theoretical list; rather, it is a practical representation of categories of material encountered at the Library of Congress and other extensive American historical collections. Standard reference sources and cataloging manuals (cited in the bibliography) were reviewed to find common vocabulary and determine relationship hierarchies. Some terms and their definitions were drawn from colleagues' personal knowledge. Other thesauri, especially the *Art and Architecture Thesaurus* (*AAT*) and the *Library of Congress Subject Headings* (*LCSH*), are always consulted for terms to incorporate into this graphic materials thesaurus. *TGM II* terms match *AAT* or *LCSH* vocabulary in order to simplify retrieval in union catalogs. A paper authority file record documents the sources or literary warrant for each *TGM II* term.

None of the consulted sources could serve as a single thesaurus for historical graphic materials. Because they are either too narrowly focused and detailed for highly diverse collections of graphic materials, too general in the terminology related to graphic materials, or incomplete in areas such as pictorial ephemera, the existing lists do not have an appropriate relationship structure for the desired universe of terms. In addition, most lack definitions or guidelines for application that would help catalogers and researchers in graphic collections use the thesaurus. It is expected that terms for genre and physical types occurring less frequently in pictorial collections (e.g., ALMANACS or DIARIES) can be taken from the authorized thesaurus most appropriate for the particular type of non-pictorial material.

## V. CATALOGING APPLICATIONS

Institutions should formulate written policies for assigning terms in their own systems. For example, users can choose, based on their institutions, whether to assign all terms to MARC field 655 or to distinguish between MARC fields 655 and 755. Automated or manual system considerations as well as indexing practices would guide this decision. Bibliographic networks may provide members with many necessary guidelines. Conformance to established book cataloging and indexing conventions is recommended for pictorial material; however, in some circumstances a departure from usual practice is justified. The guidelines here reflect practices developed and ongoing in the Library of Congress Prints and Photographs Division and may be helpful for other pictorial collections having manual files or MARC and non-MARC automated files.[8]

*TGM II* is part of a set of tools developed specifically to address various aspects of picture cataloging. Others are: the descriptive cataloging manual *Graphic Materials: Rules for Describing Original Items and Historical Collections*, which supplements the *Anglo-American Cataloguing Rules* (2nd ed. revised); the *Thesaurus for Graphic Materials I: Subject Terms* (companion to this thesaurus), which provides an extensive list of topical subject headings to be used in MARC field 650.

---

[8] More detailed explanations of these cataloging concepts can be found in the introduction to *TGM I* and in Toni Petersen and Patricia J. Barnett, ed., "Local Policy and Procedural Issues," in *Guide to Indexing and Cataloging with the Art & Architecture Thesaurus* (New York: Oxford University Press, 1994), 61-77.

# 1. Level of specificity.

**1.1.** Indexing conventions usually prescribe that the most specific term be assigned to the material being cataloged. The choice of terms also depends on the use of the collections, the degree of available information, the relationship of the material being cataloged to the rest of the institution's holdings, staff expertise, and whether the catalog record represents a single item or a group of items. Decisions about the level of specificity should also take into account the needs of a growing manual file or local automated database and the possibility of contributing records to a multi-institutional database, or other modes of record distribution.

**1.2.** If uncertain of a specific physical process, assign a broader term. Although terms are available for use when a process is recognized, one should not feel compelled to try to identify every process as specifically as possible in every case.

Example: When a color photographic print process cannot be easily identified, PHOTOGRAPHIC PRINTS--COLOR may suffice.

**1.3.** In accordance with conventional subject indexing practice, a narrower term and its broader term should not both occur in a record for a single item. However, for a group, it may be appropriate to assign both broader and narrower terms.

Example: An aquatint is indexed with: AQUATINTS. The additional broader term INTAGLIO PRINTS would be superfluous.

Example: A group that contains mostly cyanotypes, but also has a scattering of many other photo processes, may be indexed with: CYANOTYPES and the broader term PHOTOGRAPHIC PRINTS.

**1.4.** Conventional indexing rules prescribe use of the broader term when more than three of its narrower terms would be headings in the catalog record. The desire for access to examples of specific media and genre in a group may call for deviation from this practice and use of all the terms. When, however, the specific aspects are considered too numerous to index separately, either in a group or single item, the practice of using the broader term should be followed.

Example: A group containing a photographer's work includes mostly platinum prints but also has a few cyanotypes and tintypes. Each type is indexed because it is important to highlight them all in the context of the institution's holdings.

Example: The kinds of ephemera in a scrapbook are too numerous to index separately. The general term EPHEMERA is used.

Example: A drawing includes graphite, chalk, and crayon, and no one medium predominates. The general term DRAWINGS is used.

# 2. Exhaustivity in indexing.

**2.1.** It is not always necessary or appropriate to assign genre and physical characteristic terms. An institution may decide to index only selected material to exemplify a particular genre or physical type in its collections. P&P usually assigns a physical characteristic term to assist retrieval by media categories. It is based on the physical description vocabulary in MARC field 300. Pictures with clear topical subjects do not invariably need a genre term just for the sake of using the 655 field. (In fact, CITYSCAPES, GENRE WORKS, LANDSCAPES, PORTRAITS, and STILL LIFES are genre terms that are intended chiefly for assignment in the absence of other subject matter. They are not meant for every image of a city, domestic scene, mountain, or person.)

**2.2.** More than one term may be needed to express the various categories an item or group represents. The 655 and 755 fields are repeatable for this reason. Although without specified limits, selectivity in the number of terms assigned is recommended.

Example: An allegorical crayon drawing made in memory of a dead hero and intended to illustrate a magazine article, but then never published, could be indexed with: ALLEGORICAL DRAWINGS (655), MEMORIAL WORKS (655), PERIODICAL ILLUSTRATIONS (655), PROPOSED WORKS (655), and CRAYON DRAWINGS (755).

## 3. Double indexing.

**3.1.** When a genre frequently has the same physical characteristics associated with it, both aspects are not necessarily indexed.

Example: Most POSTCARDS (655) are PHOTOMECHANICAL PRINTS (755), and many CATALOGS (655) are PAMPHLETS (755). In such cases, the 655 term alone may be sufficient.

Example: For a less common combination of genre and physical characteristic, such as albumen stereographs, both STEREOGRAPHS (655) and ALBUMEN PRINTS (755) are used.

**3.2.** The same principle applies to terms for the instrument of application. Since most GRAPHITE DRAWINGS are made with pencils, it is not necessary to index under PENCIL WORKS unless there is a particular reason to draw attention to that aspect.

**3.3.** Terms are related in the thesaurus (RT) when their definitions overlap and, sometimes, when the categories frequently occur together. It is generally not necessary to index under both terms; rather, the researcher should be encouraged to use the thesaurus to be guided from one term to the other.

Example: STEREOGRAPHS, which are predominantly CARD PHOTOGRAPHS, are linked through the RT notation and are not double indexed with both terms.

## 4. Basis for cataloging.

**4.1.** Catalog the material in hand, not its original source or the broader work.

Example: An engraving of a prairie log cabin in a book about the westward expansion of the United States is indexed with: BOOK ILLUSTRATIONS (655), ENGRAVINGS (755), and LOG CABINS (650). It is not indexed by the subject(s) or genre of the larger work. An author/title added entry could be made for the book.

**4.2.** Institutions often provide photographic, microform, or quick copy reproductions of pictures as reference substitutes for originals held by the institution. In general, cataloging should be based on the original material even when only the surrogate is in hand. Information about the availability, arrangement, and type of copies is put in the note area of the catalog record (MARC fields 500 and 530), and the physical characteristics of the copy are not indexed in fields 655 and 755. An alternative approach is to catalog the item in hand, even if it is a reproduction, and link the record for the reproduction to the record for the original item. This is usually done with multiple versions of published audiovisual or microfilm material.

## 5. *TGM II* terms as subjects and in other fields of the catalog record.

**5.1.**     When an image depicts recognizable types of graphic materials, a genre or physical characteristic term may be used as a topical heading (MARC field 650).  The genre or physical type shown in the picture is its subject.

Example:  A newspaper engraving of a family viewing stereographs is indexed with: PERIODICAL ILLUSTRATIONS (655), WOOD ENGRAVINGS (755), and STEREOGRAPHS (650).

Example:  A stereograph of a family viewing stereographs is indexed with: STEREOGRAPHS (755) and STEREOGRAPHS (650).

Example:  An engraved self-portrait of an artist making a self-portrait is indexed with: SELF-PORTRAITS (655), ENGRAVINGS (755), and SELF-PORTRAITS (650).

**5.2.**     Occasionally, one genre imitates another, and the genre being imitated becomes the subject.

Example:  A cartoon designed to look like a piece of currency is indexed with CARTOONS (655) and MONEY (650).

**5.3.**     In anticipation of the need for 655 and 755 terms as subjects, all *TGM II* terms have been  incorporated in the *Thesaurus for Graphic Materials I: Subject Terms*, which is an authorized source for terms in MARC field 650.  Only the postable and lead-in terms appear, not the scope notes or full syndetic structure.

**5.4.**     For consistency in cataloging, terms are suitable for use in other areas of the record, such as the physical description (MARC field 300) or a note field (MARC field 500).  The thesaurus terms may be supplemented in the physical description and notes by uncontrolled vocabulary in order to describe material in greater detail.

## 6. Subdivisions.

**6.1.**     **General practice**.  Any term in *TGM II* may be subdivided in order to indicate certain information and to subarrange files of headings.  The MARC format provides for three types of subdivisions:

> -- general (subfield x)
> -- chronological (subfield y)
> -- geographic (subfield z).

Subdivisions need not be used with all terms, nor at all times, but a consistent practice should be developed. Although no order for these subfields is specified, the following pattern is recommended both for manual and automated catalogs: [thesaurus term]--[general subdivision]--[geographic subdivision]--[date subdivision]. Nationality and presence of color are general subdivisions that are frequently used. A suggested sequence of subdivisions has been used in most of these examples:

(1) nationality; (2) color; (3) date.

And, when reproductions are being described, this sequence is suggested:

(1) nationality; (2) date; (3) reproductions; (4) color of reproduction.

Examples:    LITHOGRAPHS--1850-1900.
               LITHOGRAPHS--FRENCH--1850-1900.
               LITHOGRAPHS--FRENCH--COLOR--1850-1900.
               LITHOGRAPHS--FRENCH--1850-1900--REPRODUCTIONS--COLOR.

**6.2.    Color.** Two general subdivisions (COLOR and HAND-COLORED) may be used with physical characteristic terms, whether or not those terms imply coloring. The subdivision COLOR refers to material in which color is an inherent part of the original creation. The subdivision HAND-COLORED refers to material to which color is applied in a later stage, by hand, stencil, or other method. When in doubt as to whether a piece is hand-colored, simply use COLOR. (This practice replaces the first edition's distinction of COLOR and COLORED.)

Examples:  ALBUMEN PRINTS--HAND-COLORED--1860-1870.
             ENGRAVINGS--COLOR--1800-1900.
             CHROMOLITHOGRAPHS--GERMAN--COLOR--1890.

**6.3.    Nationality.** The adjectival form of a country's name may also be used as a general subdivision to draw attention to the artist's nationality or the country in which the work was produced.

Examples:  POSTERS--FRENCH--1700-1750.
             ENGRAVINGS--MEXICAN--HAND-COLORED--1900-1910.
             PRINTS--AMERICAN--1900-1910.

Use the name of the country or U.S. state, possibly with a city name, to draw attention to the local place of publication or manufacture.

Example:  BROADSIDES--RHODE ISLAND--PROVIDENCE--1820.

Possible principles to follow are to subdivide by nationality in all cases; to subdivide by nationality when the material is unpublished (and by country of production when published); or to subdivide by both facets.

Examples:  TRAVEL SKETCHES--JAPANESE--1900.
             STEREOGRAPHS--ENGLAND--HAND-COLORED--1860.
             POLITICAL CARTOONS--FRENCH--FRANCE--PARIS--1700-1750.

**6.4.    Geographic subdivisions** are expressed "indirectly," i.e., with the larger jurisdiction preceding the smaller, as outlined in the Library of Congress *Cataloging Service Bulletin* 120 (1977), pp. 9-11.  The geographic place refers to where the material was made, not the place depicted.

Example:  POSTERS--INDIA--1960-1970.

**6.5.    Reproductions.**  The term REPRODUCTIONS may be used as a free-floating subdivision whenever the material being cataloged is a copy photograph, facsimile reprint, or other type of reproduction, and it is important to provide access by the medium of the original work.

Example:  A copy photograph, made in 1920, of an oil portrait painting from 1750, could be indexed with three headings.

> PORTRAIT PAINTINGS--1750--REPRODUCTIONS.
> OIL PAINTINGS--1750--REPRODUCTIONS.
> PHOTOGRAPHIC PRINTS--1920.

**6.6.    Chronological subdivision.**  Each institution must determine its own scheme for chronological subdivision. The date should be the cataloged material's date of creation, not the date of the subject depicted.  One useful practice is to use inclusive decade spans, as shown in the examples here.  Another option is to use the single year or span of years from the descriptive portion of the record, as outlined in *Graphic Materials*.

**6.7.    Manual files.**  These subdivision patterns can also be used in manual files.  In addition, some format-oriented genre headings may make useful subdivisions for topical terms to compensate for the lack of postcoordinate searching capability.  For example, TOBACCO--ADVERTISEMENTS; SLAVERY--BROADSIDES; PATENT MEDICINES--LABELS; WOMEN--PORTRAITS.

## 7. MARC Coding.

In a MARC record, terms from *TGM II* are to be entered in subfield "a" of fields 655 or 755.  Terms which do not appear in *TGM II* or other thesauri approved for 655 and 755 may not be used in these fields.  The thesaurus code (**gmgpc**) must be entered in subfield "2".  Even though the name of the thesaurus has been changed, the same code--**gmgpc**--should be used.

Examples:        655-7‡aCircus posters‡zOhio‡zToledo‡y1900-1910.‡2gmgpc
                 755  ‡aChromolithographs‡xColor‡y1900-1910.‡2gmgpc

## 8. Multiple thesauri.

Terms from *TGM II* may be used when cataloging pictorial materials in MARC formats other than Visual Materials.[9]  For example, a catalog record for an illustrated book may include such terms as PHOTOGRAVURES or WOODBURYTYPES; or a catalog record for a manuscript collection may include such terms as PORTRAITS and PHOTOGRAPHIC PRINTS.  Likewise, non-pictorial terms from other authorized thesauri may need to be used in records that describe graphic collections with non-pictorial material.  The appropriate thesaurus source code should be indicated for each heading.

---

[9] *TGM II* has been approved for rare book and special materials cataloging by the Standards Committee of the Rare Books and Manuscripts Section, Association of College and Research Libraries, American Library Association.

Examples:          655-7‡aAutobiographies.‡2rbgenr
                   655-7‡aPhotograph albums.‡2gmgpc


## VI. REVISIONS

New terms, corrections, and alterations to terms, scope notes, and references are solicited. Any new term proposal should be accompanied by notes and references. Correspondence regarding *TGM II* should be addressed to:

> Editor, TGM II/Sarah Rouse
> Prints and Photographs Division
> Library of Congress
> Washington, D.C. 20540-4840

Automated editions of *TGM II* are expected to become available through one or more of the following avenues: Internet (with Lexico software or as a text file); Cataloger's Desktop on CD-ROM; ASCII text file on diskette. No work has begun, however, to convert the terms to the USMARC Authority Format. Expressions of interest in a particular automated format would be appreciated.

## VII. EXAMPLES

Example 1.  Single print.

100   Dürer, Albrecht, 1471-1528, artist.
245   [Draftsman drawing a lute] [graphic] / AD.
260   1525.
300   1 print : woodcut.
520   Depicts draftsman drawing a lute using a device for accurate perspective drawing.
510   Illustrated Bartsch, sixteenth century German artists, Albrecht Dürer / Adam von Bartsch ; edited by Walter
      L. Strauss. New York : Abaris Books, 1981, no. 1001.347.
650   Lutes--1520-1530.
650   Drawing--1520-1530.
650   Perspective projections--1520-1530.
755   Woodcuts--German--1520-1530.

Example 2.  Group of photographs.

100     Collier, John, 1913-  photographer.
245     Home and life of Juan Lopez, majordomo (mayor), Trampas, New Mexico.
260     1943.
300     106 photographs : silver gelatin ; 8 x 10 in.
520     Photographs depict Juan Lopez, his wife Maclovia Lopez, his children, his 99 year-old grandfather Romero; domestic activities; cutting down dead tree, marked by U.S. forest ranger, for firewood; religious statues; photographs and family portraits on walls; corrals and ranch with horses.
500     Office of War Information Collection.
500     Corresponding negatives are in series LC-USW3.
530     Use microfilm for reference service.
600     Lopez, Juan--Family--New Mexico--Trampas.
650     Family life--New Mexico--Trampas--1940-1950.
650     Ranches--New Mexico--Trampas--1940-1950.
650     Tree cutting--New Mexico--Trampas--1940-1950.
650     Dwellings--New Mexico--Trampas--1940-1950.
650     Interiors--New Mexico--Trampas--1940-1950.
650     Portraits--1940-1950.
650     Photographs--1940-1950.
655     Group portraits--1940-1950.
655     Portrait photographs--1940-1950.
755     Silver gelatin prints--1940-1950.

The following examples are not accompanied by images.  They are included to show possible treatments of various genre and physical characteristics.

Example 3.  Pictorial album; MARC coding with subfields.

| | | |
|---|---|---|
| 245 | 00 | ǂaAlbum pintoresco de la Isla de Cubaǂh[graphic] |
| 260 | | ǂa[Berlin?] :ǂbB. May y Ca.,ǂc1858? |
| 300 | | ǂa1 v. (28 chromolithographs, 2 maps) ;ǂc26 x 36 cm. |
| 500 | | ǂaTitle from cover. |
| 650 | -7 | ǂaFishingǂy1850-1860.ǂ2lctgm |
| 651 | -0 | ǂaCuba. |
| 655 | -7 | ǂaAlbumsǂzGermanyǂy1850-1860.ǂ2gmgpc |
| 655 | -7 | ǂCaricaturesǂzGermanyǂy1850-1860.ǂ2gmgpc |
| 655 | -7 | ǂaLandscape printsǂzGermanyǂy1850-1860.ǂ2gmgpc |
| 655 | -7 | ǂaMapsǂzGermanyǂy1850-1860.ǂ2gmgpc |
| 710 | 21 | ǂaB. May (Firm),ǂepublisher |
| 755 | | ǂaChromolithographsǂzGermanyǂy1850-1860.ǂ2gmgpc |

Example 4.  Group of slides; physical description.

| | |
|---|---|
| 300 | 12 slides : Kodachrome ; 35 mm. |
| 755 | Dye coupler transparencies--1940-1950. |
| 755 | Slides--Color--1940-1950. |

Example 5.  Mixed media; physical description and note.

| | |
|---|---|
| 300 | 1 drawing and painting ; 12 x 15 cm. |
| 500 | Pen, pencil, ink, and graphite with blue and green paint. |
| 655 | Travel sketches--French--1960-1970. |
| 755 | Mixed media--French--1960-1970. |

Example 6.  Reproduction (fictitious item).

| | |
|---|---|
| 100 | Johnston, Mary, photographer. |
| 245 | George Washington / M. Johnston. |
| 260 | [ca. 1850] |
| 300 | 1 photograph : daguerreotype, hand-colored ; 8.5 x 6.5 cm. |
| 500 | Photograph of painting by Gilbert Stuart, dated 1795. |
| 600 | Washington, George, 1732-1799. |
| 655 | Portrait paintings--1790-1800--Reproductions. |
| 700 | Stuart, Gilbert, 1755-1828, artist. |
| 755 | Daguerreotypes--Hand-colored--1850. |

Example 7.  Extensive collection including negatives; title and physical description.

| | |
|---|---|
| 245 | U.S. News and World Report Magazine Photograph Collection (Library of Congress) [graphic]. |
| 300 | ca. 45,500 contact sheets (1,182,500 images) : b&w and some color ; 9 x 12 in. or smaller. |
| 300 | ca. 1,182,400 film negatives : b&w and some color ; 35 mm., 2 ¼ in., 5 x 7 in., and 8 x 10 in. |
| 655 | Group portraits. |
| 655 | Periodical illustrations. |
| 655 | Portrait photographs. |
| 755 | Contact sheets. |
| 755 | Film negatives--Color. |
| 755 | Film transparencies--Color. |
| 755 | Photographs. |

Example 8.  Cartoon drawing for a periodical.

| | |
|---|---|
| 100 | Bimrose, Art, 1912- artist. |
| 245 | It's spring again [graphic] / Art Bimrose. |
| 260 | 1953 April 11. |
| 300 | 1 drawing. |
| 520 | Cartoon shows boy and girl (labeled AFL and CIO) carving overlapping hearts (labeled merger talks) on a tree. Refers to renewed efforts to combine the American Federation of Labor and the Congress of Industrial Organizations in 1953. |
| 581 | Published in The Oregonian. |
| 610 | American Federation of Labor--1950-1960. |
| 610 | Congress of Industrial Organizations (U.S.)--1950-1960. |
| 650 | Labor unions--1950-1960. |
| 650 | Courtship--1950-1960. |
| 655 | Periodical illustrations--1950-1960. |
| 655 | Editorial cartoons--1950-1960. |
| 755 | Drawings--American--1950-1960. |

Example 9.  Group containing several types of photographs.

| | |
|---|---|
| 245 | Portraits of Native Americans from Plains tribes [graphic]. |
| 260 | c1882-c1949. |
| 300 | 78 photographs : silver gelatin or albumen ; 20 x 28 cm. or smaller. |
| 500 | Includes several cabinet photographs, several images on postcard stock, and several formatted for stereograph mounts. |
| 655 | Photographic postcards. |
| 655 | Portrait photographs. |
| 655 | Group portraits. |
| 755 | Albumen photographs. |
| 755 | Silver gelatin prints. |
| 755 | Cabinet photographs. |
| 755 | Stereographs. |

Example 10.  Stereograph; the object term is also the subject.

| | |
|---|---|
| 110 | Keystone View Company. |
| 245 | Still there's no place like home [graphic]. |
| 260 | Meadville, Pa. : Keystone View Company, manufacturers, publishers, c1915. |
| 300 | 1 photographic print on stereo card : stereograph. |
| 520 | Family in parlor viewing stereographs. |
| 650 | Families. |
| 650 | Stereographs. |
| 755 | Stereographs. |
| 755 | Photographic prints. |

# TGM II: BIBLIOGRAPHY

Many reference sources were consulted to select terms and compile the definitions. The selection listed here is limited to those which cover several processes or common formats. Most have illustrations and also contain additional citations which would be useful if more extensive study of particular material is desired. Thesauri authorized for fields 655 and 755 are marked with an asterisk.

*ALA Glossary of Library and Information Science*, ed. by Heartsill Young. Chicago: American Library Association, 1983.

*\*Art & Architecture Thesaurus*. 2d ed. New York: Oxford University Press, on behalf of the Getty Art History Information Program, 1994. 5 vols.

*Association of College and Research Libraries, Rare Books and Manuscripts Section, Standards Committee or Bibliographic Standards Committee. Chicago: Association of College and Research Libraries
   *Binding Terms: A Thesaurus for Use in Rare Book and Special Collections Cataloguing*. 1988.
   *Genre Terms: A Thesaurus for Use in Rare Book and Special Collections Cataloguing*. 2d ed. 1991.
   *Paper Terms: A Thesaurus for Use in Rare Book and Special Collections Cataloguing*. 1990.
   *Printing and Publishing Evidence: Thesauri for Use in Rare Book and Special Collections Cataloguing*. 1986.
   *Provenance Evidence: A Thesaurus for Use in Rare Book and Special Collections Cataloguing*. 1988.
   *Type Evidence: A Thesaurus for Use in Rare Book and Special Collections Cataloguing*. 1990.

Baldwin, Gordon. *Looking at Photographs: A Guide to Technical Terms*. Malibu, Calif.: J. Paul Getty Museum in association with British Museum Press, 1991.

Barnicoat, John. *Posters: A Concise History*. London: Thames and Hudson, 1985.

Béguin, André. *A Technical Dictionary of Print Making*, trans. by Allen J. Grieco. Brussells, Belgium: Béguin, 1981-1982. 2 vols., A-L.

Betz, Elisabeth W., comp. *Graphic Materials: Rules for Describing Original Items and Historical Collections*. Washington, D.C.: Library of Congress, 1982.

Bly, Robert W. *Create the Perfect Sales Piece*. New York: John Wiley & Sons, Inc., 1985.

*Bookman's Glossary*, ed. by Jean Peters. 6th ed. New York: Bowker, 1983.

Brenni, Vito J. *Book Illustration and Decoration: A Guide to Research*. Westport, Conn.: Greenwood Press, 1980.

Brunner, Felix. *A Handbook of Graphic Reproduction Processes* ... [English version: Dennis Qu. Stephenson] 4th ed. Teufen, Switzerland: Arthur Niggli, 1972.

Burdick, Jefferson. *The American Card Catalog: The Standard Guide on All Collected Cards and Their Values*. East Stroudsburg, Pa.: Kistler Printing, 1960.

Chenhall, Robert G. *The Revised Nomenclature for Museum Cataloging: A Revised and Expanded Version of Robert G. Chenhall's System for Classifying Man-made Objects*. Nashville, Tenn.: AASLH Press, 1988.

Clarke, Carl D. *Illustration: Its Technique and Application to the Sciences*. Baltimore, Md.: John D. Lucas Company, 1940.

Coe, Brian. *Cameras*. New York: Crown Publishers, 1978.

Coe, Brian. *Colour Photography: The First Hundred Years, 1840-1940*. London: Ash & Grant, 1978.

Coe, Brian and Mark Haworth-Booth. *A Guide to Early Photographic Processes*. London: Victoria and Albert Museum, 1983.

Darrah, William C. *Cartes de Visite in Nineteenth Century Photography*. Gettysburg, Pa.: Darrah, 1981.

Darrah, William C. *The World of Stereographs*. Gettysburg, Pa.: Darrah, 1977.

Ebert, John and Katherine. *Old American Prints for Collectors*. New York: Scribner, 1974.

Ehrenberg, Ralph E. *Archives & Manuscripts: Maps and Architectural Drawings*. Chicago: Society of American Archivists, 1982. (SAA Basic Manual Series)

*Encyclopedia of Architecture: Design, Engineering & Construction*. New York: Wiley, 1988-1989.

*Ephemera News*. Bennington, Vt.: Ephemera Society of America., 1981-    .

*Ephemerist*. London: Ephemera Society, 1975-    .

Eskind, Andrew H. and Deborah Bassel. "International Museum of Photography at George Eastman House Conventions for Cataloging Photographs." *Image* 21 (December 1978): 1-31.

*Focal Encyclopedia of Photography*. 3rd ed. Boston: Focal Press, 1993.

Gascoigne, Bamber. *How to Identify Prints: A Complete Guide to Manual and Mechanical Processes from Woodcut to Ink Jet*. [London]: Thames and Hudson, 1986.

Gill, Arthur T. *Photographic Processes, a Glossary and a Chart for Recognition*. London: Museums Association, 1978.

Goldman, Paul. *Looking at Prints, Drawings and Watercolours: A Guide to Technical Terms*. London: British Museum Publications in association with the J. Paul Getty Museum, 1988.

Haller, Margaret. *Collecting Old Photographs*. New York: Arco, 1978.

Harris, Cyril, ed. *Dictionary of Architecture and Construction*. 2d ed. New York: McGraw-Hill, 1993.

Hendricks, Klaus B. *Preservation and Restoration of Photographic Materials in Archives and Libraries: A RAMP Study*. Paris: UNESCO, 1984.

Henry Francis du Pont Winterthur Museum. *Trade Catalogues at Winterthur ... 1750 to 1980*, comp. by E. Richard McKinstry. New York: Garland Pub., 1984.

Howard, Marian B. *Those Fascinating Paper Dolls*. Unabridged, corrected edition. New York: Dover, 1981.

International Center of Photography. *ICP Encyclopedia of Photography*. New York: Crown, 1984.

International Federation of Library Associations and Institutions (IFLA) Core Programme on Preservation and Conservation. *Care, Handling, and Storage of Photographs*. Washington, D.C.: Library of Congress, 1992.

International Organization for Standardization. *Documentation and Information Vocabulary, Part 3: Iconic Documents*. ISO 5127-3, 1988.

Jones, Bernard E., ed. *Cassell's Cyclopedia of Photography*. London, New York: Cassell, 1911.

Lewis, John. *Collecting Printed Ephemera*. London: Studio Vista, 1976.

*Library of Congress. Cataloging Policy and Support Office. *Library of Congress Subject Headings*. 17th ed. Washington, D.C.: Library of Congress, 1994. 4 vol.

Luzadder, Warren J. *Fundamentals of Engineering Drawing, With an Introduction to Interactive Computer Graphics for Design and Production*. 11th ed. Englewood Cliffs, N.J.: Prentice-Hall, 1993.

Marzio, Peter C. *The Democratic Art: Pictures for a 19th-Century America: Chromolithography 1840-1900*. Boston: D. R. Godine, 1979.

Mayer, Ralph. *The Harper Collins Dictionary of Art Terms and Techniques*. 2d ed. New York: Harper Perennial, 1992.

McCulloch, Lou W. *Card Photographs*. Exton, Pa.: Schiffer, 1981.

McCulloch, Lou W. *Paper Americana: A Collector's Guide*. San Diego: Barnes, 1980.

Mintz, Patricia B. *Dictionary of Graphic Arts Terms*. New York: Van Nostrand Reinhold, 1981.

National Information Standards Organization. *Guidelines for the Construction, Format, and Management of Monolingual Thesauri*. Bethesda, Md.: NISO Press, 1994. (NISO Z39.19 1994)

Petersen, Toni, and Patricia A. Barnett. *Guide to Indexing and Cataloging with the Art and Architecture Thesaurus*. New York: Oxford University Press, 1994.

Pitts, Terence and Sharon Denton. *CREATE: A Procedure Manual for Cataloging Photographs*. 2d. ed. Tucson, Az.: Center for Creative Photography, 1984.

Quick, John. *Artists' and Illustrators' Encyclopedia*. 2d ed. New York: McGraw-Hill, 1977.

*Random House Dictionary of the English Language*. 2d ed. New York: Random House, 1987.

Range, Thomas E. *The Book of Postcard Collecting*. New York: Dutton, 1980.

Redsicker, David R. *The Practical Methodology of Forensic Photography*. New York: Elsevier, 1991.

Reilly, James. *The Albumen & Salted Paper Book*. Rochester, N.Y.: Light Impressions, 1980.

Reilly, James. *Care and Identification of 19th-Century Photographic Prints*. Rochester, New York: Eastman Kodak, 1986.

Reps, John W. *Views and Viewmakers of Urban America*. Columbia, Mo.: University of Missouri Press, 1984.

Rickards, Maurice. *This Is Ephemera: Collecting Printed Throwaways*. Brattleboro, Vt.: Gossamer Press, 1977.

Rickards, Maurice. *Collecting Printed Ephemera*. New York: Abbeville Press, 1988.

Rinhart, Floyd and Marion. *The American Daguerreotype*. Athens, Ga.: University of Georgia Press, 1981.

Ritzenthaler, Mary Lynn, et al. *Archives & Manuscripts: Administration of Photographic Collections*. Chicago: Society of American Archivists, 1984. (SAA Basic Manual Series).

Roberts, Michael J. *Construction Industry Thesaurus*. 2d ed. London: Property Services Agency, Department of the Environment, 1976.

Rosenblum, Naomi. *A World History of Photography*. New York: Abbeville Press, 1984.

Saff, Donald and Deli Sacilotto. *Printmaking: History and Process*. New York: Holt, Rinehart and Winston, 1978.

Sturgis, Russell. *A Dictionary of Architecture and Building*. New York: Macmillan, 1901-1902. 3 vols.

*Webster's New Collegiate Dictionary*. Springfield, Mass.: Merriam, 1981.

*Webster's Third New International Dictionary of the English Language, Unabridged*. Springfield, Mass.: Merriam, 1961.

Weidhaas, Ernest R. *Architectural Drafting and Design*. 6th ed. Boston: Allyn and Bacon, 1989.

Welling, William B. *Collector's Guide to Nineteenth-Century Photographs*. New York: Macmillan, 1976.

Whitehouse, P.B. *Railway Relics and Regalia*. London; New York: Hamlyn for Country Life, 1975.

Wilhelm, Henry, with Carol Brower. *The Permanence and Care of Color Photographs: Traditional and Digital Color Prints, Color Negatives, Slides, and Motion Pictures*. Grinnell, Ia.: Preservation Publishing Co., 1993.

Witkin, Lee D. and Barbara London. *The Photograph Collector's Guide*. Boston: New York Graphic Society, 1979.

Woodbury, Walter E. *The Encyclopaedic Dictionary of Photography*. New York: Scovill & Adams, 1898. Reprint. New York: Arno Press, 1979.

Woods, Robert. *Printing and Production for Promotional Materials*. New York: Van Nostrand Reinhold Company, 1987.

*World Encyclopedia of Cartoons*, ed. by Maurice Horn. New York: Gale Research, 1980. 2 vols.

Zigrosser, Carl and Christa M. Gaehde. *A Guide to the Collecting and Care of Original Prints*. New York: Crown, 1965.

# TGM II:

# GENRE AND PHYSICAL CHARACTERISTIC TERMS

**A la poupée prints**
- PN  Color prints made by simultaneously inking separate areas of the same plate or block with different colors, before printing.
- CN  MARC field 755.
- UF  Poupée prints
- BT  Prints
- RT  Intaglio prints
  - Relief prints

**A trois crayons drawings**
- PN  Chalk drawings in three colors, usually red, white, and black.
- CN  MARC field 755.
- UF  Three chalk drawings
  - Trois crayons drawings
- BT  Chalk drawings

**Äac prints**
- USE  Photochrom prints

**Abstract drawings**
- CN  MARC field 655.
- BT  Abstract works
  - Drawings

**Abstract paintings**
- CN  MARC field 655.
- BT  Abstract works
  - Paintings

**Abstract photographs**
- CN  MARC field 655.
- BT  Abstract works
  - Photographs

**Abstract prints**
- CN  MARC field 655.
- BT  Abstract works
  - Prints

**Abstract works**
- PN  Images in which the depiction of real objects has been subordinated or entirely discarded; especially non-representational images, stressing formal relationships of line, color, and shape.
- CN  MARC field 655.
- NT  Abstract drawings
  - Abstract paintings
  - Abstract photographs
  - Abstract prints

**Acetate negatives**
- PN  Acetate safety films were first introduced in the early 1900s. Various types include diacetate and triacetate and are often difficult to distinguish from one another.
- CN  MARC field 755.
- HN  Changed 6/94. Formerly, ACETATE NEGATIVES may have been indexed as CELLULOSE DIACETATE NEGATIVES or as CELLULOSE TRIACETATE NEGATIVES.
- UF  Cellulose acetate negatives
  - Cellulose diacetate negatives
  - Cellulose triacetate negatives
  - Diacetate negatives
  - Triacetate negatives
- BT  Safety film negatives

**Acrylic paintings**
- CN  MARC field 755.
- BT  Polymer paintings

**Action comics**
- USE  Adventure comics

**Adventure comics**
- PN  Comics featuring heroes and heroines involved in action-packed, danger-filled stories. Examples include Flash Gordon, Superman, and Tarzan.
- CN  MARC field 655.
- UF  Action comics
- BT  Comics
- RT  Comic books

**Advertisements**
- PN  Public notices of the availability of goods or services through purchase or other means.
- CN  Also index under BROADSIDES, HANDBILLS, POSTERS, or other appropriate form. MARC field 655.
- BT  Ephemera
- NT  Advertising cards +
  - Advertising mail
  - Display cards +
- RT  Fashion photographs
  - Fashion prints
  - Premiums
  - Publicity photographs

**Advertising cards**
- PN  Cards issued to promote goods or services. May have been distributed by merchants or enclosed as premiums with such products as bread, cigarettes, and coffee. Usually, cards bear seller or product name and a pictorial representation of the service or product. Picture may also be unrelated to the product.
- CN  MARC field 655.
- UF  Insert cards
  - Trading cards
- BT  Advertisements
  - Cards
- NT  Sailing cards +
  - Stock cards
  - Trade cards +
- RT  Business cards
  - Collecting cards
  - Sports cards

**Advertising mail**
- PN  Advertisements intended for distribution by mail.
- CN  MARC field 655.
- UF  Direct-mail advertising
  - Junk mail
- BT  Advertisements
- RT  Sales catalogs

**Aerial photographs**
- PN  Photographs taken from an air-borne vehicle within the earth's atmosphere, such as an airplane, balloon, or kite; from a camera strapped to a bird; or by a person, such as a parachutist, in flight. Use SPACE

---

BT  Broader term                    RT  Related term                    PN  Public Note
NT  Narrower term                   UF  Used for                        +  Term has NTs
HN  History Note                    CN  Catalogers Note

**Aerial photographs (cont.)**
      PHOTOGRAPHS for images taken from
      beyond the earth's atmosphere.
  CN  MARC field 755.
  BT  Aerial views
      Photographs
  RT  Space photographs
**Aerial views**
  PN  Views from a high vantage point.
  CN  MARC field 655.
  UF  Air views
      Balloon views
      Views, Aerial
  NT  Aerial photographs
  RT  Bird's-eye views
      Panoramic views
**Agfacolor transparencies**
  USE Dye coupler transparencies
**Air conditioning, heating, & ventilating drawings**
  USE HVAC drawings
**Air views**
  USE Aerial views
**Airbrush works**
  CN  MARC field 755.
  RT  Paintings
      Photographs
**Albertypes**
  USE Collotypes
**Album cards**
  PN  Collecting cards intended for display in
      albums; popular from about 1850 to 1890.
      They usually lack a publisher's name or date
      and do not have advertising on them.
  CN  MARC field 655.
  HN  Changed 10/90. Formerly, ALBUM
      CARDS may have been indexed as
      COLLECTING CARDS.
  BT  Collecting cards
**Album covers**
  PN  Containers for sound recordings; printed
      with graphic designs.
  CN  MARC field 655.
  HN  Changed 6/94. Formerly, ALBUM
      COVERS may have been indexed as
      RECORD JACKETS.
  UF  Covers, Album
      Covers, Record
      Jackets, Record
      Record covers
      Record jackets
      Sleeves, Record
  BT  Covers (Illustration)
**Albumen prints**
  PN  Predominant paper print photographic
      process in the 1800s; popular 1850s-1890s.
  CN  MARC field 755.
  BT  Silver printing-out paper prints
  RT  Crystoleum photographs
**Albumen transparencies**
  PN  Typically, glass lantern slides or
      stereographs; introduced 1849; largely
      replaced by collodion transparencies.

**Albumen transparencies (cont.)**
  CN  MARC field 755.
  UF  Hyalotypes
  BT  Glass transparencies
**Albums**
  PN  Bound or loose-leaf sets of pages. Includes
      handmade albums and published volumes of
      blank pages designed for the addition of
      images or keepsakes.
  CN  MARC field 655.
  HN  Changed 6/94. Formerly, some albums
      may have been indexed as SOUVENIR
      ALBUMS.
  UF  Souvenir albums
  NT  Photograph albums +
      Presentation albums
      Scrapbooks
      Sketchbooks
  RT  Sample books
**Allegorical drawings**
  CN  MARC field 655.
  BT  Allegories
      Drawings
**Allegorical paintings**
  CN  MARC field 655.
  BT  Allegories
      Paintings
**Allegorical photographs**
  CN  MARC field 655.
  BT  Allegories
      Photographs
**Allegorical prints**
  CN  MARC field 655.
  BT  Allegories
      Prints
**Allegories**
  PN  Representations of truths or
      generalizations about human existence by
      means of symbolic images; often of classical
      derivation.
  CN  MARC field 655.
  NT  Allegorical drawings
      Allegorical paintings
      Allegorical photographs
      Allegorical prints
  RT  Allusions
**Allusions**
  PN  Representations of or references to one
      work in another work. Does not include
      routine reproductions or works made "after"
      other works.
  CN  MARC field 655.
  RT  Allegories
**Amateur works**
  PN  Works created by people who are not
      full-time or professional practitioners in the
      medium or genre; often made for pleasure
      rather than money; does not refer to image
      quality.
  CN  MARC field 655.
  RT  Children's art
      Juvenilia

---

BT Broader term           RT Related term          PN Public Note
NT Narrower term          UF Used for             + Term has NTs
HN History Note           CN Catalogers Note

**Amateur works (cont.)**
 Snapshots
 Student works
**Ambrotypes**
 PN Direct-image photographs; the chemically
   reduced collodion glass negative packaged
   against a dark background appears as a
   positive. Commonly in a case; popular
   mid-1850s to mid-1860s.
 CN Used in a note under PHOTOGRAPHS.
   MARC field 755.
 UF Cased photographs
   Collodion positive photographs
 BT Photographs
**Anaglyphs**
 PN Photomechanical images in two
   contrasting colors, such as red and green.
   Printed either as a pair of images or as one
   image superimposed on the other but slightly
   out of registry. When viewed through a pair
   of lenses, each in the appropriate different
   color, a three-dimensional effect is created.
   Introduced in 1891; popular during the
   1920s.
 CN MARC field 755.
 BT Novelty works
   Photomechanical prints
   Stereographs
**Anamorphic images**
 PN Images produced by a distorting optical
   system or other method that renders an image
   unrecognizable unless viewed by the proper
   restoring device. Popular for prints and
   drawings in the 1600s and 1700s and for
   photographs in the 1800s. Images are often
   recorded as they appear in a convex or
   concave cylindrical mirror.
 CN MARC field 655.
 BT Novelty works
**Animation cels**
 PN Images on celluloid or polyester sheets,
   which are used to create an animated
   sequence for movie, videotape, or other
   moving image productions; usually drawings
   or paintings.
 CN MARC field 655.
 UF Cartoon cels
   Cels, Animation
**Announcements**
 PN Small notices of special occasions, such as
   weddings.
 CN MARC field 655.
 BT Ephemera
 RT Broadsides
   Invitations
**Anthropological photographs**
 USE Ethnographic photographs
**Aquatints**
 CN MARC field 755.
 BT Intaglio prints
 NT Sugar-lift aquatints
 RT Etchings

**Architectural drawings**
 PN Graphic delineations made for the design
   and construction (or documentation of design
   and construction) of sites, structures, details,
   fixtures, furnishings, and decorations, as well
   as other objects designed by an architect or
   architectural office.
 CN Also index under terms that express the
   type of projection or purpose, listed under
   PROJECTIONS and DESIGN DRAWINGS.
   Used in a note under ENGINEERING
   DRAWINGS, LANDSCAPE
   ARCHITECTURE DRAWINGS, and
   NAVAL ARCHITECTURE DRAWINGS.
   MARC field 655.
 UF Drawings, Architectural
 BT Design drawings
**Architectural photographs**
 PN Photographs made to record a structure for
   architects, architectural historians, and others
   who need clear representations of such
   aspects as construction phases, exteriors, or
   interiors. Not meant for every photo of a
   structure.
 CN MARC field 655.
 BT Photographs
 NT Progress photographs
**Aristotypes**
 PN Photographic prints made on various
   non-albumen papers. The trade name became
   a general term for prints made on collodion
   silver chloride printing-out papers (introduced
   in the 1860s) and was later applied to gelatin
   silver chloride papers (introduced in the
   1880s).
 CN MARC field 755.
 HN Changed 6/94. Formerly, ARISTOTYPES
   may have been indexed as COLLODION
   PRINTING-OUT PAPER PRINTS.
 BT Collodion printing-out paper prints
   Silver gelatin printing-out paper prints
**Armorial bearings**
 USE Coats of arms
**Armorial bookplates**
 PN Book plates bearing such heraldic devices
   as coats of arms.
 CN MARC field 655.
 UF Heraldic bookplates
 BT Bookplates
 RT Coats of arms
**Art by children**
 USE Children's art
**Art exhibition posters**
 USE Exhibition posters
**Art reproductions**
 PN Commercially published, mechanically
   printed copies of individual paintings, prints,
   drawings, and other two-dimensional works
   of art.
 CN MARC field 755.
 BT Reproductions
**Artists' devices**

---

BT Broader term      RT Related term      PN Public Note
NT Narrower term     UF Used for       + Term has NTs
HN History Note      CN Catalogers Note

**Artists' devices (cont.)**
PN    Designs, symbols, or mottoes used by
      artists to identify their creations.
CN    MARC field 755.
UF    Devices, Artists'
      Symbols, Artists'
BT    Emblems
RT    Artists' signatures
      Monograms
Artists' early works
   USE Juvenilia
**Artists' proofs**
PN    Prints which are accepted for an edition
      but are unnumbered or numbered separately
      from the edition and reserved for the artist's
      use.
CN    MARC field 755.
BT    Proofs
**Artists' signatures**
PN    Signatures of artists, photographers,
      painters, or printmakers on their own works.
CN    MARC field 755.
BT    Autographs
RT    Artists' devices
Artotypes
   USE Collotypes
**As-built drawings**
PN    Final set of working drawings
      incorporating (through revisions or
      annotations) any changes of dimensions,
      materials, form, and method of construction
      encountered in the completion of the structure
      or site.
CN    MARC field 655.
UF    Drawings, As-built
BT    Working drawings
**Auction catalogs**
CN    MARC field 655.
BT    Catalogs
**Autochromes**
PN    The Lumière brothers began marketing
      autochromes in 1907, and the color glass
      transparencies continued to be available into
      the 1930s.
CN    MARC field 755.
HN    Changed 5/89. Formerly,
      AUTOCHROMES may have been indexed as
      SCREEN COLOR GLASS
      PHOTOTRANSPARENCIES.
BT    Screen color glass transparencies
**Autographs**
PN    Names of people written in their own
      hand; stamped or printed signatures are not
      included.
CN    MARC field 755.
BT    Inscriptions
NT    Artists' signatures
Autotypes
   USE Carbon prints
Avant des lettres prints
   USE Proofs before letters
Awards of merit

Awards of merit (cont.)
   USE Rewards of merit
**Axonometric projections**
PN    Parallel orthographic projections in which
      the object or subject is tilted in relation to the
      picture plane so that three faces and axes are
      visible although not in true shape.
CN    MARC field 655.
BT    Projections
NT    Isometric projections
**Badges**
PN    Devices indicating support of a cause,
      achievements, or membership in a society or
      group. May be printed, photographic, plastic,
      metal, cloth, or other fabric; usually intended
      to be worn on the person.
CN    MARC field 655.
UF    Button badges
      Ribbon badges
BT    Ephemera
RT    Memorabilia
**Bags**
PN    Sacks, usually rectangular in shape and
      made of paper, plastic, or cloth; often printed
      with manufacturer's name or advertisement.
CN    MARC field 655.
UF    Sacks
BT    Packaging
Balloon views
   USE Aerial views
      Bird's-eye views
      Panoramic views
**Ballots**
PN    Sheets of paper, cards, or other devices
      used to cast a vote or announce a slate of
      candidates.
CN    MARC field 655.
UF    Election tickets
BT    Ephemera
**Bank note vignettes**
PN    Engraved decorations primarily designed
      for use on bank notes or other currency but
      also commonly used on stock certificates and
      other securities. Pictorial or ornamental
      images from the 1790s to the present.
CN    MARC field 655.
UF    Security engravings
BT    Vignettes
RT    Certificates
      Money
**Bank notes**
PN    Promissory notes issued by banks, payable
      to bearer on demand without interest, and
      circulating as money.
CN    MARC field 655.
BT    Money
**Banners**
PN    Sheets of cloth, plastic, or paper intended
      for hanging or other public display.
CN    MARC field 655.
BT    Signs
**Banquet camera photographs**

---

**Banquet camera photographs (cont.)**
PN   Photographs made from a fixed
       wide-angle-lens camera capable of producing
       a sharp image of great depth. Usually
       photographs of large groups of people.  One
       camera, marketed 1913-1926, produced prints
       of 7 x 17 in. (18 x 43 cm.) and 12 x 20 in. (30
       x 51 cm.).
CN   MARC field 755.
BT   Photographs
**Baptismal certificates**
CN   MARC field 655.
BT   Certificates
**Baseball cards**
PN   Advertising or collectible cards that
       feature portraits of baseball players, other
       people, or topics associated with the game.
       Introduced in 1886 or 1887 by a tobacco
       company; also popular with bubble gum
       manufacturers beginning in the 1930s.
       Common sizes include 1.5 x 2.5 inches, 2.5 x
       3.5 inches, and ca. 5 x 8 inches.  The cards
       may be actual photographs mounted on card
       stock or photomechanically printed.
CN   MARC field 655.
BT   Sports cards
Beefcake photographs
   USE Glamour photographs
Before & after views
   USE Then & now comparisons
Bellmen's verses
   USE Carriers' addresses
**Bible cards**
PN   Cards with a scriptural picture or
       quotation, or both. Sometimes issued in sets
       and often used as rewards of merit in Sunday
       schools.
CN   MARC field 655.
UF   Scripture cards
       Sunday school cards
BT   Devotional images
RT   Collecting cards
       Rewards of merit
**Billboard posters**
PN   Large multi-sheet posters; intended for
       posting on billboards, fences, or similar
       surfaces.
CN   MARC field 655.
BT   Posters
**Billheads**
PN   Documents for itemized accounts of the
       separate cost of goods sold or shipped, or
       services performed; pictorial or
       typographically decorated.
CN   MARC field 655.
BT   Stationery
Bills of fare
   USE Menus
**Bird's-eye view prints**
PN   Bird's-eye views of cities and towns that
       are lithographs, engravings, or other types of
       prints including photomechanical ones.

**Bird's-eye view prints (cont.)**
       Popular in the United States 1870-1910s, but
       also made earlier.
CN   Used in a note under BIRD'S-EYE
       VIEWS.  MARC field 655.
UF   Panoramic maps
BT   Bird's-eye views
       Prints
RT   Cityscape prints
**Bird's-eye views**
PN   Graphic representations of scenes
       portrayed as if viewed from above at an
       oblique angle.  If of a city or town, not
       generally drawn strictly to scale but showing
       street patterns, individual buildings, and
       major landscape features in perspective.
CN   For the class of engravings, lithographs,
       and photomechanical prints commonly known
       as bird's-eye views, use BIRD'S-EYE VIEW
       PRINTS. Do not use for photographs. MARC
       field 655.
UF   Balloon views
       Views, Bird's-eye
NT   Bird's-eye view prints
RT   Aerial views
       Maps
       Panoramic views
       Projections
**Birth certificates**
CN   MARC field 655.
BT   Certificates
RT   Family trees
**Birthday cards**
CN   MARC field 655.
BT   Greeting cards
Black light works
   USE Luminous works
Black line prints
   USE Diazo prints
Black-and-white prints
   USE Photographic prints
Blind embossed prints
   USE Inkless intaglio prints
**Blind stamps**
PN   Symbols or other devices embossed or
       impressed without ink onto paper or other
       material.  Often used to identify the creator,
       printer, publisher, or owner.
CN   MARC field 755.
UF   Stamps, Blind
BT   Marks
RT   Embossed works
Block prints
   USE Relief prints
Blocks, Printing
   USE Printing blocks
Blue line prints
   USE Diazo prints
**Blueprints**
PN   Cyanotypes that reproduce designs as
       white lines against a blue background.
       Introduced in the United States ca. 1876;

---

BT  Broader term                     RT  Related term                     PN Public Note
NT  Narrower term                    UF  Used for                          + Term has NTs
HN  History Note                     CN  Catalogers Note

**Blueprints (cont.)**
      predominant method for reproducing
      architectural and engineering drawings by the
      1950s; largely discontinued by 1980.
  CN  MARC field 755.
  BT  Cyanotypes
      Reproductions
**Boards, Game**
  USE Gameboards
**Bonds (Financial records)**
  PN  Interest-bearing certificates indicating
      public or private indebtedness.
  CN  MARC field 655.
  BT  Certificates
**Book covers**
  PN  Covers forming the binding or outer
      enclosure of a hardback or paperback book.
      Includes detached covers.
  CN  MARC field 655.
  BT  Covers (Illustration)
**Book illustrations**
  PN  Illustrations in books or pamphlets,
      whether photographs, photomechanical
      prints, or other media; whether still part of or
      detached from the volume. Also, drawings,
      photographs, prints, and other pictures made
      to be reproduced as illustrations, whether or
      not they were ever published.
  CN  MARC field 655.
  UF  Pamphlet illustrations
  BT  Illustrations
**Book jackets**
  PN  Detachable flexible covers, usually paper,
      designed for or published with a book.
  CN  In Binding Terms: A Thesaurus for Use in
      Rare Book and Special Collections
  —  Cataloguing, the term "Dust jackets" is used
      for "Book jackets."  MARC field 655.
  UF  Dust jackets
      Jackets, Book
  BT  Packaging
**Book plates**
  USE Bookplates
**Book & magazine posters**
  PN  Posters issued to advertise books,
      magazines, and newspapers, especially
      artist-designed posters issued in the United
      States starting ca. 1890.
  CN  MARC field 655.
  UF  Magazine posters
      Newspaper posters
      Periodical posters
  BT  Posters
**Booklets**
  USE Leaflets
      Pamphlets
      Viewbooks
**Bookmarks**
  PN  Paper, cardboard, cloth, or other markers
      used to hold a place in a book.
  CN  MARC field 655.
  BT  Ephemera

**Bookplates**
  PN  Book owners' identification labels; usually
      intended for pasting inside a book.
  CN  MARC field 655.
  UF  Book plates
      Ex libris
  BT  Labels
  NT  Armorial bookplates
  RT  Ownership marks
**Books**
  PN  Published non-periodical volumes in
      bound codex form, usually with 49 or more
      pages.  Search also under terms beginning
      with BOOK.
  CN  MARC field 755.
  RT  Leaflets
      Pamphlets
**Botanical drawings**
  USE Botanical illustrations
**Botanical illustrations**
  PN  Illustrations of plants or plant life; or
      illustrations made to document botanical
      specimens.
  CN  MARC field 655.
  UF  Botanical drawings
      Drawings, Botanical
  BT  Scientific illustrations
**Boudoir card photographs**
  PN  Card photographs; mounts measure
      approximately 8.5 x 5.5 in. (22 x 14 cm.).
      Introduced in the United States ca. 1890.
  CN  MARC field 755.
  BT  Card photographs
**Boudoir photographs**
  USE Glamour photographs
**Broadsheets**
  USE Broadsides
**Broadsides**
  PN  Single-sheet public notices that are usually
      printed on only one side. They provide
      information, commentary, proclamation, or
      other announcement or advertisement.
      Primarily posted but also distributed by hand.
      They are usually less pictorial than posters
      and have more extensive text than signs.
  CN  Used in a note under
      ADVERTISEMENTS. MARC field 655.
  UF  Broadsheets
  BT  Ephemera
  NT  Handbills
      Playbills
      Wanted posters
  RT  Announcements
      Carriers' addresses
      Fliers (Printed matter)
      Posters
      Signs
**Brochures**
  USE Leaflets
**Bromide prints**
  USE Silver gelatin prints
**Bromoil prints**

---

BT  Broader term
NT  Narrower term
HN  History Note

RT  Related term
UF  Used for
CN  Catalogers Note

PN  Public Note
+  Term has NTs

**Bromoil prints (cont.)**
PN   Bromide prints that are developed and then
     bleached and colored.  Oil base pigment(s) is
     applied with a soft brush or a brayer, usually
     in repeated applications. Introduced in 1907.
CN   MARC field 755.
BT   Photographic prints
Brownprints
USE Diazo prints
     Kallitypes
**Brush works**
CN   MARC field 755.
RT   Paintings
     Wash drawings
Bubble gum cards
USE Sports cards
**Bumper stickers**
PN   Stickers bearing printed messages and
     intended for display on automobile bumpers,
     although used in many other places.  The
     self-adhesive stickers were introduced in the
     mid-1900s and are often ca. 3 x 13 inches.
CN   MARC field 655.
BT   Stickers
Burlesque posters
USE Theatrical posters
**Business cards**
PN   Small cards that bear name and often
     address of a business or organization. Usually
     lack illustration except for a logo or emblem.
     More an information card than an
     advertisement.
CN   MARC field 655.
UF   Tradecards
BT   Cards
RT   Advertising cards
     Visiting cards
Button badges
USE Badges
Cabinet card photographs
USE Cabinet photographs
Cabinet cards
USE Cabinet photographs
**Cabinet photographs**
PN   Card photographs; mounts measure
     approximately 6.5 x 4.25 in. (16.5 x 10.5
     cm.). Introduced in the United States in 1866;
     popular until ca. 1900.
CN   MARC field 755.
HN   Changed 6/94. Formerly, CABINET
     PHOTOGRAPHS may have been indexed as
     CABINET CARD PHOTOGRAPHS.
UF   Cabinet card photographs
     Cabinet cards
BT   Card photographs
CAD drawings
USE Computer-aided designs
**Calendars**
PN   Tabular registers of days according to a
     system, usually covering one year and
     referring the days of each month to the days
     of the week.

**Calendars (cont.)**
CN   MARC field 655.
BT   Charts
NT   Perpetual calendars
     Religious calendars
Calligrams
USE Letter pictures
**Calligraphy**
PN   Elegant handwriting or penmanship.
CN   MARC field 655.
RT   Letter pictures
Calling cards
USE Visiting cards
Callitypes
USE Kallitypes
**Calotypes**
PN   In the strictest sense, paper negatives made
     by a process patented by Fox Talbot in 1841.
     Commonly, and here, also negatives made by
     the process as later modified.  More popular
     in France and England than in the United
     States; used through the 1860s.
CN   MARC field 755.
UF   Talbotypes
     Waxed paper negatives
BT   Paper negatives
**Camera lucida works**
PN   Drawings (and paintings or other works
     made from them) produced by tracing the
     image of an object or scene as it appears when
     projected through the prism of a camera
     lucida.  The device, which aids accuracy and
     enlargement or reduction, was not widely
     used until the early 1800s; replaced the
     camera obscura.
CN   MARC field 755.
RT   Tracings
**Camera obscura works**
PN   Drawings (and paintings or other works
     made from them) produced by tracing the
     image of an object or scene as it appears when
     projected through the aperture of a camera
     obscura, which is used to aid accuracy.  This
     device, available by the 1500s, may be a
     portable box with lens and mirror, or a room;
     supplanted by the camera lucida.
CN   MARC field 755.
RT   Tracings
Campaign posters
USE Political posters
**Cancellation proofs**
CN   MARC field 755.
HN   Changed 11/90. Formerly,
     CANCELLATION PROOFS  may have been
     indexed as CANCELLED PLATE PRINTS.
UF   Cancelled plate prints
BT   Proofs
RT   Restrikes
Cancelled plate prints
USE Cancellation proofs
**Carbon prints**
PN   Photographic prints made by a relatively

---

BT  Broader term                     RT  Related term                     PN Public Note
NT  Narrower term                    UF  Used for                        + Term has NTs
HN History Note                      CN  Catalogers Note

**Carbon prints (cont.)**
  permanent, non-silver process involving
  bichromated gelatin. Popular ca. 1870-1900;
  more common in Europe than United States;
  often used to reproduce art works. Typically
  carbon black, but a wide range of other
  pigments may also be used.
  CN  MARC field 755.
  UF  Autotypes
      Chromotypes
      Lambertypes
  BT  Photographic prints
  NT  Carbro prints +
**Carbon transparencies**
  PN  Transparencies made with a carbon
      process on glass.
  CN  MARC field 755.
  BT  Glass transparencies
**Carbro prints**
  PN  Photographic prints made by pressing a
      specially sensitized carbon tissue against a
      wet bromide print and subsequently
      developing the tissue. Introduced in 1905 as
      Ozobrome; popular 1920s-1930s as a way to
      make carbon prints larger than the original
      negative since the bromide print intermediary
      could be an enlargement of the negative.
  CN  MARC field 755.
  UF  Ozobrome prints
  BT  Carbon prints
  NT  Tricolor carbro prints
**Card photograph albums**
  PN  Albums designed to hold card
      photographs.
  CN  MARC field 655.
  UF  Cartes de visite albums
  BT  Photograph albums
**Card photographs**
  PN  Paper photographic prints made by a
      variety of processes on commercially
      produced cardboard mounts of standard sizes
      (with some variation). Introduced in the
      1850s. This term includes negatives and
      unmounted photographic prints intended for
      such standard mounts. Often portraits.
  CN  As desired, also index under the type of
      photographic process. MARC field 755.
  BT  Photographs
  NT  Boudoir card photographs
      Cabinet photographs
      Cartes de visite
      Imperial card photographs
      Kodak card photographs
      Panel card photographs
      Promenade card photographs
      Victoria card photographs
  RT  Photographic prints
      Stereographs
**Cards**
  PN  Pieces of thin paperboard or stiff paper,
      which are flat, usually small and rectangular,
      and designed to convey messages or other

**Cards (cont.)**
  information.
  CN  MARC field 655.
  BT  Ephemera
  NT  Advertising cards +
      Business cards
      Collecting cards +
      Comic cards
      Dance cards
      Display cards +
      Membership cards
      Playing cards +
      Postcards +
      Sentiment cards
      Speakeasy cards
      Sports cards +
      Visiting cards
  RT  Greeting cards
**Caricatures**
  PN  Cartoons that portray in a critical or
      facetious way a real individual or group, or a
      figure representing a social, political, ethnic,
      or racial type.  The effect is usually achieved
      through distortion or exaggeration of the
      features or form.
  CN  MARC field 655.
  BT  Cartoons (Commentary)
  RT  Ethnic stereotypes
      Portraits
**Carnival posters**
  USE Circus posters
**Carriers' addresses**
  PN  Verses in broadside or pamphlet format
      presented at the start of a new year by
      newspaper carriers (and sometimes by other
      trades people) to request a gratuity.
  CN  MARC field 655.
  UF  Bellmen's verses
      Newscarriers' addresses
      Newsmen's presents
  BT  Ephemera
  RT  Broadsides
      New Year cards
**Cartes de visite**
  PN  Card photographs; mounts measure
      approximately 4 x 2.5 in. (10 x 6 cm.).
      Introduced in the United States in 1859; made
      into the 1900s.
  CN  MARC field 755.
  BT  Card photographs
**Cartes de visite albums**
  USE Card photograph albums
**Cartes de visite (Visiting cards)**
  USE Visiting cards
**Cartoon cels**
  USE Animation cels
**Cartoon patterns**
  USE Cartoons (Working drawings)
**Cartoon strips**
  USE Comics
**Cartoons**
  USE Cartoons (Commentary)

---

BT  Broader term                      RT  Related term                    PN  Public Note
NT  Narrower term                     UF  Used for                        +   Term has NTs
HN  History Note                      CN  Catalogers Note

## Cartoons (Commentary)
PN Pictorial images using wit to comment on such things as contemporary events, social habits, or political trends; usually executed in a broad or abbreviated manner.
CN MARC field 655.
HN Changed 6/94. Formerly, CARTOONS (COMMENTARY) may have been indexed as CARTOONS.
UF Cartoons
Comic pictures
BT Pictures
NT Caricatures
Comic cards
Comics +
Editorial cartoons
Political cartoons
Satires
RT Humorous pictures
Protest works

## Cartoons (Working drawings)
PN Full-size preparatory drawings made to transfer a design to the working surface of a painting, tapestry, or other large work. [AAT]
CN MARC field 655.
HN Changed 6/94. Formerly, CARTOONS (WORKING DRAWINGS) may have been indexed as CARTOON PATTERNS.
UF Cartoon patterns
BT Working drawings

## Cartouches
PN Graphic delineations that are ornamental frames intended to contain an inscription, such as a map title, or a decoration, such as a coat of arms.
CN MARC field 655.
BT Decorations
RT Maps
Title pages

Cased photographs
USE Ambrotypes
Daguerreotypes
Photograph cases

## Casein paintings
CN MARC field 755.
BT Paintings

Cases, photograph
USE Union cases

## Cast paper prints
PN Paper works made since the 1970s by pouring wet, often colored, pulp into a mold. Such prints may be difficult to distinguish from embossed prints.
CN MARC field 755.
BT Prints
RT Embossed prints

## Catalogs
PN Enumerations of items arranged systematically with descriptive details. May have prices.
CN In Genre Terms ... Rare Book, this term is spelled "catalogues." MARC field 655.

Catalogs (cont.)
UF Catalogues
NT Auction catalogs
Exhibition catalogs
Sales catalogs +
RT Ephemera
Price lists
Sample books

Catalogues
USE Catalogs

## Cellocuts
PN Prints made from blocks on which the surface has been built up with liquid plastics. May be printed in intaglio or relief. They look much like linocuts.
CN MARC field 755.
BT Prints
RT Intaglio prints
Relief prints

Cellulose acetate negatives
USE Acetate negatives

Cellulose diacetate negatives
USE Acetate negatives

Cellulose nitrate negatives
USE Nitrate negatives

Cellulose triacetate negatives
USE Acetate negatives

Cels, Animation
USE Animation cels

## Censored works
PN Materials altered or prohibited because they are considered unsuitable for the general public.
CN MARC field 655.

## Ceramic photographs
PN Photographs produced by any of a variety of processes on a porcelain, earthenware, or other ceramic support.
CN MARC field 755.
UF Photoceramics
Porcelain photographs
BT Photographic prints
RT Opalotypes

## Certificates
PN Documents containing certified statements of, for example, ownership, membership, fulfilled requirements, or legal status.
CN MARC field 655.
BT Ephemera
NT Baptismal certificates
Birth certificates
Bonds (Financial records)
Death certificates
Diplomas
Insurance certificates
Marriage certificates
Membership certificates
Stock certificates
RT Bank note vignettes
Fraktur
Rewards of merit

## Chalk drawings

BT Broader term                   RT Related term                PN Public Note
NT Narrower term                  UF Used for                      + Term has NTs
HN History Note                     CN Catalogers Note

**Chalk drawings (cont.)**
- CN   MARC field 755.
- BT   Drawings
- NT   A trois crayons drawings

**Charcoal drawings**
- CN   MARC field 755.
- BT   Drawings

**Charts**
- PN   Delineations of information in tabular form.
- CN   MARC field 655.
- BT   Diagrams
- NT   Calendars +
      Family trees
      Schedules (Architectural records)
      Schedules (Time plans) +

Cheesecake photographs
   USE Glamour photographs

**Chiaroscuro woodcuts**
- PN   Woodcuts printed from two or more blocks, one of which is usually cut to print the design in black and the others to print neutral or background colors to show differences in value. Technique developed in Europe in the 1500s; often used to reproduce drawings and paintings.
- CN   MARC field 755.
- BT   Woodcuts
- RT   Reproductive prints

**Children's art**
- PN   Art produced by children. See JUVENILIA for works produced during an artist's childhood or youth.
- CN   MARC field 655.
- UF   Art by children
      Children's works
      Juvenile art
- BT   Pictures
- RT   Amateur works
      Juvenilia
      Student works

Children's works
   USE Children's art
       Juvenilia

**Chine collé prints**
- PN   Prints made by laying down a thin sheet of paper on a heavier backing. The thin sheet adheres permanently to the backing sheet during printing. Lithographic or intaglio method.
- CN   MARC field 755.
- BT   Prints
- RT   Intaglio prints
      Lithographs

Chloride prints
   USE Photographic prints
Chloro-bromide prints
   USE Silver gelatin prints

**Christmas cards**
- CN   MARC field 755.
- BT   Greeting cards

**Chromolithographs**

**Chromolithographs (cont.)**
- PN   Lithographs of the mid- to late 1800s printed in colors; often made to look like an oil painting or watercolor.
- CN   Subdivide the term LITHOGRAPHS with --COLOR for fine art prints printed in color. MARC field 755.
- BT   Lithographs
- NT   Oleographs

Chromotypes
   USE Carbon prints
Chromo-photographs
   USE Crystoleum photographs
Chronophotographs
   USE Motion study photographs
Cibachrome prints
   USE Dye destruction prints

**Cigarette cards**
- PN   Cards enclosed with cigarettes. Flourished in the United States 1885-1895 and 1909-1917; printed or photographic.
- CN   MARC field 655.
- UF   Tobacco cards
- BT   Trade cards

**Circulars**
- PN   Printed promotional pieces, frequently announcing sales; may be several pages in length; distributed widely through the mail, door to door, as newspaper inserts, or at commercial establishments.
- CN   MARC field 655.
- HN   Changed 6/94. Formerly, CIRCULARS may have been indexed as HANDBILLS or LEAFLETS.
- BT   Fliers (Printed matter)
- RT   Handbills

**Circus posters**
- PN   Includes posters for circuses as well as carnivals, and wild west shows.
- CN   MARC field 655.
- UF   Carnival posters
      Wild west show posters
- BT   Performing arts posters

Cirkut camera photographs
   USE Panoramic photographs
City planning drawings
   USE Planning drawings
City views
   USE Cityscapes

**Cityscape drawings**
- CN   MARC field 655.
- BT   Cityscapes
      Drawings

**Cityscape paintings**
- CN   MARC field 655.
- BT   Cityscapes
      Paintings

**Cityscape photographs**
- CN   MARC field 655.
- BT   Cityscapes
      Photographs

**Cityscape prints**

---

BT  Broader term                    RT  Related term                    PN  Public Note
NT  Narrower term                   UF  Used for                        +  Term has NTs
HN  History Note                    CN  Catalogers Note

**Cityscape prints (cont.)**
- CN  MARC field 655.
- BT  Cityscapes
  - Prints
- RT  Bird's-eye view prints

**Cityscapes**
- PN  General or broad views of cities and towns or sections of them. Usually made from an elevated or distant vantage point, such as a view from a roof or a view of a skyline.
- CN  MARC field 655.
- UF  City views
  - Skyline views
  - Topographic views
  - Townscapes
  - Views, City
- NT  Cityscape drawings
  - Cityscape paintings
  - Cityscape photographs
  - Cityscape prints
- RT  Panoramic views

Civil War envelopes
- USE Patriotic envelopes

**Clichés-verre**
- PN  Salted paper, albumen, silver gelatin, or other photographic prints made by exposure to a coating on a glass or film support, through which lines have been drawn or areas scraped away. Alternatively, inks can be applied to a transparent matrix in varying thicknesses to alter the amount of light reaching the sensitized paper. May resemble drawings or prints.
- CN  MARC field 755.
- UF  Glass prints
- BT  Photographic prints
- RT  Drawings
  - Prints
  - Reproductions

**Clipper ship cards**
- PN  Printed cards made to attract freight consignments or passengers to clipper ships preparing to depart; chiefly 1850s-1860s; commonly 4 x 6.5 in. (10 x 16 cm.).
- CN  MARC field 655.
- HN  Changed 6/94. Formerly, CLIPPER SHIP CARDS may have been indexed as SHIP CARDS.
- UF  Yankee clipper cards
- BT  Sailing cards

**Clippings**
- PN  Illustrations, pages, articles, or columns of text removed from books, newspapers, periodicals, or other publications.
- CN  MARC field 755.
- UF  Newspaper clippings
  - Press clippings
- NT  Tear sheets

Cloth labels
- USE Textile labels

**Cloth photographs**
- PN  Photographs produced by any of a variety

**Cloth photographs (cont.)**
- of processes on cotton, silk, or other cloth support.
- CN  MARC field 755.
- UF  Collodion positive photographs
- BT  Photographic prints

**Cloth prints**
- PN  Prints produced by any of a variety of processes on cotton, silk, or other cloth support. This term does not include printed textile design fabrics.
- CN  MARC field 755.
- BT  Prints

**Coats of arms**
- PN  Heraldic bearings, usually depicted on an escutcheon often with a crest, motto, or other adjuncts.
- CN  MARC field 655.
- UF  Armorial bearings
  - Heraldic devices
- BT  Emblems
- RT  Armorial bookplates

**Collages**
- PN  Constructions in which bits of relatively flat materials, such as newspaper or cloth, are fixed to a support for symbolic or suggestive effect.
- CN  MARC field 755.
- BT  Pictures
- RT  Mixed media
  - Photomontages

**Collagraphs**
- PN  Prints made from blocks or plates on which the image has been built up with a collage of various materials and objects. May be printed in intaglio or relief.
- CN  MARC field 755.
- UF  Collographs
- BT  Prints
- RT  Intaglio prints
  - Relief prints

**Collecting cards**
- PN  Cards issued to be sold singly, in strips, or in other sets for collecting and trading. Not available as premiums; not intended to be advertisements. Examples include cards illustrating movie stars, or wild flowers. Use TRADE CARDS for advertising cards enclosed with products.
- CN  MARC field 655.
- UF  Trading cards
- BT  Cards
- NT  Album cards
- RT  Advertising cards
  - Bible cards
  - Comic cards
  - Devotional images
  - Sports cards

**Collectors' marks**
- CN  MARC field 755.
- BT  Ownership marks

Collodion dry plate negatives

---

BT Broader term      RT Related term      PN Public Note
NT Narrower term      UF Used for      + Term has NTs
HN History Note      CN Catalogers Note

Collodion dry plate negatives (cont.)
  USE Dry collodion negatives
Collodion negatives
  USE Dry collodion negatives
      Wet collodion negatives
Collodion positive photographs
  USE Ambrotypes
      Cloth photographs
      Collodion transparencies
      Leather photographs
      Tintypes
**Collodion printing-out paper prints**
  PN  Available in the 1860s but not popular
      until late 1880s; chief commercial portrait
      medium 1895-1910. Glossy version has warm
      image hues while the matte version, which
      dominated from the mid-1890s, has
      near-neutral image hues. Usually toned with
      gold or platinum so that images show little or
      no fading. They do not exhibit silver
      mirroring.
  CN  Glossy collodion prints are virtually
      indistinguishable from SILVER GELATIN
      PRINTING-OUT PAPER PRINTS by visual
      inspection. If in doubt, use SILVER
      PRINTING-OUT PAPER PRINTS. Used in
      a note under SILVER GELATIN
      PRINTING-OUT PAPER PRINTS. MARC
      field 755.
  UF  Collodio-chloride prints
  BT  Silver printing-out paper prints
  NT  Aristotypes
**Collodion transparencies**
  PN  Typically, glass stereographs or lantern
      slides; used 1850s-1890s.
  CN  MARC field 755.
  UF  Collodion positive photographs
  BT  Glass transparencies
Collodio-chloride prints
  USE Collodion printing-out paper prints
Collographs
  USE Collagraphs
**Collotypes**
  PN  Photomechanical prints introduced
      commercially in the 1860s; commonly used in
      book illustration; can be difficult to
      distinguish from actual photographs.
  CN  Used in a note under PHOTOGRAPHIC
      PRINTS. MARC field 755.
  UF  Albertypes
      Artotypes
      Heliotypes
  BT  Photomechanical prints
Color screen transparencies
  USE Screen color film transparencies
      Screen color glass transparencies
**Color separation negatives**
  CN  MARC field 755.
  UF  Separation negatives
  BT  Film negatives
**Color separation positives**
  PN  Transparencies, usually in sets of three

Color separation positives (cont.)
      films. Each is used to make a plate for
      printing one color, in register with the others,
      to form a full-color photomechanical print.
      [AAT]
  CN  MARC field 755.
  HN  Changed 6/94. Formerly, COLOR
      SEPARATION POSITIVES may have been
      indexed as COLOR SEPARATION
      TRANSPARENCIES.
  UF  Color separation transparencies
      Positives, Color separation
      Separation positives, Color
      Separation transparencies, Color
  BT  Film transparencies
Color separation transparencies
  USE Color separation positives
Combination prints
  USE Composite photographs
**Comic books**
  PN  Cartoon strips in pamphlet form; usually
      periodicals.
  CN  MARC field 655.
  BT  Comics
  RT  Adventure comics
      Periodicals
**Comic cards**
  PN  Cards, issued individually or in sets, that
      bear a caricature or cartoon. Popular
      1850s-1900. This term does not include
      postcards.
  CN  MARC field 655.
  BT  Cards
      Cartoons (Commentary)
  RT  Collecting cards
Comic pictures
  USE Cartoons (Commentary)
      Humorous pictures
Comic strips
  USE Comics
**Comics**
  PN  Sequences of cartoons with a story line
      laid out in a series of pictorial panels across a
      page or sheet and concerning a continuous
      character or set of characters.
  CN  MARC field 655.
  HN  Changed 10/90. Formerly, COMICS may
      have been indexed as CARTOON STRIPS.
  UF  Cartoon strips
      Comic strips
  BT  Cartoons (Commentary)
  NT  Adventure comics
      Comic books
**Commemorative prints**
  PN  Prints bearing an allegorical or narrative
      image commemorating an important event or
      occasion, such as a decisive battle or the
      founding of an institution. Usually text on the
      print indicates its commemorative nature,
      e.g., in honor of, in memory of. Use
      MEMORIAL WORKS for death memorials.
  CN  MARC field 655.

---

BT Broader term        RT Related term        PN Public Note
NT Narrower term        UF Used for        + Term has NTs
HN History Note        CN Catalogers Note

**Commemorative prints (cont.)**
BT   Prints
RT   Keepsakes
       Memorial works
Commercial art design drawings
  USE Graphic design drawings
Commercial catalogs
  USE Sales catalogs
Comparisons, Then & now
  USE Then & now comparisons
**Competition drawings**
PN   Graphic delineations produced for a design
       contest or to win a construction or design
       contract. Customarily prepared according to a
       prescribed program.  In architecture, often a
       set of elevations, plans, sections, and
       renderings; often rendered or in perspective.
CN   Used in a note under ARCHITECTURAL
       DRAWINGS. MARC field 655.
UF   Drawings, Competition
BT   Design drawings
RT   Presentation drawings
       Proposed works
**Composite photographs**
PN   Photographic prints made when two or
       more separate images are optically combined
       by multiple exposures, sandwiching, or other
       means. The multiple negative images are
       printed onto the same sheet of photographic
       paper.
CN   MARC field 755.
HN   Changed 6/94. Formerly, COMPOSITE
       PHOTOGRAPHS may have been indexed as
       COMBINATION PRINTS.
UF   Combination prints
       Simulated images
BT   Photographic prints
RT   Photomontages
Composition cases
  USE Union cases
**Computer graphics**
PN   Images created within or altered with a
       computer system; may simulate photographs,
       pictorial or ornamental drawings, or other
       images.
CN   MARC field 755.
UF   Digital images
       Electronic images
       Simulated images
NT   Computer-aided designs
RT   Space photographs
**Computer-aided designs**
PN   Graphic delineations, usually design
       drawings, created with a computer drafting
       system.
CN   MARC field 755.
UF   CAD drawings
BT   Computer graphics
Concealed camera photographs
  USE Detective camera photographs
**Concert posters**
PN   Includes posters for orchestra, solo

**Concert posters (cont.)**
       instrument, ensemble, vocalist, and other
       musical performances.
CN   MARC field 655.
UF   Music posters
BT   Performing arts posters
NT   Rock posters
**Conjectural works**
PN   Images showing how something in the past
       might have appeared, such as historical
       events, places, objects, or people. Also,
       pictures of the imagined future appearance of
       real people, places, and objects.
CN   MARC field 655.
UF   Historical studies
       Imaginary views
       Recreations (Conjectural works)
BT   Pictures
RT   Reconstructions
       Then & now comparisons
Construction progress photographs
  USE Progress photographs
**Contact sheets**
PN   Proof sheets containing contact prints from
       more than one negative; often used to select
       images for individual printing.
CN   MARC field 755.
BT   Photographic prints
       Proofs
Conté crayon drawings
  USE Crayon drawings
**Contract drawings**
PN   Graphic delineations which constitute part
       of a legal contract between a client and
       craftsman, builder, architect, engineer,
       contractor, or other service provider. Signed
       or accepted by one or more parties, or
       otherwise identified as part of a contract
       agreement or set of specifications. Used
       especially from the mid- to late-1800s.
CN   MARC field 655.
UF   Drawings, Contract
BT   Design drawings
Copies
  USE Reproductions
**Copy art**
PN   Images made with photocopy machines,
       such as Xerox machines, that are original
       works rather than reproductions of other
       documents. Examples include multiple copy,
       personal use invitations as well as artists'
       works.
CN   MARC field 755.
UF   Xerographic art
BT   Photocopies
**Corner cards**
PN   Designs printed on business envelopes
       during the 1840s and 1850s; usually in the top
       left corner and embossed. The design was
       often the same one used on a business card
       showing the establishment.
CN   MARC field 655.

---

BT   Broader term          RT Related term          PN Public Note
NT   Narrower term          UF Used for              + Term has NTs
HN History Note             CN Catalogers Note

**Corner cards (cont.)**
- BT    Pictorial envelopes
- RT    Embossed works

**Costume design drawings**
- PN    Graphic delineations made for the design and production (or documentation of design and production) of costumes for theatrical and other performing arts productions and for special events, such as costume balls or Halloween.
- CN    MARC field 655.
- BT    Design drawings
- RT    Fashion design drawings

**Costume prints**
- PN    Prints made for the documentation or study of clothing, such as national dress or military uniforms; often in series.
- CN    MARC field 655.
- BT    Prints
- RT    Fashion prints
          Genre prints

Counterfeits
- USE Forgeries

**Counterproofs**
- PN    In printmaking, impressions taken from a print or drawing by passing it through a press against a sheet of damp paper.  The image appears in reverse.
- CN    MARC field 755.
- BT    Prints
          Proofs

Courtroom art
- USE Courtroom sketches

Courtroom illustrations
- USE Courtroom sketches

**Courtroom sketches**
- PN    Graphic delineations made during courtroom proceedings to illustrate newspaper, television, or other trial accounts.
- CN    MARC field 655.
- HN    Changed 6/94. Formerly, COURTROOM SKETCHES may have been indexed as COURTROOM ILLUSTRATIONS.
- UF    Courtroom art
          Courtroom illustrations
          Trial sketches
- BT    Illustrations

**Covers (Illustration)**
- PN    Illustrations and original designs for the covers of books, periodicals, pamphlets, and other graphic design works.
- CN    MARC field 655.
- UF    Illustrated covers
- BT    Graphic design drawings
- NT    Album covers
          Book covers
          Magazine covers
- RT    Illustrations
          Packaging

Covers, Album
- USE Album covers

Covers, Illustrated

Covers, Illustrated (cont.)
- USE Pictorial envelopes

Covers, Magazine
- USE Magazine covers

Covers, Patriotic
- USE Patriotic envelopes

Covers, Record
- USE Album covers

Crate labels, Fruit
- USE Fruit crate labels

**Crayon drawings**
- CN    MARC field 755.
- UF    Conté crayon drawings
- BT    Drawings

**Crayon enlargements**
- PN    Photographic portraits, usually oval in shape, often life-size enlargements, made from the 1860s to 1920s by drawing extensively in charcoal or pastel over a faint photographic print.
- CN    MARC field 755.
- HN    Changed 6/94. Formerly, CRAYON ENLARGEMENTS may have been indexed as CRAYON PRINTS.
- UF    Crayon photographic prints
          Crayon prints
- BT    Photographic prints
- RT    Drawings
          Portraits

**Crayon manner prints**
- PN    Etchings, engravings, or drypoints in which dots placed close together, usually by a roulette wheel, create lines which approximate crayon strokes. In vogue in France in the 1700s; chiefly used to reproduce drawings.
- CN    MARC field 755.
- BT    Intaglio prints
- RT    Reproductive prints

Crayon photographic prints
- USE Crayon enlargements

Crayon prints
- USE Crayon enlargements

Criblée prints
- USE Dotted prints

**Cries**
- PN    Genre works featuring peddlers hawking their wares with, usually, the text of the rhyme they cried. Introduced by the 1500s; prints, paintings, or drawings.
- CN    MARC field 655.
- UF    Street cries
- BT    Genre works

Crime photographs
- USE Forensic photographs

**Crystoleum photographs**
- PN    Photographic prints, usually albumen, the face of which is adhered to glass. The print is made transparent and hand colored, then backed with another glass (which may also be painted to add color to the photo) and a card. They give the appearance of a painting on

---

BT Broader term                                RT Related term                                PN Public Note
NT Narrower term                              UF Used for                                     + Term has NTs
HN History Note                                CN Catalogers Note

**Crystoleum photographs (cont.)**
glass.
CN   MARC field 755.
UF   Chromo-photographs
BT   Photographic prints
RT   Albumen prints
Currency
USE Money
Cut paper works
USE Paper cutouts
**Cyanotypes**
PN   Blue photographic prints employing
light-sensitive iron salts, most commonly on
paper; introduced in the 1840s but not in
general use until after 1880; often used as
proofs.
CN   MARC field 755.
BT   Monochromatic works
Photographic prints
NT   Blueprints
RT   Proofs
**Daguerreotypes**
PN   Direct-image photographs on silver-coated
copper; introduced in 1839 and in general use
until ca. 1860; distinctive mirror-like surface;
commonly in a case.
CN   Used in a note under PHOTOGRAPHS
and STEREOGRAPHS. MARC field 755.
UF   Cased photographs
BT   Photographs
**Dance cards**
PN   Cards on which names of dances and
dance partners may be written.
CN   MARC field 655.
BT   Cards
**Dance posters**
PN   Posters for dance performances; also,
posters commemorating dancers or dance
companies.
CN   MARC field 655.
HN   Changed 6/94. Formerly, DANCE
POSTERS may have been indexed as
PERFORMING ARTS POSTERS.
BT   Performing arts posters
**Dealers' marks**
PN   Marks of dealers, auction houses, or other
sellers.
CN   MARC field 755.
BT   Marks
**Death certificates**
CN   MARC field 655.
BT   Certificates
RT   Family trees
**Decals**
PN   Images made on paper specially treated so
the image can be transferred to another
surface, usually by wetting the paper, laying
it face down against the other surface, then
stripping away the backing sheet.
CN   MARC field 755.
BT   Stickers
RT   Transfer sheets

**Decorations**
PN   Images that ornament a text or picture but
do not relate specifically to its meaning.
CN   MARC field 655.
UF   Ornaments
BT   Pictures
NT   Cartouches
Scraps
RT   Illuminations
Illustrations
Title pages
**Design drawings**
PN   Graphic delineations in any medium
prepared to plan, direct, or document the
design and production of a wide range of
works in various trades, professions, and
artistic pursuits. May be sketches, diagrams,
mechanical drawings, or other formats.
CN   Used in a note under ARCHITECTURAL
DRAWINGS. MARC field 655.
UF   Drawings, Design
Production drawings
NT   Architectural drawings
Competition drawings
Contract drawings
Costume design drawings
Electrical systems drawings
Engineering drawings
Fashion design drawings
Graphic design drawings +
Industrial design drawings
Interior design drawings
Landscape architecture drawings
Measured drawings
Mechanical drawings
Mechanical systems drawings +
Naval architecture drawings
Patent drawings
Pattern books
Pattern sheets
Planning drawings
Presentation drawings
Proposed works
Renderings
Set design drawings
Site plans
Structural systems drawings +
Studies
Textile design drawings
Working drawings +
RT   Details
Diagrams
Projections
Sketches
Specifications
**Details**
PN   Small specific parts of a painting, design,
or other composition; usually at an enlarged
scale showing more information than in the
entire work. Often done in preparation for a
larger finished work, as a subject for study or
training, or as a guide for workmen or

**Details (cont.)**
artisans. This term includes photographic prints made from a portion of a negative.
CN   MARC field 655.
RT   Design drawings
Studies

**Detective camera photographs**
PN   Photographs made by cameras designed to take pictures inconspicuously. The cameras often have special shapes for concealment under a vest or elsewhere or are disguised as other objects, such as revolvers, hats, books, watches, or binoculars.
CN   MARC field 755.
UF   Concealed camera photographs
Vest camera photographs
BT   Photographs

Devices, Artists'
USE Artists' devices

**Devotional images**
PN   Pictures intended as aids to prayer or worship.  Examples include the small lace paper embossed pictures common in Europe during the 1880s that featured saints or scenes from the life of Jesus Christ.  Sometimes issued in sets or used in religious school.  May have a brief religious text.
CN   Double index under COLLECTING CARDS for appropriate images.  MARC field 655.
UF   Holy cards
Religious pictures
Sunday school cards
BT   Pictures
NT   Bible cards
Mizriha'ot
RT   Collecting cards
Ephemera
Rewards of merit

Diacetate negatives
USE Acetate negatives

**Diagrams**
PN   Delineations whose principal purpose is to explain rather than represent pictorially. May provide directions or schematic outline for construction, assembly, repair, or operation, as for electrical circuits or traffic flow.
CN   MARC field 655.
UF   Production drawings
Technical drawings
NT   Charts +
RT   Design drawings

**Diazo prints**
PN   Photographic prints made with material containing diazonium compounds, sensitive to blue and ultraviolet light; commonly developed with ammonia. Introduced in 1890; chiefly for reproducing high contrast line drawings, such as architectural drawings, on paper, cloth, or other fabric.  Lines are commonly blue or black; may be many other colors.

**Diazo prints (cont.)**
CN   MARC field 755.
UF   Black line prints
Blue line prints
Brownprints
Diazotypes
Dyelines
Ozalids
Primuline process prints
Whiteprints
BT   Photographic prints
RT   Reproductions

Diazotypes
USE Diazo prints

Digital images
USE Computer graphics
Space photographs

**Diplomas**
PN   Documents awarded to students or honorees to certify degree conferred by an educational institution.
CN   MARC field 655.
BT   Certificates

Direct-mail advertising
USE Advertising mail

**Display cards**
PN   Advertisements on cards made for use on a counter, in a window, or other commercial setting; larger than advertising cards.
CN   MARC field 655.
BT   Advertisements
Cards
NT   Lobby cards
RT   Signs
Theatrical posters

Display drawings
USE Presentation drawings

**Dotted prints**
PN   Metal relief prints in which white dots or stars, produced by punching a metal plate, punctuate otherwise dark background areas.
CN   MARC field 755.
HN   Changed 11/90.  Formerly, DOTTED PRINTS may have been indexed as METAL CUTS.
UF   Criblée prints
Manière criblée prints
BT   Metal cuts

**Drawings**
PN   Narrower terms include both physical media and genre categories but are limited to those which use drawing in the sense of a specific medium rather than in the everyday sense of graphic representation.
CN   When using a genre term that includes the word DRAWINGS, also index under a more specific physical process name, if desired. Used in a note under MIXED MEDIA. MARC field 755.
BT   Pictures
NT   Abstract drawings
Allegorical drawings

BT  Broader term
NT  Narrower term
HN  History Note

RT  Related term
UF  Used for
CN  Catalogers Note

PN  Public Note
+  Term has NTs

**Drawings (cont.)**
        Chalk drawings +
        Charcoal drawings
        Cityscape drawings
        Crayon drawings
        Figure drawings +
        Genre drawings
        Graphite drawings
        Ink drawings +
        Landscape drawings
        Marine drawings
        Metalpoint drawings +
        Pastel drawings
        Portrait drawings
        Scratchboard drawings
        Still life drawings
        Tracings
        Wash drawings
  RT  Clichés-verre
        Crayon enlargements
        Mixed media
        Pen works
        Pencil works
        Watercolors
**Drawings, Architectural**
  USE Architectural drawings
**Drawings, As-built**
  USE As-built drawings
**Drawings, Botanical**
  USE Botanical illustrations
**Drawings, Competition**
  USE Competition drawings
**Drawings, Contract**
  USE Contract drawings
**Drawings, Design**
  USE Design drawings
**Drawings, Electrical systems**
  USE Electrical systems drawings
**Drawings, Engineering**
  USE Engineering drawings
**Drawings, Exploded**
  USE Exploded drawings
**Drawings, Framing**
  USE Framing drawings
**Drawings, Landscape architecture**
  USE Landscape architecture drawings
**Drawings, Measured**
  USE Measured drawings
**Drawings, Mechanical**
  USE Mechanical drawings
**Drawings, Mechanical systems**
  USE Mechanical systems drawings
**Drawings, Medical**
  USE Medical illustrations
**Drawings, Naval architecture**
  USE Naval architecture drawings
**Drawings, Patent**
  USE Patent drawings
**Drawings, Planning**
  USE Planning drawings
**Drawings, Presentation**
  USE Presentation drawings

**Drawings, Structural systems**
  USE Structural systems drawings
**Drawings, Working**
  USE Working drawings
**Dry collodion negatives**
  PN  Negatives coated with a dry collodion solution were introduced in the 1850s. Although convenient because they could be stored until ready to be exposed, they were little used because they required long exposure times. Hand-coated emulsions made these negatives look like wet plates.
  CN  These plates are so difficult to distinguish from WET PLATE NEGATIVES that they might be indexed as wet plates. MARC field 755.
  HN  Changed 6/94. Formerly, DRY COLLODION NEGATIVES may have been indexed as COLLODION DRY PLATE NEGATIVES.
  UF  Collodion dry plate negatives
        Collodion negatives
  BT  Dry plate negatives
**Dry plate negatives**
  PN  Silver gelatin dry plate negatives were the dominant glass negative ca. 1880-1920. Dry plate negatives were made as early as the 1850s with collodion, honey, and other solutions, but they were not commercially successful and are difficult to distinguish from collodion wet plate negatives.
  CN  MARC field 755.
  UF  Gelatin dry plate negatives
        Silver gelatin glass negatives
  BT  Glass negatives
  NT  Dry collodion negatives
**Drypoints**
  CN  MARC field 755.
  BT  Intaglio prints
**Dufay color transparencies**
  USE Screen color film transparencies
**Dust jackets**
  USE Book jackets
**Dye coupler negatives**
  PN  Trade names include Kodacolor (launched in 1942 as the first commercial color negative process in the United States), and Ektacolor (1947). A chromogenic development process.
  CN  MARC field 755.
  UF  Ektacolor negatives
        Fujicolor negatives
        Kodacolor negatives
  BT  Film negatives
**Dye coupler prints**
  PN  Includes most color photographic prints (except instant camera) made since 1941. Commonly referred to as Type C if made from a negative and Type R if made from a transparency. A chromogenic development process.
  CN  MARC field 755.
  UF  Type C prints

---

BT Broader term
NT Narrower term
HN History Note

RT Related term
UF Used for
CN Catalogers Note

PN Public Note
+ Term has NTs

**Dye coupler prints (cont.)**
      Type R prints
  BT  Photographic prints
**Dye coupler transparencies**
  PN  Trade names include Kodachrome and
      Agfacolor (both introduced in 1936) and
      Ektachrome (introduced in the 1940s). A
      chromogenic development process.
  CN  MARC field 755.
  UF  Agfacolor transparencies
      Ektachrome transparencies
      Fujichrome transparencies
      Kodachrome transparencies
  BT  Film transparencies
**Dye destruction prints**
  PN  Color photographic prints made under
      various trade names including Utocolor in the
      early 1900s and Gasparcolor in the 1930s.
      Cibachrome, introduced in 1963, is the
      modern representative of the process. Valued
      in part for the relative stability of the color
      dyes.
  CN  MARC field 755.
  UF  Cibachrome prints
      Silver dye bleach prints
  BT  Photographic prints
**Dye diffusion transfer prints**
  PN  Color instant camera photographic prints.
      Polaroid was introduced commercially in
      1965; Kodak followed in 1976, and Fuji in
      1981. Commonly 3.12 x 3.12 in. (8 x 8 cm.).
  CN  MARC field 755.
  UF  Kodak instant color prints
      Polaroid instant color prints
  BT  Instant camera photographs
      Photographic prints
**Dye transfer prints**
  PN  Color photographic prints made by the
      imbibition process and techniques that begin
      with three color separation negatives, then
      dyed matrices, and a final print. Among the
      many trade names are Pinatype (introduced in
      1903) and Eastman Wash-off Relief
      (1935-1946). Kodak Dye Transfer process
      (introduced in 1946) is still in use.
  CN  MARC field 755.
  UF  Imbibition process prints
      Pinatypes
  BT  Photographic prints
**Dyelines**
  USE Diazo prints
**Easter cards**
  CN  MARC field 655.
  BT  Greeting cards
**Editions, Limited**
  USE Limited editions
**Editorial cartoons**
  PN  Cartoons offering political commentary or
      social protest and made for publication in a
      newspaper or periodical.
  CN  MARC field 655.
  BT  Cartoons (Commentary)

**Editorial cartoons (cont.)**
      Periodical illustrations
  RT  Political cartoons
**Ektachrome transparencies**
  USE Dye coupler transparencies
**Ektacolor negatives**
  USE Dye coupler negatives
**Election posters**
  USE Political posters
**Election tickets**
  USE Ballots
**Electrical systems drawings**
  PN  Graphic delineations for design, layout,
      installation, and at times operation of
      electrical systems. Examples include lighting,
      telecommunications, power, alarm, and
      detection systems.
  CN  MARC field 655.
  UF  Drawings, Electrical systems
  BT  Design drawings
**Electronic images**
  USE Computer graphics
      Transmitted images
**Electrostatic photocopies**
  USE Photocopies
**Elevations**
  PN  Graphic delineations of a vertical exterior
      or interior face of a building, structure, or
      object viewed straight on. Images usually
      seem flat but may include some sense of
      depth through shading and variations in line
      thickness.
  CN  Used in a note under ARCHITECTURAL
      DRAWINGS. MARC field 655.
  BT  Projections
**Emblem pictures**
  PN  Images that combine a picture with a
      motto or set of verses intended as a moral or
      philosophical lesson; usually prints or
      drawings.
  CN  MARC field 655.
  UF  Motto prints
  RT  Fraktur
**Emblems**
  PN  Devices or images used as identifying
      symbols.
  CN  MARC field 755.
  BT  Marks
  NT  Artists' devices
      Coats of arms
**Embossed prints**
  PN  Prints in which the image is formed largely
      by the paper being forced into relief by
      pressing it into the hollows of the printing
      plate or block, usually without ink.
  CN  MARC field 755.
  BT  Embossed works
      Prints
  NT  Inkless intaglio prints
  RT  Cast paper prints
**Embossed works**
  CN  MARC field 755.

---

BT Broader term        RT Related term        PN Public Note
NT Narrower term        UF Used for        + Term has NTs
HN History Note        CN Catalogers Note

**Embossed works (cont.)**
NT  Embossed prints +
RT  Blind stamps
    Corner cards
**Engineering drawings**
PN  Graphic delineations made for the design
    and construction (or documentation of design
    and construction) of civil, hydraulic,
    mechanical, and other engineering works or
    structural components. Distinguished from
    architectural drawings chiefly by the
    designation 'engineer' for the creator.
CN  See note under ARCHITECTURAL
    DRAWINGS. MARC field 655.
UF  Drawings, Engineering
BT  Design drawings
**Engravings**
CN  MARC field 755.
BT  Intaglio prints
NT  Stipple engravings
**Engravings, Wood**
USE Wood engravings
**Entertainment posters**
USE Performing arts posters
**Envelopes**
PN  Flat, usually paper containers, as for
    mailing a letter. Typical illustrations include
    patriotic themes or business advertisements;
    introduced for common use in the 1840s.
CN  MARC field 655.
BT  Packaging
NT  Pictorial envelopes +
RT  Stationery
**Ephemera**
PN  Transient everyday items, usually printed
    and on paper, that are manufactured for a
    specific limited use, then often discarded.
    Includes everyday items that are meant to be
    saved, at least for a while, such as
    KEEPSAKES and STOCK CERTIFICATES.
CN  MARC field 655.
UF  Printed ephemera
NT  Advertisements +
    Announcements
    Badges
    Ballots
    Bookmarks
    Broadsides +
    Cards +
    Carriers' addresses
    Certificates +
    Fans
    Fliers (Printed matter) +
    Forms
    Game pieces +
    Gameboards
    Handkerchiefs
    Invitations
    Keepsakes
    Labels +
    Lottery tickets
    Memorabilia

**Ephemera (cont.)**
    Menus
    Money +
    Packaging +
    Postage stamps
    Premiums
    Presentation albums
    Price lists
    Programs +
    Puzzles +
    Rewards of merit
    Samples +
    Schedules (Time plans) +
    Scrapbooks
    Scraps
    Signs +
    Stationery +
    Tickets
    Viewbooks
    Wallpaper
    Watch papers
RT  Catalogs
    Devotional images
    Posters
**Equipment**
PN  Three-dimensional devices used to make
    or to view graphic materials. Examples
    include engraving tools, cameras, and
    stereograph viewers.
CN  MARC field 655.
UF  Tools
NT  Printing blocks +
    Printing plates +
    Printing stones
    Printmaking equipment +
    Stencils
**Erotica**
PN  Images intended to evoke sexual responses
    in the viewer.
CN  MARC field 655.
RT  Glamour photographs
**Etchings**
CN  MARC field 755.
BT  Intaglio prints
NT  Soft-ground etchings
RT  Aquatints
    Relief printed etchings
**Ethnic stereotypes**
PN  Images that depict stereotypical traits of
    people classed according to shared racial,
    national, tribal, religious, linguistic, or
    cultural background.
CN  Also index under name of ethnic group.
    MARC field 655.
UF  National stereotypes
    Racial stereotypes
    Stereotypes, Ethnic
RT  Caricatures
**Ethnographic photographs**
PN  Photographs made for or by
    anthropologists and others involved in the
    systematic recording of human cultures.

BT  Broader term          RT  Related term          PN Public Note
NT  Narrower term          UF  Used for              + Term has NTs
HN  History Note           CN  Catalogers Note

**Ethnographic photographs (cont.)**
  CN  MARC field 655.
  UF  Anthropological photographs
      Ethnological photographs
  BT  Photographs
Ethnological photographs
  USE Ethnographic photographs
Evidence photographs
  USE Forensic photographs
Ex libris
  USE Bookplates
Exhibit posters
  USE Exhibition posters
**Exhibition catalogs**
  PN  Catalogs of items in art or other exhibits.
  CN  MARC field 655.
  BT  Catalogs
**Exhibition posters**
  PN  Posters for organized displays, including
      art exhibitions, trade shows, and world's fairs.
  CN  MARC field 655.
  HN  Changed 6/94. Formerly, EXHIBITION
      POSTERS may have been indexed as
      POSTERS.
  UF  Art exhibition posters
      Exhibit posters
  BT  Posters
Exotic works
  USE Novelty works
**Expedition photographs**
  PN  Photographs intended to gather data or to
      document the activities of geological,
      geographical, anthropological,
      archaeological, or other scientific discovery
      expeditions.
  CN  MARC field 655.
  UF  Exploration photographs
  BT  Photographs
**Exploded drawings**
  PN  Graphic delineations showing the
      individual disassembled components of a
      structure or object. The parts are shown in
      their proper relationships with respect to their
      assembled positions.
  CN  MARC field 655.
  UF  Drawings, Exploded
  BT  Projections
Exploration photographs
  USE Expedition photographs
Fabric design drawings
  USE Textile design drawings
Facsimile transmission images
  USE Transmitted images
**Facsimiles**
  PN  Copies made by someone other than the
      creator of an original image; intended to look
      the same as the original but not intended as
      forgeries.
  CN  MARC field 755.
  BT  Reproductions
Family records, Pictorial
  USE Family trees

Family registers, Pictorial
  USE Family trees
**Family trees**
  PN  Charts or other representations of family
      relationships. Includes decorated or pictorial
      charts with blank spaces for names or
      portraits.
  CN  MARC field 655.
  HN  Changed 6/94. Formerly, FAMILY
      TREES may have been indexed as
      GENEALOGICAL TABLES or as
      PICTORIAL FAMILY RECORDS.
  UF  Family records, Pictorial
      Family registers, Pictorial
      Genealogical tables
      Pictorial family records
  BT  Charts
  RT  Birth certificates
      Death certificates
      Fraktur
      Marriage certificates
      Portraits
**Fans**
  PN  Flat or folding fans with advertisements,
      souvenir or commemorative messages, or
      pictures.
  CN  MARC field 655.
  BT  Ephemera
**Fashion design drawings**
  PN  Graphic delineations made for the design
      and production (or documentation of design
      and production) of apparel and accessories.
  CN  MARC field 655.
  BT  Design drawings
  RT  Costume design drawings
**Fashion photographs**
  PN  Photographs made to sell clothing and
      accessories or show them to advantage. These
      photographs differ from GLAMOUR
      PHOTOGRAPHS, which emphasize the
      physical attractiveness of the subject, and
      PUBLICITY PHOTOGRAPHS, which are
      made for publicity or promotion purposes.
  CN  Used in a note under GLAMOUR
      PHOTOGRAPHS and PUBLICITY
      PHOTOGRAPHS. MARC field 655.
  BT  Photographs
  RT  Advertisements
      Publicity photographs
**Fashion plates**
  PN  Periodical illustrations made to advertise
      current fashion designs. Earliest date from the
      late 1700s; popular in the 1830s and later.
  CN  MARC field 655.
  BT  Periodical illustrations
**Fashion prints**
  PN  Separate prints issued by clothing
      manufacturers or haberdashers depicting or
      advertising their current designs.
  CN  MARC field 655.
  BT  Prints
  RT  Advertisements

---

BT Broader term                          RT Related term                          PN Public Note
NT Narrower term                         UF Used for                              + Term has NTs
HN History Note                          CN Catalogers Note

**Fashion prints (cont.)**
        Costume prints
**Female figure drawings**
  PN  Drawings of the human female body,
         other than portraits.
  CN  MARC field 655.
  BT  Figure drawings
**Ferrotypes**
  USE Tintypes
**Figure drawings**
  PN  Drawings of the human body, or any of its
         parts, other than portraits.
  CN  MARC field 655.
  BT  Drawings
  NT  Female figure drawings
         Male figure drawings
**Film negatives**
  PN  Negatives on a flexible base, such as
         celluloid or polyester. Introduced
         commercially in the 1880s.
  CN  MARC field 755.
  UF  Gelatin silver film negatives
         Silver gelatin film negatives
  BT  Negatives
  NT  Color separation negatives
         Dye coupler negatives
         Halftone negatives
         Nitrate negatives
         Safety film negatives +
**Film posters**
  USE Motion picture posters
**Film stills**
  PN  Still images made during the production
         of a motion picture that show scenes from the
         movie; usually for publicity purposes.
  CN  MARC field 655.
  HN  Changed 10/90. Formerly, FILM STILLS
         may have been indexed as MOTION
         PICTURE STILLS.
  UF  Motion picture stills
         Movie stills
         Production stills
         Stills
  BT  Photographs
  RT  Publicity photographs
**Film transparencies**
  PN  Transparencies on a flexible base, such as
         celluloid or polyester.
  CN  MARC field 755.
  BT  Transparencies
  NT  Color separation positives
         Dye coupler transparencies
         Radiographs
         Screen color film transparencies
         Silver gelatin film transparencies
**Fire insurance maps**
  PN  Maps intended for use in calculating fire
         insurance risks. They include data on size and
         construction materials of structures and on
         property boundaries, street widths, water
         supplies, and other features.
  CN  MARC field 655.

**Fire insurance maps (cont.)**
  BT  Maps
**Flash photographs**
  PN  Photographs made with the aid of
         magnesium, electronic, or other flash lighting
         mechanisms.
  CN  MARC field 755.
  BT  Photographs
  RT  Motion study photographs
**Fliers (Printed matter)**
  PN  Inexpensively produced single sheet
         announcements or advertisements for
         distribution among the general public.
  CN  MARC field 655.
  HN  Changed 6/94. Formerly FLIERS
         (PRINTED MATTER) may have been
         indexed as HANDBILLS or as LEAFLETS.
  UF  Flyers (Printed matter)
  BT  Ephemera
  NT  Circulars
         Handbills
  RT  Broadsides
         Leaflets
**Floor plans**
  PN  Plans that represent horizontal sections cut
         through the walls and other vertical elements
         of a building at one or more levels. They
         demonstrate the shape and disposition of
         spaces, chambers, and structural components.
         They include information on placement and
         dimensions of features, such as doors, walls,
         built-in equipment, and room names.
  CN  MARC field 655.
  BT  Plans
         Sections
**Fluorescent works**
  USE Luminous works
**Flyers (Printed matter)**
  USE Fliers (Printed matter)
**Forensic photographs**
  PN  Photographs that document physical facts
         and serve as evidence, especially in litigation.
  CN  MARC field 655.
  HN  Changed 6/94. Formerly, FORENSIC
         PHOTOGRAPHS may have been indexed as
         LEGAL PHOTOGRAPHS.
  UF  Crime photographs
         Evidence photographs
         Legal photographs
         Police photographs
         Surveillance photographs
  BT  Photographs
  RT  Identification photographs
**Forgeries**
  PN  Illegal imitations or counterfeits; fakes
         offered as genuine works; may be
         reproductions or merely in the style of a
         specific type of work and presented as
         genuine.
  CN  MARC field 755.
  UF  Counterfeits
  RT  Reproductions

---

BT Broader term
NT Narrower term
HN History Note

RT Related term
UF Used for
CN Catalogers Note

PN Public Note
+ Term has NTs

**Formation photographs**
- PN   Photographs taken from an elevated vantage point of a large group of people assembled to form a particular design, such as an eagle or the United States flag.
- CN   MARC field 655.
- BT   Group portraits
       Portrait photographs

**Forms**
- PN   Printed documents with spaces for insertion of requested information. Examples include report cards, telegrams, tax forms, checks, and summonses.
- CN   MARC field 655.
- BT   Ephemera

**Fortune telling cards**
- PN   Playing cards made specifically for forecasting the future.
- CN   MARC field 655.
- BT   Playing cards
- NT   Tarot cards

Fractur
- USE Fraktur

**Fraktur**
- PN   Illuminations typically made by the Pennsylvania Dutch, in which flowers, birds and other motifs decorate a text, such as a household motto or marriage certificate; drawn or printed.
- CN   MARC field 655.
- UF   Fractur
- BT   Illuminations
- RT   Certificates
       Emblem pictures
       Family trees

**Framing drawings**
- PN   Designs for the construction and assembly of a skeletal structural system for a floor, wall, roof, or entire building.
- CN   MARC field 655.
- UF   Drawings, Framing
- BT   Structural systems drawings

French tissues
- USE Tissue stereographs

**Frontispieces**
- PN   Illustrations placed next to the title page.
- CN   MARC field 655.
- BT   Illustrations

Fruit box labels
- USE Fruit crate labels

**Fruit crate labels**
- PN   Slips of paper for identification, description, or decoration of fruit crates.
- CN   MARC field 655.
- HN   Changed 1/94. Formerly, FRUIT CRATE LABELS may have been indexed as LABELS.
- UF   Crate labels, Fruit
       Fruit box labels
- BT   Labels

Fujichrome transparencies
- USE Dye coupler transparencies

Fujicolor negatives
- USE Dye coupler negatives

Game boards
- USE Gameboards

**Game cards**
- PN   Cards designed for use with specific games and lacking standard suit systems. Examples include Old Maid and Game of Authors.
- CN   MARC field 655.
- BT   Playing cards
- RT   Game pieces
       Toys

**Game pieces**
- PN   Objects manipulated by participants during the play of table and boardgames.
- CN   MARC field 655.
- HN   Changed 6/94. Formerly, GAME PIECES may have been indexed as GAMES.
- UF   Games
       Pieces, Game
       Playing pieces
- BT   Ephemera
- NT   Puzzles +
- RT   Game cards
       Gameboards
       Toys

**Gameboards**
- PN   Board or boardlike game accessories marked such that the progress of play can be tracked.
- CN   MARC field 655.
- HN   Changed 6/94. Formerly, GAMEBOARDS may have been indexed as GAMES.
- UF   Boards, Game
       Game boards
       Games
- BT   Ephemera
- RT   Game pieces
       Toys

Games
- USE Game pieces
       Gameboards

Gaslight prints
- USE Silver gelatin prints

Gelatin dry plate negatives
- USE Dry plate negatives

Gelatin silver film negatives
- USE Film negatives

Gelatin silver prints
- USE Silver gelatin prints

Gelatin silver transparencies
- USE Silver gelatin film transparencies
       Silver gelatin glass transparencies

**Gem photographs**
- PN   Very small tintypes that were usually mounted in a paper folder or in jewelry. Popular mid-1860s to 1880.
- CN   MARC field 755.
- HN   Changed 10/90. Formerly, GEM PHOTOGRAPHS may have been indexed as

| BT  Broader term | RT  Related term | PN  Public Note |
| NT  Narrower term | UF  Used for | +  Term has NTs |
| HN  History Note | CN  Catalogers Note | |

**Gem photographs (cont.)**
    MINIATURE WORKS.
  BT  Miniature works
      Tintypes
Genealogical tables
  USE Family trees
**Genre drawings**
  CN  MARC field 655.
  BT  Drawings
      Genre works
**Genre paintings**
  CN  MARC field 655.
  BT  Genre works
      Paintings
**Genre photographs**
  CN  MARC field 655.
  BT  Genre works
      Photographs
**Genre prints**
  CN  MARC field 655.
  BT  Genre works
      Prints
  RT  Costume prints
**Genre works**
  PN  Scenes or incidents of everyday life, such
      as domestic interiors or rural and village
      scenes; tableaux; chiefly pre-1900.
  CN  MARC field 655.
  BT  Pictures
  NT  Cries
      Genre drawings
      Genre paintings
      Genre photographs
      Genre prints
Ghost photographs
  USE Spirit photographs
Give-aways
  USE Premiums
**Glamour photographs**
  PN  Photographs portraying women or men
      and emphasizing their physical
      attractiveness.  Subjects may be scantily clad,
      but desirability is conveyed, not erotica.
      Similar to FASHION PHOTOGRAPHS,
      which emphasize the product being modeled,
      and PUBLICITY PHOTOGRAPHS, which
      are made for publicity or promotion
      purposes.
  CN  Used in a note under FASHION
      PHOTOGRAPHS and PUBLICITY
      PHOTOGRAPHS. MARC field 655.
  UF  Beefcake photographs
      Boudoir photographs
      Cheesecake photographs
      Pinup photographs
  BT  Photographs
      Publicity photographs
  RT  Erotica
      Portrait photographs
**Glass negatives**
  CN  MARC field 755.
  BT  Negatives

**Glass negatives (cont.)**
  NT  Dry plate negatives +
      Wet collodion negatives
Glass prints
  USE Clichés-verre
**Glass transparencies**
  CN  MARC field 755.
  BT  Transparencies
  NT  Albumen transparencies
      Carbon transparencies
      Collodion transparencies
      Lantern slides
      Screen color glass transparencies +
      Silver gelatin glass transparencies
Gouache drawings
  USE Gouaches
Gouache paintings
  USE Gouaches
**Gouaches**
  PN  Opaque watercolor drawings or paintings,
      commonly combined with pastels, India ink,
      and transparent watercolors.
  CN  MARC field 755.
  HN  Changed 6/94. Formerly, GOUACHES
      may have been indexed as GOUACHE
      DRAWINGS or GOUACHE PAINTINGS.
  UF  Gouache drawings
      Gouache paintings
  BT  Watercolors
**Graphic design drawings**
  PN  Graphic delineations made for the design
      and production of printed works such as book
      jackets, labels, logos, posters, and
      advertisements.
  CN  Also index under the term for the finished
      product, e.g., LABELS. MARC field 655.
  UF  Commercial art design drawings
  BT  Design drawings
  NT  Covers (Illustration) +
  RT  Illustrations
**Graphite drawings**
  CN  MARC field 755.
  BT  Drawings
Gravures
  USE Photogravures
      Rotogravures
**Greeting cards**
  PN  Cards sent or given on special occasions;
      usually bearing messages of good will.
  CN  MARC field 655.
  BT  Stationery
  NT  Birthday cards
      Christmas cards
      Easter cards
      New Year cards
      Valentines
  RT  Cards
**Group portraits**
  PN  Portraits in which two or more people are
      shown. Includes groups assembled through
      photomontage, combination printing
      techniques, or an artist's imagination.

---

BT  Broader term        RT  Related term        PN Public Note
NT  Narrower term       UF  Used for         + Term has NTs
HN  History Note        CN  Catalogers Note

**Group portraits (cont.)**
CN   MARC field 655.
BT   Portraits
NT   Formation photographs
**Gum bichromate prints**
PN   Non-silver photographic prints made by
     coating white or color paper with a
     light-sensitive gum arabic solution and any
     desired pigment color.  The print hardens
     selectively during exposure to a negative.
     Additional coatings and exposures are
     possible.  Developed in the 1850s but little
     used until the 1890s.
CN   MARC field 755.
UF   Gum prints
BT   Photographic prints
Gum prints
USE Gum bichromate prints
Gutta-percha photograph cases
USE Union cases
**Halftone negatives**
PN   Negatives in which the image appears as
     exposed through a line screen as a pattern of
     dots or squares of varying sizes. Used to
     make printing plates for halftone
     photomechanical prints.
CN   MARC field 755.
BT   Film negatives
RT   Photomechanical prints
**Halftone photomechanical prints**
PN   Prints distinguished by patterns of dots or
     circular lines, or other indication of the screen
     interposed between the original image and the
     camera. Usually used to reproduce
     continuous tone originals, such as
     photographs, in books, newspapers, or other
     publications. First commercially available in
     the 1880s.
CN   MARC field 755.
BT   Photomechanical prints
**Handbills**
PN   Small single-sheet notices, usually
     unfolded; may be printed on both sides;
     intended for wide distribution by hand,
     mailing, or other means.
CN   Also index under POSTERS when a sheet
     is partly text, partly pictorial and intended for
     both hand distribution and posting. Used in a
     note under ADVERTISEMENTS. In Genre
     Terms ...Rare Book, BROADSIDES is used
     instead of HANDBILLS. MARC field 655.
BT   Broadsides
     Fliers (Printed matter)
RT   Circulars
**Handkerchiefs**
PN   Pieces of cloth, usually square, and
     intended for wearing; printed with
     commemorative designs for use as souvenirs,
     or with political slogans for use as
     promotional material, especially during the
     mid- to late-1800s.
CN   MARC field 655.

**Handkerchiefs (cont.)**
BT   Ephemera
Head shots
USE Publicity photographs
Heating, ventilating, & air conditioning drawings
USE HVAC drawings
Heliotypes
USE Collotypes
Heraldic bookplates
USE Armorial bookplates
Heraldic devices
USE Coats of arms
**Hidden image works**
PN   Works in which images or text are hidden
     until revealed by an action, such as holding
     them to the light, heating them, or rubbing
     away a covering surface.
CN   MARC field 655.
BT   Mechanical works
NT   Hold-to-light works
RT   Picture puzzles
Historical studies
USE Conjectural works
**Hold-to-light works**
PN   Cards or sheets of paper with portions cut
     out and backed with tissue or other
     transparent material. When held up to a light
     source, a hidden picture is revealed or the
     cut-out portions (generally windows, lights,
     or the sun) appear brightly illuminated.
CN   MARC field 655.
BT   Hidden image works
RT   Transparencies
**Holograms**
PN   Photographs that present a
     three-dimensional image of a subject which
     changes as the viewing angle changes.
     Produced with laser technology; after 1960.
CN   MARC field 755.
UF   Laser photographs
     Three-dimensional photographs
BT   Photographs
Holy cards
USE Devotional images
**Humorous pictures**
PN   Images intended to be funny.
CN   MARC field 655.
UF   Comic pictures
RT   Cartoons (Commentary)
**HVAC drawings**
PN   Drawings of heating, ventilating, and air
     conditioning systems.
CN   MARC field 655.
UF   Air conditioning, heating, & ventilating
     drawings
     Heating, ventilating, & air conditioning
     drawings
     Ventilating, air conditioning, & heating
     drawings
BT   Mechanical systems drawings
Hyalotypes
USE Albumen transparencies

---

BT Broader term                RT Related term              PN Public Note
NT Narrower term               UF Used for                  + Term has NTs
HN History Note                CN Catalogers Note

Identification keys
USE Keys (Legends)
**Identification photographs**
 PN Photographs made to provide
  identification of people, animals, and plants
  for various government, legal, or commercial
  purposes.
 CN MARC field 655.
 UF Mug shots
 BT Photographs
 RT Forensic photographs
  Portrait photographs
  Wanted posters
**Illuminations**
 PN Book leaves or single sheets of text
  embellished with hand-drawn ornamental
  letters, scrolls, paintings, and other designs;
  usually gold and color; may be decorations or
  illustrations.
 CN MARC field 655.
 NT Fraktur
  Miniatures (Illuminations)
 RT Decorations
  Illustrations
Illustrated covers
USE Covers (Illustration)
Illustrated envelopes
USE Pictorial envelopes
Illustrated letter paper
USE Letterheads
  Pictorial lettersheets
**Illustrations**
 PN Images that explain or elaborate a written
  or spoken text; may be issued separately from
  the text. Published and unpublished
  illustrations are included, as are pictures made
  in one medium to be published as illustrations
  in a different medium.
 CN MARC field 655.
 BT Pictures
 NT Book illustrations
  Courtroom sketches
  Frontispieces
  Periodical illustrations +
  Scientific illustrations +
 RT Covers (Illustration)
  Decorations
  Graphic design drawings
  Illuminations
  Title pages
  Vignettes
Imaginary views
USE Conjectural works
Imbibition process prints
USE Dye transfer prints
**Imperial card photographs**
 PN Card photographs; mounts measure
  approximately 10 x 7 in. (26 x 18 cm.).
  Introduced in the United States ca. 1890.
 CN MARC field 755.
 BT Card photographs
**Industrial design drawings**

**Industrial design drawings (cont.)**
 PN Graphic delineations made for the design
  and production (or documentation of design
  and production) of utilitarian or
  machine-made objects, usually for a mass
  market. Primarily a development of the 1900s
  related to products as various as automobiles,
  lighting fixtures, furniture, and dinnerware.
 CN MARC field 655.
 BT Design drawings
**Infrared photographs**
 PN Photographs made with film that is
  sensitive to infrared light. Chiefly 1930s or
  later.
 CN MARC field 755.
 BT Photographs
**Ink drawings**
 CN MARC field 755.
 BT Drawings
 NT Marker works
 RT Wash drawings
**Inkless intaglio prints**
 PN Prints made without ink; portions of the
  paper forced into relief create the image.
 CN MARC field 755.
 UF Blind embossed prints
 BT Embossed prints
  Intaglio prints
**Inscriptions**
 CN MARC field 755.
 BT Marks
 NT Autographs +
  Monograms
Insert cards
USE Advertising cards
**Instant camera photographs**
 PN Photographs made from film packets that
  contain their own developing chemicals.
  Polaroid introduced the process in 1947.
  Chiefly photographic prints; also, negatives
  and transparencies.
 CN MARC field 755.
 UF Polaroid instant photographs
 BT Photographs
 NT Dye diffusion transfer prints
**Insurance certificates**
 PN Documents issued to certify coverage
  against loss.
 CN MARC field 655.
 BT Certificates
**Intaglio prints**
 CN Used in a note under MIXED MEDIA and
  PRINTS. MARC field 755.
 BT Prints
 NT Aquatints +
  Crayon manner prints
  Drypoints
  Engravings +
  Etchings +
  Inkless intaglio prints
  Mezzotints
 RT A la poupée prints

BT Broader term
NT Narrower term
HN History Note

RT Related term
UF Used for
CN Catalogers Note

PN Public Note
+ Term has NTs

**Intaglio prints (cont.)**
    Cellocuts
    Chine collé prints
    Collagraphs
**Interior design drawings**
  PN  Graphic delineations made for the design
    or construction (or documentation of design
    and construction) of residential and non-
    residential interiors. They include physical
    layout, support systems, furnishings, finishes,
    and fixtures.
  CN  MARC field 655.
  BT  Design drawings
**Invitations**
  PN  Requests to be present or to participate.
  CN  MARC field 655.
  BT  Ephemera
  RT  Announcements
Iron photographs
  USE Tintypes
Iron-on transfers
  USE Transfer sheets
**Isometric projections**
  PN  Axonometric projections in which all three
    faces of a three-dimensional subject are
    drawn at equally oblique angles to the picture
    plane. Horizontal projectors are drawn at an
    angle of 30 degrees, and their dimensions as
    well as those of the vertical axes are drawn to
    true scale. Plan and elevations are given
    equal prominence.
  CN  MARC field 655.
  BT  Axonometric projections
Jackets, Book
  USE Book jackets
Jackets, Record
  USE Album covers
Junk mail
  USE Advertising mail
Juvenile art
  USE Children's art
**Juvenilia**
  PN  Works produced by artists in their
    childhood or youth. See CHILDREN'S ART
    for works produced by children in general.
  CN  MARC field 655.
  UF  Artists' early works
    Children's works
  BT  Pictures
  RT  Amateur works
    Children's art
    Student works
**Kallitypes**
  PN  Introduced in 1899; commonly brown,
    sepia, or black; on paper or cloth.
  CN  MARC field 755.
  UF  Brownprints
    Callitypes
  BT  Photographic prints
  NT  Vandyke prints
**Keepsakes**
  PN  Two-dimensional works produced to mark

**Keepsakes (cont.)**
    the occasion of a gathering or event; given or
    sold to those in attendance and not usually
    otherwise available.
  CN  Used in a note under EPHEMERA.
    MARC field 655.
  UF  Souvenirs
  BT  Ephemera
  RT  Commemorative prints
    Presentation albums
    Viewbooks
Keys (Identification)
  USE Keys (Legends)
**Keys (Legends)**
  PN  Texts or diagrams that identify specific
    features or people in a picture; may be on a
    separate sheet from the picture; commonly on
    or accompanying prints.
  CN  MARC field 655.
  HN  Changed 6/94. Formerly, KEYS
    (LEGENDS) may have been indexed as
    IDENTIFICATION KEYS.
  UF  Identification keys
    Keys (Identification)
    Legends (Identification)
    Legends (Keys)
Kodachrome transparencies
  USE Dye coupler transparencies
Kodacolor negatives
  USE Dye coupler negatives
**Kodak card photographs**
  PN  Card photographs made from a Kodak no.
    1 or no. 2 camera; mounts measure
    approximately 4.25 x 5.25 in. (11 x 13 cm.).
    Produced 1888-1890s; images are circular;
    mounts marked Kodak.
  CN  MARC field 755.
  BT  Card photographs
Kodak instant color prints
  USE Dye diffusion transfer prints
**Labels**
  PN  Slips of paper, cloth, or other material
    affixed, or meant to be attached to something
    for identification, description, or decoration.
  CN  MARC field 655.
  BT  Ephemera
  NT  Bookplates +
    Fruit crate labels
    Stickers +
    Textile labels
    Tobacco package labels
Lambertypes
  USE Carbon prints
**Landscape architecture drawings**
  PN  Graphic delineations made for the design
    and construction (or documentation of design
    and construction) of landscapes, parks,
    gardens, estate grounds, planting beds,
    outdoor fountains, and other planned
    elements of scenery or building sites.
    Includes any drawings produced by landscape
    architects or firms in the course of their

---

BT  Broader term
NT  Narrower term
HN  History Note

RT  Related term
UF  Used for
CN  Catalogers Note

PN Public Note
+ Term has NTs

**Landscape architecture drawings (cont.)**
business.
CN See note under ARCHITECTURAL
DRAWINGS. MARC field 655.
UF Drawings, Landscape architecture
Planting drawings
BT Design drawings
RT Site plans

**Landscape drawings**
CN MARC field 655.
BT Drawings
Landscapes

**Landscape paintings**
CN MARC field 655.
BT Landscapes
Paintings

**Landscape photographs**
CN MARC field 655.
BT Landscapes
Photographs

**Landscape prints**
CN MARC field 655.
BT Landscapes
Prints

**Landscapes**
PN General or broad views of natural scenery;
may include figures or man-made objects, but
these are of secondary importance to the
composition. Usually made from an elevated
or distant vantage point, such as a view from
a hill; not ground level close-up views of, for
example, a tree.
CN MARC field 655.
UF Topographic views
BT Pictures
NT Landscape drawings
Landscape paintings
Landscape photographs
Landscape prints
RT Marines (Visual works)
Panoramic views
Seascapes

**Lantern slides**
PN Hand-drawn, painted, or photographic
images on glass, intended for viewing by
projection; often made in sets. Photographic
lantern slides were introduced in the United
States by 1850 and popular through World
War I; commonly 3.25 x 4 in. (9 x 10 cm.)
with a black paper mask, a cover glass, and
taped edges.
CN As desired, also index under the type of
photographic process. MARC field 755.
UF Magic lantern slides
BT Glass transparencies
Slides

Laser photographs
USE Holograms

**Leaflets**
PN Unbound volumes with fewer than five
pages.
CN MARC field 755.

**Leaflets (cont.)**
UF Booklets
Brochures
RT Books
Fliers (Printed matter)
Pamphlets

**Leather photographs**
PN Photographs on leather, such as collodion
positives on japanned leather or carbon
transfers on white or light-colored leather.
CN MARC field 755.
UF Collodion positive photographs
BT Photographic prints

Legal photographs
USE Forensic photographs

Legends (Identification)
USE Keys (Legends)

Legends (Keys)
USE Keys (Legends)

**Lenticular photographs**
PN Photographs formed and viewed through
lenticular screens (transparent sheets, usually
plastic, embossed with a pattern of tiny lens
segments). Applications include additive
color processes (introduced 1909) and
stereoscopic systems in which an image
appears to be three-dimensional.
CN MARC field 755.
UF Three-dimensional photographs
BT Photographs
RT Stereographs

**Letter pictures**
PN Designs in which words or the letters of a
word are arranged to form a picture or
decorative pattern or figure.
CN MARC field 655.
UF Calligrams
RT Calligraphy

Letter sheets
USE Letterheads

**Letterheads**
PN Printed headings on business or personal
stationery; may include a name, address, or
small illustration. Also, sheets of paper with
such a heading.
CN MARC field 655.
UF Illustrated letter paper
Letter sheets
BT Stationery
NT Pictorial lettersheets

**Letterpress works**
PN Sheets or pages of text printed from metal,
wood, or other material. May include
woodcut or photomechanical line or halftone
illustrations. Superseded for commercial use
in the mid-1900s by offset photomechanical
processes.
CN MARC field 755.
BT Relief prints

Lettersheets, Pictorial
USE Pictorial lettersheets

Lift-ground aquatints

BT Broader term
NT Narrower term
HN History Note

RT Related term
UF Used for
CN Catalogers Note

PN Public Note
+ Term has NTs

Lift-ground aquatints (cont.)
  USE Sugar-lift aquatints
Lift-ground etchings
  USE Sugar-lift aquatints
**Limited editions**
  PN  Prints, photographs, and other works
      produced in a stated number of copies after
      which no more are made. Usually numbered
      consecutively, e.g., 5/100 (the fifth print in an
      edition of 100).
  CN  In Printing & Publishing Evidence, the
      term LIMITATION STATEMENTS is used
      instead of LIMITED EDITIONS.  MARC
      field 755.
  UF  Editions, Limited
Line block prints
  USE Line photomechanical prints
**Line photomechanical prints**
  PN  Prints made from photomechanical relief
      blocks or lithographic plates of engravings,
      drawings, and other works that consist of just
      two tones: the background and the image. The
      image may be composed of solid dark areas
      as well as lines, but it lacks tonal gradations.
      No screen markings.
  CN  MARC field 755.
  UF  Line block prints
      Process line engravings
  BT  Photomechanical prints
Linen labels
  USE Textile labels
**Linocuts**
  PN  Prints made from linoleum blocks. Can be
      difficult to distinguish from cellocuts.
  CN  MARC field 755.
  UF  Linoleum cut prints
  BT  Relief prints
**Linoleum blocks**
  CN  MARC field 655.
  BT  Printing blocks
Linoleum cut prints
  USE Linocuts
Lithographic stones
  USE Printing stones
**Lithographs**
  CN  Used in a note under
      CHROMOLITHOGRAPHS. MARC field
      755.
  BT  Planographic prints
  NT  Chromolithographs +
      Lithotints
      Offset lithographs
      Zincographs
  RT  Chine collé prints
      Photolithographs
**Lithotints**
  PN  Lithographs made to look like wash
      drawings by diluting tusche (ink) with
      turpentine while creating the image on the
      stone or plate.  Introduced in the 1840s. Do
      not confuse with lithographs that have a
      background tint produced from a second

Lithotints (cont.)
      stone.
  CN  MARC field 755.
  BT  Lithographs
**Lobby cards**
  PN  Motion picture advertisements intended
      for display in a theater lobby or showcase
      window.  Often small versions of movie
      posters.  The standard size established by the
      Motion Pictures Patent Company in 1909 is
      11 x 14 inches.
  CN  MARC field 655.
  HN  Changed 10/90.  Formerly, LOBBY
      CARDS may have been indexed as DISPLAY
      CARDS.
  BT  Display cards
  RT  Motion picture posters
**Lottery tickets**
  PN  Slips of paper, cardboard, or other
      material that represent chances for winning a
      prize in a lottery.
  CN  MARC field 655.
  UF  Tickets, Lottery
  BT  Ephemera
**Luminous works**
  PN  Works that glow in the dark, including
      those that glow only when activated by
      ultraviolet light.
  CN  MARC field 755.
  UF  Black light works
      Fluorescent works
  BT  Novelty works
**Macrophotographs**
  PN  Unusually large photographs; objects
      shown are life-size or larger.
  CN  MARC field 755.
  BT  Photographs
**Magazine covers**
  PN  Illustrations and original designs for the
      covers of periodicals.
  CN  MARC field 655.
  UF  Covers, Magazine
      Periodical covers
  BT  Covers (Illustration)
Magazine illustrations
  USE Periodical illustrations
Magazine posters
  USE Book & magazine posters
Magazines
  USE Periodicals
Magic lantern slides
  USE Lantern slides
Magic posters
  USE Theatrical posters
Mailing cards
  USE Postcards
**Male figure drawings**
  PN  Drawings of the human male body, other
      than portraits.
  CN  MARC field 655.
  BT  Figure drawings
**Mammoth plates**

---

BT  Broader term                          RT  Related term                          PN  Public Note
NT  Narrower term                         UF  Used for                              +  Term has NTs
HN  History Note                          CN  Catalogers Note

## Mammoth plates (cont.)

PN   Large photographs taken during the second half of the 1800s; various sizes, including 18 x 22 in. and 20 x 24 in. Includes both the wet collodion negatives and the prints made from them.

CN   As desired, also index under the specific type of photographic process. MARC field 755.

BT   Photographs

RT   Photographic prints
Wet collodion negatives

## Manière criblée prints
USE Dotted prints

## Manufacturers' catalogs

PN   Catalogs issued by the manufacturer of the products being sold.  When made available to both general public and the trade, wholesale prices may be coded or in a separate list.

CN   MARC field 655.

HN   Changed 10/90.  Formerly, MANUFACTURERS' CATALOGS may have been indexed as COMMERCIAL CATALOGS.

BT   Trade catalogs

## Maps

PN   Graphic delineations at a set scale, of all or part of the earth or another celestial sphere indicating the relative position of selected artificial and natural features.

CN   MARC field 655.

NT   Fire insurance maps
Plats
Topographic maps

RT   Bird's-eye views
Cartouches
Plans

## Marine architecture drawings
USE Naval architecture drawings

## Marine drawings

CN   MARC field 655.

HN   Changed 6/94. Formerly, MARINE DRAWINGS may have been indexed as WATERSCAPE DRAWINGS.

UF   Waterscape drawings

BT   Drawings
Marines (Visual works)

## Marine paintings

CN   MARC field 655.

HN   Changed 6/94. Formerly, MARINE PAINTINGS may have been indexed as WATERSCAPE PAINTINGS.

UF   Waterscape paintings

BT   Marines (Visual works)
Paintings

## Marine photographs

CN   MARC field 655.

HN   Changed 6/94. Formerly. MARINE PHOTOGRAPHS may have been indexed as WATERSCAPE PHOTOGRAPHS.

UF   Waterscape photographs

BT   Marines (Visual works)

## Marine photographs (cont.)
Photographs

## Marine prints

CN   MARC field 655.

HN   Changed 6/94. Formerly, MARINE PRINTS may have been indexed as WATERSCAPE PRINTS.

UF   Maritime prints
Waterscape prints

BT   Marines (Visual works)
Prints

RT   Naval prints

## Marine views
USE Marines (Visual works)
Seascapes

## Marines (Visual works)

PN   Works depicting scenes having to do with ships, shipbuilding, or harbors. For works depicting the ocean or other large body of water where the water itself dominates the scene, use SEASCAPES.

CN   MARC field 655.

HN   Changed 6/94. Formerly, MARINES (VISUAL WORKS) may have been indexed as WATERSCAPES.

UF   Marine views
Waterscapes

BT   Pictures

NT   Marine drawings
Marine paintings
Marine photographs
Marine prints

RT   Landscapes
Panoramic views
Seascapes

## Maritime prints
USE Marine prints

## Marker works

PN   Drawings and other works made by either water-based or petroleum-based ink from a felt, nylon, or ceramic tip pen.

CN   MARC field 755.

BT   Ink drawings
Pen works

## Markings
USE Marks

## Marks

PN   Marks in, on, or applied to works; not usually considered part of the visual imagery; often an aid to dating or establishing provenance.

CN   MARC field 755.

UF   Markings

NT   Blind stamps
Dealers' marks
Emblems +
Inscriptions +
Ownership marks +
Register marks
Seals
Tax stamps
Trademarks

---

BT Broader term
NT Narrower term
HN History Note

RT Related term
UF Used for
CN Catalogers Note

PN Public Note
+ Term has NTs

**Marks (cont.)**
    Watermarks

**Marriage certificates**
    CN  MARC field 655.
    BT  Certificates
    RT  Family trees

**Matchcovers**
    PN  Covers to contain packs of matches;
        usually paper.  Introduced in 1892. Matches
        may or may not be present.
    CN  MARC field 655.
    BT  Packaging

**Measured drawings**
    PN  Drawings of an existing site or structure
        made to scale and dimensioned from site
        notes, measurements, or photogrammetric
        analysis. Often comprise a set of plans,
        elevations, sections, and details. Examples
        include the work of the Historic American
        Buildings Survey.
    CN  MARC field 655.
    UF  Drawings, Measured
        Survey drawings
    BT  Design drawings
    RT  Mechanical drawings

**Mechanical drawings**
    PN  Drawings prepared with mechanical
        devices, such as compasses, ruling pens, and
        other drafting tools, according to strict scales,
        conventions, proportions, and projection
        methods.
    CN  MARC field 655.
    UF  Drawings, Mechanical
        Technical drawings
    BT  Design drawings
    RT  Measured drawings

**Mechanical systems drawings**
    PN  Graphic delineations for design, layout,
        installation, and operation and maintenance
        of the mechanical systems in a structure.
        They include plumbing (water supply and
        sanitary waste) and transport (elevator,
        escalator, dumb waiter) systems.
    CN  MARC field 655.
    UF  Drawings, Mechanical systems
    BT  Design drawings
    NT  HVAC drawings

**Mechanical works**
    PN  Works with moving parts, such as pop-out
        or sliding sections, turning wheels, or flaps
        that unfold to reveal new aspects of a picture.
        Also, works that require an action, such as
        turning them, to reveal the whole image or
        another image.
    CN  MARC field 755.
    UF  Movable works
    BT  Novelty works
    NT  Hidden image works +
        Metamorphic pictures

**Medical drawings**
  USE Medical illustrations

**Medical illustrations**

**Medical illustrations (cont.)**
    PN  Illustrations made to document medical
        conditions or procedures; primarily used as
        instructional aids in the identification and
        treatment of disease.
    CN  MARC field 655.
    UF  Drawings, Medical
        Medical drawings
    BT  Scientific illustrations

**Megalethoscope prints**
    PN  Photographic prints on thin paper specially
        mounted on a curved frame for viewing in a
        megalethoscope, a large device with a
        magnifying lens designed for daylight or
        artificial light use. Introduced in the 1860s;
        often used for parlor entertainment; usually
        12 in. (30 cm.) wide.
    CN  MARC field 755.
    BT  Photographic prints

**Melainotypes**
  USE Tintypes

**Membership cards**
    CN  MARC field 655.
    BT  Cards

**Membership certificates**
    CN  MARC field 655.
    BT  Certificates

**Memorabilia**
    PN  Three-dimensional objects that cannot be
        otherwise categorized. Examples include
        political campaign pencils and souvenir
        paperweights.
    CN  MARC field 655.
    UF  Souvenirs
    BT  Ephemera
    RT  Badges

**Memorial works**
    PN  Prints, cards, black-edged stationery, and
        other items produced in memory of a
        deceased person. Prints marking the
        anniversary of the death of a public figure are
        included.
    CN  MARC field 655.
    UF  Mourning works
    RT  Commemorative prints

**Menus**
    PN  Lists of the dishes that may be ordered in
        an eating establishment or that are to be
        served at a banquet or other occasion.
    CN  MARC field 655.
    UF  Bills of fare
    BT  Ephemera

**Metal cuts**
    PN  Prints printed in relief from metal plates
        usually attached to wood blocks; chiefly ca.
        1450-1500.
    CN  MARC field 755.
    BT  Relief prints
    NT  Dotted prints

**Metalpoint drawings**
    CN  MARC field 755.
    BT  Drawings

---

BT  Broader term          RT  Related term          PN Public Note
NT  Narrower term        UF  Used for              + Term has NTs
HN  History Note          CN Catalogers Note

**Metalpoint drawings (cont.)**
NT  Silverpoint drawings
**Metamorphic pictures**
PN  Pictures that can be transformed into one or more other pictures by turning, folding, or sliding a section.  Also, pictures with interchangeable parts, such as sets of heads, torsos, and legs, which can be combined to make different figures.
CN  MARC field 755.
UF  Reversible head prints
    Transformation pictures
BT  Mechanical works
**Mezzotints**
CN  MARC field 755.
BT  Intaglio prints
**Microfiches**
CN  MARC field 755.
BT  Microphotographs
**Microfilms**
CN  MARC field 755.
BT  Microphotographs
**Microforms**
CN  MARC field 755.
NT  Microopaques
    Microphotographs +
RT  Miniature works
    Reproductions
**Microopaques**
PN  Microform images on opaque, white cards.
CN  MARC field 755.
UF  Microprints
    Opaque microcopies
BT  Microforms
**Microphotographs**
PN  Photographs of objects shown at greatly reduced size; require magnifying glass or other magnification device to view.
CN  MARC field 755.
BT  Microforms
    Photographs
NT  Microfiches
    Microfilms
    Stanhopes
RT  Photomicrographs
Microprints
USE Microopaques
**Miniature works**
PN  Graphic materials that are very small in comparison to the usual size of their genre or physical type.
CN  MARC field 755.
NT  Gem photographs
    Miniatures (Paintings)
RT  Microforms
**Miniatures (Illuminations)**
PN  Pictures in an illuminated manuscript; distinct from the initials and borders.
CN  MARC field 655.
HN  Changed 11/90. Formerly, MINIATURES (ILLUMINATIONS) may have been indexed

**Miniatures (Illuminations) (cont.)**
    as ILLUMINATIONS.
BT  Illuminations
**Miniatures (Paintings)**
PN  Paintings on a very small scale (usually five inches or less), especially the portraits on vellum or ivory popular in England and America from the Renaissance into the 1800s. For miniatures in manuscripts, search under MINIATURES (ILLUMINATIONS).
CN  MARC field 755.
HN  Changed 6/94. Formerly, MINIATURES (PAINTINGS) may have been indexed under MINIATURES.
UF  Portrait miniatures
BT  Miniature works
    Paintings
Minstrel posters
USE Theatrical posters
**Mixed media**
PN  Works combining techniques and materials from two or more graphic or fine art processes no one of which clearly predominates.  Examples include prints with large amounts of drawing, and photographs with heavy over-painting.
CN  For works combining more than one process within a general medium category, use the general category name. For example, for a print comprised of etching and engraving, use INTAGLIO PRINTS. For a drawing of ink, crayon, and watercolor, use DRAWINGS. MARC field 755.
UF  Multiple processes
RT  Collages
    Drawings
    Montages
    Paintings
    Photographs
    Prints
Mizrachs
USE Mizriha'ot
**Mizriha'ot**
PN  Pictures hung on the house or synagogue wall in the direction of Jersualem toward which Jews face while praying.
CN  MARC field 655.
UF  Mizrachs
BT  Devotional images
**Money**
PN  Paper money designed to circulate as medium of exchange. Examples include national and colonial government notes; bank notes; and merchant, military, and local government scrip.
CN  MARC field 655.
UF  Currency
    Paper money
BT  Ephemera
NT  Bank notes
    Scrip
RT  Bank note vignettes

BT Broader term
NT Narrower term
HN History Note

RT Related term
UF Used for
CN Catalogers Note

PN Public Note
+ Term has NTs

**Monochromatic works**
PN   Graphic delineations which are purely white, or light and dark values of a single color.
CN   Do not use for black-and-white images. Used in a note under PAINTINGS. MARC field 755.
NT   Cyanotypes +
      Vandyke prints

**Monograms**
PN   Characters or ciphers usually composed of two or more combined or interwoven letters; usually represent a name or part of a name.
CN   MARC field 755.
BT   Inscriptions
RT   Artists' devices

Monoprints
USE Monotypes

Monotype prints
USE Monotypes

**Monotypes**
PN   Prints made by painting an image on glass, metal, or other sheet, or by applying ink and wiping parts away, then transferring the image to paper. Usually no more than one or two impressions are made.
CN   MARC field 755.
HN   Changed 11/90.  Formerly, MONOTYPES may have been indexed as MONOTYPE PRINTS.
UF   Monoprints
      Monotype prints
BT   Planographic prints

**Montages**
PN   Composite pictures made by bringing together into a single composition a number of different parts of pictures and arranging these by superimposing one on another to form a blended whole. Pieces are physically rather than optically combined, but with more effort to conceal separations than in a collage.
CN   MARC field 755.
BT   Pictures
RT   Mixed media
      Photomontages

**Motion picture posters**
CN   MARC field 655.
UF   Film posters
      Movie posters
BT   Performing arts posters
RT   Lobby cards

Motion picture stills
USE Film stills

**Motion study photographs**
PN   Photographs, either single images or sets, made to record successive phases of a motion.  For example, exposures made by separate cameras set up along the path of a moving subject; successive exposures by one camera that result in separate images; exposures that result in a single image through intermittent illumination of the

**Motion study photographs (cont.)**
      subject.
CN   MARC field 755.
UF   Chronophotographs
      Multiple flash photographs
      Pulsed-light photographs
      Stroboscopic photographs
      Time-lapse photographs
BT   Photographs
RT   Flash photographs

Motto prints
USE Emblem pictures

Mourning works
USE Memorial works

Movable works
USE Mechanical works

Movie posters
USE Motion picture posters

Movie stills
USE Film stills

Mug shots
USE Identification photographs

Multiple flash photographs
USE Motion study photographs

Multiple processes
USE Mixed media

Music posters
USE Concert posters

Music sheet covers
USE Sheet music covers

**Music title pages**
CN   MARC field 655.
BT   Title pages
NT   Sheet music covers

Musical play posters
USE Theatrical posters

National stereotypes
USE Ethnic stereotypes

**Naval architecture drawings**
PN   Graphic delineations made for the design and construction (or documentation of design and construction) of ships, boats, and similar vessels.
CN   See note under ARCHITECTURAL DRAWINGS.  MARC field 655.
UF   Drawings, Naval architecture
      Marine architecture drawings
BT   Design drawings

**Naval prints**
PN   Prints that show the actions of a navy or its personnel, including naval battles, expeditions, and portraits.
CN   MARC field 655.
BT   Prints
RT   Marine prints

**Negative prints**
PN   Photographic prints in which tones or colors are the opposite of their normal values.
CN   MARC field 755.
BT   Photographic prints

**Negatives**
PN   Photographs in which the tonal values are

BT Broader term          RT Related term          PN Public Note
NT Narrower term        UF Used for              + Term has NTs
HN History Note           CN Catalogers Note

**Negatives (cont.)**
the opposite of those in the subject to which the negative was exposed. Their purpose is to be a matrix for obtaining multiple positive images of the subject.
CN  Used in a note under PHOTOGRAPHS. MARC field 755.
HN  Changed 11/90. Formerly, NEGATIVES may have been indexed as PHOTONEGATIVES.
UF  Photonegatives
BT  Photographs
NT  Film negatives +
    Glass negatives +
    Paper negatives +

**New Year cards**
CN  MARC field 655.
BT  Greeting cards
RT  Carriers' addresses

**Newscarriers' addresses**
USE Carriers' addresses

**Newsmen's presents**
USE Carriers' addresses

**Newspaper clippings**
USE Clippings

**Newspaper illustrations**
USE Periodical illustrations

**Newspaper posters**
USE Book & magazine posters

**Niello printing plates**
PN  Decorative metal plaques with incised lines that have been filled with niello and hence could also be used for printing. Predecessor of copperplate engraving; chiefly Italian, 1400s-1500s.
CN  MARC field 655.
BT  Printing plates

**Night photographs**
PN  Photographs taken at night; the primary subject may or may not be night; may involve special production techniques. Does not include daytime or indoor available-light photographs where the effect of darkness is due to limited lighting.
CN  MARC field 655.
BT  Photographs

**Nitrate negatives**
PN  Negatives with a nitrocellulose film base. Manufactured from 1887 to 1950.
CN  MARC field 755.
HN  Changed 6/94. Formerly, NITRATE NEGATIVES may have been indexed as CELLULOSE NITRATE NEGATIVES.
UF  Cellulose nitrate negatives
    Nitrocellulose negatives
BT  Film negatives

**Nitrocellulose negatives**
USE Nitrate negatives

**Novelty works**
PN  Works made with materials uncommon for their format; with unusual attachments, such as feathers or buttons; with unusual

**Novelty works (cont.)**
shapes; or with other uncommon features. Examples include leather postcards, greeting cards with tinsel, postcards that squeak, and perfumed advertisements.
CN  MARC field 755.
UF  Exotic works
NT  Anaglyphs
    Anamorphic images
    Luminous works
    Mechanical works +

**Now & then comparisons**
USE Then & now comparisons

**Offset lithographs**
PN  In original printmaking, lithographs printed by transferring an image from a printing plate or stone to an intermediate surface and then to paper or another type of sheet.
CN  MARC field 755.
BT  Lithographs

**Offset photomechanical prints**
PN  Usually a lithographic process and referred to as offset lithographs. Introduced in 1906; by the 1970s, a widely used method for publishing text and illustrations.
CN  Used in a note under PHOTOLITHOGRAPHS. MARC field 755.
BT  Photomechanical prints

**Oil paintings**
CN  MARC field 755.
BT  Paintings

**Oleographs**
PN  Chromolithographs printed on a textured surface using blocks inked with oil paint; often coated with varnish. Popular as inexpensive reproductions of oil paintings in the late-1800s.
CN  MARC field 755.
HN  Changed 11/90. Formerly, OLEOGRAPHS may have been indexed as CHROMOLITHOGRAPHS.
BT  Chromolithographs

**Opalotypes**
PN  Photographs on opal (opaque white) glass; popular in the 1880s to early 1900s. Made either by transferring a carbon print onto the glass or by exposing a light-sensitive emulsion on the opal glass to a negative.
CN  MARC field 755.
BT  Photographic prints
RT  Ceramic photographs

**Opaque microcopies**
USE Microopaques

**Opera posters**
USE Theatrical posters

**Ornaments**
USE Decorations

**Ownership marks**
CN  MARC field 755.
BT  Marks
NT  Collectors' marks

BT Broader term
NT Narrower term
HN History Note
RT Related term
UF Used for
CN Catalogers Note
PN Public Note
+ Term has NTs

**Ownership marks (cont.)**
RT   Bookplates
Ozalids
USE Diazo prints
Ozobrome prints
USE Carbro prints
Packages
USE Packaging
**Packaging**
PN   Materials for the packing or protective
      wrapping of objects; usually contain
      information about the objects.
CN   MARC field 655.
HN   Changed 6/94. Formerly, PACKAGING
      may have been indexed as PACKAGES.
UF   Packages
      Wrappers
      Wrapping materials
      Wrappings
BT   Ephemera
NT   Bags
      Book jackets
      Envelopes +
      Matchcovers
      Photograph cases +
      Ream wrappers
RT   Covers (Illustration)
**Paintings**
PN   Narrower terms include both physical
      media and genre categories.
CN   When using a genre term that includes the
      word PAINTINGS, also index under a more
      specific physical process name, if desired.
      MARC field 755.
BT   Pictures
NT   Abstract paintings
      Allegorical paintings
      Casein paintings
      Cityscape paintings
      Genre paintings
      Landscape paintings
      Marine paintings
      Miniatures (Paintings)
      Oil paintings
      Pastel paintings
      Polymer paintings +
      Portrait paintings
      Still life paintings
      Tempera paintings
RT   Airbrush works
      Brush works
      Mixed media
      Watercolors
Palladiotypes
USE Palladium prints
**Palladium prints**
PN   Photographic prints on paper sensitized
      with palladium salts. Introduced during World
      War I when platinum became prohibitively
      expensive; not commercially available after
      the 1920s.
CN   MARC field 755.

**Palladium prints (cont.)**
UF   Palladiotypes
BT   Photographic prints
Pamphlet illustrations
USE Book illustrations
**Pamphlets**
PN   Published non-periodical volumes with no
      cover or with a paper cover. Usually 5 or
      more pages and fewer than 49 pages.
CN   MARC field 755.
UF   Booklets
RT   Books
      Leaflets
**Panel card photographs**
PN   Card photographs; mounts measure
      approximately 13 x 7.5 in. (33 x 19 cm.).
      Variant sizes include 17 x 10.5 in. (43 x 27
      cm.) and 23 x 14 in. (59 x 35 cm.).
CN   MARC field 755.
BT   Card photographs
Panoramic maps
USE Bird's-eye view prints
**Panoramic photographs**
PN   Photographs which are a continuous view
      of a wider section of the horizon than could
      normally be photographed in a single
      exposure; ratio of width to height is usually
      2:1 or more. May be separate photographs
      either joined (or meant to be joined) together
      or one long piece made with a special
      camera.
CN   MARC field 755.
UF   Cirkut camera photographs
BT   Panoramic views
      Photographs
**Panoramic views**
PN   Views that cover more area than usually
      can be seen in a single glance.
CN   MARC field 755.
UF   Balloon views
      Views, Panoramic
NT   Panoramic photographs
RT   Aerial views
      Bird's-eye views
      Cityscapes
      Landscapes
      Marines (Visual works)
      Seascapes
**Pantins**
PN   Paper dolls produced in France in the
      1600s and 1700s; often jointed.
CN   MARC field 655.
BT   Paper dolls
**Paper cutouts**
PN   Images produced entirely or partially by
      cutting an outline shape or interior areas to
      form the design. Examples include hollow
      cut silhouettes and cobweb valentines.
CN   MARC field 755.
HN   Changed 11/90. Formerly, PAPER
      CUTOUTS may have been indexed as CUT
      PAPER WORKS.

BT  Broader term            RT  Related term            PN  Public Note
NT  Narrower term            UF  Used for                 +  Term has NTs
HN  History Note             CN  Catalogers Note

**Paper cutouts (cont.)**
UF   Cut paper works
       Papercuts
       Scherenschnitte
       Scissorcraft

**Paper dolls**
PN   Figures on paper or cardboard with
       several parts or different costumes; usually
       issued on one sheet or in a booklet and
       intended to be cut out.
CN   MARC field 655.
BT   Toys
NT   Pantins

Paper money
USE Money

**Paper negatives**
CN   MARC field 755.
BT   Negatives
NT   Calotypes
RT   Stats

Paper toys
USE Toys

Papercuts
USE Paper cutouts

**Pastel drawings**
PN   Drawings made with colored sticks of
       chalk in a nongreasy binder.
CN   MARC field 755.
BT   Drawings

**Pastel paintings**
PN   Paintings made with colored sticks of
       chalk in a nongreasy binder.
CN   MARC field 755.
BT   Paintings

**Patent drawings**
PN   Design drawings that describe something
       in order to obtain patent protection; often
       mechanical drawings or diagrams.
CN   MARC field 655.
UF   Drawings, Patent
BT   Design drawings

**Patriotic envelopes**
PN   Envelopes decorated with portraits of
       military leaders, camp scenes, cartoons,
       flags, and other designs.  Often in one or
       more colors.  They came into use during the
       American Civil War; a smaller number were
       used during the Spanish American War.
CN   MARC field 655.
UF   Civil War envelopes
       Covers, Patriotic
BT   Pictorial envelopes

**Pattern books**
PN   Books, pamphlets, or other volumes
       consisting of designs intended to be used as
       outlines from which to make something.
CN   MARC field 655.
BT   Design drawings

**Pattern sheets**
PN   Sheets drawn or printed with designs used
       as outlines or guides to make something.
       Examples include dress making, embroidery,

**Pattern sheets (cont.)**
       and carpentry patterns.
CN   MARC field 655.
BT   Design drawings
RT   Transfer sheets

Peep show prints
USE Vues d'optique

**Pen works**
CN   MARC field 755.
NT   Marker works
RT   Drawings

**Pencil works**
CN   MARC field 755.
RT   Drawings

**Performing arts posters**
PN   Posters issued to advertise theatrical
       performances and other entertainments.
       Also, posters generally promoting
       performers, without reference to specific
       events.
CN   MARC field 655.
UF   Entertainment posters
BT   Posters
NT   Circus posters
       Concert posters +
       Dance posters
       Motion picture posters
       Theatrical posters

Periodical covers
USE Magazine covers

**Periodical illustrations**
PN   Detached illustrations are included as well
       as original drawings, photographs, and prints
       intended for publication or actually published
       as illustrations in periodicals.
CN   MARC field 655.
UF   Magazine illustrations
       Newspaper illustrations
BT   Illustrations
NT   Editorial cartoons
       Fashion plates

Periodical posters
USE Book & magazine posters

**Periodicals**
PN   Serials usually issued at regular intervals
       and more frequently than annually.
CN   MARC field 655.
UF   Magazines
RT   Comic books

**Perpetual calendars**
PN   Calendars based on mathematical
       calculations with days and weeks arranged so
       that the correct day of the week can be
       determined for any given date for a wide
       range of years.
CN   MARC field 655.
BT   Calendars

**Perspective projections**
PN   Projections in which three-dimensional
       subjects are represented on two-dimensional
       surfaces so that the effect is the same as if the
       actual scene were observed. That is, the

BT  Broader term
NT  Narrower term
HN  History Note

RT  Related term
UF  Used for
CN  Catalogers Note

PN Public Note
+  Term has NTs

**Perspective projections (cont.)**
projectors converge towards the eye of the
observer. Frequently done without complete
dimensional accuracy.
CN   MARC field 655.
BT   Projections
RT   Renderings
Photoceramics
USE Ceramic photographs
**Photochrom prints**
PN   Color photomechanical prints produced
lithographically from photographs. The
technique was developed in Switzerland in
the 1880s by Photoglob Zurich and used until
the early 1900s. The caption is often in gold
lettering. The prints look deceptively like
color photographs unless viewed with a
magnifying glass.
CN   MARC field 755.
UF   Äac prints
BT   Photomechanical prints
**Photocopies**
PN   Typically, quick copy reproductions of
textual documents, photographs, or other
items made through an electrostatic or other
electrophotographic process. Introduced
commercially in 1948. Examples include
prints from office copiers and microfilm
readers.
CN   MARC field 755.
UF   Electrostatic photocopies
      Xerographs
BT   Photographic prints
NT   Copy art
RT   Reproductions
**Photoengravings**
PN   Limited here to prints made by
photoglyphy, photogalvanography, or other
methods of obtaining an intaglio or relief
printing plate from a photograph before the
commercial viability of the line and halftone
photomechanical print processes in the
1880s.
CN   MARC field 755.
BT   Photomechanical prints
Photoglypties
USE Woodburytypes
**Photograms**
PN   Photographs made by laying objects on
photographic paper or film and exposing them
to light.
CN   MARC field 755.
UF   Rayographs
      Schadographs
      Vortographs
BT   Photographs
**Photograph albums**
PN   Albums specially designed to hold
photographs or albums containing
photographs. Both empty and filled albums
are included.
CN   MARC field 655.

**Photograph albums (cont.)**
BT   Albums
NT   Card photograph albums
**Photograph cases**
PN   Decorative containers for one or several
photographs. Primarily made from
1840s-1860s, usually of leather,
paper-covered wood, gutta percha, or
thermoplastic material; mostly for
ambrotypes and daguerreotypes.
CN   MARC field 655.
UF   Cased photographs
BT   Packaging
NT   Union cases
**Photographic postcards**
PN   Postcards that are photographs. Kodak
introduced a sensitized postcard-size stock
with standard postcard information printed on
the back in 1902. The format remained
popular through about 1920, and is still
available. Commercial names include Velox
and Azo (from Kodak) and Cyko (from
Ansco).
CN   MARC field 655.
BT   Photographic prints
      Postcards
**Photographic prints**
PN   Photographs produced from negatives, by
transfer photo processes, or, in the case of
photograms, by the direct action of light on
light-sensitive paper. Tonal values are usually
the same as those of the subject shown. Do
not confuse with continuous tone
photomechanical prints, such as
COLLOTYPES and WOODBURYTYPES.
CN   Used in a note under PHOTOGRAPHS.
      MARC field 755.
HN   Changed 1/93. Formerly,
PHOTOGRAPHIC PRINTS may have been
indexed as PHOTOPRINTS.
UF   Black-and-white prints
      Chloride prints
BT   Photographs
NT   Bromoil prints
      Carbon prints +
      Ceramic photographs
      Clichés-verre
      Cloth photographs
      Composite photographs
      Contact sheets
      Crayon enlargements
      Crystoleum photographs
      Cyanotypes +
      Diazo prints
      Dye coupler prints
      Dye destruction prints
      Dye diffusion transfer prints
      Dye transfer prints
      Gum bichromate prints
      Kallitypes +
      Leather photographs
      Megalethoscope prints

---

BT Broader term       RT Related term       PN Public Note
NT Narrower term       UF Used for       + Term has NTs
HN History Note       CN Catalogers Note

**Photographic prints (cont.)**
  Negative prints
  Opalotypes
  Palladium prints
  Photocopies +
  Photographic postcards
  Platinum prints
  Silver gelatin prints +
  Silver printing-out paper prints +
  Stabilization prints
  RT  Card photographs
      Mammoth plates
      Photomechanical prints
      Proofs
      Stats
**Photographs**
  PN  The word PHOTOGRAPHS is a general
      designation for any photographic process.
      The narrower terms include both physical
      media and genre categories.
  CN  Whenever possible, use a more specific
      term. The basic narrower terms are
      AMBROTYPES, DAGUERREOTYPES,
      NEGATIVES, PHOTOGRAPHIC PRINTS,
      and TINTYPES. When using a genre term
      that includes the word PHOTOGRAPHS, also
      index under a more specific physical process
      name, if desired. MARC field 755.
  BT  Pictures
  NT  Abstract photographs
      Aerial photographs
      Allegorical photographs
      Ambrotypes
      Architectural photographs +
      Banquet camera photographs
      Card photographs +
      Cityscape photographs
      Daguerreotypes
      Detective camera photographs
      Ethnographic photographs
      Expedition photographs
      Fashion photographs
      Film stills
      Flash photographs
      Forensic photographs
      Genre photographs
      Glamour photographs
      Holograms
      Identification photographs
      Infrared photographs
      Instant camera photographs +
      Landscape photographs
      Lenticular photographs
      Macrophotographs
      Mammoth plates
      Marine photographs
      Microphotographs +
      Motion study photographs
      Negatives +
      Night photographs
      Panoramic photographs
      Photograms

**Photographs (cont.)**
      Photographic prints +
      Photomicrographs
      Photomontages
      Pinhole camera photographs
      Portrait photographs +
      Publicity photographs +
      Radio photographs
      Snapshots
      Solarization photographs
      Spirit photographs
      Stats
      Still life photographs
      Television stills
      Tintypes +
      Underwater photographs
      Wire photographs
  RT  Airbrush works
      Mixed media
      Space photographs
      Stereographs
      Transmitted images
      Transparencies
**Photogravures**
  PN  Prints that faithfully imitate photographs
      or other continuous tone originals.
      Hand-pulled prints from plates with an
      aquatint grain have an irregular pattern of
      dotting; prints from screened gravure plates
      have a regular pattern of dots but, unlike
      halftone prints, ink varies in density.
      Introduced in 1879.
  CN  MARC field 755.
  UF  Gravures
  BT  Photomechanical prints
  RT  Rotogravures
**Photolithographs**
  PN  Limited here to prints made directly from
      stones or zinc plates to which the image was
      photographically transferred. One such
      process was patented in the United States in
      1858. For offset photolithography, search
      under OFFSET PHOTOMECHANICAL
      PRINTS.
  CN  MARC field 755.
  BT  Photomechanical prints
  RT  Lithographs
**Photomechanical prints**
  PN  Prints made from photographically
      prepared printing surfaces. Most have a
      distinctive dot or screen pattern, but some are
      continuous tone. Usually planographic.
  CN  Used in a note under PRINTS.  MARC
      field 755.
  UF  Process prints
  BT  Prints
  NT  Anaglyphs
      Collotypes
      Halftone photomechanical prints
      Line photomechanical prints
      Offset photomechanical prints
      Photochrom prints

---

BT  Broader term
NT  Narrower term
HN  History Note

RT  Related term
UF  Used for
CN  Catalogers Note

PN  Public Note
+   Term has NTs

**Photomechanical prints (cont.)**
         Photoengravings
         Photogravures
         Photolithographs
         Rotogravures
         Woodburytypes
RT   Halftone negatives
      Photographic prints
      Planographic prints
      Stereographs
      Transmitted images

**Photomicrographs**
PN   Photographs taken through a microscope.
CN   MARC field 755.
BT   Photographs
RT   Microphotographs

**Photomontages**
PN   Photographic prints made by
      re-photographing a collage or montage of two
      or more photographic prints or pieces of
      photographic prints to which drawing,
      painting, or printing may have been added.
CN   MARC field 755.
BT   Photographs
RT   Collages
      Composite photographs
      Montages

Photonegatives
   USE Negatives

Photostats
   USE Stats

Phototransparencies
   USE Transparencies

Physiognotrace works
   USE Physionotrace works

**Physionotrace works**
PN   Drawings produced by tracing an image
      made by a physionotrace. Also, works made
      from such tracings, such as engraved
      silhouettes.
CN   MARC field 755.
UF   Physiognotrace works
RT   Tracings

**Pictorial envelopes**
PN   Envelopes with printed or hand-drawn
      designs and illustrations. William Mulready
      designed the first printed cover for Great
      Britain in 1839. Images may be portraits,
      advertisements, comic scenes, city views,
      political, or purely decorative.
CN   MARC field 655.
UF   Covers, Illustrated
      Illustrated envelopes
BT   Envelopes
NT   Corner cards
      Patriotic envelopes

Pictorial family records
   USE Family trees

Pictorial letter sheets
   USE Pictorial lettersheets

**Pictorial lettersheets**
PN   Stationery illustrated with lithographed or

**Pictorial lettersheets (cont.)**
      engraved views or other scenes. Prevalent in
      mid-1800s.
CN   MARC field 655.
HN   Changed 6/94. Formerly, PICTORIAL
      LETTERSHEETS may have been indexed as
      LETTERHEADS.
UF   Illustrated letter paper
      Lettersheets, Pictorial
      Pictorial letter sheets
BT   Letterheads

**Picture puzzles**
PN   Pictures in which some figures or objects
      are not readily apparent, for example, animal
      shapes hidden in trees or in a landscape.
CN   MARC field 655.
BT   Puzzles
RT   Hidden image works

**Pictures**
PN   Visual presentations, primarily
      two-dimensional.
CN   When possible, choose a more specific
      term. MARC field 655.
NT   Cartoons (Commentary) +
      Children's art
      Collages
      Conjectural works
      Decorations +
      Devotional images +
      Drawings +
      Genre works +
      Illustrations +
      Juvenilia
      Landscapes +
      Marines (Visual works) +
      Montages
      Paintings +
      Photographs +
      Portraits +
      Posters +
      Prints +
      Reconstructions
      Seascapes
      Still lifes +
      Transparencies +
      Vignettes +

Pieces, Game
   USE Game pieces

Pinatypes
   USE Dye transfer prints

**Pinhole camera photographs**
   CN   MARC field 755.
   BT   Photographs

Pinup photographs
   USE Glamour photographs

Placards
   USE Posters

**Planning drawings**
PN   Design drawings for local, city, regional,
      and other planning projects and their
      components. Distinguished from
      architectural, engineering, and landscape

---

BT  Broader term         RT  Related term         PN  Public Note
NT  Narrower term       UF  Used for             +  Term has NTs
HN  History Note         CN  Catalogers Note

**Planning drawings (cont.)**
architecture drawings chiefly by the
designation 'planner' for the person or firm
that produces or oversees them.
- CN   MARC field 655.
- UF   City planning drawings
  Drawings, Planning
  Urban planning drawings
- BT   Design drawings

**Planographic prints**
- CN   Used in a note under PRINTS.  MARC
  field 755.
- BT   Prints
- NT   Lithographs +
  Monotypes
  Stencil prints +
- RT   Photomechanical prints

**Plans**
- PN   Graphic delineations of a site, structure, or
  object in a horizontal projection.  Projection
  lines are parallel to the picture plane rather
  than in perspective.
- CN   MARC field 655.
- BT   Projections
- NT   Floor plans
  Site plans
- RT   Maps

**Planting drawings**
USE Landscape architecture drawings

**Plastic printing plates**
- CN   MARC field 755.
- BT   Printmaking equipment
- NT   Plastos

**Plastos**
- PN   Flexible thermosetting printing plates
  suitable for flatbed printing, stereotyping, and
  rotary printing; may have adhesive backing.
  Plastos is a commercial stock name.
- CN   MARC field 755.
- BT   Plastic printing plates

**Plates, Printing**
USE Printing plates

**Platinotypes**
USE Platinum prints

**Platinum prints**
- PN   Photographic prints on paper sensitized
  with platinum salts. Introduced commercially
  in 1879 as Platinotypes. Papers manufactured
  until World War I; revived by photographers
  who coat their own paper.
- CN   MARC field 755.
- UF   Platinotypes
- BT   Photographic prints

**Plats**
- PN   Maps showing land boundaries,
  subdivisions, ownership, and all data
  essential to describe and identify units shown
  thereon.  After about 1900, they include one
  or more certificates indicating due approval.
  They do not necessarily show relief, drainage,
  or cultural features.
- CN   MARC field 655.

**Plats (cont.)**
- BT   Maps

**Playbills**
- PN   Programs printed on one sheet for plays or
  theatrical entertainments.
- CN   MARC field 655.
- BT   Broadsides
- RT   Theater programs
  Theatrical posters

**Playing cards**
- PN   Cards made in sets of a designated number
  of cards and marked for use in playing one or
  more games or telling fortunes.
- CN   MARC field 655.
- BT   Cards
- NT   Fortune telling cards +
  Game cards

**Playing pieces**
USE Game pieces

**Plot plans**
USE Site plans

**Pochoir prints**
- PN   Prints colored by a stencil or stencil and
  brush technique; usually book illustrations or
  reproductions; extensively used in France.
- CN   MARC field 755.
- BT   Stencil prints

**Polaroid instant color prints**
USE Dye diffusion transfer prints

**Polaroid instant photographs**
USE Instant camera photographs

**Police photographs**
USE Forensic photographs

**Political cartoons**
- PN   Cartoons that present a viewpoint on a
  contemporary political issue, situation, public
  figure, or institution. They frequently employ
  wit, satire, or caricature, and may use a
  vocabulary of symbols, types, or figures to
  represent political entities, bodies, or
  principles.
- CN   MARC field 655.
- HN   Changed 6/94. Formerly, POLITICAL
  CARTOONS may have been indexed as
  CARTOONS or EDITORIAL CARTOONS.
- BT   Cartoons (Commentary)
- RT   Editorial cartoons

**Political posters**
- PN   Includes election campaign posters as well
  as posters about such social-political issues as
  the environment, health care, and civil rights.
  Also includes propaganda posters.
- CN   MARC field 655.
- UF   Campaign posters
  Election posters
  Propaganda posters
- BT   Posters
- NT   Protest posters
- RT   War posters

**Polyester negatives**
- PN   Negatives with a polyester film base;
  introduced in the mid-1950s.

---

BT  Broader term
NT  Narrower term
HN  History Note

RT  Related term
UF  Used for
CN  Catalogers Note

PN  Public Note
+  Term has NTs

**Polyester negatives (cont.)**
  CN  MARC field 755.
  BT  Safety film negatives
**Polymer paintings**
  CN  MARC field 755.
  BT  Paintings
  NT  Acrylic paintings
Porcelain photographs
  USE Ceramic photographs
**Portfolios**
  PN  Graphic materials issued in unbound sets
      with paper or board covers to contain them.
      Often have a loose title page or text
      introduction. Refers to both the container and
      its contents.
  CN  MARC field 755.
**Portrait drawings**
  CN  MARC field 655.
  BT  Drawings
      Portraits
Portrait miniatures
  USE Miniatures (Paintings)
**Portrait paintings**
  CN  MARC field 655.
  BT  Paintings
      Portraits
**Portrait photographs**
  CN  MARC field 655.
  UF  Studio portraits
  BT  Photographs
      Portraits
  NT  Formation photographs
  RT  Glamour photographs
      Identification photographs
      Publicity photographs
**Portrait prints**
  CN  MARC field 655.
  BT  Portraits
      Prints
**Portraits**
  PN  Graphic representations, especially of the
      face, of real persons, usually posed, living or
      dead.  Pictures whose purpose is the portrayal
      of an individual or several people, not
      pictures that merely include people as part of
      an event or scene.
  CN  MARC field 655.
  BT  Pictures
  NT  Group portraits +
      Portrait drawings
      Portrait paintings
      Portrait photographs +
      Portrait prints
      Self-portraits
  RT  Caricatures
      Crayon enlargements
      Family trees
      Silhouettes
Positives, Color separation
  USE Color separation positives
Post cards
  USE Postcards

**Postage stamps**
  PN  Government-authorized hand stamps,
      adhesive stamps, or meter markings intended
      as evidence of payment of postage. Also,
      stamps issued by private mail delivery
      companies to denote payment of their
      delivery fees.
  CN  MARC field 655.
  UF  Stamps, Postage
  BT  Ephemera
**Postal cards**
  PN  Postcards with preprinted postage.
  CN  MARC field 655.
  BT  Postal stationery
      Postcards
**Postal stationery**
  PN  Cards, envelopes, aerograms, and other
      stationery imprinted with postage indicating
      prepayment.
  CN  MARC field 655.
  BT  Stationery
  NT  Postal cards
**Postcards**
  PN  Cards on which a message may be written
      or printed for mailing without an envelope;
      often include a pictorial, comic, or other
      scene on one side.
  CN  MARC field 655.
  UF  Mailing cards
      Post cards
  BT  Cards
  NT  Photographic postcards
      Postal cards
  RT  Stationery
      Viewbooks
**Posters**
  PN  Single or multi-sheet notices made to
      attract attention to events, activities, causes,
      goods, or services; also, purely decorative
      posters. For posting, usually in a public
      place; chiefly pictorial. Intended to make an
      immediate impression from a distance.
  CN  Used in a note under HANDBILLS and
      ADVERTISEMENTS. MARC field 655.
  UF  Placards
  BT  Pictures
  NT  Billboard posters
      Book & magazine posters
      Exhibition posters
      Performing arts posters +
      Political posters +
      Sports posters
      Travel posters
      Wanted posters
      War posters
  RT  Broadsides
      Ephemera
      Signs
Poupée prints
  USE A la poupée prints
**Premiums**
  PN  Items available without charge or at less

BT  Broader term          RT  Related term          PN Public Note
NT  Narrower term        UF  Used for              + Term has NTs
HN  History Note         CN Catalogers Note

**Premiums (cont.)**
than the usual price with the purchase of a product or service, or as a result of a subscription or membership. May be packaged with the product or available through a coupon. Often part of an advertising promotion. Examples include insert advertising cards and cereal box prizes.
CN MARC field 655.
UF Give-aways
BT Ephemera
RT Advertisements
Sports cards

**Presentation albums**
PN Albums made to be dedicated or presented to a person or organization.
CN MARC field 655.
BT Albums
Ephemera
RT Keepsakes

**Presentation drawings**
PN Graphic representations produced to convey to a client or general audience the effect of the completed appearance and function of a project for a building, object, structure, or site. Usually comprise elevations and plans.
CN MARC field 655.
UF Display drawings
Drawings, Presentation
BT Design drawings
RT Competition drawings

Press clippings
USE Clippings

**Price lists**
PN Enumerations of costs for goods or services; usually lacking descriptive details of a catalog.
CN MARC field 655.
BT Ephemera
RT Catalogs

Primuline process prints
USE Diazo prints

Printed ephemera
USE Ephemera

**Printing blocks**
PN Wood blocks, linoleum on wood, or other materials from which relief prints are made.
CN MARC field 655.
UF Blocks, Printing
BT Equipment
Printmaking equipment
NT Linoleum blocks
Wood blocks

**Printing plates**
PN Metal plates; may be mounted on wood blocks.
CN MARC field 655.
UF Plates, Printing
BT Equipment
Printmaking equipment
NT Niello printing plates

**Printing stones**
CN MARC field 655.
UF Lithographic stones
Stones, Printing
BT Equipment
Printmaking equipment

Printing-out paper prints, Silver
USE Silver printing-out paper prints

**Printmaking equipment**
PN Tools and equipment used for printing.
CN MARC field 655.
BT Equipment
NT Plastic printing plates +
Printing blocks +
Printing plates +
Printing stones
Stencils

**Prints**
PN Narrower terms include both physical media and genre categories.
CN When using a genre term that includes the word PRINTS, also index under a more specific process name, if desired. The basic narrower terms are INTAGLIO PRINTS, PHOTOMECHANICAL PRINTS, PLANOGRAPHIC PRINTS, and RELIEF PRINTS. MARC field 755.
BT Pictures
NT A la poupée prints
Abstract prints
Allegorical prints
Artists' proofs
Bird's-eye view prints
Cast paper prints
Cellocuts
Chine collé prints
Cityscape prints
Cloth prints
Collagraphs
Commemorative prints
Costume prints
Counterproofs
Embossed prints +
Fashion prints
Genre prints
Intaglio prints +
Landscape prints
Marine prints
Naval prints
Photomechanical prints +
Planographic prints +
Portrait prints
Progressive proofs
Proofs before letters
Relief prints +
Reproductive prints
Restrikes
Still life prints
Trial proofs
Vues d'optique
RT Clichés-verre
Mixed media

---

BT Broader term
NT Narrower term
HN History Note

RT Related term
UF Used for
CN Catalogers Note

PN Public Note
+ Term has NTs

**Prints (cont.)**
    Proofs
    Register marks
    Remarques
**Process line engravings**
  USE Line photomechanical prints
**Process prints**
  USE Photomechanical prints
**Production drawings**
  USE Design drawings
    Diagrams
**Production stills**
  USE Film stills
**Programs**
  PN  Brief, usually printed outlines of the order
      to be followed, of feature(s) to be presented,
      and of person(s) participating in a public
      exercise, performance, or entertainment.
  CN  MARC field 655.
  BT  Ephemera
  NT  Theater programs
**Progress photographs**
  PN  Series of photographs made at intervals
      from generally the same vantage points
      showing construction, renovation, or
      demolition of a structure, site, or object as it
      progresses.
  CN  MARC field 655.
  UF  Construction progress photographs
  BT  Architectural photographs
**Progressive proofs**
  PN  In printmaking, sets of proofs showing
      color printing in successive stages from first
      color to finished print, with one superimposed
      over the other. Also, sets showing each color
      separately as well as in final combination.
  CN  MARC field 755.
  UF  Successive proofs
  BT  Prints
      Proofs
**Projections**
  PN  Graphic representations in which
      imaginary sight lines (projectors) extend from
      the eye of the observer to the object being
      depicted. The projectors create an image of
      the subject on an imaginary plane between the
      observer and the subject. Depending on the
      sight lines used, the subject is shown
      realistically or tilted or otherwise altered to
      emphasize particular features.
  CN  Used in a note under ARCHITECTURAL
      DRAWINGS. MARC field 655.
  NT  Axonometric projections +
      Elevations
      Exploded drawings
      Perspective projections
      Plans +
      Sciagraphic projections
      Sections +
  RT  Bird's-eye views
      Design drawings
**Promenade card photographs**

**Promenade card photographs (cont.)**
  PN  Card photographs; mounts measure
      approximately 7 x 4 or 7.5 x 4 in. (18 x 11 or
      19 x 11 cm.). Introduced ca. 1874.
  CN  MARC field 755.
  BT  Card photographs
**Promotional photographs**
  USE Publicity photographs
**Proofs**
  PN  In printmaking, impressions taken at any
      stage from a plate, block, or stone, but not
      considered part of the edition. In
      photography, photographic prints made as
      quick records of a negative or for clients to
      choose from, as with studio portraits.
  CN  MARC field 755.
  NT  Artists' proofs
      Cancellation proofs
      Contact sheets
      Counterproofs
      Progressive proofs
      Proofs before letters
      Trial proofs   .
  RT  Cyanotypes
      Photographic prints
      Prints
      Remarques
**Proofs before letters**
  PN  In printmaking, impressions complete
      except for a title or publication statement to
      be printed outside of the image area.
  CN  MARC field 755.
  UF  Avant des lettres prints
  BT  Prints
      Proofs
**Propaganda posters**
  USE Political posters
**Proposed works**
  PN  Designs for projects that have not been
      executed. Examples include architectural
      drawings for buildings that were not erected
      and book illustrations that were not
      published.
  CN  MARC field 655.
  BT  Design drawings
  RT  Competition drawings
**Protest posters**
  PN  Posters expressing criticism, negative
      social commentary or dissent. Sometimes
      such posters were issued as propaganda or in
      support of a revolutionary movement.
  CN  Used in a note under WAR POSTERS.
      MARC field 655.
  UF  Revolutionary posters
  BT  Political posters
      Protest works
**Protest works**
  PN  Works expressing political criticism,
      negative social commentary, or dissent.
  CN  MARC field 655.
  NT  Protest posters
  RT  Cartoons (Commentary)

---

BT Broader term
NT Narrower term
HN History Note

RT Related term
UF Used for
CN Catalogers Note

PN Public Note
+ Term has NTs

**Publicity photographs**
PN Photos made for publicity or promotional purposes, unlike FASHION PHOTOGRAPHS, which emphasize the product being modeled, or GLAMOUR PHOTOGRAPHS, which focus on the physical attractiveness of the subject.
CN Used in a note under FASHION PHOTOGRAPHS and GLAMOUR PHOTOGRAPHS. MARC field 655.
UF Head shots
   Promotional photographs
   Publicity stills
BT Photographs
NT Glamour photographs
RT Advertisements
   Fashion photographs
   Film stills
   Portrait photographs
   Television stills
Publicity stills
   USE Publicity photographs
Pulsed-light photographs
   USE Motion study photographs
**Puns**
PN Pictorial plays on words.
CN MARC field 655.
RT Rebuses
**Puzzles**
PN Recreational devices that present difficulties to be solved.
CN MARC field 655.
BT Ephemera
   Game pieces
NT Picture puzzles
RT Rebuses
Racial stereotypes
   USE Ethnic stereotypes
**Radio photographs**
PN Photographs scanned and converted to electrical signals, transmitted using radio waves, and then re-formed into images.
CN MARC field 755.
HN Changed 6/94. Formerly, RADIO PHOTOGRAPHS may have been indexed as TRANSMITTED IMAGES.
BT Photographs
   Transmitted images
**Radiographs**
PN Shadow images of internal structures made visible by recording the varying degrees of a subject's absorption of x-rays or gamma rays passed through it. Discovered in 1895.
CN MARC field 755.
UF X-ray photographs
BT Film transparencies
Rayographs
   USE Photograms
RC paper prints
   USE Resin-coated paper prints
**Ream wrappers**
PN Wrappers for reams of paper.

**Ream wrappers (cont.)**
CN MARC field 655.
BT Packaging
**Rebuses**
PN Messages or other texts conveyed in part through words or syllables represented by pictures of objects or symbols whose names resemble the intended words in sound.
CN MARC field 655.
RT Puns
   Puzzles
**Reconstructions**
PN Images that propose how something may have looked at a previous time; based on historical, archaeological, or similar evidence.
CN MARC field 655.
HN Changed 6/94. Formerly, RECONSTRUCTIONS may have been indexed as CONJECTURAL WORKS.
UF Re-creations
BT Pictures
RT Conjectural works
Record covers
   USE Album covers
Record jackets
   USE Album covers
Recreations (Conjectural works)
   USE Conjectural works
**Register marks**
PN Pinholes, cross marks, or other devices used to align prints passed through a press more than once.
CN MARC field 755.
HN Changed 6/94. Formerly, REGISTER MARKS may have been indexed as REGISTRATION MARKS.
UF Registration marks
BT Marks
RT Prints
Registration marks
   USE Register marks
**Relief printed etchings**
PN Etchings (which are usually intaglio prints) printed in relief.
CN MARC field 755.
BT Relief prints
RT Etchings
**Relief prints**
CN Used in a note under PRINTS. MARC field 755.
UF Block prints
BT Prints
NT Letterpress works
   Linocuts
   Metal cuts +
   Relief printed etchings
   Rubbings
   Wood engravings
   Woodcuts +
RT A la poupée prints
   Cellocuts

---

BT Broader term
NT Narrower term
HN History Note

RT Related term
UF Used for
CN Catalogers Note

PN Public Note
+ Term has NTs

**Relief prints (cont.)**
    Collagraphs
**Religious calendars**
    PN  Calendars that highlight religious
        activities and events for specific days.
    CN  MARC field 655.
    BT  Calendars
Religious pictures
    USE Devotional images
**Remarques**
    PN  Drawn, etched, or engraved designs or
        sketches on the margin of a print, printing
        plate, or stone; sometimes removed after
        proofs are made.
    CN  MARC field 755.
    RT  Prints
        Proofs
**Renderings**
    PN  Design drawings often intended for
        presentation, display, or publication. Light
        and shadow and often color heighten the
        three-dimensional appearance of the subject.
        Usually, perspectives and highly finished,
        detailed representations of a site, structure,
        building, object, or portion thereof.
    CN  MARC field 655.
    BT  Design drawings
    RT  Perspective projections
**Reproductions**
    PN  Copies that are often (but not necessarily)
        in another medium or different size from the
        original.
    CN  MARC field 755.
    UF  Copies
    NT  Art reproductions
        Blueprints
        Facsimiles
        Reproductive prints
        Restrikes
        Stats
        Thermal copies
    RT  Clichés-verre
        Diazo prints
        Forgeries
        Microforms
        Photocopies
        Transmitted images
        Vandyke prints
        Videodiscs
**Reproductive prints**
    PN  Prints (other than photomechanical) that
        are either copies of or based closely on
        two-dimensional original works in other
        media, such as paintings.
    CN  MARC field 755.
    BT  Prints
        Reproductions
    RT  Chiaroscuro woodcuts
        Crayon manner prints
**Resin-coated paper prints**
    PN  Photographic prints on a paper base coated
        on both sides with plastic to reduce

**Resin-coated paper prints (cont.)**
        processing time; introduced ca. 1970.
    CN  MARC field 755.
    UF  RC paper prints
    BT  Silver gelatin prints
**Restrikes**
    PN  In printmaking, impressions made after the
        original edition has been issued. Usually
        unsigned and unnumbered.
    CN  MARC field 755.
    BT  Prints
        Reproductions
    RT  Cancellation proofs
Revenue stamps
    USE Tax stamps
Reversible head prints
    USE Metamorphic pictures
Revolutionary posters
    USE Protest posters
Reward posters
    USE Wanted posters
**Rewards of merit**
    PN  Small printed or handwritten documents
        awarded in schools in recognition of good
        behavior or scholastic achievement. Common
        in the 1800s.
    CN  MARC field 655.
    UF  Awards of merit
    BT  Ephemera
    RT  Bible cards
        Certificates
        Devotional images
Re-creations
    USE Reconstructions
Ribbon badges
    USE Badges
Rock and roll posters
    USE Rock posters
**Rock posters**
    PN  Posters promoting rock and other popular
        music concerts or musicians. Includes works
        from the early years of rock and roll in the
        1950s, the psychedelic era of the 1960s and
        1970s, and later types.
    CN  MARC field 655.
    UF  Rock and roll posters
    BT  Concert posters
Rolls
    USE Scrolls
**Rotogravures**
    PN  Prints in which an unobtrusive cross line
        screen breaks up the image, which is then
        printed from a rotating cylinder. Introduced
        ca. 1895 and commonly used for newspaper
        illustrations. Especially suitable for long
        printing runs at high speed; inks frequently
        brown or sepia.
    CN  MARC field 755.
    UF  Gravures
    BT  Photomechanical prints
    RT  Photogravures
**Rubbings**

---

BT  Broader term                RT  Related term            PN  Public Note
NT  Narrower term               UF  Used for                +   Term has NTs
HN  History Note                CN  Catalogers Note

**Rubbings (cont.)**
- PN Impressions made by rubbing charcoal, graphite, or a similar substance across a sheet of paper placed on a surface, portions of which stand out in relief.
- CN MARC field 755.
- BT Relief prints

Sabattier effect photographs
- USE Solarization photographs

Sacks
- USE Bags

**Safety film negatives**
- PN Negatives that do not have a flammable film base; first introduced for still photography in the early 1900s. The various types are often difficult to distinguish.
- BT Film negatives
- NT Acetate negatives
  Polyester negatives

**Sailing cards**
- PN Printed cards made to attract freight consignments or passengers to ships preparing to depart. A picture of the vessel is often included; chiefly 1850s-1860s, though continued in use beyond the era of clipper ships; commonly 4 x 6.5 in. (10 x 16 cm.).
- CN MARC field 655.
- HN Changed 6/94. Formerly, SAILING CARDS may have been indexed as SHIP CARDS.
- UF Ship cards
- BT Advertising cards
- NT Clipper ship cards

**Sales catalogs**
- PN Catalogs issued by businesses and individuals offering products for sale to retailers or the public. Often include prices. Specialized catalogs, such as those for Christmas orders and seeds, are included.
- CN MARC field 655.
- HN Changed 6/94. Formerly, SALES CATALOGS may have been indexed as COMMERCIAL CATALOGS.
- UF Commercial catalogs
- BT Catalogs
- NT Trade catalogs +
- RT Advertising mail

Salt prints
- USE Salted paper prints

**Salted paper prints**
- PN Limited here to photographic prints in which the silver particles are in the paper rather than on the surface in a gelatin or other matrix; introduced in 1839; in use through 1860s.
- CN MARC field 755.
- UF Salt prints
- BT Silver printing-out paper prints

**Sample books**
- PN Albums or other volumes with type face specimens, paint chips, swatches of cloth, or other samples.

**Sample books (cont.)**
- CN MARC field 655.
- UF Specimen books
- BT Samples
- RT Albums
  Catalogs

**Samples**
- PN Books, sheets, or packages containing samples of designs or materials that can be purchased from particular manufacturers or printers. Examples include single sheets made to exhibit the type of work a commercial printer produces and small packages of advertising samples.
- CN MARC field 655.
- BT Ephemera
- NT Sample books

**Satires**
- PN Graphic commentaries critical of the failings, weaknesses, and morals of the people, governments, or organizations depicted.
- CN MARC field 655.
- BT Cartoons (Commentary)

Schadographs
- USE Photograms

Schedules
- USE Schedules (Time plans)

**Schedules (Architectural records)**
- PN Detailed tabulations on architectural and similar working drawings or on separate sheets that indicate dimensions, materials, or fixtures required at various points in the design.
- CN MARC field 655.
- HN Changed 6/94. Formerly, SCHEDULES (ARCHITECTURAL RECORDS) may have been indexed as SCHEDULES (CONTRACT DOCUMENTS).
- UF Schedules (Contract documents)
- BT Charts
  Specifications

Schedules (Contract documents)
- USE Schedules (Architectural records)

**Schedules (Time plans)**
- PN Plans or lists showing sequences of events and their respective times.
- CN MARC field 655.
- HN Changed 6/94. Formerly, SCHEDULES (TIME PLANS) may have been indexed as SCHEDULES.
- UF Schedules
- BT Charts
  Ephemera
- NT Timetables

Scherenschnitte
- USE Paper cutouts

**Sciagraphic projections**
- PN Two-dimensional graphic representations with shadows projected according to specific conventions in regard to the source of light. The projectors of the shadows are usually

BT Broader term
NT Narrower term
HN History Note

RT Related term
UF Used for
CN Catalogers Note

PN Public Note
+ Term has NTs

**Sciagraphic projections (cont.)**
fixed as the diagonal of a cube from the top left corner to the bottom rear corner and at an angle of 45 degrees in plan and elevation.
CN  MARC field 655.
UF  Shades & shadows
BT  Projections

**Scientific illustrations**
PN  Illustrations characterized by great detail and exactitude, suitable for scientific study or identification of organisms. Component parts are often labeled.
CN  MARC field 655.
UF  Technical drawings
BT  Illustrations
NT  Botanical illustrations
     Medical illustrations

Scissorcraft
USE Paper cutouts

**Scrapbooks**
PN  Albums containing or intended to contain a variety of material, especially clippings or ephemera.
CN  MARC field 655.
BT  Albums
     Ephemera

Scraperboard drawings
USE Scratchboard drawings

**Scraps**
PN  Die-cut decorations, usually embossed chromolithographs printed in sheets from which each scrap can be broken off to paste on cards or album pages. Popular from mid- to late 1800s; many made in Germany.
CN  MARC field 655.
BT  Decorations
     Ephemera

**Scratchboard drawings**
PN  White line drawings made by scratching with a stylus or other tool through a coating of black ink on a white, clay coated cardboard. Introduced in the 1800s.
CN  MARC field 755.
UF  Scraperboard drawings
BT  Drawings

**Screen color film transparencies**
PN  Additive color process transparencies introduced commercially in the 1930s. Tradenames include Filmcolor (replaced Autochromes) and Dufaycolor, which survived into the 1950s.
CN  MARC field 755.
UF  Color screen transparencies
     Dufay color transparencies
BT  Film transparencies

**Screen color glass transparencies**
PN  Additive color process transparencies available commercially from 1895-1930s.
CN  MARC field 755.
UF  Color screen transparencies
BT  Glass transparencies
NT  Autochromes

**Screen prints**
PN  Prints made by forcing ink through a fine screen stencil onto paper or another surface. Art applications date from the 1930s; commercial ones from the 1920s.
CN  MARC field 755.
HN  Changed 11/90. Formerly, SCREEN PRINTS may have been indexed as SILKSCREEN PRINTS.
UF  Serigraphs
     Silk screen prints
     Silkscreen prints
BT  Stencil prints

**Scrip**
PN  Limited here to money issued by businesses, military organizations, or local (rather than national) governments, often as payment of wages or to provide small change.
CN  MARC field 655.
BT  Money

Scripture cards
USE Bible cards

**Scrolls**
PN  Illustrated sheets of paper or cloth, much longer in one dimension than the other; meant to be rolled up when not in use.
CN  MARC field 755.
UF  Rolls

**Seals**
PN  Wax or embossed devices with a cut or raised emblem, symbol, or word; chiefly used to certify a signature or authenticate a document.
CN  MARC field 755.
BT  Marks

**Seascapes**
PN  Works depicting the ocean or other large body of water where the water itself dominates the scene. When lesser bodies of water are depicted, use LANDSCAPES. When ships, shipbuilding, or harbors are depicted, use MARINES (VISUAL WORKS). [AAT]
CN  MARC field 655.
HN  Changed 6/94. Formerly, SEASCAPES may have been indexed as WATERSCAPES.
UF  Marine views
     Waterscapes
BT  Pictures
RT  Landscapes
     Marines (Visual works)
     Panoramic views

**Sections**
PN  Graphic delineations of a vertical, horizontal, or oblique slice through a site, structure, or object. They demonstrate the shape and disposition of interior spaces, chambers, and structural or other components showing their placement, proportions, and dimensions.
CN  MARC field 655.

---

BT  Broader term
NT  Narrower term
HN  History Note

RT  Related term
UF  Used for
CN  Catalogers Note

PN  Public Note
+  Term has NTs

**Sections (cont.)**
- BT  Projections
- NT  Floor plans

Security engravings
- USE Bank note vignettes

**Self-portraits**
- PN  Images of a person created by that same person.
- CN  MARC field 655.
- BT  Portraits

**Sentiment cards**
- PN  Cards printed with a word or a brief phrase of love, friendship, or other feelings.  The size of visiting cards.
- CN  MARC field 655.
- BT  Cards

Separation negatives
- USE Color separation negatives

Separation positives, Color
- USE Color separation positives

Separation transparencies, Color
- USE Color separation positives

Serigraphs
- USE Screen prints

**Set design drawings**
- PN  Graphic delineations made for the design and production (or documentation of design and production) of stage settings for theatrical, movie, broadcast, or other performing arts productions.
- CN  MARC field 655.
- BT  Design drawings

Shades & shadows
- USE Sciagraphic projections

**Sheet music covers**
- PN  Covers or first pages of unbound songs and other pieces of music on eight or fewer pages.
- CN  MARC field 655.
- UF  Music sheet covers
- BT  Music title pages

Ship cards
- USE Sailing cards

**Signs**
- PN  Lettered boards or other displays used to give directions or information, to identify a place of business or public facility, or to give warnings or directions.  Textual or symbolic rather than pictorial.
- CN  MARC field 655.
- BT  Ephemera
- NT  Banners
- RT  Broadsides
      Display cards
      Posters

**Silhouettes**
- PN  Images shown in profile in a single hue against a contrasting background; cut, drawn, painted, printed, or photographic; often portraits.
- CN  MARC field 655.
- RT  Portraits

Silk screen prints
- USE Screen prints

Silkscreen prints
- USE Screen prints

Silver dye bleach prints
- USE Dye destruction prints

Silver gelatin film negatives
- USE Film negatives

**Silver gelatin film transparencies**
- CN  MARC field 755.
- UF  Gelatin silver transparencies
- BT  Film transparencies

Silver gelatin glass negatives
- USE Dry plate negatives

**Silver gelatin glass transparencies**
- CN  MARC field 755.
- UF  Gelatin silver transparencies
- BT  Glass transparencies

**Silver gelatin printing-out paper prints**
- PN  Introduced in the 1880s; still marketed as studio proof paper.
- CN  Virtually indistinguishable by visual inspection from the glossy COLLODION PRINTING-OUT PAPER PRINTS used in the 1880s-early 1890s.  If in doubt, use SILVER PRINTING-OUT PAPER PRINTS.  Used in a note under COLLODION PRINTING-OUT PAPER PRINTS. MARC field 755.
- UF  Studio proof paper prints
- BT  Silver printing-out paper prints
- NT  Aristotypes

**Silver gelatin prints**
- PN  Photographic prints made by several formulas; introduced in the 1880s; dominant black-and-white photographic print process since the 1890s. Includes various common developing-out papers that are very difficult to distinguish by visual inspection (e.g., bromide, chloride or gaslight, and chloro-bromide) and one printing-out process.
- CN  MARC field 755.
- UF  Bromide prints
      Chloro-bromide prints
      Gaslight prints
      Gelatin silver prints
- BT  Photographic prints
- NT  Resin-coated paper prints

**Silver printing-out paper prints**
- PN  Photographic prints that consist of a silver image produced without chemical development.
- CN  MARC field 755.
- UF  Printing-out paper prints, Silver
- BT  Photographic prints
- NT  Albumen prints
      Collodion printing-out paper prints +
      Salted paper prints
      Silver gelatin printing-out paper prints +

**Silverpoint drawings**
- CN  MARC field 755.

---

BT  Broader term                    RT  Related term                    PN  Public Note
NT  Narrower term                   UF  Used for                         +  Term has NTs
HN  History Note                    CN  Catalogers Note

**Silverpoint drawings (cont.)**
  BT  Metalpoint drawings
**Simulated images**
  USE Composite photographs
       Computer graphics
**Site plans**
  PN  Design drawings, especially architectural, landscape, and planning drawings, that are plans showing the boundaries, outlines, dimensions, contours, positions, and other characteristics of a defined area and its structures, plantings, and other physical features and improvements.
  CN  MARC field 655.
  UF  Plot plans
  BT  Design drawings
       Plans
  RT  Landscape architecture drawings
**Sketchbooks**
  PN  Albums of drawings or paintings on pages bound together before the images were created.
  CN  MARC field 655.
  UF  Sketchpads
  BT  Albums
**Sketches**
  PN  Rough drawings or paintings representing the chief features of objects or scenes; often made as quick records of a scene, object, or idea, or as a preliminary to a study for a larger work.
  CN  MARC field 655.
  NT  Travel sketches
  RT  Design drawings
       Studies
**Sketchpads**
  USE Sketchbooks
**Skyline views**
  USE Cityscapes
**Sleeves, Record**
  USE Album covers
**Slides**
  PN  Transparent materials on which there is a drawn image or a positive photographic image; intended to be bound or held in a mount and usually designed for use in a projector or viewer.
  CN  MARC field 755.
  BT  Transparencies
  NT  Lantern slides
**Snapshots**
  PN  Photographs that seem to have been made without artistic pretensions; often made quickly with amateur equipment as a remembrance of people, places, or occasions.
  CN  MARC field 655.
  BT  Photographs
  RT  Amateur works
**Soft-ground etchings**
  CN  MARC field 755.
  BT  Etchings
**Solarization photographs**

**Solarization photographs (cont.)**
  PN  Photographs in which negative and positive values have been reversed in some areas, usually as a result of a long exposure. For example, a bright street lamp at night appears as a black spot rather than a bright spot. Includes negatives and prints that exhibit the Sabattier effect caused by exposure to light during darkroom development.
  CN  MARC field 755.
  UF  Sabattier effect photographs
  BT  Photographs
**Souvenir albums**
  USE Albums
       Viewbooks
**Souvenir booklets**
  USE Viewbooks
**Souvenir viewbooks**
  USE Viewbooks
**Souvenirs**
  USE Keepsakes
       Memorabilia
**Space photographs**
  PN  Photographs taken from a vehicle or by a person beyond the earth's atmosphere. Photographs taken by astronauts with conventional cameras are included, as well as images made by digital scanners and transmitted to earth by radio signals for computer processing.
  CN  Used in a note under AERIAL PHOTOGRAPHS. MARC field 755.
  UF  Digital images
  RT  Aerial photographs
       Computer graphics
       Photographs
       Transmitted images
**Speakeasy cards**
  PN  Identification cards that admitted the bearer to a speakeasy during the American prohibition era (1920-1933). Often appear to be a club membership card or contain only cryptic markings.
  CN  MARC field 655.
  BT  Cards
**Specifications**
  PN  Textual or graphic documents, schedules, and notes that amplify working drawings and give detailed information and instruction concerning materials, finishes, and workmanship.
  CN  MARC field 655.
  NT  Schedules (Architectural records)
  RT  Design drawings
**Specimen books**
  USE Sample books
**Spirit photographs**
  PN  Photographs in which deliberate partial exposure of persons or objects causes them to appear like ghosts.
  CN  Do not use for photographs in which long

BT Broader term          RT Related term          PN Public Note
NT Narrower term        UF Used for             + Term has NTs
HN History Note         CN Catalogers Note

**Spirit photographs (cont.)**
      exposure times have caused many figures to
      be partly obliterated unintentionally.  MARC
      field 655.
  UF  Ghost photographs
  BT  Photographs
**Sport posters**
  USE Sports posters
**Sports cards**
  PN  Advertising or collecting cards issued
      since the 1880s to encourage or satisfy
      interest in sports. Examples include football,
      baseball, and basketball cards issued by
      bubble gum, bread, tobacco, and milk
      producers, among others.  Often feature
      portraits of individual athletes or teams.
  CN  MARC field 655.
  UF  Bubble gum cards
  BT  Cards
  NT  Baseball cards
  RT  Advertising cards
      Collecting cards
      Premiums
**Sports posters**
  PN  Posters issued to announce sporting events
      such as football games or boxing matches.
      Also, posters commemorating sports figures.
  CN  MARC field 655.
  HN  Changed 6/94. Formerly, SPORTS
      POSTERS may have been indexed under
      POSTERS.
  UF  Sport posters
  BT  Posters
**Stabilization prints**
  PN  Photographic prints processed rapidly in a
      machine that develops the image but does not
      provide adequate fixing and washing to
      prevent subsequent fading. Often found in
      newspaper photo morgues.
  CN  MARC field 755.
  BT  Photographic prints
**Stamps, Blind**
  USE Blind stamps
**Stamps, Postage**
  USE Postage stamps
**Stamps, Tax**
  USE Tax stamps
**Stanhopes**
  PN  Photographs mounted under a magnifying
      glass about .12 in. (.3 cm.) across.  Often in a
      ring or other jewelry; especially popular in
      the 1860s.
  CN  MARC field 755.
  BT  Microphotographs
**State proofs**
  USE Trial proofs
**Stationery**
  PN  Materials on which letters and similar
      communications are typed or written.
  CN  MARC field 655.
  BT  Ephemera
  NT  Billheads

**Stationery (cont.)**
      Greeting cards +
      Letterheads +
      Postal stationery +
  RT  Envelopes
      Postcards
**Stats**
  PN  Negative or positive image paper
      photographic reproductions made with a
      photostat machine.  Used for art layouts or
      any situation in which quickly made,
      high-contrast copies are needed whether same
      size, enlarged, or reduced.
  CN  MARC field 755.
  UF  Photostats
  BT  Photographs
      Reproductions
  RT  Paper negatives
      Photographic prints
**Stencil prints**
  CN  MARC field 755.
  BT  Planographic prints
  NT  Pochoir prints
      Screen prints
**Stencils**
  CN  MARC field 655.
  BT  Equipment
      Printmaking equipment
**Stereograms**
  USE Stereographs
**Stereographs**
  PN  Two nearly identical photographs or
      photomechanical prints, paired to produce the
      illusion of a single three-dimensional image;
      usually viewed with a stereoscope.
      Typically, photographic prints on card
      mounts, but may be daguerreotypes, glass
      negatives, or other processes.  Card mounts
      commonly 3.5 x 7 in. (9 x 18 cm.) up to 5 x 7
      in. (12 x 18 cm.). Popular in the United States
      1859-1920s.
  CN  Use even if only half of the stereograph is
      present. As desired, also index under the type
      of process, such as DAGUERREOTYPES.
      MARC field 755.
  UF  Stereograms
      Stereoscopic views
      Stereoviews
      Three-dimensional photographs
      Viewmaster cards
  NT  Anaglyphs
      Tissue stereographs
  RT  Card photographs
      Lenticular photographs
      Photographs
      Photomechanical prints
**Stereoscopic views**
  USE Stereographs
**Stereotypes, Ethnic**
  USE Ethnic stereotypes
**Stereoviews**
  USE Stereographs

BT Broader term
NT Narrower term
HN History Note

RT Related term
UF Used for
CN Catalogers Note

PN Public Note
+ Term has NTs

**Stickers**
- PN Messages or designs on slips of paper that are gummed or otherwise treated to adhere to a surface.
- CN MARC field 655.
- BT Labels
- NT Bumper stickers
  Decals

**Still life drawings**
- CN MARC field 655.
- BT Drawings
  Still lifes

**Still life paintings**
- CN MARC field 655.
- BT Paintings
  Still lifes

**Still life photographs**
- CN MARC field 655.
- BT Photographs
  Still lifes

**Still life prints**
- CN MARC field 655.
- BT Prints
  Still lifes

**Still lifes**
- PN Graphic representations of inanimate objects selected and arranged by the artist or photographer for a specific pictorial effect.
- CN MARC field 655.
- BT Pictures
- NT Still life drawings
  Still life paintings
  Still life photographs
  Still life prints

Stills
- USE Film stills
  Television stills

**Stipple engravings**
- PN Engravings in which the design consists of dots or flecks, usually in addition to line work.
- CN MARC field 755.
- HN Changed 11/90. Formerly, STIPPLE ENGRAVINGS may have been indexed as STIPPLE PRINTS.
- UF Stipple prints
- BT Engravings

Stipple prints
- USE Stipple engravings

**Stock cards**
- PN Advertising cards printed with an area left blank for local retailers to add their name or other information.
- CN MARC field 655.
- BT Advertising cards

**Stock certificates**
- PN Documents evidencing ownership of one or more shares of the capital stock of a corporation.
- CN Used in a note under EPHEMERA. MARC field 655.
- BT Certificates

Stones, Printing
- USE Printing stones
Street cries
- USE Cries
Stroboscopic photographs
- USE Motion study photographs

**Structural systems drawings**
- PN Graphic representations made for the design, construction, and assembly (or documentation of the design, construction, and assembly) of the structural support systems of a building or other structure. Features included are attributes of form (post and lintel, arch, truss) and materials (wood, masonry, and steel).
- CN MARC field 655.
- UF Drawings, Structural systems
- BT Design drawings
- NT Framing drawings

**Student works**
- PN Drawings, photographs, prints, or other works created by people for course assignments, or to gain a degree.
- CN MARC field 655.
- RT Amateur works
  Children's art
  Juvenilia

**Studies**
- PN Drawings or paintings, tending to be quite detailed, usually made in preparation for a finished composition. May also be made to explore a technique, material, or design. A more carefully detailed representation than a sketch but less finished than a completed work.
- CN MARC field 655.
- BT Design drawings
- RT Details
  Sketches

Studio portraits
- USE Portrait photographs
Studio proof paper prints
- USE Silver gelatin printing-out paper prints
Submarine photographs
- USE Underwater photographs
Successive proofs
- USE Progressive proofs

**Sugar-lift aquatints**
- PN Prints produced by an aquatint technique in which the part of the plate to be etched is exposed by dissolving the protective coating.
- CN MARC field 755.
- UF Lift-ground aquatints
  Lift-ground etchings
- BT Aquatints

Sunday school cards
- USE Bible cards
  Devotional images
Surveillance photographs
- USE Forensic photographs
Survey drawings
- USE Measured drawings

BT Broader term　　　　RT Related term　　　　PN Public Note
NT Narrower term　　　　UF Used for　　　　　　+ Term has NTs
HN History Note　　　　　CN Catalogers Note

Symbols, Artists'
  USE Artists' devices
Talbotypes
  USE Calotypes
**Tarot cards**
  PN  Pictorial playing cards made specifically
      for forecasting the future and as trumps in
      tarok games. Issued in sets of 22; depict such
      characters and forces as the the fool and the
      tower.
  CN  MARC field 655.
  HN  Changed 6/94. Formerly, TAROT
      CARDS may have been indexed as
      FORTUNE TELLING CARDS.
  UF  Tarots
  BT  Fortune telling cards
Tarots
  USE Tarot cards
**Tax stamps**
  PN  Revenue stamps affixed to various printed
      materials. Required on photographs and other
      graphics in the United States, 1864-1866.
      Also common on some playing card packs.
  CN  MARC field 755.
  UF  Revenue stamps
      Stamps, Tax
  BT  Marks
**Tear sheets**
  PN  Sheets torn or otherwise separated from
      publications to prove insertion of an
      advertisement or an image.
  CN  MARC field 755.
  UF  Tearsheets
  BT  Clippings
Tearsheets
  USE Tear sheets
Technical drawings
  USE Diagrams
      Mechanical drawings
      Scientific illustrations
Television program stills
  USE Television stills
**Television stills**
  PN  Photographs made during the production
      of a television program showing scenes from
      the program; usually for publicity purposes.
  CN  MARC field 655.
  UF  Stills
      Television program stills
      TV stills
  BT  Photographs
  RT  Publicity photographs
**Tempera paintings**
  CN  MARC field 755.
  BT  Paintings
Test proofs
  USE Trial proofs
**Textile design drawings**
  PN  Graphic delineations made for the design
      and production (or documentation of the
      design and production) of fabrics, both woven
      and non-woven.

**Textile design drawings (cont.)**
  CN  MARC field 655.
  UF  Fabric design drawings
  BT  Design drawings
**Textile labels**
  PN  Paper labels meant to identify lengths of
      cloth goods. Usually they state yardage and
      sometimes cloth type and manufacturer's
      name.
  CN  MARC field 655.
  UF  Cloth labels
      Linen labels
  BT  Labels
Theater posters
  USE Theatrical posters
**Theater programs**
  PN  Booklets with descriptions of
      performances and performers.
  CN  MARC field 655.
  BT  Programs
  RT  Playbills
**Theatrical posters**
  PN  Includes posters for plays; minstrel,
      Lilliputian, burlesque, and vaudeville shows;
      operas and operettas; revues; musicals;
      magic; specialty acts, and other stage
      performances.
  CN  MARC field 655.
  UF  Burlesque posters
      Magic posters
      Minstrel posters
      Musical play posters
      Opera posters
      Theater posters
      Vaudeville posters
  BT  Performing arts posters
  RT  Display cards
      Playbills
**Then & now comparisons**
  PN  Single images that compare the
      appearance of a person, place, activity, or
      object by showing the subject at two or more
      different time periods.
  CN  MARC field 655.
  UF  Before & after views
      Comparisons, Then & now
      Now & then comparisons
  RT  Conjectural works
**Thermal copies**
  PN  Heat-produced quick copy reproductions
      of pictorial or textual documents. Introduced
      commercially ca. 1950.
  CN  MARC field 755.
  BT  Reproductions
Thermoplastic union cases
  USE Union cases
Three chalk drawings
  USE A trois crayons drawings
Three-color carbro prints
  USE Tricolor carbro prints
Three-dimensional photographs
  USE Holograms

---

BT  Broader term
NT  Narrower term
HN  History Note

RT  Related term
UF  Used for
CN  Catalogers Note

PN  Public Note
+  Term has NTs

Three-dimensional photographs (cont.)
  Lenticular photographs
  Stereographs
**Tickets**
  PN  Slips of paper, cardboard, or other
      material used for admission or passage.
  CN  MARC field 655.
  BT  Ephemera
Tickets, Lottery
  USE Lottery tickets
Time tables
  USE Timetables
**Timetables**
  PN  Lists showing times of departure and
      arrival for a particular mode of
      transportation.
  CN  MARC field 655.
  HN  Changed 6/94. Formerly, TIMETABLES
      may have been indexed as SCHEDULES.
  UF  Time tables
  BT  Schedules (Time plans)
Time-lapse photographs
  USE Motion study photographs
**Tintypes**
  PN  Direct-image photographs in which the
      collodion negative supported by a
      dark-lacquered thin iron sheet appears as a
      positive image.  Popular mid-1850s through
      1860s; in use through 1930s.
  CN  Used in a note under PHOTOGRAPHS.
      MARC field 755.
  UF  Collodion positive photographs
      Ferrotypes
      Iron photographs
      Melainotypes
  BT  Photographs
  NT  Gem photographs
**Tissue stereographs**
  PN  Photographic print stereographs on thin
      translucent paper mounted either between
      glass plates or on cards cut out to make a
      frame; intended for viewing as a
      transparency.  Many were made in France;
      often colored.
  CN  MARC field 755.
  UF  French tissues
  BT  Stereographs
      Transparencies
**Title pages**
  PN  Pages bearing the title and usually the
      names of author and publisher, and date and
      place of publication of a book, portfolio, or
      other material.
  CN  MARC field 655.
  NT  Music title pages +
  RT  Cartouches
      Decorations
      Illustrations
Toad's-eye views
  USE Worm's-eye views
Tobacco cards
  USE Cigarette cards

**Tobacco package labels**
  PN  Slips of paper or other material affixed or
      meant to be attached to a tobacco plug or
      container for identification, description, or
      decoration.
  CN  MARC field 655.
  HN  Changed 6/94. Formerly, TOBACCO
      PACKAGE LABELS may have been indexed
      as LABELS.
  UF  Tobacco tin tags
  BT  Labels
Tobacco tin tags
  USE Tobacco package labels
Tools
  USE Equipment
**Topographic maps**
  PN  Maps that portray, identify, and locate
      natural and man-made features as precisely as
      possible; usually use contour lines to show
      variations in surface height.
  CN  MARC field 655.
  BT  Maps
Topographic views
  USE Cityscapes
      Landscapes
Tourist trade posters
  USE Travel posters
Townscapes
  USE Cityscapes
**Toys**
  PN  Sheets of paper, cardboard, or other
      material with preprinted outlines or designs
      that can be cut and folded to make toys.  Toys
      already made are included.
  CN  MARC field 655.
  UF  Paper toys
  NT  Paper dolls +
  RT  Game cards
      Game pieces
      Gameboards
**Tracings**
  CN  MARC field 755.
  BT  Drawings
  RT  Camera lucida works
      Camera obscura works
      Physionotrace works
**Trade cards**
  PN  Advertising cards issued or enclosed with
      such products as bread, cigarettes, and
      agricultural machinery.  Use COLLECTING
      CARDS for cards not intended to be
      advertisements.
  CN  MARC field 655.
  HN  Changed 6/94. Formerly, TRADE
      CARDS may have been indexed as
      ADVERTISING CARDS.
  UF  Tradecards
  BT  Advertising cards
  NT  Cigarette cards
**Trade catalogs**
  PN  Catalogs issued by manufacturers,
      retailers, and wholesalers to sell their

---

BT  Broader term                          RT  Related term                          PN  Public Note
NT  Narrower term                         UF  Used for                              +  Term has NTs
HN  History Note                          CN  Catalogers Note

**Trade catalogs (cont.)**
products.  They usually have illustrations and textual descriptions of items for sale.
CN   MARC field 655.
HN   Changed 10/90.  Formerly, TRADE CATALOGS may have been indexed as COMMERCIAL CATALOGS.
BT   Sales catalogs
NT   Manufacturers' catalogs
Tradecards
USE Business cards
Trade cards
**Trademarks**
PN   Symbols or combinations of symbols, letters, and other characters legally reserved to identify products and makers.
CN   MARC field 755.
BT   Marks
Trading cards
USE Advertising cards
Collecting cards
**Transfer sheets**
PN   Paper or other flexible sheets containing images intended for transfer to another surface by application of pressure, heat, or moisture. Examples include iron-on patterns and pictures on graphite paper.
CN   MARC field 755.
UF   Iron-on transfers
RT   Decals
Pattern sheets
Transformation pictures
USE Metamorphic pictures
**Transmitted images**
PN   Images that result from scanning other images, such as photographs, and converting them to electrical signals, which are transmitted and then recorded by electrical, thermal, or other non-photographic processes.
CN   MARC field 755.
UF   Electronic images
Facsimile transmission images
NT   Radio photographs
Wire photographs
RT   Photographs
Photomechanical prints
Reproductions
Space photographs
**Transparencies**
PN   Sheets of transparent material, such as glass, thin paper, or plastic, bearing a photographic, printed, or hand-drawn image and designed to be viewed by light shining through them; often intended for use with a projection device.
CN   MARC field 755.
HN   Changed 11/90.  Formerly, some TRANSPARENCIES may have been indexed as PHOTOTRANSPARENCIES.
UF   Phototransparencies
BT   Pictures

**Transparencies (cont.)**
NT   Film transparencies +
Glass transparencies +
Slides +
Tissue stereographs
RT   Hold-to-light works
Photographs
Transportation posters
USE Travel posters
**Travel posters**
PN   Posters that promote general tourism or advertise travel opportunities.  The means of transportation, such as railroads or ocean liners, are often depicted.
CN   MARC field 655.
UF   Tourist trade posters
Transportation posters
BT   Posters
**Travel sketches**
PN   Sketches made of places, buildings, objects, people, or events seen during a journey; often made to record a particular feature for future reference.
CN   MARC field 655.
BT   Sketches
Triacetate negatives
USE Acetate negatives
**Trial proofs**
PN   Prints made before the completion of the accepted impression.
CN   MARC field 755.
UF   State proofs
Test proofs
Working proofs
BT   Prints
Proofs
Trial sketches
USE Courtroom sketches
Trichrome carbro prints
USE Tricolor carbro prints
**Tricolor carbro prints**
PN   Photographic prints made from color separation negatives printed as three bromide prints, each of which is then pressed against a sensitized carbon tissue of the appropriate color.  The tissues are then superimposed to create the final color photograph.  Chiefly used ca. 1900-1930s.
CN   MARC field 755.
UF   Three-color carbro prints
Trichrome carbro prints
BT   Carbro prints
Trois crayons drawings
USE A trois crayons drawings
TV stills
USE Television stills
Type C prints
USE Dye coupler prints
Type R prints
USE Dye coupler prints
**Underwater photographs**
PN   Photographs made underwater with

BT Broader term   RT Related term   PN Public Note
NT Narrower term   UF Used for   + Term has NTs
HN History Note   CN Catalogers Note

**Underwater photographs (cont.)**
        waterproof equipment or from a submarine or
        other vehicle.
    CN  MARC field 755.
    UF  Submarine photographs
    BT  Photographs
**Union cases**
    PN  Thermoplastic cases introduced in the
        United States in 1852 for daguerreotypes and
        also made for ambrotypes and some tintypes
        through the 1860s.  Almost 800 design motifs
        have been recorded.  Often mistakenly
        referred to as gutta-percha cases.
    CN  MARC field 655.
    UF  Cases, photograph
        Composition cases
        Gutta-percha photograph cases
        Thermoplastic union cases
    BT  Photograph cases
Urban planning drawings
    USE Planning drawings
**Valentines**
    CN  MARC field 655.
    BT  Greeting cards
**Vandyke prints**
    PN  Photographic prints made by a formula
        introduced in the late 1800s.  Used in the
        1920s-1950s to reproduce architectural,
        engineering, and mechanical drawings.
        Mirror image white lines on a dark brown or
        sepia background were used to make blue or
        black line prints.  Revived in mid-1960s as an
        alternative photographic process.
    CN  MARC field 755.
    BT  Kallitypes
        Monochromatic works
    RT  Reproductions
Vaudeville posters
    USE Theatrical posters
Ventilating, air conditioning, & heating drawings
    USE HVAC drawings
Vest camera photographs
    USE Detective camera photographs
**Victoria card photographs**
    PN  Card photographs; mounts measure
        approximately 5 x 3.5 in. (13 x 9 cm.).
        Introduced in the United States in 1870.
    CN  MARC field 755.
    BT  Card photographs
Video disks
    USE Videodiscs
**Videodiscs**
    PN  Analog optical disks primarily intended
        for the recording of photographs, prints,
        drawings, or other still or motion pictures as
        video signals. May include sound. The
        images are recorded by a laser and can be
        displayed on a video screen
    CN  MARC field 755.
    HN  Changed 10/90.  Formerly, VIDEODISCS
        may have been indexed as VIDEO DISKS.
    UF  Video disks

**Videodiscs (cont.)**
    RT  Reproductions
**Viewbooks**
    PN  Published booklets and other volumes
        primarily consisting of views of particular
        places, events, and activities. May be
        photographs, photomechanical prints, or
        postcards; may be connected by accordion
        folds.
    CN  MARC field 655.
    HN  Changed 10/90.  Formerly, VIEWBOOKS
        may have been indexed as SOUVENIR
        VIEWBOOKS. Also changed 6/94.
        Formerly, some VIEWBOOKS may have
        been indexed as SOUVENIR ALBUMS.
    UF  Booklets
        Souvenir albums
        Souvenir booklets
        Souvenir viewbooks
        Viewbooks, Souvenir
    BT  Ephemera
    RT  Keepsakes
        Postcards
Viewbooks, Souvenir
    USE Viewbooks
Viewmaster cards
    USE Stereographs
Views, Aerial
    USE Aerial views
Views, Bird's-eye
    USE Bird's-eye views
Views, City
    USE Cityscapes
Views, Panoramic
    USE Panoramic views
Views, Toad's-eye
    USE Worm's-eye views
Views, Worm's-eye
    USE Worm's-eye views
**Vignettes**
    PN  Engravings, photographs, and other
        pictures that shade off gradually into the
        surrounding image area.  Often made to be
        combined with text or other illustration
        element.
    CN  MARC field 655.
    BT  Pictures
    NT  Bank note vignettes
    RT  Illustrations
**Visiting cards**
    PN  Small cards bearing a person's name and
        sometimes address; presented when making a
        formal social call. May have a portrait, scene,
        or decoration; may be accompanied by an
        envelope.
    CN  MARC field 655.
    UF  Calling cards
        Cartes de visite (Visiting cards)
    BT  Cards
    RT  Business cards
Vortographs
    USE Photograms

---

BT  Broader term                      RT  Related term                      PN Public Note
NT  Narrower term                     UF  Used for                          + Term has NTs
HN  History Note                      CN Catalogers Note

**Vues d'optique**
  PN  Prints intended for viewing through an
       optical system such as a zogroscope that
       enhances the effect of perspective.  Because
       the viewing device included a mirror, the
       lettering and image are usually laterally
       reversed.  Common in the late 1700s in
       Europe for peep shows.
  CN  MARC field 755.
  UF  Peep show prints
  BT  Prints
**Wallpaper**
  PN  Decorative paper intended to cover the
       walls of a room.
  CN  MARC field 655.
  BT  Ephemera
**Wanted posters**
  PN  Broadsides or posters describing criminals
       sought by law enforcement agencies.  Often
       include offers of rewards.
  CN  MARC field 655.
  UF  Reward posters
  BT  Broadsides
       Posters
  RT  Identification photographs
**War posters**
  PN  Posters issued to support military or
       civilian war efforts, including propaganda.
       Search under PROTEST POSTERS for
       posters that protest war.
  CN  MARC field 655.
  BT  Posters
  RT  Political posters
**Wash drawings**
  PN  Drawings made from diluted ink or
       watercolor applied with a brush; usually
       monochromatic or two color, such as brown
       and gray.
  CN  MARC field 755.
  BT  Drawings
  RT  Brush works
       Ink drawings
**Watch papers**
  PN  Circular papers used to ensure a tight fit
       between inner and outer cases of a pocket
       watch.  Often contain watchmaker's or watch
       owner's name.
  CN  MARC field 655.
  BT  Ephemera
Water marks
  USE Watermarks
Watercolor drawings
  USE Watercolors
Watercolor paintings
  USE Watercolors
**Watercolors**
  CN  MARC field 755.
  HN  Changed 11/90.  Formerly,
       WATERCOLORS may have been indexed as
       WATERCOLOR DRAWINGS or
       WATERCOLOR PAINTINGS.
  UF  Watercolor drawings

**Watercolors (cont.)**
       Watercolor paintings
  NT  Gouaches
  RT  Drawings
       Paintings
**Watermarks**
  CN  MARC field 755.
  UF  Water marks
  BT  Marks
Waterscape drawings
  USE Marine drawings
Waterscape paintings
  USE Marine paintings
Waterscape photographs
  USE Marine photographs
Waterscape prints
  USE Marine prints
Waterscapes
  USE Marines (Visual works)
       Seascapes
Waxed paper negatives
  USE Calotypes
**Wet collodion negatives**
  PN  Dominant glass negative process from its
       introduction in the United States ca. 1855
       until replaced by a dry plate process in the
       1880s. Its use continued for photolithographic
       printing plates until World War II.
       Distinguishable in part by creamy rather than
       grayish black tones and by presence of flow
       lines from hand coating of the emulsion.
  CN  Used in a note under DRY COLLODION
       NEGATIVES. MARC field 755.
  HN  Changed 6/94. Formerly, WET
       COLLODION NEGATIVES may have been
       indexed as WET PLATE NEGATIVES.
  UF  Collodion negatives
       Wet plate negatives
  BT  Glass negatives
  RT  Mammoth plates
Wet plate negatives
  USE Wet collodion negatives
Whiteprints
  USE Diazo prints
Wild west show posters
  USE Circus posters
**Wire photographs**
  PN  Photographs scanned and converted to
       electrical signals, transmitted over wires, and
       then re-formed into images. [AAT]
  CN  MARC field 755.
  HN  Changed 1/94. Formerly, WIRE
       PHOTOGRAPHS may have been indexed as
       TRANSMITTED IMAGES.
  UF  Wirephotos
  BT  Photographs
       Transmitted images
Wirephotos
  USE Wire photographs
**Wood blocks**
  CN  MARC field 655.
  BT  Printing blocks

---

BT  Broader term
NT  Narrower term
HN  History Note

RT  Related term
UF  Used for
CN  Catalogers Note

PN  Public Note
+  Term has NTs

Wood cuts
  USE Woodcuts
**Wood engravings**
  PN  Relief prints made from wood blocks
      incised on the end grain.
  CN  MARC field 755.
  UF  Engravings, Wood
      Xylographs
  BT  Relief prints
  RT  Woodcuts
**Woodburytypes**
  PN  Continuous tone photomechanical prints
      made by a carbon process introduced in the
      United States in 1870. Used through the
      1890s, mainly for book illustrations. Difficult
      to distinguish from actual photographic
      prints, although slight surface relief may be
      visible.
  CN  Used in a note under PHOTOGRAPHIC
      PRINTS. MARC field 755.
  UF  Photoglypties
  BT  Photomechanical prints
**Woodcuts**
  PN  Relief prints made from wood blocks
      incised on the plank side.
  CN  MARC field 755.
  UF  Wood cuts
  BT  Relief prints
  NT  Chiaroscuro woodcuts
  RT  Wood engravings
**Working drawings**
  PN  Graphic delineations showing all necessary
      information to complete a structure, system,
      or site. In architecture, an umbrella term for
      sets of drawings including elevations, plans,
      and sections provided by the architect for use
      by the builder, electrician, plumber, or other
      contractor or fabricator.
  CN  MARC field 655.
  UF  Drawings, Working
  BT  Design drawings
  NT  As-built drawings
      Cartoons (Working drawings)
Working proofs
  USE Trial proofs
**Worm's-eye views**
  PN  Views with a viewpoint well below
      normal eye level. [AAT]
  CN  MARC field 655.
  UF  Toad's-eye views
      Views, Toad's-eye
      Views, Worm's-eye
Wrappers
  USE Packaging
Wrapping materials
  USE Packaging
Wrappings
  USE Packaging
Xerographic art
  USE Copy art
Xerographs
  USE Photocopies

Xylographs
  USE Wood engravings
X-ray photographs
  USE Radiographs
Yankee clipper cards
  USE Clipper ship cards
**Zincographs**
  PN  Lithographs made from zinc plates rather
      than stones.
  CN  MARC field 755.
  BT  Lithographs

---

BT  Broader term
NT  Narrower term
HN  History Note

RT  Related term
UF  Used for
CN  Catalogers Note

PN  Public Note
+  Term has NTs